'BRADLEY'S A

LATIN PROSE COMPOSITION

'BRADLEY'S ARNOLD'

LATIN PROSE COMPOSITION

Edited and Revised, with Appendix

BY

Sir James Mountford

Published by Bristol Classical Press

General Editor: John H. Betts

Facsimile reprint of the original edition,
published 1984 with permission of Longman Group Ltd. by
Bristol Classical Press
an imprint of
Gerald Duckworth & Co. Ltd
61 Frith Street
London W1V 5TA

Reprinted 1993, 1998, 1999

A catalogue record for this book is available
from the British Library

ISBN 0-86292-150-3

Available in USA and Canada from:
Focus Information Group
PO Box 369
Newburyport
MA 01950

Printed in Great Britain by
Booksprint

PREFACE

This revision of a well-known text book, which has helped to train many generations of youthful scholars, was undertaken at the request of the publishers. They wished it to be brought into closer accord with the grammatical conceptions which have established themselves during the last half-century; and, in particular, they thought it desirable that the book should be so edited that it might be used without inconvenience alongside of the 1930 edition of Kennedy's *Revised Latin Primer*.

The general plan of the book has not been modified in any essential; and it will be found that in the great majority of instances the corresponding paragraphs of the old and new editions deal with identical topics. In the Preface to his revision of Mr. Arnold's original book, Dr. Bradley defended the order in which the various subjects were treated and explained the reason for the apparent lack of scientific principle:

'I have not hesitated,' he wrote, 'to invite the learner, who will follow the guidance of the present work, to leave at a very early period the artificially smoothed waters of such simple sentences as are carefully framed with a view to exclude the most ordinary forms of speech in both English and Latin, and to face as soon as possible the constructions of the Infinitive Mood, of the Relative and Interrogative Pronoun, of the Conjunctional Clause, and some of the main uses of the Subjunctive Mood, and of the Latin, as compared with the English, Tenses. It appears to me that after thus obtaining some firm grasp of the great lines in which the Latin language is modelled under the influence of that great instrument of thought, the Verb, he will be far more likely to notice and retain a permanent impression of the usages and mutual relations of other parts of speech, than if he had followed step by step an opposite system under the guidance of a synthetically arranged Syntax. At the same time, as some amount of systematic arrangement is desirable even on practical grounds, the Exercises have been arranged, as a glance at the Table of Contents will show, in groups of closely related subjects.'

Other arrangements of the material are doubtless possible and may be no less effective in the training of students; but it is obvious that any violent departure from the order of treatment adopted by Dr. Bradley would have destroyed the very foundation of the book.

Many teachers have felt that the English sentences set for translation in the Exercises are often dull and uninteresting in content and not always felicitous in expression. These sentences, however, were carefully planned and have proved to be excellent for giving pupils a practical familiarity with Latin grammatical usages. I have therefore not felt justified in attempting to re-cast them wholesale; but here and there I have tried to smooth away some angularities in the English, and have occasionally modified a sentence so that the circumstances in which it could have been uttered by a rational human being will be more immediately obvious. The Supplementary Exercises (except No. 15, which is omitted) have been brought forward from the end of the book and inserted in their appropriate places. The General Vocabulary has been slightly revised and new Indexes have been compiled.

The Latin examples have been retained, wherever possible, with the orthography modernised. It has seemed worth while also to mark the quantity of all long vowels; for even though one may admit that correct quantities are most easily learned by imitating the habits of a good teacher, nevertheless an observant pupil can do much to correct his own errors if, in a book of this kind, he is helped by visual indications.

The need for revision was most obvious in the enunciation of grammatical rules and in the explanations of the nature of Latin usages. The sections on Verbs of Fearing, on the Subjunctive Mood, on *se* and *suus*, on *cum*-clauses, and on Conditional Sentences have been entirely rewritten; and relatively few paragraphs have been left without alteration. Many of the changes introduced may seem to be concerned with matters of detail or with nicety of expression; but in bulk they represent a considerable modification of the attitude to grammatical phenomena which was current when the book was first written. So far as the writing of correct Latin Prose is concerned, these changes may effect little; but in this country, where the reading of classical authors and the writing of Latin exercises have long been closely associated, many students derive more of their knowledge of Latin Syntax from a book on composition than from a formal grammar. It is therefore important that the doctrines presented in such a book as this should not be based on grammatical conceptions which the majority of scholars have abandoned.

In order to increase the usefulness of the book, an Appendix on Continuous Prose Composition has been added. Of the 125 English passages for translation into Latin, more than half deal with interesting and important events and persons of Roman History, arranged in a chronological sequence. The passages are also graduated in difficulty, so that pupils who have worked through the detached sentences will at once be able to attempt continuous pieces of English. The later passages will provide practice for pupils who are preparing for Higher School Certificate Examinations or for a Pass Degree at a University. The few pages of Preliminary Hints at the beginning of the Appendix are not intended to be exhaustive; but they are based on experience gained in teaching continuous composition, and are designed to focus attention on the points which are most frequently found to be causes of stumbling.

In the reading of proofs I have been fortunate in securing the valuable help of Mr. C. J. S. Addison, Mr. S. F. Bonner, and Mr. F. W. Walbank, all of the University of Liverpool; of Mr. R. J. Getty of St. John's College, Cambridge; of Miss A. Woodward of the Royal Holloway College; and of Mr. J. W. Bartram. For their vigilant attention and pertinent criticisms I am deeply grateful; they have rid the book of more than misprints.

J. F. Mountford.

Liverpool,
August 1938.

PUBLISHERS' NOTE

The original edition of this book was by Thomas Kerchever Arnold. Dr. G. G. Bradley, Master of Marlborough, later Master of University College, Oxford, and Dean of Westminster, revised this so thoroughly that it was known as 'Bradley's Arnold' for many years. Now Professor Mountford has edited and revised 'Bradley's Arnold' in accordance with present day practice.

CONTENTS

PAGE

INTRODUCTION—The Parts of Speech 1
Analysis of the Sentence 11
Order of Words and Clauses 16

EXERCISES—

I. Elementary Rules 23

II. III. Meaning of Words and Phrases 28, 33

IV. Agreement of Subject and Verb 36

V. VI. Accusative with Infinitive, *Ōrātiō Oblīqua* . . 39, 42

VII. Nominative with Infinitive 45

VIII. Adjectives—Agreement, Use as Nouns, etc. . . . 49

IX. Adjectives and Adverbs 55

X. XI. The Relative 59, 63

XII. Correlatives 66

XIII. The Infinitive as a Noun 70

XIV. Final Clauses—Sequence of Tenses 74

XV. Consecutive Clauses 77

XVI. *Ut, Nē,* introducing a Noun Clause 83

XVII. *Quōminus, Quīn*—Verbs of Fearing 89

XVIII. Commands and Prohibitions 93

XIX. Remarks on Moods—Subjunctive used independently . 96

XX. Interrogative Sentences—Direct 101

XXI. XXII. Interrogative Sentences—Dependent or Indirect 107, 111

XXIII. Tenses of the Indicative 115

PAGE

XXIV. How to translate *Can, Could, May, Might, Shall, Must,* etc. 121

XXV. Remarks on the Cases—the Nominative 125

XXVI. Apposition 129

XXVII. XXVIII. The Accusative 132, 136

XXIX.-XXXII. The Dative 139, 143, 146, 148

XXXIII.-XXXV. The Ablative . . . 151, 156, 159

XXXVI.-XL. The Genitive . . . 163, 166, 168, 171, 173

XLI. Place, Space 178

XLII. Expressions of Time 182

XLIII. Prepositions—General Remarks; Prepositions with Accusative 186

XLIV. Prepositions with Ablative 191

XLV. Pronouns, Personal and Demonstrative 194

XLVI. Pronouns, Reflexive and Emphatic 199

XLVII. Pronouns, Indefinite 203

XLVIII. A and B. Pronouns—*Īdem, alius,* etc. . . 207, 211

XLIX. L. Gerund and Gerundive 214, 218

LI. The Supines 222

LII. Participles 224

LIII. The Ablative Absolute 230

LIV. Temporal Clauses—General Rules, *Cum* 233

LV. Temporal Clauses—*Dum, Dōnec, Priusquam,* etc. . . 238

LVI. *Ōrātiō Oblīqua* 241

LVII.-LIX. Conditional Clauses 246, 251, 256

LX. Concessive Clauses 262

LXI. Causal and Explanatory Clauses 265

LXII. Comparative Clauses 268

PAGE

LXIII. *Quī*-Clauses : Final and Consecutive 276

LXIV. *Quī*-Clauses : Causal and Concessive 280

LXV. Reported Speeches in *Ōrātiō Oblīqua* 283

LXVI. Numerals 289

LXVII. The Roman Calendar 294

Appendix : Continuous Prose Composition—
Preliminary Hints 299
Passages for Translation 308

General Vocabulary 385

Index of Subjects 431

Latin Index 437

INTRODUCTION

WHAT, it may be asked, is the object of studying Latin Prose Composition?

Until comparatively recent times Latin was an important means of communication between men of different nationalities. During the Middle Ages it was extensively used as the international language of Europe, both for speaking and writing; and within more modern times, until the end of the eighteenth century, theologians, philosophers, and men of science composed their chief works in Latin.

Although Latin is not now used so widely for such practical purposes, Prose Composition is still studied because it is an invaluable means of acquiring a real mastery of the language. Sound progress is not achieved in any language until some successful effort is made to use the language as a medium of expression. Latin Prose Composition helps, firstly, to fix in the memory the various inflexions of nouns and verbs and the rules of Latin syntax; it gives us a closer insight into the workings of the Roman mind; like composition in any foreign language, it trains the student to penetrate beneath the superficial appearances of words to the meanings they are intended to convey; and, finally, when a student has himself employed the language as a tool, he is better able to appreciate the achievements of the great Roman writers.

In this Introduction will be found information about some grammatical terms and ideas of fundamental importance, about types of sentences, and about the order of words and clauses in Latin. To these sections the student should frequently refer.

THE PARTS OF SPEECH

1. By Parts of Speech we mean the various classes, or headings, under which all words used in speaking or writing may be arranged.

2. In Latin, as in English, the Parts of Speech are eight in number :—

(i) Noun (or Substantive).
(ii) Adjective.
(iii) Pronoun.
(iv) Verb.
(v) Adverb.
(vi) Preposition.
(vii) Conjunction.
(viii) Interjection.

3. English has a Definite Article, *the*, and an Indefinite Article, *a*, *an* ; both of them are classed as Adjectives.

Latin has no Article ; thus *lūx* may mean either *the light*, *a light*, or simply *light*.

4. In Latin five of the eight Parts of Speech (*i.e.* all except Prepositions, Conjunctions, and Interjections) have inflexions, that is to say, changes in form (most often at the end of a word) whereby various grammatical relationships are indicated.

It is assumed that all who use this book are thoroughly familiar with these inflexions.

(i) Nouns

5. A Noun is the name which we give to any person (*Caesar*), place (*Rōma*), thing (*mēnsa*), or conception of the mind (*virtūs*).

6. Nouns are sometimes called Substantives because they denote what was once called the *substantia*, or essential nature of a person or thing.

7. Nouns denoting the names of persons or places, such as *Cicerō*, *Metellī*, *Rōma*, *Italia*, are called **proper** nouns.

All other nouns are called **common** nouns, and they may be classified as :—

(*a*) **Concrete** nouns, which denote any object we can perceive with any one of our five senses. In the plural they designate a whole class of objects, and in the singular any individual of that class : *vir*, *virī* 'a man, men' ; *arbor*, *arborēs* 'a tree, trees.'

(*b*) **Collective** nouns, or nouns of multitude, which in the singular denote a group of individuals who can be regarded as forming a unity : *exercitus* 'an army' ; *senātus* 'the senate.'

(c) **Abstract** nouns, which denote some quality, or state, or action as 'withdrawn' (*abstractum*) from the person or thing in which we see it embodied, and looked on as existing by itself. Thus *candor* is the quality of 'whiteness,' wherever that quality is found; *servitium* is the state of 'servitude' which we see existing in a number of *servī*.

(ii) Adjectives

8. An ADJECTIVE is a word which we add or apply to a noun to denote some *one quality* possessed by a person or thing: *bonus* 'good,' *candidus* 'white,' *parvus* 'small.'

9. Adjectives may be divided into :—

Adjectives of **quality**, as *bonus* 'good,' *malus* 'bad,' *fortis* 'brave.'

Adjectives of **quantity** and **number**: *multī* 'many,' *paucī* 'few,' *ducentī* 'two hundred.'

There is also a large number of **pronominal** adjectives closely connected with pronouns: *meus* 'mine,' *tuus* 'thine,' *ūllus* 'any.'

10. When an adjective is *attached* to a noun in order to define it more closely, it is called an **attributive** adjective; thus in *equī albī* 'white horses,' *hominēs bonī* 'good men,' the adjectives are used **attributively.**

11. When a quality denoted by an adjective is *asserted* to belong to a noun, the adjective is said to be used **predicatively**; thus in *hominēs sunt bonī*, the adjective is a **predicative** adjective.

12. Though an adjective is primarily used for *attaching to* or *being predicated* of a noun, yet, where no ambiguity can arise, it is capable of being used by itself as a noun: *bonī* 'good men,' *bona* 'good things.'

(iii) Pronouns

13. PRONOUNS are words used in place of nouns to *indicate* or *point to* a person or thing without naming that person or thing: *ille* 'he.'

14. Pronouns may be classified as :—

(*a*) Personal. *ego* 'I,' *tū* 'thou,' *nōs* 'we,' *vōs* 'you.'
(*b*) Reflexive. *sē* 'himself.'
(*c*) Demonstrative. *hic* 'this'; *is, ille, iste,* 'that.'
(*d*) Definitive. *īdem* 'the same.'
(*e*) Intensive. *ipse* '-self.'
(*f*) Relative. *quī* 'who,' *quīcumque* 'whoever.'
(*g*) Interrogative. *quis* 'who,' *quī* 'what sort of,' *quot* 'how many.'
(*h*) Indefinite. *quis* 'any,' *aliquis* 'someone,' *quīdam* 'a certain one.'

15. All these pronouns except the Personal, Reflexive, and Relative are also used as adjectives : *hic vir* 'this man.'

16. A personal pronoun is not used as the subject of a verb except for emphasis: *dīcō* 'I say'; but *ego dīcō* 'it is I who say.' (See **55.**)

(iv) Verbs

17. A Verb denotes an *action* or *state*.

Valēs 'you are well'; *currō* 'I run'; *hostēs vincuntur* 'the enemy are being conquered'; *Rōma manet* 'Rome remains.'

18. The distinctions between the following different kinds of verb must be carefully attended to in composition :—

19. **Transitive** verbs are those denoting an action which necessarily *affects* some person or thing, or *produces some result* : thus, *interficiō* 'I kill' and *aedificō* 'I build' are not complete in sense until it is clear *whom* 'I kill' and *what* 'I build.'

20. The person or thing that is directly *affected* or *effected* by the action is called the **direct object** of the verb, and is always in the **accusative** case : *latrōnem interfēcī* 'I killed the robber,' *templum aedificant* 'they build a temple.'

21. But in appropriate contexts many Latin transitive verbs may be used **absolutely** (*i.e.* without an expressed object) : *vincō* 'I conquer (my enemies),' *scrībō* 'I am writing (a letter or a book).'

22. **Intransitive** verbs are those denoting an action which has no direct object : *Stō* 'I stand,' *currō* 'I run,' *cadō* 'I fall,' *sum* 'I exist.'

23. Many intransitive verbs, however, denote an action which *indirectly* affects some person or thing which is then indicated by the **dative** case. Thus in *tibi noceō* 'I am hurtful to you,' *mihi pāret* 'he is obedient to me,' *tibi* and *mihi* are the **indirect objects** of intransitive verbs.

24. It is important to realise that in some instances the nearest English equivalent to a Latin intransitive verb is transitive. We feel that 'I spare' is transitive; the Romans felt that *parcō* was intransitive. Furthermore, approximately the same idea may be expressed in Latin sometimes by an intransitive, sometimes by a transitive verb. Thus *noceō* 'I hurt, I am hurtful,' and *placeō* 'I please, I am pleasing' are intransitive, but *laedō* and *dēlectō* are transitive.

25. The **Active Voice** of a verb expresses what the subject of the verb is or does: *valeō* 'I am well,' *amō* 'I love.'

26. The **Passive Voice** of a verb either expresses what is done *to* the subject of the verb, or it expresses the verbal activity regarded impersonally. In *interficit* 'he kills,' the subject 'he' performs the action; but in *interficitur* 'he is being killed,' the subject 'he' is no longer the actor but the recipient or sufferer of the action.

27. It is only transitive verbs that have a full passive voice. If we think carefully about the meaning of intransitive verbs like *currō* 'I run, *vīvō* 'I live,' it will be obvious that forms like *curror, vīvor* can have no meaning.

28. But the third person singular passive of intransitive verbs is frequently used (without any identifiable subject) to denote that the action described by the verb is produced or effected; *Hāc ītur* 'there is a going (*i.e.* men go) in this direction'; *tibi nocētur* 'harm is done to you (*i.e.* you are injured).' Owing to the large number of verbs which, like *noceō*, are intransitive in Latin, this impersonal construction is of great importance. (See **5.**)

29. **Deponent** verbs are those which have an *active meaning* though most of their *forms* are *passive.* Of these, some are transitive, some intransitive.

Tē sequor 'I follow you'; *tibi īrāscor* 'I am angry with you.'

30. Semi-deponent verbs have an active form in the present stem, a passive form in the perfect stem, but an active meaning in both.

Gaudeō 'I rejoice'; *gāvīsus sum*. *Audeō* 'I dare'; *ausus sum*.

31. It is important to remember that deponent and semi-deponent verbs differ from other Latin verbs in having both a present and a past participle with an active sense.

Proficīscor 'I set out'; *proficīscēns* 'setting out' and *profectus* 'having set out.'

(See **14**.)

32. **Impersonal** verbs are those which have only the third person singular of each tense, Infinitives, and a Gerund.

The subject of such verbs is not a person, but either (*a*) unidentifiable (like the English 'it'), or (*b*) an infinitive, or (*c*) a clause, or (*d*) a neuter pronoun :—

Mē pudet. It shames me.
Haec fēcisse piget. It is painful to have done this.
Accidit ut abessem. It happened that I was absent.
Hoc rēfert. This is of importance.

33. By **Auxiliary** verbs we mean verbs used as aids (*auxilia*) to enable other verbs to form moods and tenses which they cannot express within the compass of a single word. Thus in the English 'I have fallen', 'have' has lost the sense of possession, and only serves as an auxiliary to the verb 'fall.' Such verbs abound in English—*may*, *would*, *should*, *shall*, *will*, *let*, etc.—to express what can be expressed in Latin by the form of the verb itself. Compare 'I was loving' with *amābam*; 'let him go' with *eat*.

In Latin the only auxiliary verb is *esse*, 'to be,' which is used largely in the passive voice and future infinitive : *audītus sum*, *audītūrum esse*.

34. Some Latin verbs[1] have as their object the infinitive of another verb.

Possum (*nequeō*, *dēsinō*, *volō*) *haec dīcere*.
I am able (unable, cease, wish) to say this.

(See **42**.)

[1] Such verbs are sometimes called modal verbs, and the infinitive used with them is sometimes called a **prolative infinitive** because it 'carries on' (*prōfert*) their construction.

35. **Copulative** or **Link** verbs are those which simply unite the subject and some noun, pronoun, or adjective which is asserted or predicated of that subject.

Caesar est dictātor. Caesar is dictator.

Note.—The principal of these is the verb *sum*; others are: *appāreō* 'I appear,' *videor* 'I seem,' *audiō* 'I am called.'

When *sum* means 'I am,' 'I exist,' it is called a *substantive* verb, because it expresses the idea of existence, *substantia*.

When it merely joins together the subject and a predicative noun or adjective, as above, it is called a *copulative* verb.

When it forms part of the compound tenses of another verb, it is called an *auxiliary* verb. (See 33.)

36. **Factitive** verbs are those which express the idea of *making* by deed, word, or thought. In the passive they are used as copulative verbs:

fiō, I am made, I become.
appellor, I am called.
creor, I am created.
dēclāror, I am declared.
feror, I am reported.
legor, I am chosen.
putor, I am thought.
vocor, I am called.

Caesar fit (creātus est) dictātor.
Caesar becomes (was created) dictator.

37. Those parts of verbs which are defined by person and number are called **finite**: *sedet* 'he sits,' *vēnimus* 'we have come.'

(v) Adverbs

38. The ADVERB is so called because its main use is to qualify the *verb* by adding some particular as to the *manner*, *amount*, *time*, or *place* of the state or action denoted by the verb.

Fortiter pugnāvit. He fought bravely.
Tum excessit. Then (at that time) he went out.
Ibi cecidit. He fell there (in that place).

39. But adverbs, especially those of *amount* or *degree*, may also qualify *adjectives*, or other *adverbs*.

Satis sapiēns. Sufficiently wise.
Admodum neglegenter. Very carelessly.

(vi) Prepositions

40. PREPOSITIONS are words which are joined with, and almost invariably *placed before* (*praeposita*), nouns and pronouns, to define their relation to other words in the sentence.

Ad mē vēnit.	*Ā Caesare victus est.*	*Prō patriā morī.*
He came to me.	He was conquered by Caesar.	To die for one's native land.

41. In Latin a case alone will often express what in English must be expressed by a noun with a preposition.

Ēnse mē percussit.	*Rōmam Narbōne rediit.*
He struck me with a sword (instrument).	He returned to Rome from Narbonne (motion from and to a town).

42. Prepositions were originally adverbs, and some of them were used in classical Latin both as adverbs and as prepositions.

Ante tē nātus sum.	*Hoc numquam ante vīderam.*
I was born before you (prep.).	I had never before seen this (adverb).

43. Many prepositions are prefixed to and compounded with verbs and modify their meaning.

Pugnō, I fight; *oppugnō*, I assault (a place).

Because of these changes of meaning, some intransitive verbs which had neither direct nor indirect object may, when compounded, have a direct object (compare *pugnō* and *oppugnō* above); others may have an indirect object (*veniō* 'I come,' *tibi subveniō* 'I aid you'); and some transitive verbs which had only a direct object may, when compounded, take an indirect object also (*pontem fēcit* 'he made a bridge,' *cōpiīs lēgātum praefēcit* 'he put a general in charge of the forces'). (See 252, 253.)

In Old English also, prepositions were closely compounded as prefixes with verbs, and we still use *over*come, *with*stand, *gain*say. In later English the preposition is placed after the verb: He is *sent for*, I am *laughed at*.

(vii) Conjunctions

44. CONJUNCTIONS are indeclinable words which join together (*coniungō*) words, phrases, and sentences.

Caelum suspiciō ut lūnam et sīdera videam.
I look up to the sky that I may see the moon and stars.

They are divided into two classes : *Co-ordinating* and *Subordinating* conjunctions.

45. **Co-ordinating** conjunctions join together words and sentences on equal terms. Sentences so connected are of equal grammatical rank, or co-ordinate (*ōrdō* 'rank') ; each is grammatically independent of the other.

Tū abīs et (sed) ego sequor.
You go away and (but) I follow.

46. **Subordinating** conjunctions attach to a sentence or clause another clause which holds a grammatically subordinate position.

Hoc fēcī nē tibi displicērem.
I did this in order not to displease you.

47. The chief Co-ordinating conjunctions in Latin are :—

Connective :	*et* *-que* *atque* *ac*	and.	*neque* *nec*	nor, and not.
			etiam *quoque* *item*	also.
Separative :	*aut* *vel* *-ve*	or, either.	*sīve* *seu*	whether, or.
Adversative :	*sed* *at*	but.	*autem*	but, however.
	atquī *tamen*	but, yet.	*cēterum* *vērum* *vērō*	but, moreover.
Causal :	*nam, namque* *enim, etenim*	for.	*enimvērō*	for indeed.
Conclusive :	*ergō* *itaque* *igitur*	therefore.	*quārē* *quam ob rem* *quāpropter* *quōcircā*	wherefore.

48. *Et* simply joins words and clauses; *-que* couples words to form one whole (*sē suaque* 'himself and his belongings'), or couples two closely related clauses; *atque* connects with emphasis: 'and also, and I may add.' *Ac*, a shorter form of *atque*, is not used before words that begin with a vowel.

49. *Aut* marks a sharp distinction, and *aut . . . aut* exhausts the possible alternatives: *hoc aut vērum est aut falsum* 'this is either true or false.' *Vel* and *-ve* treat the difference as unimportant, and *vel . . . vel* does not necessarily exhaust the possible alternatives: *hoc velim vel vī vel clam faciās* 'I would have you do this either by force or secretly (as you prefer).'

50. Frequently the relative pronoun *quī* is used in the sense of *et is* and is then the equivalent of a co-ordinating conjunction and a demonstrative pronoun.

Fīlium vīdī quī haec mihi nārrāvit.
I saw your son and he told me this news.

51. The chief Subordinating conjunctions in Latin are :—

Final:	*ut*, in order that. *nē*, that . . . not, lest. *quō*, whereby.	*nēve*, *neu*, and that . . . not. *quōminus*, whereby . . . not.
Consecutive:	*ut*, so that. *ut . . . nōn*, so that . . . not.	*quīn*, that . . . not.
Temporal:	*cum*, *ut*, *ubi*, *quandō* } when. *dum*, *dōnec*, *quoad* } while, so long as, until.	*antequam*, *priusquam* } before that. *postquam*, after that. *simul ac*, as soon as. *quotiēns*, as often as.
Causal:	*quod*, *quia* } because. *cum*, *quoniam*, *quandō* } since.	*quippe* { seeing that, for as much as. *siquidem*, *sī quidem* } in as much as.
Conditional:	*sī*, if. *sīve*, *seu*, whether, or if. *sī modo*, if only.	*sīn*, but if. *nisi*, *nī*, unless. *sī nōn*, if not.

Concessive :	*etsī*, *etiamsī*, even if, although.	*tametsī*, although.
	quamquam, *utut*, although.	*quamvīs*, although, however much.
	ut, *licet*, granting that.	*cum*, whereas, although.
Comparative :	*ut*, *utī*, *velut*, *velutī*, *sīcut*, *sīcutī*, as.	*quōmodo*, *quem ad modum*, as, how.
	utpote, as being.	*quam*, than, as.
	quasi, *quam sī*, *ut sī*, *velut sī*, as if.	*tamquam*, as though.
Interrogative :	*num*, *utrum*, whether.	*cūr ?* why ?
	an, or.	*ubi ?* where ?
	necne, or not.	*quandō ?* when ?
		quem ad modum ? how ?

52. The relative pronoun *quī* is often used to introduce final, consecutive, causal, or concessive clauses. (See **498-513.**)

(viii) Interjections

53. **Interjections** are so called because they are words inserted or *thrown in among* (*interiecta*) the other words of a sentence to express some feeling or emotion. Such are : ***heu, vae***, alas ! woe !

ANALYSIS OF THE LATIN SENTENCE

THE SIMPLE SENTENCE

54. By a **sentence**, whether in Latin or in English, we mean a grammatical combination of words which either (1) makes a *statement*, or (2) asks a *question*, or (3) conveys a *command*, or (4) expresses a *desire*.

Every such sentence, however long or however short, involves two elements :—

55. First, a **subject** who (or which) performs an action or is in a certain state ; secondly, a **predicate** which indicates the action or state of the subject.

Veniō.	*Venitne ?*	*Venī !*	*Utinam adesset !*
I come.	Is he coming ?	Come !	Would he were here !

In these Latin sentences the subject is not expressed, because the form of the verb sufficiently indicates whether the subject is first, second, or third person; and personal pronouns are used only for emphasis. (See 16.)

56. But such short sentences are comparatively rare in all languages.

The following is a more frequent type :—

Hī omnēs linguā, īnstitūtīs, mōribus, inter sē differunt.
These all (*or* all of these) differ from one another in language, institutions, and habits.

Here *Hī omnēs* 'these all' is the *subject*; all the rest is the *predicate*. The main part of the predicate is the verb *differunt*, the remainder being *adjuncts* or additions to the verb, explaining and limiting it, telling us *from whom* all of these differ, and *in what points*.

57. A sentence of this kind, which has only one predicate, is called a **simple sentence**.

58. The **subject**, when expressed, is a noun or its equivalent. The equivalent may be a pronoun (13), an adjective (12), a participle, an infinitive, or some combination of words used as a substantive. (See Examples in 61.) But when the meaning is clear from the context, the subject is not expressed.

59. The subject of a sentence is said to be *compound* when it consists of several parts united by conjunctions.

Caesar et Pompeius inimīcī erant.
Caesar and Pompey were enemies.

60. The subject may be *enlarged* by the addition of *adjectives, adjectival phrases,*[1] *pronouns*, words in *apposition*, etc.

Bonī rēgēs amantur. Good kings are loved.
Gaius, vir optimus et magnae auctōritātis, interfectus est.
Gaius, an excellent man and one of great influence, was slain.

---

[1] By an adjectival phrase we mean a combination of words used in place of an adjective :—

vir summae fortitūdinis = *vir fortissimus.*
(*haec rēs*) *tibi magnae erit dēlectātiōnī* = *grātissima tibi erit.*

61. The **predicate** either consists of a verb or contains a verb.

Caesar vīxit. Caesar has lived.

Sapientēs sunt beātissimī. Wise men are the happiest.

Hic rēx est. He (this man) is king.

Agrum colere mihi grātum est. Cultivating the land (*or* farming) is a delight to me.

62. The predicate may not only consist of a verb and the nouns which express its direct and indirect objects, but these nouns may have various adjuncts, such as adjectives or other substantives in apposition.

Pater fīliō, puerō cārissimō, librum pretiōsissimum Rōmae ēmptum, dōnō dedit. The father gave his much-loved son a present of a costly book bought at Rome.

Pater 'the father' is the subject; all the rest is the predicate.

Note.—The verb *dedit* says of the father that he *gave* something. The dative case *dōnō,* closely combined with the verb, explains (by a special use of that case) that he gave the book *as,* or *for, a present.* The dative case *fīliō* does the regular work of the dative, *i.e.* specifies the *indirect object* of the 'giving,' the son who benefited by it; the substantive and adjective in apposition, *puerō cārissimō,* give some further particulars as to that indirect object.

The accusative case *librum* is the *direct object* of the idea expressed by *dōnō dedit.* This is in turn made more distinct by its combination with an adjective, *pretiōsissimum,* and by a participle combined with the locative case of a noun, *Rōmae ēmptum.* These tell us its value and the place where it was purchased.

But the main and essential parts of the predicate are the verb *dedit* with its two accompanying cases *fīliō* and *librum.*

63. Again, the action described by the verb may be explained and made distinct by the addition of *adverbs,* of *cases of nouns* used adverbially (especially the ablative and locative cases), or of *adverbial phrases.*

Diū vīxit. He lived long.

Vīxit nōnāgintā annōs. He lived ninety years.

Famē interiit. He died of hunger.

Summā cum celeritāte vēnit (=*celerrimē vēnit*). He came with the utmost speed.

Londinī vīxit. He lived at London.

64. When the predicate contains a copulative verb (see 35, 36), the predicative noun or adjective is in the same case as the subject: *ego cōnsul erō* 'I shall be consul'; *rēx Numa appellātur* 'the king is named Numa.'

THE COMPOUND SENTENCE

65. Simple sentences are in English and in Latin rather the exception than the rule.

In Latin, as in English, we can neither converse nor write without using sentences which are either combined with other sentences, or contain within themselves other sentences as part of their subject or predicate.

66. A **Compound** sentence is a combination of two or more simple sentences linked together by one or more Co-ordinating conjunctions. (See 47.)

Domum ībō et ibi cēnābō sed nōn dormiam.
I shall go home and take a meal there but I shall not sleep.

67. Sometimes co-ordinate sentences are placed side by side without any conjunction.

Vēnī, vīdī, vīcī. I came, I saw, I conquered.
Contempsī Catilīnae gladiōs, nōn pertimēscam tuōs.
I despised the sword of Catiline, I shall not dread yours.

68. The syntax of the co-ordinate sentence will cause no special difficulty. The characteristic of a co-ordinate sentence is that it *does not grammatically depend on another*; it is a sentence combined with another, but on an *independent footing*. The mood and tense of its verb, the case of its noun or nouns, are in no way dependent upon any other sentence.

THE COMPLEX SENTENCE

69. A **Complex** sentence consists of a Simple sentence (called the **Main Sentence**) on which another sentence (called a **Subordinate Clause**) is grammatically and logically dependent. The main sentence and the subordinate clause (or clauses) are generally linked by Subordinating conjunctions. (See 51.)

Fabius, quī paucās cōpiās habuit, dēclārāvit sē pugnāre nōn posse, nisi senātus subsidia mitteret.
Fabius, who had few troops, asserted that he could not fight unless the senate sent aid.

Here the main sentence is *Fabius dēclārāvit* ; all the rest consists of subordinate clauses.

70. Such subordinate clauses will answer to the three different parts of speech—the noun, the adjective, and the adverb—which form with the verb the chief component parts of a sentence.

(i) Noun Clauses

71. A **Noun Clause** is an Indirect Statement, Command, Wish, or Question standing, like a noun, in some case-relation (generally that of nominative or accusative) to the verb of the main sentence.

(*a*) *Sē rēgem esse dīxit.*	He said that he was a king.
(*b*) *Ut abīrem imperāvit.*	He commanded me to go away.
(*c*) *Quid fieret quaesīvit.*	He asked what was being done.

In each of these Latin sentences the main clause consists of a single word, the verbs *dīxit, imperāvit, quaesīvit* ; but each has appended to it a subordinate clause, answering to an accusative case, and containing (*a*) a statement, (*b*) a command, (*c*) a question.

(ii) Adjectival Clauses

72. An **Adjectival clause** qualifies some noun or pronoun (called the **antecedent**) in the main sentence like an *attributive* adjective (see 10).

For *Bonī rēgēs amantur* we may say *Rēgēs, quī bonī sunt, amantur.*

For *Servōrum fidēlissimum mīsī* we may say *Servum mīsī, quem fidēlissimum habuī.*

(iii) Adverbial Clauses

73. An **Adverbial clause** qualifies the main sentence like an adverb, answering such questions as *how? when? where? why?* Compare—

Hoc cōnsultō fēcī,	with	*Hoc fēcī ut tibi placērem ;*
I did this purposely,	with	I did this in order that I might please you ;

where the adverbs *cōnsultō* and 'purposely' are replaced by *adverbial clauses.*

74. Adverbial clauses are divided into seven classes—

1. Final, those which denote a		*purpose.*
2. Consecutive,	"	*result.*
3. Temporal,	"	*time.*
4. Causal,	"	*reason* or *cause.*
5. Conditional,	"	*supposition.*
6. Concessive (or adversative),		*contrast.*
7. Comparative,	"	*comparison* or *proportion.*

75. They are connected with the main clause sometimes by subordinating conjunctions, a list of which has been given above (see 51), sometimes by the relative *quī*, the use of which in Latin is far wider and more varied than the use of 'who,' 'which' in English.

76. The following are instances :—

Final . .	*Hūc vēnī, ut tē vidērem.* I came here in order to see you.
Consecutive .	*Humī sīc cecidit ut crūs frēgerit.* He fell on the ground so that he broke his leg.
Temporal .	*Cum haec dīxisset, abīre voluit.* When he had spoken thus, he wished to depart.
Causal . .	*Quod haec fēcistī, grātiās tibi agō.* I return thanks to you for acting thus.
Conditional .	*Sī hoc fēceris, poenās dabis.* If you do this you will be punished.
Concessive .	*Quamquam festīnō, tamen hīc morābor.* Though I am in haste, yet I will delay here.
Comparative .	*Proinde ac meritus es, tē ūtar.* I will deal with you as you have deserved.

ORDER OF WORDS AND CLAUSES IN A LATIN SENTENCE

77. The order of words in a Latin sentence differs, in many important respects, from the English order. There are very few sentences in which the natural order of the one language corresponds to that of the other. There is much greater freedom and variety in Latin, especially as regards nouns, adjectives, pronouns, and verbs. For these parts of speech are each susceptible of a great variety of

changes in their terminations, called *inflexions*. It is these inflexions, and not the place of a word in the sentence, which mark the relation of one word to another. As we have far fewer inflexions in English, we are obliged to look for the precise meaning of a word not to its *form* but to its *position*.

78. If we take the English sentence, 'The soldier saw the enemy,' we cannot invert the order of the two nouns, and write 'The enemy saw the soldier,' without entirely changing the meaning; but in Latin we may write *mīles vīdit hostem*, *hostem vīdit mīles*, or *mīles hostem vīdit*, without any further change than that of shifting the emphasis from one word to another.

But for all this, the following general principles should be carefully attended to in writing Latin, and variations from them noticed in reading Latin prose authors.

ARRANGEMENT OF WORDS

79. The **subject** of the sentence stands, as in English, at the beginning of or early in the sentence.

Caesar (or *Tum Caesar*) *exercitum in Aeduōrum fīnēs dūcit.*
Compare—Thereupon Caesar leads his army into the territory of the Aedui.

80. The **verb** (or if not the verb, some important part of the predicate) comes last of all, as *dūcit* in the sentence above.

Ea rēs mihi fuit grātissima.
That circumstance was most welcome to me.

Note.—*Sum*, when used as a link verb, rarely comes last.

81. But if great stress is laid on the verb it is placed at the beginning, and the subject removed to the last place.

Tulit hoc vulnus graviter Cicerō. Cicero doubtless felt this wound deeply.

Est caeleste nūmen. There really is (*or* there exists) a heavenly power.

The position of *sum* often distinguishes its *substantive* from its *copulative* and *auxiliary* uses. (See 35, *Note*.)

82. It must always be remembered that :—

The degree of **prominence** and **emphasis** to be given to a word is that which mainly determines its position in the sentence. And :—

The two emphatic positions in a Latin sentence are the *beginning* and the *end.* By the former our attention is raised and suspended, while the full meaning of the sentence is rarely completed till the last word is reached.

Hence, from the habit of placing the most important part of the predicate, which is generally the verb, last of all, we rarely see a Latin sentence from which the last word or words can be removed *without destroying the life,* so to speak, of the whole sentence.

This can easily be illustrated from any chapter of a Latin author.

83. The more **unusual** a position is for any word, the more emphatic it is *for that word.* Thus :

> *Arborēs seret dīligēns agricola, quārum adspiciet bācam ipse numquam.*—(*Cic.*)

Here the adverb is made emphatic by position ; in English we must express the emphasis differently, as by 'though the day will never come when he will see their fruit,' or 'though never will he see.'

A word that generally stands close by another receives emphasis by *separation* from it ; especially if it be thus brought near the beginning or end of a sentence.

> *Voluptātem percēpī maximam.* Very great was the pleasure I felt. *Aliud iter habent nūllum.* They have no other route at all. *Equitēs ad Caesarem omnēs revertuntur.* The cavalry return to Caesar without exception.

84. As regards the interior arrangement of the sentence, the accusative or dative, expressive of the direct or indirect objects of verbs, come usually *before* the verb. In this Latin differs markedly from English.

> *Hunc librum fīliō dedī.*
>
> Contrast—I gave this book to my son.

But a genitive usually follows the word on which it depends : *fīlius rēgis, tribūnus plēbis.*

85. Adjectives, when used as attributes (see 10), are oftener than not placed *after* the noun with which they agree; but demonstrative and interrogative pronouns, numerals, and adjectives denoting *size* or *quantity* come *before* the noun they qualify.

Vir bonus; cīvitās opulentissima; pater meus; but: *haec opīniō; permultī hominēs.*

When a noun is combined both with an adjective and a genitive, the usual order is this—

Vēra animī magnitūdō. True greatness of mind.

86. A word in apposition generally stands, as does an adjective, after the word to which it relates.

Q. Mūcius augur; M. Tullius Cicerō cōnsul; Pȳthagorās philosophus. Luxuria et ignāvia, pessimae artēs.

87. Adverbs and their equivalents, such as ablative and other cases, and adverbial phrases, come *before* the verbs which they qualify.

Hic rēx diū vīxit. This king lived long.
Agrum ferrō et ignī vastāvit. He laid waste the land with fire and sword.
Libenter hoc fēcī. I did this cheerfully.
Trīgintā annōs rēgnāvit. He reigned thirty years.

88. The adverbs of time *tum* and *deinde* are often the first word in a sentence.

Tum eōs vehementer hortātus sum.
Then I vigorously exhorted them.

89. *Enim, vērō, autem, quoque, quidem* (with the *enclitics*,[1] *-que, -ve, -ne*), cannot be the first words of a clause; *enim, vērō,* and *autem* are generally second word; *quoque* and *quidem* immediately follow the words they emphasise.

90. The negative adverbs *nōn, haud, neque,* are placed always before the words which they qualify. *Nē* . . .

[1] An enclitic is a word which does not stand by itself, but is added at the end of another word: *-ne* (interrogative), *-que* (=and), *-ve* (=or), are the commonest Latin enclitics.

quidem 'not even' always enclose the word which they emphasise : *nē hic quidem* 'not even he.'

91. It may be well to add that a repeated word, or a word akin to another in the sentence (such as one pronoun to another), is generally placed as near to that word as possible.

Nūlla virtūs virtūtī contrāria est. No kind of virtue is opposed to virtue.

Tēne ego aspiciō? Is it you whom I see?

Aliīs aliunde est perīculum. Danger threatens different men from different quarters.

Timor timōrem pellit. Fear banishes fear.

We see that Latin has a great advantage in this respect over English.

ARRANGEMENT OF CLAUSES

Noun Clauses

92. No general rule applies to **noun clauses**. But indirect questions and noun clauses introduced by *ut, nē, quōminus,* and *quīn* generally follow the main sentence, especially if the noun clause is long or important.

Quaeris cūr hōc homine tantō opere dēlecter. You ask why I am so greatly pleased by this person.

Ōrō ut mē, sīcut anteā, attentē audiātis. I beg you to listen carefully to me, as previously.

Adjectival Clauses

93. Though a **relative clause** usually comes after the word it qualifies (as in English), it may be placed earlier and more in the centre of the sentence than is possible in English.

In hīs, quae nunc īnstant, perīculīs.
In these dangers which now threaten us.

The relative pronoun is placed at the beginning of the clause it introduces unless it depends upon a preposition.

Patriam, prō quā pugnāvī, nōn dēseram.
I will not desert my country for which I have fought.

Adverbial Clauses

94. Temporal, causal, conditional, concessive, and comparative clauses usually come before the main sentence; but final and consecutive clauses usually follow it (as in English).

95. The following are examples of the *usual* order :—

Cum haec dīxisset, abiit (temporal).	Having said this, he departed.
Quoniam vir es, congrediāmur (causal).	Since you are a man, let us close in fight.
Sī futūrum est, fiet (conditional).	If it is to be, it will come to pass.
Rōmānī, quamquam fessī erant, tamen obviam prōcessērunt (concessive).	The Romans advanced to meet (them) in spite of their fatigue.
Ut sēmentem fēceris, ita metēs (comparative).	You will reap as you have sown.
Ēsse oportet, ut vīvās (final).	You should eat to live.
Quis fuit tam ferreus, ut meī nōn miserērētur (consecutive).	Who was so hard-hearted as not to pity me?

96. When a word is the common subject or object of both main sentence and subordinate clause, it generally is placed before both.

Aeduī, cum sē dēfendere nōn possent, lēgātōs ad Caesarem mittunt.
Since the Aedui could not defend themselves, they sent ambassadors to Caesar.

97. When several clauses depend on one main sentence and on one another, Latin so arranges them that a succession of verbs is avoided. In the following sentence :

Imperātor, quamquam ōrātiōnem lēgātōrum quī aderant audīverat, prōgressus est,
The commander set forth although he had heard the speech of the ambassadors who were present,

the position of every word is in accordance with the general principles mentioned above. But the following order would be preferable in the circumstances :

Quamquam lēgātōrum quī aderant ōrātiōnem audīverat, imperātor prōgressus est.

98. Of two corresponding *clauses* or *groups* of words of parallel construction, the order of the first is often *reversed* in the second, so that two of the *antithetical* words are as *near* as possible.

> *Fragile corpus animus sempiternus movet. Ratiō nostra cōnsentit; pugnat ōrātiō. Quae mē mōvērunt, mōvissent eadem tē profectō.*

99. To many of these rules exceptions may be found. For the order in Latin is determined not only by general principles, but also by considerations of **emphasis, clearness, sound, rhythm,** and **variety.**

As a general rule, **in any but the shortest clause, the English order is sure to be ill adapted to a Latin sentence.**

EXERCISES

EXERCISE I

ELEMENTARY RULES

1. A finite verb (see Intr. 37) agrees with its *subject* in *number* and *person*.

Avis canit.	The bird sings.
Avēs canunt.	The birds sing.

2. An adjective, pronoun, or participle agrees with the noun to which it is attached, or of which it is predicated, in *gender*, *number*, and *case*.

Rēx ille, vir iūstissimus, plūrima foedera pactus est.
That just king contracted many treaties.

3. When to a noun or personal pronoun there is added a noun explaining or describing it, the latter is said to be placed in *apposition* to the former, and must agree *in case* with the noun to which it is added.

Alexander, tot rēgum atque populōrum victor.
Alexander, the conqueror of so many kings and nations.

4. A **transitive** verb, whether active or deponent, takes an **accusative** of the *direct object*; that is to say, of the *person* or *thing acted upon* or *result produced*.

Sacerdōs hostiam cecīdit. The priest struck down the victim.
Alius alium hortātur. One man exhorts another.
Pontem fēcērunt. They made a bridge.

This rule is invariable; **every really transitive verb governs an accusative.**

5. But many verbs that are transitive in English must be translated into Latin by verbs that are really intransitive. Such verbs take a **dative** of the person (or thing) *interested in* the action of the verb, *i.e.* an *indirect object.* (Intr. 24.) Thus—

I favour you,	*tibi faveō,*	(I am favourable *to* you.)
I obey you,	*tibi pāreō,*	(I am obedient *to* you.)
I persuade you,	*tibi persuādeō,*	(I am persuasive *to* you.)
I please you,	*tibi placeō,*	(I am pleasing *to* you.)
I spare you,	*tibi parcō,*	(I am sparing (merciful) *to* you.)

In the passive voice these verbs cannot be used otherwise than impersonally.

You are favoured,	*tibi favētur,*	(Favour is shown to you.)
You are spared,	*tibi parcitur.*	etc.
You are pardoned,	*tibi ignōscitur.*	
You are persuaded,	*tibi persuādētur.*	
You are obeyed,	*tibi pārētur.*	

6. The dative of the indirect object is sometimes, but by no means always, marked in English by the preposition *to* or *for.*

But the dative does not express *to* in the sense of *motion to.*

'I gave this to my father' is: *Hoc patrī meō dedī* ;

but

'I came to my father' is: *Ad patrem vēnī.*

Note.—For *to* in the sense of motion to a town, see **9**, *b.* *For,* when it means 'in defence of,' 'in behalf of,' is expressed by *prō* with the ablative.

Prō patriā morī. To die for one's country.

7. The verb *to be*, and such verbs as *to become, to turn out, to continue,* etc., passive verbs of *being named, considered, chosen, found,* and the like, do not govern any case, but act as links between the subject and predicate, and therefore have the same case after as before them. (See Intr. 35, 36.)

Gaius est iūstus. Gaius is a just man.

Scio Gaium iūstum fierī. I know that Gaius is becoming just.

Gaius imperātor salūtātus est. Gaius was saluted as Imperator.

8. (*a*) With passive verbs and participles, the thing *by which* or *with which* (the instrument) the action is performed, stands in the **ablative** ; the person *by whom* (the agent), in the **ablative with the preposition** *ā* **or** *ab.*

Castra vallō fossāque ā mīlitibus mūnīta sunt. The camp has been fortified by the soldiers with a rampart and ditch.

(*b*) But when English 'with' means 'together *or* in company with' the preposition *cum* must be used with the ablative.

Cum tēlō vēnit. He came with a weapon.
Cum Caesare hoc fēcī. I did this with Caesar.

Note.—Cum is written after, and as one word with, the ablatives of the personal and reflexive pronouns (*mēcum, tēcum, sēcum, nōbīscum, vōbīscum*), and sometimes after the relative, as *quibuscum.*

9. (*a*) The ablative also expresses the time *at* or *in* which a thing takes place, the accusative the time *during which* it lasts.

Hōc mēnse quīndecim diēs aegrōtāvī. I have been ill for fifteen days in this month.

Trēs ibi diēs commorātus sum, quārtō diē domum rediī. I stayed there three days, I returned home on the fourth day.

(*b*) The ablative of names of **towns** (without a preposition) is used to express motion *from.*

Rōmā vēnit, 'he came from Rome'; but *ex* or *ab Italiā,* 'from Italy.'

Motion *to* a town is expressed by the accusative without a preposition.

Neāpolim rediit, 'he returned to Naples'; but *ad* or *in Italiam,* 'to Italy.'

The ablative and accusative of *domus* and of *rūs* are used in the same way without a preposition.

Domō vēnit 'he came from home'; *rūs abiit* 'he went off to the country.'

10. A noun in close connexion with another which it qualifies is put in the **genitive** case.

Hortī patris. The gardens of my father=my father's gardens.
Laus ducis. The praise of the general.
Fortium virōrum facta. The deeds of brave men.

This case corresponds often to the English 'possessive' case.

11. (*a*) A nominative pronoun is not used as the subject of a sentence, except for the sake of *clarity* or *emphasis.*

This is because the termination of the verb indicates

sufficiently the first, second, and third persons, and singular and plural number. (See Intr. 55.)

Ego hoc volō. For myself I wish this.

(*b*) When there is a distinction or contrast between persons to be expressed, the personal pronouns must be used.

Tū Tarentum āmīsistī, ego recēpī. You lost Tarentum, I retook it.

(*c*) A *possessive* adjective is also omitted when there can be no doubt as to *whose* the thing is.

Tum ille dextram porrigit. Then he (the other) holds out his right hand.

But it must be used when emphatic, or when its omission would cause a doubt as to the meaning.

Suō sē gladiō vulnerāvit. He wounded himself with his (own) sword.

Patrem meum vīdī. I have seen my father.

(*d*) *He, she, it, they,* and their oblique cases, when they carry no emphasis, but merely *refer* to some person or thing already named, should be translated by *is, ea, id,* not by *ille*. *Ille* is much more emphatic, and often means 'the other' in a story where two persons are spoken of; and sometimes it means 'that distinguished person.' *Iste* is 'that of yours,' and often implies scorn or depreciation.

(*e*) But when *him, her, them* denote the same person as the subject of the verb, the reflexive *sē* must be used.

He says he (himself) will do it. *Hoc sē factūrum esse ait.*

The possessive adjective *suus* also refers to the subject of the verb.

12. The relative pronoun *quī* agrees in *gender* and *number* with a noun or demonstrative pronoun in a preceding sentence. Its *case* depends on the construction of its own clause. The noun to which it thus *refers* is called its **antecedent**. (See Intr. 72.)

Ille est equus, quem ēmī. Yonder is the horse which I have bought.

13. A relative clause is often used where English prefers a co-ordinate sentence. (See Intr. 50.)

Dīvitiās optat, quās adeptūrus est numquam. He is praying for riches, but will never obtain them.

14. As compared with English, Latin is deficient in participles; and in writing Latin prose it is essential to keep clearly in mind the following facts :—

(*a*) The Latin past participle is passive and not active (except when derived from a deponent verb : see Intr. 31) : *amātus* means 'having *been* loved,' not 'having loved.'

(*b*) The present and future participles are always active.

The lack of a past participle active is especially troublesome when turning English into Latin; but there are two common ways in which the difficulty can be surmounted.

Either (i) a subordinate clause may be used; for 'having heard this, he returned' we may write : *cum hoc audīvisset, rediit.*

Or (ii) advantage may be taken of the past participle passive itself, by using a construction known as the **Ablative Absolute.** In this construction a noun (or pronoun) and a past participle passive are put in the ablative case to show in what circumstances the action of a finite verb takes place. Thus, for 'having heard this, he returned,' we may write : *hōc audītō* (literally 'this having been heard'), *rediit.*

15. Where in English two finite verbs are coupled by *and* we may often substitute a Latin participle in the proper case for one, and omit the *and.*

They marvelled and went away. *Admīrātī abiēre.*
He attacked and took the city. *Urbem oppugnātam cēpit.*

Note.—Observe that *admīrātī* in the first example has an active sense because it is derived from a deponent verb. (See **14.**)

Exercise 1

1. I have been elected consul by the votes of the Roman people; you are favoured by the enemies of the human race. 2. The town had now been blockaded for three days; it was taken by assault on the fourth day. 3. I sent three messengers to you in the month (of) January.[1] 4. If you are (*fut.*) obeyed, I shall be spared. 5. That

[1] *Iānuārius*, an adjective.

district had been laid waste by the enemy[1] with fire and sword. 6. I am envied, but you are despised. 7. Fortune favours the brave (*pl.*), but sometimes envies the fortunate. 8. Having arrived at the city at daybreak, he sent for the chiefs. 9. I never injured you, but you have always envied me, and you hate my friends. 10. Having heard this, he halted for three hours, but at mid-day began his march again. 11. Having spoken thus[2] and having stretched forth his right hand, he showed him the way.

EXERCISE II

MEANING OF WORDS AND PHRASES

16. Though Latin words answering to all the English words in the following Exercises will be found in the Vocabulary, yet continual care and thought will be necessary.

The same English word is often used in very different senses, some **literal,** some **figurative.** It is most unlikely that a single word in Latin will answer to all the various meanings of a single English word.

(*a*) Thus we use the word 'country' (connected through the French with the Latin *contrā*, 'opposite to us') in a great variety of meanings: 'rural districts,' as opposed to 'town'; 'our native land,' as opposed to a foreign country; 'the territory' of any nation; 'the state,' as opposed to an individual; even 'the inhabitants or citizens of a country.' Each of these senses is represented by a different word in Latin. Thus:—

Rūs abiit. He went into the country.
Prō patriā morī. To die for one's (native) land or country.

---

[1] Plural; the singular *hostis,* however, is used sometimes like our 'enemy,' as a collective noun. (Intr. 7, *b.*)

[2] *I.e.* 'these things,' neut. pl. of *hic.*

In fīnēs (or *in agrōs*) *Helvētiōrum exercitum dūxit.* He led his army into the country of the Helvetii.

Reī pūblicae (or *cīvitātī*), *nōn sibi cōnsuluit.* He consulted the interests of the country, not of himself.

Cīvibus omnibus cārus fuit. He was dear to the whole country (or nation).

No Vocabulary or Dictionary therefore will be of any real use, unless we clearly understand the precise **meaning** of the English.

(*b*) Again, we might meet with the word 'world' in an English sentence; but we cannot translate it into Latin till we know whether it means 'the whole universe,' or 'this globe,' or 'the nations of the world,' or 'people generally,' or 'mankind,' or 'life on earth.'

Num cāsū factus est mundus? Was the world (sun, moon, stars, and earth) made by chance?

Lūna circum tellūrem movētur. The moon moves round the world (this planet).

Orbī terrārum (or *omnibus gentibus*) *imperābant Rōmānī.* The Romans were rulers of the world.

Omnēs (*hominēs*) *īnsānīre eum crēdunt.* The whole world thinks him out of his mind.

Nēmō ūsquam. No one in the world.

Multum hominibus nocuit. He did the world much harm.

In hāc vītā numquam eum sum vīsūrus. I shall never see him in this world.

Since many words are used in various senses we must ask ourselves their precise meaning. Assistance will be given in the present book; but the learner cannot too soon accustom himself to dispense with this kind of aid, and to think for himself.

17. There are a great many **metaphorical expressions** in English which we cannot possibly render literally into Latin. We say, 'His son ascended the throne,' or 'received the crown,' or 'lost his crown'; and we might be tempted to translate such phrases literally after finding out the words for 'to ascend,' for 'a throne,' for 'to receive,' for 'a crown,' and so on.

But the fact is that these words when so combined **mean** something quite different from what they **appear to say**, and to translate the actual words literally would be to say in Latin something quite different from the idea which the English conveys.

Fīlius solium ascendit, or *cōnscendit*, would (except in a poem) merely mean that his son 'went up,' or 'climbed up,' a throne; *Fīlius corōnam accēpit* that he 'received a (festal or other) garland.' A Roman would certainly say *rēgnum excēpit*, 'received in turn (inherited) the sovereignty.'

This is only a specimen of the kind of mistake which we may make by not asking ourselves what words *mean* as well as what they say.

Compare such common expressions as 'he held his peace,' 'he took his departure,' answering to *conticuit*, *abiit*. Mistakes in such phrases as these are more likely to occur in translating longer passages without the aid afforded in these Exercises; but the warning cannot be given too early.

18. There are many English words whose **derivation from Latin words** is obvious. We are apt to think that if we know the parent word in Latin we cannot do better than use it to represent the English descendant, which so much resembles it in sound and appearance; but we can hardly have a worse ground than that of the similarity of *sound* in Latin and English words on which to form our belief that their **meaning** is identical. Most of these words have come to us through French. The Latin language spoken by Roman soldiers and settlers was borrowed from them by the Gauls; the Gauls in turn communicated the dialect of Latin which they spoke to their German conquerors; from these the Normans, a Scandinavian people, learnt, and adopted, what was to them a foreign tongue, with words from which, after conquering England, they enriched the language spoken by our English or Saxon forefathers. It would be strange if the meanings of words had not altered greatly in such a process.

When, therefore, we meet such a word as 'office' in an Exercise we must beware of turning it by *officium*, which means 'a duty,' or an 'act of kindness.' We shall learn in time, by careful observation, when the English and Latin kindred words correspond in meaning, and when they differ; but we cannot too early learn that they **generally differ.**

19. Thus—

'Acquire' is not *acquīrere* (=add to), but *adipīscī, cōnsequī.*
A man's 'acts' are not *ācta* (=transactions), but *facta.*
'Attain to' is not *attinēre ad*, or *attingere ad* (=appertain to), but *pervenīre ad*, or *cōnsequī.*
'Famous' is not *fāmōsus* (=infamous), but *praeclārus.*
'Mortal' (wound) is not (*vulnus*) *mortāle* (=liable to die), but *mortiferum.*
'Nation' is not *nātiō* (=a tribe), but *cīvitās, populus, rēs pūblica, cīvēs.*
'Obtain' is not *obtinēre* (=hold fast), but *cōnsequī, adipīscī*, etc.
'Office' is not *officium* (=duty), but *magistrātus.*
'Oppress' is not *opprimere* (=overwhelm), but *vexāre*, etc.
'Perceive' is not *percipere* (=take possession of), but *intellegere.*
'Receive' is not *recipere* (=regain, retake), but *accipere.*
'Ruin' (as a metaphor) is not *ruīna* (=a falling), but *perniciēs, interitus*, etc.
'Secure' (safe) is not *sēcūrus* (=free from care), but *tūtus.*
'Vile' is not *vīlis* (=cheap), but *turpis.*

These are only specimens. The Vocabulary will afford guidance, but the learner cannot too early be on his guard against a fruitful source of blunders, or learn too soon to lay aside, as far as possible, the use of vocabularies and similar aids, and trust to his own knowledge as gained from reading Latin.

Exercise 2

A

1. I was made king by the votes of the whole nation. 2. He attained to the highest offices in (his) native country. 3. I hate the din of cities; the country is always most pleasing to me. 4. Our forefathers acquired this district by the sword. 5. The whole world was at that time obedient to the empire of Rome. 6. He reigned long; the crown which he had acquired by violence he held to[1] the great advantage of the nation. 7. He was a most famous orator, and all the world admired him greatly.

---

[1] Use *cum* with abl.

8. He was most dear to the whole nation, for he was ever ready to do all things for the country. 9. He received a mortal wound (while) fighting for his native land. 10. At last he held his peace; he had said much (*neut. pl.*), and (spoken) long. 11. He succeeded to the crown (while) a boy; (as) king he attained to the highest glory. 12. He never attained to his father's glory, but all things that were vile he always hated. 13. He foretold the ruin of his country.

B

1. Not even [1] the vilest of mankind wished to injure his own father. 2. Yesterday he returned from Naples,[2] to-morrow he will set out from Italy to Spain. 3. No one in the world is more secure against [3] violence; for no one [4] ever consulted to such [5] a degree the interests of the country. 4. Having obtained the throne by violence, he yet became before long [6] most dear to the whole nation; for no one [4] ever less consulted his own interests. 5. On the fourth day after his father's death he ascended the throne, on the fifth he was saluted Emperor by the soldiers, on the sixth, having led his army into the enemy's country, he was wounded by his own sword while he was mounting [7] his horse. 6. No one was ever more famous, and no one ever attained to higher (*greater*) rank, or acquired such wealth; yet he was dear to few, hated by many, and no one ever did his country greater harm. 7. You are obeyed by no one, yet your father was the ruler [8] of a mighty nation. 8. That [9] deed of yours will never be pardoned by your countrymen.

---

[1] Intr. 90. [2] See **9**, *b*. [3] *ā*, *ab*.

[4] *neque enim quisquam* (see **358**, i, *Note*); *nōn* is but rarely used before *enim*.

[5] *tantum*, adv. [6] = soon. [7] Tense? (See **180** and **411**.)

[8] *imperō*, *-āre*. (See **25**.) [9] *iste*. (**11**, *d*.)

EXERCISE III

MEANING AND USE OF WORDS—*Continued*

VERBS

20. In translating an English verb into Latin, it is most important to be sure of the precise sense in which the English verb is used.

We have in English a large number of verbs which are used in two senses: sometimes **transitively** with an expressed object, and sometimes **absolutely** (Intr. 21), or **intransitively.**

We say 'he changed his seat,' and 'the weather is changing'; 'he moved his arm,' and 'the stars move'; 'we dispersed the mob,' and 'the fog dispersed'; 'he turned his eyes,' and 'he turned to his brother'; 'he collected books' and 'a crowd collected'; 'he joined this to that,' 'he joined his brother,' 'the two ends joined.'

But in translating such verbs into Latin, we must carefully distinguish between these different senses of the same verb.

21. If the English transitive verb is used *absolutely* (see Intr. 21), as in 'the crowd *dispersed,*' we must either (*a*) use the passive of the Latin verb, or (*b*) insert the reflexive pronoun *sē*, or (*c*) use a different verb.

Thus—

(*a*)	He changed his seat.	*Sēdem mūtāvit.*
	The weather is changing, *or* altering.	*Mūtātur tempestās.*
	He broke up the crowd.	*Multitūdinem dissipāvit.*
	The fog broke up.	*Dissipāta est nebula.*
	He moved his arm.	*Bracchium mōvit.*
	The moon moves round the earth.	*Lūna circā tellūrem movētur.*
	He rolled down stones.	*Lapidēs dēvolvit.*
	The stones roll down.	*Dēvolvuntur lapidēs.*
(*b*)	He will surrender the city.	*Urbem dēdet.*
	The enemy will surrender.	*Sē dēdent hostēs.*
(*c*)	Riches increase.	*Crēscunt dīvitiae.*
	He increased his wealth.	*Opēs suās auxit.*
	He collected books.	*Librōs collēgit.*
	A crowd was collecting.	*Conveniēbat multitūdō.*

22. Many English verbs, usually intransitive, become transitive by the addition of a preposition: 'to hope, to hope *for*'; 'to wait, to wait *for*'; 'to sigh, to sigh *for*'; similarly 'to gaze *on*,' 'to look *at*,' 'to smile *at*,' and many others.

To determine whether the preposition really belongs to the verb, the verb may be turned into the passive; if the preposition *remains attached to the verb*, we may be sure that the two words form one transitive verb.

Thus, 'to wait' is converted by the addition of the preposition 'for' from an intransitive to a compound transitive verb, 'to wait for.'

He waits for his brother.	*Frātrem exspectat.*
His brother is waited for.	*Frāter exspectātur.*

23. Examples of such words are—

I aim at distinctions (high office).	*Honōrēs petō.*
I crave for leisure.	*Ōtium dēsīderō.*
I hope for peace.	*Pācem spērō.*
I listen to you.	*Tē audiō.*
I look *or* wait for you.	*Tē exspectō.*
I look up at the sky.	*Caelum suspiciō.*
I pray for (*i.e.* greatly desire) this.	*Hoc optō.*

The number of such English verbs is very large.

24. In Latin (as in older English: 'I *fore*go, I *be*speak') an intransitive verb very often becomes transitive by composition with a preposition prefixed to the verb. (See Intr. 43.)

Sedeō, I sit, *obsideō*, I blockade (a town); *vehor*, I am carried, *or* I ride, *praetervehor*, I ride past; *veniō*, I come, *conveniō*, I have an interview with (as: *Caesarem convēnī*).

25. A single Latin verb will often indicate what English expresses by a *verbal phrase*, *i.e.* a combination of a verb with a noun or other words. Thus—

Taceō, I keep silence; *abeō*, I take my departure; *nāvigō*, I take, *or* have, a voyage; *īnsāniō*, I am out of my senses; *minor*, I utter threats; *colloquor*, I have a conversation; *tē līberō*, I give you your liberty; *adeō mortem pertimēscit*, such is his terror of death.

Exercise 3

A

Verbs marked in *italics* are to be expressed by participles, and the conjunction that follows is to be omitted (**15**).

1. We were all craving for peace, for we had carried on a long and bloody war. 2. They at last surrendered the city, which-had-been-besieged (*part.*) for eight months (**9**, *a*). 3. He prays for peace and leisure, but [1] he will never obtain these things. 4. All the world is looking for war, but heaven will bestow upon us the peace for which we pray. 5. Then he *turned* (*part.*) towards his friends, and in vain endeavoured to look up at them. 6. He looked round for his friends, but all for whom he looked round (*imperf.*) had deserted him. 7. The enemy *had swarmed* out of the gates and were mingling with our soldiers. 8. The multitude which had gathered together in the morning dispersed before noon. 9. Many rocks were rolling down from the mountains, and one of our guides *was struck* by a vast mass and received a mortal wound. 10. On that fatal day I craved for you, but you were absent in the country. 11. A vast multitude had flocked together, and was now waiting for the return of the exiles.

B

1. For three days [2] we waited for you (*pl.*) and hoped in vain for your arrival. On the fourth day the Indians, who were blockading our camp, dispersed and [3] took their departure : a [4] circumstance which gave us freedom from long-continued fear and anxiety. 2. You (*pl.*) crave for freedom, and are going [5] to fight for [6] your native land, for your altars and hearths ; these (men) pray for peace,

---

[1] Relative neut. pl. = 'which things.' (See **13**.)
[2] 9, *a*. [3] **15**. [4] See **67**.
[5] Fut. part. [6] *prō*. (See **6**, *Note*.)

and are afraid of the hardships and toils of war. You I honour, them [1] I despise. 3. Your riches increase daily, but they neither increase your leisure nor bring you (243) either happiness or peace of mind. 4. Your native land, which was once the ruler of many nations, is now most cruelly oppressed by the vilest enemy, whom lately you both despised and hated. 5. I am waiting here in vain for the arrival of the soldiers whom I sent for yesterday; the enemy's forces are increasing daily, and we shall soon despair of peace. 6. By a bloody and long-continued war we have freed our country and repelled from our walls a haughty foe; we now pray for peace. 7. Having [2] advanced into the thick [3] of the battle, he received a mortal wound; while [4] dying, he foretold the ruin of his nation and the triumph of the enemy.

EXERCISE IV

AGREEMENT OF THE SUBJECT AND VERB

26. If one verb is predicated of a compound subject (see Intr. 59) whose parts refer to different *grammatical* persons, it will be in the plural number, and agree with the first person rather than the second, and with the second rather than the third.

> ***Et ego[5] et tū manūs sustulimus.*** Both you and I raised our hands.
>
> ***Et tū et frāter meus manūs sustulistis.*** Both you and my brother lifted up your hands.

---

[1] *ille.* (11, *d.*)
[2] 14, *a.*
[3] 'midst of.' (See **60.**)
[4] See **406, i,** and *Note.*
[5] For 'Gaius and I,' the Romans, putting 'I' first, said *Ego et Gaius.* When therefore Cardinal Wolsey said '*Ego et rēx meus,*' he was a good grammarian but a bad courtier. Similarly the Romans placed the second person before the third; 'Your brother and you' would be: ***Et tū et frāter tuus.***

27. But sometimes in Latin authors a verb which has a compound subject is singular, especially when it is placed immediately before or after the first part of the compound subject.[1]

Et tū ades et frāter tuus. Both you and your brother are here.

28. If a single verb is predicated of several subjects of the third person, it is normally plural ; but it sometimes agrees with a singular noun nearest itself.

Appius et soror eius et frāter meus manūs sustulērunt. Appius and his sister and my brother lifted up their hands.

Nunc mihi nihil librī, nihil litterae, nihil doctrīna prōdest. Now neither do books avail me, nor letters, nor does learning.

29. After the conjunctions *neque* (*nec*) . . . *neque* and *aut* . . . *aut*, though either construction may be used, a singular verb is much more usual and more logical.

Neque tū neque frāter tuus adfuistis ; or *Neque tū adfuistī neque frāter tuus.* Neither you nor your brother were present.

30. A singular collective noun (see Intr. 7, *b*), especially if it denotes a united body which acts as one man, is followed by a singular verb.

Vult populus Rōmānus. It is the wish of the Roman people.

Exercitus ē castrīs profectus est. The army started from the camp.

Senātus dēcrēvit. The senate decreed.

But it may be followed by a plural verb if the writer has in mind the separate individuals.

Magna pars fūgēre. A large proportion of the men fled.

Note.—The singular is always used with *Senātus populusque ;* the two words are looked on as forming one idea.

Exercise 4

A

1. If the army and you are in good health, it is well.
2. Both you and I have waged many wars for our country.

---

[1] So also in English : 'For thine is the kingdom, the power, and the glory.'

3. The Gauls were conquered by Caesar before the end of the summer. 4. The flock returned home safe the next day. 5. Neither you nor your brother have ever done this. 6. A great number of my countrymen were at that time in exile. 7. Both you and I have been made consuls by the votes and by the kindness of the Roman people. 8. I have spared my countrymen, you the Gauls. 9. Having settled [1] these matters, he returned home on the third day. 10. Clitus was killed by Alexander with a sword. 11. The Roman people and senate decreed many honours to you and to your father. 12. Neither you nor I had looked for this reward of all our toil.

B

1. Both your brother and you were at that time in exile; my father and I were at home, exposed to the fury and cruelty of our deadliest [2] enemies. We had provoked no one either by words or acts, yet we endured much; long and sorely [3] we sighed in vain for freedom and safety; now you and I are secure and free from care, and no [4] one will any longer [5] inflict on us injury or wrong. 2. Freed from the barbarous tyranny of an alien race, we have spared those [6] who had most cruelly oppressed our country, (and) we have pardoned [7] those who in (the face of) national ruin had neglected [8] the welfare of the nation, and were consulting merely their own interests; but neither you nor I will any longer [9] consent to forgive the offences of these [10] men, or to listen to those who, having obtained rank and riches by the vilest arts, are now urging upon us a dishonourable peace.

---

[1] Abl. abs. (See **14.**)
[2] *inimīcissimī.*
[3] *multum diūque.*
[4] **358, i,** *Note.*
[5] *iam.* (See **328,** *a.*)
[6] *is.* (**70.**)
[7] See **5.**
[8] Abl. abs. (**14.**)
[9] *diūtius.* (See **328,** *a.*)
[10] *iste*, contemptuous. (See **338,** *Note* 2.)

EXERCISE V

ACCUSATIVE WITH INFINITIVE

Ōrātiō Oblīqua

31. One of the most noteworthy features of the Latin language is the use of dependent noun clauses (see Intr. 71) whose verb is an **infinitive** and whose subject is an **accusative**.

Such clauses are especially used :

(*a*) as the **subject** of impersonal verbs and phrases like *piget* 'it grieves,' *pudet* 'it shames,' *taedet* 'it wearies,' *paenitet* 'it causes regret,' '*libet* 'it pleases,' *oportet* 'it is one's duty,' *cōnstat* 'it is agreed,' *appāret* 'it is evident,' *manifēstum est* 'it is plain.'

Haec mē fēcisse pudet (*paenitet*). I am ashamed (I repent) of having done this.

Cōnstat Rōmam nōn sine labōre conditam esse. It is agreed that Rome was not built without toil.

Manifēstum est nivem esse albam. It is plain that snow is white.

(*b*) As the **object** after active verbs of *saying, thinking, knowing, believing, feeling* (**verba sentiendī ac dēclārandī**).

Hostēs adesse dīxit. He said that the enemy was near.

Respondit sē esse itūrum. He answered that he would go.

Frātrem tuum fortem esse intellegō. I perceive that your brother is a brave man.

Rem ita sē habēre videō. I see that the fact is so.

Sentīmus calēre ignem. We perceive-by-our-senses that fire is hot.

Instead of an infinitive with subject accusative, English generally uses a subordinate clause beginning with *that* and having a finite verb. But in turning such sentences into Latin, *that* must be omitted. The English *nominative* must be turned into the *accusative*, and the English verb into the *infinitive*.[1]

---

[1] We are not quite without this idiom in English: 'I saw *him to be a knave*' (='I saw *that* he was a knave').

The statement made by the noun clause dependent upon a verb of 'saying, thinking,' etc., is said to be in **ōrātiō oblīqua,** because it is not made directly (*ōrātiō rēcta*), but indirectly and in dependence upon another verb. (See also Exercises LVI and LXV.)

32. Cautions.—(*a*) Beware of ever using *quod* or *ut* to represent *that* after any verb or phrase *sentiendī vel dēclārandī*.

Never say *Scio quod errās* 'I know that you are wrong'; but always *tē errāre scio.*

(*b*) In English we often express a statement or an opinion as though it were a fact, but with such words as *he said, he thought,* etc., inserted in a parenthesis.

> You were, *he said,* mistaken. You were absent, *he thought,* from Rome. He is, *it is plain,* quite mad.

In Latin this construction must not be used; such expressions as *he said, he thought, it is plain,* must become main sentences on which an accusative with infinitive depends.

We must write—not *tū, dīxit, errāstī,* but *tē errāre dīxit*; not *Rōmā, crēdidit, aberās,* but *Rōmā tē abesse crēdidit.*

The only exception to this rule is dealt with in **40.**

33. Where English *say* introduces a negative clause, Latin transfers the negative and uses the verb *negō.*

> He says that he is not ready. *Sē parātum esse negat.*
> He said he would never do this. *Sē hoc umquam esse factūrum negāvit.*
> He says he has done nothing. *Negat sē quidquam fēcisse.*

34. The personal or demonstrative pronouns which are not used, except for clarity or emphasis (see Intr. 16), as the subject of a verb in *ōrātiō rēcta,* must always be inserted in *ōrātiō oblīqua.*

> *Currit* 'he runs'; but: *sē currere ait* 'he says he is running.'
> *Furit* 'he is mad'; but: *sē furere simulat* 'he pretends to be mad.'

He, she, they must be translated by the reflexive pronoun *sē* (11, *e*) whenever one of these pronouns stands for the *same person* as the *subject* of the verb of 'saying' or 'thinking.'

Hoc sē fēcisse negat. He says that he (himself) did not do this.

Eum or *illum* would be used if the second 'he' denoted a different person from the first 'he.' Latin is therefore much less ambiguous than English, as it carefully distinguishes the different persons denoted by 'he.'

Tenses of the Infinitive

35. The tenses of the Latin infinitive do not indicate time absolutely but only in reference to the verb on which they depend. Thus, in relation to the verb of 'saying,' etc., the *present infinitive* indicates a *contemporaneous* action, the *perfect infinitive* a *prior* action, and the *future infinitive* a *subsequent* action.

36. Therefore in translating the verb in an English *that*-clause dependent on a verb of 'saying,' we must attend carefully to the following rule :—

An English *past* tense in the *that*-clause will be translated by the *present* infinitive, if the time denoted by the verb of the subordinate clause is the same as that of the main verb.

Sē in Asiā esse dīcit. He says that he is in Asia.
Sē in Asiā esse dīxit. He said that he was in Asia. (When ?—at the time of his speaking.)

The perfect infinitive will be used only if the verb in the *that*-clause denotes a time *prior* to that of the verb *sentiendī vel dēclārandī*.

Sē in Asiā fuisse dīcit. He says he was (*or* has been) in Asia.
Sē in Asiā fuisse dīxit. He said that he had been, *or* was, in Asia. (When ?—at some time earlier than that at which he was speaking.)

The future infinitive (*-ūrum esse*) will be used if the verb in the *that*-clause denotes a time subsequent to that of the verb of 'saying,' etc.

He says that he will go. } *Sē itūrum esse* { *dīcit.*
He said that he would go. } *Sē itūrum esse* { *dīxit.*

The English *would have* in a dependent statement is represented in Latin by *-ūrum fuisse*. (See also **472.**)

> He says (said) that he would have gone. *Sē itūrum fuisse dīcit* (*dīxit*).

Verbs that have no future infinitive are dealt with in **38.**

Exercise 5

1. He had waged many wars, he answered, and was now sighing for peace and repose. 2. He says that he has not sinned. 3. Both you and your brother, he replied, were in good health. 4. He perceived that the enemy [1] would soon attack the city. 5. He says that Caesar will not break the laws. 6. It is plain that the place pleases you. 7. It was plain that the place pleased you. 8. It was plain that the place had pleased you. 9. Pompey believed that his countrymen would, one and all, follow him. 10. The soldiers said that they had not taken up arms against their country and the laws. 11. Brave men, remember, are trained by toils. 12. The soldiers answered that they would have gladly attacked the town in the preceding year, but that now they hoped for repose. 13. Having returned to the camp, he said that he had ridden past the enemies' line, and had an interview with their [2] general.

EXERCISE VI

ACCUSATIVE WITH INFINITIVE—*Continued*

37. Verbs of 'hoping' (*spērō*), 'promising' (*prōmittō, polliceor*), 'swearing' (*iūrō*), 'threatening' (*minor*) generally have reference to a subsequent action. In Latin, therefore, the infinitive of a verb dependent upon them is **future.**

---

[1] Sing.

[2] Gen. pl. of *is*: why would *suus* be wrong? (See **11**, *d* and *e*.)

Since the English equivalents of such verbs often have a present infinitive associated with them, special care must be taken when translating into Latin.

Spērat plērumque adulēscēns diū sē victūrum (esse).[1] A young man generally hopes to live a long time.
Hoc sē factūrum esse minātus est. He threatened to do this.

38. When the verb in a dependent statement is an active one which has no future infinitive, Latin is compelled to use *futūrum esse* or *fore* (the future infinitive of *esse*) with the subjunctive of the verb concerned introduced by *ut*.

Spērāvit fore ut id sibi contingeret. He hoped that this would fall to his lot.

This periphrastic construction is also generally used when the dependent verb is passive, and is sometimes used even as a substitute for the ordinary construction.

Spērō fore ut dēleātur Carthāgō. I hope that Carthage will be annihilated.

Note.—The *tense* of the subjunctive after *fore* depends upon that of the verb of 'hoping,' etc.; after the present, perfect with *have*, future, and future perfect, the present subjunctive is used; after a past tense, the imperfect subjunctive is used.

39. In a dependent statement, the present infinitive *posse* is often used with future meaning.

Hoc sē facere posse spērat. He hopes he will be able to do this.

40. The great exception to the construction of *verba dēclārandī* is *inquam, inquit,*—'say I,' 'says he.'

Inquit always quotes the *exact words used*, and never stands first.

Domum, inquit, redībō. 'I will,' says he, 'return home.'
Domum sē reditūrum esse dīcit. He says he will return home.

Inquit therefore is always used with *ōrātiō rēcta*; all other words of *saying* with *ōrātiō oblīqua*.

Note.—*Aiō* is occasionally used, like *inquam*, parenthetically in *ōrātiō rēcta*.

---

[1] The *esse* which normally forms part of the future active infinitive is frequently omitted.

41. The infinitive with subject accusative is used also as the *object* of—

(*a*) A small number of verbs of 'commanding' (*iubeō*), 'allowing' (*sinō, patior*), and 'forbidding' (*vetō, prohibeō*).

Mīlitēs abīre iussit (*sīvit, vetuit*). He ordered (allowed, forbade) the soldiers to depart.

(*b*) The verbs *volō, nōlō, mālō, cupiō*, **but** only when the subject of the infinitive is different from that of the main verb. (Contrast **45.**)

Tē venīre nōlō. I do not wish you to come.

(*c*) Verbs expressing 'joy, sorrow, indignation, wonder.'

Tē incolumem rediisse gaudeō (*mīror*). I rejoice (am surprised) that you have returned safely.

Exercise 6

A

1. Solon pretended to be out of his mind. 2. I will pretend, says he, to be out of my mind. 3. He promised to come to London shortly. 4. I hope that you will have a satisfactory voyage. 5. He hopes to obtain the crown presently. 6. He was pretending to be quite mad. 7. Caesar threatened to lay waste our country with fire and sword. 8. He replied that he had had a satisfaetory voyage. 9. He swore to finish the business by force. 10. He says that he will not return home earlier than the fifth day. 11. He replied that he had not yet seen his sister, but (that he) hoped to find both her and her husband at home. 12. The army hoped that the land of the enemy would now be laid waste with fire and sword. 13. He hopes soon to attain to the highest honours, but [1] I believe that he will never win them. 14. I rejoice greatly that your nation, (which has been) so long oppressed by a cruel foe, has at last asserted its freedom by the sword. 15. I have not, says she, yet seen my sister, but I hope to find both her and her [2] husband at home.

---

[1] See **13.** [2] *Eius.* Why not a case of *suus*? (See **11**, *e.*)

B

1. You and I were, he replied, in the country with [1] your brother, and would not return to Naples on the first [2] of August. I believe that he made [3] a great mistake, and that [4] not designedly but by pure [5] accident; for I do not imagine that he would have endeavoured to deceive a friend and guest; but we shall, it is plain, be looked for in vain both by your father and my relations. 2. He ascertained that the weather had changed,[6] and that the crowd, which had gathered together in the morning, would soon disperse. He hoped therefore before night to be able to leave his house, and reach our camp in safety. Having arrived there,[7] he wished to have an interview with Caesar, whom he hoped to join, and from whom he was anxious to obtain safety and assistance; for he hoped by his [8] aid to attain to the highest rank and office in his [8] own nation.

EXERCISE VII

NOMINATIVE WITH INFINITIVE

42. (i) There is in Latin, as in English, a large number of verbs which generally have as their object the infinitive of another verb. (See Intr. 34.)

Such are verbs of—

(*a*) Possibility (or the reverse). *Possum, nequeō.*

(*b*) Duty, habit. *Dēbeō; soleō, assuēscō, cōnsuēvī.*

---

[1] *i.e.* 'in the house of,' *apud.* (**331**, 4.)

[2] *Kalendīs Sextīlibus.* (See **538**.)

[3] Use *multum* or *vehementer* with a verb.

[4] *neque id.* (Cf. **344**.)

[5] Use two adverbs with *ac.* (See Vocab., under *chance.*)

[6] Abl. abs. (**14**.)

[7] 'Whither when he had arrived.' (**14**.)

[8] See **11**, *d* and *e*.

(*c*) Wish,[1] purpose, daring, endeavour. *Volō, nōlō, mālō, cupiō, optō ; statuō, cōnstituō ; audeō ; cōnor.*

(*d*) Beginning,[2] ceasing, continuing. *Coepī, incipiō ; dēsinō, dēsistō ; pergō, persevērō.*

(*e*) Hastening, hesitating. *Festīnō, properō, mātūrō ; dubitō.*[3]

(*f*) Learning, knowing how. *Discō, doceō ; scio.*[4]

(ii) When, as often happens, the infinitive is accompanied by a **predicative** noun or adjective referring to the subject of the governing verb, that noun or adjective is **nominative** (*not* accusative).

Cīvis Rōmānus fierī (*vocārī*) *cupiō.* I am anxious to become (to be called) a citizen of Rome.

Soleō (*incipiō, festīnō*) *ōtiōsus esse.* I am accustomed (I am beginning, I am making haste) to be at leisure.

Morī mālō quam servus esse. I had rather die than be a slave.

43. A similar construction is used with the **passives** of verbs of 'saying' and 'thinking,' which in Latin are used *personally* rather than impersonally.

Dīcitur Cicerō cōnsul fuisse. Cicero is said to have been consul.

If *dīcitur* were regarded as impersonal, 'it is said,' it would be followed by an accusative with infinitive clause ; but the Romans preferred to regard *dīcitur* as personal, 'he is said,' and consequently used with it an infinitive and (where necessary) a nominative noun or adjective in the predicate. *Dīcitur Cicerōnem cōnsulem fuisse* would be bad Latin.

Note 1.—When a first or second person is involved, special care is necessary. For 'it is said that I am just' we must write *dīcor iūstus esse*, **not** *dīcitur mē iūstum esse.*

Note 2.—The passive of *videō* is also used personally with a similar construction: *videor esse fortis* 'I seem to be brave'; *vidētur esse caecus* 'he seems to be blind.' Consequently 'It seems that I am dear to you' should be rendered by *videor tibi cārus esse*, **not** by *vidētur mē tibi cārum esse.*

---

[1] Sometimes expressed by the termination *-uriō*: *edō*, I eat ; *ēsuriō*, I am hungry. Such verbs are called *desiderative.*

[2] Sometimes expressed by the termination *-scō* of the verb : *senēscō*, I begin to grow old. Such verbs are called *inchoative.*

[3] *Dubitō* takes an infinitive only when it means 'I hesitate' and is also negatived or used in an interrogative sentence. See also 136.

[4] Distinguish between *scio nāre* 'I know *how* to swim' and *scio tē fortem esse* 'I know that you are brave.'

44. But very common is the use of the active forms *ferunt, dīcunt, trādunt,* 'they *or* men say,' followed by the accusative and infinitive. So that for 'There is a tradition that Homer was blind,' we may say either *Trāditur Homērus caecus fuisse,* or *Trādunt Homērum caecum fuisse,* but **not** *Trāditur Homērum caecum fuisse.*

45. Verbs of *wish* and *purpose* obviously can have this infinitive with nominative construction only when *the subject of the infinitive is the same as that of the main verb.*

Cōnstituit (voluit) Caesar cōnsul fierī. Caesar determined (wished) to become consul.

But

Cōnstituit Caesar ut Antōnius cōnsul fieret. (See **118,** *d.*)
Voluit Caesar Antōnium cōnsulem fierī. (See **41,** *b.*)
Caesar determined (wished) that Antony should be made consul.

46. EXCEPTIONS

(*a*) The **perfect** passive of verbs of 'saying' and 'thinking' is often used impersonally, and is consequently followed by the accusative and infinitive.

Caesarī nūntiātum est adesse Gallōs. News was brought to Caesar that the Gauls were at hand.

(*b*) *Vidētur* can be used impersonally, but means, not 'it seems,' but 'it seems *good.*'

Haec mihi facere vīsum est. It seemed good to me (I resolved) to do this.

(*c*) Impersonal verbs and phrases (see **31,** *a*), from their very nature, cannot take the nominative with infinitive construction, but must be followed by the accusative and infinitive.

Exercise 7

A

1. I had rather keep my promises than be the richest man in the world. 2. I begin to be troublesome to you. 3. Cease then to be cowards and begin to become patriots. 4. He resolved to return at once to Rome and become a good member of the state. 5. It seems that he was unwilling to become king, and preferred to be a private

person. 6. It is said that by the verdict of the jury you had been freed from all blame. 7. Having [1] resolved to be a candidate for office, I ventured to return home and ask for your votes. 8. We would rather die free than live (as) slaves. 9. There is a tradition that he refused to accept the crown (when) offered by the nation and (its) chief men. 10. It was clear [2] that the destined day was now at hand; but the townsmen were unwilling either to despair or to surrender. 11. He said that he had neither broken his word nor deceived the nation. 12. The senate [3] and people resolved that ambassadors should be sent to Pyrrhus.

B

1. News was now brought to me that my brother, having been struck by a javelin, and exhausted by many [4] serious wounds, was no longer able either to keep [5] the saddle, or lead his men [6] against the enemy. Having [7] heard this, I was much affected, for I could neither hurry to him as [8] I wished to do, nor did I expect that he would be able any longer to keep the enemy in check. It seemed, moreover, that the soldiers who were with [9] me were losing heart, and it was said that the enemy was expecting large reinforcements before night, and would soon take the offensive. I resolved therefore to try to finish the matter by a single charge. 2. Your brother was, he said, a man of [10] kindly heart, and abounded [11] in wealth and resources; and he was sure that he would never desert his friends, nor wish such a blow to be inflicted on his own relations. 3. It seems that he had resolved to become consul in that year, but that he pretended to be craving for repose and quiet. 4. He was unwilling, he replied, to despair, but would rather be in exile than be a slave.

---

[1] See **14**. [2] Imperfect tense. [3] See **30**, *Note*.
[4] See below, **56**. [5] *in equō haerēre*. [6] *suī*. (See **50**.)
[7] See **14**. [8] **67**, *Note*. [9] **8**, *Note*.
[10] Abl. (See **271**.) [11] *abundō* or *circumfluō*. (**284**.)

EXERCISE VIII

ADJECTIVES

Agreement of Adjectives

47. When a single adjective or participle is **predicated of several nouns,** much variety of construction is allowed.

(*a*) If several *persons* are spoken of, the adjective is generally in the *plural,* and the masculine gender takes precedence over the feminine.

Et pater mihi et māter mortuī sunt. Both my father and mother are dead.

(*b*) But the predicate may agree both in *gender* and *number* with the substantive nearest to itself, especially when it precedes the compound subject. Thus a brother might say for 'Both my sister and I had been summoned to the praetor,' either *Et ego et soror mea ad praetōrem vocātī erāmus,* or *Vocātus eram ad praetōrem ego et soror mea.* Compare the use of a singular verb with a compound subject (27).

48. (*a*) If the nouns are not persons but *things,* the adjective or participle is usually in the plural, and agrees in gender if all the nouns are of the same gender.

Fidēs tua et pietās laudandae sunt. Your good faith and dutifulness are to be praised.

But *laudanda est* or *laudanda sunt* would also be allowable. (See *c* and *d*.)

(*b*) If they are of different genders the adjective is generally in the *neuter.*

Glōria, dīvitiae, honōrēs incerta ac cadūca sunt. Glory, riches, and distinctions are uncertain and perishable (things).

(*c*) Where the subject consists of **abstract nouns** (Intr. 7, *c*), the neuter is common in the predicate, even if the nouns are of the same gender.

Fidēs et pietās laudanda sunt. Good faith and a sense of duty are to be praised.

The neuter *laudanda* means '*things* to be praised' (as *incerta ac cadūca* in *b*).

(*d*) Sometimes, but more rarely, the predicate agrees in gender and number with the substantive nearest itself.

Spernendae igitur sunt dīvitiae et honōrēs. Riches then, and distinctions, are to be despised.

Mihi prīncipātus atque imperium dēlātum est. The sovereignty and chief power were offered to me.

49. When a single adjective is used as the **attribute** of two or more substantives of different genders, it usually agrees with the one nearest itself. Either *Terrās omnēs et maria perlūstrāvit*, or *Terrās et maria omnia perlūstrāvit* 'He travelled over all lands and seas.'

It is sometimes repeated with each : *terrās omnēs, maria omnia*, etc.

These rules will cause very little real difficulty, as the freedom which they allow is great. The Exercise will be mainly on what follows.

Adjectives used as Nouns

50. Where English uses the nouns 'men,' 'things,' qualified by an adjective, Latin frequently uses an adjective as a noun ; for the inflexions of the Latin adjective are a sufficient indication of gender. (See Intr. 12.)

Bonī[1] *sapientēsque* (*ex*)[2] *cīvitāte pelluntur.* The good and wise men are being banished (*literally*, driven from the state).

Iam nostrī aderant. Our men (*or* soldiers) were now at hand.

Omnia mea mēcum portō. I am carrying all my property with me.

51. Hence many adjectives, pronominal adjectives, and participles, both singular and plural, masculine and neuter, are used precisely as nouns, and may even have other adjectives attached, or *attributed* to them.

---

[1] *Bonī* thus used means generally, 'the well-affected,' 'the patriotic party'; opposed to *improbī* 'the disaffected.'

[2] The ablative may be used here without the preposition.

(*a*) Masculine—

(Singular) *adulēscēns*,[1] *iuvenis* (young man), *amīcus*, *inimīcus*; *aequālis* (a contemporary, one of the same age), *candidātus*, *socius*.

(Plural) *nōbilēs*,[2] *optimātēs* (the aristocracy), *maiōrēs*[3] (ancestors), *posterī* (posterity), *dīvitēs* (the rich), and many others.

(*b*) Neuter—

factum, a deed; *dictum*, a saying; *bona*, property; *dēcrētum*, a decree; *prōmissa*, promises; *ēdictum*, a proclamation; *senātūs cōnsultum*, a vote or resolution of the senate, etc.

(*c*) Also the neuter adjectives *honestum*, *ūtile*, *commodum*, *vērum*, are used in the singular, and still more in the plural, for the English abstract words 'duty,' 'expediency,' 'advantage,' 'truth.'

Note.—But when an oblique case or an adjectival qualification is needed the abstract nouns *honestās*, *ūtilitās* are preferred.

52. Ambiguous expressions must be avoided in Latin, no less than in English. Consequently an adjective is not used as a noun when it would be doubtful whether 'men' or 'things' was meant. In such circumstances we must use *rēs* 'thing' with a feminine adjective, or *vir* (*homō*) with a masculine adjective. So—

Futūra, the future; but *rērum futūrārum*, of the future; *bonī*, the good, *or* well-affected; but *bonōrum virōrum*, of the well-affected.

53. The neuter *plural* of Latin adjectives is constantly used in the nominative and accusative cases where we use a *singular* noun.

So *Vēra et falsa*. Truth and falsehood.
Vēra dīcēbat. He was speaking the truth.

---

[1] *Adulēscēns* denotes a younger age than *iuvenis*—it embraces the period from boyhood to the prime of life; *iuvenis* is used of all men fit to bear arms.

[2] *Nōbilēs* 'nobles,' *i.e.* men whose ancestors had borne a curule office; opposed to *novī hominēs* 'self-made men.' *Nōbilis* never means 'noble' in a moral sense. *Optimātēs*, the aristocracy, as opposed to the popular party, or *populārēs*.

[3] *Patrēs*, *avī*, are never used in prose for 'forefathers,' but denote 'men of the last generation' and 'of the last but one.' *Minōrēs*, *nepōtēs*, etc., are used for 'posterity' only in poetry.

Words similarly used are—

Multa, much.
Permulta, very much.
Pauca, little.
Perpauca, very little.
Omnia, everything.
Haec omnia, all this.

54. Such plural neuter adjectives are used as nouns in Latin where we use not 'things,' but some more specific noun, as *property*, *objects*, *possessions*, *performances*, *thoughts*, *reflections*, etc.

His hopes were high.	*Magna spērābat.*
He was revolving many thoughts.	*Multa cōgitābat.*
He ventured on those enterprises.	*Illa ausus est.*
He told many falsehoods.	*Multa mentītus est.*

The neuter of pronouns is also used in this way.

This was his object.	*Haec secūtus est.*
What falsehoods has he told?	*Quae mentītus est?*

These are some of the many instances in which the English noun cannot be translated literally into Latin.

Note.—Observe from the above examples that Latin often uses a *verb* of strong and distinctive meaning where English uses a strong and distinctive *noun*.

55. The fact that adjectives and participles can be used sometimes as nouns and sometimes as true adjectives or participles, makes possible some variety of expression. So we can say :—

Cicerōnis est amīcus (substantival), 'he is the friend of Cicero,' or *Cicerōnī est amīcus* (adjectival), 'he is friendly to Cicero.'

Multa fuēre eius et praeclāra facta (substantival), 'many and distinguished were his deeds,' or *multa ab eō praeclārē facta sunt* (participial), 'many distinguished things were performed by him.'

Other uses of Adjectives

56. In English we join the adjective *many* with another adjective, 'many excellent men.' In Latin we should insert a conjunction : *hominēs multī optimīque ; multī atque optimī hominēs ;* or . . . *multī, iīque optimī.*

Of course we can say *adulēscentēs multī* or *amīcī multī*, because these words are used as substantives.

If an adjective is so constantly united with its noun as

to form a single expression, the whole phrase may be qualified by another adjective without a conjunction.

Multae nāvēs longae. Many ships of war.

57. (*a*) The superlative degree of adjectives and adverbs is often used in Latin to mark merely a high degree of a quality.

Optimus, excellent; *praeclārissimus*, famous *or* noble.

Hoc molestissimum est. This is exceedingly, *or* very troublesome.

Hoc saepissimē dīxī. I have said this repeatedly, *or* again and again.

(*b*) So also the comparative degree is often used, without any direct idea of comparison, to express a *considerable*, *excessive*, or *too great* amount. It may then be translated by 'rather,' 'somewhat,' 'too,' etc., or by a simple adjective in the positive degree.

Saepius, somewhat often; *asperius*, with excessive harshness; *morbus gravior*, a serious illness.

Exercise 8

A

1. He said that he would never [1] banish the good and wise. 2. We are all ignorant of much. 3. He said that courage and cowardice were contrary to each other. 4. It appears that he was banished with you, not by the dictator himself, but by a praiseworthy vote of the senate. 5. He resolved to abandon the aristocratic and to join the popular party. 6. He said that rashness and change of purpose were not to be praised. 7. He was an excellent youth, and a most faithful friend to me; he had much conversation with me that day about the future. 8. Having returned to Rome, he promised to transact everything for [2] his father. 9. The army was led by Hannibal through many pathless defiles, and across many broad rivers, many lofty mountains, and unhealthy [3] marshes, into the

[1] See 33. [2] See 6, *Note*. [3] Superl. (See 57, *a*.)

country of the enemy. 10. You will scarcely venture to deny that duty was sometimes at variance with interest. 11. I know that your forefathers ventured on many glorious enterprises. 12. He makes many promises, many threats, but I believe that he will accomplish very little.

B

1. You, said he, were meditating on the past; I was attempting to foretell the future. I now perceive that both you and I were mistaken. 2. He tells (us) that he has been driven by these brothers, his deadly enemies, from his throne and native land; that they are persecuting with unjust [1] proclamations and decrees all the well-affected, all the wise; that no one's property or good name is [2] spared; that rich and poor are alike oppressed. 3. I hope to write a list of the many striking sayings of your grandfather. 4. These objects, said he, did our forefathers pursue; these hopes did they form; these traditions have they handed down to posterity. 5. It is allowed that many noble deeds were done by him. 6. I rejoice that you spoke little and thought much. 7. It is said that many merchant vessels were shattered and sunk or driven on shore by many violent storms last winter.

C

1. He talked very little about the past; about the future his hopes were high, but he perceived that he was at variance on this question [3] with many excellent men; and he preferred being [4] silent to disagreeing [4] with them. Neither you nor I can think that he was mistaken, for we know that his good sense, honesty, and courage were worthy of all praise. 2. He promised to send me [5] a letter on the 15th of March, [6] and made many other fine pretences [7];

---

[1] Superl. [2] See 5. [3] *in hāc causā*, lit. 'in this suit.'
[4] Infinitive. (See 42 and 94.)
[5] *ad mē*. (See 6.) [6] See 538. [7] See 54.

but he has neither kept his promises, nor does he any longer venture to make a secret of having purposely broken his word. 3. He threatens, they say, to take from me all the distinctions which I have obtained from the senate and people of Rome; for myself,[1] I hardly think he will succeed in this design. 4. He would rather, he replied, obey the most unjust laws than be at variance with true patriots and disagree with every sensible[2] man. 5. We scarcely dare to hope that your brother will return to Rome and imitate the noble acts of his forefathers; but all his contemporaries can guarantee[3] that he will never desert his friends, or break his word, or join the enemies of his native land.

EXERCISE IX

ADJECTIVES—*Continued.* ADVERBS

58. In Latin, as in English, the meaning of a noun is sometimes qualified not by an adjective but by the genitive case of another noun; so with 'the royal palace,' compare 'the king's army.' But though the relation between adjective and genitive case is very similar in both languages, the Latin usages are not precisely identical with the English.

(i) The Latin adjective is often used where in English we employ the preposition 'of' with a noun. Thus—

Rēs aliēnae. The affairs of others.
Condiciō servīlis. The condition (*or* state) of slavery.
Vir fortis. A man of courage.

So often with proper names—

Pugna Cannēnsis (not *Cannārum*). The battle of Cannae.
Populus Rōmānus (never *Rōmae*). The people of Rome.

Note.—So *vir fortissimus* 'a man of the greatest courage.' In Latin an adjectival genitive of quality may be used only when the genitive itself is qualified by an adjective or pronoun. We can say *vir summae fortitūdinis;* not *vir fortitūdinis.* (See 303.)

---

[1] *ego* or *equidem.* (11, *a.*)
[2] Superlative with *quisque.* (375.)
[3] Use *spondeō.*

59. (ii) Sometimes we must use a genitive because the adjective is wanting, or rarely used, in Latin.

Corporis (animī) dolor. Bodily (mental) pain.

Omnium iūdiciō (sententiīs). By a unanimous verdict, *or* unanimously.

In hōc omnium lūctū. In this universal mourning.

Meā ūnīus sententiā. By my single vote.

Post hominum memoriam. Within human memory.

60. (iii) Certain Latin adjectives are used where we use a noun expressing *whole, end, middle, top,* etc., followed by 'of.' Thus—

Summus mōns. The top of the mountain.

In mediam viam. Into the middle (*or* centre) of the road.

Reliquum opus. The rest of the work.

Īma vallis. The bottom of the valley.

Novissimum agmen. The rear of the line of march.

Tōta Graecia. The whole of Greece.

Summa temeritās. The height of rashness.

Note.—These adjectives, especially where, as with *summus, medius,* etc., ambiguity might arise, generally stand before the substantive, not, as the attribute usually does, after it. (See Intr. 85.)

61. (iv) An adjective in agreement with the subject (or object) of the sentence is often used where in English we should use either an *adverb* or an *adverbial phrase, i.e.* a preposition and noun.

Invītus haec dīcō. I say this unwillingly, *or* with reluctance, *or* against my will.

Tacitus haec cōgitābam. I was meditating silently, *or* in silence, on these subjects.

Imprūdēns hūc vēnī. I came here unawares.

Incolumis rediī. I returned safely, *or* in safety.

Absēns condemnātus est. He was condemned in his absence.

Tōtus dissentiō. I disagree wholly (*or* entirely).

Frequentēs convēnēre. They came together in crowds.

Vīvus. In his lifetime. *Mortuus.* After his death.

Diversī fūgēre. They fled in opposite directions.

62. (v) The adjectives *sōlus* (*ūnus*), *prīmus* (*prior* if of two), *ultimus,* are used in agreement with the *subject* of a sentence to express 'only,' 'first,' 'last,' where we should add a relative clause, or an infinitive mood, and put the adjective in the *predicate* of the main sentence.

Prīmus haec fēcit. He was the first who did this, *or* to do this.
Sōlus mala nostra sēnsit. He was the only person who perceived our evils.
Ultimus vēnisse dīcitur. It is said (43) that he was the last to come.

63. Certain nouns also, especially those which relate to *time*, *age*, and *office*, are used in apposition to the subject (or object) of a verb, where in English we should use an adverbial phrase.

Hoc puer (adulēscēns, senex) didicī. I learned this lesson (54) in my boyhood (youth, old age).
Hoc cōnsul vōvit. He made this vow in his consulship, *or* as consul.
Victor rediit. When victorious (in the hour of triumph), he returned.

64. A single adverb in Latin will often represent a whole adverbial phrase in English; and on the other hand an English adverb will often require a Latin phrase, or whole clause, or combination of words. Thus—

Piē. With a good conscience.
Dīvīnitus. By a supernatural interposition.
Omnīnō. Speaking in general, as a general rule, etc.

Easily. *Nūllō negōtiō.*
Indisputably. *Dubitārī nōn potest quīn* . . . (See 135.)
Fortunately. *Opportūnē accidit ut* . . . (See 126.)
Possibly. *Fierī potest ut* . . .
You are obviously mistaken. *Errāre tē manifēstum est.*
You are apparently unwell. *Aegrōtāre vidēris.*

It must therefore never be taken for granted that an adverb in one language can be translated by the same part of speech in the other.

Exercise 9

A

1. He said that the management of other people's affairs was always exceedingly[1] troublesome. 2. In this universal panic your brother was the first to recover himself. 3. I

[1] To be expressed by superlative adj. (See 57.)

obeyed, said he, the law [1] in my youth; I will not break it in my old age. 4. I was the first to venture on these enterprises; I will be the last to relinquish them. 5. In his lifetime we neglected this poet; after his death we honour him with a state funeral, a marble tomb, many beautiful [2] monuments, and every kind of distinction. 6. The king, having been (**14**) the first to reach the summit of the mountain, looked down in silence on the fair plains spread beneath his eye (*pl.*). 7. He turned [3] to his companions and pointed out the farmhouse in which he had been born, and brought up in his boyhood; too late, said he, has fortune changed. 8. He promised to supply the army of Rome with food and clothing. 9. I read through the whole of this proclamation in silence; it seemed to me that he who wrote and posted it up (when) written was out of his mind. 10. He was unanimously acquitted, and returned home in safety; the next year he attained with universal consent to the highest office in the nation. 11. The soldiers, having gathered together in crowds, listened to his speech in silence. 12. I entrust myself wholly to your good faith and kindness. 13. No one can with a good conscience deny that your brother returned home in safety by a miraculous interposition.

B

1. You (*pl.*) have come here [4] manifestly with reluctance, and you say that you will not [5] wait any longer for the arrival of your friends, who will, you think,[6] be far from [7] secure in our camp. For myself, I have promised you again and again to say nothing about the past, and I have resolved both to pardon you, and to spare them. But you

---

[1] Plural. *Lēx* (sing.) is seldom used in an *abstract* sense; it means *a* law.

[2] Superl. (**57.**) [3] Participle. (See **15.**)

[4] Why not *hīc*? *Hūc* is used after verbs of motion.

[5] **33.** [6] **32,** *b.* [7] *parum* 'but little.'

apparently expect that in the hour of triumph I shall break my word and act [1] towards [2] you and them with the height of treachery. I know that you can scarcely believe that I am speaking the truth, and that you are silently despairing both of your own and your children's safety. What falsehood [3] have I ever told ? When have I ever broken my word ? 2. It is said that the king himself was the only one of [4] the whole of his army to ride in safety past the fatal marsh (*pl.*), and the first to reach the foot of the mountains, whence on the next day he mournfully and reluctantly led back his troops. He never [5] again ventured to form such high hopes or embark [6] on such great enterprises. It seemed that as [7] he had been the first to hope for the best,[8] so he was the first to abandon his undertaking ; he preferred to appear fickle and cowardly rather than to bring ruin and destruction on his country.

EXERCISE X

THE RELATIVE

65. The relative pronoun *quī* which introduces an adjectival clause (see Intr. 72) agrees in number and gender with its antecedent, but its case depends on the construction of its own clause.

> *Mulierem aspiciō quae piscēs vēndit.* I see a woman who is selling fish.
>
> *Ubi est puer cui librum dedistī ?* Where is the boy to whom you gave the book ?
>
> *Adsum quī fēcī.* I, who did the deed, am here.

---

[1] 'employ (*ūtor* with abl.) treachery.'
[2] *in vōbīs* 'in your case.' [3] See **54.** [4] *ē, ex* 'out of.'
[5] *nec umquam posteā.* Never join *et* with *numquam*, or any negative word.
[6] Metaphor. Use *mōlīrī*, and see **54.**
[7] *sīcut . . . ita*, or *et . . . et.* [8] Neut. pl.

66. Where there is more than one antecedent, the rules for the number and gender of the relative are the same as those for predicative adjectives. (See **47**, **48**.)

Pater eius et māter quī aderant. His father and mother who were present. (**47**, *a*.)

Dīvitiae et honōrēs quae cadūca sunt. Riches and distinctions, which are perishable (things). (**48**, *b*.)

67. Sometimes a relative clause refers not to a single word, but to the *whole statement* made by the main sentence. When this is the case, the main sentence is summed up in an appositional *id* (or *rēs*), to which the *quod* (or *quae*) of the subordinate clause refers.

Tīmoleōn, id quod difficilius putātur, sapientius tulit secundam quam adversam fortūnam. Timoleon, though this (*lit.* a thing which) is thought the more difficult (task), bore prosperity more wisely than adversity.

Multae cīvitātēs ā Cȳrō dēfēcērunt, quae rēs multōrum bellōrum causa fuit. Many states revolted from Cyrus; and this (see **13**) (circumstance) was the cause of many wars.

Note.—*As* is often used in English as equivalent to *a thing which*, or *which*, in reference to a whole clause.

He, as you have heard, died at Rome. *Ille, id quod audiistī, Rōmae mortem obiit.*

68. A relative pronoun in the accusative case is frequently omitted in English, but never in Latin.

This is the man I saw. *Hic est quem vīdī.*

He found the books he wanted. *Librōs quōs voluit repperit.*

69. In English an adjective which refers to the antecedent is kept in the main sentence; but in Latin a *superlative* adjective, or any *emphatic* adjective (especially those of *number* or *amount*) which refers to the antecedent, is placed in the relative clause.

Volscī cīvitātem, quam habēbant optimam, perdidērunt. The Volsci lost the best city they had.

Equitēs, quōs paucōs sēcum habuit, dīmīsit. He sent away the few mounted men whom he had with him.

Note.—Frequently in Latin we find parenthetic relative clauses like: *quā es prūdentiā* 'such is your prudence.' They arise from the placing of the logical antecedent (*prūdentiā*) in the relative clause. So *animī benignitāte, quā erat, omnibus veniam dedit* becomes *quā erat animī benignitāte, omnibus veniam dedit*, 'Such was his kindliness, he pardoned all.'

Use of *quī* with *is*

70. The demonstrative pronoun which corresponds to *quī*, as 'he' to 'who,' is not *ille*, but *is*. *Ille* is used only when great emphasis is laid on the 'he'; 'that *well known*, or that *other* person.' *Is* may be thus used of all three persons.

I am the man I always was. *Is sum quī semper fuī.*

71. When the antecedent *is* would be in the same case as the relative, it is generally omitted; but otherwise it must be used.

Quī haec vidēbant, flēbant. Those who saw this (the spectators) wept.

Eīs, quī adstābant, īrāscēbātur. He was angry with those who stood by (the bystanders).

72. *Is*, *iī*, etc., often answer to our 'one,' 'men,' 'a man,' when used to denote a class of persons.

Eum quī haec facit ōdī. I hate one who (*or* a man who) does this.

Eōs quī haec faciunt ōdī. I hate men who do this.

Is, however, is omitted under the conditions mentioned in 71.

Quī haec faciunt, peiōra facient. Men who are doing this will do worse.

73. A relative clause, however, is not the only way of denoting a class of persons; for the oblique cases of a participle, especially the genitive and dative, are often used to represent 'him who,' 'those who.'

Adstantium clāmōre perterritus. Alarmed by the shouts of the bystanders (*or* of those who stood by, *or* of those standing by).

Interrogantibus respondit. He replied to those who questioned him (*or* to those questioning him, *or* to his interrogators).

74. But we must never combine any case of *is* with a participle to denote a class. *Eōrum adstantium, eōs adstantēs*, is very bad Latin for 'those who stood by,' *or* 'those standing by.' (See **346.**)

75. Sometimes the force of the demonstrative in *is quī*, and similar combinations, *hic quī*, etc., is emphasised by placing the relative clause first, and the demonstrative pronoun with the main sentence afterwards.

> *Quī tum tē dēfendit, is hodiē accūsat.* He who (the very man who) then defended you is to-day accusing you. Your former advocate is your present accuser.

This construction is always to be used where a strong contrast is dwelt on.

76. Observe how often an English noun has to be expressed in Latin by a clause beginning with *quī, is quī, ea quae*, etc., *i.e.* by an *adjectival clause*. Thus—

> *Quī mē cēpērunt*, my captors; *quī mē vīcit*, my conqueror; (*ea*) *quae vēra sunt*, the truth.

(See **175.**)

Exercise 10

1. Those [1] who were in agreement with you yesterday, to-day entirely disagree (with you). 2. Both you and I despise one who [1] would rather be a slave with [2] riches than free with poverty. 3. We know that he, concerning whom you have told us this story, expects to attain to the highest offices, the greatest distinctions; but [3] I hope that he will never obtain them, for I know the man. 4. I who [4] repeatedly opposed you in your youth, will gladly come to your assistance in your old age and helplessness. 5. I sent you the best and bravest foot-soldiers that I had with me; and having promised [5] to send them back, you reluctantly kept your word. 6. He ordered those standing by (him) to follow him; but they were dismayed by the shouts of those who were coming to meet (him). They first halted, and then suddenly scattered and fled in different directions. 7. The woman for whom you were seeking is present; I will therefore [3] hear and dismiss her. 8. The best institutions and laws you have set at nought, and this [6] will be your ruin to-day. 9. The things [4] which I treated lightly in my boyhood, I value

---

[1] Place the relative clause first, and use *is* in the main sentence. (See **75.**)
[2] See **8,** *b*.
[3] See **13.**
[4] See **75.**
[5] See **14.**
[6] See **67.**

highly in my old age. 10. I who[1] was the last to come to your assistance on that occasion, will be the first to join you to-morrow.

EXERCISE XI

THE RELATIVE—*Continued*

77. When the relative *quī* introduces a clause which merely states a **fact** about the antecedent, the verb is indicative.

> *Est flūmen quod appellātur Tamesis.* There is a river which is called the Thames.

Note.—But if the verb in the main sentence is in *ōrātiō oblīqua*, *i.e.* is an infinitive after a verb of *saying* or *thinking*, the verb in the *quī*-clause (as in all other types of subordinate clause) will be *subjunctive.*

Thus *Mulierem aspiciō quae piscēs vēndit.* (*Ōrātiō rēcta.*) I see a woman who is selling fish.

But *Ait sē mulierem aspicere quae piscēs vēndat.* (*Ōrātiō oblīqua.*) He says that he sees a woman who is selling fish.

Quī-clauses which have a subjunctive verb even in *ōrātiō rēcta* are dealt with in Exercises LXIII, LXIV.

78. A *quī*-clause is often used in Latin where English uses a co-ordinating conjunction (*and, but, so, therefore,* etc.) and a demonstrative, to connect together co-ordinate sentences. (See **13.**)

> *Ad rēgem vēnī, quem cum vīdissem. . . .* I came to the king, and when I had seen him. . . .

Note.—Such clauses are sometimes called co-ordinating *quī*-clauses, and the *quī* which introduces them is equivalent to *et is.*

79. Indeed the Latin *relative* is often used where we should use a *demonstrative* only. Thus nothing is commoner than for Latin sentences to begin with—*Quibus audītīs,* having heard this; *Quod ubi vīdit,* when he saw this; *quam ob rem,* and therefore, *or* therefore. But in all such sentences the Latin relative refers to what has gone before.

---

[1] See **75.**

Note.—When a relative clause that is felt to be co-ordinate in *thought* to the main sentence forms part of *ōrātiō oblīqua,* its verb is put in the infinitive like the verb of the main sentence.

Dīxit prōditōrem esse eum . . . quem brevī peritūrum esse. He said that he was a traitor . . . and that he would soon perish.

80. '*But*' after universal negatives, such as 'nobody' (in Latin *nēmō, nūllus*), is equivalent to 'who not,' and should be translated by *quī nōn*, or by *quīn* [1] if the relative is in the *nominative* (or occasionally the *accusative*) case; and the verb in such a clause should be subjunctive. (See **505.**)

Nēmō est quīn tē dēmentem putet. There is no one but thinks you mad; *or* the whole world thinks, etc.

Nēmō fuit quīn vīderim. There was no one whom I did not see (but *quem nōn* is more usual).

81. It has been already said (**62**) that where English uses a relative with a word such as *only, first, last* as its antecedent, Latin uses not a relative clause, but an adjective in agreement with the subject of the sentence.

He was the first who did this. *Prīmus haec fēcit.*

82. An emphatic order of words often expresses in Latin what English can express only by a relative clause following a main sentence which begins with the impersonal *it.*

Agricolam laudat iūris lēgumque perītus. It is the farmer whom the lawyer praises.

Note.—For other examples of this English usage, see **156,** *Note.*

83. When a relative clause contains a predicative noun, the relative itself is often attracted into the gender of the predicative noun instead of agreeing with its antecedent.

Thēbae, quod Boeōtiae caput est. Thebes, which is the capital of Boeotia.

Note.—A demonstrative pronoun used as a subject is also attracted to the gender of a predicative noun.

Ea (not *id*) *vēra est pietās.* That is true piety.

---

[1] For *quīn,* see **133.**

Exercise 11

A

In the following Exercise the italics indicate the use of the co-ordinating relative, 78, *Note*.

1. He pretended that he had met the man [1] who had killed the king by poison. 2. There is no one but knows that one who does not till his land will look in vain for a harvest. 3. The exiles believed that they had reached the locality from which (whence) their forefathers were sprung. 4. I hope to avert this ruin from my country *and therefore* I am willing to venture on or endure anything. 5. He promised to lead his troops into the country of the Remi, *and* (said) that he hoped he could [2] soon recall *them* to their allegiance. 6. Having heard *this*, he perceived that the ambassadors spoke the truth [3] and that the danger was increasing. 7. He said that he had never preferred expediency to duty, *and* (that) *therefore* he would not abandon allies whom he had promised to succour. 8. Having ascertained *this* fact, he promised to break up the crowd which had gathered around the king's [4] palace. 9. He pretended that it was not for the sake of gain but of friendship that he had given me all the books which his brother had left. 10. He said that the friends for whom you were looking round were all safe, *and therefore* that he for his part was free from anxiety. 11. He pretends to reject glory, which is the most honourable reward of true virtue. 12. All the world [5] knows that the moon moves round the earth.

B

1. As [6] I was making my way through the lowest part of the valley, I fell unawares into an ambush of brigands. My captors [7] had, it seemed, been long expecting my arrival,

---

[1] *Is*. (71.) [2] See 39. [3] That which (pl.) was true. (76.)
[4] Adjective. (58.) [5] See 80.
[6] *dum* with pres. indic. (See 180.) [7] 76.

and having seized [1] and made [1] me fast with chains, and dragged me from the road [2] into the neighbouring forest, they again and again threatened me with (**244**) torture and death. At last, when I promised to send a large amount [3] of gold within four days, my chains [4] were struck off and I was set at liberty, and in company [5] with two armed guards, returned to the place [6] whence I had set out. 2. He had now, he said, ceased to hope for much, for he had lost (he said) the best friends he had,[7] and was going to live with men who had always been his deadly enemies, by whom he had been both accused and condemned in his absence, and who had reluctantly spared his life. 3. Your accusers [8] will, I expect, reach the city to-morrow ; I hope that you will be (**38**) unanimously acquitted. 4. You [9] who once set at nought bodily (**59**) pain (*pl.*), are now apparently dismayed by it. It is [10] with reluctance that I say this of (*dē*) the son of so great a man. 5. You obviously treat lightly the affairs of others ; I hope that you will value highly the good opinion of your countrymen.

EXERCISE XII

CORRELATIVES

84. The relative pronouns and pronominal words, *quī* (who), *quālis* (of what *kind*), *quantus* (of what *size*), *quot* (how many), answer respectively to the demonstratives *is* (he), *tālis* (of such a *kind*), *tantus* (of such a *size*), *tot* (so many).

It will be observed that when they answer to demonstratives, all relatives except *quī* (and even *quī* when it answers to *īdem*) are to be translated by the English 'as.'

---

[1] Acc. of participle pass. (**15.**)
[2] *dē viā.*
[3] *pondus, n.*
[4] Abl. abs.
[5] **8**, *b.*
[6] *eō . . . unde.* (See **89.**)
[7] Mood ? (See **77**, *Note.*)
[8] Not *accūsātōrēs* (see **76.**)
[9] See **75.**
[10] See **82.**

Tālis est quālis semper fuit. He is such as (of the same character as) he has ever been.

Tantam[1] *habeō voluptātem quantam tū.* I have as much pleasure as you.

Tot erant mīlitēs quot maris flūctūs. The soldiers were as many as the waves of the sea.

Idem est quī semper fuit. He is the same as (*or* that) he has always been.

Rēs perācta est eōdem modō quō anteā. The thing has been done in the same manner as before.

85. When thus used, the two pronouns which correspond with each other are called **correlative,** or corresponding, words.

Note.—Just as a relative *quī*-clause is sometimes placed before the main sentence and its demonstrative (see **75**), so a clause introduced by *quālis, quantus, quot* is often placed first.

This is in accordance with the general tendency of Latin to place the most emphatic part of a sentence at or near the end. (Intr. 82.)

Quot adstābant hominēs, tot erant sententiae. There were as many opinions as there were men standing by.

Quālis fuit domina, tālem ancillam inveniēs. You will find the maid of the same character as her mistress was.

86. '*Such*' in English is often used where *size* or *amount* is meant rather than *kind* or *quality*. *Such . . . as* should then be translated into Latin by *tantus . . . quantus,* not by *tālis . . . quālis*.

Note.—We must therefore always ask ourselves whether 'such' means 'of such a kind' or 'so great.' Thus, in 'the storm was such as I had never seen before,' 'such' evidently means 'so violent' or 'so great'; in 'his manners were such as I had never seen,' 'such' evidently means 'of such a kind.' In the former case we must use *tantus,* in the latter *tālis.*

87. When 'such' means 'of such a kind,' the place of the demonstrative *tālis* is often taken by *eius modī, huius modī, istīus modī,* 'of such a kind, of such a kind as this, of such a kind as you speak of.'

Huius modī hominēs ōdī. I hate such men (as these).

Note.—*Modī* is here a genitive of quality (see **58,** *Note*).

---

[1] *Tantus* is sometimes used in a limiting sense, 'just as (only as) much as'; *tantum faciet quantum coāctus erit,* 'he will do no more than he is compelled (to do).'

88. 'Such' in English is often an adverb qualifying an adjective: 'such good men,' 'such a broad river.' *Tālis* and *tantus* cannot of course be used as adverbs. We must say: *tam bonus vir*, or *tālis tamque bonus vir*; *tam lātum flūmen*, or *tantum tamque lātum flūmen*; **not**, *tālis bonus vir*, *tāle lātum flūmen*.

Note.—But *tantus* and *tālis* are often combined with *hic*, sometimes with *ille*; *haec tanta multitūdō* 'this great number of men,' *or* 'so great (*or* such) a multitude as this.' In such instances *tantus* or *tālis* with the noun is felt to form a single concept. Similarly when *tam* qualifies an adjective, the whole phrase may be further defined by *hic* or *ille*.

Hic tam bonus vir. So good a man as this *or* this good man.

89. The following pairs of words correspond as relatives and demonstratives.

Ubi (where) to *ibi*, *illīc* (there), *hīc* (here).
Unde (whence) to *inde* (thence), *hinc* (hence).
Quō (whither) to *eō*, *illūc* (thither), *hūc* (hither).
Quā (in the direction in which) to *eā*, *hāc* (in that *or* this direction).

Inde vēnistī, unde ego. You have come from the same place as I.
Eō rediit, unde profectus erat. He returned to the place from which he had set out.

90. Observe also that *īdem* is frequently followed by *ac*[1] (*atque*) instead of *quī*.

Eadem ac (=*quae*) *tū sentiō.* My views (54) are the same as yours.

91. *Alius*, *contrā*, *aliter*, and words signifying *contrast*, are almost always followed by *ac* (or *atque*).

Aliter ac tū sentiō. My views are different from yours.

But sometimes *quam* is used instead of *ac*.

Rēs aliter quam (or *atque*) *exspectāvī ēvēnit.* The matter turned out contrary to my expectation.

(See Comparative Clauses, Ex. LXII.)

92. Where a strong *difference* is pointed out, a repeated *alius* is often used; *aliud est dīcere, aliud facere*, 'there is all the difference between speaking and acting'; 'speaking is one thing, acting another.'

---

[1] See Intr. 48.

93. What has been said (77) about the mood of the verb in *quī*-clauses applies equally to every kind of relative clause, whether introduced by a relatival or pronominal *adjective*, such as *quālis*, etc., or by a relatival *adverb*, such as *ubi*, *unde*. Thus—

Ubi tū es, ibi est frāter tuus. Your brother is in the same place as you.

Note.—But, of course, the verb of such a clause in *ōrātiō oblīqua* will be subjunctive (see **77**, *Note*).

Quālis fuerit frāter tuus, tālem tē esse dīcunt. They say that you are of the same character as your brother was.

Exercise 12

A

This Exercise (A) contains examples of various *relative* constructions; instances of relative clauses in *ōrātiō oblīqua* will be found in B.

1. This is the same as that. 2. You are of the same character as I have always believed you to be. 3. All the world knows that the past cannot be changed. 4. The waves were such as I had never seen before. 5. He died in the place where he had lived in boyhood. 6. He was the first who promised to help me. 7. I will send the most faithful slave I have with me.[1] 8. There is no one but knows that the Gauls were conquered by Caesar. 9. The island is surrounded by the sea which you (*pl.*) call ocean. 10. The Gauls are the same to-day as they have ever been. 11. He was the first to deny the existence of gods. 12. I was the last to reach Italy. 13. That expediency and honour are sometimes contrary to each other (is a fact that)[2] all the world knows. 14. I believe him to have been the first within human memory[3] to perpetrate such a monstrous crime; and I hope he will be the last to harm his country in such a way.

This Exercise may be also varied by placing 'he said' before 2, 4, 7, 10, and altering the sentence accordingly; thus:—'he said that you were of the same character as he had always believed you to be.

---

[1] **8**, *Note*. [2] Omit in Latin. [3] See **59**.

B

1. All the world allows that you are of the same character as your father and grandfather. 2. The scouts having returned to the camp, brought back word that the enemy, who had flocked together in crowds the-day-before, were now breaking up and stealing away in different directions. 3. He said that he would never abandon such good and kindly men, who had so often come to his aid in adversity. 4. My objects [1] are different from yours, nor are my hopes [1] the same as yours. 5. He said that he himself [2] was the same as he had ever [3] been, but that both the state of the nation and the views of his countrymen had gradually changed, and that the king, the nobles, and the whole people were now exposed to dangers such as they had never before experienced. 6. Many ships of war were shattered and sunk by the violence of the storm ; a single merchantman returned in safety to the point from [4] which it had set out.

EXERCISE XIII

THE INFINITIVE AS A NOUN

94. The infinitive is a verbal noun of the neuter gender. Thus—

Sedēre mē dēlectat. To sit, *or* sitting, delights me.

Note.—The English word 'sitting' is here a verbal noun, and must be carefully distinguished from the participle, which has an identical form. Compare '*sitting* rests me' with 'he rested *sitting* on a bank.'

---

[1] Express by neut. pl. of adj. (See 54.)
[2] *Quidem* after 'he' (he *at least*, he *on the one hand*).
[3] Ever = always, as in the preceding Exercise, A, 10.
[4] = whence. (89.)

95. But the infinitive may be used as a noun in two cases only : *nominative* and *accusative.*

(i) In the **nominative** :—

(*a*) As the subject of an impersonal verb, or of a verb used impersonally, or of *est, fuit,* etc., with a neuter predicative adjective.

Nihil agere mē dēlectat. Doing nothing is a pleasure to me.
Turpe est mentīrī. It is disgraceful to lie, *or* lying is disgraceful.

(*b*) Occasionally as a predicative nominative.

Homō cui vīvere est cōgitāre. Man, to whom living is thinking (to live is to think).

(ii) In the **accusative** :—

(*a*) As the object of verbs mentioned in **42.**

(*b*) As one of two accusatives depending on a factitive verb (see Intr. 36).

Errāre, nescīre, et malum et turpe dūcimus. To err, to be ignorant, we deem both unfortunate and disgraceful.

Note.—Obviously when the infinitive is the antecedent to a relative pronoun, the relative will be in the neuter gender.

Laudārī, quod (or *id quod*) *plērisque grātissimum est, mihi molestissimum est.* To be praised, which is very pleasant to most men, is to me most disagreeable.

96. But though the infinitive is thus used as a noun, it retains some characteristics of a verb. For—

(*a*) It is qualified, not by an adjective, but by an adverb.

'Good writing' is *bene scrībere,* not *bonum scrībere.*

Bene arāre est bene colere. Good ploughing is good farming. (See **95,** (i) *b.*)

(*b*) It takes the case constructions of the verb to which it belongs.

Haec perpetī et patriā carēre, miserrimum est. To endure these things and to be deprived of one's country, is most wretched.

(*c*) It has three tenses.

Haec facere (*fēcisse, factūrum esse*). The doing (the having done, the being about to do) this.

(*d*) It may have a subject (which is *always* in the **accusative** case).

Tē hoc dīcere mihi est grātissimum. Your saying this is most welcome to me.

Note.—In English, when an infinitive (or a sentence introduced by ' that ') is the nominative to a verb, it generally *follows* the verb, and the pronoun 'it' is used as its representative before the verb: 'It is pleasant to be praised.' 'It is strange that you should say so.' In Latin we simply write: *Laudārī iūcundum est. Tē hoc dīcere mīrum est.*

97. In the accusative and infinitive constructions (see **31**), the infinitive with its subject accusative is the subject or object of the governing verb. In *tē mentīrī dīcō, tē* is subject accusative to *mentīrī* and *tē mentīrī* is the object of *dīcō.* In *dīxit turpe esse mentīrī,* the object of *dīxit* is *turpe esse mentīrī* and *mentīrī* is the (accusative) subject of (*turpe*) *esse.*

98. The infinitive, either by itself or with other words, can often be used to render English *abstract* nouns. Thus—

(*a*) *Sibi placēre* 'self-satisfaction'; *suīs rēbus contentum esse* 'contentment'; *mentīrī* 'falsehood'; *cūnctārī* 'procrastination' (=*cūnctātiō*); *improbōs laudāre* 'praise of the bad'; *fēlīcem esse* 'success'; *prosperīs rēbus ūtī* 'prosperity.'

(*b*) Thus, since Latin has no single word to express 'happiness' or 'gratitude,' the infinitive is mostly used.

Beātē vīvere, or *beātum esse*=*vīta beāta,* happiness.
Grātiam habēre=*grātus animus,* the feeling of gratitude.
Grātiās agere, the returning thanks, *or* expression of gratitude.
Grātiam dēbēre, the being under an obligation.
Grātiam referre, the returning a favour, *or* the showing gratitude.

Notice that these are instances of the general tendency of Latin to prefer direct and simple to more general and abstract modes of expression.

99. The infinitive cannot be used as a genitive, dative, or ablative; nor can it be used as an accusative governed by a preposition. These cases and prepositional uses are supplied by another verbal noun, the Gerund. (See Exercise XLIX.)

Pugnāre, to fight, *or* fighting; but *pugnandī cupidus,* desirous *of* fighting; *ad pugnandum parātus,* prepared *for* fighting; *pugnandō vincēmus,* we shall win the day *by* fighting.

Exercise 13

A

1. It is always delightful [1] to parents that their children should be praised. 2. He said that it was disgraceful to break one's word, but keeping one's promises was always honourable. 3. Both your brother and you [2] have told many falsehoods [3]; falsehood is always vile. 4. It is one thing to be praised, another to have deserved praise. 5. To be praised by the unpatriotic is to me almost the same thing as to be blamed by patriots. 6. Feeling gratitude, says [4] he, is one thing, returning thanks another. 7. Procrastination, which in all things was dangerous, was, he [5] said, fatal in war. 8. Pardoning the wicked is almost the same thing as condemning the innocent. 9. Procrastination in showing gratitude is never praiseworthy; for myself,[6] I prefer returning kindness to being under an obligation. 10. Happiness is one thing; success and prosperity another. 11. Brave fighting, says [4] he, will to-day be the same thing as victory; by victory we shall give freedom to our country.

B

1. It is generally [7] agreed among historians that this king, trained by toil (*pl.*) and accustomed to bear with patience the frowns [8] of fortune, showed [9] in the midst of disaster (*pl.*) and ruin the same character as in prosperity. As he had been the first to help his country in its hour [10] of distress, so he was the last to despair of it (when) conquered and down-trodden. But he preferred being an exile in his old age to living in safety at home, and obeying one whom the

---

[1] Use the intensive superlative of this and of many of the other adjectives in this exercise. (See **57**, *a*.)

[2] See **26**.

[3] See **54**.

[4] See **40**.

[5] See **32**, *b*.

[6] See **11**, *a*.

[7] *satis* or *ferē*.

[8] Metaphor; say 'adverse fortune.'

[9] See **240**, *Note* **1**.

[10] Simply pres. part. of *labōrō, -āre*.

rest of the world, almost without exception, believed would keep his word. 2. There is all the difference between returning thanks and showing gratitude. As I was the last to believe that you would have set at nought honour, honesty, and the good opinion of your countrymen, so to-day I refuse to think that you have proved [1] to be of such a character as the rest of the world represent [2] you to be ; and it is with reluctance that I yield to those who deny that you are the same man as I once fancied you were.

EXERCISE XIV

FINAL CLAUSES

100. A subordinate clause which expresses the *purpose* or *end in view* (*fīnis*) of the action of the main verb is called a **Final Clause.**

101. In English, purpose can be expressed either by the infinitive (preceded sometimes by 'in order to'), or by a clause introduced by 'that, in order that, *or* so that' and containing an auxiliary verb ('may, might, should').

In Latin prose, purpose is never expressed by the infinitive,[3] but most generally by a clause (introduced by *ut*) whose verb is subjunctive.

> *Multī aliōs laudant, ut ab illīs* [4] *laudentur.* Many men praise others, that they may be praised by them (*or* to be praised by them, *or* in order to be praised by them).
>
> *Multī aliōs laudābant, ut ab illīs laudārentur.* Many men were praising others, in order to be praised by them.

---

[1] See **240** *Note* 1. [2] 'assert.'

[3] Hence such parenthetic clauses as 'not to mention,' 'so to say,' 'not to be tedious,' must never be translated by the Latin infinitive, but by *nē dīcam, ut ita dīcam, nē longus sim.*

[4] *Illīs* is here used in place of the less emphatic *eīs*, as a marked distinction between *themselves* and *others* is intended. (11, *d.*)

Note 1.—Purpose may, however, be expressed in various ways in Latin. Although 'he sent ambassadors *to sue* for peace' is never expressed in Latin prose by *lēgātōs mīsit pācem petere*, it may be expressed by :—

(*a*) *lēgātōs mīsit, ut pācem peterent* (Final Clause),
(*b*) „ *quī pācem peterent* (Relative Clause),
(*c*) „ *ad pācem petendam* (Gerundive),
(*d*) „ *pācis petendae causā* (Gerundive),
(*e*) „ *pācem petītum* (Supine).

Note 2.—The subjunctive in a final clause is jussive (see **149**).

But when the purpose is a negative one and the subordinate clause indicates that which the action of the main verb seeks to avoid, the subordinate clause is introduced by the negative conjunction *nē*, instead of *ut*.

Gallīnae avēsque reliquae pennīs fovent pullōs, nē frīgore laedantur. Hens and other birds cherish their young with their feathers, that they may not be hurt by the cold.

Gallīnae avēsque reliquae pennīs fovēbant pullōs, nē frīgore laederentur. Hens and other birds were cherishing their young with their feathers, that they might not be hurt by the cold.

Note 3.—The combination *ut . . . nōn* must *never* be used in a final clause; and for *ut . . . nēmō* and *ut . . . numquam*, we must use *nē . . . quis* and *nē . . . umquam*. (See **109**.)

102. When the final clause contains a comparative adjective or adverb, the conjunction used is *quō = by which*; but *quō* must never be used to introduce a final clause unless it contains a comparative adjective or adverb.

Medicō puto aliquid dandum esse, quō sit studiōsior. I think that something should be given to the physician, that he may be the more attentive (*or* to make him more attentive).

103. When a final clause is followed by a negative one, the conjunction **nēve** (or **neu**), not *neque*, connects the two clauses.

Hoc fēcī nē tibi displicērem nēve amīcīs tuīs nocērem. I did this to avoid displeasing you, or injuring your friends.

Sequence of Tenses

104. The tenses of the Indicative and Subjunctive moods are classified as Primary and Secondary (or Historic) in the following manner :—

	Indicative	*Subjunctive.*
Primary.	Present.	Present.
	Future.	—
	Perfect (with *have*).	Perfect.
	Future Perfect.	—
Secondary.	Imperfect.	Imperfect.
	Perfect (without *have*).	—
	Pluperfect.	Pluperfect.

Note.—The Latin perfect indicative has two meanings corresponding to two English tenses ; *fēcī* may mean 'I have done' (primary) *or* 'I did' (secondary). (See **187.**)

105. When the verb of the main sentence is a Primary tense, the tense of a subjunctive verb in a subordinate clause is also Primary ; and when the verb of the main sentence is a Secondary tense, the tense of a subjunctive verb in a subordinate clause is also Secondary.

This is the rule for **Normal Sequence of Tenses.**

Haec scrībō (scrīpsī, scrībam, scrīpserō) ut bonō sīs animō. I write (have written, shall write, shall have written) this, in order that you may be in good spirits.

Haec scrībēbam (scrīpsī, scrīpseram) ut bonō essēs animō. I was writing (wrote, had written) this, in order that you might be in good spirits.

In Primary sequence the Present subjunctive, and in Secondary sequence the Imperfect subjunctive are used for actions contemporaneous with or subsequent to that of the main verb ; the Perfect and Pluperfect subjunctive (according to sequence) are used for actions prior to that of the main verb.

Note. 1.—Since the Latin Perfect Indicative may be either Primary or Secondary, the tense of the subjunctive in a subordinate clause generally depends upon the sense in which the Perfect Indicative form is used. (See example of *scrīpsī* given above.)

Note 2.—A little reflection will show that the action of the verb in a Final clause can never take place before the action of the main sentence. Consequently, only the present or imperfect subjunctive can be used in Final clauses.

Note 3.—A Perfect infinitive (or Perfect subjunctive), even when dependent on a Present tense, is itself often followed by Secondary sequence: *Dīcō eum vēnisse ut pācem peteret,* I say he came to seek peace.

Exercise 14

1. In order not to be driven into exile, I shall pretend to be mad. 2. That you might not be punished for this crime, both your brother and you told many falsehoods. 3. He pardoned, it is said,[1] the wicked, in order to obtain a reputation for clemency. 4. He spared the best patriots when he was[2] victorious, in order that his own crimes might be forgiven. 5. He praised your countrymen again and again in their presence in order to be praised by them in his absence. 6. The enemy will, they say,[1] be here to-morrow with[3] a vast army in order to[4] besiege our city. 7. That he might not be condemned in his absence, he hastened to go to Rome. 8. It is said that he told many falsehoods to make[5] himself seem younger than he really was. 9. It seems that he wishes to return home in order to[6] stand for the consulship. 10. There is a tradition that he refused to accept the crown to avoid displeasing his brother or injuring the lawful heir. 11. In order to testify his zeal and loyalty, he hastened in his[7] old age to Rome, and was the very first[8] to pay his respects to the new king.

EXERCISE XV

CONSECUTIVE CLAUSES

106. A subordinate clause which expresses the *result* of the action of the main verb is called a **Consecutive Clause.**

---

[1] See **32**, *b*; **43**. [2] See **63**. [3] **8**, *b*.
[4] Gerundive with *ad*. (See **101**, *Note* 1.) [5] See **102**.
[6] **101**, *Note* 1. [7] See **63**. [8] *I.e.* 'the first of all.' (See **62**.)

Note.—For the difference between a final and a consecutive clause, compare :—

(*a*) I ran against him *in order to throw* him down (Final) ;
(*b*) I ran against him with *such* force *that I threw* him down (Consecutive).

In the former sentence, (*a*), nothing is said of the *result* , only the end in view, or *motive*, is mentioned. In the latter, (*b*), nothing is said of the *motive* ; only the *result* is named.

107. In English, result can be expressed either by an infinitive (preceded by 'so as to'), or by a clause introduced by 'that, so that.'

In Latin, result is expressed by a clause (introduced by *ut*) whose verb is subjunctive ; but **never** by an infinitive.

Nēmō tam potēns est ut omnia efficere possit. Nobody is so powerful as to be able to perform everything.

Note.—It is the peculiarity of Latin that the verb should be subjunctive, even though the result is presented as an actual fact :

Tanta vīs probitātis est ut eam vel in hoste dīligāmus. Such is the force of honesty that we love it even in an enemy.

'That we love it' is stated as a *fact*, and would be indicative in other languages ; but in Latin *dīligimus* would never be used in a consecutive clause.

108. *Note* 1.—Although both final and consecutive clauses in Latin are introduced by *ut* (when positive) and have a subjunctive verb, the context will almost always prevent ambiguity. In such a sentence as *puer humī prōlāpsus est ut crūs frangeret*, 'the boy fell down so as to break his leg,' *intention* would be absurd. Furthermore, a final clause will very often correspond to some such word or phrase as *idcircō, eō cōnsiliō, ob eam causam*, etc., in the main sentence ; and a consecutive clause to *adeō, tam, ita, tantus*, or *tālis*.

Contrast : *Hoc eō cōnsiliō dīxī ut tibi prōdessem.* I said this to be of use to you (*or* with the intention of being of use).

with : *Hoc ita dīxī ut tibi prōdessem.* I said this so as to be of use to you (*or* in such a manner that I was of use to you).

Note 2.—Remember that *ut* is used to introduce various kinds of clauses, not final and consecutive clauses only. Particular care is necessary when translating into Latin to distinguish a *comparative* clause introduced by *ut* and having its verb in the *indicative*, from a consecutive clause.

Ut multitūdō solet, concurrunt. They are running together, as a multitude is wont to do.

Contrast: *Tālis fuit ut nēmō eī crēderet.* He was of such a character that no one believed him.

with: *Tālis fuit quālem nēmō anteā vīderat.* He was of such a character as no one had seen before.

109. A consecutive clause is negatived by the adverb *nōn.*

Tanta fuit virī moderātiō ut repugnantī mihi nōn īrāscerētur. The self-control of the man was so great, that he was not angry with me when I opposed him.

Consequently the following differences between negative final and negative consecutive clauses are **most important**:

	Final	Consecutive
That not	*nē*	*ut nōn*
That nobody	*nē quis*	*ut nēmō*
That nothing	*nē quid*	*ut nihil*
That no . . .	*nē ūllus*	*ut nūllus*
That never	*nē umquam*	*ut numquam*
That nowhere	*nē ūsquam*	*ut nūsquam*

Contrast: The gates were shut that no one might leave the city. *Portae clausae sunt nē quis urbem relinqueret.*

with: The fear of all men was so great that no one left the city. *Tantus fuit omnium metus ut nēmō urbem relīquerit.*

110. When a consecutive clause is followed by a negative one, the conjunction **neque (nec)** (not *nēve*; contrast **103**) connects the two clauses.

Note.—Consequently: and no one is *nec quisquam.*
and nothing „ *nec quidquam.*
and no „ *nec ūllus.*
and never „ *nec umquam.*
and nowhere „ *nec ūsquam.*

111. Sometimes a consecutive clause has a *limiting* force. Such clauses often correspond to an *ita* in the main sentence; and when negative they can frequently be translated by the English 'without . . .'

Ita bonus est ut interdum peccet. He is good to this extent (*or* he is only so far good), that he makes mistakes sometimes.

Nec perīre potes ut nōn aliōs perdās. Nor can you be ruined without ruining others.

Note.—With the first example above, compare the use of *tantus* in a limiting sense. (See **84**, *footnote.*)

Tenses in Consecutive Clauses

112. The tense of a subjunctive verb in a consecutive sentence is in accordance with the rule for normal sequence (**105**), with *two exceptions* :—

(i) After a Secondary tense in the main sentence, a Present Subjunctive is used in the result clause if the result is still true at the time of writing.

Hoc eum adeō terruit ut vix hodiē prōdīre audeat. This so terrified him that he scarcely ventures to come forward to-day.

Verrēs Siciliam ita perdidit ut ea restituī nōn possit. Verres so ruined Sicily that it cannot now be restored.

113. (ii) After a Secondary tense in the main sentence, a Perfect Subjunctive is used to stress the result as something completed.

Tanta fuit pestis ut rēx ipse morbō absūmptus sit. The pestilence was so great that the King himself was cut off by the disease.

114. If the meaning of the result clause is such that stress is laid on its futurity, we must use the future participle in *-ūrus* with a subjunctive tense of the verb *sum.*

Adeō territī sumus ut numquam posthāc pugnātūrī sīmus. We were so frightened that we shall never fight again.

So in *ōrātiō oblīqua* :—

Dīxit sē adeō territōs esse ut numquam posteā pugnātūrī essent. He said that they (himself and his companions) had been so frightened that they would never fight again.

115. When the English result clause contains the words *would have,* they must be translated by the future participle in *-ūrus* with the *perfect subjunctive* of *sum.*

Tanta fuit caedēs ut . . . nēmō superfutūrus fuerit. The slaughter was such that no one would have survived.

(See **474**.)

116. The following examples should be studied :—

Hoc ita faciō (fēcī, faciam) ut tibi displiceam. I do (am doing, have done, will do) this in such a way as to displease you.

Hoc ita fēcī (faciēbam, fēceram) ut tibi displicērem. I did (was doing, had done) this in such a way as (then) to displease you.

Hoc ita fēcī ut tibi displiceam (rare). I did this in such a way as to be displeasing to you now.

Hoc ita fēcī ut tibi displicuerim. I did this in such a way as to have now displeased you (*or* so that, as a matter of fact, I displeased you).

Dīxit sē hoc ita fēcisse ut tibi displicēret. He said that he did this in such a way as to displease you.

Hoc ita fēcī ut tibi displicitūrus sim. I have done this in such a way that I shall displease you.

Exercise 15

A

1. I have lived, said [1] he, so virtuously that I quit life with resignation. 2. He had lived, he said,[1] so virtuously as to quit life with resignation. 3. I will endeavour, said he, to live so as to be able to quit life with resignation. 4. He said that he had lived so as to be able to quit life with resignation. 5. The charge of the enemy was so sudden that no one could find his arms or proper rank. 6. Thereupon the enemy made a sudden [2] charge in order to prevent any of our men from finding either his arms or proper rank. 7. Thereupon he [3] began to tell many [4] falsehoods with the intention of preserving his life. 8. He told so many falsehoods that no one believed him then and (that) no one has ever put faith in him since. 9. He was so good a king that his subjects loved him in his lifetime, sighed for him after his death, honour his name and memory to-day with grateful [5] hearts, and will never forget his virtues. 10. The waves were such as to dash over the whole of [6] the ship, and the storm was of such a

---

[1] See **40**.
[2] Use adverb : *suddenly made a charge.*
[3] *Ille* (*the other*), **11**, *d.*
[4] See **54**.
[5] Superlative. (See **57.**)
[6] See **60**.

kind as I had never seen before. 11. The cavalry charged so fiercely that had [1] not night interfered with the contest, the enemy would have [2] turned their backs. 12. You cannot, said he, injure your country without [3] bringing loss and ruin upon yourself and your own affairs. 13. I said this with the intention of benefiting you and yours, but the matter has so turned out that I shall injure you whom I wished to benefit, and benefit those whom I wished to injure. 14. So little did he indulge even a just resentment that he pardoned even those who had slain his father.

B

On the next day the king, to avoid wearying by a long march his soldiers (who were) exhausted with a long and indecisive battle, kept his men within their lines. Meantime the enemy, having sent for reinforcements, were waiting for an attack (on the part) of our men, so that they seemed by no means desirous of fighting. After noon-day the king, seeing [4] that the strength and spirits of his men were now so much restored, that they were likely to shrink from no danger, and were well prepared for fighting,[5] threw open [6] two gates, and having made a sudden [7] sally, surprised the enemy (who were taken) unawares and looking for nothing of the [8] kind. Great numbers they surrounded and slew, and so great was the slaughter that out of (*ex*) more than [9] 3000 soldiers scarcely 500 escaped unwounded; and, had [10] not night interposed, not even these would have survived. So (entirely) did fortune change (sides), that those who quite lately [11] were on the point of winning the day, were now stealing away and praying for night and darkness, and those who but lately [12] were despairing of their safety, and looking for death or slavery, were exulting in victory and freedom.

---

[1] *Nisi* with pluperf. subj.
[2] **115.**
[3] See **111.**
[4] See **412.**
[5] **99.**
[6] Abl. abs.
[7] Use adverb.
[8] **87.**
[9] **275,** *Note.*
[10] *nisi* with pluperf. subj.
[11] *paulō ante.*
[12] *modo.*

EXERCISE XVI

Ut, Nē, INTRODUCING A NOUN CLAUSE

117. One of the main difficulties in translating English into Latin is to know when to represent the English infinitive by a Latin infinitive, and when to use a subordinate clause containing a finite verb.

Note 1.—We have already seen that the Latin accusative and infinitive construction is used where English has a *that*-clause after verbs of *saying, thinking,* etc. (**31-32**).

On the other hand we have seen that the Latin infinitive must never be used to express either a *purpose* or a *result* (**101, 107**).

In English, a verb which implies an **act of the will** (' command, entreat, urge, persuade,' etc.) or a **wish,** is followed sometimes by an infinitive and sometimes by a *that*-clause.

> ' I command you to go.' ' The senate decreed that he should lead the army.'

In Latin, such verbs have dependent upon them a clause introduced by *ut* (if positive) or *nē* (if negative) and having its verb in the subjunctive. The dependent clause is substantival (see Intr. 71) and is an indirect command (or wish).

> *Tē rogō atque ōrō ut eum iuvēs.* I ask and beg you to help him.

Note 2.—These noun clauses after a verb of will are very similar to final clauses, for both express the intention or end in view of the main verb. But a final clause is *adverbial* to the main sentence whereas the *noun* clause stands in the same relation to the main verb as would an accusative case. Thus the final clause in *haec dīcō ut intellegās* performs a function similar to the adverb in *haec cōnsultō dīcō* ; but the noun clause in *rogō ut veniās* corresponds to the accusative in *hoc rogō.*

118. The commonest verbs implying an act of the will or a wish are :—

(*a*) 'Command, entreat' : *imperō, mandō, praecipiō, ēdīcō, oportet, necesse est ; rogō, ōrō, petō, postulō, obsecrō, precor.*

(*b*) ' Exhort, urge ' : *hortor, exhortor ; suādeō, moneō.*

(*c*) ' Persuade, induce ' : *persuādeō ; impetrō, impellō.*

(*d*) 'Resolve': *cēnseō, dēcernō, cōnstituō.*

(*e*) 'Take care': *cūrō, videō, caveō, operam dō, id agō.*

(*f*) 'Permit': *permittō, concēdō.*

(*g*) 'Wish': *optō* (and *volō, nōlō, mālō, cupiō;* but see **120**).

Mihi nē quid facerem imperāvit. He ordered me to do nothing.

Hoc tē rogō, nē dēmittās animum. I beg of you not to be disheartened (*literally*, not to let your mind sink).

Magnō opere tē hortor ut hōs librōs studiōsē legās. I earnestly advise you to read these books attentively.

Helvētiīs persuāsit ut exīrent. He persuaded the Helvetii to depart.

Cōnsulī permissum est ut duās legiōnēs scrīberet. The consul was permitted to enrol two legions.

119. The tense of the subordinate clause follows the rule for normal sequence (**105**); and the use of *nē, nē quis*, etc., is identical with the use in final clauses. (See **109.**)

Note.—A second clause of this type if negative is joined to the first by *nēve.* (See **103.**)

120. But the following verbs implying an act of the will take the accusative and infinitive construction and must be carefully noted: **iubeō** 'I command,' **patior, sinō** 'I allow.' (See also **41** *a*.)

Cōnsul mīlitēs pedem referre iussit (*passus est*). The consul ordered (allowed) the soldiers to retreat.

The following verbs of wishing sometimes have a dependent subjunctive clause, but most frequently they take an infinitive (**42**, i *c*), or an accusative and infinitive (**41** *b*): **volō, nōlō, mālō, cupiō.**

121. With many verbs of will (especially *rogō, moneō, suādeō, imperō, cūrō, oportet, necesse est*) and with *velim, nōlim, mālim,* 'I should wish, not wish, prefer,' the subjunctive clause is used without the conjunction *ut*, especially when the verb of the subordinate clause is second person singular.

Culpam fateāre necesse est. You must needs avow your fault.

Hoc faciās velim. I would have you do this.

122. Special care must be taken to use the proper case with verbs implying an act of the will. If the person commanded is mentioned in the main sentence, the **accusative** case is used with *rogō, ōrō, obsecrō, oportet, hortor, exhortor, impellō;* but the **dative** is used with *imperō, mandō, ēdīcō, praecipiō, suādeō, persuādeō,* *permittō, concēdō* (and these verbs are used in the passive only impersonally); and **ā** with the **ablative** is used with *petō, postulō, impetrō* (and sometimes with *poscō, flāgitō,* and *precor*).

123. *Iubeō* expresses our 'bid,' and may be used in a wide sense. *Salvēre tē iubeō = salvē.* It may express the wish of equals, superiors, or inferiors.

Imperō implies an order from a higher authority, as from a commanding officer.

Ēdīcō, a formal order from someone in office, as a praetor, etc.

Praecipiō, a direction or instruction from one of superior knowledge.

Mandō, a charge or commission entrusted by anyone.

Permittō differs from *sinō,* as meaning rather to give leave *actively*; *sinō,* not to prevent. *Permittō* sometimes means 'entrust wholly to,' 'hand over to.'

124. It is important to observe that some verbs may be used in two senses, and therefore with two constructions.

If a verb is used as a verb of 'saying,' 'thinking,' etc., it will take the accusative and infinitive (**31**) of *indirect statement*; if it is used as a verb of will, it will be followed by a subjunctive clause of *indirect command* (**117**). Thus—

(*a*) *Moneō adesse hostem.* I warn you that the enemy is at hand.

Nē hoc faciās moneō. I warn you not to do this.

(*b*) *Mihi persuāsum est* (5) *fīnem adesse.* I was persuaded (*i.e.* convinced) that the end was near.

Mihi persuāsum est nē hoc facerem. I was persuaded not to do this.

(*c*) *Mihi scrīpsit sē ventūrum esse.* He wrote me word that he would come.

Mihi scrīpsit nē ad sē venīrem. He wrote to me (to order or beg me) not to come to him.

Note.—Observe that in the above instances the English verbs have two senses and a double construction; but where we use the conjunction 'that' Latin uses the infinitive, and Latin uses a conjunction where we use the infinitive.

125. A subjunctive clause introduced by *ut* (or *nē*) is the object of *faciō* and its compounds when they are used in the sense of 'bring it about, succeed in.'

Effēcit nē ex urbe exīrent. He prevented their leaving the city.

Effēcit nē poenās daret. He contrived not to be punished.

Note.—The conjunction ***ut*** is often omitted (see **121**): ***Fac veniās*** 'Be sure to come.'

126. Many **impersonal** verbs and phrases which express 'happening, occurrence' (*accidit, ēvenit, fit, fierī potest*) have as their *subject* a noun clause (introduced by *ut*) whose verb is subjunctive.

Accidit ut nēmō senātor adesset. It happened that no senator was present (*or* no senator happened to be present).

Ex quō factum est ut bellum indīcerētur. The consequence of this (**79**) was that war was declared (*or* the result was a declaration of war).

Note 1.—The clauses mentioned in **126** are analogous to consecutive clauses (**106**); hence *ut nēmō*, not *nē quis*, in the first example. (See **109**.) Compare them with the noun clauses mentioned in **117** (and see **117**, *Note* 2).

Note 2.—Never translate 'it happened to him to be absent' *or* 'he happened to be absent' by *accidit eī abesse*, but by *eī accidit ut abesset*, or else by *is forte āfuit.*

127. The following are examples of the commonest verbs and phrases which have a subjunctive noun clause as their subject :—

(*Cāsū*) *accidit.* It happens (by chance).
Ēvenit. It happens.
Ita fit. Thus (hence) it happens.
Quī (old abl.) *fit?* How happens it, how is it?
Fierī potest. It can happen, it is possible, possibly.
Nūllō modō fierī potest. It is quite impossible.
Sequitur, proximum est. It follows, the next thing is.
Reliquum est, restat. It remains.

128. *Tantum abest* 'so far is it from' is always used impersonally, and is followed by two *ut*-clauses, of which one is *substantival* and subject to *abest*, and the other is an *adverbial* consecutive clause explaining *tantum abest.*

Tantum abest ut nostra mīrēmur, ut nōbīs nōn satisfaciat ipse Dēmosthenēs. So far are we from admiring our own works, that Demosthenes himself does not satisfy us.

Ut nostra mīrēmur is a noun clause, standing as the subject to *abest*. *Ut nōbīs nōn satisfaciat ipse Dēmosthenēs* is a consecutive clause which qualifies *tantum abest* like an adverb of degree or quantity.

The same idea might also be expressed by using *adeō nōn . . . ut*, or *nōn modo nōn . . . sed*, as :—

(*a*) *Adeō nōn nostra mīrāmur ut nōbīs nōn satisfaciat*, etc.; or,

(*b*) *Nōn modo nōn nostra mīrāmur, sed nōbīs nōn satisfacit. . . .*

Notice carefully the moods used in (*a*) and (*b*).

Exercise 16

A

1. I entreated him not to do this, but urged him to trust his father. 2. He exhorted the soldiers not to be disheartened on account of the late disaster. 3. He made it his aim to avoid injuring any one of his subjects, but to consult the good of the whole nation. 4. He gave orders to the soldiers to get ready for fighting, and exhorted them to fight bravely. 5. The senate passed a resolution that the consuls should hold a levy. 6. I resolved to warn your brother not to return to Rome before night. 7. To prevent him from telling any more falsehoods, I bade him hold his peace. 8. It happened (on) that day [1] that the consuls were about to hold a levy. 9. I prevailed on him to spare the vanquished (*pl.*), and not [2] to allow his (soldiers) to massacre women and children. 10. I was the first to warn him not to put faith in the falsest and most cruel of mankind. 11. You [3] and I happened that day to be in the country; the consequence [4] of this was that we have been the last [5] to hear of this disaster. 12. He said that he would never allow himself to promise to betray his allies.

B

1. Thereupon he earnestly implored the bystanders not to obey men [6] who were (*subj.*) ready to betray both their allies and themselves in order to avoid incurring a trifling loss. 2. He succeeded at last in persuading the Spaniards that it was quite impossible to leave the city, (which was [7]) blockaded on all sides by the enemy. 3. He says [8] that he never asked you to pardon the guilty or condemn the innocent. 4. I will not, said he, allow myself to be the last to greet my king after so heavy a disaster. 5. The jury were at last persuaded that

---

[1] See **9**, *a*. [2] *Nēve* or *neu*. (See **119**, *Note.*)
[3] See **26**, *footnote*. [4] See **126**, example 2. [5] See **62**.
[6] See **72**. [7] Omit relative and use participle. [8] See **33**.

my brother was innocent; they could not be persuaded to acquit him by their verdict, such was their terror [1] of the mob. 6. News has been brought to me in my absence that the city has been taken; it remains (for me) to retake it by the same arts as [2] those by which I have lost it. 7. So far am I from praising and admiring that king, that it seems [3] to me that he has greatly injured not only his own subjects, but the whole human race. 8. So far am I from having said everything, that I could take up the whole of the day in speaking; but I do not wish to be tedious.[4] 9. It never before happened to me to forget a friend in his absence, and this [5] circumstance is a great consolation to me to-day.

C

Thereupon, he sent [6] for their chief men, and exhorted them not to be disheartened on account of such a serious disaster. He had warned them, he said,[7] that the enemy was at hand, but it had been impossible to persuade them not to put faith in idle rumours and fictitious messages. The Indians earnestly implored him to forgive them [8] for this great error; they succeeded at last by their prayers or tears in persuading him that they would never again [9] allow themselves to be so easily over-reached and entrapped (*caught*). While [10] they were thus [11] conversing, it happened that a [12] prisoner who professed to be one [13] of the king's [14] bodyguard, was brought to Cortes. The general ordered his fetters to be struck off and himself to be set at liberty, and sent him back with a letter to the king. He did this with the intention of appearing to be anxious for a truce; but so far was he from wishing for anything [15] of the kind, that he was ready to reject any [16] conditions,

---

[1] See **25**, last example. [2] See **84**.
[3] See **43**, *Note* 2. [4] See **42**, ii. [5] See **67**.
[6] Acc. part. pass. (**15**.) [7] Avoid parenthesis. (**32**.)
[8] Pronoun? (See **349**.) [9] *posteā*. [10] *dum*: tense? (**180**.)
[11] *haec*. [12] *quīdam*. (**361**.) [13] *ūnus ē*. (See **529**.)
[14] Adj. (**58**.) [15] Neut. of *quisquam*. (**358**.) [16] **359**.

and preferred to put the fortune of war a second time to the test (rather) than to accept from the king even the most honourable peace.

EXERCISE XVII

Quōminus, Quīn. Verbs of *Fearing*

129. Verbs of 'hindering, preventing, and forbidding' (*impediō, dēterreō, retineō, obstō, obsistō ; interdīcō, recūsō, prohibeō*) take a noun clause of Indirect Command which is introduced by *nē*, *quōminus* ('whereby the less'), or *quīn* ('whereby not') and whose verb is subjunctive.

Atticus, nē qua sibi statua pōnerētur, restitit. Atticus opposed having any statue raised to himself.

Nāvēs ventō tenēbantur quōminus in portum redīrent. The ships were prevented by the wind from returning into harbour.

Note.—If *imperō ut veniās* means 'I command you to come,' why should not *prohibeō ut veniās* mean 'I forbid you to come'? The reason is that originally these clauses were independent of the verb of 'commanding' or 'forbidding.' (*Ut*) *veniās, imperō* meant 'You are to come; I command it'; and *nē veniās, prohibeō* meant 'You are not to come; I forbid it.' Consequently the **negative** conjunction is necessary with the verbs mentioned above.

130. *Vetō* (always) and *prohibeō* (often) have an accusative and infinitive clause instead of a subjunctive clause.

Caesar mīlitēs pedem referre vetuit. Caesar forbade his soldiers to retreat.

Recūsō (from *re-* and *causa*) means properly 'I protest against, give reasons against,' and consequently as a verb of 'hindering' it takes a subjunctive clause introduced by *nē, quōminus*, or *quīn.* But *nōn recūsō* is sometimes used with a meaning approximating to that of *volō* and consequently takes an infinitive (see **42**): *nōn recūsō abīre* 'I do not object to going.'

131. If the verb of 'preventing,' etc., is itself positive the conjunction is either *nē* or *quōminus* ; if it is negative, or virtually negative (see **132**), the conjunction is either *quōminus* or (more usually) *quīn*.

> *Plūra nē dīcam impedior.* I am prevented from saying more.
>
> *Per tē stetit quōminus vincerēmus.* You were the cause of our not winning the day.
>
> *Nōn recūsābō quōminus tē in vincula dūcam.* I will not object to taking you to prison.
>
> *Germānī retinērī nōn poterant quīn tēla conicerent.* The Germans could not be restrained from hurling their weapons.

Note.—These clauses correspond to the English verbal noun in *-ing* with a preposition.

132. A verb or sentence is said to be virtually negative if it is qualified by such a word as *vix, aegrē* 'scarcely, with difficulty,' or if it is a question which expects a negative answer.

> *Vix inhibērī potuit quīn saxa iaceret.* He could scarcely be prevented from throwing stones.
>
> *Num quis obstat quīn vēra dīcas?* Does anyone prevent your telling the truth?

133. *Quīn* is derived from an old ablative form *quī* and the interrogative particle *-ne*, and originally meant 'why not?' as in *quīn tū tacēs* 'why do you not keep silent?' It was also associated with commands: *quīn Deciōs aspice* (Virgil, *Aen.*, 6, 824) 'Look at the Decii (why not?)' and sometimes was used as an emphatic particle = 'nay.' But its commonest use in classical Latin is as a conjunction.

134. *Quīn* is often, but not invariably, used instead of *ut nōn* to introduce negative consecutive clauses (both adverbial, **106**, and substantival, **126**), when the main verb is also negative, or virtually so.

> *Nihil tam difficile est quīn investīgārī possit.* Nothing is so difficult that it cannot be discovered. (Adverbial clause.)
>
> *Nec multum āfuit quīn interficerēmur.* And we were not far from losing our lives. (Noun clause.)
>
> *Nūllō modō fierī potest quīn errem.* It is quite impossible that I am not mistaken, *or* but that I am, etc. (Noun clause.)
>
> *Facere vix potuī quīn tē accūsārem.* It was scarcely possible for me not to accuse you. (Noun clause.)

Note.—In *nec eum umquam adspexit, quīn frātricīdam compellāret,* 'And she never beheld him without calling him a fratricide,' we have a consecutive clause used in a limiting sense (see **111**), dependent upon a negative main verb.

135. A clause introduced by *quīn* and having its verb in the subjunctive is used as the subject or object of negative and interrogative expressions of 'doubt.'

> *Nōn dubium erat quīn plūrimum Helvētiī possent.* There was no doubt that the Helvetii were the most powerful.
>
> *Quis dubitat quīn hoc fēcerīs?* Who doubts (=no one doubts) but that (*or* that) you did this?

136. When *dubitō* means 'I doubt' and is interrogative or negatived, it takes a *quīn*-clause; when it means 'I hesitate' and is interrogative or negative, it takes an infinitive (see **42**, i. and *footnote*); when it means 'I am uncertain' it takes an Indirect Question (see **172**): *dubitō num veniat,* 'I am uncertain whether he is coming.'

Verbs of Fearing

137. The constructions used in Latin after verbs of 'fearing' are quite different from that which follows verbs of 'hoping.' (See **37**.)

But they will cause no difficulty if the student grasps the fact that the subordinate noun clause dependent on such a verb in Latin is an Indirect Wish, and that the verb of the main sentence (naturally) *fears the reverse of the wish.*

Note 1.—'May he live! I fear he will *not*,' is a logical sequence of ideas; 'May he live! I fear he will' would be nonsense. Similarly 'May he not come! I fear he *will*' is reasonable; but 'May he not come! I fear he will not' is not reasonable.

Consequently, what we fear **will happen** is expressed in Latin by a subjunctive clause introduced by **nē**; and what we fear **will not happen** by a subjunctive clause introduced by **ut.**

> *Vereor nē veniat.* I fear that he will come (*or* I fear *or* am afraid of his coming).
>
> *Vereor ut veniat.* I fear that he will not come (*or* I am afraid of his not coming).
>
> *Veritus sum ut venīret.* I feared that he would not come.
>
> *Perīculum erat nē hostēs urbem expugnārent.* There was a danger of the enemy's taking the city.

Note 2.—Observe that whereas English concentrates attention on the positive or negative *happening,* Latin keeps in mind the positive or negative nature of the *wish.*

Note 3.—Occasionally *nē . . . nōn* is used instead of *ut*: *Vereor nē exercitum firmum habēre nōn possit,* 'I fear he cannot have a strong army.'

138. The tense of the verb in the subordinate clause is determined by the rule for normal sequence (105).

But where stress is laid on the idea of futurity, the future participle with a tense of *sum* is used.

Vereor ut hoc tibi prōfutūrum sit. I am afraid that this is not going to do you good.

139. Verbs of 'fearing' sometimes approximate in meaning to *nōlō*; and then they take an infinitive instead of a subjunctive clause.

Caesar timēbat flūminī exercitum obicere. Caesar feared (was unwilling) to expose his army to the river.

Exercise 17

1. I never beheld him without imploring him to come to the aid of his oppressed and suffering country; but I fear that he will never listen to my prayers. 2. I cannot refrain from blaming those who were ready to hand over our lives, liberties, rights, and fortunes to our deadliest enemies. 3. All the world believes that you did wrong, and I am afraid that it is quite impossible that all mankind have been of one mind with me in a blunder. 4. He pretends that I was the cause of my countrymen not defending the homes of our allies. 5. The soldiers could not be restrained from hurling their darts into the midst of the mob. 6. He promises to leave nothing undone to persuade your son not to hurry away from the city to the country.[1] 7. We were within a very little of all being killed, or at least of being wounded or cut off either by famine or by disease. 8. Nothing,[2] he said, had ever prevented him [3] from defending the freedom and privileges of his countrymen. 9. What circumstance prevented you from keeping your word and coming to my aid with

---

[1] See 9, *b*. [2] See 33. [3] *i.e.* himself (11, *e*).

your army, as you[1] had promised to do? 10. I will no longer then protest against your desiring to become a king, but I am afraid you will not be able to obtain your desire. 11. What reason is there why he should not be ready to return in his old[2] age to the scenes which he left unwillingly in his boyhood?[2] 12. Such was his terror[3] of Caesar's victory, that he could scarcely be restrained from committing suicide. 13. He could not, he replied,[4] help waging war by land and sea. 14. News has been brought me that our brave general has been struck by a dart, and I fear that he has received a mortal wound. 15. He was not afraid, he replied, of our being unable to reach Italy in[5] safety; the danger was[6] of our being unable ever to return.

EXERCISE XVIII

COMMANDS AND PROHIBITIONS

Imperative Mood

140. The **imperative mood** is used freely in Latin, as in English, in commands and entreaties, in the *second* person singular and plural.

Ad mē venī. Come to me. *Audīte*[7] *hoc.* Hear this.

141. But, especially in the singular, where one person, an equal, is addressed, there are many substitutes for so peremptory a mode of speaking.

For example, instead of *scrībe* we might say :—

tū, quaesō (obsecrō), ad mē scrībe.
cūrā ut scrībās (see **118**).
scrībās velim (see **121**).
scrībe sīs (= *sī vīs* 'please').
fac scrībās (see **125**, *Note*).

---

[1] See **67**, *Note*. [2] **63**. [3] See **25**. [4] **32**, *b*.
[5] See **61**. [6] Inf., dependent on 'he replied.'
[7] The forms *venītō*, *venītōte* (second person), and *venītō*, *veniuntō* (third person), sometimes called future imperatives, are used in *wills* and *laws*, and sometimes elsewhere for emphasis.

142. For commands, entreaties, and exhortations in the *first* and *third* persons, Latin uses the present subjunctive (in a jussive sense ; see **149**).

Moriāmur, let us die ; *abeat*, let him go ; *nē sim salvus*, may no good befall me ; *nē exeat urbe*, let him not go out of the city. In older English and in poetry we have 'turn we to survey,' 'hallowed be thy name.'

Note.—A (jussive) subjunctive is sometimes used instead of the imperative in the second person singular where no definite person is addressed, but a general maxim given.

Postrēmus loquāris : prīmus taceās. Be you (*or* a man should be) the last to speak, the first to be silent.

143. Negative commands or **prohibitions** in the *second* person are expressed most commonly in Latin by the imperative of *nōlō* (i.e. *nōlī*, *nōlīte*) and an infinitive ; or by the imperative of *caveō* and *videō* with a dependent subjunctive clause (see **118**) introduced by *nē*.

Nōlī hoc facere. Cavē nē hoc faciās. 'Do not do this.'

Note 1.—In English also (though in older English and in poetry we constantly find 'go not,' 'fear not,' etc.) we generally use the infinitive with the imperative of an auxiliary verb : *do* not go, *do* not fear.

Note 2.—When *cavē* is used, the conjunction *nē* is often omitted.

Less frequently the second person of the *perfect subjunctive* with *nē* is used.

Nē dubitāverīs. Do not hesitate.

Note 3.—The second person *present* subjunctive is used for general maxims.

Nē multa discās, sed multum. Do not learn many things, but learn deeply.

Note 4.—The imperative with *nē* is not used to express a negative command in prose.

144. Prohibitions in the (*first* and) *third* persons are expressed by *nē* and the *present* subjunctive.

Nē veniat. Let him not come.

145. When a (subjunctive) prohibition follows another prohibition or a command, *nēve* (*neu*) is used as the conjunction.

Exeat nēve plūra dīcat. Let him go out and say no more.
Hoc facitō ; illud nē fēcerīs, nēve dīxerīs. Do this ; do not do or say that.

Note.—Two infinitives dependent on *nōlī* (**143**) are connected by *ac*, *aut*, or (somewhat illogically) *nec*.

146. *Vīderis* and *vīderint* are sometimes used in the sense of 'you, they, must look to it.'

Dē hāc rē tū vīderis, or *vīderint sapientiōrēs.* I leave this to you, *or* to wiser men ; do you, *or* let wiser men, decide.

These forms are probably future perfect indicatives, not perfect subjunctives. A statement of what will have happened has here the force of a polite command.

Exercise 18

A

1. Do not then lose (*sing.*) such an opportunity as[1] this, but rather let us, under your leadership, crush the eternal enemies of our country. 2. Do not, my countrymen, fear the foes who are threatening you with massacre and slavery ; let them rather meet the same lot which they are preparing for us. 3. Pardon (*sing.*) this fault of mine ; and be sure you remember that I, who have done wrong to-day, have repeatedly brought you help before. 4. Let us then refuse to be slaves, and have the courage not only to become free ourselves, but to assert our country's freedom also. 5. Therefore[2] do not object to[3] enduring everything on behalf of your suffering country and your exiled friends. 6. I exhort you, my countrymen, not to believe that I, who have so often led you to the field of battle, am afraid to-day of fortune abandoning me. 7. Let us be the same in the field (of battle) as[4] we have ever been ; as[5] to the issue of the battle let the gods decide.

---

[1] See **88**, *Note*.
[2] See **79**.
[3] See **130**.
[4] See **84**.
[5] Prep. *dē* with abl.

B

I am afraid that this letter will not reach you across the enemies' lines. We have now been [1] invested here for a whole month (321), and I cannot help beginning to despair of the whole state [2] of affairs. The numbers [3] of the enemy are such as we had never dreamed of,[4] and as [5] all the roads are closed, no supplies can be brought up; scarcely any letters reach us, so that it is impossible to doubt that we are involved in very serious danger. Do you therefore not hesitate to write to the general to hasten to bring us assistance, and do not allow yourself to think that I am writing thus with the intention of calling [6] him away from his great designs and bringing him here for the sake of our safety. I fear that the enemy (if once) victorious here, will soon become formidable to him also; and I do not think that we can be crushed without [7] drawing others into the same ruin.

EXERCISE XIX

REMARKS ON MOODS: THE SUBJUNCTIVE USED INDEPENDENTLY

147. By a **Mood** we mean a group of verb-forms which (either by themselves or in relation to a given context) represent a verbal activity (or state) as being *real*, *willed*, *desired*, or *hypothetical*. These forms mark the manner (*modus*) in which the speaker is viewing the verbal activity.

Note 1.—No language has a separate mood for every conceivable aspect of verbal activity; for example, Latin (unlike Greek) has no separate mood to express wish, as distinct from command. On the other hand, one aspect of verbal activity may be expressed by more than one mood; for example, in Latin both the Imperative and the Subjunctive are used to express command.

---

[1] Tense? (See **181.**) [2] *summa rēs.* [3] *multitūdō* (sing.).
[4] Metaphor; say, 'fancied would come together.'
[5] Abl. abs. (**420.**) [6] See **15.** [7] See **111.**

The functions of the Latin moods are as follows :—

The **Indicative** makes a statement or enquiry about a fact, or about something which will be a fact in the future.

Amō 'I love'; *amatne?* 'does he love?'; *sī vēnerit, vidēbit* 'if he comes, he will see'; *nōn ēmit* 'he did not buy.'

The **Imperative** expresses the will of the speaker as a command, request, entreaty.

Amā 'love thou'; *mihi ignōsce* 'pardon me'; *valē* 'farewell.'

The **Subjunctive** represents a verbal activity as willed, desired, conditional, or prospective.

Istam nē relīquerīs 'do not leave her!'; *dī prohibeant* 'may the gods forbid'; *sī veniās, videās* 'if you were to come, you would see.'

Note 2.—In modern English the subjunctive mood has largely fallen into disuse, although it is still found in clauses like: 'though he *fail*'; 'if it *be* so.'

148. The **Subjunctive** is used in Latin (*a*) in simple sentences and in the main sentence of a complex sentence; (*b*) in subordinate clauses. This Exercise is mainly concerned with its use in simple sentences.

Note.—The mood takes its name from the fact that it is used in many types of subordinate (or *subjoined*) clauses. But many subordinate clauses were originally independent of the verb which, in classical Latin, seems to 'govern' them (see **129**, *Note* and **137**, *Note* for striking examples); and the subjunctive in such clauses is used not to indicate subordination, but because the subjunctive is the only mood to express the precise meaning required.

For the use of the subjunctive simply as a mood of subordination see, *e.g.* **164**, *Note.*

149. The **Subjunctive of Will** (sometimes called the Volitive or Jussive Subjunctive) has various uses in simple sentences :—

(*a*) It is used (in the present and perfect tenses) to express *commands* and *exhortations*, and (with the negative *nē*) *prohibitions*. (See **142, 143, 144.**)

Abeat. Let him go away.
Amēmus patriam. Let us love our country.
Nē dubitāverīs. Do not hesitate.
Nē veniat. Let him not come.

Note 1.—It is a subjunctive of this type which is used in Final clauses (**101**) and in Indirect commands (**117**). Originally such subjunctives were felt to be merely placed by the side of another sentence, so that *hoc faciō : nē veniās* meant 'I do this : you are not to come,' and *imperō : nē veniās* meant 'I give an order : you are not to come.' This juxtaposition of sentences of which neither is yet felt to be subordinate is called **parataxis.** Later the subjunctive of will was felt to be subordinate to the verb of the other sentence and the use of the subordinating conjunction *ut* (when the subjunctive was not negatived by *nē*) became common, but not invariable. (See **121.**)

(*b*) The Subjunctive of Will is also used (in the present and perfect tenses, sometimes in the imperfect) in *concessions* and *suppositions* (negative *nē*).

Sit fūr. Granted that he is a thief.
Fuerit malus cīvis. Suppose he was a bad citizen.

(*c*) The Subjunctive of Will is also used (in the present and imperfect tenses, sometimes in the pluperfect) to express what ought to be done or was to be done as a matter of *obligation* or *propriety.* In this usage the negative is *nōn* (**not** *nē*).

Quō mē nunc vertam ? Where am I now to turn ?
Nōnne argentum redderem ? nōn redderēs. Ought I to have returned the money ? you ought not.

Note. 2.—When, as is often the case, a subjunctive of this type is in an interrogative sentence, it is sometimes called **a deliberative** subjunctive.

Note 3.—Obligation can also be expressed by using the Gerundive (see **387-92**).

150. The **Subjunctive of Desire** (sometimes called the Optative Subjunctive) expresses a *wish* or a *prayer.* The present (and sometimes the perfect) expresses a wish for the future : the imperfect a wish that something were so now ; the pluperfect a wish that something had been so in the past. Such wishes are often introduced by *utinam* when positive, and by *nē* or *utinam nē* when negative.

Sīs fēlīx ! May you be happy !
Utinam adessēs ! Would that you were here !
Utinam potuissem ! Would I had been able !
Quod utinam nē faciātis ! And may you never do this !

Note.—A subjunctive of desire is used in subordinate clauses dependent upon: (*a*) verbs of 'wishing' like ***optō, cupiō, velim*** (see **120**), and (*b*) verbs of 'fearing' (see **137**). The tense of the subjunctive verb in such subordinate clauses, however, follows the normal rule for sequence (**105**).

151. The **Subjunctive of Conditioned Futurity** expresses one verbal activity as being dependent upon the fulfilment of another. It is negatived by *nōn* (**not** *nē*).

(*Hanc viam sī asperam esse negem*), *mentiar.* (If I were to deny that this road is rough), I should lie.

Note.—Subjunctives of this type are so called because the verbal activity is 'future' in so far as it has not yet taken place, and its fulfilment is conditioned by the fulfilment of another action. The English 'would' (and 'should') are generally to be translated by such a subjunctive.

The present (and sometimes the perfect) tense denotes what would happen (in a vague future) if some imagined condition of the present or future were fulfilled.

The imperfect and pluperfect tenses denote what would be happening or would have happened if some imagined condition of the past were being fulfilled or had been fulfilled. The reference of the imperfect is generally to the present, that of the pluperfect always to the past.

(*Sī faciās*), *peccēs.* (If you were to do it), you would sin.

(*Sī facerēs*), *peccārēs.* (If you were doing it), you would be sinning.

(*Sī fēcissēs*), *peccāvissēs.* (If you had done it), you would have sinned.

152. Subjunctives of Conditioned Futurity are most frequently used in the main sentence of a conditional statement (see **455-8**); but sometimes the condition is taken for granted and therefore not expressed.

Hoc tū dīcere audeās? Would you dare to say this (*e.g.* if you realised what you were doing)?

Migrantēs cernās (Virg.). One would see them leaving (if one were there).

Crēderēs victōs (Livy). You would think (have thought) they were vanquished (*e.g.* if you had seen them).

Three common types of expression in which the condition is not expressed are—

(*a*) ***Dīcat aliquis.*** Someone would say (*e.g.* if he gave his opinion).

Note 1.—This phrase often introduces an imaginary objection, which the writer proposes to forestall.

(*b*) *Vix crēdiderim.* I should scarcely believe (*e.g.* if I were sane).

Note 2.—Such phrases are sometimes called **modest assertions;** thus *ausim* (an old Perf. Subj.) means 'I am inclined to venture.'

(*c*) *Velim adsīs.* I (should) wish you were here (*e.g.* if wishes counted for anything).

Vellem adessēs (*adfuissēs*). I wish you were (had been) here.

Note 3.—In this type, the *velim* or *vellem* amounts to little more than a polite expression for *volō.* (See **150,** *Note.*) The *adsīs* and *adessēs* are dependent wishes (see **120, 121**).

Note 4.—It is quite legitimate in many contexts to translate such phrases as those given above by the English 'may' and 'could': *Dīcat aliquis* 'someone may say'; *vix crēdiderim* 'I could scarcely believe'; *velim* 'I could wish.' But it must be clearly understood that the Subjunctive cannot *of itself and apart from a particular context* express such ideas as 'may' (=may possibly), 'may' (=am permitted), 'can' (=am able). 'He may (possibly) come' is to be expressed in Latin by *fortasse veniet, forsitan veniat* (**169**), or *fierī potest ut veniat* (**127**); 'he may (=is permitted to) come' by *eī venīre licet*; 'he can (=is able to) come' by *venīre potest.* See the whole of Exercise XXIV.

153. An indicative instead of a subjunctive of conditioned futurity is used when a verb of 'duty' or 'possibility' is involved.

Potuī hoc facere. I might have (could have) done this.

Hoc dēbuistī facere. You should (ought to) have done this.

Note 1.—The reason for this apparent exception is that the *duty* or *ability* is not conditioned by the fulfilment of another action; what is conditioned is the *accomplishment* of the possible or obligatory activity. (See further **461.**)

Note 2.—Observe that the idea of past time in such Latin phrases is expressed by the tense of the finite verb, and not by the tense of the infinitive.

The indicative of *sum* is also used (instead of the subjunctive of conditioned futurity) when the predicate consists of that verb and a gerundive or a neuter adjective. (See **463**.)

Ille interficiendus erat, sī hoc fēcisset. He ought to have been killed if he had done this.

Haec omnia dīcere longum (*melius, satius*) *est.* It would be a lengthy task (better, preferable) to tell the whole story.

Exercise 19

1. This at least I would venture to say, that as [1] I was the first to urge you to undertake this work, so [1] I promise to be the last to advise you to abandon the undertaking. 2. What was I to do, said he, what to say? Who would care to blame me because I refused to listen to such [2] abandoned men? 3. I would neither deny nor assert that he had looked forward to all this (*pl.*), but he should have provided against the country being overwhelmed by such disasters. 4. On that day my brother was reluctantly absent from the battle at your suggestion; would that he had been [3] there! For it would have been better to fall on the field of battle than to submit to such dishonour. 5. In return [4] then for such acts of kindness, I would have you not only feel but also show your gratitude. 6. I could have wished that you had sent me the best [5] soldiers that you had with you. 7. The soldiers stood (*imperf.*) drawn up in line, eager for the fight,[6] with [7] eyes fixed on the foe, clamouring for the signal. 8. I have consulted, as [8] I ought to have done, your (*pl.*) interests rather than my own; may you not ever impute this to me as a fault!

EXERCISE XX

INTERROGATIVE SENTENCES

I. Direct (Single and Alternative)

154. Interrogative sentences or questions are either Direct or Indirect.

Note.—A **direct question** is a simple sentence which differs from a *statement* or a *command* inasmuch as the connexion between the subject and the predicate is not *stated*, or *willed*, but only *enquired about*.

---

[1] as . . . so, *et* . . . *et*.
[2] See **88.**
[3] Use *adsum*.
[4] *prō*, with abl.
[5] See **69.**
[6] Gerund, **99.**
[7] Abl. abs., 'their eyes fixed.'
[8] See **67**, *Note*.

The **indicative** mood is used in all direct questions except those whose meaning requires a deliberative subjunctive (**149**, *Note* 2) or a subjunctive of conditioned futurity (**151**).

Cūr vēnit? Why did he come?
Quid faciam? What am I to do?
Num id fēcissēs? Would you have done it?

155. In English we mark a question by the order of the words, and sometimes by the insertion of an auxiliary verb. Compare 'Saw ye?' with 'you saw'; 'Is he well?' with 'he is well'; 'Did you see?' with 'you saw'; and in French 'Va-t-il?' with 'il va.'

But in Latin, where the order of the words would have no such effect (Intr. 78), an interrogation is usually indicated by an interrogative particle (*-ne, num, nōnne, an*), or by interrogative *pronoun* or pronominal *adverb*.

Note.—Occasionally, the interrogative particle is omitted when the context provides sufficient indication that a question is being asked.

156. The interrogative particles used in Direct Single Questions are: *-ne, num, nōnne.*

(*a*) **-ne** (enclitic, see Intr. 89, *Note*) is used in questions that ask simply for information, and to which the answer may be either 'yes' or 'no.'

Scrībitne Gaius? Is Gaius writing? (The person who asks the question does not expect one answer more than another.)

Note.—*Ne* is always attached to the emphatic word placed at the beginning of the sentence.

Praetōremne accūsās? Is it a praetor whom you are accusing?
Mēne fugis? Is it from me that you are fleeing?

Notice here how English emphasises a noun by making it the predicate of a sentence whose subject is 'it,' and puts the less important verbal notion into a subordinate clause. For another example of this English usage, see **82.**

(*b*) **Num** expects the answer 'no.'

Num putās? Do you fancy? = Surely you don't fancy, do you? (expected answer 'no').

(*c*) **Nōnne** expects the answer 'yes.'

Nōnne putās? Don't you fancy? = Surely you do fancy, don't you? (expected answer 'yes').

157. Other interrogative words are either (i) Pronouns, or (ii) Adverbs.

(i) The interrogative Pronouns are :—

quis, quid, who, what ?	*quālis*, of what kind ?
quī, quae, quod, what sort of ?	*quantus*, how great ?
ecquis, ecquid, is there any who ?	*quantum*, how much ?
quisnam, quaenam, quidnam, who, pray ?	*quot*, how many ?
uter, which of the two ?	*quotus*, which in a series ?

Note 1.—Distinguish carefully between *quis* (*quid*) which is a pronoun and *quī* (*quae quod*) which is a pronominal adjective.

Quid fēcit ? What has he done ?

Quod facinus admīsit ? What (sort of) crime has he committed ?

Note 2.—*Num* is frequently associated with *quis*: *num quis est quī* . . . 'Is there anyone who . . .'

Note 3.—*Quantum* is followed by a partitive genitive: *quantum cibī* 'how much food ?' (See **294.**)

Note 4.—*Quotus quisque* is used to imply 'few' or 'none': *quotus quisque est disertus* 'how few men are eloquent' (*i.e.* 'in what order (of merit) is each one eloquent,' implying that few or none take any rank as orators).

(ii) The interrogative Adverbs are :—

ubi, where ?	*quōmodo* / *quem ad modum* } how, in what manner ?
unde, whence ?	*cūr, quārē*, / *quam ob rem* } why, wherefore ?
quō, whither ?	*quantum, quantopere*, how greatly ?
quā, by what way ?	*quoūsque*, how long, how far ?
quandō, when ?	*quam*, how ? (with adjectives and adverbs)
quotiēns, how often ?	
quamdiū, how long ?	

Note 5.—The adverb *tandem* is often placed immediately after an interrogative word to give emphasis.

Quoūsque tandem ? To what point, I ask ?

Quae tandem causa ? What possible cause ?

Note 6.—The old ablative form *quī* 'how' is used in the phrase *quī fit ut* . . . ? 'how comes it that . . . ?' (See 127.)

Note 7.—Observe that *cum* 'when' is never used as an interrogative.

Alternative Direct Questions

158. In English two or more questions may be combined by the disjunctive conjunction 'or', so that an affirmative answer to the one negatives the other or others. These are called **alternative, disjunctive,** or **double** questions.

'Are you going to Germany, *or* (are you going) to Italy, *or* to France?'

We have here simple sentences joined together by *co-ordination.* (See Intr. 66.)

In English the first question has no interrogative particle ('whether' being obsolete in *direct* questions), the second and any further questions are introduced by 'or,' which however is sometimes, where the verb is suppressed, confined to the last.

'Did you mean me, *or* think of yourself, *or* refer to some one else?'

'Did you mean me, him, *or* yourself?'

159. In Latin the first question is introduced by *utrum,* or the enclitic *-ne*; the second, or any further question, by *an* (**never** by *aut* or *vel*).

Utrum hostem, an ducem, an vōsmet ipsōs culpātis? Is it the enemy, or your general, or yourselves that you blame?
Servīne estis an līberī? Are you slaves or freemen?

But frequently, as in English, no interrogative particle introduces the first question; and the second question is then introduced by *an,* or *anne,* or (more rarely) by the enclitic *-ne.*

Erum vīdistī an ancillam? Did you see the master or the maid?
Hoc illudne fēcistī? Did you do this or that?

Or not?' in a direct question should be translated by **annōn.** Contrast with **168.**

Īvitne annōn? Did he go, or not?

160. Thus alternative questions are introduced by:—

1. *utrum,* }
2. *-ne,* . } . . . . *an, anne, annōn?*
3. —— }

161. *Num* is occasionally used for *utrum* where a negative answer is expected.

An is sometimes found before a single question. But there is always an *ellipsis,* or suppression of a previous question, so that even here *an* means 'or is it that?' 'can it be that?' In such circumstances the answer 'no' is generally expected.

An servī esse vultis? (Or is it that) you wish to be slaves?

Answers to Questions

162. The affirmative or negative answer is rarely given in Latin so simply as by the English 'yes' and 'no.'

An affirmative answer may be indicated by *etiam*, *ita vērō*, *sānē*; and a negative by *minimē*, *minimē vērō*, *nēquāquam*, *nōn*.

But more often some emphatic word is repeated from the interrogative sentence (with or without *etiam*, etc.); such a question as *dāsne hoc mihi?* could be answered by *dō*, *dō vērō* (='yes'); or by *nōn dō*, *minimē ego quidem* (='no'). Other types of answer may be illustrated by:

Vīsne hoc facere? velle sē, nōlle sē, respondit. Are you ready to do this? he answered 'yes,' 'no.'

Num hoc fēcistī? Have you then done this? *Negō.* I answer 'no.' *Fēci, inquam.* I answer 'yes.' *Aiō.* I say 'yes'.

Exercise 20

A

1. Is it possible for a true patriot to refuse to obey the law [1]? 2. Where, said he, did you come from, and whither and when do you hope [2] to start hence? 3. Can we help fearing that your brother will go away into exile with reluctance? 4. What crime, what enormity, has my client [3] committed, what falsehood has he told, what, in short, has he either said or done that you, gentlemen of the jury, should be ready to inflict on him either death or exile by your verdict? 5. Will any one venture to assert that he was condemned in his absence in order to prevent his pleading his cause at home, or impressing the jury by his eloquence? 6. Was it by force of arms, or by judgment, courage, and good sense, that Rome was able to dictate terms to the rest of the world? 7. Does it seem [4] to you

[1] See Ex. 9A, sentence 3. [2] 37.
[3] Simply *hic*, 'this man.' (See 338, *Note* 1.) [4] See 43, *Note* 2.

that death is an eternal sleep, or the beginning of another life? 8. Are you ready to show yourselves men of courage, such as the country looks for in such a crisis as this? You answer 'yes.' Or are you ceasing to wish to be called Roman soldiers? 'No,' you all reply. 9. Do you believe that the character of your countrymen is altering for the better, or for the worse? 10. Whom am I to defend? Whom am I to accuse? How much longer shall I pretend to be in doubt? Was it (**156**) by accident or design that this murder was committed? 11. What am I to believe? Did the enemy or our men win the battle yesterday? Do not tell more falsehoods on such [1] an important question. 12. Was he not a prophet of such a kind that no one ever believed [2] him?

B

Are we to say that Caesar was foully [3] murdered or that he was rightfully [4] slain? That either one [5] or the other is true is most certain. Do you (*sing.*) then choose whichever [6] you like; but do not say now this, now that, and [7] do not to-day look on Brutus as a patriot, to-morrow as an assassin. Did Caesar pay the penalty of his crimes? You answer 'No'; then let his slayers be either banished or put [8] to death as traitors. Or [9] did Brutus speak the truth, when [10] (while) raising aloft the bloody dagger, he exclaimed that the nation's freedom was recovered? 'Yes,' you reply. Then why do you heap abuse on one to whom alone [11] you are indebted for your freedom? Or [7] do you think that what Brutus did was in [12] itself right and a benefit [13] to the nation, but that he himself acted criminally, and should be punished [14] with banish-

[1] **88.** [2] See **113.** [3] 'criminally.'
[4] *iūre caesus*, a legal phrase.
[5] *hic, ille.* (See **340**, ii.) [6] *utervīs.* (**379.**) [7] **145.**
[8] 'He is put to death, etc.,' *mōre maiōrum in eum animadvertitur*, a *euphemism* for scourging and beheading. [9] *An.* (**161.**)
[10] *tum . . . cum.* (**431.**) [11] *ūnus.* (**529.**) [12] *per sē.*
[13] Use neut. of *ūtilis*; *beneficium* means 'a kindness, a favour.'
[14] Gerundive of *multō, -āre*, with abl.

ment, or imprisonment, or death ? For myself I decline to meddle with so nice [1] a question : I leave it (146) to philosophers.

EXERCISE XXI

INTERROGATIVE SENTENCES—*Continued*

II. Dependent or Indirect

163. The **dependent** or **indirect question is a** *noun clause* dependent upon a verb of 'asking, enquiring, telling, knowing,' etc., and introduced by an Interrogative Pronoun, Adverb, or Particle.

Quis es? 'who are you ?'; *Cūr hoc fēcistī?* 'why have you done this ?' are direct questions, and each is a simple sentence.

But *rogō quis sit*, 'I ask who he is'; *dīc mihi cūr hoc fēceris*, 'tell me why you did this,' are two complex sentences. Neither *taken as a whole* is a question : the first is a *statement*, the second a *command*; but each *contains* an indirect question.

164. In Latin the verb in an indirect question is invariably subjunctive. It is of the utmost importance to remember this, as the subjunctive mood is not used in such clauses in English.

Compare the English and Latin moods in—

Quis eum occīdit? Who killed him ?
Quis eum occīderit quaerō. I ask who killed him.

Note.—The subjunctive in such clauses is simply the mood of subordination ; it has here no distinctive meaning of its own (see **148**, *Note*). Indeed, in early Latin the indicative was used in indirect questions.

165. An indirect question may depend not only on a verb like *rogō* which has no other meaning except that of 'enquiry,' but also upon any verb or phrase which in a given context *implies* a question.

Quid faciendum sit moneō monēbōque. I warn and will warn you what you ought to do.

Quandō esset reditūrus metuī. I had fears as to when he would return.

---

[1] *subtīlis*, or *difficilis*.

Cūr haec fēcerit mīror. I wonder why he did this.

Incertum (difficile dictū est, magnī rēfert) num hoc vērum sit. It is uncertain (difficult to say, of great importance) whether this is true.

Note.—This illustrates the important principle that many Latin verbs do not have a fixed construction; for the construction of a verb is not determined mechanically, but by its **meaning**. If it has several shades of meaning, it may have several constructions. With the construction of *moneō* above, compare its use as a verb of 'command' (**118**); and with the construction of *metuō* above, compare its use as a verb of 'fearing' (**137**).

166. In English the interrogative nature of a subordinate clause is not always obvious; and this point must be kept in mind when translating into Latin. Thus, 'I know what you have found' contains not a relative clause (*quod invēnistī*) but an indirect question (*quid invēnerīs*). There is ambiguity in 'Tell me when your father arrives'; for according to the context the subordinate clause is either temporal (*cum*) or an indirect question (*quandō*).

167. Single Indirect Questions are introduced in the same ways as Single Direct Questions (**155-7**), except that *num* does not imply a negative answer and *nōnne* is used only after *quaerō*.

Epamīnōndās quaesīvit salvusne esset clipeus. Epaminondas asked whether his shield was safe.

Dīc mihi num eadem quae ego sentiās. Tell me if you have the same opinion as I.

Quaesierās ex mē, nōnne putārem, etc. You had inquired of me whether I did not suppose, etc.

Note.—In English an indirect question is often introduced by 'if' (see second example above). When 'if' is so used, it must *not* be translated by *sī*.

Alternative Indirect Questions

168. Alternative Indirect Questions are introduced like Alternative Direct Questions (**159**), except that *anne* is rare, and **necne** is used instead of *annōn*.

Thus, 'It matters not whether you are slaves or free' may be rendered by:

Utrum servī sītis an līberī,
Servīne sītis an līberī,
Servī sītis an līberī, } *nihil rēfert.*

Note.—It is important to remember that 'or not' in an indirect question is necne.

Itūrus sit necne, rogābimus. We shall ask whether or not he is about to go.

169. (i) *An* normally introduces a second or third question; but *haud scio* 'I know not' is followed by an indirect question introduced by *an* because a first question is suppressed (see **161**).

Difficile hoc est, tamen haud[1] *scio an fierī possit.* This is difficult, yet perhaps (I incline to think that) it is possible.

(ii) *Forsitan* (=*fors sit an* 'it would be a chance whether') is also followed by an indirect question.

(iii) Both *haud scio an* and *forsitan* mean little more than 'perhaps, possibly.'

(iv) *Nescio quis* when used as if one word forms an indefinite pronoun (see **362**) and the *nescio* is not then regarded as governing an indirect question. Contrast:—

Nescio quis venit. Someone is coming; with—
Nescio quis veniat. I do not know who is coming.

(v) Similarly *nescio quī* (adjectival) is used for 'some sort of' and *nescio quō modō* for 'somehow.'

170. *Forte* is not 'perhaps,' but 'by accident.'

Forte cecidit is 'he happened to fall,' not 'perhaps he fell.'
Forte abest, 'he is accidentally absent.'

'Perhaps' may be expressed in the following ways:—

Forsitan absit, 'perhaps (it may be that) he is absent.'
Nescio (haud scio) an absit, 'perhaps (I incline to think that) he is absent.'
Fortasse abest, 'perhaps (it is likely that) he is absent.'

171. Notice how the English 'if,' 'whether,' and 'or,' are rendered in the following sentences; and observe that *sī*,[2] *sive, seu, aut*,[3] *vel*, are not used as *interrogatives* in Latin.

(*a*) You shall die if (conditional) you do this. *Moriēre sī haec fēceris* (fut. perf. ind.).

---

[1] *Haud* is mostly used with *scio*; and with adjectives and adverbs in the sense of 'far from,' when a negative idea is substituted for a positive, as *haud difficilis* for *facilis*, etc.

[2] For the special use of *sī*, 'in hopes that,' after *exspectō, cōnor*, and similar verbs, see Conditional Clauses, **475**.

[3] For the difference between *aut* and *vel*, see Intr. **49**.

(*b*) I ask if (interrogative) you did this. *Num haec fēceris* (subj.) *rogō.*

(*c*) He shall go, whether he likes it or no (alternative condition). *Seu vult seu nōn vult, ībit.*

(*d*) I ask whether he likes it or no (alternative question). *Utrum velit an nōlit rogō.*

(*e*) He is either a wise man or a fool (disjunctive sentence). *Aut sapiēns est aut stultus.*

(*f*) I don't know whether he is a wise man or a fool. *Utrum sapiēns sit an stultus nescio.*

Exercise 21

1. Whether Caesar was rightfully put to death, or foully murdered, is open to question. It [1] is allowed by all that he was killed on the 15th [2] of March by Brutus and Cassius and the rest of the conspirators. 2. It is still uncertain whether our men have won the day or no; but whether they have won or lost it, I am certain that they have been false neither to their allies nor to their country. 3. It is hard to say whether he injured the world [3] or benefited it most; it is unquestionable that he was a man, alike in his ability (*abl.*) as in his achievements, such as we cannot hope to see again in this world. 4. It is scarcely credible how often you and I have advised that (friend) of yours [4] not [5] to break his word; but it [6] seems that we shall lose our labour to-morrow, as yesterday and the day before. 5. Be sure you write me word when the king will start for [7] the army. He is perhaps lingering purposely in order to raise an army and increase his resources. I am afraid he will not [8] effect this,[9] for people are either alarmed or disaffected. 6. Some one has warned me not to forget how much you once injured me in my boyhood. Whether you did so (this) or not matters little; what [10] is of importance to me is whether you are ready

[1] *Illud, i.e.* 'the following.'
[2] *Īdibus Mārtiīs.*
[3] 16, *b.*
[4] See 11, *d.*
[5] See 118.
[6] See 43, *Note* 2.
[7] *Ad.*
[8] See 137.
[9] Relative.
[10] Lit., 'the following (*illud*) is of importance.'

to be my friend now. 7. As[1] he felt himself sinking (*inf.*) under a severe wound, he asked first if his shield was safe; they answered yes; secondly, if the enemy had been routed; they replied in the affirmative. 8. They asked if it was not better to die than to live dishonourably. 9. He was the dearest to me of my soldiers, and perhaps the bravest of (them) all.

EXERCISE XXII

DEPENDENT INTERROGATIVE—*Continued*

Mood and Tense—Interrogative Clauses for English Nouns

172. As has been explained, the mood used in direct questions is *generally* the indicative (**154**), and in indirect questions it is *always* subjunctive in classical Latin (**164**).

If the meaning of a direct question is such that the subjunctive mood is required, no change of mood *can* take place when such a question becomes indirect. Thus a deliberative question is expressed by the subjunctive (**149**, *Note* 2): *quid faciam?* 'What am I to do?' When a deliberative question is dependent upon a verb of 'enquiring' it can often not be distinguished from an indirect question relating to fact. Thus *rogās quid faciam* may mean either 'you ask what I am doing' or 'you ask what I am to do.' When it was necessary to bring out the second meaning, the Romans made use of the gerundive, which could express obligation: *rogās quid mihi faciendum sit* (**388, 390**).

For subjunctives of conditioned futurity which are themselves in an indirect question see **474**.

173. The tense of a subjunctive verb in an indirect question is generally determined by the rule for normal sequence of tenses (**105**).

Note 1.—The application of this rule sometimes involves difficulties. How are we to render 'tell me what you were doing'? If we write: *dīc mihi quid fēceris*, the perfect subjunctive will

---

[1] *Cum* with imperf. subj.

imply that the activity was not continuous but completed; but if we write: *dīc mihi quid facerēs,* we shall violate the rule for normal sequence. The Romans sometimes avoided the difficulty by keeping the question independent: *dīc mihi! quid faciēbās?* Sometimes they neglected the sequence for the sake of the sense :—

Quaerō abs tē cūr Cornēlium nōn dēfenderem. I ask you why I was not to defend Cornelius.

Quid causae fuerit postrīdiē intellēxī. I realised next day what the reason was.

But in the majority of instances the normal sequence is followed.

Note 2.—If the question is such that stress is laid on the future, we must use the future participle and a tense of *sum* :—

Quandō esset reditūrus rogāvī. I asked when he would return.

174. Indirect questions introduced by *quis* (*quī*), *quālis, quantus, quot, quandō, cūr,* etc., are very often used in Latin where in English we use a single word, such as *nature, character, amount, size, number, date, object, origin, motive,* etc.

Latin does not use nearly so many *abstract terms* as English. Thus—

(*a*) *Quot essent hostēs, quantās habērent opēs, quandō domō profectī essent, rogāvit.* He asked the number of the enemy, the magnitude of their resources, the date of their departure from home.

(*b*) *Quāle ac quantum sit perīculum dēmōnstrat.* He explains the nature and extent of the danger.

(*c*) *Quālis sit, quem ad modum senex vīvat, vidētis.* You see the kind of man he is, his manner of life in his old age (63).

(*d*) *Haec rēs quō ēvāsūra sit, exspectō.* I am waiting to see the issue of this matter.

(*e*) *Quam repentīnum sit hoc malum intellegō, unde ortum sit nescio.* I perceive the suddenness of this danger, its source I know not.

These are only a few of the many instances where Latin prefers simple and direct modes of expression to the more abstract and general forms of noun with which we are familiar in English. (See **54.**)

175. For the same reason, as well as from a lack of substantives in Latin to express *classes* of persons, and also of verbal substantives denoting *agents*, such English substantives must often be translated into Latin by a **relative** (adjectival) clause (see 76). Thus—

> 'Politicians,' *quī in rēpūblicā versantur;* 'students,' *quī litterīs dant operam;* 'my father's murderers,' *quī patrem meum occīdērunt;* 'my well-wishers,' *quī mē salvum volunt;* 'the government,' *quī reīpūblicae praesunt;* 'his predecessors on the throne,' *quī ante eum rēgnāverant.*

For the use or omission of *iī* with this use of *quī* see 71.

176. Remember, however, that the difference between these two kinds of dependent clause, the *relative* (adjectival) and the *indirect interrogation*, will be marked by the use of the *indicative* in the one, the *subjunctive* in the other. Thus in:

> (*a*) *Hī sunt quī patrem tuum occīdērunt.* These are your father's murderers;

the relative *quī* introduces an *adjectival* clause; but in:

> (*b*) *Quī patrem suum occīderint nescit.* He knows not who were his father's murderers;

the interrogative *quī* (pl. of *quis*) introduces a dependent question. Similarly, in:

> (*a*) *Quae vērē sentiō dīcam,* I will utter my real sentiments;

quae is a relative; but in:

> (*b*) *Quae vērē sentiam dīcam,* I will tell you what are my real sentiments;

quae is interrogative.

Exercise 22

A

1. I am waiting to see why this crowd has gathered and what will be the issue of the uproar. 2. I wish [1] you would explain to me his manner of life in boyhood; I know pretty well the kind of man that he is now. 3. We perceived well enough that danger was at hand; of its source, nature, character, and extent, we were ignorant. 4. Do but reflect on the greatness of your debt to your country and your forefathers; remember who you are and the position that you occupy. 5. I knew not (*imperf.*) whither to turn, what to do, how to inflict punishment on my brother's

[1] 152, *c*.

murderers. 6. Who did this evil deed I know not, but whoever he was, he shall be punished. 7. The reason why politicians do not agree with the commanders of armies is pretty clear. 8. I wonder who were the bearers of this message, whether (they were) the same as the perpetrators of the crime or no. 9. He was superior to all his predecessors on the throne in ability ; but he did not perceive the character of the man who was destined to be his successor. 10. The government was aware of the suddenness of the danger, but they did not suspect its magnitude and probable [1] duration.

B

The king summoned his staff and set before them the nature and extent of the danger, the numbers of the enemy, the magnitude of their resources, their aims,[2] designs,[2] and hopes. For my part, said he, I will utter my real sentiments and will not hide the fact [3] that I have no doubt that all (of) you and I myself are to-day involved in the greatest danger. I know that it is difficult to say [4] whether the reinforcements which we look for will ever reach us, or whether we shall perish first,[5] overwhelmed by the weapons of this enormous [6] host. But whether [7] we live or die, I venture to feel confident of this at least, that no one of us will allow himself to think it a light [8] matter, whether our countrymen are to be grateful to us in our graves [9] or to scorn (despise) us while we still live. We need deliberate on one single question: by what [10] course of action or what endurance we shall best benefit our country. Possibly we can consult our own safety by remaining here, sheltered and preserved by these walls ; and perhaps this [11] is the safer plan ; but it sometimes happens that

---

[1] 173, *Note* 2.
[2] 174. Use the verbs *petō* and *mōlior*. [3] *illud*. (341.)
[4] Supine in *-ū*. (404.) [5] *prius*. [6] Simply *tantus*. (88.)
[7] 171, *c*. [8] *parvī facere*. (305.)
[9] Metaphor; use *mortuus*. (61.)
[10] 'By doing what, enduring what.' (398.) [11] Relative.

the most daring[1] course is the safest; and I hope to persuade you that it will so turn out to-day.

EXERCISE XXIII

TENSES OF THE INDICATIVE

177. The Latin indicative tenses express two things: (*a*) a **time** at which the action of the verb takes place (Present, Future, or Past); (*b*) a **kind** of action, either Momentary, Continuous, or Completed. The tenses may therefore be arranged thus:—

Kind of Action	Time of Action: Present	Past	Future
Momentary	Present **rogō,** *I ask.*	Historic Perfect **rogāvī,** *I asked.*	Future **rogābō,** *I shall ask.*
Continuous	Present **rogō,** *I am asking.*	Imperfect **rogābam,** *I was asking.*	Future **rogābō,** *I shall be asking.*
Completed	Present Perfect **rogāvī,** *I have asked.*	Pluperfect **rogāveram,** *I had asked.*	Future Perfect **rogāverō,** *I shall have asked.*

Note **1.—It will be seen (i) that some tenses (Present and Future) can express either momentary or continuous action; (ii) that the Perfect can express either an action completed from the point of view of the present (Present Perfect) or a momentary action in the past (Historic Perfect); (iii) that there are no tenses corres-**

[1] See 375, *footnote*.

ponding to 'I have been asking,' 'I had been asking,' 'I shall have been asking.'

Note 2.—The tenses which denote Present and Future time (Present, Present Perfect, Future, and Future Perfect) are called **Primary** tenses; those which denote past time (Historic Perfect, Imperfect, and Pluperfect) are called **Secondary** or Historic. (See **104**.)

The Present

178. The Latin **Present** tense corresponds to both forms of the English present; *scrībō* = 'I write' (momentary), and 'I am writing' (continuous).

179. In English and (far more commonly) in Latin, the *Present* tense is often, in an animated narrative, substituted for the *Historic Perfect*. The writer visualises the events as taking place in the present.

So far as tense sequence is concerned this **Historic Present** is sometimes regarded as Primary, sometimes as Secondary.

Sulla suōs hortātur ut fortī animō sint. Sulla exhorts (=exhorted) his men to be stout-hearted. (Primary Sequence.)

Subitō ēdīcunt cōnsulēs ut ad suum vestītum senātōrēs redīrent. The consuls suddenly publish (=published) an edict, that the senators were to return to their usual dress. (Secondary Sequence.)

180. The Historic Present is always used when a temporal clause introduced by **dum** ('while') denotes a period of time *within which* something else happened.

Dum Rōmānī tempus terunt, Saguntum captum est. While the Romans were wasting time, Saguntum was captured.

181. Since the Latin Perfect cannot express 'I have been doing' (see **177**, *Note* 1), the Romans used the Present in its continuous sense and expressed the idea of the past by the adverbs *iamprīdem, iamdiū, iamdūdum.*

Iamprīdem cupiō abīre. I have long been desiring to depart.

Similarly, since the Latin Pluperfect cannot express 'I had been doing,' the Romans used the Imperfect (a continuous tense of past time) with the adverbs *iamprīdem*, etc.

Cōpiae quās iamdiū comparābant, aderant. The forces which they had long been collecting, were at hand.

Note.—Both Greek and French have a similar idiom: *πάλαι λέγω. Depuis longtemps je parle.*

182. The present is used sometimes, but far less widely than in English, in an *anticipatory* sense for the future.

> *Hoc nī properē fit.* . . . Unless this is done at once. . . .
> *Antequam dīcere incipiō.* . . . Before I begin to speak. . . .

See **190**, *Note*.

The Imperfect

183. The Latin **Imperfect** tense denotes an action which was continuous in the past, and corresponds to the English 'I was doing.'

184. It is the tense of *description* as opposed to mere *narrative* or *statement*.

Thus it is often used to describe the circumstances, or feelings, which accompany the main fact as stated by a verb in the historic perfect :—

> *Caesar armīs rem gerere cōnstituit, vidēbat enim inimīcōrum in diēs maiōrem fierī exercitum, reputābatque, etc.* Caesar decided to have recourse to arms, for he saw the army of his personal enemies increasing daily and he reflected, etc.

Notice how we use the same tense for all three verbs ; *decided, saw, reflected* ; but the two last explain the *continued* circumstances which accounted for the *single fact* of his decision.

185. For the same reason, the imperfect often expresses ideas equivalent to '*began to*,' '*proceeded to*,' '*continued to*,' '*tried to*,' '*were in the habit of*,' '*used to*,' '*were wont to*,' sometimes even to the English '*would*.' It must therefore often be used where we loosely use a preterite, and we must always ask ourselves the precise meaning of the English past tense before we translate it.

> *Barbarī saxa ingentia dēvolvēbant.* The barbarians began to (*or* proceeded to) roll down huge stones.
> *Stābat imperātor immōtus.* The general continued to stand motionless (*or* was seen to stand, as if in a picture).
> *Haec puerī discēbāmus.* When we were boys we used to learn (*or* we learned) this.
> *Huius modī hominēs adulēscens admīrābar.* These were the men whom I admired (*or* would admire) in my youth.

186. What is called the *Historic Infinitive* is often used as a substitute for the imperfect, especially when a *series of actions* is described. The subject of such an infinitive is always nominative.

Interim cottīdiē Caesar Aeduōs frūmentum flāgitāre ; . . . diem ex diē dūcere Aeduī . . . dīcere, etc. Meanwhile Caesar was daily importuning the Aedui for provisions; they kept putting off day after day, asserting, etc.

The Perfect

187. The Latin **Perfect** represents two English tenses. (See **177.**) *Fēcī* is both 'I did' (Historic Perfect), and 'I have done' (Present Perfect).

The Historic Perfect indicates that an action took place in the past, and it differs from the Imperfect in that it does not imply continuous action. It is the ordinary tense used in simply narrating or mentioning a past event.

The Present Perfect indicates that from the point of view of present time an action is completed. It represents an act as past in itself; but in *its result* as coming down to the present. '*I have been* young, and now am old.' So: *vixērunt*, 'they have lived,' *i.e.* and 'are *now dead*.' We should say of a recent event, with the result still fresh in the mind, 'My friend has been killed'; we should not say, 'Cain has killed Abel.'

Though in Latin the same word *dīxī* may mean 'I have spoken,' *i.e.* 'I have finished my speech,' or 'I spoke,' the context will generally make it quite clear in which sense the Latin tense is used.

Note.—The English auxiliary *am, are*, etc., with a past participle, may mislead. 'All *are* slain' may be either *occīsī sunt* (=have been killed *or* were killed), or *occīduntur* (=are being killed), according to the context.

188. Sometimes the verb *habeō*, 'I have,' or 'possess,' is used in combination with a participle (especially of verbs of 'knowing') in a use approaching that of the English auxiliary 'have.'

Hoc compertum, cognitum, explōrātum habeō. I have found out, ascertained, made sure of this.

Hunc hominem iamdiū nōtum habeō. I have long known this man.

Future and Future Perfect

189. The Latin **Future** indicates what will happen in the future; it has both momentary and continuous meanings. *Scrībam* is 'I shall write' and 'I shall be writing.'

The Latin **Future Perfect** indicates that which will be a completed action at some time in the future. *Scrīpserō*, 'I shall have written.'

190. The Latin future and future perfect are used in many circumstances where English uses a present.

Note.—There was no true future in Old English, and we are obliged to use the auxiliaries *shall* and *will* to indicate futurity. We still say, 'I *return* home to-morrow,' whereas Latin says *crās domum redībō* (or *reditūrus sum*).

191. (i) If the indicative verb of a subordinate clause refers to an action which is genuinely future, the future tense is used in Latin.

Dum hīc erō tē amābō. As long as I am here I shall love you.

Facitō hoc ubi volēs. Do this when you please.

Tum, quī poterunt, veniant. Then let those come who are able to.

192. (ii) If the indicative verb of a subordinate clause refers to an action which, although genuinely future, is also prior to the action of the main verb, the future perfect is used in Latin.

Sī tē rogāverō aliquid, nōnne respondēbis? If I put any question to you, will you not answer?

Cum Tullius rūre redierit, ad tē eum mittam. When Tullius returns from the country, I will send him to you.

Quodcumque imperātum erit, fīet. Whatever is ordered shall be done.

Note 1.—In English the perfect is sometimes used where Latin has a future perfect.

Quae cum fēcerō, Rōmam ībō. When I have done this, I shall go to Rome.

Note 2.—For *vīderis, vīderint*, see **146**.

Pluperfect

193. The Latin **pluperfect** indicates that which from the point of view of the past was completed; it does not differ materially from the corresponding English tense, 'I had done.' So *dīxerat* 'he had spoken, he had finished speaking.'

Note 1.—Observe that Latin indicates by the pluperfect in a subordinate clause that an action prior to the main verb was already completed.

Cum eō vēnerat, locō dēlectābātur. As often as (**432**) he came there, he was charmed with the situation.

Quōs vīderat ad sē vocābat. Whomsoever he saw he summoned to him.

Note 2.—For the use of the perfect indicative instead of the pluperfect after *postquam*, etc., see **428**, *Note* 1.

194. Further examples of the use of Latin tenses :

1. *Dum haec inter sē* loquuntur, advesperāscēbat.
2. *Iamdiū tē* exspectō ; . . . *iamprīdem* exspectābam.
3. *Dīxī, iūdicēs ; vōs, cum* cōnsēderō, *iūdicāte.*
4. *Signum pugnandī* datum est ; stābant *immōtī mīlitēs,* respicere, circumspicere ; *hostēs quoque parumper* cūnctātī sunt ; *mox sīgna* īnferre ; *et iam prope intrā tēlī iactum* aderant, *cum subitō in cōnspectum* veniunt *sociī.*
5. *Sī mihi* pārēs, *salvus eris.*
6. *Sī mihi* pārēbis, *salvus eris.*
7. *Sī hoc* fēceris, *moriēre.*
8. *Veniam, sī* poterō.
9. *Quemcumque* cēperat *trucīdārī* iubēbat.

Exercise 23

A

1. I have long been anxious to know the reason why you were so afraid of the nation forgetting [1] you. 2. Both my father and I had for some time been anxious to ascertain your opinion on this question. 3. When you come to Marseilles, I wish [2] you would ask your brother the reason of my having received no letter from him. 4. My speech is over, gentlemen, and I have sat down, as [3] you see. You must now decide on this question. For myself, I hope, and have long been hoping, that my client will be acquitted by your unanimous [4] verdict. 5. While the Medes were making these preparations, the Greeks had already met at the Isthmus. 6. Up to extreme old age your father would learn something fresh daily. 7. As often as the enemy stormed a town belonging [5] to this ill-starred race, they would spare none ; women, children, old men, infants, were butchered, without [6] any distinction being made either of age or sex.

---

[1] 137. [2] See 152, *c*. [3] See 67, *Note*. [4] See 59.
[5] Use a possessive genitive. [6] Abl. abs.: 'no distinction made.'

B

1. He promises to present the man [1] who shall be the first to scale the wall, with a crown of gold.[2] 2. When I have returned from Rome, I will tell you [3] why I sent for you. 3. The Gauls had long been refusing [4] either to go to meet our ambassadors, or to accept the terms which Caesar was offering. 4. Suddenly the enemy came to a halt, but while they [5] were losing time, our men raised [6] a cheer, and charged into the centre of the line of their infantry. 5. The general had for some time seen that his men were hard pressed by the superior numbers of the enemy, who hurled darts and arrows, and strove to force our men from the hill. 6. I have now finished my speech, judges: when you [7] have given your verdict it will be clear whether the defendant is going to return home with impunity, or to be punished for his many crimes.

EXERCISE XXIV

HOW TO TRANSLATE *Can, Could, May, Might, Shall, Must, etc.*

195. The ideas of **possibility, permission, duty, necessity,** are expressed in English by auxiliary verbs, 'can,' 'may,' 'ought,' 'should,' 'must,' etc. (Intr. 33.)

Note.—These words have, in modern English, owing to their constant use as mere auxiliaries, ceased to be used as independent verbs. In Latin no verb has been reduced to this merely auxiliary function, though the verb *sum* is largely used as an auxiliary. (Intr. 35, *Note.*)

---

[1] See 72. [2] See 58.
[3] Of course dative: 'you' is the indirect object of 'tell.'
[4] Use *negō* here, because their refusal was expressed in words.
[5] Use *illī*, to distinguish the enemy from our men. (See 70.)
[6] See 186. [7] *Vōs*, to be placed first. (See 11.)

These ideas are expressed in Latin in the following ways :—

196. Possibility is expressed by *possum* 'I am able,' which is followed by an infinitive.

(*a*) *Hoc facere possum* (*poterō*). I can do this (*now, or in the future*).

(*b*) *Hoc facere poteram* (*potuī*). I could have (*or* might have) done this (*past*).

Note 1.—*Fēcisse,* the literal translation of our 'have done,' would be quite wrong, for it would mean '*have finished* doing' (see **153,** *Note* 2).

Note 2.—*Potest* cannot be used impersonally (=' it is possible') except when the infinitive of an impersonal passive depends upon it (see **219**). Hence we must render 'It is possible to see you' by *vidērī potes,* not by *tē vidēre potest.*

197. The English words 'possible,' 'impossible,' 'possibility,' 'impossibility,' are often used in a sense which is near to 'practicable,' 'impracticable.' In such circumstances, we should translate them into Latin by *fierī potest, fierī nōn potest* with a noun clause introduced by *ut* or *quīn.* (See **127, 134.**)

There was a possibility of our escaping. *Fierī potuit ut effugerēmus.*

It is impossible for us not to do this. *Fierī nōn potest quīn hoc faciāmus.*

When 'possibly' means no more than 'perhaps,' *haud scio an* or *forsitan* with an indirect question is used. (See **169** (iii), **170.**)

198. Permission is expressed by the impersonal verb *licet,* which is constructed with the *dative* and *infinitive.*

(*a*) *Hoc mihi facere licet* (*licēbit*). I may do this (*now* or *hereafter*).

(*b*) *Hoc mihi facere licēbat* (*licuit*). I might have done this (*past*).

Note 1.—Here again, *facere* and not *fēcisse* is used as in the example in **196.**

Note 2.—*Licet* is also used with the subjunctive. (See **118, 121.**)

Hoc faciās licet. You may do this.

Note 3.—'*May,*' '*might,*' must be translated by *possum* or *licet* according as they mean 'I have the *power,*' or 'have *permission.*'

Note 4.—A very common construction is :

Hoc tibi per mē facere licuit. You might have done this, so far as I was concerned, *or,* I should have allowed you to do this.

Hoc per mē faciās licēbit. I shall leave you free to do this.

199. To express **duty, obligation** ('ought,' 'should,' etc.), three constructions may be used :—

(i) The personal verb *dēbeō*.

(*a*) *Hoc facere dēbēs* (*dēbēbis*). **You ought to do this, you should do this** (*present* **and** *future*).

(*b*) *Hoc facere dēbuistī* (*dēbēbās*). **You ought to** (*or* **should) have done this** (*past*).

(ii) The impersonal verb *oportet* [1] with the accusative and infinitive (see **31,** *a*).

(*a*) *Hoc tē facere oportet* (*oportēbit*). **You ought to do this.**

(*b*) *Hoc tē facere oportēbat* (*oportuit*). **You ought to have done this.**

Note.—*Oportet* is also used with the subjunctive (see **118, 121**).

Hoc facerēs oportuit. You should have done this.

200. (iii) The gerundive used impersonally (neuter nominative) if the verb is intransitive, or used as a predicative adjective if the verb is transitive. (See Exercises XLIX and L.)

The person *on whom the duty lies* is in the dative except when an intransitive verb is itself constructed with the dative ; in such circumstances the person is indicated by the ablative with *ā*.

Impersonal use :—

(*a*) *Tibi currendum est.* You must run.

(*b*) *Tibi currendum fuit.* You ought to have run.

(*c*) *Cīvibus ā tē cōnsulendum est.* You ought to take heed for your fellow citizens.

Predicative use :—

(*a*) *Haec tibi facienda sunt* (*erunt*). **You ought to do this** (*present* **and** *future*).

(*b*) *Haec tibi facienda erant* (*fuērunt*). **You ought to have done this** (*past*).

201. To express **necessity,** use either the gerundive, which implies both *duty* and *necessity*—

(*a*) *Tibi moriendum est* (*erit*). **You must die (will have to die).**

(*b*) *Tibi moriendum fuit* (*erat*). **You had to die.**

---

[1] *Oportet* expresses a duty as binding *on oneself* ; *dēbeō* the same duty, but rather as owed *to others*, 'I am bound to,' 'under an obligation to.' The gerundive implies both *duty* and *necessity*, and is commoner than either *oportet* or *necesse est*.

Or, more rarely, *necesse est* with the infinitive or a subjunctive clause as its subject.

(*a*) *Tibi morī necesse est;* or *moriāre necesse est.*

(*b*) *Tibi morī necesse erat;* or *morerēre necesse erat.*

Note.—With *necesse est* and a subjunctive clause the conjunction *ut* is generally not used. Compare **121.**

202. *Licet* and *necesse est* both take a dative of the person to whom something is permitted or for whom something is necessary. Consequently when *licet* or *necesse est* has as its subject the infinitive of a copulative verb which is accompanied by a predicative noun or adjective, the case of that noun or adjective is also dative.

Aliīs licet ignāvīs esse, vōbīs necesse est virīs fortibus esse. Others may be cowards, you must needs be brave men.

Exercise 24

1. We ought long ago to have listened to the teaching of so great a philosopher [1] as this. 2. Was it not your duty to sacrifice your own life and your own interests to the welfare of the nation? 3. The conquered and the coward (*pl.*) may be slaves; the defenders of their country's freedom must needs be free. 4. I blush at having persuaded you to abandon this noble undertaking. 5. You had my leave to warn your friends and relations not to run headlong into such danger and ruin. 6. It was impossible for a citizen of Rome [2] to consent to obey a despot of this kind. 7. You might have seen what the enemy was doing, but perhaps you preferred to be improvident and blind. 8. This (is what) you ought to have done; you might have fallen fighting in battle; and you were bound to die a thousand deaths rather than sacrifice the nation to your own interests. 9. Are you not ashamed of having in your old age,[3] in order to please your worst enemies, been false to your friends and betrayed your country? 10. I shall gladly give you leave to come to Rome as often as you please; and when you come [4] there [5] be sure you stay in my house if you can.

---

[1] **88,** *Note.* [2] **58.** [3] **63.** [4] Tense? (See **191.**)

[5] For 'and . . . there' use 'whither,' *quō.* (See **78.**)

EXERCISE XXV

CASES

General Remarks

203. There is nothing in which Latin differs more from English than in what are called its **cases.**

A **Case** is a form of a noun, adjective, pronoun, or participle standing in a particular relation to other words in a sentence.

204. In English the relation of a noun, etc., to the rest of the sentence is shown, not by its ending (except when it is possessive), but by its position in the sentence or by the aid of a preposition.[1]

205. In Latin the order of the words will tell us little or nothing of the relation of a noun to the rest of the sentence; the form of a noun tells us a great deal. But as there are only six or at most seven cases, and the number of relations which language has to express is far greater than six or seven, the case-system is largely assisted by a great number of *prepositions*, which help to give precision and clearness to the meaning of the case.

206. The word 'case' is an English form of a Latin word, *cāsus* (Gk. πτῶσις), used by grammarians to denote a *falling*, or deviation, from what they held to be the true or proper form of the word. The nominative was called, fancifully enough, the *cāsus rēctus*, as that form of the word which stood *upright*, or in its natural position. The other cases were called *cāsūs oblīquī*, as *slanting* or falling over from this position; and by *dēclīnātiō*, or 'declension,' was meant the whole system of these deviations, or, as we call them, *inflexions*.

207. The Latin cases are six in number: the **Nominative, Accusative, Dative, Ablative, Genitive, Vocative.** Besides these there is a case, nearly obsolete in the classical period of Latin, the **Locative.**

208. (i) The **Nominative** indicates the subject of the verb.

Without a subject, expressed or understood, a verb is meaningless. The nearest approach to the absence of a subject is in such im-

---

[1] The English language once possessed, as German does still, a case-system; but this only survives in the strictly *possessive* case, 'King's speech,' etc., and in certain pronouns, *he, him; who, whose, whom*, etc.

personal forms of intransitive verbs as *curritur*, 'there is a running,' *pugnātum est*, 'there was fighting.' (See Intr. 28.)

209. (ii) In its commonest use, the **Accusative** completes the meaning of a transitive verb by denoting the immediate (direct) object of its action. *Tē videō*, I see you. (Intr. 19.)

210. The object in English is usually indicated by its position after the verb; the subject by its position before the verb: 'The sun illuminates the world'; 'the world feels the sunlight.' In Latin the object (accusative) usually precedes the verb. (Intr. 84.)

211. (iii) The **Dative** is mainly used to represent the remoter (indirect) object, or the person or thing *interested in* the action of the verb.

For the great importance and wide use of the Dative with intransitive verbs which are represented in English by verbs really or apparently transitive, see Intr. 23, 24.

212. (iv) The **Ablative** gives further particulars as to the mode of action of the verb in addition to those supplied by its nearer and remoter objects. Its functions are very wide, for it can express the *source*, *cause*, *instrument*, *time*, *place*, *manner*, *circumstances*, of the action of the verb, as well as the point *from* which *motion* takes place.

Hōrā eum septimā vīdī. I saw him at the seventh hour.
Gladiō eum interfēcī. I slew him with a sword.
Rōmā profectus est. He set out from Rome.

213. (v) The **Locative** case, answering to the question, *where? at what place?* has a form distinct from the ablative only in certain words.

Rōmae, at Rome; *Londinī*, at London.

214. (vi) The **Genitive** is most commonly used in Latin to define or qualify another noun, pronoun, adjective, or participle to which it is closely attached, or of which it is predicated.

Hence its extremely common use as a substitute for the adjective.

Vir summae virtūtis = vir optimus.

Its use with certain verbs (*meminī*, *oblīviscor*, *indigeō*) is treated in Exercise XL.

215. (vii) The **Vocative** case indicates the person to whom a remark is addressed, and is always parenthetic.

The Nominative

216. There is no special difficulty in the syntax of the nominative.

The object (*accusative*) of an active verb becomes the subject (*nominative*) when the verb is changed to the passive.

> *Brūtus Caesarem interfēcit.* Brutus killed Caesar;

but

> *Caesar ā Brūtō interfectus est.* Caesar was killed by Brutus.

Note.—It is often advisable in translating from English into Latin, and *vice versā*, to substitute one voice for the other. Thus, to prevent ambiguity, 'I know that Brutus killed Caesar,' should be translated by *scio Caesarem ā Brūtō interfectum esse,* not by *Caesarem Brūtum interfēcisse. Aiō tē, Aeacidā, Rōmānōs vincere posse* ('I say that you, Pyrrhus, can overcome the Romans' *or* 'that the Romans can overcome you') is an instance of oracular ambiguity which should be carefully avoided in writing Latin.

217. It has been already explained that many English *transitive* verbs are represented in Latin by *intransitive* verbs, *i.e.* verbs which complete their sense, not by the aid of the *accusative*, but by that of the *dative*. (See Intr. 24.)

The passive voice of such verbs can only be used *impersonally* (see 5); hence the subject of an English passive is often represented in Latin by the *dative*.

> *Nēminī ā nōbīs nocētur.* No one is hurt by us.
>
> *Puerō imperātum est ut rēgem excitāret.* The servant was ordered to wake the king.
>
> *Tibi ā nūllō crēditur.* You are believed by no one.
>
> *Glōriae tuae invidētur.* Your glory is envied.

Note.—Similarly, an impersonal construction is used in the passive with those intransitive verbs which complete their sense by a preposition and substantive.

> *Ad urbem pervēnimus.* We reached the city.
>
> *Iam ad urbem perventum est.* The city was now reached.

218. This impersonal construction is frequently used where English has an abstract or verbal noun.

In urbe maximē trepidātum est. The greatest confusion reigned in the city.
Ad arma subitō concursum est. There was a sudden rush to arms.
Ācriter pugnātum est. The fighting was fierce.

Note.—In such phrases the English *adjective* will be represented by a Latin *adverb.*

219. (i) When this impersonal passive construction becomes an infinitive dependent on *possum, coepī,* or *dēsinō, potest* is used impersonally (see **198,** *Note* 2) and *coepī* and *dēsinō* themselves have the impersonal passive form (*coeptum, dēsitum est*).

Huic culpae ignōscī potest. It is possible to pardon this fault.
Resistī nōn potuit. Resistance was impossible.
Iam pugnārī coeptum (*dēsitum*) *est.* The fighting has now begun (ceased).

(ii) When the passive infinitive of a transitive verb depends upon *coepī* and *dēsinō,* these verbs themselves are put into the personal passive.

Urbs obsidērī coepta est. The siege of the city was begun.
Veterēs ōrātiōnēs legī dēsitae sunt. The old speeches ceased to be read.

220. The use of a predicative nominative with an infinitive has been dealt with in **42-6**; these sections should be read again before translating the following sentences.

Exercise 25

A

1. Your goodness will be envied. 2. Liars are never believed. 3. As for you [1] (*pl.*), do you not want to be free? 4. Do not become slaves; slaves will be no more pardoned than freemen. 5. It seemed that you made no answer to his [2] question. 6. So far from being hated by us, you are even favoured. 7. For myself,[3] it seems to me that I have acted rightly; but you possibly take a different view. 8. I will ask which of the two is favoured by the king. 9. The fighting has been fierce to-day; the contest will be longer and more desperate to-morrow.

---

[1] *Vōs vērō;* 'as for' is simply emphatic. The emphasis is given in Latin by the *use* and place of *vōs.* (**11,** *a.*)
[2] 'To him questioning.'
[3] *Equidem.*

B

1. Thereupon a sudden [1] cry arose in the rear, and a strange [1] confusion reigned along [2] the whole line of march. 2. When I said 'yes' you believed me; I cannot understand why you refuse to trust my word when I say 'no.' 3. When [3] a boy, I was with difficulty persuaded not to become a sailor and face the violence of the sea, the winds, and storms; as an old man I prefer sitting at leisure at home to either sailing or travelling; you perhaps have the same views.[4] 4. You ought to have been content with such good fortune as this, and never to have made it your aim to endanger everything by making excessive demands.[4] 5. So far from cruelty having been shown in our case, a revolt and rebellion on the part of our forefathers has been twice over pardoned by England. 6. It seems that your brother was a brave man, but it is pretty well allowed [5] that he showed himself rash and improvident in this matter. 7. It seems that he was the first of [6] that nation to wish to become our fellow-subject, and it is said that he was the last who preserved in old age the memory of (their) ancient liberties.

EXERCISE XXVI

APPOSITION

221. Apposition is not confined to the nominative; but it is more often used with the nominative and accusative than with other cases.

The general rule was given in **3**; see also **227**.

Note.—A noun in apposition stands in an adjectival relation to the noun with which it is combined; in *Thēbae, Boeōtiae caput,*

---

[1] Adjectives will become adverbs. (See **218**, *Note.*)
[2] 'Along' may be expressed here by the ablative of place.
[3] See **63**.
[4] 'Views,' etc., not to be expressed, see **54**: cf. **91**.
[5] =agreed on.
[6] *ex.*

the words in apposition define *Thebes* by adding the special quality of its being *the capital of Boeotia.*

Tē ducem sequimur. We follow you as[1] (*or* in the capacity of) our leader.

222. A noun in apposition agrees not only in case but, if possible, in gender also with the noun to which it is in apposition.

Ūsus, magister ēgregius. Experience, an admirable teacher.

But

Philosophia, magistra mōrum. Philosophy, the teacher of morals.

223. Where a geographical expression, such as 'city,' 'island,' 'promontory,' is defined in English by 'of' with a proper name, apposition is used in Latin. Thus—

Urbs Veiī, the city of Veii; *īnsula Cyprus,* the island of Cyprus; *Athēnās, urbem inclutam,* the renowned city of Athens.

Note 1.—*Rēs* with a qualifying adjective is frequently used appositively.

Lībertās, rēs pretiōsissima. The precious possession of freedom.

Note 2.—Some substantives are very frequently used in apposition and have a markedly adjectival relation to the nouns they accompany.

Cum exercitū tīrōne. With a newly levied army.

Nēmō[2] *pictor,* no painter; always *nēmō* (never *nūllus*) *Rōmānus,* no Roman.

224. The Romans did not combine, as we do, an adjective of praise or blame with the actual name of a person (and rarely with a word denoting a person). They employed *vir* (or *homō*) with an adjective, in apposition.

'The learned Cato' is *Catō, vir doctissimus.*

'Your gallant (excellent) brother' is *Frāter tuus, vir fortissimus* (*optimus*).

'The abandoned Catiline' is *Catilīna, homō perditissimus.* (See **57**, *a.*)

Note 1.—Occasionally an adjective was added as a permanent *cognōmen* or title to a person's name: *C. Laelius Sapiēns.*

---

[1] We must always ask what '*as*' means. 'We follow you as (=*as though*) a God' is: *tē quasi Deum sequimur.*

[2] *Nēmō* is a substantive: *nūllus* (which supplies *nēmō* with genitive, ablative, and often dative) is an adjective.

Note 2.—The appositional use of *vir* or *homō* with an adjective often supplies the place of the absent participle of *esse*.

Haec ille, homō[1] *innocentissimus, perpessus est.* This is what he, being (*i.e.* in spite of being) a perfectly innocent man, endured.

Note 3.—Sometimes it represents our ‘so good (bad, etc.) as.’

Tē hominem[2] *levissimum* (*virum optimum*) *ōdit.* He hates so trifling a person (so good a man) as you; *or* one so good. etc., as you.

225. A noun is often used in apposition to an unexpressed personal pronoun.

Māter tē appellō. I your mother call you; *or* it is your mother who calls you.

Hoc facitis Rōmānī. This is what you Romans do.

226. The verb (and predicative adjective, if any) will agree not with the appositive noun, but with the noun to which the apposition applies.

Brūtus et Cassius, spēs nostra, occidērunt. Brutus and Cassius, our (only) hope, have fallen.

Note.—But if *urbs, oppidum,* etc., is used in apposition to the name of a town which is plural, the verb is singular, in agreement with *urbs*, etc.

Thēbae, Boeōtiae caput, paene dēlētum est. Thebes, the capital of Boeotia, was nearly annihilated.

227. Single words are used in apposition to all cases of nouns; phrases, *i.e.* combinations of words, only if they define a nominative or accusative; when other cases are to be defined, a *quī*-clause is preferred to a phrase.

Exstīnctō Pompeiō, quod huius reīpūblicae lūmen fuit. After the death of Pompey who was the light of this commonwealth.

Ad Leucopetram, quod agrī Rēgīnī prōmunturium est. Near Leucopetra which is a promontory in the territory of Regium.

Notice in both examples the attraction of the relative to the gender of the predicate. (See **83**.)

---

[1] The word in apposition generally follows, unless unusual emphasis is to be conveyed. *Rēx* comes before the proper name as applied to hereditary kings, *prō rēge Dēiotarō*.

[2] *Homō* is ‘a human being’ as opposed to an animal or a god: *vir* ‘a man’ as opposed to a woman or child. Hence *homō* is joined with adjectives of either praise or blame; *vir* with adjectives of strong praise, *fortissimus, optimus*, etc.

Exercise 26

1. Philosophy, he says, was (32) the inventor of law,[1] the teacher of morals and discipline. 2. There is a tradition that Apiolae, a city of extreme [2] antiquity, was taken in this campaign. 3. It is said that your gallant father Flaminius founded in his consulship the flourishing colony of Placentia. 4. I earnestly implore you, my countrymen, he said, not to throw away the precious jewels of freedom and honour, to humour a tyrant's caprice. 5. The soldier, in spite of his entire innocence, was thrown into prison; the gallant centurion was butchered then and there. 6. There is a story that this ill-starred king was the first of his race to visit the island of Sicily, and the first to have beheld from a distance the beautiful city of Syracuse. 7. I should scarcely believe that so shrewd a man as your father would have put confidence in these [3] promises of his.

EXERCISE XXVII

ACCUSATIVE

228. The **accusative** is used most commonly as the case of the direct or nearer object of a transitive verb.

Tē videō ; tē sequimur ; tē piget.

Note.—When we say that in Latin the words *pāreō* 'I obey,' *ūtor* 'I use,' *meminī* 'I remember,' govern a *dative, ablative,* and *genitive* respectively, we really mean that the Romans put the ideas which we express by these English verbs into a shape different from that which we employ; and that in none of the three they made use of a transitive verb, combined with a direct object. In the first case we say, 'I obey *you*'; they said, *tibi pāreō* 'I am obedient *to* you.' In the second we say, 'I use *you*'; they said, *ūtor vōbīs* 'I serve *myself with* you.' In the third we say, 'I remember *you*'; they said, *tuī meminī* 'I am mindful *of* you.' On the other hand, where the Romans said *tē sequimur,* the Greeks

---

[1] See Exercise 9A, *footnote* 2. [2] Use adjective: 'most ancient.'
[3] 'In him making (*participle*) these promises.' (54.)

said σοὶ ἑπόμεθα, 'we are followers *to you*.' They looked, that is, on the person followed as *nearly interested in*, but not, as the Romans did, as the *direct object of* the action described by the verb (ἑπόμεθα).

229. The meaning of intransitive verbs in Latin, as in English, is modified when they are compounded with a preposition; and in consequence the compound verb is often transitive. (See also Intr. 43, and 24.)

Note 1.—This is especially the case with verbs that express some bodily movement or action.

Urbem oppugnō, expugnō, obsideō, circumsedeō. I assault, storm, blockade, invest, a city.

Caesarem conveniō, circumveniō. I have an interview with, overreach *or* defraud, Caesar.

Compare 'I *out*ran him,' 'I *over*came him,' etc.

Note 2.—Such transitive compound verbs are of course used freely in the passive: *Ā tē circumventus sum* 'I was defrauded by you.'

Note 3.—Verbs compounded with *trāns* may have two accusatives, one the object of the verb and the other depending on the preposition. *Cōpiās Hellēspontum trānsdūxit* 'He led his forces over the Hellespont.'

In the passive, the accusative dependent on the preposition is retained. *Cōpiae Rhēnum trāiectae sunt* 'The forces were transported across the Rhine.'

Trāicere means not only 'transport something across,' but also 'cross over'; hence *trāiectō Rhēnō* 'the Rhine having been crossed.'

230. Certain verbs of 'teaching' (*doceō*), 'concealing' (*cēlō*), 'demanding' (*poscō, flāgitō*), 'asking questions' (*rogō, interrogō*), may take two accusatives, one of the *person*, another of the *thing*.

Quis mūsicam docuit Epamīnōndam? Who taught Epaminondas music?

Nihil nōs cēlat. He conceals nothing from us.

Verrēs parentēs pretium prō sepultūrā līberum poscēbat. Verres used to demand of parents a payment for the burial of their children.

Meliōra deōs flāgitō. I implore better things of the gods (122).

Racilius mē prīmum rogāvit sententiam.[1] I was the first whom Racilius asked for his opinion.

---

[1] *Sententiam rogāre* is a technical expression: 'to ask a senator for his opinion and vote.' The acc. *sententiam* is preserved in the passive: *prīmus sententiam rogātus sum* 'I was asked my opinion first.'

231. But this double-accusative construction is commonest when the *thing* is indicated by a neuter pronoun, *hoc*, *illud*, or by *nihil*; otherwise *very frequently* (and with some verbs *always*) either the *person* or the *thing* is indicated by an ablative with a preposition.

Thus *doceō* always takes the accusative of the *person*, but prefers the ablative with *dē* for the *thing* about which information is given. After *petō* and *postulō*, and *sometimes* after the other verbs of *begging*, the *person* is put in the *abl.* with *ā*; and after *rogō*, *interrogō*, etc., the *thing* often stands in the *abl.* with *dē*.

Dē hīs rēbus Caesarem docet. He informs Caesar of these facts.

Haec ā vōbīs postulāmus atque petimus. We demand and claim this of you.

Haec abs tē poposcī. I have made this request of you.

Haec omnia ā tē precāmur. We pray for all these things from you.

Dē hāc rē tē rogō. I ask you about this.

Hoc or (*dē hāc rē*) *tē cēlātum volō.* I want you kept in the dark about this.

232. Some verbs which are usually intransitive are used occasionally in a transitive sense; such as *horreō* (oftener *perhorrēscō*) 'I shudder,' used for 'I fear,' and *sitiō* 'I am thirsty,' used as 'I thirst *for*,' with accusative. But these constructions are far commoner in poetry than in prose and should not be imitated.

Pars stupet innūptae dōnum exitiāle Minervae.—VIRGIL. Some are amazed at the deadly gift of virgin Minerva.

233. (i) An accusative indicating the *thing put on*, or the *part affected*, is used frequently in poetry with passive *forms* (the past participle, in particular) of verbs of 'dressing,' etc.

Longam indūtus vestem. Having put on a long garment.

Ōs impressa torō. Having pressed (*or* pressing) her face upon the couch.

The accusative is the direct object and the passive forms are used semi-reflexively like the forms of the Greek middle voice. The construction is not to be imitated in writing Latin prose.

(ii) In poetry also an accusative of *specification* or *respect*, partly imitated from the Greek, is used with participles which are passive in meaning (as well as in form) and with adjectives.

Trāiectus femur trāgulā. Having had his thigh pierced with a dart.

Ōs umerōsque deō similis. Like a god in face and shoulders.

This usage also is to be avoided in prose.

234. The accusative of the person is used with the following impersonal verbs: *decet, dēdecet; piget, pudet, paenitet, taedet, miseret.*

An infinitive is used as the impersonal subject of *decet* and *dēdecet.*

> *Ōrātōrem īrāscī minimē decet, simulāre nōn dēdecet.* It by no means becomes an orator to feel anger, it is not unbecoming to feign it.

With the last five the cause or object of the feeling is denoted by the genitive.

> *Eum factī suī neque pudet neque paenitet.* He feels neither shame nor remorse for his deed.

235. With verbs of 'movement' the bare accusative was originally capable of indicating the *goal* or *motion towards.* But with certain definite exceptions, *motion towards* is expressed in classical Latin not by the bare accusative but by the accusative and a preposition (*ad, in, sub*) which helps to define the meaning of the case.

The exceptions are :—

(i) Names of towns and small islands: *Rōmam eō.*

(ii) A few words and phrases: *domum* 'homewards,' *rūs, forās* 'out of doors,' *vēnum dō* 'I sell,' *īnfitiās eō* 'I deny.'

(iii) The Supine in *-um* which is used to express purpose.

> *Mē hās iniūriās questum mittunt.* They send me to complain of these wrongs.

Note.—With the accusative of names of towns the preposition *ad* is used to indicate 'to (*or* in) the neighbourhood of.'

Exercise 27

1. As the army mounted up the highest part of the ridge the barbarians attacked its flanks with undiminished vigour. 2. I have repeatedly warned your brother not to conceal anything from your excellent father. 3. You ought surely to have been the first to encounter death, and to show yourself the brave son of so gallant a father. Why then were you the first to be horrified at a trifling danger ? 4. If Caesar leads (**192**) his troops across the Rhine there will be the greatest agitation throughout

the whole of Germany. 5. Our spies have given us much information as to the situation and size of the citadel; it seems that they wish to keep us in the dark as to[1] the size and character of the garrison. 6. Having[2] perceived that all was lost, the general rode in headlong flight past the fatal marsh (*pl.*), and reached the citadel in safety. 7. In order to avoid the heavy burden of administering the government, he pleaded his age and bodily[3] weakness. 8. Many have coasted along distant lands; it is believed that he[4] was the first to sail round the globe. 9. I should be sorry for you to be kept in the dark about my journey, but this request I make of you, not to forget me in my absence. 10. About part of his project he told me everything; the rest he kept secret even from his brother.

EXERCISE XXVIII

ACCUSATIVE II

Cognate and Predicative

236. Many verbs, which are otherwise intransitive, take an accusative (called **cognate**) containing the same idea as the verb and often etymologically connected (*cognātus*) with it.

Hunc cursum cucurrī. I ran this race.
Multa proelia pugnāvī. I have fought many battles.

Thus we say in English, 'I struck him *a blow*.'

237. A noun used as a cognate accusative generally, but not always, has an adjective or its equivalent attached to it.

Longam vītam vīxī. Long is the life I have led.
Hās notāvī notās. I set down these marks.

---

[1] 'What is the size,' etc. (See **174**.)
[2] See **14**.
[3] See **59**.
[4] 'He' is emphatic = 'this man' (*hic*).

But in prose the cognate accusatives most commonly used are neuter pronouns (as *hoc, illud, idem*), neuter plural adjectives (as *pauca, multa*), and the word *nihil*.

Illud tibi assentior, in this I agree with you. *Nihil mihi succēnset*, he is in no way angry with me. *Idem glōriātur*, he makes the same boast. *Multa peccat*, he commits many sins (see **54**). *Hoc laetor* (=*hāc rē laetor*), this is the cause of my joy.

238. This accusative is the origin of many constructions :—

(i) The adverbial use of *multum, minimum, nescio quid, quantum*.

(ii) The *poetical* use of the neuter singular and plural of many adjectives : *dulce rīdentem*, sweetly smiling. Even in prose we find : *maius exclāmat*, he raises a louder cry.

(iii) Such adverbial expressions as *id temporis*, at that time ; *cum id aetātis puerō*, with a boy of that age ; *tuam vicem doleō*, I grieve for your sake.

(iv) The accusative of *space*, of *time*, and of *distance*. *Trēs annōs absum*, I have been away for three years ; *tria mīlia (passuum) prōcessī*, I advanced three miles.

239. Factitive verbs (Intr. 36) have an accusative of the direct object and another accusative (called **predicative**) agreeing with the object.

Mē mātrem tuam appellant. They call me your mother.
Mē cōnsulem creant. They make me consul.
Sē virum bonum praestitit.[1] He proved himself a good man.

Note.—Remember that the passives of factitive verbs are used as copulative verbs (see Intr. 36).

Ego māter tua appellor. I am called your mother.

240. Examples of predicative accusatives :—

Haec rēs mē sollicitum habuit. This made me anxious.
Mare īnfēstum habuit. He infested (*or* beset) the sea.
Haec missa faciō. I dismiss these matters.
Hoc cognitum (compertum, mihi persuāsum) habeō. I am certain (assured, convinced) of this. (See **188**.)

---

[1] *Praestāre*, when it means 'to be superior,' takes a dative (or an accusative, in authors other than Caesar and Cicero) of the person to whom one is superior, and an ablative (with or without *in*) of that in which one is superior : *quantum gēns genti virtūte praestat !* 'how much one race excels another in courage !'

Note 1.—*Sē mōnstrāre* and *sē ostendere* are not used in Latin in the sense of 'show one's self to be something,' *i.e.* they are not used as factitive verbs. 'He showed himself a man of courage' or 'he showed courage' can be rendered by: *virum fortem sē praestitit* (or *praebuit*), or *fortissimē sē gessit*, or *fortissimus exstitit.*

Note 2.—In place of the predicative accusative a phrase may often be used.

I consider you as my friend. *Tē amīcōrum in numerō habeō.*
I look on this as certain. *Hoc prō certō habeō.*
I behaved as a citizen. *Mē prō cīve gessī.*

241. An accusative noun or pronoun accompanied by an adjective is used in exclamations: *Miserum hominem!* 'Wretched man!'; *Ō spem vānissimam!* 'Foolish hope!'

Exercise 28

Before doing this Exercise read carefully **54**; also, for the different senses of 'such,' **86**.

1. Perhaps he is himself going to commit the same fault as his ancestors have repeatedly committed. 2. He makes many complaints, many lamentations; at this one thing he rejoices, that [1] you are ready to make him your friend. 3. For myself, I fear he will keep the whole army anxious for his safety, such [2] is his want of caution and prudence. 4. England had long covered the sea with her fleets; she now ventured at last to carry her soldiers across the Channel and land them on the continent. 5. The rest of her allies Rome left alone; the interests of Hiero, the most loyal of them all, she steadily consulted. 6. Whether he showed himself wise or foolish I know not, but a boy of that age will not be allowed to become a soldier; this at least I hold as certain. 7. This is the life that I have led, judges; you possibly feel pity for such a life. For myself, I would [3] venture to make this boast, that I feel neither shame,[4] nor weariness, nor remorse for it. 8. He behaved so well at this trying crisis that I hardly know whether to admire his courage most or his prudence.

---

[1] See **41**, *c*. [2] **69**, *Note*. [3] See **152**, *b*. [4] **234**.

EXERCISE XXIX

DATIVE

I. Dative with Verbs

242. The **Dative** indicates the person or thing which, though not the direct object, is *interested in*, or *affected by*, the state or action described by the verb.

As the accusative answers the question, *whom? what?* so the dative answers the question, *to* or *for whom* or *what?*

243. Many relations expressed by the dative in Latin are expressed in English by '*to*' and '*for*.' But very often English dispenses with these prepositions. 'He built *me* a house'; 'he saddled *him* the horse'; 'I paid *them* their debt'; 'I told *him* my story'—are just as correct sentences as 'He built a house *for* me'; 'I told my story *to* Caesar,' etc. In translating into Latin, therefore, we must look to the **meaning** of the English.

244. Some transitive verbs (especially those of 'giving,' 'showing,' 'saying') take not only an accusative of the direct object but a dative of the indirect object *also*.

Frūmentum eīs suppeditāvit. He supplied corn to them.
Haec tibi mōnstrō (*dīcō, polliceor*). I show (say, promise) this to you.
Poenās mihi persolvet. He shall pay me the penalty.

Note 1.—Observe that in the following instances the *person* is the indirect object of the Latin verb but is the direct object of the English verb of approximately similar meaning.

Mortem mihi minātus est. He threatened me with death.
Hanc rem tibi permīsī or *mandāvī.* I entrusted you with this.
Haec peccāta mihi condōnāvit. He pardoned me for these offences.
Facta sua nūllī probāvit. He won no one's approval for his acts.

Note 2.—A dative is also used with *adimō* 'I take away.'

Vītam nōbīs adimunt. They are robbing us of life.

245. The Latin equivalents of many transitive English verbs are intransitive, and complete their meaning not by an accusative but by a dative *alone*. (See **217.**) Verbs of this kind which are most frequently used are :—

(*a*) Verbs of **aiding, favouring, obeying, pleasing, serving.**

Auxilior, medeor ('heal'), *opitulor, subveniō; faveō, studeō; pāreō, obsequor, oboediō; placeō, indulgeō; serviō.*

(*b*) Verbs of **injuring, opposing, displeasing.**

Noceō; adversor, obstō, repugnō; displiceō.

(*c*) Verbs of **commanding, persuading, trusting, distrusting, sparing, pardoning, envying, being angry.**

Imperō, praecipiō; suādeō, persuādeō; fīdō; diffīdō; parcō; ignōscō; invideō; īrāscor, succēnseō.

Fortibus favet fortūna. It is the brave whom fortune favours.
Haec rēs omnibus hominibus nocet. This fact injures the whole world.
Lēgibus pāruit cōnsul. He obeyed the law in his consulship (**63**).
Victīs victor pepercit. He spared the vanquished in the hour of victory (**63**).

Note 1.—Remember that these verbs must be used impersonally in the passive.

Mihi repugnātur. I am resisted.
Tibi diffīditur. You are distrusted. (See **217**.)

Note 2.—Verbs of 'commanding' and 'persuading' often have a noun clause as their direct object (see **117, 118**). When *imperō* is used in the sense of 'demand' it has a direct and an indirect object: *Pecūniam nōbīs imperāvit* 'he demanded money from us (ordered us to supply, exacted from us).'

Note 3.—Observe: *nūbō virō* 'I marry a husband'; but *dūcō uxōrem* 'I marry a wife.'

Note 4.—*Cōnfīdō* is used with a dative of the *person* but with an ablative of the *thing* relied on.

246. Some Latin verbs whose meaning is similar to that of verbs given in **245** are transitive.

aid, *iuvō, adiuvō;* heal, *cūrō;* please, *dēlectō;* harm, *laedō, offendō;* command, *iubeō;* exhort, *hortor.*

Fortūna fortēs adiuvat. Fortune helps the bold.
Librīs mē dēlectō. I amuse myself with books.
Offendit nēminem. He offends nobody.
Haec laedunt oculōs. These things hurt the eyes.

247. The impersonal verbs *accidit, contingit, expedit, libet, licet, placet,* take a dative of indirect object (contrast **234**).

Hoc tibi dīcere libet. It is your pleasure, suits your fancy, to say this.

248. Many Latin verbs have various shades of meaning according to which they take an accusative alone, a dative alone (either of the indirect object or of the person interested), or both accusative and dative. No general rule can be given and the student should continually observe the actual usages of the Latin authors whom he is reading. The following examples, however, should be studied:

Hostēs timet 'he fears the enemy'; *fīliō timet pater* 'the father fears for his son'; *fūrem pōmis timet agricola* 'the farmer fears the thief for his apples.'

Senātum cōnsulit 'he consults the senate'; *reīpūblicae cōnsulit* 'he considers the interests of the state.'

Fossās cavet 'he is on his guard against the ditches'; *veterānis cāverat* 'he had taken care for the veterans'; also: *caveō abs tē* 'I am on the lookout against you.'

Tempestātem prōspicit 'he foresees a storm'; *sibi prōspicit* 'he looks out for himself.'

Crēdō hoc tibi 'I entrust this to you'; *crēdō tibi* 'I believe you'; *crēdō tē hoc fēcisse* 'I believe you have done this.'

Note.—Observe the distinction between *philosophiae vacat* 'he has leisure for philosophy' and *culpā vacat* 'he is free from fault.'

249. *Temperō* and *moderor* in the sense of 'to govern' or 'direct' take the *accusative*; when they mean 'to set limits to' they have the *dative*. *Temperāre* in the sense of 'to abstain from,' 'to spare,' takes either the dative or *ā* with the ablative.

Hanc cīvitātem lēgēs moderantur. This state is governed by law. (216, *Note.*)

Fac animō moderēris. Be sure you restrain your feelings, *or* temper. (125, *Note.*)

Ab inermibus or *inermibus* (dative) *temperātum est.* The unarmed were spared. (The past participle of *parcō* is rare.)

250. *Dōnō* takes either a *dative* of the *person* and an *accusative* of the *thing*, or an *accusative* of the *person* and an *ablative* of the *thing*.

Cicerōnī immortālitātem dōnāvit; or *Cicerōnem immortālitāte dōnāvit.* (The Roman people) conferred immortality on Cicero.

So in English we may say either 'I present this to you' or 'I present you with this.'

Circumdō has a similar variety of construction:

Circumdat mūrum urbī or *circumdat urbem mūrō.* He surrounds the city with a wall.

Exercise 29

A

1. I have long been warning you whom it is your duty to guard against, whom to fear. 2. I know that one so good as [1] your father will always provide for his children's safety. 3. It is impossible [2] to get any one's approval for such [3] a crime as this. 4. On my asking [4] what I was to do, whether and how and when [5] I had offended him, he made no reply. 5. Is it [6] your country's interest, or your own that you (*pl.*) wish consulted ? 6. I pardoned him for many offences ; he ought not to have shown such cruelty toward you. 7. In his [7] youth I was his opponent ; in his age and weakness I am ready to assist him. 8. I foresee many political storms, but I fear neither for the nation's safety nor for my own.

B

1. It is said that he wrenched the bloody dagger from the assassin, raised [8] it aloft, and flung it away on the ground. 2. Do not (*pl.*) taunt with his lowly birth one who has done such good service to his country. 3. It matters not whether [9] you cherish anger against me or not. I have no fears for my own safety and you may [10] henceforth threaten me with death daily, if you please.[11] 4. You were believed, and must have [12] been believed ; for all were agreed (*imperf.*) that you had never broken your word. 5. He complained that the office with which the nation had just entrusted [13] him had not only been shared with others, but would be entirely taken away from him, by this law. 6. You have deprived us of our liberties and

---

[1] See **224**, *Note* 3.
[2] See **196**, *Note* 2.
[3] **88**, *Note*.
[4] 'To me asking,' *participle*.
[5] Why not *cum* ? (See **157**, *Note* 7.)
[6] See **156**.
[7] **63**.
[8] Participle passive. (**15**.)
[9] See **168**.
[10] Future of *licet*. (See **198**.)
[11] See **191**.
[12] See **201**.
[13] Mood ?

rights in our absence (61), and perhaps to-morrow you will wrench from us our lives and fortunes. 7. The soldiers were all slain to a man, but the unarmed were spared.[1] 8. We are all of us[2] ignorant of the reason[3] for so gentle a prince as ours exacting from his subjects such enormous quantities of corn and money. 9. He never spared any one[4] who had withstood him, or pardoned any who had injured him. 10. I have always wished your interests protected; but I did not wish one so incautious[5] and rash as you to be consulted on (*dē*) this matter.

EXERCISE XXX

DATIVE—*Continued*

II. Dative with Verbs

251. The verb *sum* is either a copulative verb (Intr. 35), an auxiliary verb, or means 'I exist'; in none of these senses can it have a direct object. But the person who is interested is indicated by the dative.

Erat eī domī fīlia. He had a daughter at home.
Mihi hoc ūtile est. This is useful for me.

The compounds of *sum* are intransitive verbs and may take a dative.

Mihi adfuit, hīs rēbus nōn interfuit. He gave me the benefit[6] of his presence, he took no part in these matters.

Note.—*Īnsum*, however, is frequently followed by the ablative with the preposition *in*; and *absum* by the ablative with *ā*, *ab*.

252. When a simple verb is compounded with a preposition, with *re-*, or with the adverbs *satis*, *bene*, *male*, its meaning is changed. Whether the compound verb is

---

[1] See 249. [2] See 225. [3] See 174.
[4] Use *nēmō umquam*. [5] Use *incautus*. (224, *Note* 3.)
[6] A very common meaning of *adsum* with dative, 'I am at hand to aid.'

transitive or intransitive does not depend upon the transitive or intransitive nature of the simple verb but upon the meaning of the compound verb itself.

No infallible rule can therefore be given about the construction used with compound verbs. The most that can be said is that very many compound verbs, because of their meaning, take a dative of the indirect object, and that many of them take an accusative of the direct object as well.

253. (i) Many compound verbs are intransitive and take a dative of the indirect object only. Such are :—

> *Assentārī*, to flatter; *imminēre*, to hang over, be threatening; *cōnfīdere* (see **245**, *Note* 4), to trust in; *īnstāre*, *īnsistere*, to press on, urge; *intercēdere*, to put a veto on; *obstāre*, *repugnāre*, to resist; *occurrere* (=*obviam īre*), to meet; *obsequī*, to comply with; *satisfacere*, to satisfy; *maledīcere*, to abuse. (See also **245**.)

(ii) Some are intransitive but complete their meaning not by a dative but by another case with a preposition.

> *Ad urbem pervēnit.* He reached the city.

(iii) Many are transitive, and have both direct and indirect objects.

> *Tē illī posthabeō.* I place you behind him (=*illum tibi antepōnō*, I prefer him to you).
>
> *Sē perīculīs obiēcit.* He exposed himself to dangers.
>
> *Mortem sibi cōnscīvit.* / *Vim sibi intulit.* } He committed suicide, laid violent hands on himself.
>
> *Tē exercituī praefēcērunt.* They have placed you in command of the army.
>
> *Bellum nōbīs indīxit* (*intulit*). He declared (made) war against us.

(iv) Others are transitive and have only a direct object. (See **229**.)

> *Āversārī*, to loathe; *attingere*, to touch lightly; *alloquī*, to speak (kindly) to; *inrīdēre*, to deride.

(v) Some take a direct object and complete their meaning by a case with a preposition.

> *Hoc mēcum commūnicāvit.* He imparted this to me.
>
> *Ad scelus nōs impellit.* He is urging us to crime.

Exercise 30

1. Possibly one so base as you [1] will not hesitate to prefer slavery to honour. 2. He says [2] that as a young man he took no part in that contest. 3. He promises never to fail his friends. 4. To my question who was at the head of the army he made no reply. 5. All of us know well the baseness of failing [3] our friends in a trying crisis. 6. I pledge myself not to fail our general, or [4] to neglect so great an opportunity; but possibly fortune is opposing our designs. 7. It is said that Marcellus wept over the fair city of Syracuse.[5] 8. For myself, I can scarcely believe [6] that so gentle a prince as ours could have acted so sternly. 9. In the face of these dangers, which are threatening the country, let all of us devote ourselves to the national cause. 10. It concerns his reputation immensely for us to be assured whether he fell in battle or laid violent hands on himself. 11. You ought to have gone out to meet your gallant brother; but you preferred to sit safely at home. 12. I would fain know whether he is going to declare and make war on his country, or to sacrifice his own interests to the nation. 13. To prevent his urging others to a like crime, I reluctantly laid the matter before the magistrates. 14. He never consented either to fawn upon the powerful, or to flatter the mob; he always relied on himself, and would [7] expose himself to any danger. 15. Famine is threatening us daily and the townsmen are urging the governor to surrender the city to the enemy; but he refuses to impart his decision to me, and I am at a loss what to do.

---

[1] **224**, *Note* **3**; *tū* should be expressed. (See also **334**, ii.)
[2] See **33**.
[3] See **94**, **95**.
[4] 'Or,' after 'not' will be *neque*.
[5] See **223**.
[6] **152**, *b*.
[7] Imperfect. (See **185**.)

EXERCISE XXXI

DATIVE—*Continued*

III. The Dative with Adjectives and Adverbs

254. The dative is used not only with *verbs*, but also with **adjectives** (and even **adverbs**), to mark the person or thing *affected by the quality* which the adjective denotes.

The adjectives (and adverbs) so qualified are, in general, those whose English equivalents are followed by 'to' or 'for'; *e.g.* adjectives signifying: *advantage, agreeableness, usefulness, fitness, facility, nearness*, and *likeness* (with their *opposites*). So—

Rēs populō[1] *grāta.* A circumstance pleasing to the people.
Puer patrī similis. A child like his father.
Cōnsilium omnibus ūtile. A policy useful to all.
Tempora virtūtibus īnfēsta. A time fatal to virtues.
Convenienter nātūrae vīvendum est. We should live agreeably to (*or* in accordance with) nature.

255. But some of these adjectives have alternative constructions.

Thus, with *similis* the genitive is also used (especially of a *pronoun*, and usually of a *proper name*).

Pompeiī similis, 'resembling Pompey'; *vērī simile*, 'probable'; *nūlla rēs similis suī manet*, 'nothing remains like itself.'

The genitive or dative is used also with *affīnis* 'akin,' *aliēnus* 'foreign,' *commūnis* 'common,' *pār* 'equal,' *proprius* 'peculiar (to),' *superstes* 'surviving.'

Hoc quidem vitium nōn proprium senectūtis est. This vice is not the special property of old age.

Adjectives of 'fitness' are sometimes qualified by the accusative with *ad*. *Aptus* (*idōneus, ūtilis*) *ad rem*.

Adjectives of 'disposition' may take *in* or *ergā* with the accusative. *Benevolus ergā aliquem*.

---

[1] But *in vulgus grāta*; for the form *vulgō* is used only as an adverb.

Aliēnus may be qualified also by the ablative with *ā* (see also **265**). *Aliēnus ā litterīs* 'unversed in literature.'

The participles *assuētus, assuēfactus,* like the verbs to which they belong, take an ablative; but *insuētus* usually takes a genitive.

256. Some adjectives which are qualified by a dative may also be used as nouns (*e.g. aequālis, affīnis, vīcīnus, fīnitimus, propinquus, amīcus, inimīcus*). As nouns they are qualified by the genitive, or by a possessive pronoun (*meus, tuus,* etc.).

Thus, *nōbīs vīcīnī* 'near us,' but *vīcīnī nostrī* 'our neighbours.'

The construction of such words therefore varies according as they are regarded as adjectives or substantives. (See **55.**)

Exercise 31

1. I could not doubt that falsehood was most inconsistent with your brother's character. 2. All of us are apt to love those [1] like ourselves. 3. I fear that in so trying a time as [2] this so trifling a person [3] as your friend will not show [4] himself the equal of his illustrious father. 4. This [5] circumstance was most acceptable to the mass of the people, but at the same time [6] most distasteful to the king. 5. He had long been an opponent of his father's policy, whom in (*abl.*) almost every point he himself most closely resembled. 6. He was both a relation of my father and his close friend from boyhood; he was also [6] extremely well disposed to myself. 7. For happiness, said he, which [7] all of us value above every blessing, is common to kings and herdsmen, rich and poor. 8. To others he was, it seemed,[8] most kindly disposed, but he was, I suspect,[8] his own worst enemy. 9. He is a man far removed from all suspicion of bribery, but I fear that he will not be acquitted by such an unprincipled judge as this. 10. It was, he used to say,[9] the special peculiarity of kings to envy men [10] who had done [11] the state the best service.

---

[1] See **346**.
[2] **88**, *Note*.
[3] **224**, *Note* **3**.
[4] **240**, *Note* 1.
[5] Relative. (See **78**.)
[6] See **366**.
[7] **95**, *Note*, and **98**, *b*.
[8] **32**, *b*, and **43**, *Note* **2**.
[9] Tense? (**185**.)
[10] **72**.
[11] Mood? (See **77**, *Note*.)

EXERCISE XXXII

DATIVE—*Continued*

IV. Further Uses of the Dative

257. (i) A dative of the **possessor** is used with *esse* when more stress is laid on the thing possessed than on the possessor.

Est mihi frūmentī acervus. I have a heap of corn.

(ii) With other verbs than *esse* a dative of the person interested in or affected by the action (see **211**) is used where English uses a possessive.

Tum Pompeiō ad pedēs sē prōiēcēre. Then they threw themselves at Pompey's feet.
Hoc mihi spem minuit. This lowered my hopes.
Gladium eī ē manibus extorsit. He forced the sword out of his hands.

258. The dative sometimes indicates the person who is interested in the action to the extent of being its **agent** :—

(i) In association with the Gerundive it indicates the person on whom a duty or necessity for action lies (see **200, 201**).

Haec rēs tibi facienda fuit. This ought to have been done by you.

(ii) The dative is sometimes used with passive participles (especially those of verbs of *seeing, thinking, hearing, planning*) to indicate the agent.

Haec omnia mihi perspecta et cōnsīderāta sunt. All these points have been studied and weighed by me.
Hoc mihi probātum ac laudātum est. This has won my approval and praise=has been approved of and praised by me.

(iii) The use of a dative to mark the agent with other forms of passive verbs is occasionally found in poets, but must be avoided in writing Latin prose.

259. (i) The dative is also used (especially in military language) to express a purpose or end in view, and is often accompanied by another dative of the person interested.

Receptuī canere. To sound the trumpet for retreat.
Caesarī cōpiās auxiliō (subsidiō) addūxit (mīsit). He led (sent) forces to be an aid (a support) to Caesar.

(ii) A dative (called **predicative**) is also used instead of a predicative nominative or accusative (i) after *sum* 'I am, I serve as'; (ii) after verbs like *habeō, dūcō, vertō, ēligō* 'I consider as, reckon as, chose as.' Such a dative is almost invariably accompanied by another dative indicating the person interested.

Haec rēs eī magnō fuit dēdecorī. This was (*or* proved) a great disgrace to him.

Ipse sibi odiō erit. He will be odious (*or* an object of dislike) to himself = be hated by himself.

Nōlī hanc rem mihi vitiō vertere. Do not impute this to me as a fault.

Haec rēs salūtī nōbīs fuit. This fact saved us (proved our salvation).

Quaerere solēbat cui bonō fuisset. He used to ask to whom it had been advantageous.

Note 1.—Hence the English 'proves,' 'serves,' etc., may often be rendered by *sum* with a predicative dative; and sometimes an English predicative adjective may be rendered by a noun in the dative: *hoc mihi ūsuī est* 'this is useful to me.'

Note 2.—The predicative dative is never itself qualified unless by an adjective of quantity or size.

Note 3.—A word denoting a person must not be put into the predicative dative, but must agree with the object of the verb: *tē ducem ēligimus* 'we choose you as our leader.'

260. Examples of common phrases containing predicative datives:—

To impute as a fault, *culpae dare; vitiō vertere.*
To give as a present, *dōnō (mūnerī) dare.*
To consider as a source of gain, *habēre quaestuī.*
To be very dishonourable *or* discreditable, *magnō esse dēdecorī.* (*Note* 1.)
To be hated by, to be hateful, *odiō esse.* (*Note* 2.)
To be a hindrance, *impedīmentō esse.*
To be creditable *or* honourable, *honōrī esse.*
To be hurtful *or* detrimental, *dētrīmentō (damnō) esse.*
To cause pain *or* sorrow, *dolōrī esse.*
To be a proof, *argūmentō (documentō) esse.*
To profit, to be profitable, *bonō esse.*
To be a reproach *or* disgraceful, *opprobriō esse.*

Note 1.—When an English predicative adjective is rendered by a predicative dative in Latin, the accompanying adverbs 'very,' 'how,' will be represented in Latin by the adjectives *magnō* (*summō*), *quantō*.

Quantō hoc tibi sit dēdecorī vidēs. You see how disgraceful this is to you.

Note 2.—The phrase *odiō esse* forms a passive voice to *ōdī*. Thus Hannibal, when at the close of his life he expresses to Antiochus his hatred of the Romans, says (Livy xxxv. 19) :—

Ōdī odiōque sum Rōmānis. I hate the Romans and am hated by them.

261. The dative in the predicate with *licet*, etc., has been noticed (**202**).

Liceat nōbīs quiētīs esse. Let us be allowed to be at rest.

The actual name of a person which is used with the phrases *alicui nōmen* (*cognōmen*) *est* (*addō, dō, additur, datur*) often agrees, not with *nōmen*, but with the dative *alicui*.

Puerō cognōmen Iūlō additur. The surname of Iulus is given to the boy.

Exercise 32

Words and phrases marked * will be found in **259-60.**

A

1. He promises to come shortly to the assistance * of your countrymen. 2. Thereupon he forced the bloody dagger out of the assassin's [1] hand. 3. I fear that these things will not prove very creditable * to you. 4. I don't quite understand what your friends [2] have said. 5. It is very honourable * to you to have been engaged in such (**86**) a battle. 6. Such (**87**) superstition is undoubtedly a reproach * to a man. 7. I fear that this will prove both detrimental * and dishonourable * to the government. 8. Cassius was wont to ask [3] who had gained by the result. 9. It is vile to consider politics a source * of gain. 10. I would fain inquire what place you have chosen for your dwelling. 11. I am afraid that this will be very painful * and disgraceful * to you. 12. I will warn the boy what (*quantus*) a reproach * it is to break one's word. 13. He promised to give them the island of Cyprus as a present *.

---

[1] Genitive not to be used. (See **257.**) [2] **338**, *Note* 2.

[3] Frequentative form, *rogitō*. Tense ? (See **185.**)

14. I hope that he will perceive how odious * cruelty is to all men. 15. Then the ambassadors of the Gauls threw themselves at Caesar's feet. 16. It seems that he hates our nation and is hated * by us. 17. I hope soon to come to your aid with three legions.

B

1. He gives his word to take care that the ambassadors shall be allowed to depart home in safety. 2. To this prince, owing to a temperament (which was) almost intolerable to the rest of the world, (men) had given the name of the Proud. 3. This circumstance is a proof * that no [1] Roman took part in that contest. 4. So many and so great are your illustrious brother's (224) achievements that they have by this time been heard of, praised, and read of by the whole world. 5. We know that the name of deserters is hated * and considered execrable by all the world; but we earnestly implore that our change of sides may bring us neither reproach * nor credit.* 6. Not even (Intr. 90) in a time of universal [2] joy were we allowed to enjoy repose. 7. I can scarcely believe that so monstrous a design as this has been heard of and approved by you. 8. This circumstance, which is now in every one's mouth, he communicated to me yesterday; I suspect it concerns you more than me. 9. When my colleague comes [3] to my assistance * I can [4] supply you with provisions and arms.

EXERCISE XXXIII

THE ABLATIVE

262. The **Ablative** answers the questions *whence? by what means? how? from what cause? in what manner? when?* and *where?*

---

[1] See 223, *Note* 2. [2] See 59. [3] See 192. [4] Tense? (191.)

263. Its various meanings may be thus classified :—

(i) Separation ; *from.*

(ii) Instrumentality or Means ; *by*, *with.*

(iii) Accompaniment ; *with*, etc.

(iv) Locality ; *at* or *in* a *place* or *time.*

264. An ablative of **separation** is used with verbs meaning 'keep away from, free from, deprive, lack.'

Abstinēre iniūriā, to abstain from wrong ; *abīre magistrātū*, to go out of office ; *dēsistere cōnātū*, to abandon (*or* cease from) an attempt ; *cēdere patriā*, to leave one's native land ; *pellere cīvitāte*, to banish ; *solvere lēgibus*, to exempt from the laws.

Note.—The ablative with *ā* is commonly used with *līberō* and with compounds of *dis-*, *sē-*, *ab-* (e.g. *discernō, sēparō, abhorreō*).

Discēdant ab armīs. Let them depart from arms.
Abhorret ab eius modī culpā. He is far removed from such blame.

265. An ablative of **separation** (often with *ā* or *ab*) also qualifies **adjectives** signifying 'want' or 'freedom from.'

Metū vacuus. Free from fear.
Loca sunt ab arbitrīs lībera. The locality is free from witnesses.
Ab eius modī scelere aliēnissimus. Quite incapable of (removed from) such a crime.

266. An ablative of separation is used (generally without *ā* or *ab*) with verbs (chiefly past participles) indicating 'origin' or 'descent.'

Cōnsulārī familiā ortus. Sprung from a consular family.
Homō optimīs parentibus nātus. A man of excellent parentage.

Note.—Ablatives of this type are sometimes called ablatives of origin.

267. The ablative (always **with** *ā* or *ab*) is used with a passive verb to indicate the **agent** by whom an action is done. (See **8,** *a.*)

Clītus ab Alexandrō interfectus est. Clitus was killed by Alexander.

Note 1.—This ablative is one of separation and marks that *from which* the action proceeds.

Note 2.—A secondary agent, *i.e.* a *person* used as an instrument, is expressed by *per* with an accusative or by *operā* with a genitive or a possessive pronoun.

Haec per explōrātōrēs cognita sunt. These facts were ascertained by means of scouts.

Tuā, non illīus, operā haec facta sunt. By your instrumentality, not his, were these things done.

268. The ablative (always **without** *ā* or *ab*) indicates the **instrument** with which an action is performed.

Clītus gladiō interfectus est. Clitus was killed by (with) a sword.

Note 1.—This ablative is one of instrumentality.

Note 2.—A similar ablative (without *ā* or *ab*) is used to denote cause.

Iam vīrēs lassitūdine dēficiēbant. Their strength was now beginning to fail through (from) weakness.

Note 3.—*Propter* and *ob* with the accusative are also used to express the *cause.* The ablative is mostly used when a bodily, or mental, or other property of the *subject of the verb* is concerned. *Tuā fortitūdine hoc meruistī,* 'by (*or* through) your courage you deserved this'; but, *propter tuam fortitūdinem hoc dēcrēvit senātus,* 'because of your courage the senate decreed this.'

269. The ablative of **accompaniment** or association (with the preposition *cum*) is used with verbs of motion to denote 'in company with.'

Cum frātre meō vēnī. I came with my brother.
Cum tēlō vēnit. He came with a weapon.
Tēcum (mēcum, nōbīscum) ībit. He will go with you (me, us). (See **8**, *Note.*)

270. The ablative of **manner** (which is nearly related to the ablative of accompaniment) is used with *cum*; but *cum* may be omitted if the noun in the ablative is qualified by an adjective or a demonstrative.

Cum dignitāte morī satius est quam cum ignōminiā vīvere. It is better to die with honour than to live in disgrace.
Summā haec dīligentiā fēcī. I did this with the greatest care.

Note 1.—A few words are used as ablatives of manner without an adjective or *cum*: *cāsū* 'by chance'; *cōnsiliō* 'by design';

cōnsultō 'deliberately'; *forte* 'by chance'; *fraude* 'deceitfully'; *iūre* 'rightly'; *iniūriā* 'unjustly'; *silentiō* 'in silence'; *vī* 'by force.'

Note 2.—The words given in *Note* 1 are used exactly as adverbs; they differ from adverbs only in being more obviously what most other adverbs were originally, oblique cases of nouns.

Note 3.—With a number of common phrases *cum* is never used: *hōc cōnsiliō* 'with this intention'; *hōc modō, hāc ratiōne* 'in this way'; *summō opere* 'earnestly, energetically'; *aequō animō* 'calmly'; *iussū tuō* 'at your command'; *iniussū Caesaris* 'without Caesar's permission'; *bonā tuā veniā* 'with your kind permission'; *nūllō negōtiō* 'without trouble'; *nescio quō pactō* 'in some way or other.'

Note 4.—The preposition *in* is never used with ablatives of manner: *in hōc modō* would be bad Latin.

271. The ablative of **quality** (which also is an ablative of accompaniment) is used without *cum* but is always defined by an adjective.

Eximiā fuit corporis pulchritūdine. He was a man of great personal beauty.

Note.—For the Genitive of quality and the distinction between it and the ablative, see **303**.

Exercise 33

A

1. He replied that nearly the whole of the army was annihilated, and [1] that it made no difference whether it had been overwhelmed by famine, or by pestilence, or by the enemy. 2. Having been chosen king not only by his own soldiers, but also by the popular [2] vote,[3] he aimed at establishing and securing by the arts of peace a throne gained by the sword [4] and violence. 3. Sprung as he was from an illustrious family, he entered public life as [5]

---

[1] *Nec quidquam interesse.* (See **110, 310.**) [2] 'Of the people.' (See **59.**)
[3] Plural. [4] Why not *gladiō*? (See **17.**)
[5] 'As' is not to be expressed; why would *velut* or *quasi* be wrong? (See **221.**)

a young man, and retired at last from office as an old one. 4. Freed from the fear of foreign war, the nation was now [1] able to drive traitors from its territory and show its gratitude to patriots. 5. Whether [2] your unprincipled relation has abandoned this attempt, or intends to persevere in it, I know not; but whether [2] he means to take one course [3] or the other, it seems to me that he is not yet willing to abstain from wrong. 6. So far is my unfortunate brother from having been freed from debt, that he is even now leaving his country for [4] no other cause.

B

1. I would fain ask, with your kind permission, whether it [5] was by accident, or by design that you acted [6] thus. 2. We set forth from home with tears, with wailing, and with the deepest anxiety; we reached the end of our journey relieved of a load of cares, free from fear, and amidst great and universal rejoicing. 3. He is a man of the most spotless character, and so far removed from such a crime that for my part, I wonder [7] how he can have been suspected of such monstrous impiety. 4. We had rather die with honour than live as slaves (42, ii); but we refuse to perish in this manner for the sake of such [8] a person as this. 5. I might have [9] faced death itself without trouble, but I cannot endure such a heavy disaster as this [10] with resignation. 6. He was so transported with passion that he threatened not only his brother, but all the bystanders, with death.

---

[1] *Iam; nunc* is 'at *this present* moment.'

[2] See 171.

[3] =to do this or that.

[4] *Propter* with accusative.

[5] See 160.

[6] =did this; avoid using *agere* for 'to act.'

[7] Mood?

[8] See 87. *Tālis* is rarely used contemptuously.

[9] See 196.

[10] 88, *Note.*

EXERCISE XXXIV

ABLATIVE—*Continued*

272. The ablative of **place** and **time** indicates 'where' or 'when' an action takes place.

Proximā aestāte in Graeciā mortuus est. He died in Greece in the following summer.

Note.—These functions of the ablative originally belonged to the **locative** case, which is almost extinct in Latin as a separate form. When so used, the ablative may be described as **local.**

273. A preposition (*in, ex, ā, ab*) is generally used with words denoting place, but not with words denoting time (See **311, 320.**)

Note 1.—The following expressions of 'place where' are regularly used without a preposition: *terrā marīque* 'by land and sea'; *hōc locō* 'in this place'; *dextrā, laevā* 'on the right, left.'

Note 2.—Distinguish between *tālī tempore* 'at such a time' and *in tālī tempore* 'in such circumstances, in spite of (in the face of) such a crisis.'

274. The ablative of **respect** or **limitation** (which is related to the ablative of accompaniment) denotes that 'in respect of which.'

Linguā, mōribus, armōrum genere inter sē discrepābant. They differed from one another in language, habits, and type of arms.

Note.—Very common are: *speciē* 'in appearance'; *rē ipsā* 'in reality'; *nōmine* 'in name'; *maior nātū* 'elder (in age).'

An ablative of this type is used also with adjectives.

Alterō saucius bracchiō. Wounded in one arm.
Dignus (indignus) laude. Worthy (unworthy) of praise.

275. In English, a comparative adjective or adverb is connected by the conjunction 'than' with the clause or word with which the comparison is made: He is older *than* he was; He is more *than* twenty years old.

In Latin, *quam* is the regular particle of comparison. As it is a *conjunction*, and not a *preposition*, things compared by *quam* will be in the same case.

Eurōpa minor est quam Asia. Europe is smaller than Asia.

Dīxit Eurōpam minōrem esse quam Asiam. He said that Europe was smaller than Asia.

Ā nūllō libentius quam ā tē litterās accipiō. I receive a letter from no one with more pleasure than from you.

Note.—With numerals, *plūs, minus, amplius, longius* are often used as the equivalents of *plūs quam, minus quam*, etc.

Minus quīnque mīlia prōcessit. He advanced less than five miles.

276. Instead of the *quam* construction, Latin often uses an ablative of **comparison.**

Hōc homine nihil contemptius esse potest. Nothing can be more despicable than this man.

Haec nōnne lūce clāriōra sunt? Are not these things clearer than daylight?

Note 1.—This ablative is one of separation and denotes the point *from which* the comparison is made.

Note 2.—The ablative of comparison is used **only** when the other noun is nominative or accusative; otherwise the *quam* construction **must** be used.

Tuī studiōsior sum quam illīus. I am fonder of you than of him.

Tuī studiōsior illō sum. I am fonder of you than he is.

Note 3.—For ‘ than those of,’ see **345.**

277. The ablatives of *spēs, opīniō, fāma, exspectātiō, iūstum,* and *aequum* are frequently used after comparative adjectives and adverbs.

Spē omnium celerius vēnit. He came sooner than any one had hoped.

Nōlī plūs iūstō dolēre. Do not feel undue pain.

278. Notice how this construction may be used to render the English ‘ superior to,’ ‘ inferior to.’

Omnia virtūte īnferiōra dūcit. He counts everything inferior to (of lower rank than) goodness.

Negant quemquam tē fortiōrem esse. They say that no one is superior to you in courage.

Note.—*Nēmō tibi virtūte praestat* (where *virtūte* is an ablative of respect) would also be good Latin for ‘ no one is superior to you in courage.’ (See 239, *footnote.*)

279. An ablative (instrumental) is often used with comparatives to indicate **measure of difference.**

Multō mē doctior. Greatly my superior in learning.

Homō paulō sapientior. A man of somewhat more wisdom than is common (of fair, *or* average, wisdom).

Senātus paulō frequentior. A somewhat crowded senate.

Note.—These ablative forms, *paulō, multō, eō, tantō,* etc., must **never** be used with adjectives or adverbs in the positive degree.

But they may be used with words which, though not comparative in form, imply comparison.

Paulō ante. A little before, *or* earlier.

Multō tibi praestat. He is much superior to you.

280. The ablative of **price** (instrumental) is used with verbs of 'buying' and 'selling.'

Vīgintī talentīs ūnam ōrātiōnem Īsocratēs vēndidit. Isocrates sold one oration for twenty talents.

Note 1.—A similar ablative is used with verbs of 'exchanging.'

Pācem bellō mūtāvit. He exchanged peace for (at the cost of) war.

Note 2.—The adjectives *magnō, parvō, nimiō, quantō,* etc., are used by themselves to indicate price.

Vēnditōrī expedit rem vēnīre quam plūrimō. It is for the interest of the seller that the thing should be sold for as high a price as possible.

Multō sanguine victōria nōbīs stetit (cōnstitit). The victory cost us much blood.

Note 3.—Verbs of 'valuing, esteeming,' etc., as distinct from actual *buying,* take the genitive. (See **305.**)

Exercise 34

1. It is pretty well agreed on by all of you that the sun is many times [1] larger than the moon. 2. I have known this man from boyhood; I believe him to be greatly your superior in both courage and learning. 3. The general himself, while he was [2] fighting in front of the foremost line of battle, was wounded in the head. In spite of this [3] great confusion and universal panic, he refused to with-

[1] = by many parts. [2] See **180.** [3] **88,** *Note.*

draw from the contest. 4. By this means he rightly became dear to the nation,[1] and reached the extremity of old age, in name a private citizen, in reality almost the parent of his country. 5. This [2] crime must be at once atoned for by your blood; for your [3] guilty deeds are clear and plain as [4] this sun-light, and [5] it is quite impossible that any citizen can wish you to be pardoned. 6. It seems [6] to me, said he, that all of you are soldiers in name, deserters and brigands in reality. 7. The battle [7] was now much more desperate, and on the left our men were beginning to fail through weariness. The general, himself wounded in one arm, was the first to become aware of this. 8. You might [8] but lately have exchanged war for peace; too late (*adv.*) are you repenting to-day of your blunder. 9. I was anxious yesterday for your safety; but the matter has turned out much better than I had looked for. 10. How much better would [9] it have been in the presence of such a crisis to have held all considerations inferior to the national safety!

EXERCISE XXXV

ABLATIVE—*Continued*

281. An (instrumental) ablative is used to complete the sense of the following verbs:

***Fungor*, *fruor*, *ūtor*, *potior*, *vēscor*, and their compounds.**

Hannibal, cum victōriā posset ūtī, fruī māluit. Hannibal at a time when [10] (although) he might have used his victory preferred enjoying it.

Mortis perīculō dēfūnctī sumus. We have got over the danger of death.

Nostrī victōriā potītī sunt. Our soldiers gained the victory.

---

[1] Or 'country.' (See **16**, *a*.) [2] See **79**. [3] See **338**.
[4] See **276**. [5] =nor can any . . . .
[6] **43**, *Note* 2. [7] **218**. [8] **196**, **197**. [9] **153**.
[10] Or, 'instead of using his victory, preferred to enjoy it.'

Note.—The ablative is used with these verbs because of their meaning: *ūtor,* I serve myself *with*; *fruor,* I enjoy myself *with*; *vēscor,* I feed myself *with*; *potior,* I make myself powerful *with*; *fungor,* I busy myself *with.* (See **228,** *Note.*)

282. *Potior* sometimes takes the genitive, 'I am master of.' *Ūtor* qualified by an adverb is a convenient verb for rendering many English expressions: *male, perversē, immoderātē ūtor,* 'I make a bad, or immoderate use of,' = 'I abuse.'

Tē familiāriter, tē amīcō ūsus sum. I was on intimate terms with you, I found a friend in you.

Note.—Instrumental ablatives are sometimes used also with *glōrior* 'I boast, glorify myself with,' *nītor* 'I rely on, support myself with,' *cōnfīdō* 'I trust.' But *glōrior* sometimes takes an ablative with *in* or *dē, nītor* an ablative with *in,* and *cōnfīdō* (see **245,** *Note* 4) the dative of a word referring to a person.

283. Observe that in the following instances what is the direct object of the English verb is indicated by an ablative of the instrument with the Latin transitive verb. (Compare **244,** *Note* 1.)

Honōre (*praemiō*) *tē affēcī.* I conferred on you a distinction (a reward).
Poenā (*suppliciō*) *eum afficiam.* I will inflict punishment on him (=*poenās dē eō sūmam*).
Honōribus tē cumulāvimus. We have heaped (showered) honours on you.
Omnī observantiā eum prōsecūtus sum. I have paid him every kind of respect.

284. Verbs of 'filling, abounding,' and their opposites, such as verbs of 'depriving of, emptying of, lacking,' take an ablative.

Such verbs are *complēre, onerāre, refercīre, cumulāre* (*honōribus*), *abundāre*; *carēre, egēre, vacāre* (*culpā*), *orbāre, prīvāre, fraudāre.*

Nāvēs mīlitibus onerat. He loads the ships with soldiers.
Flūmen piscibus abundat. The river is full of fish.
Mortuī cūrā et dolōre carent. The dead are free from anxiety and pain.

Note 1.—*Egeō, indigeō* (especially), *complēre, replēre* sometimes take a genitive.

Rēs maximē necessāriae nōn tam artis indigent quam labōris. The most necessary things do not require skill so much as labour.

Note 2.—The ablative used with verbs of 'filling' and 'abounding' is instrumental; that used with verbs of 'depriving,' 'lacking,' etc., is one of separation (see **264**).

285. The ablative in many of its various senses is also used to qualify adjectives. (See **265, 274.**)

Vir omnī honōre dignus. A man worthy of every distinction. (**274.**)

Vir maximō ingeniō praeditus. A man endowed with remarkable ability.

Dīvitiīs opibusque frētus. Relying on his wealth and resources.

Note 1.—Adjectives of 'fulness' take either a genitive (see **301**) or an ablative; but *plēnus* generally takes a genitive.

Note 2.—Remember that *dignus* takes an ablative (see **274**), not a genitive.

286. An (instrumental) ablative is used also with *opus* and *ūsus* when they bear the sense of 'need of.'

Ubi rēs adsunt, quid mihi verbīs opus est? When facts are here, what need have I of words?

Ait sibi cōnsultō opus esse. He says he has need of deliberation.

Note.—Sometimes the thing needed is the subject to *opus est.*

Dux nōbīs et auctor opus est. We need a leader and adviser.

This indeed is the rule with neuter pronouns and adjectives:—*Quae nōbīs opus sunt; pauca tibi opus sunt; omnia, quae ad vītam opus sunt,* 'all the necessaries of life.' The infinitive is also used as the subject (see **95**, i).

Quid haec scrībere opus est? What need is there to write this?

Exercise 35

A

1. I have now lived long on most intimate terms with your son; it seems to me that he resembles his father in ability and in character, rather than in features or in personal appearance. 2. Do[1] not deprive (*pl.*) of well-earned distinction and praise one who has made so good and so sensible a use[2] of the favours of heaven. 3. I

[1] **143.** [2] **282.**

cannot but believe[1] that it is by your instrumentality that I have surmounted this great danger. 4. All of us, your well-wishers, make this one prayer, that you may be permitted to discharge the duties of your office with[2] honour and advantage to yourself; we all rely on your honesty and self-control, and are all proud of your friendship. 5. Relying on your support, I have ventured to inflict severe punishment on the rebels. 6. He always put confidence in himself, and in[3] spite of humble means and scanty fare preferred contentment (**98**, *a*) to resting[4] on other men's resources. 7. He preferred dispensing with all the necessaries of life (as) a free man, to abounding in riches in the condition of a slave.

B

1. He promises to supply us with everything that is[5] necessary. 2. We have need of deliberation rather than haste, for I fear that this victory has already cost us too much. 3. In my youth I enjoyed the friendship of your illustrious father; he was a man of remarkable abilities, and of the highest character. 4. He hopes to visit with condign punishment the murderers of his father and those who conspired against their sovereign. 5. I fear that he seems far from worthy of all[6] the compassion and indulgence of which he stands in need to-day. 6. Nothing can ever be imagined more happy than my father's lot in life; he discharged the duties of the highest office without[7] failing to enjoy the charms of family life. 7. Relying on your good-will, I have not hesitated[8] to avail myself of the letter which you sent me by[9] my son. 8. Can any one be more worthy of honour, more unworthy of punishment, than this man?

---

[1] *Facere nōn possum quīn*. . . . See example in **134**.
[2] **270**. [3] **273**, *Note* 2. [4] See **94**.
[5] Mood? See **77**, *Note*. [6] *Tantus* . . . *quantus*.
[7] See **111**, 'so discharged as to enjoy.' [8] See **136**. [9] **267**, *Note* 2.

EXERCISE XXXVI

GENITIVE

The Possessive Genitive

287. The commonest function of the genitive is to define or complete the meaning of another noun on which it depends.

288. It does this in various ways; and the relation between one noun and another, as denoted in Latin by the genitive, may be very variously expressed in English: by the '*possessive*' *case*, by various *prepositions*, and by the *adjective*. Thus—

Librī Cicerōnis, Cicero's books; *hominum optimus*, the best of men; *mortis fuga*, flight from death; *Helvētiōrum iniūriae populī Rōmānī*, the wrongs done by the Helvetii to the people of Rome; *mortis remedium*, a remedy against death; *fossa quīndecim pedum*, a trench fifteen feet wide; *lēgum oboedientia*, obedience to law; *corporis rōbur*, bodily strength; *āmissī fīliī dolor*, pain for the loss of his son.

289. The genitive thus used to define a noun is similar to an adjective; it may be called the **adjectival case**, and in fact often corresponds exactly to an adjective. (See **58.**)

Caesaris causā, meā causā, on behalf of Caesar, on my behalf; *tuā* (*illīus*) *operā*, with your (his) aid; so *Sullānī mīlitēs* =*Sullae mīlitēs*, the soldiers of Sulla.

290. The **possessive** use of the genitive answers to the English 'possessive' case in '-s,' to the preposition 'of,' to the *possessive pronoun*, and to the *adjective*.

Pompeiī aequālis ac meus. Pompey's contemporary and my own.
Noster atque omnium parēns. Our own, and the universal parent.
Scēptrum rēgis (or *rēgium*). The king's sceptre.
Illud Platōnis. That saying of Plato.

Note 1.—Observe that Latin prefers to use a possessive adjective rather than the genitive of a personal pronoun: *meā grātiā* 'for my sake,' rather than *meī grātiā*.

Note 2.—The genitive used in such expressions as the following is possessive: *tuī similis, Cicerōnis inimīcissimī* (see **256**); *Pompeiī causā, grātiā*, 'in the interest of, for the sake of, Pompey.'

Note 3.—The genitive in *suī iūris, suae diciōnis facere* 'to bring under one's own jurisdiction or power' is either possessive or partitive (293).

Note 4.—A demonstrative pronoun is not qualified in Latin by a possessive genitive. (See 345.)

291. Not far removed in sense from the possessive is the genitive of **characteristic.** This genitive is used as a predicate with a copulative verb to denote such ideas as English expresses by 'property,' 'duty,' 'part,' 'mark,' etc.

Tālia dīcere sapientis (*stultitiae, rēgis*) *est.* It is the mark of a wise man (of folly, of a king) to speak thus.

Note 1.—The genitive of those third declension adjectives that have the same termination for masculine and neuter in the nominative singular, is almost invariably preferred to the predicative use of the neuter nominative. (Contrast carefully with 295, *a.*)

'It is foolish' may be translated by *stultum est* or by *stultī est*; but 'it is wise' is always *sapientis* (or *sapientiae*) *est*, never *sapiēns est.*

Note 2.—But in place of the genitive of personal pronouns the neuter of the possessive adjective is used. (Compare 290, *Note* 1.)

Meum (not *meī*) *est*, it is my part (duty), it is for me to, etc.

Note 3.—Observe that various English phrases may be rendered by this construction :—

It is characteristic of; it is incumbent on; it is for (*the rich,* etc.)*; it is not every one who; any man may; it demands or requires; it betrays, shows,* etc.*; it belongs to; it depends upon; it tends to,* etc.

292. Examples—

1. *Imbēcillī animī est superstitiō.* Superstition is a mark of (*or* betrays) a weak mind.
2. *Iūdicis est lēgibus pārēre.* It is the part (*or* duty) of a judge to obey the law.
3. *Ingeniī hoc magnī est.* This requires great abilities.
4. *Cuiusvīs hominis est errāre.* Any man may err.
5. *Meum est.* It is my business (duty).
6. *Summae est dēmentiae.* It is the height of madness.
7. *Temporī cēdere semper sapientis est habitum.* It has always been held a wise thing to yield to circumstances (to temporise).
8. *Hoc dēmentiae esse summae dīxit.* He said that this showed the height of madness.

9. *Hoc suī esse arbitriī negāvit.* He said that this did not depend upon his own decision.

10. *Hoc ēvertendae esse reī pūblicae*[1] *dīxit.* He said that this tended to the destruction of the constitution. (But this use of the gerundive is rather rare; see **399**, *Note* 2.)

Exercise 36

1. Whether you (*pl.*) will be[2] slaves or free, depends upon your own decision. 2. We know that any man may err, but it is foolish to forget that error is one thing, persistency (**98**, *a*) in error another. 3. He brought under his own jurisdiction, sooner than he had hoped, the privileges and liberty of all his countrymen. 4. Living[3] for the day only, and making no provision for the future was, he said,[4] rather the characteristic of barbarians than of a free nation. 5. Your father's contemporaries were,[5] he said, his own, and none of them had[5] been dearer to him than your uncle. 6. In my absence I did not cease to do everything in your interest and (that) of your excellent brother. 7. A sensible man will[6] yield, says he, to circumstances, but it is the height of folly to pay attention to threats of this kind. 8. Whether we have won the day or no (**168**, *Note*), I hardly dare[7] say; it is, I know,[8] a soldier's duty to wait for his general's orders. 9. It will be[9] for others to draw up and bring forward laws, it is our part to obey the law. 10. You were, he said, evading the law which you had[10] yourself got enacted; a course which, he believed, tended to[11] the overthrow of the constitution.

---

[1] The various meanings of this phrase *rēs pūblica* (often written as one word) should be carefully noticed. It should never be translated by ' republic ' but by ' the constitution,' ' the nation,' ' the state,' 'politics,' ' public life,' etc., according to the context, and should never be used in the plural unless it means more than one ' state ' or ' nation.'

[2] **173**, *Note* 2.

[3] See **94**.

[4] **32**, *b*.

[5] ' Were.' For tenses, see **35**, **36**.

[6] =it is the part of a, etc.

[7] Subjunctive. (**152**, *b*.)

[8] See **32**, *b*.

[9] 291, *Note* 3.

[10] Mood? (See **77**, *Note*.)

[11] **292**, 10.

EXERCISE XXXVII

GENITIVE—*Continued*

The Partitive Genitive

293. A word in the genitive often indicates that whole of which a part is mentioned. This is called the **partitive genitive.**

Note.—This genitive defines not only words meaning 'a part,' as in: *magna pars exercitūs*, but is also used with *comparative* and *superlative adjectives* and *adverbs*, with interrogative and other *pronouns*, with *numerals*, and with any word which can denote in any way *a part of a larger whole*, such as *nēmō, quisquam, multī, paucī, uterque, quisque*, etc. Thus—

> *Ūnus*[1] *omnium īnfēlīcissimus*, the most unfortunate of all mankind; *tū maximē omnium*, you most of all; *uterque vestrum*, each of you two; *multī hōrum*, many of these; *duo hōrum*, two of these; *quotus quisque* (see **157**, *Note* 4) *philosophōrum*, how few (*of*) philosophers.

294. A partitive genitive is also used with the **neuter singular** of adjectives and pronouns which express *quantity* or *degree*, and with *plūs, nihil, satis, nimis, parum.*

Compare Latin and English in—

> *Quantum voluptātis*, how much pleasure; *plūs dētrīmentī*, greater loss; *nihil praemiī*, no reward; *satis* (*parum*) *vīrium*, sufficient (insufficient) strength; *quid novī?* what news? *nimium temporis*, too much time; *hoc ēmolumentī*, this (of) gain; *quid hoc reī est?* what is the meaning of this?

Note.—This genitive is even used with **adverbs**: *eō audāciae*, to such a pitch of boldness; *ubi gentium*, where in the world? and in such adverbial phrases as *cum id aetātis puerō*, with a boy of that age; *ad id locōrum*, up to that point (of time). (See **238**, iii.)

295. Cautions in the use of the partitive genitive.

(*a*) The genitive of an adjective of the second declension used as a noun may be employed as a partitive genitive: *aliquid bonī;* but the genitive of third declension adjectives is not so used:

---

[1] Note this intensive use of *ūnus* with the superlative.

aliquid humile 'something degrading,' not *aliquid humilis*. (Contrast carefully with **291**, *Note* 1.)

(*b*) Adjectives expressing 'whole, middle, top,' etc., are not used as nouns with a partitive genitive depending on them. So: *tōta* (*media*) *urbs*, not *urbis tōtum* (*medium*), for 'the whole,' 'middle of the city.' (See **60**.)

(*c*) The partitive genitive is used to define neuter pronouns or adjectives *only* if they are nominative or accusative without a preposition.

Ad multam noctem (not *ad multum noctis*). To a late hour.

Tantō sanguine (not *tantō sanguinis*). At the cost of (**280**) so much blood.

296. With **numerals**, and words expressing *number*, as *nēmō*, *multī*, *ūnus*, *paucī*, etc., and even with superlatives, the *ablative* with *ex*, *ē*, *dē*, or the *accusative* with *inter*, is often used instead of a partitive genitive: *multī* (*nēmō*, *ūnus*) *ē vōbīs*, for *multī* (etc.) *vestrum*.

Note.—Where *the whole* is itself a numeral, or contains a numeral or an adjective expressing number or quantity, a prepositional construction is always used.

Dē tot mīlibus vix paucī superfuēre. Of so many thousands scarcely a few survived.

297. **Further Cautions.**—The partitive genitive is only used to denote a larger amount than the word which it qualifies.

If the two words denote the **same persons**, or the **same amount**, *apposition* is used. (*Nōs*) *omnēs*, 'all of us' (*i.e.* 'we all'). *Equitēs, quī paucī aderant*, 'the cavalry, few of whom were there' (lit. 'who were there in small numbers'). (See **69** and **225**.)

298. (*a*) *Uterque* 'each of two' is used as a noun governing a partitive genitive *only* if the genitive is a pronoun; otherwise it is treated as an adjective.

Uterque vestrum; but *frāter uterque*.

(*b*) The genitive in the following phrases is partitive:

Nihil reliquī fēcit. He left nothing remaining.

Nihil pēnsī habuit. He cared not at all.

Exercise 37

1. There was [1] nothing mean in this sovereign, nothing base, nothing degrading; little learning (but [2]) fair ability,

---

[1] Either *sum* or *insum*. [2] Express by order of words. (Intr. 98.)

some experience of life and a dash of eloquence, much good sense, abundance of honesty and strength of mind. 2. Of the many [1] contemporaries of your father and myself, I incline to think that no one was more deserving than he of universal praise and respect. 3. Which of you two has caused greater loss and [2] injury to the nation it is hard to say. I hope and trust that you will [3] both before long repent your crimes. 4. Fate has left us nothing [4] except either to die with honour or to live in disgrace. 5. The battle [5] has been most disastrous. Very few of us out of so many thousands survive, the rest are [6] either slain or taken prisoners, so that I greatly fear that (138) all is lost. 6. Where in the world are we to [7] find a man like him [8]? It would [9] be tedious to enumerate, or express in words his many [10] good qualities; and [11] would that he had been [12] here to-day! 7. So much blood has this victory cost us, that for myself I doubt whether the conquerors or the conquered have sustained [13] the greater loss.

EXERCISE XXXVIII

GENITIVE—*Continued*

Subjective and Objective Genitive

299. The genitive case always implies a close relation between the noun in that case and another noun.

(i) Sometimes that relation is such that, if the other noun were converted into a **verb**, the word now in the genitive would become the *subject* of that verb.

---

[1] Use *tot*. (Compare the use of *tantus*, **88**, *Note.*)

[2] Repeat 'greater'; this repetition of a word already used is very common in Latin in place of a conjunction.

[3] The fut. participle of *paenitet* is rare. What is the substitute? (**38.**)

[4] See **298** (*b*) and **127.**

[5] See **218.**

[6] See **187**, *Note.*

[7] See **149**, *c.*

[8] Use *ille*, why? (**339**, iii.)

[9] Mood? (See **153.**)

[10] *Tot.*

[11] *Quī.* (**78.**)

[12] See **150.**

[13] *Accipiō.*

Thus: *post fugam Pompeiī=postquam fūgit Pompeius.* Such a genitive is called **subjective.**

(ii) Sometimes the relation of a genitive to its governing noun resembles that of an object to its verb.

Thus: *propter mortis timōrem=quod mortem timuit.* Such a genitive is called **objective.**

300. The **objective genitive** is very common in Latin and often depends upon a noun whose verbal cognate takes, not the accusative, but the dative or ablative, or some prepositional construction. It represents therefore many English phrases besides those containing the preposition 'of.'

Instances are—*Litterārum studium* (*studēre litterīs*), devotion to literature; *dolōris remedium* (*dolōrī mederī*), a remedy against pain; *reī pūblicae dissēnsiō* (*dē r. p. dissentīre*), a disagreement on political matters, *or* a political disagreement; *Pyrrhī rēgis bellum* (*cum Pyrrhō bellum gerere*), the war with, *or* against, King Pyrrhus; *suī fīdūcia* (*sibi cōnfīdere*), confidence in one's-self; *lēgum oboedientia* (*lēgibus oboedīre*), submission to law; *deōrum opīniō* (*dē dīs aliquid opīnārī*), an impression about the gods.

301. An objective genitive is used also with **adjectives** in which a verbal notion is prominent.

(i) Such adjectives are those which signify *desire, knowledge, recollection, fear, fulness, participation,* and their *opposites*; and those which end in *-āx.*

Rērum novārum cupidus, desirous of change; *mīlitiae ignārus,* ignorant of warfare; *imperiī capāx,* with a capacity for rule.

(ii) Many of these adjectives such as *cupidus, ignārus, memor,* etc., answer to English adjectives which are followed by the preposition 'of,' and will cause no difficulty; with others the Latin genitive represents various English prepositions and constructions. (See **300.**)

Reī pūblicae perītus (*imperītissimus, rudis*). Skilled (most unskilled, unversed) in the management of the state.

Pugnandī īnsuētus. Unaccustomed to fighting.

Litterārum studiōsissimus. Most devoted to literature.

Huius sceleris particeps (*expers, affīnis*). With part in (free from, connected with) this guilt.

Beneficiī immemor. Apt to forget a favour.

Note 1.—*Plēnus* sometimes takes the ablative (**285,** *Note* **1**); *prūdēns* and *rudis* sometimes take *in* with ablative.

Note 2.—*Certiōrem facere* (=to inform) has a double construction. 'He has informed me of his plan' is either *Certiōrem mē suī cōnsiliī fēcit* or *Certiōrem mē dē suō cōnsiliō fēcit.*

302. An objective genitive is used to qualify the **present participle** of transitive verbs, when the latter is used as an adjective, *i.e.* to denote a *permanent quality*, not a *single act.*

Thus *rēgnum appetēns*='while aspiring to the crown,' but *rēgnī appetēns*=aspiring to kingly power (habitually, or by character).

Note 1.—These present participles, when thus used, admit, as adjectives, of degrees of comparison: *tuī amantissimus*, etc.

Note 2.—An objective genitive is used with a past participle in *iūris cōnsultus* 'one consulted on the law.'

Exercise 38

1. He was most devoted to literature, and at the same time (**366**) most uncomplaining under toil, cold, heat, want of food and of sleep. My fear,[1] however, is that he consents to allow himself too little repose and rest. 2. Such was the soldiers' ardour for the fight,[2] such the universal enthusiasm, that they refused to obey the orders of their general, who was thoroughly versed in warfare of that kind. Full of self-confidence and contempt for the enemy, and cheering each other on, they advanced as [3] to certain victory, but fell unawares into an ambuscade. 3. In spite of the greatest disagreement on politics, the friendship [4] which existed [5] between your gallant father and myself remained firm longer than either (*et*) he or I had hoped.[6] 4. He had [7] enough wealth and to spare, but he was at the same [8] time most inexperienced in political life, with but little desire for fame, praise, influence, or

---

[1] *Illud vereor.* (See **341**.) [2] Gerund, **99**.

[3] Note carefully the different meanings of 'as.' '*As* he does this' (time), *dum haec facit*; '*As* (though) to victory' (comparison), *tamquam* . . .; 'I did this *as* a boy,' *puer hoc faciēbam.* (**63**.)

[4] Insert *tamen*, 'yet.'

[5] 'Which *was* to me *with* your,' etc. (Intr. 35, *Note.*)

[6] See **277**. [7] See **257**. [8] See **366**.

power, and very averse to (265) all competition for office [1] or distinction.[1] 5. But these [2] men (though) they have borne [3] no part in all these toils, craving only for pleasure and repose, most indifferent to the public interest, devoted to feasting and gluttony, have reached such a pitch of shamelessness, that they have ventured in my hearing to taunt with luxury an army that has borne uncomplainingly [4] all the hardships of a prolonged warfare.

EXERCISE XXXIX

GENITIVE—*Continued*

Quality and Definition

303. The resemblance of the Latin genitive to the adjective is to be further noticed in its next use, the **genitive of quality.**

(i) A Latin noun in the genitive often defines another noun by denoting some quality.

Vir summae fortitūdinis. A man of the greatest courage.

(ii) A genitive of quality invariably has an **adjective** attached to it. 'A man of courage' is not *homō fortitūdinis*, but *homō fortis*; 'a man of good sense' is *homō prūdēns*, not *homō prūdentiae*.

Note.—Since the ablative can also be used to denote quality (**271**), it is important to remember :—

(i) If *number, amount, precise dimensions, age,* or *time* is to be denoted, the genitive and not the ablative is used.

Septuāgintā nāvium classis, a fleet of seventy ships; *vīgintī pedum erat agger*, the embankment was twenty feet high; *puer tredecim annōrum*, a boy thirteen years old; *prōvectae* (*exāctae*) *aetātis homō*, a man advanced (far advanced) in

---

[1] Plural. Latin would not represent either word here by an *abstract term* in the singular. [2] *Istī.* (See 338, *Note* 2.)

[3] Use adjective *expers* (301, ii) in apposition with 'these men.'

[4] Use a single word: 'most uncomplaining under.'

years; *tot annōrum fēlīcitās*, so many years of good fortune; *quīndecim diērum supplicātiō*, a thanksgiving of fifteen days' duration.

(ii) The **genitive** is used mainly to express *permanent* and *inherent* qualities: *optimae speī adulēscēns*, a youth of the highest promise; the **ablative** is used to express both these and *external* characteristics of dress or appearance: *senex cānīs capillīs et veste sordidā* (not *cānōrum capillōrum*), an old man with white hair and unclean garments. The ablative is also used for any state or feeling of the *moment*: *fac bonō sīs animō* 'be of good cheer.'

304. A **defining** or **appositional** genitive is sometimes added to another substantive to *explain* or *define* its sense: *Virtūs iūstitiae*, the virtue of justice; *glōriae praemium*, a reward consisting in glory.

Note.—**Cautions.**—The resemblance of the uses of the Latin genitive to those of an English noun with the preposition 'of' is obvious, but it must be remembered that—

(i) After such words as *urbs*, *īnsula*, etc., apposition is used, not the **defining** genitive, to express the English 'of' with the proper name.

Urbs Saguntum, the city of Saguntum; *īnsula Britannia*, the island of Britain. (See **223**.)

(ii) Latin often uses an adjective instead of the possessive genitive of names of **towns** or **countries**.

Rēs Rōmānae, the affairs of Rome; *cīvis Thēbānus*, a citizen of Thebes. (See **58**.)

(iii) Remember also: *media urbs*, the middle of the city (**295**, *b*); *quot estis?* how many of you are there? (**297**).

Exercise 39

1. It is said that serpents of vast size are found in the island of Lemnos. 2. No one denies that he was a man of courage[1]; the real question is whether he was (one) of good sense,[1] and experience.[1] 3. It seems that your son is a boy of the highest promise and of great influence with[2] those of his own age. 4. After three days'[3] procrastination he at last set out with a fleet of thirty ships;

[1] 303, ii. [2] *Apud* (with *acc.*). [3] 303, *Note* (i).

but being [1] far advanced in life, he was scarcely competent to carry out so difficult a task. 5. I would have [2] you therefore be of good cheer. Do not on account of a short-lived panic throw away the result of so many years of toil. 6. As all of us know, he is a person[3] of old-world, and perhaps of excessive, sternness: but at the same time a man [3] of justice and honesty and of the most spotless life. 7. Gallant fighting [4] and an honourable death in the field becomes citizens of Rome; let the few therefore of us [5] who survive show ourselves worthy alike of our ancestors and of the nation of Rome. 8. It seemed that there stood by him in his sleep an old man far advanced in years, with white hair, and kindly countenance, who bade him be of good cheer and hope for the best,[6] and promised that he would reach in safety the island of Corcyra after a voyage of some [7] days.

EXERCISE XL

GENITIVE—*Continued*

Genitive with Verbs

The genitive is also used to complete or define the sense not only of nouns but of certain **verbs**.

305. A genitive of value is used with verbs of 'valuing' and 'buying,' etc., especially the former.

Magnī, maximī, plūris; parvī, minōris, minimī; tantī, quantī, nihilī, are used with *factitive* verbs such as *faciō, habeō, aestimō,* etc.; and ***plūris, minōris, tantī,*** and *quantī* are used with ***emō*** and ***vēndō.*** (Compare **280.**)

> ***Tē in diēs plūris faciō.*** I value you more highly every day.
>
> ***Rempūblicam nihilī habet, salūtem suam maximī.*** He sets no value on the national cause, the highest on his own safety.

---

[1] Use *homō* in apposition. (See **224**, *Note* 2.)
[2] *Fac* or *velim.* (141.)
[3] See **224**, *Note* 3, *footnote.*
[4] **96**, *a.*
[5] **297.**
[6] Neut. plur.
[7] *aliquot.*

Ēmit hortōs tantī quantī Pȳthius voluit. He bought the pleasure-grounds at the full (*or*, exactly at the) price that Pythius wished for.

Note.—This genitive of value is also used as a predicate with copulative verbs, such as *sum, fīō.*

Tua mihi amīcitia plūris est quam cēterōrum omnium plausūs. Your friendship is of more value to me than the applause of all the world besides.

306. Verbs of **accusing, condemning, acquitting,** such as *accūsāre, arguere, reum facere, condemnāre, absolvere,* take a genitive defining the **charge.**[1]

Prōditiōnis accūsāre, reum facere. To accuse, to prosecute, for treachery.

Fūrtī ac repetundārum condemnātus est. He was condemned for (found guilty of) theft and extortion.

Parricīdiī eum incūsat. He taxes him with parricide.

Sacrilegiī absolūtus est. He was acquitted of sacrilege.

Note.—Instead of the *genitive*, the *ablative* with *dē* is often used.

Dē pecūniīs repetundīs damnārī. To be condemned for extortion.

Aliquem dē ambitū reum facere. To bring an action against a man for bribery.

So: *Dē vī, dē sacrilegiō, dē caede, dē venēficiīs,* etc., *sē pūrgāre.* To clear oneself of assault, sacrilege, murder, poisoning.

Notice also—*Inter sīcāriōs accūsātus est.* He was accused of assassination.

307. The **punishment** is sometimes expressed by the *genitive*; far oftener by the *ablative.*

Capitis (or *capite*) *damnātus est.* He was capitally condemned, *i.e.* to death or exile.

Octuplī condemnātus est. He was condemned to pay eightfold.

But: *Morte, exsiliō condemnātus* (*multātus*) *est.* He was condemned to (punished with) death, exile.

308. The genitive is also used to complete the sense of verbs of **remembering, reminding, forgetting, pitying.**

---

[1] Sometimes the genitive depends on *crīmine* 'on the charge (of)' or *nōmine* 'under the heading (of)'; but the simple genitive construction with these verbs is not only the more frequent but the earlier, and did not arise from the *omission* of *crīmine* or *nōmine*.

Such are *meminī*; *admoneō*, *commonefaciō*; *oblīvīscor*; *miserēscō*, *misereor*.

Note 1.—*Meminī* takes the genitive of a personal pronoun, but the accusative of other words referring to persons; either the genitive or accusative of words referring to things may be used.

Cicerōnem meminī; *rērum praeteritārum* ('the past') *meminī*.

Note 2.—Even an impersonal phrase equivalent to a verb of remembering is followed by a genitive.

Venit mihi in mentem eius diēī. I have a recollection of that day.

Note 3.—*Recordor* 'I recall to my thoughts' generally takes an accusative.

Note 4.—With verbs of 'reminding', the person concerned is indicated by the accusative, and the thing by the genitive. But if the thing of which some one is reminded is indicated by a neuter pronoun, the accusative is used for it also.

Foederis tē admoneō 'I remind you of the treaty'; but *hoc*[1] (*illud*) *tē admoneō*.

Note 5.—*Miserārī* 'to express pity for,' 'to bemoan the lot of,' takes an accusative. Thus—

Cāsum nostrum miserābātur. He bemoaned our disaster.

The Genitive with Impersonal Verbs

309. The impersonals, *pudet*, *piget*, *paenitet*, *taedet*, *miseret*, take an **accusative** of the *person feeling*, a **genitive** of what *causes* the feeling.

Ignāvum paenitēbit aliquandō ignāviae. The slothful man will one day repent of his sloth.

Mē nōn sōlum piget stultitiae meae, sed etiam pudet. I am not only sorry for my folly, but also ashamed of it.

Taedet mē vītae. I am weary of my life.

Tuī mē miseret; *meī piget*. I pity you; I am vexed with myself.

Note 1.—Instead of a genitive, we often find an infinitive, or an indicative clause introduced by *quod*, or a neuter pronoun used as the impersonal subject of the verb.

Taedet eadem audīre mīlitēs. The soldiers are tired of hearing the same thing.

Paenitet nōs { *haec fēcisse.* / *quod haec fēcimus.* } We are sorry that we acted so.

Hoc pudet, illud paenitet. This causes shame, that causes regret.

---

[1] This may be looked on as a cognate accusative (236, 237).

Note 2.—The genitive with *pudet* is also used for the person *before whom* the shame is felt.

Pudet mē veterānōrum mīlitum. I blush before the veterans.

310. The constructions used with the impersonals *interest,* 'it makes a difference, it matters' and *rēfert* 'it concerns,' should be carefully noticed.

(i) The **person** to whom something is of importance is either (*a*) put in the genitive, or (*b*) is referred to by the ablative singular feminine of a possessive adjective (*meā, tuā,* etc.).[1]

Interest omnium rēctē facere. It is the interest of all to do right.
Quid nostrā interest (*rēfert*)*?* Of what importance is it to us? (*or* What does it signify to us?)

(ii) The **thing** that is of importance is the impersonal subject of these verbs and may be either (*a*) an infinitive, or (*b*) a neuter pronoun (*hoc, id, illud, quod*) or (*c*) a noun clause (infinitive with subject-accusative, indirect question, or even an indirect command).

(iii) The **degree of importance** is expressed either (*a*) by a genitive of value (*magnī, tantī, plūris*), or (*b*) by an adverb (*magnopere, vehementer, magis, parum*), or (*c*) by an accusative neuter used adverbially (*multum, plūs, nihil, nimium, quantum,* etc.).

(iv) The *thing* with reference to which something else is of importance is sometimes indicated by the accusative with *ad.*

Examples.—The following examples of the usages with *interest* should be well studied and analysed :—

Multum interest quōs quisque cotīdiē audiat. It is of great consequence whom a man listens to every day.
Illud[2] *meā plūris interest tē ut videam.* It is of more consequence to me that I should see you.
Vestrā interest, commīlitōnēs, nē imperātōrem pessimī faciant. It is of importance to you, my comrades, that the worst sort should not elect your commander.
Hoc et tuā et reīpūblicae interest. This concerns both yourself and the nation.

---

[1] The *rē-* in *rēfert* was regarded as the ablative singular of *rēs*; hence the feminine ablatives *meā, tuā,* etc., were used in agreement. The use of such ablatives with *interest* is due to the fact that this verb resembles *rēfert* in meaning. The genitive of the person concerned is presumably possessive; but it is in fact rarely used with *rēfert.*

[2] The substantival *ut*-clause is often used in apposition to an *illud* or *hoc* at the beginning of the sentence.

Nihil meā interest quantī mē faciās. Your estimate of me is of no concern to me.

Magnī interest ad laudem cīvitātis haec vōs facere. Your doing this is of great importance to the credit of the state.

Note.—Cicero and Caesar prefer to use *interest* rather than *rēfert.*

Exercise 40

1. He was a man of moderate abilities, but of the highest character, and in the greatest crisis of a perilous war he was valued more highly in his old age than any [1] of (his) juniors. 2. He was a man of long-tried honour and rare incorruptibility; yet at that time he was taxed with avarice, suspected of bribery, and prosecuted for extortion. You all know that he was unanimously acquitted of that charge. Who is there of you but remembers [2] that day on which he not only cleared himself of an unjust accusation, but exposed the malice and falsehoods of his accusers? None [3] of those who were present in the court that day will easily forget his magnificent address; nothing ever made a deeper impression on his audience.[4] 3. The whole nation has long [5] been weary of the war, regrets its own rashness, and blushes for the folly and incompetence of its general. 4. I remember well the man [6] whom you mention. He was a person of very low origin, of advanced age, with white hair, mean dress, of uncultivated and rustic demeanour. Yet no one was ever more skilled in (301, ii) the science of war, and his being made general [7] at such an emergency was of the utmost importance to the welfare of the state. 5. It makes no difference to us, who are waiting for your verdict, whether the defendant be acquitted or condemned; but it is of general interest that he should not in his absence and unheard be sentenced to either exile or death.

---

[1] *Quisquam.* (See 358, ii.) [2] 308, *Note* 2. [3] *Nēmō.*

[4] 'The mind (*pl.*) of his audience.' Either genitive of present participle of *audiō* or a relative clause. (73, 76.)

[5] Tense? (See 181.) [6] *Ille.* (339, iii.) [7] 310, ii, *a.*

EXERCISE XLI

PLACE, SPACE

Locative Case

311. Place at which is generally expressed by the **local ablative** (272) with the **preposition** *in* : *in Italiā, in urbe.*

But the ablatives of a few words (**273**, *Note* 1) express place where ' without a preposition; and the preposition is sometimes omitted when a noun is qualified by an adjective : *mediā urbe, tōtā Italiā.*

312. But, whenever it exists, the locative case is used to express ' place where.'

Vīxī Rōmae, Tarentī, Carthāginī. I lived at Rome, Tarentum, Carthage.

Note 1.—There is a distinct locative singular form of names of towns and small islands of the first and second declensions, and occasionally of the third. *Domī* ' at home,' *bellī* ' at war,' *mīlitiae* ' on service,' *rūrī* ' in the country,' *humī* ' on the ground,' are also locative forms.

Note 2.—The noun in *pendēre animī* ' to be in suspense ' is possibly a locative also.

313. Place to which is generally expressed by the **accusative** with the **prepositions** *ad, in* : *In* (*ad*) *Italiam rediit.*

But the accusative of names of towns and small islands (and of *domus* and *rūs*) is used without a preposition (see **235**) : *Syrācūsās* (*Rōmam, domum, rūs*) *rediit.*

Note.—When a town is mentioned, *ad* with the *accusative* expresses ' in the neighbourhood of.'

Ad (sometimes *apud*) *Cannās pugnātum est.* There was a battle at (near) Cannae.

Notice also : *Ad* [1] *urbem est.* He is in the neighbourhood of (outside) the city.

---

[1] This phrase is often used of Roman generals, who could not enter the city without laying down their *imperium.*

314. Place from which is usually expressed by the **ablative** with the **prepositions** *ē* (*ex*), *ā* (*ab*) : *ā Pyrrhō*, *ex Italiā*, *ab Āfricā*, *ē nāve*, *ab urbe*.

But the ablative of names of towns and small islands (and of *domus* and *rūs*) are used without a preposition.

Rōmā venit, he comes from Rome ; *Tarquiniōs Corinthō fūgit*, he fled (went into exile) to Tarquinii from Corinth ; *rūre rediit*, he returned from the country.

315. In English we say 'He came to his father *at* Rome,' or 'from Carthage *in* Africa.' But in Latin, with verbs of motion, all such phrases must follow the rules for motion *to* or *from*, given above. Thus—

He returned home from his friends at Corinth. *Corinthō ab amīcīs domum rediit.*

He sent a despatch to the senate at Rome. *Rōmam ad senātum litterās mīsit.*

He returned to his friends in Africa. *In Āfricam ad amīcōs rediit.*

316. (i) When the name of a town or small island is qualified by an adjective, the ablative is used for 'place at which' because the adjective has no locative form. So: *tōtā Corinthō* 'in the whole of Corinth.'

(ii) When *urbs*, or *oppidum*, comes before the proper name (see **223**), the preposition must be used.

In urbe Londiniō, in the city of London ; *ad urbem Athēnās*, *ex urbe Rōmā*.

(iii) When a possessive adjective qualifies the locative *domī* it also has a locative form. But when other adjectives are involved, the ablative (*or* accusative) of *domus* is used with a preposition.

Domī meae (or *apud mē*) *commorātus est.* He stayed at my house.

But *In vetere domō*, *ad veterem domum.* In, *or* to, his old home.

317. An adjective is not directly applied to the name of a town (compare the construction used with the names of persons : **224**).

The name of the town is placed first, in either the *locative*, *accusative*, or *ablative*, according to the meaning ; then follows the word *urbs* or *oppidum* qualified by the adjective, with or without a preposition according to the rules already given. Thus—

Archiās Antiochīae nātus est, celebrī quondam urbe (local ablative). Archias was born in the once famous city of Antioch.

Athēnās, in urbem praeclārissimam vēnī. I reached the illustrious city of Athens.

Syrācūsīs, ex urbe opulentissimā, profectus est. He set out from the flourishing city of Syracuse.

318. (i) **Space covered** (in answer to the question **how far ?**) is generally expressed by the **accusative.**

Triduī iter prōcessit. He advanced a three days' march.

Ab officiō cavē trānsversum, ut aiunt, digitum discēdās. Do not swerve 'a finger's breadth' from your duty.

(ii) For **distance from** (question, **how far off ?**), either the **accusative** (238, iv) or **ablative** (279) is used.

Ariovistus vix duo mīlia (or *duōbus mīlibus*) *passuum aberat.* Ariovistus was at a distance of scarcely more than two miles.

(iii) **Dimension** (question, **how high, deep, broad ?**) is generally expressed by the **accusative.**

Mīlitēs aggerem lātum pedēs trecentōs exstrūxērunt. The soldiers threw up a mound three hundred feet broad (*or* in breadth).

Note.—Occasionally the **genitive** of quality (**303**, *Note*) is used for the actual measurement, and the idea of 'length, depth,' etc., is left unexpressed: *fossa quīndecim pedum,* a ditch fifteen feet deep (*or* wide).

319. In English the name of a town or country is often personified and used for the nation or people: 'Spain,' 'France,' 'England,' etc. This is much rarer in Latin prose. (Cf. **17.**)

'The war between Rome and Carthage' is *Bellum, quod populus Rōmānus cum Carthāginiēnsibus gessit.*

For 'Rome' in this sense we may use *Populus Rōmānus, rēs pūblica Rōmāna,* or *Rōmānī,* but rarely *Rōma.*

Exercise 41

1. After living [1] many years [2] at Veii, **a town at that** period of great population [3] and vast resources, he removed

[1] 'After living,' *i.e.* 'having lived.' (**14.**)

[2] Case ? (See 321.)

[3] May be turned either by 'flourishing (superlative of *flōrēns*) with a multitude of citizens and vast resources,' or by 'most populous and wealthy.'

thence late in life to the city[1] of Rome, which was at a distance of about fourteen miles from his old home. 2. His parents, sprung originally from Syracuse, had been[2] long resident at Carthage. He himself was sent[3] in boyhood to his uncle at Utica, and was absent from home for full three years; but after his[4] return to his mother, now[5] a widow, at Carthage, he passed the rest of his youth at his own home. 3. The enemy (*pl.*) was now[5] scarcely a single day's march off. The walls of the fortress, scarcely twenty feet high, surrounded by a ditch of (a depth of) less than six feet, were falling into ruin from age. The general, after waiting[6] six days for reinforcements, sent a despatch by[7] a spy to the governor at Pisa, earnestly imploring[8] him not to waste time any longer, but to bring up troops to[9] his aid without delay. 4. Born and brought up in the vast and populous city of London, I have never before had permission to exchange the din and throng of the city for the repose and peace and solitude of rural life. But now I hope shortly to travel to my son at Rome, and from Italy to sail, before the middle of winter, to the city of Constantinople, which I have long been eager to visit. You, I fancy,[10] will winter at Malta, an island[11] which I am not likely ever to see. In the beginning of spring I have decided to stay in the lovely city of Naples, and to betake myself to my old home at London in the month of May or June. 5. Caesar shows himself, I fancy, scarcely less tenacious of his purpose at home than in the field. It is said[12] that he is outside the city waiting for his triumph, and wishes to address the people. 6. Exasperated and

---

[1] *Urbs* may be removed into the relative clause: 'which city.'
[2] Tense? (See **181.**) [3] Participle; and omit 'and.' (**15.**)
[4] Use verb and *postquam.* (**14.**)
[5] Why not *nunc*? (See **328,** *b.*)
[6] 'After waiting,' *i.e.* 'having waited.' (**14.**)
[7] Why not *ab*? (See **267,** *Note* 2.)
[8] '(in) which he implored.' Why not participle? (See **411.**)
[9] For construction, see **259.** Is 'his' *ei* or *sibi*? (See 349.)
[10] See **32,** *b.* [11] 'Which island.' [12] See **43, 44.**

provoked by the wrongs and insults of Napoleon, Spain turned at last to England, her ancient foe.

EXERCISE XLII

EXPRESSIONS OF TIME

320. In answer to the question **when? at what time?** Latin uses the **local ablative (272)** of words which in themselves denote *time*.

Vēre, autumnō, nocte, sōlis occāsū, prīmā lūce, etc.

But the preposition *in* is generally used with words which do not *in themselves* denote time, unless they are qualified by an adjective. (Compare **311.**)

In bellō 'in time of war,'

But *Bellō Pūnicō secundō* 'in the second Punic war.'

Note 1.—If the time is simply indicated as 'before' or 'after' some other event, *ante* or *post* with the accusative is used: *ante noctem, post proelium.*

Note 2.—For the difference made by the preposition *in,* see **273,** *Note* 2. *In tempore* means 'at the right moment,' but *Alcibiadis temporibus,* 'at the time (in the days) of Alcibiades.'

321. In answer to the question **how long?** the **accusative** is used. (See **238,** iv.)

Multōs iam annōs hīc domicilium habeō. I have now been living (**181**) here for many years.

Note 1.—Sometimes the idea of duration is emphasised by the addition of *per: Per tōtam noctem, per hiemem.*

Note 2.—The answer to **for how long past?** is often expressed by a singular noun with an *ordinal* adjective.

Annum iam (or *hunc*) *vīcēnsimum rēgnat.* He has been king for the last twenty years.

322. In answer to **how long before? how long after?** two constructions may be used.

(*a*) The word, or words, expressing the length of time may be in the ablative of *measure of difference* (**279**) associated with *post* or *ante* used **as an adverb.** Or:

(*b*) *Post* or *ante* may be used as a **preposition** with the **accusative** of a word or words denoting an amount of time.

For example, for the phrase 'the fleet returned after three years,' we may write either: *tribus post annīs* (*tertiō post annō*) *classis rediit*, or *post trēs annōs* etc.

Note.—In *paucīs diēbus ante eius mortem* 'a few days before his death,' *ante eius mortem* indicates vaguely the 'time when' (**320**, *Note* 1), and *paucīs diēbus* is the ablative of difference. In *haec fēcit paucīs ante diēbus quam ē vītā excessit*, the compound conjunction *antequam* is separated (as often) into its elements, and *ante* functions within its own sentence as an adverb. (See also **443**.)

323. The following examples should be studied :

(*a*) Three hundred and two years after the foundation of Rome.

1. *Annō trecentēnsimō alterō quam Rōma condita est.* Or :
2. *Post trecentēnsimum alterum annum quam Rōma condita est.*

(*b*) *Prīdiē quam excessit ē vītā.* The day before his death.
Postrīdiē quam ā vōbīs discessī. The day after I left you.
Posterō annō quam, etc. The year after, etc.
Priōre annō quam, etc. The year before, etc.

324. How long ago?, reckoning from the present time, is answered by the adverb *abhinc* in association with the **accusative.**

Abhinc annōs quattuor Vergilium vīdī. I saw Virgil four years ago.

Note.—*Abhinc* is placed before the accusative. The use of *abhinc* and an ablative of difference (which would seem to us a natural construction) is rare in classical Latin.

325. Within what time? is answered by the **ablative,** or by *intrā* and the accusative.

Decem annīs (or *intrā decem annōs*) *urbem capiēmus.* We shall take the city in (*or* within) ten years.

Note 1.—A singular noun with an *ordinal* adjective is often used instead of a plural noun with a *cardinal* numeral.

Intrā decem annōs or *intrā decimum annum.*

(Compare **321**, *Note* 2.)

Note 2.—Observe the following expressions : *Hīs tribus diēbus*, in (*or* for) the last three days (from the *present* time) ; *illīs*, etc, from a *past* time ; *hōc bienniō*, within two years from this time.

Note 3.—The ablative with *in* is sometimes used for time 'within which.'

326. *In* with the **accusative** denotes a time *for* which provision or arrangements or calculations are made:

In diem vīvere, to live for the day (only); *in sex diēs indūtiae factae sunt,* a truce was made for six days; *ad cēnam mē in posterum diem invītāvit,* he invited me to supper for the next day.

Ad with the accusative denotes an exact date in the future: *ad Kalendās solvam,* I will pay on, or by, the 1st; *ad tempus,* at the appointed time, punctually.

Ex or *ab* with the ablative denotes the time at which a period begins: *Ex eō diē ūsque ad extrēmum vītae diem,* from that day to the very end of his life.

327. In answer to the question **how old?** the usual construction is *nātus* with the accusative.

Annōs quīnque et octōgintā nātus excessit ē vītā. He died at the age of eighty-five.

Note 1.—The accusative here is similar to that used to express dimensions (**318**, iii).

Note 2.—*Cum annōs quīnque et octōgintā habēret,* or *cum annum octōgēnsimum quīntum ageret,* would be equally good Latin.

Note 3.—A genitive of quality (**303**) may also be used: *puer ūndecim annōrum.*

Note 4.—'Under (over) twenty years,' may best be expressed by an adjectival or temporal clause: *quī nōndum vīgintī annōs habēbat; cum vīcēnsimum annum nōndum ageret.*

Notes on Adverbs of Time

328. The correct use of certain adverbs of time is important.

(*a*) **No longer** is only *nōn diūtius* when a long time has already passed, otherwise *nōn iam*; 'no one any longer' is *nēmō iam,* or (with 'and') *nec quisquam iam.*

(*b*) **Now.** *Nunc* is 'at the present moment,' or 'as things are now.' It cannot be used of the past. 'Caesar was now tired of war' is: *iam Caesarem bellī taedēbat.* Occasionally, if the 'now' of the past is very precise: *tum. Iam* can be used also of the future: *quid hoc reī sit, iam intellegēs,* 'you will soon be aware of the meaning of this.'

(*c*) **Daily** is generally *cottīdiē*; *in diēs* (or *in singulōs diēs*) is used only in association with comparatives, or verbs of *increasing* or the reverse. *Diem dē diē*, day after day; *dē nocte*, after night has begun. The adjective *diurnus* is 'daily' as opposed to *nocturnus*; *cottīdiānus* is 'daily' in the sense of 'everyday.'

(*d*) **Not yet** is *nōndum, necdum*; 'no one yet' *nēmō umquam*, or, where the present is opposed to the future, *adhūc nēmō*.

(*e*) **Still** (=even now) is *etiam nunc* (or *etiam tunc* in reference to the past).

(*f*) *Iam diū* is 'now for a long while' simply; *iam prīdem* looks back rather to the *beginning* of the time that is past; *iam dūdum* 'for *some*, or a considerable, time.'

(*g*) **Again.** *Rūrsus*, 'once more'; *iterum*, 'a *second* time,' opposed to *semel* or *prīmum*; *dē integrō*, 'afresh' as though the former action had not taken place; *saepe, saepissimē*, 'again and again.' (57, *a*.)

Exercise 42

1. Mithridates, who in a single day had butchered so many citizens of Rome, had now been on the throne two and twenty years from that date. 2. It seems that here too the swallows are absent in the winter months. I at least have seen not a single [1] one for the last three weeks. 3. He died at the age of three and thirty. When less than thirty years old he had already performed achievements unequalled [2] by any of his predecessors or successors. 4. The famine is becoming sorer daily. Exhausted by daily toil (*pl.*), we shall soon be compelled [3] to discontinue the sallies which up to this day we have made both by night [4] and by day. Day after day we look in vain for the arrival of our troops. 5. He promised to be by my side by the first of June; but for the last ten years I have never once known [5] him to be present in good time. 6. Nearly three years ago I said that I had never yet seen any one [6] who surpassed [7] your brother in character or

---

[1] ='not even one.' (Intr. 90.)
[2] 'Such as (86) not even one (had performed).'
[3] 'The sallies must be,' etc. (See 200.)
[4] Use adjectives. (328, *c*.)
[5] *Cognōscō*, 'I find or ascertain.' [6] 328, *d*.
[7] Mood? (77, *Note* and 505, *Note* 1.)

ability, but in the last two years he seems to be growing daily sterner and harsher, and I no longer value him as highly as I did before. 7. I saw your father about three weeks after [1] his return from India. Years [2] had not yet dulled the keenness of his intellect or the vigour of his spirit; in spite of his advancing years, he had been in command of an army within the last six months, and had won a great victory. 8. Misled by a mistake in the date,[3] I thought you had stayed at Athens more than six months. 9. I have spoken enough on this question, and will detain you no longer; six months ago I might [4] have spoken at greater length.[5]

EXERCISE XLIII

PREPOSITIONS

329. (i) **Prepositions** are indeclinable words which, besides other uses, are placed before substantives and pronouns to define their relation to other words. (Intr. 40-43.)

(ii) Since the number of cases is not nearly sufficient to mark all the different relations of a noun to other words, prepositions are used to make the meaning of the cases more definite and clear (see **205**). Thus, to take the simplest instance, the use of the preposition distinguishes the relation of the *agent* from that of the *instrument* (**267, 268**).

(iii) Prepositions were originally adverbs which, because of their frequent association with a given case (*or* cases), were eventually felt to 'govern' that case. (See also Intr. 42.)

(iv) In Latin, as in modern languages, they come, as a rule, before [6] the noun, and all (except *tenus*) are used exclusively with the *accusative* and *ablative* cases.

---

[1] See **322**. [2] *i.e.* age. [3] Genitive. (**300**.)
[4] See **196**, *b*. [5] 'Said more.' (**53**.)
[6] For the position of *cum* in *tēcum*, etc., see **8**, *Note*; *tenus* also follows its noun (*Alpibus tenus*, as far as the Alps), as does *versus*, and occasionally *propter* and others.

Note.—The ablatives *grātiā*, *causā*, are used as *quasi-prepositions* with the *genitive*, and resemble such English *prepositional phrases* as 'in consequence of,' 'in spite of,' etc. (see **290**, *Note* 2).

330. (i) The following prepositions are used with the **accusative only** :—

(Those marked with an asterisk are used also as *adverbs*.)

*ante**, *apud*, *ad*, *adversus**,
*circum**, *circā**, *citrā**, *cis*,
ergā, *contrā**, *inter*, *extrā**,
*infrā**, *intrā**, *iuxtā**, *ob*,
penes, *pōne**, *post** and *praeter*,
*prope**, *propter**, *per*, *secundum*,
*suprā**, *versus*, *ultrā**, *trāns*.

(ii) The following are followed by the **ablative only** :—

ā (*ab*, *abs*), with *cum* and *dē*,
*cōram**, *prō*, with *ex* or *ē*,
palam, *sine*, also *prae*.

(iii) The following are joined with the *accusative* when they express *motion towards* ; otherwise with the *ablative* :—

in, *sub*, *subter**, and *super**.

331. Their meanings are so various that no attempt will be made to illustrate more than some of the most important. The *local* meaning, however, is generally the earliest, and from it the other meanings have developed.

Prepositions with Accusative

1. **Ad**, 'towards,' 'to,' used after verbs of motion, and transferred to various other uses. *Ad tē scrīpsī*, 'I wrote to you'; *ad haec respondit*, 'he replied in answer to this'; *ad Cannās*, 'in the neighbourhood of (near) Cannae'; *hoc ad nōs cōnservandōs pertinet*, 'this tends to our preservation'; *diēs ad urbis interitum fātālis*, 'the day destined for the ruin of the city'; *ad ūnum*. 'to a man (=all)'; *ad hoc*, 'moreover.'

2. **Adversus, adversum**, 'opposite to.' *Adversus castra nostra*, 'opposite to our camp'; *adversus tē contendam* (=*contrā tē* or *tēcum*), 'I will strive against (with) you.'

3. **Ante**, 'before' (place and time). *Ante aciem*, 'before the battle line'; *ante mē*, 'before my time.' Often used adverbially (see **322**, *a*).

4. **Apud,** 'close by.' *Apud Cannās,* 'near (*or* at) Cannae.' But mostly in such phrases as: *apud mē,* 'in my house'; *apud Xenophōntem,* 'in the writings of Xenophon'; *apud vōs contiōnātus est,* 'he made a speech in your hearing'; *apud mē,* 'in my judgment'; *apud vōs ille plūs valet,* 'he has more influence with you.'

5. **Circum, circā,** 'round.' *Circā tellūrem,* 'round the earth'; *circā viam,* 'on both sides of (along) the road'; *circā prīmam lūcem,* 'about dawn.' *Circā* as a preposition (and *circiter* as an adverb) are used with numerals to express 'approximately.'

6. **Cis, citrā,** 'this side,' in contrast to *trāns* ('the other side'). *Cis* (*citrā*) *flūmen Rhēnum,* 'on this side of the Rhine.'

7. **Contrā,** 'facing.' *Contrā urbem,* 'opposite the city.' But oftener = 'against': *contrā rempūblicam facere,* 'to act unconstitutionally'; *contrā nōs bellum gerit* (= *nōbīscum*), 'he wages war against (with) us'; *contrā* (*praeter*) *spem* (*opīniōnem*), 'contrary to expectation.'

8. **Ergā,** 'towards' (but not in a local sense in classical Latin). *Ergā mē benevolentissimus,* 'full of kindness towards me.'

9. **Extrā,** 'outside of.' *Extrā urbem,* 'outside the city'; *extrā culpam,* 'free from blame'; *extrā ōrdinem,* 'out of his proper order,' 'extraordinarily.'

10. **Inter,** 'amongst,' 'between.' *Inter hostium tēla,* 'amid the enemy's weapons'; *inter mē ac vōs hoc* (or *illud*) *interest,* 'this is the difference between me and you'; *inter sē dīligunt* (reciprocal), 'they love each other'; *inter omnēs cōnstat,* 'all are agreed.'

11. **Īnfrā,** 'below': *omnia īnfrā sē esse iūdicat,* 'he holds that he is superior to all things.'

12. **Intrā,** 'within.' *Intrā tēlī iactum,* 'within the cast of a javelin'; *intrā diem decimum* (**325,** *Note* 1), 'within ten days.'

13. **Iuxtā,** 'close to,' 'near': *iuxtā mūrum,* 'near the wall.' Often used adverbially: *iuxtā cōnstitī,* 'I stood near by.'

14. **Ob,** 'before, opposite to.' *Ob oculōs,* 'before one's eyes.' Also = 'on account of,' *ob dēlictum,* 'because of his fault'; *quam ob rem* = 'wherefore (therefore).'

15. **Penes,** 'in the power of.' *Penes tē hoc est,* 'this depends on you'; *penes tē es?* 'are you in your senses?'

16. **Per,** 'through' (place and time). *Per prōvinciam,* 'through the province'; *per hōs diēs,* 'during the last few days' (**325,** *Note* 2); *per mē licet,* 'you have my leave, you may (do it) as far as I am concerned'; *per speculātōrēs,* 'by means of spies' (**267,** *Note* 2); *per vim,* 'by violence, violently.'

17. **Post, pōne,** 'behind,' 'after.' *Post tergum,* 'behind one's back'; *post hominum memoriam,* 'since the dawn of history,' 'within human memory.' Prose writers generally use *post* rather than *pōne.* (For the adverbial use of *post,* see **322,** *a.*)

18. **Praeter,** 'past.' *Praeter castra,* 'beyond the camp'; *fortis praeter cēterōs,* 'brave beyond the rest'; *praeter spem,* 'contrary to hope'; *praeter tē ūnum omnēs,* 'all except you alone.'

19. **Prope (propius, proximē),** 'near to': *prope mē,* 'near to me'; *propius urbem,* 'nearer to the city.' Often used adverbially.

20. **Propter,** 'close to.' *Propter mūrum,* 'hard by the wall.' Often = 'because of': *propter sē,* 'for its own sake'; *propter tē salvus sum* (= *tuā operā*), 'I am safe, thanks to you.'

21. **Secundum,** 'along.' *Secundum flūmen,* 'following the river'; *secundum nātūram,* 'in accordance with nature'; *secundum pugnam,* 'next to (immediately after) the fight'; *secundum deōs,* 'next to the Gods.'

22. **Suprā,** 'above,' 'beyond.' *Suprā terrram,* 'above the earth'; *suprā vīrēs,* 'beyond his strength.'

23. **Trāns,** 'on the other side, across'; in contrast to *cis*: *trāns Rhēnum,* 'across the Rhine.'

24. **Versus,** only with *domum* and names of towns; placed after the substantive: *Rōmam versus,* 'in the direction of Rome.'

25. **Ultrā,** 'beyond.' *Ultrā flūmen*; *ultrā vīrēs,* 'beyond his strength.'

In, sub, subter, super, *with accusative*

26. **In,** 'into,' 'to.' *Athēnās in Graeciam exsulātum abiit,* 'he went into exile at Athens in Greece' (**315**); *exercitum in nāvēs impōnere, in terram expōnere,* 'to embark, disembark, an army'; *in orbem sē colligunt,* 'form a circle (for defence)'; *in quārtum diem in hortōs ad cēnam invītāvit* (**326**), 'he gave an invitation to supper in his grounds four days from that time'; *in praesēns,* 'for the present'; *in diēs,* 'daily' (**328,** *c*); *in posterum,* 'for the future'; *in mē invectus est,* 'he inveighed against me'; *in rempūblicam merita,* 'services to the nation' (but *dē r. p. merērī*); *in hunc modum locūtus est,* 'he spoke in this way, after this fashion.'

27. **Sub,** 'up to' (motion). *Sub ipsōs mūrōs adequitant,* 'they ride close up to the walls.' Also used of time: *sub lūcem,* 'just before dawn'; *sub haec,* 'just after this.'

28. **Subter,** 'below, underneath.' *Subter mūrōs venīre,* 'to come close up to the walls.'

29. **Super,** 'above.' *Super ipsum,* '(next) above the host at table'; *aliī super aliōs,* 'one after another.'

Exercise 43

1. Next to heaven,[1] I ascribed this [2] great favour mainly to you and your children. 2. I hope that when once [3] he has reached Rome he will stay in my house. 3. It seems that this year is destined for the ruin of the nation. 4. He is generally believed to be free from blame, and no one supposes that such [4] a good patriot would have [5] done anything unconstitutionally. 5. He drew up his line on the other side of the Danube. Our men, who had now for some time been [6] marching along the river, halted close to the other bank opposite the enemies' camp. 6. You had my leave to return home to your friends in London. Whether [7] you have gone away or no depends on yourself. 7. There is this difference between you and others : with them (**339,** iv) my client has, thanks to his many [8] services to the nation, great weight ; with you, for the same reason, he has absolutely none. 8. It seems that he invited your son to supper with him three days from that time at his house. Since that date none of his friends has seen him anywhere. 9. The enemy had now disembarked, and had come within the reach of missiles. Our men hurled [9] their javelins and tried [9] to drive their opponents back to the ships. 10. Such was their joy for the present, such their hopes [10] for the future, that no one suspected the real state of affairs.[11] 11. Having inveighed against me with the utmost fury, he sat down. In answer to his long speech I made a very few [12] remarks. 12. Having ridden past the many [13] tall trees which stood along the road, I halted at last close to the gate.

---

[1] Why not *caelum* ? (See **17.**) [2] **88,** *Note.*
[3] Express 'once' by the right tense. (**192,** *Note* 1.)
[4] **88.** [5] **36.**
[6] **181.** [7] See **171.** [8] =*So* many : *tot.* (Cf. **88,** *Note.*)
[9] Historic infinitive. (See **186.**)
[10] Singular. In Latin prose *spēs* is very rarely used in the plural.
[11] '*What* was really happening' (*fīō*), see **174** ; or '*that* which,' etc., see **176.**
[12] 'Said very little.' (See **53, 54.**) [13] See **56** and **69.**

EXERCISE XLIV

PREPOSITIONS WITH THE ABLATIVE

332. Here also the *local* meaning is the earliest.

1. **Ā, ab,** 'from.' (Before vowels and *h*, and sometimes before consonants, *ab* is used. The form *abs* is rare.) *Ab Āfricā*, 'from Africa'; *ā puerō*, 'from boyhood'; *ab urbe conditā*, 'from (after) the foundation of the city'; *ā dextrō cornū*, 'from (on) the right wing'; *ā fronte*, 'in front'; *ā senātū stāre*, 'to take the side of the senate'; *sēcūrus ab hoste*, 'free from care as to the enemy'; *ā rē frūmentāriā labōrāre*, 'to be in distress for provisions'; *ā tē incipiam*, 'I will begin with you'; *cōnfestim ā proeliō*, 'immediately after the battle.'

2. **Cum,** 'with' (opposed to *sine*). *Tēcum Romam rediī*, 'I returned to Rome in company with you'; *cum gladiō, cum sordidā veste*, 'having (wearing) a sword, a squalid garment'; *cum febrī esse*, 'to suffer from fever'; *cum imperiō esse*, 'to be invested with military power'; *tēcum mihi amīcitia (certāmen) est*, 'I have friendship (rivalry) for (with) you'; *tēcum* (or *contrā tē*) *bellum gerō*, 'I am waging war against you'; *hoc mēcum commūnicāvit*, 'he imparted this to me'; *maximō cum damnō meō*, 'to my great loss.'

3. **Cōram,** 'in the presence of'; *cōram populō*, 'in the presence of the people.'

4. **Dē,** 'down from,' and various derived meanings. *Dē moenibus dēturbāre*, 'to drive in confusion from the walls'; *dē spē dēicere*, 'to disappoint'; *homō dē plēbe*, 'a man of (taken from) the people'; *dē tē āctum est*, 'it is all over with (concerning) you'; *dē viā languēre*, 'to be tired after a journey'; *dē industriā*, 'on purpose'; *bene merērī dē nōbīs*, 'to deserve well of us'; *poenās sūmere dē aliquō*, 'to punish someone.'

5. **Ex** (before all letters), **ē** (only before consonants), 'out of,' and many derived meanings. *Ex equō pugnāre*, 'to fight on horseback'; *ē rēbus futūrīs pendēre*, 'to depend upon the future'; *ex sententiā*, 'according to one's wish *or* views'; *ē rēpūblicā* (opposed to *contrā rem p.*), 'in accordance with the constitution'; *ex imprōvīsō*, 'unexpectedly.'

6. **Prae,** 'in front of'; but the commonest uses are metaphorical. *Prae sē ferre*, 'to avow,' 'make no secret of'; *prae clāmōre vix audīrī potuit*, 'he could scarcely be heard for the shouting'; *prae nōbīs beātus est*, 'he is happy compared with us.'

7. **Prō**, 'in front of.' *Prō tribūnālī dīcere*, 'to speak (in front of) from the magistrate's tribunal'; *prō ārīs et focīs*, 'in defence of our altars and hearths'; *ūnus ille mihi prō exercitū est*, 'that one man is as good as (in place of) an army to me'; *prō certō habēre*, 'to feel sure of,' 'to consider as certain'; *prō meritīs eius grātiam reddere*, 'to render thanks in proportion to his deserts'; *prō prūdentiā tuā*, 'in accordance with your prudence'; *prō potestāte*, 'in virtue of your power'; *caedēs minor quam prō tantā victōriā*, 'slaughter small in proportion to the greatness of the victory.'

8. **Sine**, 'without': *sine dubiō*, 'doubtless.' But *sine* is not used nearly so often as the English preposition, which may be rendered by many constructions such as the following: *Nūllō negōtiō*, 'without trouble'; *rē īnfectā*, 'without result'; *nūllō repugnante*, 'without resistance'; *imprūdēns*, 'without being aware.' (See **425**.) *Stetit impavidus neque locō cessit*, 'he stood undismayed, without yielding ground'; *nōn potes mihi nocēre quīn tibi ipsī noceās*, 'you cannot hurt me without injuring yourself.'

In, sub, subter, super, *with ablative*

9. **In**, 'in,' 'among.' *In bonīs dūcere*, 'to reckon among blessings'; *in dēlīberandō*, 'whilst deliberating'; *quae in oculīs sunt*, 'what is before our eyes'; *in armīs esse*, 'under arms'; *quantum in mē est*, 'to the utmost of my power'; *satis ut in rē trepidā impavidus*, 'with fair courage considering the critical state of things'; *in tantō discrīmine*, 'in the face of such a crisis.' (See **273**, *Note* 2.)

10. **Sub**, 'under.' *Sub terrā*, 'under the earth'; *sub armīs*, 'under arms.' This preposition must never be used with the ablative after verbs of motion towards. Its metaphorical use (*e.g.* 'under a leader *or* king') is rare in Latin prose; thus: 'under his guidance' is *eō duce*.

11. **Subter**, 'beneath.' *Subter lītore*, 'close to the shore.' This preposition is used with the ablative only in poetry.

12. **Super**, 'upon'; *super focō* 'upon the hearth.' In the sense of 'concerning' (*super hāc rē*) it is rarely used by Cicero, never by Caesar.

333. Absque, 'without,' is rare. It is used mostly in Early Latin in phrases like: *absque nōbīs esset*, 'were it not for us . . .'

Clam, 'secretly,' is most commonly used as an adverb. As a preposition 'unknown to,' it is very rarely used with the ablative, and even with the accusative (*clam nostrōs*, 'unknown to our men') it is not common in prose.

Palam, 'before, in the sight of' (*palam omnibus*), is used only as an adverb by Cicero and Caesar.

Tenus, 'as far as,' follows its noun. It is used with the ablative (particularly of words denoting a part of the body: *pectoribus tenus*, 'as far as the chest') and (less frequently) with the genitive. The word is most frequent in the compound adverbs: *hāctenus* 'to this extent,' *aliquātenus* 'to some extent.'

Exercise 44

1. In the midst of this dire confusion and tumult, the emperor was seen with his staff on the left wing. He was now [1] free from care about the enemy's cavalry, and his words of encouragement were drowned in shouts of joy and triumph. 2. I fear that [2] it is all over with our army; for [3] ten successive days there has been the greatest want of provisions. In front, in flank, in rear, enemies are threatening (them). All the neighbouring tribes are in arms; on no side is there any prospect of aid. Yet, for myself,[4] in the face of these great dangers, I am unwilling wholly to despair. 3. Immediately after the battle they bring out [5] and slay the prisoners; they begin with the general. None [6] are spared; all are butchered to a man. 4. I will begin, then,[7] with you. You pretend that your countrymen are fighting for their homes and hearths; and yet [8] you avow that they have repeatedly made raids upon our territory, and wasted our land with fire and sword without provocation or resistance. 5. I have known this young man from a boy; both his father and he have again and again in my father's lifetime stayed under our roof. I esteem him most highly. 6. In virtue of the power with which my countrymen have entrusted me, I intend to reward all who have deserved well of the nation;

[1] See **328**, *b*. [2] **137**. [3] Turn in two ways. (See **321**, *Note* 2.)
[4] **334**, i. [5] Accusative of passive participle. (See **15**.)
[6] Use *nēmō*; case? [7] = 'therefore.' [8] Use *idem*. (See **366**.)

the rest I shall punish in proportion to their crimes. 7. I will aid you to the utmost [1] of my power ; but I fear that it is all over with your hopes. 8. I should be sorry to disappoint you, but I fear that your brother has returned without result. 9. Considering the greatness of the danger, he displayed great courage, and we ought all to show him gratitude in proportion to his many services to us and to the nation. 10. We should [2] all of us look at what is before our eyes ; to depend on the future is useless.

EXERCISE XLV

PRONOUNS

Personal and Demonstrative

334. The termination of a Latin verb indicates whether the subject is singular or plural and whether it is first, second, or third person. The nominative of a personal pronoun is therefore used only for special reasons. (See **11,** *a.*)

(i) *Ego* often begins a sentence in which the speaker is giving an account of his own conduct or feelings.

Ego cum prīmum ad rempūblicam accessī. For myself, when first I entered on political life.

(ii) *Tū* (especially) is often used indignantly.

An tū praetōrem accūsās? Are you (one like you) bringing a charge against a praetor?

(iii) *Ego, tū,* and even *ille* are often inserted without any special emphasis side by side with the oblique case of the same or another pronoun. (Intr. 91.)

Hīs ego perīculīs mē obiēcī. These were the dangers to which I exposed myself.

(iv) *Ego, tū,* and *ille* are often joined closely with *quidem* and *equidem,* and inserted in a clause where an admission is made in contrast with a statement which follows.

Vir optimus tū quidem, sed mediocrī ingeniō. You are an excellent man, but of moderate abilities.

---

[1] (See **332,** 9.) Tense? (See **191.**) [2] *Oportet.* (See **199,** ii.)

Is, ille, hic, iste

335. Latin has many words which answer to our 'he,' 'she,' 'they.' In '*he* says that *he* has not done wrong,' the second 'he' might be expressed in Latin by *sē*, *eum*, *hunc*, *istum*, or *illum*, according to the precise meaning of 'he' in the English sentence. The first 'he' might be either unexpressed, or translated by *is*, *hic* *iste*, *ille*, according to circumstances.

336. Is is the pronoun of **mere reference.** It is regularly used, especially in the oblique cases, for 'he,' 'she,' 'him,' 'her,' 'it,' as an unemphatic pronoun referring to some person or thing *already mentioned*, or *to be mentioned*.

Is is, in all cases, the regular pronoun corresponding to *quī*. The other demonstrative pronouns have each a special force of their own, in addition to that of mere reference to some person or thing indicated.

337. Hic is the demonstrative of the *first person*. '*This* person, or thing, *near me*' (the speaker or writer).

Haec patria, this our country; *haec vīta*, this present life; *haec omnia*, everything around us; *piget haec perpetī*, it is painful to endure the present state of things; *hīs sex diēbus*, in the last six days; *hīs cognitīs*, after learning this (which I have just related).

338. Iste on the other hand is the demonstrative of the *second person* (the person addressed): 'that *near you*.'

Cūr ista quaeris? why do you put that question of yours?; *opīniō ista*, that belief of yours; *Epicūrus iste*, your friend Epicurus; *cāsus iste*, your present disaster.

Note 1.—In the language of the law-court *hic* is often opposed to *iste*. *Hic* then means 'the man near me,' 'my client[1] and friend here,' and is opposed to *iste*, 'the man near you,' 'my opponent,' 'the defendant.'

Note 2.—This meaning 'that of yours' often, but by no means always, gives *iste* a meaning of contempt: *ista nōvimus*, 'we know that story'; *istī*, 'those friends of yours (whom I think lightly of).'

---

[1] *Cliēns* is never used in this sense; either *hic*, or, if more emphatic, *hic cuius causam suscēpī*, *hic quem dēfendō*, etc.

339. Ille is the demonstrative of the *third person*, 'that *yonder*,' 'that *out there*.' Hence come various uses.

(i) The remote in *time* as opposed to the present: '*Illīs temporibus*, 'in those days'; *antīquitās illa*, 'the far-off past,' 'the good old times.'

(ii) The 'distinguished,' as opposed to the common: *Catō ille*, 'the great Cato.'

(iii) The *emphatic* 'he,' the 'he' of whom we are all thinking or speaking or whom we all know. Thus *ille* is used instead of *is*, where a well-known person is meant, even when followed by *quī*: *illī quī*, 'those (whom we all know) who,' not merely 'men who.'

(iv) So, 'he' in the sense of 'the other' of two parties; often substituted for a proper name in a narrative.

340. Hic and **ille** are often opposed to each other.

(i) Of two persons or things already mentioned, *hic* relates to the *nearer*, the *latter*; *ille* to the *more remote*, the *former*.

Rōmulum Numa excēpit; hic pāce, ille bellō melior fuit. To Romulus succeeded Numa; the latter excelled in peace, the former in war.

(ii) So, of persons or things already mentioned or implied.

Neque hoc neque illud. Neither the one nor the other.
Et hic et ille (=*uterque*). Both one and the other.

(iii) Sometimes they answer to 'some . . . others.'

Hī pācem, bellum illī volunt. Some desire peace, others war.

341. *Illud* is often used to introduce a quotation or emphasise a following clause.

Nōtum illud Catōnis. . . . The well-known saying of Cato. . . .
Illud vereor, nē famēs in urbe sit. My real fear is (*or* what I fear is) lest there should be hunger in the city.

It sometimes answers to the English 'this,' 'the following.'

Nē illud quidem intellegunt . . . They do not even perceive this, that . . .

342. *Is*, as the **pronoun of reference,** is the regular correlative to *quī*, and may refer to any one of the three grammatical persons.

Read again **70-76**, and study the following examples:—

(*a*) *Quī hoc fēcerint* (**192**), *iī poenās dabunt.*
(*b*) *Dē eīs quī hoc fēcerint, poenās sūmam.*
(*c*) *Quī ōlim terrārum orbī imperāvimus, iī hodiē servīmus.*

(*d*) *In eōs quī dēfēcerant saevītum est.* The rebels[1] (175) were treated with severity.

343. For the difference between *cum eō rēs est quī nōs semper contempserit* (subjunctive), and the same sentence with *contempsit*, see **504**, *Note.*

It will be enough to say here that

Is sum quī fēcī, is 'I am the man who did (it).'

Nōn is sum quī faciam, is 'I am not such a person as to do it.'

344. *Et is, isque, idque*, etc., are often used to draw attention to some important detail.

Decem captī sunt, et iī Rōmānī. Ten men have been taken, and (what is more) those were Romans.

Litteris operam dedī, idque ā puerō. I have been a student, and that from my boyhood.

345. A demonstrative pronoun is not qualified in Latin by a possessive genitive; and care must be taken when translating the English 'that of,' 'those of.'

'Our own children are dearer to us that those of our friends,' is *nostrī nōbīs līberī cāriōrēs sunt quam amīcōrum*; never *quam iī amīcōrum.*

If, as in the above example, the pronoun (*iī*) would be in the same case as the noun (*līberī*) to which it refers, it is simply omitted; otherwise the noun itself is repeated.

Līberī nostrī amīcōrum līberīs cāriōres sunt.

346. So also it must again be noticed (see **74**) that *is* and *ille* (unlike the English demonstrative) cannot define a participle, adjective, or phrase.

'Those near him' is not *eōs prope eum*, but *eōs quī prope eum erant* or *stābant*; 'to those questioning him' is not *eīs interrogantibus*, but either *interrogantibus*, or *eīs quī interrogābant*; 'those like ourselves' is not *eōs nostrī similēs*, but *nostrī similēs*, or *eōs quī nostrī sunt similēs.*

347. When a demonstrative or relative pronoun (*is, hic*, or *quī*, etc.) is the *subject* of a copulative verb, it generally agrees with the predicative noun in gender. (See **83**, *Note.*)

Ea (not *id*) *dēmum est vēra fēlīcitās.* This and this only is true good fortune.

---

[1] *Dēfector* is first used in Tacitus. Observe that the Latin nouns in *-tor, -sor*, generally express a more permanent and inherent quality than the English nouns in *-er*: *gubernātor* is not the pilot of the moment, but the *professional pilot.*

Note.—*Fēlīcitās* never means 'happiness' (see **98**, *b*), but 'good luck' or 'fortune.' Note also the use of *dēmum*, which emphasises the word it follows.

348. Both *ille* and *is* sometimes represent the English *the* (which itself is demonstrative in origin).

I remember the day on which . . . *Venit mihi in mentem diēī illīus, quō . . .*

The friendship which existed between you and me. *Ea quae mihi tēcum erat amīcitia.*

Exercise 45

1. Those friends of yours are in the habit of finding fault with the men, the institutions, and the manners of the present [1] day, and of sighing for, and sounding the praises of, the good old times; possibly you yourself have sometimes fallen into that mistake. 2. There is the greatest disagreement on [2] political matters in my house; some of us wish everything changed, others nothing. For myself, I believe neither of the two parties to be in the right. 3. He [3] always showed himself proof against these perils, these bugbears; do [4] not you then appear unworthy of your noble forefathers. 4. Of this at least I am convinced, that that belief of yours as to [2] the antiquity of this custom is groundless; it is for you to consider [5] its origin.[6] 5. The saying of Caesar is pretty well known, that chance has the greatest influence in war. 6. When just on the point of pleading his cause, my client was ready to be reconciled with the defendant; and this design [7] he accomplished. 7. To the question why he preferred being an exile to living in his own home, the other replied that he could not return yet without violating the law, (and) must [8] wait for the king's death. 8. This only, it is said,[9] is true wisdom: to command oneself. 9. I value

[1] See **337**. Repeat the pronoun with each word. (See **49**.)
[2] See **300**.
[3] **334**, iii.
[4] See **143**.
[5] See **146**.
[6] See **174**, *a*.
[7] *Id quod.* (See **67**.)
[8] **200**.
[9] See **32**, *b* and **44**.

my own reputation more highly than you (do) yours, but I am ready to sacrifice my freedom to that of the nation. 10. I who[1] twenty years ago never quailed even before the bravest foe, now in the face[2] of an inconsiderable danger am alarmed for my own safety and that of my children. 11. To those who asked why they refused to comply with the royal caprice, they replied that they were not men[3] to quail before pain or danger. 12. You have been praised by an excellent man, it is true,[4] but by one most unversed in these matters.

EXERCISE XLVI

PRONOUNS—*Continued*

Reflexive and Emphatic Pronouns—*Sē, suus, ipse*

349. The third person Reflexive pronoun **sē** and the possessive adjective **suus** are used to refer:

(i) to the subject of the sentence or clause in which they stand:

Brūtus pugiōne sē interfēcit suō. Brutus killed himself with his dagger.

(ii) to the subject of the main sentence, *if* the clause in which they stand represents something in the mind of that subject:

Mīlitēs exhortātus est ut sē sequerentur. He exhorted the soldiers to follow him.

(iii) to the subject of the verb of 'saying, thinking,' etc., which introduces *ōrātiō oblīqua*:

Dīxit sē suīs amīcīs sua omnia datūrum. He said that he would give to his friends all his property.

Note 1.—*Sē* is a third person pronoun only. For the first and second persons, *mē* and *tē* are used as reflexives (sometimes em-

[1] See 75 and 342, c.
[2] 273, *Note* 2.
[3] See 343.
[4] 334, iv.

phasised by a case of *ipse*): *An tē* (or *tēmet*) *ipse* (or *ipsum*, agreeing with *tē*) *contemnis?* Is it that you despise yourself?

Note 2.—Subordinate clauses which represent something in the mind of the subject of the main verb are: indirect commands, prohibitions, and wishes; indirect questions; final clauses.

Scīre voluit vērum falsumne sibi esset relātum. He wished to know whether what had been reported was true or false.

Note 3.—Other types of adverbial clause and purely adjectival clauses do not represent the thought or desire of the main verb.

Mīlitēs, quī sē suaque omnia hostī trādiderant, laudāre nōluit. He was unwilling to praise soldiers who had surrendered themselves and all that belonged to them to the enemy.

350. It is obvious from **349** that in some kinds of subordinate clause and in *ōrātiō oblīqua*, *sē* and *suus* may legitimately be used to refer to any one of two or more different persons; but in a context arranged with moderate skill, no ambiguity need arise.

Ariovistus ad Caesarem lēgātōs mittit utī ex suīs (=*Caesaris*) *aliquem ad sē* (=*Ariovistum*) *mitteret.* Ariovistus sent ambassadors to Caesar to ask that Caesar should send some one of his (Caesar's) men to him (Ariovistus).

In the above example *suīs* refers to the subject of *mitteret*, whereas *sē* refers to the subject of the main verb *mittit*.

Note.—Occasionally the intensifying pronoun *ipse* is used to refer to the subject of the main verb.

Rogāvit Caesar cūr dē suā virtūte aut dē ipsīus dīligentiā dēspērārent. Caesar asked why they despaired of their own valour or of his zeal.

In the above example, the genitive singular *ipsīus* makes it clear that the reference is to the subject of *rogāvit*; and by contrast (as well as from the context) *suā* is taken to refer to the subject of *dēspērārent*.

351. When translating into Latin, the following points should be observed: (1) within a simple sentence or a subordinate clause, the subject of that sentence or clause *must* be referred to by *sē*; (2) within a subordinate clause of the kind mentioned in **349**, *Note* 2, the subject of the main verb *must* be referred to by *sē*; (3) within *ōrātiō oblīqua*, the subject of the verb of 'saying, thinking,' etc., *must* be referred to by *sē*; (4) *ipse* should be used only if there is some emphasis, and not simply because the writer doubts whether *sē* or *eum* would be correct; (5) if ambiguity arises from the application of these rules, the passage must be remodelled.

352. *Sē* and *suus* are also used with the meaning 'oneself, one's own' in sentences whose subject is undefined.

Dēfōrme est dē sē ipsum praedicāre. It is unseemly to brag about oneself.

Aliēnīs iniūriīs vehementius quam suīs commovērī. Being moved more deeply by other men's wrongs than by one's own.

In the following common phrases, *sē* is used without reference to anything but the nearest word: *per sē*, 'in itself'; *propter sē*, 'for its own sake'; *fīdūcia suī*, 'self-confidence'; *quantum in sē fuit*, 'to the utmost of his ability'; *suī compos*, 'master of himself.'

Tum illum vix iam suī compotem esse videt. Then he sees that he (the other) is scarcely any longer master of himself.

Haec omnia per sē ac propter sē expetenda esse ait. All these things, he says, are desirable in themselves and for their own sake.

353. *Sē* is sometimes used as a third person reciprocal pronoun; and *inter sē* is frequently so used.

Fūrtim inter sē aspiciēbant. They would look stealthily at each other.

Note.—For a similar use of *alius alium*, see **371**, iv.

354. The following points in the use of *suus* should be noticed:

(i) It is often used as a possessive in reference to *quisque* even though *quisque* is not the subject.

Suus cuique erat locus attribūtus. To each man his own place had been assigned.

(ii) Sometimes, when no ambiguity is likely to arise, *suus* refers in a simple sentence to something other than the subject of the sentence.

Senātum ad suam sevēritātem revocāvī. I recalled the senate to its strictness.

(iii) *Suī* is often used for a man's 'friends,' 'party,' 'followers.'

Auctōritās Pausistratī, quae inter suōs maxima erat . . . The influence of Pausistratus, which was predominant amongst his followers . . .

(iv) *Suus* corresponds to 'his own' rather than to 'his'; consequently it is not used in many circumstances where we use the unemphatic English 'his.'

Animum adveritit, 'he turned his attention'; *fīliī mortem dēplōrābat*, 'he was lamenting his son's death.'

But *suus* is often used emphatically as opposed to *aliēnus*: *suō tempore*, 'at the time that suited him'; and always in the phrase *suā sponte*, 'of his own free will.'

355. The intensifying pronoun **ipse** emphasises the word to which it refers.

Quid ipsī sentiātis velim fateāminī. I would fain have you confess your own sentiments.

Note 1.—Observe from the following instances how *ipse* may be used to render various English expressions :

Ipsīs sub moenibus. Close beneath the walls.

Illō ipsō diē. On that very day.

Adventū ipsō hostēs terruit. He frightened the enemy by his mere arrival.

Ipse hoc vīdī. I saw this with my own eyes.

Ipse fēcī. I did it unaided.

Ipsī venient. They will come of their own accord.

356. (i) *Ipse* is often inserted in Latin for the sake of clearness or contrast where we should hardly express it.

Dīmissīs suīs ipse nāvem cōnscendit. He dismissed his followers and embarked.

(ii) It very often denotes the leading person : the 'host' as opposed to the guests, 'the master' as opposed to the disciples.

(iii) The genitive (singular or plural as the sense requires) of *ipse* is used to emphasise a possessive adjective.

Meā ipsīus culpā, vestrā ipsōrum culpā. Through my own, *or* your own, fault.

Exercise 46

1. Many evils and troubles befall us through our own fault, and it [1] is often the lot of men to atone for the offences of their boyhood in mature life. 2. Having thus spoken, he sent back the officers to their several regiments. Then, telling [2] the cavalry to wait for his arrival under shelter of the rising ground, he started at full gallop and encouraged by voice and gesture the infantry, who had retreated quite up to the camp, to turn back [3] and follow him. 3. You are one whom your countrymen will entrust [4] with office from the mere impression of your goodness. 4. It is a king's duty (291) to have regard not only to him-

---

[1] 'It' emphatic. (341.) [2] Why not present participle ? (See 411.)
[3] Participle, see 15 ; for mood of 'follow,' see 118.
[4] Mood ? (343.)

self, but to his successors. 5. I heard him with my own ears deploring the untimely death of his son, a calamity which [1] you pretend that he treated very lightly. 6. We ought, says he, to be scarcely more touched by our own sorrows than by those of our friends. 7. Having returned to his countrymen, he proceeded [2] to appeal to them not to surrender him at the conqueror's bidding to men who were [3] his and their [4] deadliest enemies, to his father's murderers and their [4] betrayers, but rather to brave [5] the worst, and perish in the field. 8. He intends, he says, to lead his men out to fight [6] at his own time, not at that of the Germans. 9. Any one [7] may be dissatisfied with himself and his own generation; but it requires [7] great wisdom to perceive how we can retrieve the evils of the past, and treat with success the national wounds. 10. To those who asked what advantage he had reaped from such numerous friends, he replied that friendship was to be cultivated in itself [8] and for its own sake. 11. Taking [9] his seat, he sent [5] for the ambassadors of the allies, and asked them why they were ready to desert him, and betray their own liberties at such a crisis.

EXERCISE XLVII

PRONOUNS—*Continued*

Indefinite Pronouns—*Quisquam, aliquis*, etc.

There are many **indefinite** pronouns in Latin. We may divide them into: (1) those that correspond to the English 'any' and (2) those that correspond to the English 'some.'

---

[1] 'Which calamity.' [2] See **185**.
[3] Mood? (**77**, *Note*.) [4] Use a case of *ipse*.
[5] Participle, see **15**; for mood of 'perish,' see **118**.
[6] *Ad* with Gerund. [7] See **292**, **4**, and **291**, *Note* 3. [8] See **352**.
[9] Use *cōnsīdō*. Why not present participle? (See **411**.)

357. Quis (pronoun) and **quī** (adjective), ' any,' the least definite of the pronouns, are used after *sī*, *nisi*, *num*, *nē*, *quō*, *quantō*.

Sī quis ita fēcerit, poenās dabit. If any one does (192) so, he will be punished.

Num quis īrāscitur īnfantibus? Does anybody feel anger towards infants?

Nē quis aedēs intret, iānuam claudimus. We shut the door to prevent any one from entering the house.

Quō quis versūtior, eō suspectior. The more shrewd a man (any one) is, the more is he suspected.

Note.—The indefinite *quis* does not begin a sentence.

358. (i) **Quisquam** (pronoun) and **ūllus** (adjective) ' any at all,' are used after a **negative particle** (*nec*, *vix*, *etc*.), or **a verb** of ' denying, forbidding, preventing,' or in a **question**, or in a **sī**-clause where a negative is implied.

Haec aiō, nec quisquam negat. This I say, and no one denies it.

Negant sē cuiusquam imperiō esse obtemperātūrōs. They refuse to obey any one's command.

Et est quisquam? And is there any one? (It is implied that there is no one.)

Vetat lēx ūllam rem esse cuiusquam quī lēgibus pārēre nōlit. The law forbids that anything should belong to any one who refuses to obey the laws.

Note.—*Nec quisquam* is always used for *et nēmō*.

(ii) Since *quisquam* and *ūllus*=' any *at all*,' they are naturally used in *comparisons*.

Fortior erat quam amīcōrum quisquam. He was braver than any of his friends.

Sōlis candor illūstrior est quam ūllīus ignis. The brightness of the sun is more intense than that of any fire.

359. Quīvīs and **quīlibet**, ' any one (or thing) *you please*,' are used in affirmative sentences.

Quodlibet prō patriā, parentibus, amīcīs adīre perīculum oportet. We ought to encounter any danger (*i.e.* all dangers) for our country, our parents, and our friends.

Mihi quidvīs satis est. Anything is enough for me.

Note.—*Quīvīs* expresses a more deliberate, *quīlibet* a more blind or capricious choice (*voluntās* contrasted with *libīdō*).

360. '**Some**' is *aliquis* (*aliquī*), *quispiam*, *quīdam*, *nescio quis*. We might say for 'some one spoke,' *locūtus est aliquis*, *quīdam*, *nescio quis*, according to our precise meaning.

(i) **Aliquis** (pronoun) and **aliquī** (adjective) represent 'some,' 'someone,' as opposed to 'none,' 'no one.'

Dīxerit aliquis. Someone (no definite person thought of) will say (have said).

Senēs quibus aliquid rōboris supererat. Old men who had still some strength remaining.

(ii) **Quispiam,** 'someone,' is not so often used, and is vaguer.

Dīcet quispiam. Someone will say.

(iii) 'Some,' when used in an emphatic and yet indefinite sense is often to be rendered by *sunt quī*, *erant quī*, with a **subjunctive** verb (see **506**).

Sunt quī dīcant. Some say. *Erant quī dīcerent.* Some said.

(iv) **Nōnnūllī** is 'some few,' 'more than one,' as opposed to 'one' or 'none.'

Disertōs cognōvī nōnnūllōs, ēloquentem nēminem. I have met with several clever speakers, but not a single man of eloquence.

361. Quīdam is 'a certain one,' or simply 'a.' It indicates someone sufficiently known to the speaker for the purpose in hand, but not further described.

Quīdam ex (or *dē*) *plēbe ōrātiōnem habuit.* A man of the commons made a speech.

Quōdam tempore. At a certain time (I need not go on to give the date).

Cīvis quīdam Rōmānus. A (certain) citizen of Rome.

Note 1.—*Quīdam* also is very commonly used as an adjective to qualify a strong expression, or to introduce some metaphorical language; it corresponds in use to *ut ita dīcam*, 'so to speak.' (See **101**, *footnote*.)

Erat in eō virō dīvīna quaedam ingeniī vīs. There existed in that man almost a divine, *or* a really heroic, force of character.

Prōgreditur rēspūblica nātūrālī quōdam itinere et cursū. The state advances in a natural path and progress.

Note 2.—As English uses metaphorical expressions much more readily than Latin, the Latin *quīdam*, or some qualifying phrase (*tamquam*, 'as if,' etc.), will often be used where no such phrase is required in English.

362. Nescio quis and **nescio qui**, used as if they were single words, play the part of indefinite pronouns. (See **169.**) When used of a person **nescio quis** is often contemptuous, and therein it differs from *quīdam.*

Alcidamās quīdam, 'one Alcidamas (whom I need not stop to describe further).'

But *Alcidamās nescio quis,* 'an obscure person called Alcidamas.'

363. The phrases *nescio quid, nescio quō modō, nescio quō pactō* (also *quōdam modō*), are used to indicate something that is not easily defined or accounted for.

Inest nescio quid in animō ac sēnsū meō. There is something (which I cannot define) in my mind and feelings.

Bonī sunt nescio quō modō tardiōrēs. Good people are somehow or other rather sluggish.

Nescio quō pactō ēvēnit ut . . . Somehow or other it happened that . . .

364. Quicumque, quisquis, 'whoever,' are indefinite relatives, and as such introduce clauses whose verb is indicative, unless there is some particular reason for the subjunctive.

Crās tibi quodcumque volēs dīcere licēbit. To-morrow you may say whatever you like.

Quisquis hūc vēnerit, vāpulābit. Whoever comes here shall be beaten.

Exercise 47

1. Do not,[1] says he, be angry with any one, not to mention[2] your own brother, without adequate grounds. 2. Scarcely any one[3] can realise the extent and nature of this disaster, and perhaps[4] it can never be retrieved. 3. Your present disaster might have[5] befallen any one, but it seems to me that you have been somehow more unlucky than any of your contemporaries. 4. No one ever attained to any such goodness without, so[6] to speak, some divine inspiration, and no one ever sank to such a depth of wickedness without any consciousness of his own guilt.

---

[1] Use *cavē.* (143.)

[2] *Nē dīcam* used parenthetically. The case of 'brother' will be determined by its relation to 'be angry.'

[3] 291, *Note* 3.

[4] ='which perhaps.' (See 169.)

[5] See 196.

[6] 361, *Note* 1.

5. Some believed that after the defeat of Cannae the very name of Rome [1] would disappear, and no one imagined that the nation would have [2] so soon recovered from so crushing a calamity. 6. It seems to me, to express [3] myself with more accuracy, that this nation has long been advancing in learning and civilisation, not of its own impulse, but by what I may call [4] divine aid. 7. Some one of his countrymen once said that my client was naturally disposed to laziness and timidity; to me it seems that he is daily becoming somehow braver, firmer, and more uncomplaining under any toil or danger. 8. In the [5] army that was investing Veii was a [6] Roman citizen who had been induced to have a conference with one or other of the townsmen. He [7] warned him that a terrible disaster was threatening the army and people of Rome, and that scarcely a soul would return home in safety.

EXERCISE XLVIII

A

PRONOUNS—*Continued*

Īdem, alius, alter, cēterī

365. Īdem, 'the same.' It has been already said (**84**) that 'the same *as*' is usually expressed in Latin by *īdem quī*, occasionally by *īdem atque* (or, before consonants only, *ac*).

> *Īdem sum quī* (or *ac*) *semper fuī.* I am the same as I have always been.
>
> *Incidit in eandem invidiam quam pater suus.* He fell into the same odium as his father.

366. *Īdem* also serves to join together two predicates or two attributes applied to the same person or thing. It may then be translated by 'also, at the same time, yet, notwithstanding.'

---

[1] Adjective. (**58** and **319.**)
[2] See **36.**
[3] See **101**, *footnote.*
[4] *Quīdam.* (See **361**, *Note* 1.)
[5] See **348.**
[6] **361.**
[7] **339**, iv.

Quidquid honestum est, idem est ūtile. Whatever is right, is also expedient.

Accūsat mē Antōnius, īdem laudat. Antonius accuses and at the same time praises me.

Note.—*Īdem* generally precedes the second attribute or predicate; but sometimes it is used with both.

Īdem vir fortissimus, īdem ōrātor ēloquentissimus. At once a man of the highest courage and the most eloquent of speakers.

367. Alius, 'another.' To express 'different from,' *alius ac* (*atque*) is used. **(91.)**

Aliō ac tū est ingeniō. He is of a different disposition from you.

Note.—The adverb *aliter* has a similar use.

Aliter atque sentit loquitur. His language is different from his (real) sentiments.

368. *Alius*, 'another' (of any number), should be distinguished from **alter,** 'the other of two,' or 'second' or 'one of two' (as opposed to the other).

Cōnsulum alter domī, alter mīlitiae, fāmam sibi parāvit. One of the consuls won glory at home, the other in war. (**312.**)

Duōrum frātrum alter mortuus est. One of the two brothers is dead.

Amīcus est tamquam alter īdem. A friend is a second self. (**361,** *Note* 2.)

Diēs ūnus, alter, plūrēs intercesserant. One, two, several, days had passed.

369. A repeated **alius** is used in *four* common constructions.

(i) In a distributive sense: 'some . . . some . . . others.'

Tum aliī Rōmam versus, in Etrūriam aliī, aliī in Campāniam, domum reliquī dīlābuntur. Thereupon they disperse, some towards Rome, some, etc.

Note.—Of course, of two persons, *alter . . . alter,* or *ūnus . . . alter,* will be used for 'one . . . the other,' and sometimes *hic . . . ille.* (See **340.**)

370. (ii) When used as a predicate in separate clauses a repeated *alius* marks an essential difference. **(92.)**

Aliud est maledīcere, accūsāre aliud. There is a vast difference between reviling (**94**) and accusing.

Aliud loquitur, aliud facit. His language is irreconcilable with his actions.

371. (iii) When *alius* is repeated *in different cases* in the same clause, it answers to a common use of the English 'different,' 'various.'

> *Hī omnēs alius aliā ratiōne rempūblicam auxērunt.* All of these by different methods promoted the interests of the nation.

Note 1.—The cognate adverbs have a similar use: *Aliī aliunde congregantur,* 'they flock together from various quarters'; *omnēs alius aliter sentīre vidēminī,* 'all of you, it seems, have different views.'

Note 2.—When used in this sense, the repeated *alius* is generally singular, even though the subject is plural. (See example in *Note* 1.)

Note 3.—Avoid using *dīversus* or *varius* loosely in this sense. *Dīversus* is rather 'opposite'; *varius,* 'varying.'

> *Dīversī fugiunt* is 'they fly in opposite directions.'

(iv) Sometimes a repeated *alius* (or of *two* persons *alter*) supplies the place of the **reciprocal** 'each other.' (Compare 353.)

> *Tum omnēs alius alium intuēbāmur.* Thereupon all of us began to look at each other.
>
> *At frātrēs alter alterum adhortārī. . . .* But the (two) brothers began (186) to encourage each other, etc.

372. Cēterī and **reliquī** mean 'the rest.'

Reliquī is opposed to 'the mass,' those who (or that which) remain after many have been deducted.

Cēterī is 'the rest,' as *contrasted* with some one or more already named or indicated.

Thus either *cēterī* or *alter* will answer to our 'others,' 'your neighbours,' 'fellow-creatures,' as opposed to 'yourself.'

> *Quī cēterōs* (or *alterum*) *ōdit, ipse eīs* (or *eī*) *odiō erit.* He who hates his neighbours will be hated by them.

Note.—*Cēterī* has no singular masculine nominative; in other forms it may be used in the singular, but only with collective nouns: *cētera multitūdō.*

Exercise 48

A

1. Human beings pursue various objects; of these brothers, the one devoted himself to the same tastes and

studies as his distinguished father, the other entered political life in quite early manhood. 2. Your judgment in this matter has been quite different from mine. You might [1] have shown [2] yourself a true patriot, and lived in freedom in a free country; you preferred riches and pleasure [3] to the toil and danger which freedom involves. 3. All of [4] these men in different ways did good service to the human race; all of them preferred being of use to their neighbours to studying their own interest. 4. We have different aims; some are devoted to wealth, others to pleasure; others place happiness in holding [5] office,[3] in power, in the administration of the state, others again [6] in popularity, interest, influence. 5. Hearing this, the soldiers began to look [7] at each other, and to wonder silently what the general wished them to do, and why he was angry with them rather than with himself. 6. You pay me compliments in every other (377) word, at the same time you tax me with the foulest treachery. I would like you to remember that speaking the truth is one thing, speaking pleasantly another. 7. The enemy now fled [7] in opposite directions. Of the fugitives the greater part were slain, the rest threw down their arms [8] and were taken prisoners to a man. Few asked for quarter, none obtained it. 8. We, most of us, came to a stand, looking silently at each other, and wondering which of us would be [9] the first to speak. But Laelius and I held our peace, each waiting for the other. 9. After raising [8] two armies, they attack the enemy's camp with one; with the other they guard the city. The former returned without success, and a sudden panic attacked the latter.

---

[1] 196. [2] 240, *Note* 1.

[3] *Plural*; so also for 'toil,' 'danger,' 'office'; why? Latin uses *abstract* terms much less than English. (See 174.)

[4] 297. [5] Gerundive.

[6] *Dēnique* =lastly; used often in enumerations.

[7] Historic inf. (See 186.) [8] Abl. abs.

[9] 173, *Note* 2, and 62.

EXERCISE XLVIII—Continued

B

PRONOUNS—*Continued*

Quisque, uterque, singulī, etc.

373. Quisque is 'each one,' as distinct from *omnis* 'every one.' It is associated particularly with **relative, interrogative,** and **reflexive** pronouns, with **superlatives** and **comparatives,** and with **ordinal** numerals; and it is generally placed after such words.

Note 1.—It is very rarely used in the plural in prose, but often stands in the singular in apposition to a plural noun. (Cf. *alius* and *alter*, **371,** iii, *Note* 2, and **371,** iv.)

Rōmānī domum, cum suā quisque praedā, redeunt. The Romans return home, each with his own booty.

Note 2.—It is sometimes emphasised by prefixing *ūnus*: *ūnus quisque*, 'each and every one.'

Note 3.—In the neuter, the form *quidque* is substantival, *quodque* adjectival.

374. In association with **pronouns** its use is simple, if its proper place in the sentence is remembered.

Mīlitēs, quem quisque vīderat, trucīdābant. The soldiers would butcher whomever any of them saw. (**193,** *Note* 1.)

Nōn meum est statuere quid cuique dēbeās. It is not for me (**291,** *Note* 2) to determine your debt to each.

Suum cuique tribuitō. Give to every one his due. (Cf. **354,** i.)

375. It is used in agreement with **superlative** adjectives, almost always in the *singular*,[1] to express 'all,' or 'every.'

Haec optimus[2] *quisque sentit.* These are the views of all good men, *or* of every good man.

Beware of writing *bonus quisque*, or *optimī quīque*.

376. Latin frequently expresses the idea of *proportion* by using *quisque* with a superlative as the subject and another superlative in the predicate.

Optimum quidque rārissimum est. Things (*or* all things) are rare in proportion to their excellence.

---

[1] In the *neuter* the plural is occasionally used: *fortissima quaeque cōnsilia tūtissima sunt*, 'the bravest plans are always the safest.'

[2] This phrase is generally used in a *political* sense:—'all good patriots, all the well-disposed.'

Quisque with a **superlative** is also used in one of a pair of co-ordinate sentences connected by *ut* and *ita*, to express proportion :—

Ut quisque est sollertissimus, ita fermē labōris est patientissimus. In proportion to a man's skill is, as a rule, his readiness to endure toil. (See **497**, *a.*)

When *quō* (*quantō*) and *eō* (*tantō*) are used to indicate proportion, *quisque* is used with a **comparative** adjective or adverb :—

Quō quisque est sollertior, eō est labōris patientior.

377. *Quisque* is also used with **ordinal numerals** ; *quīntō quōque annō*, 'each fifth year = every five years' ; *decimus quisque*, 'every tenth man' ; *quotus quisque*, 'how few.' (See **157**, *Note* 4.)

Prīmum quidque videāmus. Let us look at each thing in turn, take each (in turn) as first.

Prīmō quōque tempore. At the earliest opportunity possible.

378. (i) **Uterque** is 'both,' in the sense of 'each *of two*,' and denotes two things or persons looked on *separately*.

Propter utramque causam. For both reasons, *i.e.* for each of the two.

Ambō is 'both,' but it is used of two individuals as forming *one whole* ; 'both together.'[1]

Quī utrumque probat, ambōbus dēbet ūtī. He who approves of each of these (separately) is bound to use them both (together).

Note 1.—*Alter ambōve* is 'one or both.'

Note 2.—*Uterque* (like *nēmō*) is used with the genitive of *pronouns* ; but in apposition to *nouns*.

Hōrum uterque, 'each of these' ; but *fīlius uterque.* Compare : *hōrum nēmō*, but *nēmō pictor.*

Note 3.—*Uterque* is used in Latin with *interest*, where we should use 'the two.'

Quantum inter rem utramque intersit, vidēs. You see the great difference between the two things.

Note 4.—*Uterque* can be used in the **plural** only where it denotes not two single things or persons, but each of two *parties* or *classes* already represented by a plural word.

Stābant īnstrūctī aciē Rōmānī Samnītēsque ; pār utrīsque pugnandī studium (each felt the same ardour for the fight).

---

[1] For example, in an election in which there are three candidates, the victor who has a bare majority has more votes *quam uterque* ; if he has an absolute majority, he has more votes *quam ambō*.

379. As *uterque* unites two and = *ūnus et alter*, so **utervīs** and **uterlibet** disjoin them and = *ūnus vel alter*, 'whichever of the two you like,' *i.e.* excluding the other. (See **359**, *Note*.)

Uter is generally interrogative, 'which of two?'; but it is also used as a relative 'whichever of two.' Different cases of *uter* are often used in the same sentence.

Uter utrī plūs nocuerit, dubitō. I am doubtful which of the two injured the other most.

380. Singulī (-ae, -a) is **only used in the plural,** and has two main uses.

(*a*) As a distributive numeral, 'one apiece,' 'one each.' (See **532.**)

Cum singulīs vestīmentīs exeant. Let them go out each with one set of garments.

Eius modī hominēs vix singulī singulīs saeculīs nāscuntur. Such men come into the world scarcely once in a century (one in each century).

(*b*) As opposed to **ūniversī**, 'the mass,' 'all,' looked on as forming one class, *singulī* denotes 'individuals,' 'one by one.'

Rōmānōs singulōs dīligimus, ūniversōs āversāmur. While we feel affection for individual Romans, we loathe the nation, *or* them as a nation.

Nec vērō ūniversō sōlum hominum generī, sed etiam singulīs prōvīsum est. Nor is it only mankind in general (as a whole), but the individual that has been cared for.

381. 'A single person,' where 'single' is emphatic, may be turned by *ūnus aliquis*: *ad ūnum aliquem rēgnum dētulērunt*, 'they offered the crown to a single person.' 'Not a single,' = an emphatic 'no one,' is *nē ūnus quidem*.

Note.—*Singulāris* is generally used of *qualities*, and denotes 'rare,' 'remarkable.'

Exercise 48

B

1. As a nation we praise the poet whom as individuals we neglected. 2. All true patriots and wise men are on our side, and we would fain have those whom we love and admire hold the same sentiments as ourselves. 3. Men are valued by their countrymen in proportion[1] to their

[1] May be done in two ways. (See 376.)

public usefulness. This man was at once a brave[1] soldier and a consummate statesman; for both reasons therefore he enjoyed the highest praise and distinction. 4. It is often the case that men are talkative and obstinate in exact[2] proportion to their folly and inexperience. 5. It is a hackneyed saying that all weak characters[3] crave for different things at different times. 6. It now seemed that the enemy would attack our camp at the first possible opportunity, but that at the same time they were afraid of losing many men. 7. We are one by one deserting and abandoning the man who saved us all. 8. All good patriots are, I believe, convinced of this,[4] that it is quite impossible for us to effect anything by hesitation (**94, 99**), procrastination, and hanging back. I therefore feel sure that there is need of haste rather than of deliberation. 9. He found a difficulty in persuading his countrymen that[5] their enemies and allies were powerless separately, most powerful in combination. 10. Thereupon all, each in turn, answered the consul's questions; and the greater part besought the senate, appealing[6] to the whole body and to individuals, that one or both the consuls should at the earliest opportunity bring them relief.

EXERCISE XLIX

GERUND AND GERUNDIVE

382. The **Gerund** is a verbal noun, active in meaning: *ad faciendum* 'for the doing.' Its nominative is not used, and it has no plural.

Note.—The infinitive, which is also a verbal noun, has different forms for different tenses (see **35**); the gerund simply denotes the verbal activity without specific reference to time.

---

[1] 57, *a*.
[2] Use *quantō . . . tantō*. (See **376**.)
[3] 'Characters' is of course not to be expressed literally in Latin: it = 'men.'
[4] **341.**
[5] See **124.**
[6] Past participle of *obtestor*. (See **416.**)

383. Because of its verbal nature, the gerund (*a*) may be qualified by adverbs; (*b*) is followed by the same case as the verb from which it is derived.

> *Ad bene vīvendum,* 'for living well'; *parcendō hostibus,* 'by sparing the enemy'; *orbem terrārum subigendō,* 'by conquering the world.'

384. The infinitive is used only as a nominative and as an accusative (without a preposition); the gerund supplies the other cases, and its accusative is used instead of the infinitive when a preposition is required.

> *Docēre mihi iūcundum est,* 'teaching is pleasant for me.'

But: *Ars docendī,* 'the art of teaching'; *homō ad agendum nātus est,* 'man was born for action.'

385. The use of the gerund with a direct object is, in general, avoided unless the object is a neuter pronoun or adjective; in its place the gerundive is preferred. (See **395.**)

> *Cupiditās plūra habendī,* 'the desire to possess more.'

But: *Ad pācem petendam vēnērunt,* 'they came to seek peace,' rather than: *ad pācem petendum vēnērunt.*

386. The **Gerundive** is a verbal adjective, passive in meaning [1]: *vir laudandus,* 'a man to be praised.'

387. In the nominative (and sometimes in the accusative) the gerundive is used to express *obligation* and *necessity*; in the oblique cases it is used as a passive participle.

> *Carthāgō dēlenda est.* Carthage ought to be (must be) destroyed.

---

[1] The commonly accepted view of the origin of the gerund and gerundive and of the relation between them is as follows. The gerundive was at first an adjective which implied a vague connection with the verbal activity and was not distinctively passive in meaning. The idea of a vague connection, however, gave rise, especially when a transitive verb was involved, to the idea of 'fit to be, bound to be.' So *vir laudandus* 'a man with whom one associates the idea of praise, a man for praising,' was felt to imply 'a man fit to praise, fit to be praised, bound to be praised, who ought to be praised.' Thus was evolved the idea of *obligation* which, in classical Latin, the gerundive may be used to express. The gerund is either the neuter of the gerundive, retaining an active sense, or (less probably) it originated from a form in *-dō* (= to, at). On this latter theory, *agen-dō* would mean originally 'towards doing, in doing'; and when this form was felt to be a dative or ablative case, other case-forms would be analogically evolved.

Studiōsus est pācis petendae. He is eager to seek peace (for peace being sought).

Caesare interficiendō rempūblicam restituere cōnātī sunt. They tried to restore the constitution by slaying Caesar (by Caesar being slain).

Illī violandīs lēgātīs interfuēre. They took part in the outrage on the ambassadors (in the ambassadors being harmed).

388. The nominative of the gerundive of a transitive verb is used as a predicative adjective in agreement with the subject to express *obligation* and *necessity.*

Amīcī tibi cōnsōlandī sunt. You must console your friends.

Omnia ūnō tempore erant agenda. Everything had to be done at one and the same time.

389. But if the verb is intransitive or is used intransitively, the nominative neuter of the gerundive is used with a tense of *esse* in an impersonal construction.[1]

Hostibus parcendum est. One must spare the enemy.

Occāsiōne ūtendum fuit. The opportunity ought to have been used.

Note 1.—The gerundive thus used impersonally takes the same case as the verb to which it belongs.

Note 2.—The two types of gerundive construction with transitive and intransitive verbs are well illustrated by *cōnsulō.* Since *cōnsulō Gaium* means 'I ask Gaius for advice,' and *cōnsulō Gaiō* means 'I consult the interests of Gaius,' we must say: *Gaius cōnsulendus est* for 'Gaius must be consulted,' and *Gaiō cōnsulendum est* for 'the interests of Gaius must be consulted.'

390. When the gerundive is used to express obligation and necessity the person on whom the duty lies is in the dative. (See **258**, i.)

Hostēs tibi vincendī sunt. You must overcome your enemies.

Suō cuique iūdiciō ūtendum est. Each man must use his own judgment.

---

[1] The neuter gerundive of a *transitive* verb is sometimes, but very rarely, found with an accusative object: *agitandumst vigiliās* 'one must keep watch'; *aeternās poenās in morte timendum est* 'one must fear eternal punishment in death.'

On the other hand the gerundives of *ūtor, fruor, fungor, potior,* and *vēscor* (see **281**) sometimes have a personal construction, because in early Latin these verbs were often used as transitives: *haec ūtenda (fruenda) sunt* 'these things must be used (enjoyed).'

391. But when the verb whose gerundive is being used itself takes a dative, the agent is indicated by the ablative with *ā* (or *ab*).

Cīvibus ā tē cōnsulendum est. You must consult the interests of the citizens.

Hostibus ā nōbīs parcendum erat. We ought to have spared the enemy.

392. The gerundive with the various tenses of *sum* forms a periphrastic conjugation expressing duty and necessity.

Mihi, tibi, eī, etc., *scrībendum est, fuit, erit.* I, you, he, etc., must write, should have written, shall have to write.

Hostēs tum dēbellandī fuēre. The enemy should have been conquered then.

Dīxit sibi scrībendum esse (fuisse). He said that he had (had had) to write.

Dīxit rem perficiendam fuisse. He said that the matter should have (=ought to have) been finished.

393. The gerundive is sometimes used as an *attributive* adjective with a sense of *necessity, fitness,* etc., even in the *oblique cases.*

Cum haud irrīdendō hoste pugnāvī. I have fought with no despicable foe (no fit object for ridicule).

394. Caution.—Neither gerund nor gerundive denotes **possibility.** The English 'is to be' requires caution, as it may mean either *possibility* or *duty.*

'Your son was not to be persuaded' is not *fīliō tuō nōn fuit persuādendum* (=your son should not have been persuaded), but *fīliō tuō persuādērī nōn potuit.*

But sometimes in association with a *negative* word the gerundive approaches the idea of possibility.

Calamitās vix toleranda. A scarcely endurable calamity.

Exercise 49

The gerundive to be used exclusively for 'ought,' 'should,' etc.

1. He ought voluntarily to have endured exile, or else died on the field of battle, or done anything [1] rather than this. 2. Ought we not to return thanks to men to whom we are under an obligation? 3. The soldiers should have

[1] 359.

been ordered[1] to cease from slaughter, and to slay no unarmed person; women at least and children ought to have been spared, to say nothing[2] of the sick and wounded. 4. I do not object to your exposing your own person to danger, but you ought in the present emergency to be careful for your soldiers' safety. 5. This is what one so sensible[3] as yourself should have done, and not left that undone. 6. Seeing[4] that he must either retreat, or come into collision on the morrow with a far from contemptible enemy, he decided on forming line and fighting at once. 7. Nor should we listen to men (72) who tell us that we ought to be angry with a friend who refuses[5] to flatter and fawn upon us. 8. Your son was wise enough[6] not to be persuaded to think that the matter should or could be forgotten. 9. We shall all have to die one day: when[7] and how each will have to meet the common and universal doom, is beyond[8] the power of the wisest of mankind to foresee or to foretell. 10. It seems that you have one and all come to me in[9] the king's palace from two motives, partly for the sake of consulting me, partly to clear yourselves[10]; you must therefore seize the opportunity, and plead your cause while the king is present (*abl. abs.*).

EXERCISE L

GERUND AND GERUNDIVE—*Continued*

Oblique Cases

395. The gerundive construction is, in general, preferred to a gerund with an accusative. *Epistulae scrībendae*

[1] Do in two ways, *i.e.* use both *iubeō* and *imperō*. (See **120**.)
[2] Use *nē dīcam* (**101**, *footnote*) parenthetically; see Ex. 47, *Note* 2.
[3] 224, *Note* 3.
[4] *Cum vidēret*. (See **430**, *Note*.)
[5] Mood? (See **77**, *Note*.)
[6] Turn: 'your son, being most wise, was not,' etc. (**224**, *Note* 2.)
[7] Not *cum*. (See **157**, *Note* 7.)
[8] 'Not even the wisest of mankind can,' etc.
[9] See **315**.
[10] See **399**, *Note* 1.

studiōsus is more frequent than *epistulam scrībendī studiōsus.*

(i) The gerund with a direct object is especially avoided if the gerund would itself be governed by a preposition or would be dative.

Ad Gallōs īnsequendōs, 'for pursuing the Gauls'; not *ad Gallōs īnsequendum.*

Ūtile bellō gerendō, 'useful for waging war'; not *ūtile bellum gerendō.*

(ii) To avoid ambiguity, however, the genitive or ablative of the gerund is used when the object is a neuter pronoun or adjective.

Studium plūra cognōscendī. Zeal for learning more.

Honestum petendō glōriam cōnsecūtus est. He won glory by pursuing virtue.

Plūrium cognōscendōrum and *honestō petendō* might be taken for masculines.

(iii) To avoid the repetition of the endings *-ārum, -ōrum,* an accusative object is used with the genitive of the gerund.

Arma capiendī facultās. . . . The chance of taking arms. . . .

396. The **accusative** of both the gerund and gerundive is chiefly used with *ad,* but rarely with other prepositions. When used with *ad* it is a substitute for a **final** *clause.*

Gerund.—*Ad cōnsultandum hūc vēnimus.* We have come here to deliberate.

Gerundive.—*Ad pācem petendam missī sumus.* We have been sent for the purpose of asking for peace.

Note 1.—The genitive of the gerund and gerundive dependent on *causā* or *grātiā* is also used to express purpose: *cōnsultandī causā; pācis petendae grātiā.*

Note 2.—Do not imitate such rare uses as: *inter lūdendum, ob iūdicandum,* 'in the midst of play,' 'for the sake of giving a verdict.'

397. The **dative** of the gerund and gerundive is used after a few verbs and adjectives such as *praeficere, praeesse, dare operam, impār,* etc., and occasionally to express aim or purpose.

Gerund.—*Legendō dabat operam.* He was giving his attention to reading.

Gerundive.—*Bellō gerendō mē praefēcistis.* You put me in control of the conduct of the war.

Gerundive.—*Comitia cōnsulibus creandīs.* The meeting for the election of consuls.

Note.—*Solvendō nōn esse,* 'not to be able to pay one's debts,' is a common technical phrase.

398. The **ablative** of the gerund and gerundive is mainly used to denote *instrument* and *cause*; or is dependent on the prepositions *ā*, *dē*, *ex*, and *in*.

Ūnus homō nōbīs cūnctandō restituit rem. One man restored our fortunes by his delays.

Ōrātōribus legendīs dēlector. I find delight in reading orators.

Ex discendō capiunt voluptātem. They gain pleasure from learning.

Note.—The ablative of the gerund and gerundive is not used with *prō* and *sine* to represent our 'instead of,' 'without,' followed by the verbal substantive; you cannot say *prō sequendō, sine sequendō* for 'instead of,' *or* 'without following.' (See **332**, 8.)

399. The **genitive** of the gerund and gerundive is frequently used with nouns and adjectives in an objective (**300**) or in an appositional sense (**304**), and in dependence on *causā* and *grātiā* (**396**, *Note* **1**).

Cupidus urbis videndae. Desirous of seeing the city.

Quī hic mōs obsidendī viās? What sort of a way is this of blocking up the roads? (For *viās*, see **395**, iii.)

Note 1.—The genitive *singular* of the gerundive is used with *suī, nostrī, vestrī,* even to denote a number of persons: *suī purgandī causā adsunt,* 'they are here to clear themselves.' The reason is that these words were regarded as neuter singulars: *suum* 'his (their) self.'

Note 2.—Notice such phrases as *respīrandī spatium,* a breathing space; *suī colligendī facultās,* an opportunity of rallying; *pācis faciendae auctor et prīnceps fuī,* I suggested and was the leader in making peace. The rare construction *hoc cōnservandae lībertātis est,* 'this tends to the preservation of freedom,' has been noticed above. (**292**, 10.)

400. After some verbs, such as **dō, cūrō, trādō,** the gerundive is used predicatively in agreement with the object to indicate that something is caused to be done.

Obsidēs Aeduīs custōdiendōs trādit. He hands over the hostages to the Aedui, to keep in guard.
Agrōs eīs habitandōs dedit. He gave them lands to dwell in.
Caesar pontem faciendum cūrāvit. Caesar had a bridge made.

Exercise 50

1. These men came, it is said, to our camp for the purpose of praising themselves [1] and accusing you (*pl.*); they are now intent on pacifying you, and clearing themselves of a most serious indictment. 2. The matter must on no account be postponed; you must on this very day come to a decision, as to whether your actions will destroy or preserve your ancient constitution. 3. Such gentleness and clemency did he show in the very hour of triumph, that it may be questioned whether he won greater [2] popularity by pardoning his enemies or by relieving his friends. 4. There can be no question that in point [3] of consulting his country's interests rather than his own, of sacrificing his own convenience (*pl.*) to that [4] of his friends, of keeping in check alike his temper and his tongue, this young man far outdid all [5] the old. 5. All the spoil which the defendant had obtained by sacking temples, by confiscating the property of individuals, and by levying contributions on so many communities, he secretly had [6] carried out of the country. 6. It was by venturing on something, he said, and by pressing on, not by delay and hanging back, nor by much [7] discussion and little action, that they had effected what they had hitherto achieved.[8] 7. It was I who suggested following up the enemy (*sing.*), in order to leave [9] him no breathing space, no [10] opportunity of rallying or of ascertaining the nature [11] or number of his assailants.

---

[1] 399, *Note* 1. [2] *Plūs.* (See 294.)
[3] Simply abl. of limitation. (274.) [4] See 345.
[5] Use *quisque.* (375.) [6] *Cūrō.* (400.)
[7] 'Much,' 'little,' with gerund. (See 53.)
[8] Repeat the same verb; mood? (See 77, *Note.*)
[9] Use the passive. (216, *Note.*)
[10] Use *ūllus* after *nē*, as more emphatic than *quī* (adj.). (See 357, 358.)
[11] See 174.

EXERCISE LI

THE SUPINES

401. The **Supines** in **-um** and **-ū** are oblique cases of a **verbal substantive** of the fourth declension.

402. The **Supine** in **-um** (accusative) is used only with *verbs of motion* to express the purpose of the motion. It is thus one of the various Latin ways of expressing purpose or design mentioned in **101,** *Note* 1.

It so far keeps its verbal nature as to govern the same case as the verb from which it is formed.

Pācem nōs flāgitātum vēnērunt (**230**). They have come to importune us for peace.

Note 1.—This supine is one of the few instances of *motion towards* being expressed by the accusative without a preposition. (See **235.**)

Note 2.—This supine is used most frequently with the verbs *īre* and *venīre.*

403. This supine, in association with the impersonal (passive) form *īrī*, is sometimes used by the Romans as a way out of the difficulties caused by the lack of a future passive infinitive.

Rūmor vēnit datum īrī gladiātōrēs. The rumour came that a show of gladiators was going to be given.

In the above example, *datum* is the accusative of motion after *īrī* ('that a movement is being made'); and *gladiātōrēs* is the direct object after *datum.*

But most commonly the future active infinitive *fore* with a dependent clause containing a passive subjunctive is preferred. (See **38.**)

Rūmor vēnit fore ut gladiātōrēs darentur.

404. The **Supine** in **-ū** is used to qualify adjectives denoting 'ease, difficulty, pleasure, displeasure, belief,' (*e.g. facilis, difficilis, iūcundus, crēdibilis*), and the nouns *fās, nefās.*

Difficile est dictū quantō sīmus in odiō. It is hard to say how hated we are.

Nefās est dictū tālem senectūtem miseram fuisse. It is sacrilege to say that such an old age was wretched.

Note 1.—Only a few supines in *-ū* are in common use; *i.e.* those derived from verbs of 'speaking' (*dictū*, *memorātū*) and verbs denoting the five senses (*audītū*, *tāctū*, etc.).

Note 2.—Unlike the supine in *-um*, the supine in *-ū* does not take a noun as its direct object. 'It was easy to hear him' is not *eum audītū facile erat*, but *facile audiēbātur* or *eum audīre facile erat*. But, as in the examples given above, an indirect question or statement may be associated with it.

Note 3.—It is uncertain whether the supine in *-ū* was originally a dative or an ablative. As a dative, its use is analogous to that of the dative with adjectives (see **254**); as an ablative it is one of Respect (see **274**).

Exercise 51

1. Ambassadors came from the Athenians to Philip at Olynthus [1] to complain of wrongs done to their countrymen. 2. He set out to his father at [1] Marseilles from his uncle at [1] Narbonne to see the games; but within the last [2] few days has been killed, either by an assassin or brigands, while [3] on his journey. 3. Do you (*pl.*) remain within the camp in order to take food and rest and all else that you require; let us, who are less exhausted with fighting—for did we not arrive fresh and untouched immediately after the contest?—go out to get food and forage. 4. We have come to deprecate your (*pl.*) anger, and to entreat for peace; we earnestly hope that we shall obtain what (*pl.*) we seek. 5. He sent ambassadors to the senate to congratulate Rome [4] on her victory. 6. It is incredible how repeatedly and how urgently I have warned [5] you to place no reliance in that man. 7. It is not easy to say whether this man should be spared and be sent away with his companions, or whether he should at once be either slain or cast into prison.

---

[1] See **315**.
[2] See **325**, *Note* **2.**
[3] Either *dum* (see **180**), or present participle (**410**).
[4] Why not *Rōma*? (See **319.**)
[5] Mood? (See **165**, **166.**)

EXERCISE LII

PARTICIPLES

General Remarks

405. Participles are verbal adjectives. Like finite verbs, they express tense and voice, they may be qualified by adverbs, and some of them may govern a case. As adjectives, they are inflected and may be attached to a noun (or pronoun) attributively or (as in the compound tenses) predicated of it.

> *Rēs abstrūsa ac recondita* (attribute). A deep and mysterious question.
>
> *Multī occīsī sunt* (predicate). Many were slain.

406. (i) The most characteristic use of a participle is to stand in **apposition** to some noun or pronoun and so form a substitute for a *subordinate clause*, either adjectival or adverbial. Thus—

> *Caesar haec veritus.* Caesar fearing (=who, *or* as he, feared) this.
>
> *Haec scrībēns interpellātus sum.* I was interrupted while I was writing this.
>
> *Urbem oppugnātūrus cōnstitit.* He halted when he was on the point of assaulting the city.
>
> *Nōbilēs, imperiō suō iamdiū repugnantēs, ūnō proeliō oppressit.* He crushed in a single battle the nobles, who had long been contesting his sovereignty.

Note.—Remember that the conjunctions *dum, cum,* etc., introduce a subordinate clause which has a finite verb. The English 'when coming, while writing,' cannot therefore be translated into Latin by *cum veniēns, dum scrībēns.*

Sometimes the Latin participle represents not a *subordinate*, but a *co-ordinate*, clause.

> *Mīlitem arreptum trahēbat.* He seized the soldier and began to drag him off. (See **15.**)
>
> *Patrem secūtus ad Hispāniam nāvigāvit.* He followed his father and sailed to Spain.

407. (ii) Participles may also be used precisely as **adjectives,** and as such admit of comparative and superlative degrees.

(*a*) Past participles such as ***doctus, ērudītus, parātus, ērēctus***, etc., are constantly so used.

(*b*) So also present participles such as ***abstinēns, amāns, appetēns, fīdēns, flōrēns, nocēns, sapiēns***, etc. The present participle of a transitive verb, however, when used as an epithet, takes an objective genitive in place of an accusative: ***patriae amantissimus***. (See **302**.)

(*c*) Some participles are even compounded with the negative prefix *in-* (which is never joined with the verb): ***innocēns, impotēns, īnsipiēns, indomitus, invictus, intāctus***.

Note.—Although this use of the participle as an epithet is common in both languages, we must be cautious in translating English *participial adjectives* literally: 'a moving speech' is ***ōrātiō flēbilis***; 'a smiling landscape,' ***aspectus amoenus***; 'burning heat,' ***aestus fervidus***.

408. (iii) Some participles are frequently used as **nouns**. (See **51**.)

Such are—***Adulēscēns***, 'a youth'; ***īnfāns***, 'a child'; ***senātūs cōnsultum***, 'a decree of the senate'; ***candidātus***, 'one in a white toga, a candidate'; ***praefectus***, 'a governor'; ***īnstitūtum***, 'a fixed course, a principle' (sing.), 'institutions' (pl.); ***ācta***, 'measures, proceedings'; ***facta***, 'deeds'; ***merita*** (*in*), 'services (towards)'; ***peccātum, dēlictum***, 'wrong-doing, crime.'

Note.—The variety of construction which this substantival use of participles makes possible has been mentioned in **55**.

409. Latin verbs have three participles only: Present, Future, and Past. The present and future participles are always active; the past is passive except when it is derived from a deponent or semi-deponent verb. (See **14**.)

Present Participle

410. The **present participle** (always **active**), when used as a participle (not as a mere adjective), denotes **incompleted action contemporaneous with** that of the verb of the sentence in which it is used.

Haec dīxit moriēns. He said this while dying.

Prōvinciā dēcēdēns[1] ***Rhodum praetervectus sum***. In the act of (*or* while) returning home from my province, I sailed past Rhodes.

---

[1] ***Dēcēdere*** is the technical word for ***to return home*** from holding the government of a province.

Ad mortem euntī obviam factus sum. I met him as he was going to death.

Note.—After *audiō* and *videō* the accusative of a present participle is used (instead of an infinitive) when emphasis is laid on the actual presence of the one who hears or sees.

Audīvī tē dīcentem.[1] I heard you say.
Aedēs flammantēs vīdit. He saw the house blaze.

411. Hence its use is far more limited than that of the English present participle, which is often used *vaguely*, as regards even time, and *widely* to represent other relations than those of mere time. Thus—

'*Mounting* (*i.e.* after mounting) his horse, he galloped off to the camp'; '*arriving* (*i.e.* having arrived) in Italy, he caught a fever'; '*hearing* this (*i.e.* in consequence of hearing), he ordered an inquiry.'

In all these cases the Latin present participle would be entirely wrong; *equum cōnscendēns* would mean that he galloped to the camp while *in the act of* mounting; *in Italiam perveniēns*, that the fever was caught at *the moment of reaching* Italy; *haec audiēns*, that the inquiry was ordered *while he* was listening to a story—all of which would of course be wrong or absurd.

In these three instances *cum* should be used with the pluperfect subjunctive: *cum equum cōnscendisset*; *cum pervēnisset*; *cum haec audīvisset* (or *hīs audītīs*).

412. The Latin present participle, unlike the English, should not be used as a substitute for a causal clause.

'Caesar, hoping soon to win the day, led out his men,' should be: *Caesar, cum sē brevī victūrum esse spērāret* (or *quod . . . spērābat*), *suōs ēdūxit*; not *Caesar spērāns*, etc. (See Exercise LXI.)

Though this rule should be strictly observed, it is not without exceptions, especially in Caesar.

Note.—The present participle is sometimes used instead of a *concessive* clause. (See Exercise LX.)

Rē cōnsentientēs, verbīs discrepāmus. Though we agree (while agreeing) in substance, we differ in words.

413. But the oblique cases (especially the **dative** and **genitive**) of present participles are also used to indicate a

[1] Sometimes: *audīvī tē, cum dīcerēs.*

whole class of persons or a member of a class, without any stress on contemporaneous activity. (See **73.**)

Vērum (or *vēra*) *dīcentibus semper cēdam.* I will always yield to those who speak the truth; *or* to men if they speak the truth (not merely 'while they are speaking').

Pugnantium clāmōre perterritus. Alarmed by the shouts of the combatants, *or* of those who were fighting.

Nescio quem prope adstantem interrogāvī. I questioned some bystander, *or* one who was standing by (not simply 'while he was . . .').

Note.—The nominative of a present participle, however, is not to be used in this way. 'Men doing this,' or 'those who do this,' should be translated by *quī hoc faciunt. Hoc facientēs laudantur* would mean, not 'men who do this are praised,' but 'they are praised while doing this,' and *iī hoc facientēs*, 'those doing this' (οἱ ταῦτα ποιοῦντες) is not Latin at all. (See **346.**)

414. This freer use of the genitive and dative of a present participle often affords a neat rendering of an English noun.

Interrogantī mihi respondit. He replied to my question.

Lūgentium lacrimae, tears of mourning; *grātulantium clāmōrēs*, shouts of congratulation.

Vōx eius morientis, his dying voice *or* words; *adhortantis verba*, his cheering words, *or* words of encouragement.

Note.—Beware of translating 'tears of grief' by *lūctūs lacrimae*, or 'cries of pain' by *vōcēs dolōris*; for *lūctūs* and *dolōris* do not conform to any of the normal uses of the possessive genitive or the genitive of quality.

Past Participle

415. The **past participle**, which is **passive** in meaning (except when derived from a deponent or semi-deponent verb), denotes an action which is prior to that of the verb of the sentence in which it stands.

Haec locūtus aciem īnstrūxit. Having spoken (when he had spoken) thus, he drew up his battle line.

Urbem captam incendit. He burned the city which he had taken.

Note 1.—Special care should be taken when translating into Latin not to use the past participle passive as if it were active. *Audītus* can never mean 'having heard.'

Note 2.—The ways in which Latin surmounts the difficulties caused by the lack of an active past participle are mentioned in **14.**

416. But the **past participles** of **deponent** and **semi-deponent verbs**, such as *veritus, ratus, ausus, cōnfīsus, diffīsus, ūsus, prōgressus* (advancing), *āversātus* (expressing disgust at), *indignātus* (feeling indignation at), and those of verbs whose passives are used in a *reflexive* sense, as *conversus* (turning), *prōiectus* (throwing himself), *humī prōvolūtus* (rolling on the ground), often denote an action which is partly prior to and partly contemporaneous with the action of the verbs of the sentence.

Metellum esse ratī, portās clausēre. Having thought (and still thinking) it was Metellus, they closed the gates.

417. Latin sometimes uses a (concrete) noun qualified by a past participle, where English uses an abstract noun connected with another noun by the preposition 'of.'

Post urbem conditam. After the foundation of the city.
Violātī foederis poenās dabis. You shall be punished for the violation of the treaty.
Nūntiāta clādēs. The news of the disaster.

Note.—This usage, together with those noticed in **54, 174, 387,** and **414,** illustrates how Latin is able to overcome its comparative poverty in abstract nouns.

Future Participles

418. The **future participle** (always **active**) denotes an action which is subsequent to that of the verb of the sentence in which it stands. It is most frequently used with a tense of *sum* to form periphrastic tenses, *e.g. locūtūrus eram* 'I was about to speak.' The following examples will recall some of its uses.

Hoc sē umquam factūrum fuisse negat. He says he would never have done this. (**36.**)
Numquam futūrum fuisse ut urbs caperētur respondit. He replied that the city would never have been taken. (**38, 472.**)
Adeō territī sunt ut arma facile trāditūrī fuerint. They were so terrified that they would have easily delivered up their arms. (**115, 474.**)
Nōn vereor nē domum numquam sīs reditūrus. I am not afraid that you will never return home. (**138.**)

Note.—In poets, and in prose writers after Cicero, the future participle is used not only in the sense of 'about to,' but also in the sense of 'intending to' or even 'destined to.' This latter usage should not be imitated when translating from English.

Exercise 52

The asterisk* means that a participial construction is to be used.

1. Are we [1] then to spare those who * resist (us) and hurl darts at us? 2. Are we to spare these men even though * they resist (us)? 3. I heard you ask more than once whether we were going to return to [2] my home, or to see your father in London. 4. I heard the whole city ring with the shouts of joy [3] and triumph. 5. Returning in his old age from India, he died in his own house; his sons and grandsons stood round his sick-bed, gazed sadly on his dying countenance, and retained in their memories his prophetic words. 6. To my complaint that he had broken his word, he said that he had done nothing of the kind, but was ready to pay the penalty of having caused [4] such a loss. 7. I saw the soldiers brandishing their weapons throughout the city; I heard the voices of joy and triumph; I recognised the clear proofs of the announcement of a victory. 8. Throwing themselves at the king's [5] feet, they solemnly appealed to him not to give over to certain destruction men who * were not guilty up to that time, and who * would be of the utmost value to the nation one day. 9. Embarking at Naples, and fearing for the safety of himself and his family,[6] he took refuge with my father at Marseilles. 10. His words alike of praise [3] and of rebuke [3] were drowned in shouts of indignation, and in groans and outcries of disapproval. 11. Distrusting my own sense of hearing, I asked some [7] one who * was standing nearer you whether I had heard aright; he answered my question in the affirmative.[8] 12. Are you not ashamed and sorry for the abandonment of your undertaking, the desertion of your friend, and the violation of your word?

---

[1] See 388. [2] 316, iii. [3] 414, *Note*.
[4] =of the causing of . . . (417.) [5] See 257.
[6] *Sui.* (354, iii.) [7] *Nescio quis.* (362.) [8] See 162.

EXERCISE LIII

THE ABLATIVE ABSOLUTE

419. One of the commonest uses of the Latin present and past participles is in a construction called the **Ablative Absolute.**

The ablatives of a participle and a noun (or pronoun) together form a substitute for a subordinate clause. *Caesar, acceptīs litterīs, proficīscī cōnstituit,* 'Caesar, letters having been received, decided to set out.' *Acceptīs litterīs* is here the equivalent in meaning of such a clause as *cum litterās accēpisset.*

Note.—This construction is called ablative absolute because the words in the ablative seem to stand apart, as if set free (*absolūtus*) from the main construction of the sentence. These ablatives were originally ablatives of accompaniment (**263**) indicating the attendant circumstances. In classical Latin the construction is widely used to indicate such ideas as *cause* or *time.*

420. This ablative absolute construction may be translated into English, sometimes by an active participle in apposition to some word in the sentence; sometimes by such phrases as 'on,' 'after,' 'in consequence of,' 'in spite of,' 'without,' 'instead of,' followed by a verbal substantive in *-ing*; sometimes by a subordinate clause introduced by 'after,' 'when,' 'while,' 'because,' 'although,' 'if,' etc.; and sometimes by a co-ordinate clause (**406,** ii). Thus—

Hīs audītīs rediit, having heard (*or* hearing) this he returned; *tē praesente,* in your presence; *hōc compertō scelere,* in consequence of discovering this crime; *tē repugnante,* in spite of (in the teeth of) your resistance; *illō manente,* as long as he remains; *Antōniō oppressō,* if Antony is crushed; *patefactā portā ērūpit,* he had the gate opened and sallied forth.

421. Owing to the absence of a past participle active in Latin, the use of this construction is exceedingly frequent. (See **14.**)

422. Cautions.—The **ablative absolute,** however, is not always admissible.

(*a*) Care must be taken not to use a past participle passive as if it were active. We cannot say *Caesare perventō* for 'Caesar having arrived'; instead we must write: *Caesar cum pervēnisset.*

(*b*) Since transitive verbs alone have a personal passive construction, the ablative of the perfect passive participle of an intransitive verb cannot be used with the ablative of a noun in this construction. 'Caesar having been persuaded' cannot be translated by *Caesare persuāsō*, but by *Caesarī cum persuāsum esset.*

(*c*) The construction must never be used if the person or thing involved is either the subject or object of the verb of the sentence.

'Caesar having taken the enemy massacred them' is not *captīs hostibus Caesar eōs trucīdāvit*, but *Caesar captōs hostēs trucīdāvit.* 'As I was reading this I saw you' is not: *mē haec legente tē vīdī*, but *haec legēns tē vīdī.*

423. (*d*) A participle forming part of an ablative absolute may take the normal case construction of the verb to which it belongs: *haec mē dīcente*; but for so long a combination as *Caesare ā mīlitibus imperātōre salūtātō*, a *cum*-clause should be substituted.

(*e*) The past participle of a deponent or semi-deponent verb, being active in meaning, often affords an alternative mode of expression. *Haec locūtus rediit* is as good Latin as *hīs dictīs rediit.*

(*f*) The future participle is very rarely used in the best prose in the ablative absolute construction.

424. Since the verb *sum* has no present or past participle, an ablative absolute construction sometimes consists simply of a noun (or pronoun) and a predicative adjective or noun.

Mē invītō, against my will; *tē duce*, with you for leader, under your leadership (332, 10); *mē auctōre*, at my suggestion; *salvīs lēgibus*, without violating the law; *honestīs iūdicibus*, if the judges are honourable men.

Note.—Sometimes the place of a noun in the ablative absolute construction is taken by a clause.

Missīs quī rogārent. Having sent people to ask.
Compertō eum aegrōtāre. Having ascertained that he was ill.

425. When the ablative absolute involves a negative, it may be translated by the English 'without' and a verbal noun. (See 398, *Note.*) Thus—

Tē nōn adiuvante, without your assistance; *nūllō exspectātō duce*, without waiting for any guide; *rē īnfectā*, without success; *nūllō respondente*, without receiving an answer from any one; *causā incognitā*, without hearing the case; *indictā causā condemnātur*, he is being condemned without pleading his cause.

426. The proper place for the ablative absolute is early in, or at the very beginning of, a sentence.

Exercise 53

1. Thereupon, after saluting the enemy's general, he turned to his companions, and setting spurs to his horse, rode past the ranks of the Germans without either waiting for his staff or receiving an answer [1] from any one. 2. It was at my suggestion, to prevent your voice and strength failing you, that you suspended for a while the speech which you had begun. 3. For myself, fearing that glory and the pursuit of honour had but little effect with you, I abandoned such topics [2] and tried to work upon your feelings by a different method. 4. All this he did at the instigation of your brother, without either receiving or hoping for any reward. 5. It was most fortunate for me that, fighting [3] as I did against your wishes and advice, not to say in spite of your opposition and resistance, I gained the victory without the loss of a single [4] soldier, and with few wounded. 6. After attacking the camp for several hours, the barbarians were so exhausted by the heat and overcome by fatigue, that having lost more than 1200 men they abandoned the attempt and returned home without success. 7. It was at your suggestion, not only against my will, but in spite of my opposition, resistance, and appeals to heaven and earth, that your countrymen were persuaded to condemn a whole people without a hearing. 8. This I am persuaded of, that you will not pass this law without violating the constitution. 9. As I was thus speaking, the news of the enemies' arrival, and the handing in of a despatch from the king, filled my audience [5] with mingled rage and panic; but some,[6]

[1] =or any one replying.
[2] Simply *ista*. (**54**.)
[3] Present participle. (**412**, *Note*.)
[4] See **381**.
[5] 'The minds (*animī*) of my audience.' (See **17**.)
[6] Use *erant quī*. (**360**, iii.)

judging that haste was necessary, seized their arms and hastened to go down to meet the foe. 10. So long as you survive and are unharmed, I feel sure that my children will never be orphans. 11. Under your leadership I would have taken up arms; but hearing [1] that you were ill, I resolved to remain behind at home without [2] taking part in that contest.

EXERCISE LIV

TEMPORAL CLAUSES

427. Temporal clauses are adverbial clauses which qualify the statement made by the verb in the main sentence in respect of time. They are introduced by temporal conjunctions.

Note.—One or other of the participial constructions given in the last two exercises may often be used as an alternative to a temporal clause, *e.g. haec locūtus, hīs dictīs* are exactly equivalent to *haec cum dīxisset.*

428. Ubi, ut 'when,' **postquam** 'after,' **simul ac, cum prīmum** 'as soon as,' **quotiēns** 'as often as,' introduce temporal clauses whose verb is *indicative.*

> *Quae ubi (postquam, simul atque* [3]) *audīvit, abiit.* When (after, as soon as) he heard (or had heard) this he took his departure.
>
> *Quae postquam audierit* (192), *abībit.* After he hears this, he will go away.

Note 1.—The perfect indicative, and not the pluperfect, is generally used in a temporal clause introduced by the conjunctions mentioned above if a single act in the past is referred to; but the pluperfect indicative is used after *ubi, ut, simul ac, quotiēns* to express the repeated occurrence of an act; and sometimes after *postquam* if a definite interval is mentioned.

> *Hostēs, ubi aliquōs ēgredientēs cōnspexerant, adoriēbantur.* Whenever the enemy saw (had seen) any soldiers disembarking, they attacked them.

---

[1] 424, *Note.* [2] Use 'and not to': *neque.* (332, 8.)
[3] *Simul ac* only before consonants.

Ūndecimō diē postquam ā tē discesseram, litterās scrīpsī. Ten days after I (had) left you, I wrote a letter.

Note 2.—The subjunctive, of course, is used in such clauses when they form part of *ōrātiō oblīqua.*

Note 3.—*Quotiēns* is used only when the idea of '*every* time that' is strongly emphasised.

Cum

429. Special attention must be paid to temporal clauses introduced by **cum** 'when,' which is the commonest of the temporal conjunctions.

(1) When the clause introduced by *cum* refers to a *present* or to a *future* action, the verb in the *cum*-clause is indicative.

Cum vidēbis, tum sciēs. When you see, you will know.

Poenam luēs, cum vēnerit (192) *solvendī diēs.* You will pay the penalty when the day of payment comes.

Note.—Observe expressions like *decem sunt annī* (or *decimus hic est annus*) *cum haec facis,* 'You have been doing this (181) for the last ten years.'

430. (2) When the clause introduced by *cum* refers to a *past* action the verb is generally subjunctive.

Caesar, cum haec vidēret, mīlitēs impetum facere iussit. Caesar, seeing this, ordered his troops to charge.

Lēgātī, cum haec nōn impetrāssent, domum rediērunt. The ambassadors having failed to obtain this, returned home.

Note.—Whereas the other temporal conjunctions introduce clauses which express *only* a relation of time, clauses introduced by *cum* and referring to a past action are felt to express, in addition to the relation of time, the circumstances which led up to and even accounted for and caused the fact stated by the verb of the main sentence.

431. But in some circumstances a *cum*-clause referring to a past action has an indicative verb.

(*a*) When the relation between the clause and the main sentence is *solely* one of time. This relation is often impressed on the reader by the presence of *tum* or *eō tempore* in the main sentence.

Cum tū ibi erās, tum ego domī eram. At the time you were there, I was at home.

Note.—As the cause must come *before* the effect, the presence of *tum* excludes from the *cum*-clause any notion of cause, and underlines, as it were, the purely temporal meaning.

432. (*b*) When *cum* is used in the sense of 'whenever' and the action of the clause is frequentative.

If the principal verb is past, the verb in the *cum*-clause is **pluperfect**; if the principal verb is present, the verb in the *cum*-clause is **perfect**.

> *Cum rosam vīderat, tum vēr esse arbitrābātur* (**185**). Whenever he saw the rose in bloom (*i.e.* year after year), he judged that it was spring-time.
>
> *Cum ad vīllam vēnī, hoc ipsum nihil agere mē dēlectat.* As often as I come to my country-house, this mere doing nothing (**94**) has a charm for me.

Note.—The indicative is also used in frequentative clauses introduced by *sī quandō, ubi, ut quisque*, and the relatives *quī, quīcumque.*

> *Ut quisque hūc vēnerat, haec loquēbātur.* Whenever any one came here, he would use this language.
>
> *Quōs cessāre vīderat, verbīs castīgābat.* Whomever he saw hanging back, he made a point of rebuking.

But in Livy often, in Tacitus regularly, the subjunctive is used in such clauses.

> *Id fētiālis ubi dīxisset, hastam immittēbat.* As soon as (in every case) the herald had uttered this, he would launch a spear.

433. (*c*) The indicative is also used where, by an inverted construction, what would otherwise be the principal assertion is stated in a subordinate clause introduced by *cum.*

> *Iam vēr appetēbat, cum Hannibal ex hībernīs*[1] *mōvit.* Spring was already approaching, when Hannibal left his winter quarters.

Note 1.—The same sense could be expressed by: *Cum vēr iam appeteret, Hannibal ex hībernīs mōvit*; or by: *Vēre iam appetente Hannibal ex hībernīs mōvit.*

Note 2.—The *cum* which introduces such a clause is sometimes called *cum inversum.* It generally follows the main sentence.

---

[1] The neut. pl. adjective *hīberna* is used as a military term; the noun *castra* must be supplied.

434. A *cum*-clause in which the idea of *cause* predominates over the idea of time has a subjunctive verb, no matter whether the action is present or past.

Quae cum ita sint, Rōmam ībō. Seeing that these are the circumstances, I will go to Rome.

Similarly, a *cum*-clause which expresses a *concession* always has a subjunctive verb.

Cum līber esse possit, servīre māvult. Although he might be free, he prefers to be a slave.
Cum dīcere dēbēret, conticuit. Although he ought to have spoken (*or* instead of speaking), he held his peace.

435. When *tum* appears in the main sentence, a *cum*-clause often differs little in meaning from a co-ordinate sentence. *Cum . . . tum* then mean 'both . . . and,' 'not only . . . but also,' 'on the one hand . . . but on the other.'

(i) If the verb is common to both clauses, the indicative is used.
Cōnsilia cum patriae tum sibi inimīca capiēbat. He conceived plans that were harmful both to his country and to himself.

(ii) If there is not a common verb, the verb of the *cum*-clause is indicative if it denotes an action contemporaneous with that of the main verb.

Cum tē semper amāvī, tum meī amantissimum cognōvī. Not only have I always felt affection for you, but I have found you most affectionate towards myself.

(iii) But when the action of the *cum*-clause is prior to that of the main sentence, an idea of concession is often present, and the verb of the *cum*-clause is subjunctive.

Cum tē semper dīlēxerim, tum hodiē multō plūs dīligō. Not only I have always loved you, but I love you far more now; *or* although . . . yet . . .

Exercise 54

The asterisk * means that one of the various constructions of *cum* is to be used.

1. This * being the case, he was reluctant to leave the city, and openly refused,[1] in the governor's presence, to

[1] *Negō* with accus. and fut. inf.

do so. 2. As * I was wearied with my journey, I determined (45) to stay at home the whole day and do nothing. 3. No sooner was he made aware, by the hoisting of a flag from the summit of the citadel, that the advance guard of the enemy was approaching, than, taking advantage [1] of the darkness [2] of the night, he caused a gate to be thrown open and sallied out boldly into their midst. 4. No sooner had he heard of the landing of the enemy's forces, than, instead of remaining quietly at home, he determined to take up arms and do his utmost [3] to repel the invasion. 5. Seeing * that his prayers and entreaties were of no avail with the king, he brought his speech to an end. No sooner was he (*quī*) silent, than the door was opened and two soldiers entered, each [4] armed with a sword. 6. At the moment when * the enemy was entering the gates of your crushed and ruined city, not one of you so much as heaved a groan ; when * even worse than this (*pl.*) befalls you, who will [5] pity you ? You will bewail, I fear, your [6] destiny in vain. 7. Whenever * he heard anything of this kind, he would instantly say that the story was invented by some neighbour. 8. Whomever he saw applauding the conqueror he would blame, and exhort not to congratulate their country's enemies 9. For the last five years the enemy has been [7] sweeping in triumph through the whole of Italy, slaughtering our armies, destroying our strongholds, setting fire to our towns, devastating and ravaging our fields, shaking the allegiance of our allies, when * suddenly the aspect of affairs is changed, and he sends ambassadors, and pretends to wish for peace, tranquillity, and friendship with [8] our nation.

---

[1] *Ūtor* (416.) [2] =night and darkness. [3] See 332, 9.
[4] Why not *quisque* ? (378.) [5] 309. [6] *Iste.* (338.)
[7] 429, *Note.* [8] Genitive. (288.)

EXERCISE LV

TEMPORAL CLAUSES—*Continued*

Dum, dōnec, priusquam, etc.

436. The other temporal conjunctions will cause little difficulty, if the remarks on Tenses are carefully read, especially those in **190-2**.

The general rule is that the indicative is used unless (*a*) the clause forms part of *ōrātiō oblīqua*, or (*b*) some other idea than that of time is introduced.

437. When *dum* (*dōnec*) 'while,' *quamdiū* or *quoad* 'as long as' introduces a clause whose action is co-extensive in time with that of the main verb, the indicative is used in the subordinate clause.

Haec fēcī, dum licuit. I did this as long as I was permitted.

Vīvet eius memoria, dum erit haec cīvitās. His memory will live as long as this country exists.

Note 1.—*Quamdiū* implies a *long* period; *quoad* means 'to the last point,' and is not limited to *time*: *quoad potuī*, 'to the utmost extent of my power'=*quantum in mē fuit*. (332, 9.)

Note 2.—*Dōnec* in the sense of 'while' is rare in Caesar and Cicero.

438. But the verb in a *dum*-clause which denotes a longer period, **during part of which** something else has happened, is a historic present **(180)**, even when past time is referred to.

Dum haec geruntur, hostēs discessērunt. While these things were being done, the enemy departed.

Note 1.—The historic present indicative is retained in such a clause even in *ōrātiō oblīqua*.

Allātum est praedātōrēs, dum lātius vagantur, ab hostibus interceptōs. News was brought that the plunderers, while they were wandering too far, had been cut off by the enemy.

Note 2.—'While' is constantly used in English without any idea of *time*, simply to place two statements side by side, generally with the idea of *contrast*: 'while you hate him, we love him.' *Dum* is never used in this sense in Latin: we must write either *tū quidem eum ōdistī, nōs vērō amāmus*; or simply *tū eum ōdistī, nōs amāmus*. (See also **406**, *Note*.)

439. *Dum* sometimes introduces a clause which, although related in time to the main sentence, itself contains a jussive subjunctive (negative *nē*). *Dum* then means 'so long as' in the sense of 'if, provided that,' and the clause is sometimes called a **clause of proviso.**

Ōderint, dum metuant. Let them hate, let them fear the while (*i.e.* provided they fear).

Veniant igitur, dum nē nōs interpellent. Let them come then, provided they don't interrupt us.

Note.—Clauses of proviso are also introduced by *modo* and *dummodo.*

Maneant ingenia senibus, modo permaneat studium et industria. Let the aged retain their faculties provided their zeal and industry persist.

440. When *dum, dōnec, quoad* mean 'until,' their mood is determined by the rule in **436.** If nothing more than time is indicated they take the **indicative** (except in *ōrātiō oblīqua*).

Manē hīc, dum ego redierō (*redībō*). Remain here till I return. (191-2.)

In senātū fuit quoad (or *dōnec*) *senātus dīmissus est.* He was in the senate till the moment when it was adjourned.

441. But if some further idea of *purpose* or *expectation* is involved, the **subjunctive** is used.

Num exspectātis dum testimōnium dīcat? Are you waiting till he gives his evidence? *i.e.* with a view to hearing him.

Note 1.—Thus in *Epamīnōndās ferrum in corpore retinuit, quoad renūntiātum est vīcisse Boeōtiōs,* 'Epaminondas retained the spear in his body, till it was reported to him that the Boeotians were victorious,'—the two facts are related in time, but by nothing else. *Esset* in place of *est* would indicate that he retained the spear *with the purpose of* waiting till the news should be (have been) brought.

Differant, dōnec īra dēfervēscat. Let them put off till their anger cools; *i.e.* let them put off with the *purpose* that their anger may cool.

Dēfervēscet would mean simply 'till the *time when* their anger *shall be cooling*'; *dēferbuerit*, 'has (shall have) cooled.' (191-2.)

Note 2.—The subjunctive in these clauses is jussive in origin. But since the idea of purpose is weaker than it is, for example, in final clauses, such subjunctives are sometimes called **Prospective or Anticipatory.**

442. Similarly, when *antequam* and *priusquam* 'before' introduce a clause denoting simple *priority of time*, the indicative is used.

Quārtō ante diē quam hūc vēnī litterās accēpī. I received the letter four days (**323,** *b*) before I came here.

But when the idea of an *end in view*, *motive*, or *result prevented*, is added to that of time, the subjunctive is invariably used.

Priusquam ē pavōre reciperēmus animōs, impetum fēcērunt hostēs. The enemy made a charge before we should recover from the panic, *i.e.* to prevent us from recovering (*end in view*).

Note.—The subjunctive is also used when the second person (used in an indefinite sense) is the subject of a *priusquam* clause.

Priusquam incipiās, cōnsultō opus est. Before men begin, they require deliberation.

443. *Priusquam* and *antequam* are compound conjunctions whose two parts may be placed in separate clauses; *prius* (or *ante*) may be placed in the main sentence if it precedes (and especially when it is negative), leaving the *quam* to introduce the following subordinate clause. See also **322,** *Note.*

(i) So used, they are often equivalent to *not . . . until.*

Nōn prius respondēbō quam tacueris. I will not answer until you are silent.

(ii) They may also sometimes be used to translate 'without.' (See **425.**)

Nōn prius abiit quam iūdicum sententiās audīvit. He did not go without hearing the verdict of the jury.

Note.—'Not until' may often be expressed by *tum dēmum* (or *dēnique*).

Tum dēmum respondēbō, cum tacueris. I will not answer till you are silent.

Exercise 55

The asterisk * means that *dum* is to be used in one of its various constructions. ** *Antequam* or *priusquam* is to be used.

1. I am ready to pay you the greatest possible honour, so * long as you are ready to estimate at its proper value all the slander and detraction of my rivals. 2. The [1] launching of this handful of cavalry against the enemy's

[1] 417.

left wing caused such universal panic that, while * the king was inquiring of his staff what was happening, even the centre began [1] to fall into confusion. Before worse [2] befell us, night intervened, so that fighting ceased [3] on both sides. 3. And now before we could reap the fruit of a contest which had cost us so much bloodshed, a second army came on the scene, so that, while * our general was sleeping in his tent, the battle had to be [4] begun anew. 4. He will be dear to his countrymen as long * as this nation exists, nor will his memory die out of the hearts of men till ** all things are (192) forgotten. 5. He did not enter political life till [5] by the death [6] of his father he was able, as [7] he had long desired, to join the ranks [8] of the aristocratic party. 6. Let them venture on anything,[9] provided * they do not injure the influence and authority of those with whom rests the administration of the nation. 7. As long [10] as I believed you were studying these matters for their own sake, so long [10] I honoured you highly; now I estimate you at your true value. 8. As long * as those who are to command our armies are chosen either by chance or on grounds of interest, the nation can never be served successfully.

EXERCISE LVI

ŌRĀTIŌ OBLĪQUA

444. In reporting another person's language two methods may be used.

(i) The historian may name the speaker, and give the words he used in the precise form in which he spoke them, *e.g.*:

To this Caesar replied, 'I will come if you are ready to follow.'

---

[1] 'Ĕven in the centre confusion began.' (See 219.)
[2] Neut. pl.
[3] Impersonal construction. (219.)
[4] Gerundive.
[5] See **443**, *Note*.
[6] Abl. abs.; use *mortuus*.
[7] 67.
[8] Why not *ōrdinēs*? (See 17.)
[9] See 359.
[10] *Quamdiū* (437, *Note*) . . . *tamdiū*.

Such professedly *verbatim* reports are spoken of as being in *ōrātiō rēcta*, as coming, as it were, *directly* from the lips of the speaker.

This method is used in Latin, sometimes in a formal report of long speeches in the senate or elsewhere, sometimes in reporting a short saying, if very memorable or striking. In the latter case particularly, *inquit* 'he says, he said' is inserted after the first or second word of the speech or saying. (See **40.**) Such speeches, being in *ōrātiō rēcta*, should never be preceded by verbs like *dīxit*, *respondit*.

(ii) But the more usual method in Latin, more common even than it is in English, is not to profess to give the speaker's words in the form in which they were spoken, but to prefix [1] a verb of *saying* (*dīxit*, *respondit*), and then to report the substance of what was said in the third person, that is, in **ōrātiō oblīqua.** All the principal verbs will now be dependent on a verb of *saying*, expressed or understood; and the personal and demonstrative pronouns and possessive adjectives are adjusted to the point of view of the person making the report. Thus, instead of Caesar's own words: 'I will go, if you are ready to follow,' we have in English *ōrātiō oblīqua*: 'Caesar replied that *he* would go, if *he* were ready to follow.'

445. In *ōrātiō oblīqua* all simple sentences and main sentences of *ōrātiō rēcta* become noun clauses. (Intr. 71.)

(i) Statements which were in the indicative become dependent statements in the accusative and infinitive. (See **31.**) The use of the tenses of the infinitive in *ōrātiō oblīqua* has been explained in **35.**

Ōrātiō rēcta	*Ōrātiō oblīqua*
Rōmulus urbem condidit. Romulus founded a city.	(*Dīcunt*): *Rōmulum urbem condidisse.* They say that Romulus founded a city.

[1] An actual verb of 'saying,' such as *dīcō*, is often omitted when it is implied in the immediate context.

Lēgātōs ad Caesarem mittunt: sēsē parātōs esse portās aperīre. They send ambassadors to Caesar (who said:) 'We are ready to open the gates.'

Colōnīs trīste respōnsum redditum est: facesserent properē ex urbe. The colonists received a severe answer: 'Begone at once from the city.'

(ii) Direct commands, prohibitions, real questions, and wishes become dependent commands, prohibitions, questions, and wishes; and their verbs become subjunctive.

Ōrātiō rēcta	*Ōrātiō oblīqua*
Creāte cōnsulēs. Elect consuls.	(*Hortātus est*) : *creārent cōnsulēs.* His advice was that they should elect consuls.

446. An accusative and infinitive construction of *ōrātiō rēcta* is retained in *ōrātiō oblīqua*; but all[1] other subordinate clauses have a subjunctive verb in *ōrātiō oblīqua*.

Ōrātiō rēcta	*Ōrātiō oblīqua*
Cōnstat tē patriam amāre. It is agreed that you love your country.	(*Dīxērunt*) : *cōnstāre illum patriam amāre.* They said that it was agreed that he loved his country.
Stultus est quī hoc facit. He who is doing this, is foolish.	(*Dīcō*) : *eum stultum esse quī hoc faciat.* I say that he who is doing this, is foolish.
Simul atque hostem vīdērunt, fūgēre. As soon as they saw the enemy, they fled.	(*Dīcunt*) : *eōs simul atque hostem vīderint, fūgisse.* They say that as soon as the others saw the enemy, they fled.

447. The tense of a subjunctive verb in *ōrātiō oblīqua* in general follows the rule for normal sequence (**105**), and is determined by the tense of the verb of 'saying' which introduces the *ōrātiō oblīqua*.

Ōrātiō rēcta	*Ōrātiō oblīqua*
Quī hoc fēcerint, poenās dabunt. Those who do (shall have done) this, will pay the penalty.	(*Dīxit*) : *eōs quī illud fēcissent, poenās datūrōs esse.* He said that those who did this, would pay the penalty.

Note 1.—Observe that a future perfect of *ōrātiō rēcta* is represented in *ōrātiō oblīqua* after a past verb of 'saying' by a pluperfect subjunctive.

Note 2.—For exceptions to the normal sequence of tenses see **524, 525.**

---

[1] The verb in a *dum*-clause of the type mentioned in **438** is an exception to this rule.

Virtual Ōrātiō Oblīqua

448. Even when there is no verb of 'saying' expressed or clearly implied in the context, the subjunctive is frequently used instead of the indicative in an adjectival or adverbial clause which the writer wishes to present, not as his own statement, but as the reported statement of someone else.

> *Supplicātiō dēcrēta est, quod Italiam bellō līberāssem.* A thanksgiving was decreed because (as they said) I had saved Italy from war.

Such clauses are said to be in **virtual ōrātiō oblīqua**; and in translating them we can insert some such words as 'as he said.'

Note.—This is a convenient way of distinguishing what the writer or speaker (A) states on his own responsibility, from that for which he declines to be responsible, and which he tacitly shifts to (B).

Thus in the fable: 'The vulture invited the little birds to a feast which he was going to give them,' *quod illīs datūrus erat* would mean that he really *was* going to give them the feast and the narrator vouched for the fact; but *quod illīs datūrus esset* would mean that the vulture only *said* he was going to do so, and the writer does not vouch for the truth of the statement.

So with the verbs of *accusing*, the charge is often expressed by a *quod*-clause with a *subjunctive* verb, because the *accusers alone are made to assert* that the crime has been committed; the *indicative* would make the historian or speaker assert, and be *responsible for*, the truth of the charge. Thus—

> *Sōcratēs accūsātus est quod corrumperet iuventūtem.* Socrates was accused of corrupting the young men.

Quod corrumperet throws the responsibility for the charge on the accuser. *Corrumpēbat* would imply that the historian agreed with the charge.

(See below, **484.**)

449. Sometimes a subordinate *quī*-clause is introduced in the midst of *ōrātiō oblīqua* by a writer as an explanatory parenthesis of his own; and since such a clause is not part of what the writer is reporting, the verb is indicative.

Themistoclēs certiōrem eum fēcit, id agī, ut pōns, quem ille in Hellēspontō fēcerat, dissolverētur. Themistocles sent him word that the intention was to break down the bridge, which he (Xerxes) had made over the Hellespont.

The words *quem ille in Hellēspontō fēcerat* are inserted by the historian; they do not belong to the words reported as used by Themistocles.

Similarly, in such a sentence as: 'he ordered him to send for the troops who were in the rear,' the *who*-clause would, in Latin, have a *subjunctive* verb if it were part of the order given, but an *indicative* verb if a mere definition of the troops were meant, and inserted as such by the *historian*.

Exercise 56

1. Then turning to Cortes, he made a vehement attack upon the Spaniards, who, without any adequate justification, were invading his territory, and were either inviting or compelling his subjects to rebel. 2. He gave orders not to spare a single (**358**) person who had been present at the massacre of the prisoners or the outrage on the ambassadors. 3. Then the gallant and undaunted chief, though surrounded on all sides by armed men, turned to the conqueror and denounced the cowardice of his countrymen, who by surrendering him to the Spaniards had flung away the priceless possessions [1] of freedom and of honour. 4. He promised not to leave the city till they had brought safely within the walls all who had survived from the massacre of yesterday. 5. He asked the many [2] bystanders whether those who wished for their king's safety were ready to follow him, and, using [3] all speed, to inflict chastisement on those who had violated their allegiance and their oath. 6. On reaching the summit of the mountain he called to him his staff, and pointed out the streams which (he said) flowed down towards Italy. 7. He said that he would not allow himself to put faith in men who had not only showed themselves cowardly and disloyal, but were still, in the face of such a political emergency, on the point of sacrificing everything to their own comfort and interest.

[1] See **223**, *Note* 1. [2] See **69**. [3] Abl. abs.; use *adhibeō*.

EXERCISE LVII

CONDITIONAL CLAUSES

450. Conditional (or conditioned) **statements** consist of two parts: (1) a subordinate clause, called the **Protasis,** which is introduced by *sī* 'if' or *nisi* 'unless,' and contains a condition; and (2) a main sentence, called the **Apodosis,** which expresses what is (was, will be, would be, or would have been) true *if* the condition of the protasis is (or was, will be, etc.) fulfilled.

Sī hoc dīcit, errat. If he says this, he is making a mistake.
Sī hoc dīcat, erret. If he were to say this, he would be wrong.

Note.—In 'If it has lightened there will be thunder,' that 'there will be thunder' is dependent, as an *inference,* on whether or no 'it has lightened.' But *grammatically* 'there will be thunder' is the main sentence, qualified by the subordinate clause 'if it has lightened.'

451. Conditional statements can be divided into three main types according to the kind of condition expressed in the protasis.

Type I. The condition may be so expressed that there is no implication about its fulfilment or probability of fulfilment. Such conditions are said to be **Open Conditions.**

Sī spīrat, vīvit. If he is breathing, he is alive.
Sī ēmī, meum est. If I bought it, it is mine.

Note.—A sentence like: *sī valēs, gaudeō* 'if you are well, I am glad,' simply expresses a logical relation between (A) *valēs* and (B) *gaudeō*; if (A) is true, then (B) is true; but not the slightest hint is given whether (A) is, in fact, true or not. Similarly when Cicero says: *Parcite Lentulī dignitātī, sī ipse fāmae suae umquam pepercit,* 'Show respect for the rank of Lentulus, if he ever showed respect for his own reputation,' the orator does not assert or deny the truth of *pepercit*; he merely makes it a necessary antecedent to *parcite.* Both Cicero and his hearers knew that, in fact, *pepercit* was not true; but it is ironically made an open condition.

452. In Open Conditions the verb of the protasis is indicative; the verb of the apodosis may be either indicative, imperative, or a subjunctive of will or desire.

Sī eum occīdī, rēctē fēcī. If I slew him, I did rightly.

Excitāte eum, sī potestis, ab īnferīs. Raise him from the underworld, if you have the power.

Moriar, sī vēra nōn loquor. May I die, if I am not speaking the truth.

453. When translating a subordinate clause of condition into Latin, special attention must be paid to the use of the future and future perfect indicative where English uses a present indicative (see **191, 192**).

Note 1.—'If you do this, you will be punished' is: *Hoc sī fēceris, poenās dabis*; because the 'doing this' will be a completed action in the future time at which the punishment is applied. *Sī facis* would mean 'if you are now doing' and in some circumstances might be a logical condition; *sī faciēs* 'if you shall be doing' could scarcely be logical since the 'doing' must be prior to the punishment and the simple future does not express that priority; *sī faciās* 'if you were to do' would be a wholly illogical condition to an apodosis in the future indicative.

Note 2.—If a command in the apodosis does not have reference to the immediate moment, the future indicative must be used in the protasis. 'Give me the cup, if you have it' is: *dā mihi pōculum, sī habēs*; but 'Come to-morrow, if you can' is: *venī crās, sī poteris.*

454. When the apodosis is an Imperfect indicative, and the action of the protasis is prior to it, the verb of the protasis is Pluperfect indicative. (See also **193**, *Note* 1, and **432**.)

Sī quem cessāre vīderat, nōn verbīs sōlum sed etiam verberibus castīgābat. If he saw that any one was hanging back, he would correct him, not with words only, but with a flogging.

455. Type II. The condition may be conceded only as a supposition, which may or may not be fulfilled. Such conditions are sometimes called **Ideal Conditions.**

Note.—A sentence like: *Sī veniās, gaudeam,* 'If you were to come, I should be glad,' not only expresses a logical relation between (A) *veniās* and (B) *gaudeam,* but *also* implies a doubt about the fulfilment of (A).

456. In Ideal Conditions, the verb of both protasis and apodosis is generally Present subjunctive.

Hanc viam sī asperam esse negem, mentiar. If I were to deny that this road is hard, I should lie.

Note.—But sometimes a Perfect subjunctive is used in the protasis to denote an act as hypothetically completed and prior in time to the apodosis.

> *Sī gladium quis apud tē sānā mente dēposuerit, repetat īnsāniēns, reddere peccātum sit, officium nōn reddere.* If a man in sound mind were to have deposited a sword with you and reclaim it when mad, it would be wrong to return it, right not to return it.

457. Type III. The condition may be one which is represented as being contrary to known facts, or as impossible of fulfilment. Such are called **Unreal Conditions.**

Note.—A sentence like: *Sī vēnissēs, gāvīsus essem,* 'If you had come, I should have been glad,' not only expresses the logical relation between (A) *vēnissēs* and (B) *gāvīsus essem,* but *also* implies that (A) *vēnissēs* has not taken and cannot now take place.

458. In Unreal Conditions the verb of both protasis and apodosis is subjunctive. The Imperfect expresses something continuing even into the present time, the Pluperfect expresses something completed in the past.

> *Sī amīcī adessent, cōnsiliī nōn indigērem.* If my friends were here to help, I should not be in need of a plan.
>
> *Sī ibi tē esse scīssem, ad tē ipse vēnissem.* If I had known you were there, I should have come myself.

Note.—When the meaning and context require it, the Imperfect can be used in one clause and the Pluperfect in the other.

> *Sī ad centēnsimum annum vīxisset, senectūtis eum suae paenitēret?* If he had lived to his hundredth year, would he be regretting his old age?
>
> *Nisi ante Rōmā profectus essēs, nunc eam certē relinquerēs.* If you had not previously left Rome, you would certainly leave it now.

459. Caution.—Remember that *sī* is never used in Latin as an interrogative particle. 'He asked him *if* he was well,' is: *ex eō, num valēret, quaesīvit.* (167.)

Note.—*Sī* begins a sentence less commonly in Latin than 'if' does in English. *Sī* often follows a name or pronoun: *Caesar sī,* etc., *Ego sī,* etc. Often *quod* is prefixed to a *sī*-clause to connect it with the previous sentence: *quod sī*=' *but* if,' sometimes '*and* if'; literally it means '*as to which,* if.'

Exercise 57

A

1. If you love me, be sure to send a letter to me at Rome. 2. I am not yet sure whether [1] you have returned; but if you are at home I hope soon to receive a letter from you. 3. Were your countrymen to use this language to [2] you, would they not expect a favourable answer? 4. If I am speaking falsely, Metellus, refute me; if I am speaking the truth, why do you hesitate [3] to put confidence in me? 5. Were virtue denied this reward, yet she [4] would be satisfied with her own self. 6. Time [5] would fail me were I to try to reckon up all his services to the nation. 7. If ever any [6] one was indifferent to empty fame and vulgar [7] gossip, it [8] is I. 8. If any one were to make this request of you, he would be justly ridiculed. 9. If you are desirous of entering political life, do not [9] hesitate to count me among your friends. 10. Had he been a man of [10] courage, he would never have declined this contest. 11. If you have any regard, either for your own safety or your private property, do not [11] delay your reconciliation with the conqueror. 12. But if you are aiming at the crown, why do you use the language of a citizen,[12] and pretend to sacrifice everything to the judgement and inclination of your countrymen?

B

1. If the enemy had with a veteran army invaded our territory, and routed our army of recruits, no [13] German would have survived to-day. 2. If I either decline the contest or show [14] myself a coward and a laggard, then you may [15] taunt me if you will, with my lowly birth, then

---

[1] 167. [2] '*With* you' (*tēcum*). [3] Use *nōlō*.
[4] See **356.** [5] 'The day,' *diēs*. [6] See **357.**
[7] Gen. of *vulgus*. (See **59.**) [8] = 'I am he'; use *is*. (See **70.**)
[9] See **143**, *Note* 1. [10] **303**, ii. [11] *Cavē*. (**143.**)
[12] Adj. *cīvīlis*. (See **58.**) [13] See **223**, *Note* 2.
[14] *Praebeō*. (**240**, *Note* 1.) [15] *Licet* with subj. (**198**, *Note* 2.)

call [1] me, if you choose, the basest and meanest of mankind. 3. If once [2] the enemy throws his army across the Rhine, I am afraid that [3] no one will be able to stand in his way on this side of the Vistula. 4. If we have had [4] enough of fighting to-day, let us recall the soldiers to their several (**354**, i) standards, and hope for better things for [5] the morrow. If to-morrow resistance [6] is manifestly no longer possible, let us yield, however [7] reluctantly, to necessity, and bid each take care [8] of himself. 5. If, when you have got to Rome, you care [9] to receive a letter from me, mind you are the first [10] to write to me. 6. When once Italy is reached,[11] I will either lead you (*pl.*), said he, at once to Rome, if you wish, or having let you sack such [12] wealthy cities as Milan and Genoa, will send you home, if you prefer it, laden with plunder and spoil. 7. If they saw any of our soldiers running forward from (*ex*) the line of march, or left behind by his comrades, they would all hurl their darts at him. 8. It is haste,[13] said he, not deliberation, that we need; had we used it [14] earlier, we should have had [15] no war to-day. 9. These men, had you permitted it, would have been alive to-day, and been maintaining with the sword the national cause. 10. Had you asked me yesterday if I feared so worthless a person as your brother, I should have answered no; to-day the news of this defeat makes [16] me so anxious, that, were you to ask the same question, I should answer yes.

---

[1] Imperat. of *dico*.
[2] Need not be expressed if the right tense of the verb is used. (**192.**)
[3] *Ut quisquam*. (See **137.**)
[4] See **218.**
[5] *In*. (See **326.**)
[6] **219**, i.
[7] *Quamvīs*. (**480**, *Note* 2.)
[8] Use *cōnsulō*. (**248.**)
[9] *Volō*.
[10] *Prior*. (See **62.**)
[11] **217**, *Note*.
[12] Use *urbs* in apposition. Compare use of *homō* in **224**, *Note* 3. (See **317.**)
[13] Use past participle of *properō*, and see **286**.
[14] Relative.
[15] Use *sum*. (**251** and **257.**)
[16] See **240.**

EXERCISE LVIII

CONDITIONAL CLAUSES—*Continued*

460. In the apodosis of conditional statements of Types II and III an indicative, and not a subjunctive, is sometimes used.

461. (i) If the verb of the apodosis is one of 'possibility, obligation *or* necessity,' the indicative is generally used.

Dēlērī tōtus exercitus potuit, sī fugientēs persecūtī victōrēs essent. The whole army might have been destroyed, if the victors had pursued the fugitives (*which they did not do*).

Bonus vātēs poterās esse, sī voluissēs. You might have been a good prophet, if you had cared to be one.

Hunc hominem, sī ūlla in tē esset pietās, colere dēbēbās. If you had had any natural affection (*as you had not*), you ought to have respected this man.

Note.—The reason for such apparent exceptions to the general rule is that what is contrary to fact (see **457**) is not the *possibility* or the *obligation*, but the *fulfilment* of *dēlērī*, *bonus esse*, and *colere*. The verbs *potuit*, *poterās*, *dēbēbas* superimpose upon the contrary to fact *dēlētus esset*, *bonus fuissēs*, *coluissēs* a statement of a possibility or obligation which *is in no way conditioned* by the protasis ; and it is *this statement alone* which finds expression in such sentences.

Similarly, *erat* and *fuit* are used in the apodosis with a gerundive, expressing obligation.

Sī ūnum diem morātī essētis, moriendum omnibus fuit. If you had delayed a single day, you must all have died.

Hōs nisi manū mīsisset, tormentīs etiam dēdendī fuērunt. If he had not set these men free, they must have been given up to torture.

462. (ii) In place of the logical apodosis expressed by a verb in the subjunctive, an indicative statement of an *allied fact* is sometimes substituted.

(*a*) *Quod nī ita sit, quid venerāmur deōs?* And if this were not so, why do we honour the gods?

(*b*) *Pōns iter paene hostibus dedit, nī ūnus vir fuisset.* The bridge almost gave a passage to the enemy, had it not been for one man.

(c) *Sī frāctus illābātur orbis, impavidum ferient ruīnae.* If the vault of heaven should break and fall, its crash will smite him unafraid.

Note.—In example (*a*) above, the logical apodosis would be *nōn venerēmur deōs* 'we should not honour the gods.' In its place we have a *question* about a fact which is true apart from the condition. In (*b*) the logical apodosis would be *pōns iter dedisset,* 'the bridge would have afforded a passage.' In its place we have a *statement* concerning the event which was actually prevented by the fulfilment of the condition. In sentences of this type the apodosis generally contains some adverb like *paene* or *vix.* In (*c*) the logical apodosis would be *impavidum feriant,* 'would strike him unafraid.' In its place we have a *prophecy* enunciated with an illogical disregard of the condition.

463. When the predicate of an apodosis consists of a future participle or a neuter adjective with *sum,* the indicatives *est, erat,* and *fuit* are commonly used instead of a subjunctive.

Relictūrī agrōs erant, nisi Metellus litterās mīsisset. They were about to abandon the territory had not Metellus sent a message.

Aliter sī fēcissēs, idem ēventūrum fuit. Had you acted otherwise, the result would have been the same.

Melius erat, sī numquam vēnissēs. It would have been better if you had never come.

Note.—In such sentences, the apodosis is suppressed in favour of a statement of an *allied fact* which (like the substitution in **462,** *a*) is true apart from the condition.

464. Nisi 'if not,' 'unless,' negatives a protasis *as a whole* ; the negative in **sī . . . nōn** applies to a *single word.*

Moriētur, nisi medicum adhibuerit. Unless he calls in (*or* if he does not call in) a physician, he will die.

Moriētur, sī medicum nōn adhibuerit. He will die, if he *fails*-to-call-in a physician.

Note 1.—*Sī nōn* is regularly used if:

(*a*) the apodosis contains *tamen, at . . . tamen,* or *certē* :

Dolōrem sī nōn potuerō frangere, tamen occultābō. If I cannot suppress my sorrow, yet I will hide it.

(*b*) the positive of the same verb precedes :

Sī fēceris, habēbō grātiam, sī nōn fēceris, ignōscam. If you do it, I shall thank you ; if not, I shall pardon you.

Note 2.—**Nī** is sometimes used (but rarely by Cicero) for *nisi.* See examples in 462.

465. Sīn 'but if' has only a restricted use. When two conditions exclude each other and each has its own apodosis, the first is introduced by **sī** and the second by **sīn.**

Sī lūna clāra est, domō exeunt, sīn obscūrior, domī manent. If the moon is bright, they leave their houses, but if it is at all dim (57, *b*), they stay at home.

Note.—But if the second condition is merely the negative of the first, either *sī nōn* with the verb, or *sī minus* without the verb is used.

Sī haec fēcerit, gaudēbō, {*sī nōn fēcerit,* / *sī minus,*} *aequō animō feram.* If he does this, I shall be glad; if he does not (*or* if not), I shall take it quietly.

466. *Sī, nisi, sī nōn, sī minus* sometimes connect single words.

(*a*) *Nihil aliud discere est, nisi recordārī.* Learning is nothing else than recollecting.

(*b*) *Cum spē, sī nōn optimā, at aliquā tamen vīvit.* He lives with some hopes, if not the highest.

(*c*) *Iūrāvit sē, nisi victōrem, numquam reditūrum.* He swore never to return, unless victorious.

Note.—This usage originated with the omission of a verb. In (*a*) we could write *discere nihil aliud est, nisi recordārī est*; and in (*b*) *cum spē vīvit, sī nōn cum optimā spē vīvit.* But in (*c*) *nisi victōrem* is used for *nisi victor esset,* and the omission of the verb has led to an adjustment of the case of *victor.* (Compare 494, *Note* 2.)

467. Sīve (seu) 'or if' introduces two or more alternative conditions which have a common apodosis.

Sīve adhibueris medicum, sīve nōn adhibueris, convalēscēs. You will get well, whether you call in a physician or no.

Note.—Great care must be taken to distinguish *sīve . . . sīve* (*seu . . . seu*) from *utrum . . . an,* and *aut . . . aut.*

(*a*) *Sīve . . . sīve* introduce **adverbial** clauses (alternative conditions).

(*b*) *Utrum . . . an* introduce **substantival** clauses (alternative questions).

(*c*) *Aut . . . aut* introduce **co-ordinate** clauses.

(*a*) *Seu legit, seu scrībit, nihil temporis terit.* Whether he reads or writes, he wastes no time.

(*b*) ***Utrum legat an scrībat nescio.*** I do not know whether he is reading or writing.

(*c*) ***Aut legit aut scrībit.*** He is either reading or writing.

The manner, therefore, in which 'whether' and 'or' are to be translated into Latin depends entirely on the sense in which they are used, that is, on the nature of the clause which they introduce.

468. The English 'on condition that' generally introduces, not a conditional clause, but a clause of proviso or a restrictive clause.

(*a*) ***Ōderint, dum metuant*** (see **439**). Let them hate provided (on condition that) they fear.

(*b*) ***Maneat, modo taceat*** (see **439**, *Note*). Let him remain provided he holds his tongue.

(*c*) ***Ita maneat, ut mihi pāreat*** (see **111**). Let him remain provided (on condition that) he obeys me.

Exercise 58

A

1. Had he listened to your warnings, had he endured everything in silence, the result would have been the same then as to-day. 2. Had you been in office during the same year as my father, had you encountered the same political storms as he did, you would have shown,[1] if not[2] as great self-control, yet as much good sense as he did. 3. Had I said this with the intention of being of use to him and pleasing him, yet I should have had to put up with his abuse and insults. 4. Had your father said this with the intention of displeasing you, yet you should have remembered that he was your father, and have endured his angry mood calmly and in silence. 5. This is the course, which, had I been born in the same position as you, I should have had to take; but happily I have never had to undertake such a task. 6. Had the son been of the same character as the father, I might have touched his heart by prayer[3] and entreaty; but in truth he is so inhuman and cruel, that, had all mankind

---

[1] Use *adhibeō*, 'I employ, call in.' [2] See **466**, *b*. [3] Gerund.

endeavoured to soften him, no one would [1] have prevailed. 7. If you wish to see me before I leave the city, I would have [2] you write to your father not [3] to summon me to the army till you have come to Rome. 8. If you had been persuaded [3] to pardon him his offences, and not to exact punishment for so many crimes, would any [4] one impute that to you as a fault, or taunt you with your clemency and gentleness? It might perhaps have been [5] better not to have listened to him; but error is one thing, wrong-doing another.

B

1. If you fail to return at the end of a week, you will greatly injure your own [6] cause. 2. I should not have written thus [7] had I not been convinced that your father took the same view on this question as I. 3. He was a man of the highest ability and character, and of respectable, if humble, origin. 4. If I obtain my request, I shall be most grateful; if not, I will do my best [8] to bear it with resignation. 5. In the morning he [9] promised and bound himself by oath never to return from the field, unless victorious; yet [10] in the evening I saw him with my [11] own eyes walking in the park, with countenance unmoved and calm, if not cheerful. 6. Let him speak out his whole mind, his whole wishes; provided that he is silent for the future, it matters little what he says at present. 7. You shall obtain your request, but only on [12] condition that you depart at once, and never more return. 8. Whether you were absent intentionally, or by chance, concerns yourself, and is of no small importance to your own reputation; what [13] we have to decide is whether you were absent or present. If you were absent during the battle, whether it happened by design or by mere chance,

---

[1] See **115**. [2] **121**. [3] **124**, *c*. [4] **358**. [5] **463**. [6] See **356**, iii.
[7] *Haec*. So 'to act *thus*' is *haec* (or *hoc*) *facere*, never *ita agere*.
[8] See **332**, 9. [9] *Iste*. (See **338**, *Note* 2.)
[10] *Eundem* for 'yet him.' (See **366**.) [11] *Ipse*. (**355**, *Note*.)
[12] *Ita . . . ut*. (**468**, *c*.) [13] **341**.

you will be condemned, and that[1] deservedly, by a unanimous verdict; for you ought never to have[2] left the camp. 9. Whether you will do me this favour or not, I do not yet know, but whether you consent to do it or no, I shall always be grateful to you for[3] your many kind deeds, and will show my gratitude if I can. 10. Whether this bill is constitutional or unconstitutional may be questioned; but whether it is constitutional or unconstitutional, I venture to say this, that if not indispensable, it is so beneficial, so useful to the nation in the face[4] of the present crisis, that it has been approved of by every patriot.

EXERCISE LIX

CONDITIONAL CLAUSES in Ōrātiō oblīqua, etc.

469. When a Conditional Statement forms part of *ōrātiō oblīqua* in dependence on a verb of 'saying': (i) the main sentence becomes a dependent statement in the accusative and infinitive construction (see **31**); and (ii) the verb of the subordinate conditional clause, no matter whether the sentence is of Type I, II, or III (see **451-7**), is subjunctive.

470. Little difficulty should arise in converting sentences of Type I (**451**), provided the meanings of the tenses of the infinitive (**35**) are kept clearly in mind. The tense of the verb in the protasis depends on that of the verb of 'saying,' in accordance with the rule for normal sequence of tenses (**105**).

(1) Thus after a verb of 'saying' in the present or future—

Ōrātiō rēcta		*Ōrātiō oblīqua*
(*a*) *Sī hoc faciō, errō*	becomes (*dīcit*):	*sē, sī hoc faciat, errāre.*
(*b*) *Sī hoc faciēbam, errābam*	,,	[See *Note* 1.]

[1] *Idque.* (See **344.**)

[2] Tense? (**153**, *Note* 2.)

[3] *Propter tot.*

[4] **273**, *Note* 2.

Ōrātiō rēcta		*Ōrātiō oblīqua*
(*c*) *Sī hoc fēcī, errāvī*	becomes	(*dīcit*) : *sē, sī hoc fēcerit, errāvisse.*
(*d*) *Sī hoc faciam* (fut.), *errābō*	„	(*dīcit*) : *sē, sī hoc faciat, errātūrum esse.*
(*e*) *Sī hoc fēcerō, errābō*	„	(*dīcit*) : *sē, sī hoc fēcerit, errātūrum esse.*

(2) After a verb of 'saying' in a past tense :—

Ōrātiō rēcta		*Ōrātiō oblīqua*
(*f*) *Sī hoc faciō, errō*	becomes	(*dīxit*) : *sē, sī hoc faceret, errāre.*
(*g*) *Sī hoc faciēbam, errābam*	„	(*dīxit*) : *sē, sī hoc faceret, errāvisse.*
(*h*) *Sī hoc fēcī, errāvī*	„	(*dīxit*) : *sē, sī hoc fēcisset, errāvisse.*
(*i*) *Sī hoc faciam* (fut.), *errābō*	„	(*dīxit*) : *sē, sī hoc faceret, errātūrum esse.*
(*k*) *Sī hoc fēcerō, errābō*	„	(*dīxit*) : *sē, sī hoc fēcisset, errātūrum esse.*

Note 1.—In converting (*b*), it is clear that since *errābam* is prior to *dīcō*, it must be represented by *errāvisse*. But the treatment of *faciēbam* is not so obvious. If it is converted to *fēcerit*, the distinction between (*b*) and (*c*) is submerged; yet *faciat* would be illogical and meaningless; and *faceret* would violate the normal sequence of tenses. The Roman writers themselves wrote *faceret* when they felt it essential to preserve the distinction between (*b*) and (*c*); but actual instances are rare.

Note 2.—The Future Perfect in a *protasis* is represented by the Perfect Subjunctive after a present verb of 'saying' and by the Pluperfect Subjunctive after a past verb of 'saying': see (*e*) and (*k*) above.

Note 3.—The periphrasis of *fore ut* and a subjunctive (see 38) must be used in the apodosis of sentences like (*d*), (*e*), (*i*), and (*k*) above, if the verb has no future participle, and is generally used instead of the supine with *īrī* (see 403) if the verb is passive. Thus: *Nisi Caesar subvēnerit, urbs capiētur* 'unless Caesar comes to help, the city will be captured' becomes: (*Dīxit*) : *nisi Caesar subvēnisset, fore ut urbs caperētur* (rarely *urbem captum īrī*).

471. The verb in the apodosis of an Ideal Condition (Type II, **455**) becomes a Future Infinitive in *ōrātiō oblīqua*; and the protasis, in accordance with the rule for normal sequence (**105**), is Present Subjunctive after a present or future verb of 'saying,' and Imperfect Subjunctive after a past verb of 'saying.'

Thus:

Sī hoc faciam, errem 'If I were to do this, I should be wrong,' becomes:

(*a*) (*Dīcit*) *: sē, sī hoc faciat, errātūrum esse ;*

(*b*) (*Dīxit*) *: sē, sī hoc faceret, errātūrum esse.*

Note 1.—Observe that in *ōrātiō oblīqua* both (i) *Sī hoc faciam* (fut.), *errābō* and (ii) *Sī hoc faciam* (subj.), *errem* are represented by (*Dīcit*) *: sē, sī hoc faciat, errātūrum esse* or by (*Dīxit*) *: sē, sī hoc faceret, errātūrum esse ;* and consequently the distinction between them is obliterated.

Note 2.—The periphrasis of *fore ut* and a subjunctive must be used in the apodosis of a sentence of Type II if the verb has no future participle, and is generally used instead of the supine with *īrī* (see **403**) if the verb is passive. Thus—
Sī hoc faciam, pūniar becomes: (*Dīxit*)*: sī hoc faceret, fore ut pūnīrētur.*

472. The verb in the apodosis of an Unreal Condition (Type III, **457**) is represented in *ōrātiō oblīqua* by *fuisse* with the accusative of the future participle; and the tense of the subjunctive verb in the protasis is unchanged (even if the verb of 'saying' is present or future).

(*a*) *Sī hoc facerem, errārem* becomes (*Dīcit* or *dīxit*) *: sē, sī hoc faceret, errātūrum fuisse.*

(*b*) *Sī hoc fēcissem, errāvissem* " (*Dīcit* or *dīxit*) *: sē, sī hoc fēcisset, errātūrum fuisse.*

Note.—The use of *errātūrum fuisse* in *ōrātiō oblīqua* to represent *errāvissem* is something of a compromise. *Errāre* would express neither the past idea nor contingency ; *errāvisse* would express only the past idea ; and *errātūrum esse* only an idea of futurity nearly allied (within such a context) to that of contingency. The future participle with *fuisse*, therefore, is as near as Latin could possibly get to combining the two ideas in an infinitive form.

Notice however that a future participle with *erat* and *fuī* is a common substitution of an allied fact for the real apodosis in *ōrātiō rēcta* (see **463**) ; and *errātūrum fuisse* is the form which *errātūrus fuī* would properly take in *ōrātiō oblīqua.*

Note 2.—The use of *errātūrum esse* to represent *errārem* is very rare.

473. If the verb of the apodosis of a sentence of Type III has no future participle or is passive, the periphrasis *futūrum fuisse ut* with an imperfect subjunctive is used.

(*Dīcit* or *dīxit*) : *sī hoc fēcisset, futūrum fuisse ut pūnīrētur.*
(*Dīcit* or *dīxit*) : *nisi Caesar subvēnisset, futūrum fuisse ut urbs caperētur.*

Note.—Distinguish between this periphrasis and that used when the sentence is of Type I or II (see **470,** *Note* 3 and **471,** *Note* 2).

474. When a Conditional Statement of Type III is itself a Result clause, an Indirect Question, or dependent on *nōn dubitō quīn*, the tense of the protasis is unchanged (even in violation of the rule for sequence). In the apodosis also the subjunctive is unchanged except that an Active Pluperfect becomes *-ūrus fuerim.*

(*a*) *Honestum tāle est ut, vel sī ignōrārent id hominēs, esset laudābile.* Virtue is such that it would be worthy of praise even if men did not know of it.

(*b*) *Dīc mihi quidnam factūrus fuerīs, sī eō tempore cēnsor fuissēs.* Tell me what you would have done if you had been censor at that time.

(*c*) *Nec dubium erat quīn, sī tam paucī simul obīre omnia possent, terga datūrī hostēs fuerint.* There was no doubt that, if it were (and had then been) possible for so few to manage everything, the enemy would have fled.

Note.—The use of a future participle with the perfect subjunctive *fuerit* in such circumstances is a compromise analogous to the use of *-ūrum fuisse* in *ōrātiō oblīqua* (see **472**).

475. Sometimes a protasis without any expressed apodosis is used in Virtual *ōrātiō oblīqua* (**443**).

(*a*) *Mortem mihi dēnūntiāvit pater, sī pugnāssem.* My father threatened me with death if I fought.

(*b*) *Exspectābat Caesar sī hostēs posset opprimere.* Caesar was waiting in the hope of crushing the enemy.

Note.—In (*a*), *sī pugnāssem* is the protasis, not to *dēnūntiāvit* (which is quite unqualified), but to an apodosis implied in *mortem* : (*dēnūntiāvit*) *fore ut perīrem* (*sī pugnāssem*). The father's words were : *sī pugnāveris, moriēre*; and *pugnāveris* is represented by *pugnāssem.*

In (*b*), *sī posset* is the protasis, not to *exspectābat* (which is quite unqualified), but to an unexpressed apodosis that was in Caesar's mind : 'I will seize every chance (if I can crush the enemy).' *Sī*-clauses of this kind are frequently associated with verbs of expectation and endeavour (*e.g. cōnor*) ; after such verbs English uses a clause introduced by 'in case that, in the hope that.'

476. Some additional examples are added for careful observation.

1. *Dēbuistī enim, etiam sī falsō in suspīciōnem vēnissēs, mihi ignōscere.* You ought to have forgiven me (it would have been your duty to forgive me), even if you had been falsely suspected. (**461.**)
2. *Atrōx certāmen aderat, nī Fabius rem expedīvisset.* A desperate contest was at hand (would have taken place), had not Fabius solved the difficulty. (**462.**)
3. *Ibi erat mānsūrus, sī īre nōn perrēxisset.* It was there he would have stayed, had he not continued his journey. (**463.**)
4. *Quid enim futūrum fuit, sī rēs agitārī coepta esset?* What would have happened, if once the question had begun to be discussed? (**463.**)
5. *Neque hostem sustinēre poterant, nī cohortēs illae sē obiēcissent.* And they could not have maintained themselves against the enemy, but for those cohorts' exposure of themselves. (**461.**)
6. *Virginēs sī effūgissent, implētūrae urbem tumultū erant.* Had the maidens escaped, they would have spread disorder through the whole city. (**463.**)
7. *Praeclārē vīcerāmus, nisi hostēs sē recēpissent.* We should have won a splendid victory, had not the enemy retreated. (**462.**)
8. *Sī in hōc errāvī, id mihi velim ignōscās.* If I have blundered in this, I beg you to forgive me. (**452.**)
9. *Circumfunduntur hostēs sī quem aditum reperīre possent.* The enemy swarm (historic pres.) round, in hopes of finding some means of approach. (**475.**)
10. *Praemium prōposuit, sī quis ducem interfēcisset.* He offered a prize (*i.e.* said that he would give a prize) in case any one should kill the leader. (**475.**)
11. *Nūntium ad tē mīsī, sī forte nōn audīssēs.* I sent you a messenger, in case you had not heard. (We must supply *ut audīrēs.*) (**475.**)
12. *Nōn recūsāvit quōminus vel extrēmō spīritū, sī quam opem reīpūblicae ferre posset, experīrētur.* He did not flinch from trying even with his latest breath whether he could not give some aid to his country (*lit.* from making the experiment in hopes that he could). (**475.**)

Exercise 59

A

1. Did you imagine that, if all the rest were cut off either by the sword or by famine, you alone would be saved? 2. He feared, he said, that unless he consented to do everything that the king should command, he would never be allowed to return to his native land. 3. He will cheerfully bear, he says, his own destitution and that [1] of his family, if once he be freed from this degrading suspicion. 4. He warned them of the extent [2] and suddenness [2] of the crisis, saying that they could win if they were ready to show themselves brave men and worthy of their forefathers; but that if they hesitated or hung back, all the neighbouring tribes would soon be in arms. 5. He felt convinced of this, that if once he crushed the barbarians who had long been [3] infesting the mountains, the way to Italy would be open to himself and his soldiers. 6. He said that he would never have imparted this story to you, had he not when [4] leaving home promised his father to conceal nothing from such dear friends as [5] yourselves. 7. He felt convinced, he said, that unless they had placed so experienced a general as yourself at the head of a veteran army, the city would have been stormed within a week. 8. He said he would never have pardoned you so monstrous a crime, had not your aged father thrown [6] himself at his feet and implored him to spare you.

B

1. I scarcely imagine that you are at Rome; but if you are, please write to me at once. 2. If the enemy reaches the city, there will be reason [7] to fear a dreadful massacre. 3. I sent you a letter of Caesar's, in case you wished to read it. 4. He declared that it was absolutely impossible

---

[1] See **345**.

[2] See **174**, *b* and *c*.

[3] Tense? (See **181**.) Mood? (See **446**.)

[4] See **406**, *Note*.

[5] **224**, *Note* 3.

[6] See **257**. Use passive participle.

[7] 'must (*tense?*) be feared.'

for the Germans to win the day, if they engaged in battle before the new moon. 5. If you are ready to make some exertion, you will take the city. 6. If you once exert yourselves, you will take the city. 7. He said that if they once exerted themselves, they would take the city. 8. As the neighbouring tribes were all jealous of his fame, he felt that if he and his people surrendered their arms, their doom [1] was certain. 9. If anything falls out amiss,[2] we shall make you responsible. 10. He threatened him with violence and every kind [3] of punishment, if he entered the senate-house. 11. It was certainly [4] a wonderful speech; I could not imitate it if I would; perhaps I would not if I could. 12. The Dictator announced a heavy penalty in case any one should fight without his permission. 13. They feared that if they once departed without success, they would lose everything for the sake of which they had taken up arms. 14. They now at last perceived that if, at his suggestion, they had consented to abandon the popular party and join the nobles, they would have lost all their privileges and their freedom, if not their lives. 15. If you do this, you will possibly incur some loss; if you do not, you will undoubtedly have acted dishonourably; it is for [5] you to decide which of the two you prefer to do. 16. If any one evades military service, he shall be declared infamous; if any one has fears for his own safety, let him at once lay down his arms, and leave his native land safe and sound.

EXERCISE LX

CONCESSIVE CLAUSES

Quamquam, quamvīs, etc.

477. By **concessive clauses** we mean such adverbial clauses as are introduced in English by 'although' and the

[1] 'were doomed to certain destruction.'
[2] *Secus* (= otherwise than well).
[3] Simply *omnis.*
[4] *Sānē*, 'certainly,' in the sense of making an *admission.*
[5] 291, *Note* 2.

like, in Latin by the conjunctions ***etsī, tametsī, etiamsī*** 'even if'; *quamquam, quamvīs, licet* 'although.'

Such clauses are called *concessive* because they admit or *concede* something, in spite of which the statement made in the main sentence is true; its truth is emphasised by the contrast.

478. Etsī, tametsī, etiamsī are compounds of *sī* and introduce a particular kind of conditional clause (protasis) which, in its context, amounts to a concession. The use of mood and tense in such clauses is therefore governed by the principles given in **452, 456, 458.**

Etiamsī nōn adiuvēs, haec facere possim. Even if you were not to help, I should be able to do this.

Vēra loquī, etsī meum ingenium nōn monēret, necessitās cōgit. Even if my disposition did not bid me, necessity compels me to speak the truth.

Note.—*Etsī* is also used in the sense of 'although.'

Etsī mōns Cevenna iter impediēbat, tamen ad fīnēs Arvernōrum pervēnit. Although the Cevennes were in the way of his march, he reached the territory of the Arverni.

479. Quamquam (a double *quam*, 'to what extent so ever') is used to introduce a clause expressing what is admitted as a fact; the verb of such a clause is therefore indicative.

Rōmānī quamquam itinere et aestū fessī erant, tamen obviam hostibus prōcēdunt. Though the Romans were fatigued with the march and the heat, yet they advanced (historic present) to meet the enemy.

Note 1.—*Tamen*, 'yet,' 'still,' is often inserted in the main sentence to mark the contrast.

Note 2.—*Quamquam* is often used to introduce an entirely fresh sentence in contrast with what precedes it, and is then = 'and yet.'

Note 3.—The verb in a *quamquam*-clause is sometimes subjunctive in writers later than Cicero; but this usage should not be imitated.

480. (i) **Quamvīs** introduces a clause whose verb is a subjunctive of will. (See **149,** *b*.)

Quamvīs sit magna exspectātiō, tamen eam vincēs. Although expectations are great, you will surpass them.

Note 1.—*Quamvīs* = *quam vīs*, 'as you will,' was originally a separate clause, and the force of the above sentence is 'Let expectations be as great as you please, you will surpass them.'

Note 2.—*Quamvīs*, like *nisi* (**466**), is sometimes closely associated with a single word (adjective or adverb): *quamvīs audāx*, 'however bold,' 'whatever his boldness.'

Note 3.—In the poets the verb in a *quamvīs*-clause is often indicative; but this usage should not be imitated. (Compare **479**, *Note* 3.)

(ii) **Licet** 'although' is simply the impersonal verb, 'it is granted,' and is followed by a subjunctive clause without a conjunction. (See **121.**)

Licet undique pericula impendeant, tamen subībō. Though dangers threaten me on every side, I will face them.

481. Observe the following ways in which concession may also be expressed. 'Though he is an excellent man, he does wrong sometimes,' may be translated not only by: *Quamquam homō optimus est, tamen interdum peccat*, but by *Homō optimus ille quidem, sed interdum peccat* (**334**, iv); or *Ita homō optimus est ut interdum peccet*, *i.e.* 'so far only,' etc. (**111**); or *Sit* (jussive) *homō ille optimus, tamen interdum peccat.* Very commonly concession is indicated by the use of *sānē* in one clause, and an *adversative particle* in the other,—*rēs sānē difficilis, sed tamen investīganda*, 'though a difficult question, yet still one that demands investigation'; or by a participle,—*hōc crīmine absolūtus, fūrtī tamen condemnātus est*, 'though acquitted on this charge he was found guilty of theft.'

For the use of a *quī*-clause to express concession, see **510**, *b*.
,, *cum*-clause ,, ,, 435.
,, *sīcut . . . ita* ,, ,, 492 (i).

Exercise 60

1. Though he feels neither remorse nor shame for this deed, yet he shall pay me the penalty of his crime. 2. Even though it were quite impossible to pardon his fault, yet you ought [1] to have taken into account his many services to the nation. 3. Whatever his guilt,[2] whatever his faults, no one has a right to accuse him in his absence and to condemn him unheard. 4. Entirely guilty as he is, and absolutely deserving of condign punishment, yet I cannot help comparing his present fallen and low condition

---

[1] Gerundive. [2] Use adjective.

with his former good fortune and renown. 5. Miserable as it is for an innocent man to be suspected and charged, yet it is better for the innocent to be acquitted than for the guilty not to be accused. 6. However criminal he had been, however worthy of every kind of punishment, yet it would have [1] been better for ten guilty persons to be acquitted, than for one innocent man to be found guilty. 7. In spite of having had the sovereignty and supreme power offered and entrusted to him by the unanimous vote [2] of his countrymen, he long refused to take any part in politics, and was the only person in my day who attained to the highest distinctions against his will, and almost under compulsion. 8. Though [3] freed from this apprehension, I was soon suspected of a darker [4] crime, and perhaps, had you not come to my aid, I might have fallen a victim [5] to the hatred and schemes of my enemies. 9. Many [6] as are the evils that you have endured, you will one day, I still believe,[7] not only enjoy good fortune, but a rarer gift,[8] happiness.

EXERCISE LXI

CAUSAL AND EXPLANATORY CLAUSES

482. Clauses which give a **reason** or **explanation** for the statement, etc., made by the verb in the main sentence are introduced in English by 'because,' 'inasmuch as,' 'seeing that,' 'whereas,' 'considering that,' etc.

483. In Latin, the conjunctions *quod*, *quia*, 'because,' *quoniam*, *quandō*, 'since,' introduce an adverbial clause whose verb is indicative when the speaker or writer vouches for the reason.

> ***Hostēs, quoniam iam nox erat, domum discessērunt.*** The enemy, since it was now night, departed homewards.

---

[1] Mood? (153.)
[2] Number?
[3] Use a participle. (See 481.)
[4] Metaphor. (See Vocab.)
[5] Metaphor: =' been crushed by.'
[6] 'Although . . . so many.'
[7] 32, *b*.
[8] 'Gift' is a metaphor: =' that which (67) more rarely falls to men's lot.'

Note 1.—A *demonstrative* particle or phrase in the main sentence often points to the causal clause.

Idcircō (*eō, hanc ob causam*, etc.) *ad tē scrībō quod mē id facere iussistī.* The reason of my writing is that you told me to do so.

Nūllam aliam ob causam . . . quam quod, etc. The one and only cause or motive . . . is that, etc.

Note 2.—Other examples of the way in which Latin likes to bind together the parts of a complex sentence will be found in **108, 479,** *Note* **1.**

484. All these conjunctions however introduce a subjunctive clause of Virtual *ōrātiō oblīqua* (see **448**) if the speaker does not himself vouch for the reason.

Discessērunt, quoniam fessī essent. They departed because (as they alleged) they were tired.

Note.—This use of the subjunctive in a *quod*-clause is exceedingly common after words of *praising, blaming, accusing, admiring, complaining, wondering.*

Rēx cīvibus odiō erat, quod lēgēs violāvisset. The king was hated by his subjects, because (they felt that) he had broken the law.

Violāverat would be a statement made and accredited by the historian: 'for having (as, in fact, he had) broken the law.'

Mihi īrāscitur, quod eum neglēxerim. He is angry with me because (as he says *or* fancies) I have neglected him.

In *neglēxerim* the responsibility for the statement is shifted from the speaker or writer to the subject of the principal verb.

485. A reason which is mentioned only to be set aside, is introduced by *nōn quod, nōn quō*, 'not that,' *nōn quīn*, 'not but what,' and the verb is always **subjunctive.**

Sometimes the *accepted* reason follows in a clause introduced by *sed quod* and having an **indicative** verb.

Haec fēcī, nōn quō tuī mē taedeat (or *nōn quīn mē amēs*) *sed quod abīre cupiō.* I did this, not that I am tired of you (*or* not but what you love me), but because I am anxious to depart.

486. When a causal clause is introduced by **cum,** the verb is always subjunctive. (See **434.**)

Cum sīs mortālis, quae mortālia sunt, cūrā. Since you are mortal, look to the things that are mortal.

Note.—For the use of a *quī*-clause to express reason, see **510.**

487. Quod 'that' often answers to the English 'the fact that,' and introduces a noun clause whose verb is indicative. Such clauses are used (*a*) as the subject of impersonal verbs or phrases where a fact is stressed, (*b*) as the object of verbs like *addō*, *mittō*, *omittō*, *praetereō*, and verbs of 'rejoicing' and 'grieving,' and (*c*) in apposition to a preceding demonstrative.

(*a*) ***Magnum est quod victor victīs pepercit.*** It is no small thing that he spared the vanquished when victorious.

Peropportūnē accidit quod vēnistī. Your coming was very fortunate.

Accēdit quod domī nōn est. There is the additional reason that he is not at home.

(*b*) *Adde quod īdem nōn hōram tēcum esse potes.* Besides, you cannot keep your own company for an hour.

Omittō illud, quod rēgem patriamque prōdidit. I pass over the fact of his having betrayed his king and country.

Gaudē quod spectant oculī tē mīlle loquentem. Rejoice that a thousand eyes behold you as you speak.

(*c*) ***Hōc praestāmus maximē ferīs, quod loquimur.*** We excel beasts most in this respect, that we speak.

Note 1.—Such *quod*-clauses will be found very useful in translating the English verbal **substantive** of the present or perfect tense, *e.g.* 'your saying *or* having said this,' and such **abstract nouns** as 'circumstance,' 'fact,' 'reason,' 'reflection.'

Of course it cannot be used for 'that' after verbs **sentiendī et dēclārandī.** (See **32,** *a.*) *Illud dīcō, quod patriam prōdidistī* would mean, not 'I say that you have betrayed your country,' but, 'I mean the fact of your having betrayed,' etc.

Note 2.—An indicative *quod*-clause is used with *accidit* only if this verb is qualified by an adverb. See example in (*a*) above.

Note 3.—With verbs of rejoicing, etc., there is no perceptible difference between the infinitive (**41,** *c*) and the *quod*-clause: *Tē rediisse gaudeō=quod rediistī gaudeō.*

Exercise 61

1. The reason of my somewhat disliking in my youth one so attached to me as [1] your excellent relative, was that I was unable to bear his want of steadiness and principle. 2. I am hated by every [2] bad citizen for having been the

[1] **224,** and *Note* 3. [2] **375.**

very last to uphold the national cause, and because I have constantly disdained to flatter the conqueror. 3. I received [1] the thanks of parliament and the nation for having been alone [2] in not despairing of the commonwealth. 4. It was scarcely possible [3] for you not to incur the hatred [4] of your countrymen,—not that you had been guilty of betraying your country, but because you had the courage to be the advocate of a burdensome and distasteful, though [5] necessary, peace. 5. All honoured your gallant father for having sacrificed the unanimous offer [6] of a throne to the true and more substantial glory of giving [6] freedom to his country. 6. Though the whole world is angry with me for having pardoned (as they say [7]) my father's murderers, yet I shall never be ashamed of the fact that I spared the vanquished in the hour of victory. 7. As for your having still a grudge against me, under the impression [7] that six years ago I injured you in your absence and sacrificed your interests to my own gain (*pl.*), my only motive in wishing to refute such a charge is that I count your friendship worth seeking. 8. And now, in spite of his being incapable of any such baseness, he was the object of universal unpopularity, as having [7] supplied the enemy with funds, and treated the office with which the nation had entrusted him as a source of disgraceful gain.

EXERCISE LXII

COMPARATIVE CLAUSES

Proportion

488. Comparative clauses are adverbial clauses which express *likeness*, *agreement*, or the *opposite*, with what is stated, asked, or ordered, in the main sentence.

---

[1] ='thanks were returned to me by . . .'

[2] See **62**, and **484**, *Note*. [3] **132**.

[4] *Pl.*, why? Because 'countrymen' is plural.

[5] Use *sī . . . at tamen* (**466**, *b*) or *quamvīs* (**480**, *Note* 2).

[6] Same construction as that in **417**. [7] See **484**.

Instances of such clauses in English are: He acted *as I had ordered him*; Why was he treated worse *than he deserved?* Do *as I bid you*; He behaved *as though he were mad.*

In Latin the number of **conjunctions** or **conjunctional phrases** used to introduce such clauses is very large: *ut, sīcut, quem ad modum, atque (ac), quam, quasi, velut, velut sī, tamquam, tamquam sī, ac sī.* (Intr. 51.)

They correspond also to a number of **demonstrative adverbs** or phrases, such as *ita, sīc, prō eō, perinde, pariter, potius, aliter, secus,* etc., which stand to them in the same relation as *is* to *quī, tantus* to *quantus, idcircō* (or *adeō*) to *ut, tamen* to *quamquam,* etc.

489. All such clauses, both in English and Latin, fall naturally into **two classes.**

Class I.—Those in which the comparison made in the subordinate clause is *stated* as something *real*; for example :—

> He was punished as he deserved. *Perinde ac meritus est, poenās persolvit.*

Class II.—Those in which such comparison is introduced as a mere *conception* of the mind, something *imaginary* or *unreal,* not stated as a *fact*; as—

> He was punished as though he had deserved it. *Perinde ac sī (ut sī, quasi) meritus esset, poenās persolvit.*

In Class I the **indicative** is the rule (except in *ōrātiō oblīqua*), in Class II the **subjunctive.**

Class I.—Comparative Clauses (Indicative)

490. Observe that in Latin, as in English, the ideas of *likeness, equality, difference,* etc., which are often expressed by *adverbial* clauses, may also be expressed in other ways.

(i) In Latin we often have an adjectival (correlative), instead of an adverbial, clause.

> *Tanta est tempestās, quantam numquam anteā vīdī.* The storm is greater than I ever saw before, *or* is unparalleled in my experience. (See **84, 85.**)

(ii) In Latin (though not as frequently as in English) an adverbial **phrase** within a simple sentence expresses the same meaning as an adverbial **clause** of comparison.

Thus the comparison between a man's punishment and what he deserves may, in both languages, be expressed in three different ways: (1) by an *adverbial* clause; (2) by an *adjectival* clause; (3) by an *adverbial phrase* or an *adverb*.

(1) *Perinde ac meritus est, poenās persolvit.* He was punished as he deserved.

(2) *Poenās quās dēbuit persolvit.* He paid the penalty which he merited.

(3) *Prō meritīs (meritō, prō scelere) poenās persolvit.* He was punished in accordance with his guilt, *or* deservedly.

General Rule

491. In Class I, 'likeness' and 'difference' are expressed by using in the main sentence an adjective or adverb of *likeness* or *difference* and introducing the (indicative) comparative clause by *ut*, *atque*, or *quam*. Thus:

	Main Sentence	Comparative Conjunction
Likeness	*ita, sīc, perinde.*	*ut.*
	perinde, pariter, aequē, iuxtā, prō eō.	*atque.*
Difference	*aliter, secus.*	*atque.*
	contrā.	*atque, quam.*
	a comparative adjective or adverb.	*quam.*

Ut sunt, ita nōminantur senēs. Their title 'old men' corresponds to the fact.

Prō eō ac (perinde ac) dēbuī, fēcī. I have acted in accordance with my duty.

Aliter ac (nōn perinde ac) meritī sumus, laudāmur. We are not praised in proportion to our deserts.

Contrā quam pollicitus es fēcistī. You have acted in violation of your promises.

Peiōrēs sumus quam fuērunt maiōrēs. We are worse than our ancestors.

Note.—A very strong contrast may be marked by a double *aliter.*

Aliter tum locūtus es, aliter tē geris hodiē. Your behaviour to-day is most inconsistent with your language at that time.

Special Usages

492. A comparative clause introduced by **ut** 'as' may have various shades of meaning:—

(i) Sometimes the clause marks a contrast with the main sentence: 'as *or* while (see **438**, *Note* 2) one fact is true, so, on the other hand, is another,' and is virtually *concessive*.

Ut fortasse honestum est hoc, sīc parum ūtile. Though this is perhaps right, yet it is scarcely expedient.

(ii) Sometimes such a clause is used in a *restrictive* sense, and is virtually *conditional*.

Ita vīvam, ut tē amō. May I live so far only as I love you, *i.e.* may I die if I do not love you.

(iii) Or it may make a *general remark* in accordance with which a particular fact is noticed.

Tum rēx, ut erat nātūrā benignus, omnibus veniam dedit. Thereupon the king, in accordance[1] with the kindness of his nature, forgave them all.

(iv) Or it may be parenthetic: *ut fit*, 'as (often) happens'; *ut aiunt*, 'as the proverb says.'

But such parentheses as: *ut crēdō, ut arbitror, ut vidētur*, are far rarer in Latin than in English, and are used in an *apologetic* and self-depreciatory sense, 'I think,' or else are *ironical*, as is almost invariably the parenthetic *crēdō*. (See **32**, *b*.)

(v) Sometimes the verb of such a clause is not expressed when either of the two following ideas is involved:—

(*a*) 'As you would expect':

Magnus pavor, ut in rē imprōvīsā, fuit. The panic was great, as was natural in so unexpected an occurrence.

(*b*) 'So far as could be expected':

Satis intrepidē, ut in rē imprōvīsā, sē gessit. He showed considerable presence of mind, considering the unexpected nature of the occurrence.

493. Quam regularly introduces an indicative clause of comparison when the main sentence contains a comparative adjective or adverb or a word involving the idea of comparison. (See **275**.)

Nec ultrā saeviit quam satis erat. Nor did he show more severity than was necessary (*i.e.* any needless severity).

Note 1.—Frequently the verb of the comparative clause is understood from that of the main sentence.

---

[1] The same idea might be expressed by *quā erat animī benignitāte* (see **69**, *Note*), or *prō solitā eius benignitāte*, or *homō nātūrā benignissimus*. All these are substitutes for the much needed present participle of *esse*. (**224**, *Note* 2.)

Tūtior est certa pāx quam spērāta victōria. A definite peace is safer than an anticipated victory.

Note 2.—When the point of the comparison is *the degree to which* two adjectives (*or* adverbs) are applicable to a common noun (*or* verb), the comparative of one adjective (*or* adverb) is used in the main sentence and the comparative of the other in the *quam*-clause.

Pestilentia mināclor fuit quam perniciōsior. The pestilence was more alarming than fatal.

Hoc bellum fortius quam fēlīcius gessistis. You have carried on this war with more courage than good fortune.

Note 3.—Equality of degree is expressed by using *tam* with the positive of one adjective (*or* adverb) in the main sentence, and the positive of another adjective in the *quam*-clause.

Tam timidus hodiē est quam tum fuit audāx. He is as cowardly to-day as he was then bold.

Class II.—Comparative Clauses (Subjunctive)

494. To Class II belong comparative clauses of three different types :—

(i) The comparative clause is itself the protasis of a conditional statement whose apodosis is suppressed. Such clauses are introduced by *quasi*, *quam sī*, *ut sī*, *tamquam sī*, *velut sī* (or simply by *tamquam* or *velut*) ; and the main sentence contains some word which looks forward to the comparison.

Ita sē gessit quasi cōnsul esset. He behaved as though he were consul (*i.e.* as he would behave if he were consul).

Note 1.—The tense of the subjunctive in such clauses is usually determined by the rule for normal sequence (**105**), and not by the principles which apply to conditional sentences of Types II and III (**456**, **458**). But sometimes normal sequence is abandoned : *eius negōtium sīc velim suscipiās, ut sī esset rēs mea*, 'I wish you would undertake his business just as if it were my affair.'

Note 2.—*Tamquam*, *velut*, and *quasi* are often associated with a single word (noun or adjective) or phrase when the verb can be inferred from the context.

Eum tamquam pater amō. I love him as (though I were) his father.

But in : *eum tamquam hostem ōdī* 'I hate him as a public enemy,' *tamquam hostem* is used for *tamquam sī hostis sit*, and the omission of the verb has led to an adjustment of the case of *hostis*. (Compare **466**, *Note*.)

These conjunctions are constantly so used in Latin to **qualify a strong expression or metaphor**, and must often be inserted when there is nothing answering to them in English (where metaphors are much more freely used). (See **17**.)

'The soul flies forth from the prison-house of the body.' *Ē corpore, velut ē carcere, ēvolat animus.*

'Do not suffer yourself to be overwhelmed by the tide of business.' *Nēve tē obruī, tamquam flūctū, sīc magnitūdine negōtiī, sinās.*

Remember that *quīdam* (**361**, *Notes* 1, 2), *quōdammodo*, and *ut ita dīcam* are often used to qualify a metaphor.

495. (ii) The comparative clause sometimes refers to an action which is mentioned only to be rejected. Such clauses are introduced by *quam* and have a subjunctive verb; and some such word as *potius*, *prius* in the main sentence draws attention to the action which is preferred.

Dēpugnā potius quam serviās. Fight to the death rather than be a slave.

Nōs potius hostem aggrediāmur quam ipsī eum prōpulsēmus. Let us take an aggressive, rather than a merely defensive, attitude.

Note.—The subjunctive in such *quam*-clauses is *prospective* (see **441**, *Note* 2).

496. (iii) Sometimes the comparative clause itself involves the result of the action of the main sentence. Such clauses follow a comparative adjective or adverb in the main sentence and are introduced by *quam ut*.

Īsocratēs maiōre ingeniō est quam ut cum Lysiā comparētur. Isocrates is too great a genius to be compared with Lysias.

Nihil ultrā commōtus est quam ūt abīre eōs iubēret. He was only so far moved as to bid them depart.

Note.—Such clauses afford a convenient rendering for English expressions containing 'too . . . to . . .'

497. Proportion. The ideas expressed in English by a clause introduced by 'in proportion as,' by the phrase 'in proportion to,' or by a double 'the' with the comparative ('*the* more . . . *the* more'), may be best translated into Latin by one of two constructions :—

(*a*) By the use of two co-ordinate sentences which are connected by *ut* . . . *ita*, and each of which contains a superlative (see **376**).

Ut quisque est vir optimus, ita difficillimē aliōs esse improbōs suspicātur. In proportion to a man's excellence is his difficulty in suspecting others to be evil-minded, *or*: the better a man is, the greater his difficulty in, etc., *or*: those whose character is the highest will find most difficulty, etc.

(*b*) By the use of two co-ordinate sentences which are connected by *eō . . . quō* or *tantō . . . quantō*, and each of which contains a comparative.

Quō dēlictum maius est, eō poena est tardior. The greater the fault, the slower the punishment.

Note.—The ablatives *eō, quō*, etc., express the measure of difference (see **279**).

Exercise 62

The asterisk * indicates that the *phrases* are to be translated by a Latin *clause*. (See **490**, ii.)

1. The soldiers having now reached the summit of the mountain, and seeing a vast level plain, fertile territory, and rich cities spread beneath their eyes, crowded round their leader, and as though they had already triumphed over every obstacle, congratulated him on the conquest [1] of Italy. 2. He behaved differently from what I hoped and you expected. For in violation * of his repeated promises,[2] as though he made no account of the ancient tie which had long existed between his own father and mine, instead [3] of coming to my aid in my adversity, he has rejected up to this day my friendship, and has paid no attention to my more than once repeated and solemn appeals.[4] 3. May each and every one of you, when the hour of battle arrives, conduct himself in accordance * with his duty, and may each fare in accordance * with his deserts. 4. Let us endure everything rather than act in this matter contrary to * our promises. 5. We should [5] abide by the most oppressive conditions, rather than break our word and

[1] See **417.**
[2] **491**; 'repeated' will of course be turned by an *adverb.*
[3] See **398**, *Note*, and use one of the constructions given in **128.**
[4] *i.e.* 'to me more than once solemnly *appealing*.'
[5] Gerundive; and for second clause see **495.**

brand our country with dishonour. 6. Then, with his usual [1] passion and want of self-control, he ordered the ambassadors to be brought before him. As though their mere sight had added fuel to his [2] fury, after declaring that their king had acted in defiance * of his promise and oath, he ordered them to be dragged to prison. The next day he showed more gentleness than was consistent [3] with the ferocity of his language of the day before, and, after apologising for his outrage on the rights of hospitality, invited them to a banquet on [4] the next day as though he had done nothing strange [5] or unusual. Their answer showed [6] more daring than caution, considering the [7] perilous ground on which they stood. 7. Then, putting spurs to his horse, he dashed, with his usual [8] eagerness for battle, into the thick of the contest, as though it were the part of a good general to act with spirit [9] rather than with deliberation. 8. The longer the war is protracted, the more oppressive will be the conditions of peace which will be imposed upon us. Do not wonder then why the truest patriots are always the most ardent advocates of peace. 9. The more hidden a danger is, the greater will be the difficulty [10] in avoiding it, and those [11] among our enemies (*gen.*) are likely to be the most formidable who are readiest in dissembling their ill-will. 10. And it seemed to me that, considering the importance [12] of the matter, he spoke with some want of energy, as though he were ashamed to speak in the presence of the conqueror with greater warmth and emotion than became [3] either his former rank or his recent disaster.

---

[1] **492**, iii. [2] Participle of *ardeō* (with *īrā*). (**414.**)

[3] *Quam prō.* (See **332**, 7.) [4] **326.** [5] *Novus.* Case? (See **294.**)

[6] 'Showed.' Avoid *ostendit.* (See **240**, *Note* 1.) 'They answered with more daring (*adv.*) than caution.' (**493**, *Note* 2.)

[7] 'Ground,' etc., a metaphor. (See **492**, v, *b.*)

[8] Use *ut* with *semper.* (**492**, iii.)

[9] Two comparative adverbs.

[10] Substitute *adverb.*

[11] Use *ut quisque.* (**497**, *a.*) [12] *Tanta rēs.*

EXERCISE LXIII

Quī-CLAUSES WITH SUBJUNCTIVE VERB

498. (i) **Recapitulatory.**—It has been already said that when the **relative** *quī* introduces a clause which states a *fact* about the antecedent, the verb is indicative. (See **77.**)

> *Quī bonī sunt, īdem sunt beātī.* Those who are good are also happy. (**366, i.**)

(ii) It has been also pointed out that if such a clause forms part of *ōrātiō oblīqua,* the verb must be **subjunctive.** (**446.**)

(iii) Remember also that a *quī*-clause in virtual *ōrātiō oblīqua* (**448**) has a subjunctive verb.

> *Omnia, quae pater suus relīquisset, mihi lēgāvit.* He bequeathed to me everything which his father had left.

Lēgāvit means: 'he bequeathed in the terms of his will,' *quae relīquisset,* 'which the will spoke of as left by his father.'

499. The verb of a **co-ordinating** *quī*-clause (see **78**) is indicative if it states a fact.

> *Frātrem tuum, virum praeclārissimum, valdē admīror, quī brevī cōnsul fiet,* 'I profoundly admire your distinguished brother who (=and he) will soon be made consul'; but: *quī utinam brevī cōnsul fīat,* 'and may he soon be made consul.'

500. But *quī* often introduces clauses which do not simply state a fact about the antecedent, but express some *purpose, result, cause,* or *concession.*

RULE.—The verb of a final or consecutive *quī*-clause is *invariably* subjunctive; the verb of a causal or concessive *quī*-clause is *generally* subjunctive.

Final *quī*-Clauses

501. When a *quī*-clause expresses a **purpose,** the verb is always subjunctive; and the relative is equivalent to *ut is.*

> *Lēgātōs mīsit, quī pācem peterent.* He sent ambassadors to sue for peace (*lit.* who were to sue for peace).
>
> *Equitēs in castrīs relīquit, quī ērumperent.* He left cavalry behind in the camp, to make a charge.

Note 1.—If the verb in the *quī*-clause were indicative, the meaning would be quite different.

Lēgātōs mīsit, quī pācem petiērunt. He sent ambassadors, who sued for peace.

Equitēs in castrīs relīquit, quī ērūpērunt. He left cavalry behind in the camp, who made a charge.

Here *quī* is equivalent to *et iī*, 'and they.'

Note 2.—*Quō*, the ablative of the relative, is used (as the equivalent of *ut eō*) to introduce a final clause when that clause contains a comparative adjective or adverb. (See **102**.)

Consecutive *quī*-Clauses

502. When a *quī*-clause expresses a **consequence,** the verb is always subjunctive.

Habētis eum cōnsulem quī pārēre vestrīs dēcrētīs nōn dubitet. You have a consul such as does not hesitate to obey your decrees.

503. Especially common are consecutive *quī*-clauses which define a *quality* of the antecedent.

Is est quī haec dīcat. He is the sort of man to say this.

Note.—Such clauses are sometimes called **clauses of characteristic.** The action expressed by the verb is not presented *primarily* as a fact (though it may be one) but as a result of the antecedent's being the sort of person he is.

504. Such clauses are used :—

(i) After a demonstrative, especially *is*.

Ea est Rōmāna gēns quae victa quiēscere nesciat. The race of Romans is one (of a kind) that knows not how to rest under defeat.

Note.—A *quī*-clause following *is* has an indicative verb if it states a fact, a subjunctive verb if it defines a quality. Compare *Is sum quī fēcī*, 'I am the man who did it,' with *nōn is sum quī haec fēcerim*, 'I am not the sort of person to have done this.'

505. (ii) When one of the negatives *nēmō, nihil, nūllus*, or an indefinite or interrogative pronoun, or *sōlus*, or *ūnus*, is the subject of a verb indicating 'existence.'

Nēmō est (quis est ?) quī haec faciat. There is no one (who is there ?) who would do this.

Nihil est quod magis deceat quam cōnstantia. Nothing is more becoming than consistency.

Sōlus es, Caesar, cuius in victōriā ceciderit nēmō. You are the only one, Caesar, in whose victory no one has fallen.

Quotus quisque est (invenītur) quī haec facere audeat. How few there are (are met with) who venture to do this.

Note 1.—A characterising *quī*-clause is inevitable after *nēmō (nihil) est*; for a statement of fact cannot be made about what does not exist: *nēmō est quī haec facit* 'there is no one and he does this' is nonsense. Nor do indefinite and interrogative pronouns refer to any definite person about whom a *quī*-clause containing a statement of fact could be made. *Sōlus* and *ūnus* call for a clause which should define the quality in which a person is unique.

Note 2.—*Quīn* is often used instead of *quī nōn* after *nēmō est, quis est?* (Compare **134.**)

Nēmō est quīn sciat. All the world knows, *i.e.* there is no one of such a kind as not to know.

Note 3.—When the *est* in *nēmō est, quis est,* etc., is used as a link verb and not to indicate 'existence,' a following *quī*-clause is not necessarily one of characteristic. Compare *nihil est bonum quod glōriam minuat,* 'no good thing exists which lessens glory,' with *nihil est bonum quod glōriam minuit,* 'nothing is good which lessens glory (*i.e.* if it lessens glory).' Compare also *quis est quī haec dīcat,* 'who is there (=exists) who says this?' with *quis est quī haec dīcit,* 'what is the name of the man who says this?'

506. (iii) After *est (sunt)* 'there exists,' used of an indefinite subject.

Erant quī putārent. Some fancied (there were people of such a kind as to fancy).

Note 1.—*Multī sunt* also is often followed by a clause of characteristic.

Multa sunt quae mentem acuant. There are many things to sharpen the wits.

Note 2.—But *est quī, sunt quī* introduce an indicative clause if they refer to definite antecedents.

Multī (trecentī, duo, quīdam) sunt quī haec dīcunt. There are many (three hundred, two, certain) persons who say this.

507. A consecutive *quī*-clause is also used :—

(i) After *dignus, indignus, idōneus:*

Dignus est quī amētur. He deserves to be loved (*lit.* He is worthy that he should be loved).

Indignus erat cui summus honōs tribuerētur. He was not a proper person to receive the highest mark of distinction.

(ii) After **comparatives** followed by *quam:*

Quae beneficia maiōra sunt quam quibus grātiam referre possim. These favours are greater than I can requite (too great for me to requite).

508. A consecutive *quī*-clause is sometimes used in a *corrective* or *limiting* sense. (Compare **111.**)

Nēmō, quod sciam, no one to my knowledge; *nēmō, quī quidem paulō prūdentior sit,* no one, at all events no sensible man. (57, *b.*)

509. The relatival adverbs *ubi, unde,* can also be used to introduce final and consecutive clauses.

Massiliam īvit ubi exsulāret. He went to Marseilles to live in exile there.

Cupit habēre unde solvat. He wishes to have means to pay.

Note.—Contrast: *Massiliam īvit, ubi diū vīxit,* 'he went to Marseilles and lived long there.'

Exercise 63

1. Caesar, seeing that the tide of battle [1] was turning, and that he must take advantage of the critical [2] moment, sent forward all his cavalry to attack the enemy's infantry in the rear. He himself, with the rest of his soldiers, whom wounds, heat, and fatigue left [3] scarcely capable of supporting their arms, hastened to charge them in front. 2. He was one who was worthy of every kind of distinction; for no one, within my knowledge, has governed the nation in this generation, whose public services have been equal to his, and who has been satisfied with so moderate a reward for his exertions. How few there are who have been, or will be, like him. 3. The chiefs of the enemy easily perceived that in the recent rebellion and mutiny their offences had been too great [4] to be pardoned. At the same time (366), in spite of this great defeat, they were too high-spirited to ask for mercy, and too powerful to

[1] Use the phrase *rēs inclīnātur.*
[2] Simply *tempus.*
[3] Use *possum* with *prae.* (332, 6.)
[4] Use *maiōra dēlinquere,* or *peccāre.* (See 54.)

obtain it. 4. He is not, so far as I know, one who hesitates to follow his own line in a discussion, or prefers to bow to the opinion[1] of others. 5. Who is there in the whole world so stony-hearted as not to be ashamed of having, in order to please his worst enemies, abandoned his friends, and of having betrayed his country to win the favour of its most ancient foes? 6. We have[2] to carry on war with an enemy who has no respect for any treaty, or armistice, or promise, or agreement; unless we conquer him in the field, there will be nothing which can keep him back from our shores, or repel him from our walls and homes.

EXERCISE LXIV

Quī-CLAUSES: CAUSAL AND CONCESSIVE

510. Quī is also used to introduce **causal** and **concessive** clauses in which the verb is *generally* subjunctive.

(*a*) *Mē miserum, quī haec nōn vīderim!* Unhappy that I am in not having seen this!

Here the *quī*-clause is obviously **causal**=*quod haec nōn vīdī.*

(*b*) *Ego, quī sērus advēnissem, nōn tamen dēspērandum esse arbitrātus sum.* For myself, though I had arrived late (*or* in spite of my having, etc.), yet I did not think I need despair.

Here the *quī*-clause is obviously **concessive**=*quamquam sērus advēneram.*

511. Sometimes, however, a writer uses an indicative in such a clause because he prefers to emphasise the **reality** of the statement which *quī* introduces, and to leave the reader to infer the relation of **cause** or **contrast** in which it stands to the other clause.

Grātiam tibi habeō, quī vītam meam servāvistī, is as good Latin as, though less usual than, *grātiam . . . servāverīs*, for: 'I am grateful to you for having saved my life.'

So: *Caesar fertur in caelum, quī contrā tē bellum comparāvit*, 'Caesar is extolled to the skies (by you), although he (*or*, and yet he) levied war against you.' *Comparāverit* would be more usual,

[1] *Auctōritās* (=an opinion which has weight).

[2] Gerundive.

but the indicative **emphasises the fact,** and leaves the reader to draw the **contrast.**

512. An exceedingly common use of causal or concessive *quī*-clauses is to represent the **circumstances** *in which*, or *in spite of which* the action of the principal verb takes place.

Tum Caesar, quī haec omnia explōrāta habēret, redīre statuit. Then (or thereupon) Caesar, having full knowledge of all this (though he had, etc.), decided to return.

Tum ille, quī homō esset iūstissimus, etc. Then he (the other) being a just man (because he was), etc.

Note.—When a *quī*-clause is concessive, this is generally made clear by a *tamen* in the main clause.

Tum Caesar, quī hoc intellegeret, tamen redīre statuit. Then Caesar, in spite of his being aware of this, yet, etc.

513. The **causal** force of a *quī*-clause is sometimes made more clear by prefixing *quippe*, sometimes *utpote*, or *ut*.

Eum semper prō amīcō habuī, quippe quem scīrem meī esse amantissimum. I always looked on him as a friend, for I knew that he bore me the warmest affection.

Note.—Cicero always uses the subjunctive in a clause introduced by *quippe quī*; Livy uses either the indicative or the subjunctive with *quippe quī*, but is particularly fond of using *ut quī* to introduce a subjunctive clause.

Nec cōnsul, ut quī id ipsum quaesīvisset, moram certāminī fēcit. Nor did the consul, as this was the very object at which he had aimed, delay the contest.

Exercise 64

The asterisk * indicates that a causal or concessive *quī*-clause is to be used.

1. Thereupon the messenger, seeing * that it was impossible by fair [1] words to succeed in persuading the Spaniards not to advance further, aimed at producing [2] the same effect by menaces (*gerund*) and appeals to fear. The forces, he said,[3] which were gathering and concealed

[1] 'By pleading gently.'
[2] *Idem efficere.*
[3] Beware of this parenthesis. (32, *b*.)

on the other side of the mountain, were too numerous (**507**, ii) to be counted, while [1] those who were already assembled, and were visible close at hand, were veteran soldiers, too brave and well trained to be routed, as [2] the Spaniards seemed to hope, in the first onset of a single fight. 2. Who is there of you, who in any way is worthy of this assembly and this nation, that does not cherish and value highly the memories [3] of the heroes [4] of the past, even though he has never seen them?* 3. There are things which I fear still [5] more. In your absence your brother, since* his influence with your faction is unrivalled, will be still more formidable; as long as he lives, will the party [6] of disorder, do you [7] suppose, ever lack a standard round which to rally? 4. Thereupon he dismissed the council, and ordered the Indian [8] chiefs to be brought before him. The unhappy men, as * they had no suspicion of his intentions,[9] hurried in joyfully [10]; for there was none among [11] them who had any fears either for [12] his freedom or his safety, or was aware of the extent [13] of the danger which threatened them, or of the [13] character of the host with whom they were to have an interview. Even he, though * he blushed at no treachery, and felt remorse for no crime, was, it seemed, somewhat touched by the confidence and friendliness of those whom he (felt [14] that he) was on the point of betraying.

---

[1] Why not *dum*? (**438**, *Note* 2): *et* or *vērō* would do.

[2] **67**, *Note*.

[3] *Memoria* is never used in the pl.

[4] Not *hērōs*, a Greek word = demigod; say 'of illustrious men, and those (**344**) ancient (ones).'

[5] Rarely expressed in Latin.

[6] Use *improbī* (*cīvēs*); this is Cicero's usual term for those opposed to the *bonī*.

[7] Beware of this parenthesis. (**32**, *b*.)

[8] 'Of the Indians.'

[9] 'As to what he would do.' (**174**.)

[10] Adj. (**61**.)

[11] **296**.

[12] **248**.

[13] **174**.

[14] See **448**.

EXERCISE LXV

REPORTED SPEECHES IN *ŌRĀTIŌ OBLĪQUA*

514. The general principles of *ōrātiō oblīqua* have been explained in Exercises V and LVI. The present Exercise will recapitulate what has already been given, and will introduce some new points not previously mentioned.

Pronouns

515. Personal and demonstrative pronouns and possessive adjectives are adjusted to the point of view of the person making the report. In most contexts, therefore, pronouns and possessive adjectives of the third person must be substituted for those of the first and second persons. So :—

ego, nōs,	become	*sē.*
meus, noster,	,,	*suus.*
tū, vōs,	,,	*ille, illī* (or accusative if the subject of an infinitive).
tuus. vester,	,,	*illīus, illōrum.*
hic, iste,	,,	*ille* or *is* (or accusative if the subject of an infinitive).

Suppose Caesar met Pompey and said: 'I am on your side,' (*ego*) *tibi faveō.* This might be 'reported' in various ways: (i) when C. reminded P. of the incident: *dīxī mē tibi favēre*; (ii) when P. reminded C.: *dīxistī tē mihi favēre*; (iii) when C. reported it to X.: *dīxī mē illī favēre*; (iv) when P. reported it to X.: *dīxit sē mihi favēre*; (v) when X. reminded C.: *dīxistī tē illī favēre*; (vi) when X. reminded P.: *dīxit sē tibi favēre*; and (vii) when X. told Y.: *dīxit sē illī favēre.* Of all these reports, (vii) is that which is most frequently required by the circumstances.

Note 1.—The insertion of the *sē* will often be necessary where no pronoun is required in *ōrātiō rēcta*: compare *tibi parcō* with *dīxit sē eī parcere.*

Note 2.—Latin has here an advantage over English; 'I' and 'you' have, in English *ōrātiō oblīqua,* both to be expressed by *he*; hence constant obscurity. In Latin the 'I' generally becomes *sē,* the 'you' *ille.*

Note 3.—*Ille* will be in very constant use in place of *is*, as it is more distinctive, and opposes the *other party* to the speaker; sometimes, as in English, a proper name will be introduced.

Adverbs

516. When (as is usually the case) a reported speech depends on a *past* verb of 'saying,' **adverbs** of **present** time must be changed into those of **past** time, and adverbs of place must be accommodated to the sense. So:—

nunc	becomes	*tunc.*	*hīc*	becomes	*ibi.*
hodiē	„	*illō diē.*	*hūc*	„	*illūc.*
heri	„	*prīdiē.*	*hinc*	„	*ex eō locō.*
crās	„	*posterō diē.*			

Note.—There are similar changes in English. '*I* say that *I* will speak to *you now* and *here*' would in English be converted into '*He* said that *he* would speak to *them then* and *there*.'

Main Sentences

517. In all of these the **indicative** will entirely disappear.

Statements and **denials** will be expressed by the accusative and infinitive. *Nihil doleō* 'I feel no pain,' will become: *nihil sē dolēre* 'he felt no pain'; *hoc faciam* will become: *id sē factūrum esse,* etc. For the use of the tenses of the infinitive, see **35.**

Note.—A **co-ordinate** *quī*-clause also becomes accusative and infinitive.

Adsunt hostēs, īnstat Catilīna, quī brevī scelerum poenās dabit.
Adesse hostēs, īnstāre Catilīnam, quem brevī scelerum poenās datūrum esse.

518. The verb in the apodosis of a **Conditional Statement** of Types II and III, which in *ōrātiō rēcta* is a subjunctive of conditioned futurity, becomes an infinitive with subject accusative in *ōrātiō oblīqua.* (See **469-73.**)

519. Real Questions (*i.e.* those to which an answer is expected) are expressed by the **subjunctive**; and if, as is usual, the narrative is in past time, the necessary adjustment of tense is made.

Nōnne audītis? will become: *nōnne audīrent?*
Quid vultis? quid optātis? will become: *Quid vellent? quid optārent?*

520. Deliberative Questions (see **149**, *Note* 2) remain in the **subjunctive**; but the *tense* is altered if, as is usual, it is necessary.

Quid faciam? 'what am I to do?' after *dīxit* will become: *quid faceret?* 'what was he to do?'

Quō eāmus? 'whither are we to go?' will become: *quō īrent?* 'whither were they to go?'

Note.—In *ōrātiō oblīqua* the distinction between 'what am I doing' (*quid faciō*) and 'what am I to do' (*quid faciam*) is obscured, since both become *quid faciam* or *quid facerem*. But see **521**, *Note.*

521. But **Rhetorical Questions** (*i.e.* those that do not expect an answer) are expressed by the accusative and infinitive.

Ecquis umquam eius modī mōnstrum vīdit? 'Did any one ever see such a monster?' will become: *Ecquem umquam eius modī mōnstrum vīdisse?*

Num haec tolerāre dēbēmus? will become: *Num illa sē tolerāre dēbēre?*

Note.—A deliberative question of *ōrātiō rēcta* may be represented in *ōrātiō oblīqua* by a rhetorical question containing a gerundive (**388, 389**). *Quō eāmus* 'where are we to go' may become: *quō sibi eundum esse?* (See **520**, *Note.*)

522. Commands, prohibitions, and **wishes,** expressed in *ōrātiō rēcta* by the imperative or subjunctive, will be expressed by the **subjunctive** with the necessary alteration of **tense** and **person.**

Ōrātiō rēcta	*Ōrātiō oblīqua* (after *dīxit*)
Festīnāte; utinam salvī sītis.	*Festīnārent; utinam salvī essent.*
Nōlīte cūnctārī; nē dēspexeris.	*Nē cūnctārentur; nē dēspiceret.*

Note.—The **hortative** 1st person (and even other forms of command) is often represented by a dependent statement in which the obligation is expressed by the gerundive (**388, 389**).

Nihil temere agāmus, may become: *nihil sibi temere agendum esse.*

Subordinate Clauses

523. Moods.—An accusative and infinitive construction of *ōrātiō rēcta* is retained in *ōrātiō oblīqua*; but the verb of all other subordinate clauses is subjunctive. (See **446.**)

Note 1.—Remember that a *quī*-clause which is equivalent to a co-ordinate sentence becomes an accusative and infinitive. (See **517**, *Note*.)

Note 2.—A historic present indicative in a *dum*-clause is retained in *ōrātiō oblīqua*. (See **438**, *Note* 1.)

Note 3.—Explanatory parentheses of the writer, such as are mentioned in **449**, form no part of *ōrātiō oblīqua*.

524. Tenses.—The tenses of the subjunctive depend, in general, on that of the verb of 'saying,' according to the rule for normal sequence (**105**).

Note 1.—But an imperfect or pluperfect subjunctive in the protasis of a Conditional Sentence of Type III (**458**) is retained even though the verb of 'saying' is present. (See **472**.)

Note 2.—The future perfect indicative becomes perfect subjunctive after a present verb of 'saying,' and pluperfect subjunctive after a past. (See **470**, *Note* 2.)

525. After a past verb of 'saying,' the exclusive use of imperfect and pluperfect subjunctives is grammatically correct, and conforms to the practice of Cicero. But (in Livy especially) a present subjunctive is frequently used (instead of an imperfect) when the *ōrātiō rēcta* had a present indicative, and a perfect subjunctive (instead of a pluperfect) when the *ōrātiō rēcta* had a perfect indicative. This usage, which gives a greater liveliness to the reported speech by retaining at least the tenses used by the speaker, is called **repraesentātiō**.

> *Dīxērunt indignum vidērī ab eīs sē obsidērī quōrum exercitūs saepe fūderint.* They said that it seemed degrading to be besieged by men whose armies they had (*lit.* have) often routed.

In *ōrātiō rēcta* the word used would have been *fūdimus*—'we have routed.'

526. The following example of *ōrātiō oblīqua* should be carefully studied :—

Away then with such follies! Do you not see that your liberty and lives are at stake to-day! Why do you obey a few centurions, still fewer tribunes, who can do nothing against your will? When will you dare to demand redress? It is of the utmost importance what you do. Awake at last, and follow me! Remember the ancestors from whom you are sprung. If you let slip this opportunity, you will deservedly be slaves, and no one will give you a thought, or feel compassion for your present condition.

Ōrātiō rēcta	*Ōrātiō oblīqua*
Pellantur igitur, inquit, ineptiae istae; nōnne vidētis dē lībertāte, dē vītīs vestrīs, agī hodiē? Cūr paucīs centuriōnibus, pauciōribus tribūnīs, quī nihil invītīs vōbīs facere possunt dictō audientēs estis? quandō remedia exposcere audēbitis? Maximī quid faciātis rēfert. Expergīsciminī aliquandō, et mē sequiminī. Maiōrum quibus ortī estis reminīsciminī. Hanc occāsiōnem si praetermīseritis, meritō serviētis, nec quisquam vel ratiōnem vestrī habēbit, vel istīus fortūnae miserēbitur.	(*Dīxit*): *Pellerentur igitur ineptiae illae; nōnne illōs vidēre dē lībertāte ipsōrum, dē vītīs, eō diē agī? Cūr paucīs centuriōnibus, pauciōribus tribūnīs, quī invītīs illīs nihil facere possent, dictō audientēs essent? quandō remedia exposcere ausūrī essent? Maximī rēferre quid facerent. Expergīscerentur aliquandō, et sē sequerentur. Maiōrum quibus ortī essent reminīscerentur. Eam occāsiōnem si praetermīsissent, meritō servītūrōs esse, nec quemquam vel ratiōnem eōrum habitūrum esse vel fortūnae illīus miseritūrum.*

Exercise 65

A

The following sentences are all to be converted into *ōrātiō oblīqua*; the tenses to be altered throughout from *primary* to *historic*. It may be well to begin by converting the sentences into English *ōrātiō oblīqua*.

1. Can any [1] one endure this? Ought we to abandon this great undertaking? It would have been better to fall on the field with honour, than to submit to such slavery. 2. Do not delay then; a few soldiers will suffice. We have no other allies anywhere, no other hopes; whither can we turn if you should abandon us? But if you wish for our safety, you must away [2] with all niceties of argument [3]; it is haste, not deliberation, that is needed. 3. What are you doing? what are you wishing for? Are you waiting till the enemy is at hand, till you hear their shouts,

[1] Use *ecquis*. [2] Use *pellō*. (See 526.) [3] Gerund.

till you see their standards ? Even now [1] resistance is possible, provided you do not linger or hesitate. 4. It is possible that I on my part [2] have made the same mistake as you ; if the case is so, I pray, forget the past,[3] and in union with your king consult the national interests. Is there any thing in the world which we ought to value more highly ? 5. What am I to do in this crisis ? Do you bid me to go to meet the enemy ? I would do so most gladly, if it could be done without ruin to the nation. But what could be more foolish, what more fatal, than with an army of recruits to engage in conflict with veteran soldiers trained in twenty years [4] of battle ? 6. How many of you are there, whence do you come, and what do you demand or hope for ? When do you expect to be allowed to enjoy freedom, (and) to return home ? Possibly the time is even now at hand, provided you do not let slip the opportunity or injure your cause by putting off the contest. But if you refuse to take up arms till [5] I assist you, you will ruin the common cause, and sigh in vain for the [6] freedom which brave men assert by arms.

B

To be translated into *ōrātiō oblīqua* after *dīxit.*

In vain therefore do you appeal to Spain.[7] It makes no difference whether you intend to make an alliance with the rebels, or to threaten them with war. I shall neither rely on your friendship, nor dread your enmity. For what could be more despicable than your policy and schemes, seeing that within the last five years you have thrice abandoned your allies, twice joined your enemies like [8] deserters, and have not sent ambassadors to me to sue for a peace of which you are unworthy, until [9] you

---

[1] See **516.** [2] See **355,** *Note* 1. [3] Use *rēs.*
[4] 'Battles of twenty years.' (See **303,** *Note* (i).)
[5] *Prius . . . quam.* (**443,** 1.) [6] **348.**
[7] **319.** [8] *Velut.* [9] **443,** *Note.*

have made sure that, unless you can get over this danger with our aid, you are doomed to inevitable destruction? Would any one have put trust in such allies? Would any one in the future feel gratitude to such friends? If you wish to find a remedy and shelter against[1] your present[2] dangers, return home, lay down your arms, throw open the gates of your cities and strongholds, and place yourselves at the mercy of the sovereign against whom you have been so long waging an unnatural war. Possibly I may be touched by your prayers; I shall pay no attention to your envoys and orations.

EXERCISE LXVI

NUMERALS

527. Numerals are in Latin, as in English, mainly **adjectives** and **adverbs.**

Cardinal numerals answer the question 'how many?' *quot?*

Ūnus, duo, trēs, quattuor; ūndecim, duodecim, tredecim (decem et trēs); duodēvīgintī (decem et octō), ūndēvīgintī (decem et novem); vīgintī, ūnus et vīgintī (vīgintī ūnus), duodētrīgintā (28), *quadrāgintā, nōnāgintā octō (octō et nōnāgintā), centum (et) ūnus* (101); *ducentī (-ae, -a), trecentī (-ae, -a), quadringentī, quīngentī, sescentī, septingentī, octingentī, nōngentī, mīlle, duo mīlia, ūnum et vīgintī mīlia, centum mīlia, quīngenta mīlia, deciēns centēna mīlia* (1,000,000). The full list will be found in any Grammar.

528. The **first three** are (as in many kindred languages) declinable *adjectives*; the rest, including *vīgintī*, are indeclinable up to *ducentī* (*-ae, -a*): this, and the series of hundreds, are plural declinable adjectives; *mīlle* is an indeclinable adjective in the singular (*exercitus mīlle mīlitum*, 'an army *of* 1000'), but it is declined in the

[1] See 300. [2] *Hic* in *ōrātiō rēcta.* (337.)

plural and is used as a **noun** (*cum duōbus mīlibus mīlitum*).

As in English, so in Latin, a compound number from 20 to 100 may be arranged in two ways, 'one-and-twenty' or 'twenty-one'; above 100 the higher number stands first; 28,455 is *duodētrīgintā mīlia quadringentī quīnquāgintā (et) quīnque.*

529. Notice the following uses of *ūnus:*

(*a*) It often represents the English 'one of' (a class) without any stress on the numeral: *ūnus ex captīvīs*, 'one of the prisoners.'

(*b*) In the predicate it often answers to our 'belonging to the class of': *ūnus ex fortūnātīs hominibus esse vidētur*, 'he seems to be one of (*i.e.* to belong to the number of) fortune's favourites.'

(*c*) 'One or two' is *ūnus vel (aut) alter, ūnus alterve.*

(*d*) *Ūnus* is often used emphatically for *sōlus*: *ūnus maiōra fēcistī quam cēterī omnēs*, 'you by yourself have done greater things than all the rest.'

(*e*) It is used to strengthen *quisque*; *ūnus quisque*, 'each one, each and every' (373).

(*f*) It emphasises **superlatives.** *Ducem praestantissimum āmīsimus*, 'we have lost one of our best leaders, *or* a distinguished leader,' but *Ducem ūnum praestantissimum āmīsimus*, 'we have lost the very best of our leaders.'

(*g*) *Nōn ūnus* is not the equivalent of *nūllus*; it means 'more than one'; *nōn ūnō proeliō dēvictus sum*, 'I have been overcome in several battles.' 'Not one' is *nē ūnus quidem.*

530. Ordinal numerals answer the question 'in what order?' *quotus?*

They are all *declinable adjectives*; only a few will be enumerated. *Prīmus* (or *prior*); *secundus* or *alter*; *tertius decimus* (13th), *duodēvīcēnsimus* (*octāvus decimus*) (18th), *ūnus* (*prīmus*) *et vīcēnsimus* (21st), *ūndētrīcēnsimus* (29th), *alter* (*secundus*) *et trīcēnsimus* (*trīcēnsimus alter*) (32nd), *quadrāgēnsimus* (40th), *quīntus et nōnāgēnsimus* (*nōnāgēnsimus quīntus*) (95th), *centēnsimus prīmus* (*prīmus et centēnsimus*) (101st), *millēnsimus*, *bis millēnsimus* (2000th), *deciēns millēnsimus* (10,000th), *semel et vīciēns millēnsimus* (21,000th), etc.

531. Notice that: (*a*), as in English, the two first **ordinals** are not derived from the corresponding **cardinals**; and that *alter* is largely used for 'second.' *Secundus* is rather 'following' next in *time* or in *rank.*

Alter īdem is 'a second self'; *alterō tantō*, 'by as much again.'

(*b*) *Ūnus* often takes the place of our 'first' in enumerating.

Huius reī trēs sunt causae, ūna, altera (or *alia*), *tertia*: 'first, second, third.'

(*c*) The ordinal is often used in reckoning a period of time.

Ūndēvīcēnsimum iam annum bellum gerēbātur. The war had now been going on for 19 years. (See **321**, *Note* 2.)

(*d*) The ordinal is always used in giving *dates*; and the point from which the reckoning commences is expressed by the ablative with *ā*.

Annō ab urbe conditā millēnsimō. In the 1000th year after the foundation of the city.

532. The **Distributive** numerals answer the question 'how many at a time?' *quotēnī?* or 'how many each?' Among these are—

Singulī, bīnī, sēnī (6); *ternī dēnī* (13); *vīcēnī singulī* (21); *centēnī, singula mīlia, centēna mīlia.*

(*a*) *Ex singulīs* (or *bīnīs*) *familiīs singulōs* (*bīnōs, ternōs*) *obsidēs ēlēgimus.* We selected one (two, *or* three) hostages from each separate household (*or* each pair of households).

(*b*) They are also used instead of **cardinal** numerals with words that have no singular; but *ūnī* (*-ae, -a*) takes the place of *singulī* in such circumstances.

In ūnīs aedibus bīnae fuēre nūptiae. There were two weddings in one house.

(*c*) For the special uses of *singulī* as opposed to *ūniversī* and *singulāris*, see **380, 381.**

533. The numeral **adverbs** answer the question, 'how often?' 'how many times?' *quotiens?* Such are—

Semel, once; *bis*, twice; *ter*, thrice; *sexiēns*, 6 times; *ter deciēns*, 13 times; *vīciēns*, 20 times; *bis et vīciēns*, 22 times; *trīciēns*, 30 times.

Sexiēns cōnsul factus est. He was made consul six times (but: *sextum*, for the sixth time; see **534.**)

(*a*) They are coupled with *distributives* in the multiplication table.

Bis bīna sunt quattuor. Twice two is four.

(*b*) Distinguish between *bis* 'twice,' 'on two occasions,' and *iterum* 'a second time.' 'Once or twice' is *semel et iterum*; 'once and again,' 'more than once,' is *semel ac saepius*; 'again and again,' is *saepissimē.*

534. Ordinal adverbs of time are *prīmum*, *iterum*, *tertium*, etc., 'for the first, second, third, time,' etc. Except *iterum*, they are the neut. acc. of ordinal numerals (**530**).

Iterum (*quārtum*) *cōnsul factus est.* He was made consul for the (second *or* fourth) time.

Tum prīmum iūstō proeliō interfuit. That was the first occasion on which he took part in a regular engagement.

Note.—'In the first place,' 'secondly,' 'lastly,' are expressed in a narrative or argument by: *prīmō* (or *prīmum*); *deinde* (*deinceps*), *tum*, or *post*; *dēnique*, *postrēmō*, *ad extrēmum*.

535. Fractions are expressed thus:

(*a*) One-half, *dīmidium* or *dīmidia pars*.

(*b*) Others, where the *numerator* is 1, by ordinals with *pars*: $\frac{1}{3}$, *tertia pars*, $\frac{1}{1000}$, *millēnsima pars*; 'tithes,' *decumae* (*i.e. partēs*).

(*c*) $\frac{2}{3}$, *duae partēs*; $\frac{3}{4}$, *trēs partēs*; $\frac{3}{5}$, *trēs quīntae* (*i.e. partēs*).

(*d*) *Dīmidio plūrēs*, 'half as many again'; *duplō plūrēs* 'twice as many.'

Dīmidium exercitūs quam quod accēperat, redūxit. He brought back half the army which he had received.

536. (*a*) The cardinal numerals, like many adjectives, can be used as nouns and be defined by a partitive genitive or by the ablative with *ex*.

Ducentī mīlitēs 'two hundred soldiers,' and *ducentī mīlitum* (or *ex mīlitibus*) 'two hundred of the soldiers.'

(*b*) *Mīlia* is sometimes used in apposition; so either *nostrōrum duo mīlia* or *nostrī duo mīlia*.

(*c*) When *mīlia* refers to men, a predicative adjective or participle is sometimes masculine: *peditēs duo mīlia caesī sunt*.

(*d*) Approximation to a number is expressed by *ad* with the accusative.

Cum annōs ad quadrāgintā nātus esset. . . . When he was about forty years old. . . .

But sometimes *ad* is used *adverbially* with a numeral: *occīsis ad hominum mīlibus quattuor* (Caesar); *ad duo mīlia et trecentī occīsī* (Livy).

(*e*) In comparisons involving numerals, *quam* is often omitted after *plūs*, *minus*, *amplius*, and *longius*. (See **275**, *Note.*)

(*f*) *Sescentī* is often used for any large indefinite number.

Exercise 66

A

1. In his ninety-second [1] year he was still [2] able to answer those who [3] asked his opinion. 2. I ask first whence you come, secondly, whither you are going, thirdly, why you are armed, lastly, why you are in my house. 3. The generals met at the river side, each with an interpreter and ten soldiers. 4. One, two, three days had now passed, yet [4] no agreement had been come to as regards the conditions of peace. 5. In prosperity I thought your father one of Fortune's favourites; in these dark [5] days I see that he belongs, and always has belonged, to the class of great men.[6] 6. He stayed at Milan, one of the richest and most populous of cities, one or two days; yet out of 100,000 citizens, not one thanked him for the preservation [7] of the city and the repulse of the enemy from its walls; and perhaps [8] not one single soul felt the gratitude which he owed. 7. There has been a disastrous [9] battle; 2500 [10] of our men have been slain. It is said that half as many again are taken prisoners, and that one or two of [11] the four generals are missing. 8. We have lost an excellent man, if not the very best of his class, yet at all events one of those who come but once [12] in a generation. 9. I have received two [13] letters from you to-day, one yesterday; the rest I have looked for in vain, though I have waited for them one or two days, and sent to enquire,[14] not once,[15] but twice. 10. This is the nineteenth day from the commencement of the siege. The commander of the garrison is demanding two hostages from every [16] household, to pre-

---

[1] Either: . . . *annō aetātis*, or as in 327.
[2] 'Still' need not be expressed.
[3] Part. pres. (413.)
[4] *Nec tamen quidquam.*
[5] Simply *tempora*.
[6] Use *vir* with *summus*.
[7] See 417.
[8] Use *haud scio an*. (169.)
[9] Impersonal, 218.
[10] 536, *c*.
[11] *Ex*, *ē*.
[12] 380, *a*.
[13] 532, *b*.
[14] Supine of *sciscitārī*. (402.)
[15] 533, *b*.
[16] 532, *a*.

vent [1] any rising on the part of the townspeople, who are mostly [2] armed and who outnumber his troops by two to one.

Exercise 66

B

At the age of scarcely nineteen he had again and again taken part in regular engagements, and had more than once slain an enemy in single combat, and was now [3] on the point [4] of engaging an army half as large again as that which he [5] commanded. Yet in the face of such a crisis, he did not hesitate to detach more than 1600 infantry to defend [6] his allies against an irruption of the Indians, although two-thirds of his army consisted of recruits,[7] who [8] were now to fight their first battle. But he preferred to die a thousand [9] deaths, rather than turn his back on barbarian foes, who if once they won the day would, he well [10] knew, afflict his country with every kind of wrong.

EXERCISE LXVII

THE ROMAN CALENDAR

537. The Roman months consisted (after the reform of the Calendar by Julius Caesar) of the same number of days as the English months; but the days were numbered quite differently.

538. The *first* day of the month was called *Kalendae* (the **Kalends**); the **Nones** (*Nōnae*) fell on the *fifth* or

---

[1] 'That no rising of . . . may take place.'

[2] Use *plērīque* in app.; often so used where *the whole* and a *part* are not contrasted. (297.)

[3] 328, *b*.

[4] Use fut. participle.

[5] 356, i.

[6] 'To repel from his allies.'

[7] *Tīrō mīles*, sing. (223, *Note* 2.)

[8] Use fut. participle.

[9] 536, *f*.

[10] 32, *b*.

seventh ; the **Ides** (*Īdūs, -uum, f.*) were always eight days after the **Nones**, that is, the *thirteenth* or *fifteenth*.

'In March, July, October, May,
The Nones were on the seventh day.'

(The **Ides** therefore on the 15th.)

To these three names of days, the names of the months were attached as *adjectives* [1]: *ad Kalendās Maiās*, 'by the 1st of May' (326) ; *in Nōnās Iūniās*, 'for the 5th of June'; *Īdibus Mārtiīs*, 'on the 15th of March.'

539. The other days of the month were indicated by reckoning *backwards*, and *inclusively*, from these three fixed points, *i.e.* both days were counted in.

Days between the Kalends and the Nones were reckoned by their distance from the Nones; those between the Nones and the Ides by their distance from the Ides; those after the Ides by their distance from the Kalends of the *following month*.

To suit this Roman way of reckoning, we must subtract the given day from the *number of the day* on which the Nones or Ides fall *increased by one*. If the day be one before the Kalends, we must subtract from *the last day* of the month *increased by two*, as the Kalends fall within the next month.

Thus take the 3rd, 9th, 23rd of June :—

(1) In June the Nones are on the *fifth* ; therefore three must be subtracted from *six* (5+1) ; and the remainder being 3, the day is 'the *third* day before the *Nones* of June.'

(2) In June, the Nones being on the *fifth*, the Ides are on the *thirteenth*, and the subtraction must be from *fourteen*; Hence subtract 9 from 14 ; the remainder being 5, the day is the *fifth* day before the Ides of June.

---

[1] These forms are, *Iānuārius, Februārius, Mārtius, Aprīlis, Maius, Iūnius, Quīntīlis* (or *Iūlius*), *Sextīlis* (or *Augustus*), *September, Octōber, November, December*. The last four are adj. of 3rd decl. (gen. *-bris*.)

The months of July and August were called *Quīntīlis, Sextīlis*, respectively (=the *fifth* and *sixth* month, reckoning from March, the old beginning of the year), till those names were altered to *Iūlius* and *Augustus* in honour of the first two Caesars.

(3) Since June has *thirty* days, we must subtract from *thirty-two.* Hence subtract 23 from 32; the remainder being 9, the day is the *ninth* day before the *Kalends of July.*

So December 30th is not the *second,* but the *third* day before the Kalends of January.

540. A date such as 'on the 29th of April' may be expressed in several ways :—

(*a*) by the ablative of time : *tertiō diē ante Kal. Maiās.*

(*b*) as in (*a*) except for the conventional omission of *diē* and *ante* : *tertiō Kal. Maiās.*

(*c*) most commonly in Cicero and Livy by : *ante diem tertium Kal. Maiās,* shortened to *a. d. iii Kal. Mai.*[1]

This *ante-diem* phrase came to be treated as an indeclinable substantive, and the prepositions *ad, in, ex* were prefixed to it, as to other substantives of time : *ad a. d. iv Kal. Oct.* 'up to the 28th of September.'

The last day of the month is *prīdiē Kalendās.*

The following are examples.

1. *Nātus est Augustus ix Kal. Oct.* (*nōnō Kalendās Octōbrēs*), *i.e.* on the 23rd of September.
2. *Kalendīs Augustīs nātus est Claudius, iii Īd. Oct.* (*tertiō Īdūs Octōbrēs*) *excessit.* (1st of August and October 13th.)
3. *Meministī mē a. d. xii Kal. Nov. sententiam dīxisse in senātū?* Do you remember my speaking in the Senate on the 21st of October?
4. *Quattuor diērum supplicātiō indicta est ex a. d. v Īd. Oct.* A four days' public thanksgiving has been proclaimed from the 11th of October.
5. *Cōnsul comitia in a. d. iii Nōn. Sext. ēdīxit.* The consul fixed the 3rd of August for the elections.

---

[1] The explanation usually given for this strange construction is that originally the expression was *ante diē tertiō Kal.,* in which *ante* was a preposition associated with *Kalendās* and *tertiō diē* either a (parenthetic) ablative of measure of difference 'by the third day,' or an ablative of time at which 'on the third day'; and that through the proximity of the ablative to *ante* it was changed to the accusative.

6. *In ante diēs octāvum et septimum Kalendās Octōbrēs comitiīs dicta diēs.* The dates fixed for the elections are the 24th and 25th of September.

Exercise 67

1. We have been looking for you day [1] after day from the third of March to the tenth of April. Your father and I [2] begin to fear that something has happened amiss. 2. Your father parted from us at [3] Rhodes on the 14th of July; he seemed to be suffering seriously both from sea-sickness and home-sickness. We have not [4] yet received any letter from him, but we hope that he will reach home safe and sound by [5] the twelfth of August. The day after [6] he left us we heard that he ought to have started three days earlier [7] if he wished [8] to be at home in good time. 3. You promised six months ago to stay in my house [9] from the 3rd to the 21st of April. I hope that you will do your utmost to keep your word; you have been looked for now these ten [10] days. 4. Instead of keeping his word by starting to his father at Rome on the last day of August, he preferred to linger in the fair city [11] of Naples for over twenty days. He scarcely reached home by the 25th of September; a circumstance [12] of which he repented, I believe, from that day to the latest day of his life.

---

[1] 328, *c.* [2] See 26, *footnote.* [3] See 315.
[4] *Nūllus adhūc.* (See 328, *d.*) [5] *Ad.* (326.)
[6] 323, *b.* [7] 322, *a.*
[8] Mood? [9] 316, iii. [10] 321, *Note* 2.
[11] 317. [12] *Quae rēs.* (67.)

APPENDIX

CONTINUOUS PROSE COMPOSITION

PRELIMINARY HINTS

The sentences contained in the preceding Exercises have been intended, in the main, to provide the student with opportunities for practice in those grammatical points with which a particular Exercise was concerned. The student's chief task, therefore, has been to apply the grammatical knowledge recently acquired, and he has been in no doubt about the problem he had to solve. Furthermore, the footnotes often gave additional help and warnings and frequently reminded him about other matters which he had previously learned but might have forgotten.

The continuous passages of English given in this Appendix differ from the earlier Exercises in two important ways. Firstly, the student is offered no guidance about the constructions he should use; he has now to decide for himself what Latin constructions will best express the meaning of the English; and when, as sometimes is the case, there are two or more possible ways of expressing what is required, he must make his own choice. Secondly, the sentences are not detached from one another in thought. Each passage is a unity and must be rendered into Latin in a way which will not obscure the sequence of ideas. The manner in which the first sentence of such a passage is rendered may influence the manner of rendering the following sentences. Not infrequently it will be found that more satisfactory Latin will be written if several English sentences are combined into a single period. Consequently it may be taken as a golden rule, never to be broken, that before commencing to translate any continuous passage of English, we should read it through carefully to grasp the full meaning of the whole and the relation between the separate sentences; and before writing a single word of Latin, we should consider how far we intend to combine the English sentences into periods, and what constructions we propose to use.

When translating a continuous passage of English into Latin, the student should set before himself, as his ideal, the writing of a piece of Latin which would have been intelligible, and perhaps even pleasing, to a Roman. To achieve this aim, constant attention must be paid to three things :—

(i) correctness of expression ;
(ii) lucidity of thought ;
(iii) elegance of style.

Correctness in accidence, in syntax, and in choice of words is obviously of fundamental importance ; and the previous Exercises will already have helped the student to make progress in this direction. But it is possible to compose a series of sentences in none of which there is anything contrary to the rules of syntax or unusual in vocabulary, and yet to leave the passage obscure and difficult to understand as a whole. Such obscurity arises, for example, when the sequence of thought and the relation of one sentence to another have been neglected, or when the separate clauses of a compound sentence have not been arranged harmoniously. The lucidity of a Latin rendering can often be tested by asking oneself whether one would have been able to translate it easily into English if it had been set as an exercise in Latin unseen translation.

Elegance of style is a virtue which comes only with practice and experience, and it can be built only on the sure foundation of correctness and lucidity. Remember that elegance is not synonymous with over-elaboration ; and a false elegance which is achieved at the expense of correctness or lucidity is to be avoided at all costs. From the very first, however, the student should endeavour to avoid such obvious faults of style as the following :—

(i) an unrelieved series of simple or co-ordinate sentences ;
(ii) the monotonous use of one or two constructions ;
(iii) combinations of words which would give an ugly sound ;
(iv) needless changes of subject in neighbouring clauses or sentences ;
(v) strings of relative clauses all relating to the same antecedent or depending one upon another ;
(vi) ill-balanced sentences in which some trailing subordinate clause makes the reader lose the thread of the main sentence.

When you have finished a Latin composition, ask yourself whether a listener could reasonably be expected to understand it if you read it aloud to him; that will provide a simple test both of lucidity and of elegance.

The following paragraphs contain a number of hints and warnings arranged under a few general headings. The student will find it well worth while to read them through before commencing a continuous prose passage; it will be worth his while to glance at them again before putting the finishing touches to a composition; and he should not cease to read them until he can trust himself to apply them automatically.

(i) **Avoid errors of syntax.** No one would deliberately contravene the rules of Latin syntax; but when one is occupied with all the little problems which arise in rendering a piece of English into Latin, it is very easy to forget some of the most elementary matters and to neglect some of the most striking differences between English and Latin syntax. Preoccupation with the meaning of the English often causes slips in Latin grammar, and no piece of Latin composition should be regarded as finished until the work has been checked, word by word, for possible grammatical blunders. The errors which most frequently occur are those which arise from a temporary forgetfulness of the following ten points :—

(i) Many Latin verbs take a dative though their English equivalents are transitive (see **5**; **242–8**). The verbs *faveo, ignosco, irascor, parco,* and *servio* are frequent pitfalls.

(ii) Verbs which take a dative are not used personally in the passive (see **217**).

(iii) Verbs of 'saying' and 'thinking' are used personally in the passive (see **43**).

(iv) Latin frequently employs the imperfect indicative, the future, and the future perfect where English does not (see **183–5**; **189–92**).

(v) Present participles, especially when in the nominative case, generally have a definite temporal significance and are not used vaguely like the English present participle (see **410–12**).

(vi) Past participles are not active in meaning unless they are derived from deponent verbs; and future participles are not passive in meaning (see **415–18**).

(vii) The uses of *sive . . . sive, utrum . . . an,* and *aut . . . aut* are quite distinct (see **467** *Note*).

(viii) The presence of an indirect question is not always obvious from the English (see **166**).

(ix) *Oratio Obliqua* is often introduced into a narrative passage, even in English, without any introductory verb of 'saying' (see **444**, *footnote*).

(x) The poets use a number of constructions which are not found in the best Latin prose writers and should not be imitated.

You will find it useful to keep a small book in which to make a note of words, phrases, and constructions which your own experience indicates as stumbling-blocks.

(ii) **Avoid poetic, unusual, or late words.** (i) In the course of reading Latin poetry the student becomes acquainted with a number of words which are not commonly used, if at all, in the best prose writers. The poets, for example, use *ensis* where prose writers use *gladius*; *sonipes* for *equus*; *pontus*, *pelagus*, or *aequor* for *mare*; *inclutus* for *praeclarus*; *longaevus* for *senex*. The poets select such words because they do not carry with them the commonplace associations of prose; and if we introduce them into a Latin prose passage we create as stilted an effect as we should by using 'steed,' 'agèd sire,' or 'trusty blade' in a piece of English.

(ii) Unusual words like *iactator* 'a boaster,' and late words like *politicus*, sometimes find their way into a composition when the student has had recourse to an English-Latin dictionary or some similar aid (see § x below). So far as possible, the student should confine himself to the vocabulary he has acquired in his reading of Latin prose authors; and he should never use a word which is not familiar to him unless he has taken the trouble to ascertain that it is employed by Caesar, or by Cicero (in his speeches), or by Livy. These three great prose writers had occasion to describe every human emotion and almost every kind of human experience; and they consequently provide a vocabulary which is sufficient for all the ordinary needs of prose composition.

(iii) It sometimes happens that a piece of English deals with some modern concept such as 'bullets' or 'House of Lords' for which the Romans had no word at all. Do not waste time inventing a word or trying to evolve some descriptive periphrasis, but use your knowledge of Roman civilisation and adopt a word which will be a reasonable equivalent. There are few contexts in which *sagittae* will not be an adequate rendering for 'bullets' or *senatores* for 'House of Lords' (see § iv below).

(iii) **Use words in their normal Latin meaning.** (i) The poets not only use words not found in prose; they also employ prose words with special meanings, as when they use *ratis* 'a raft' or *puppis* 'a poop' instead of *navis*, or use *carbasus* 'linen' for *velum* 'a sail.' Such usages are to be avoided in prose.

(ii) Special care needs to be taken to avoid the fallacy that English derivatives can be translated by their Latin originals. Two important paragraphs (**18–19**) have already been devoted to this topic. They should be carefully studied, and in the course of reading Latin every opportunity should be taken to add to the list of examples given in those paragraphs.

(iii) No type of Latin noun needs more care than those of the third declension that end in *-io*. Some of them like *legio, oratio, ratio,* are in common use. But some like *amissio* are rare and others like *fractio* are used only by late authors. Furthermore, all except the most common correspond to English nouns in *-ing*; they indicate an activity and not the result of an activity. Thus *petitio* is not 'a petition' but 'the act of seeking,' and in particular 'a candidature'; *possessio* is not 'a thing which one owns' but is 'the act of taking possession' or 'possessing' in the abstract; *solutio* is not 'the solution of a problem' but 'an act of freeing' or 'the paying out of what one owes.'

(iv) It should be remembered also that for many English words there is no single Latin word exactly equivalent. The use of a relative clause is sometimes the best way of rendering such English words. Thus, for 'audience' we can use *qui audiunt*; for 'politicians' *qui rei publicae operam dant.* Look again at the examples in **175** where this point was mentioned.

(v) It is a very useful plan to collect in a notebook groups of words which are likely to be wrongly used or confused with one another. Here are examples of such groups :—

> *Acies, agmen, exercitus—augeo, cresco—bellum, proelium, pugna—caedes, clades—calidus, callidus—diligo, deligo, delego—error, culpa—expers, expertus, peritus—honor, pudor—ignavus, ignarus, ignotus—ignoro, ignosco—interdum, interea—invidus, invisus—magis, maius, plus, potius—memini, memoro—post, postea, postquam—religio, cultus deorum—securus, tutus.*

(iv) Translate thoughts, not words. (i) In all languages there are many words which have various shades of meaning; and the way an English word is to be rendered into Latin depends upon the shade of meaning it has in a particular context. Nothing leads so easily to the writing of grotesque and unintelligible Latin as the neglect of this simple fact.

In **16** the various meanings of 'country' and of 'world' have been examined, and in **20–5** there are some important remarks on the translation of English verbs into Latin. These paragraphs should be studied carefully and the student should constantly ask himself whether he is allowing himself to be deluded by the superficial meaning of the English.

(ii) A special warning may be given about adjectives which in English are often applied figuratively to nouns to which they could not apply literally. An 'angry speech' is not *oratio iracunda,* since a speech is neither angry nor black nor white; in Latin it would be *oratio irascentis*; and a 'treacherous plan' is *consilium perfidorum* rather than *consilium perfidum.*

(iii) Neglect of this principle of translating thoughts rather than words almost inevitably leads to the use of Latin words in wrong senses, as when 'public men' is rendered by *viri publici* (which would mean 'men owned by the state').

(iv) Some English expressions verge on redundancy and should not be translated literally. In most contexts 'I succeed in doing' does not differ from 'I do'; 'I am occupied in besieging the city' means that I am besieging it; 'I find it impossible' is simply *non possum*; and a 'sinister threat' is generally no more than a threat.

(v) Nevertheless, though English is sometimes not as economical as it might be, do not rush to the other extreme of omitting some detail of importance. Prune English verbiage, but prune it judiciously.

(v) Prefer the concrete to the abstract. (i) Latin is very far from being devoid of abstract words like *ardor, ignavia, magnitudo, odium, prudentia, virtus*; but it has fewer abstract words than English and those which it does possess it uses less frequently than English. It is consequently a safe principle to think carefully before you translate an English abstract noun by a Latin one. 'The obscurity of his origin prevented his elevation to the consulship' is not *obscuritas originis elevationem eius ad consulatum impedivit*; but rather *ille quod loco obscuro natus erat ad consulatum pervenire non potuit.* 'Bravery and consideration for others characterised him' will be *fortem se praestitit, aliis semper consuluit.* 'There was a widespread impression that . . .' is simply *multi opinabantur.* 'The enemy made only a faint show of resistance' is *hostes vix restiterunt.*

(ii) A heedless rendering of English abstract nouns will often lead you into the use of rare and late words like *impossibilitas* or even into the invention of words like *incertitudo.*

(iii) Some useful hints which will help you to avoid abstract expressions will be found in **54** (the use of neuter plural adjectives: *multa mentitus est* 'he told many falsehoods'); in **98** (the use of infinitives: *beate vivere* 'happiness'); in **174** (the use of clauses: *qualis sit videtis* 'you see the sort of man he is'); in **414, 417** (the use of participles: *querentibus satisfecit* 'he attended to their complaints'; *nuntiata clades* 'the news of the disaster'); and in **420** (the use of an ablative absolute: *me praesente* 'in my presence').

(vi) Beware of English metaphors. (i) English abounds in metaphors, many of which are used so commonly that we no longer recognise them as such. If we render them literally into Latin we shall often be guilty of translating words instead of meanings and even of using Latin words in unusual senses. Think carefully about the English, extract its plain meaning and translate that. Here are a few English metaphors and simple renderings of them into Latin :—

This blow of fortune plunged them into despair: *haec res omnem spem eis ademit.*—Bowing to the stern law of necessity, he adopted an entirely new plan: *necessitate coactus, novum cepit consilium.*—He cast amorous eyes on her: *eam amare coepit.*—This task bristles with difficulties: *hoc opus difficillimum est* or *difficile erit hoc opus perficere.*—Many of the enemy bit the dust: *multi interfecti sunt.*

(ii) Latin has its own metaphors, especially such as are derived from natural phenomena, from war, and from navigation. Some of them do in fact correspond to English metaphors, as :—

Oratio libere fluebat 'his style flowed freely'—*accusatorem rebus armo* 'I equip the prosecutor with facts'—*ad gubernacula reipublicae sedere debet* 'he ought to be seated at the helm of state'—*naufragium fortunarum* 'the shipwreck of one's fortune.'

Others, however, do not correspond so closely to common English usage :—

Illum neque periculi tempestas neque honoris aura potuit de suo cursu demovere 'neither danger nor the allurement of public honours could deflect him from his course—*tempestas invidiae nobis impendet* 'a wave of prejudice confronts us'—*virtutibus et beneficiis floruit* 'he was eminent for his virtues and his good deeds'—*odium incendit* 'he arouses hatred'—*omnium animi ad ulciscendum ardebant* 'all were eager for vengeance'—*infamiam exstinguo* 'I wipe out the disgrace.'

To draw up a long list of Latin metaphors would only tempt the student to use stereotyped phrases in a haphazard fashion. He should make a note of all the metaphors with which he becomes acquainted in his own reading of Latin authors and then introduce them judiciously into his composition.

(iii) Though the Romans had metaphors of their own, they were less liberal in the use of them than English; and they often soften the metaphor into a simile or apologise for it by *ut ita dicam, quasi, tamquam*; thus: *philosophia artium omnium quasi parens est* 'philosophy is the mother of all the arts'; *hinc, tamquam a fonte rivus, omnia mala oriuntur* 'all evils flow from this source.'

(vii) Observe the rules of Latin word order. (i) A separate paragraph is devoted to this point because English word order differs so greatly from that of Latin that special care is continually needed if we are to avoid an order of words which would have puzzled a Roman. The rules for Latin word order have been given in the Introduction §§ 79–91. There is no need to repeat them here; but constant reference should be made to them until the student has developed so strong a sense of Latin word order that he adopts it automatically.

(ii) Deviations from the normal Latin word order have been discussed in the Introduction §§ 83–4. It is worth pointing out that such deviations can be of great service in the cause of lucidity if they are sparingly used and are designed to secure appropriate emphasis. Deviations from the normal which are dictated by a mistaken striving after false elegance should be avoided.

(viii) Link your sentences together. (i) Any writer who knows the first elements of his art, no matter whether he is composing a speech, a historical narrative, or a philosophical treatise, will arrange his sentences in a logical order and will make the sequence of thought clear to his reader. In English, however, the relation between one sentence and another is frequently left, quite legitimately, to the intelligence of the reader; in Latin such relationships are generally made explicit by the use of connecting words or by subordinating one sentence grammatically to another. When translating into Latin therefore we must frequently introduce distinctive connecting words where none is expressed in the English, or combine two or more English sentences into a single Latin one.

(ii) The English 'and' is often used as a vague connective and joins sentences which are not really parallel in thought. 'He spared the soldiers and sent them back to their country' could be translated by *militibus pepercit et in patriam dimisit*; but 'he spared the soldier and killed the general' needs a different connective: *militibus pepercit sed ducem interfecit.* Frequently one of two sentences connected in English by 'and' must be made subordinate in Latin; thus: 'the king summoned his friend and gave him the command of the army' will be *rex, cum amicum ad se vocavisset, exercitui praefecit* or *rex amicum quem ad se vocaverat exercitui praefecit.*

(iii) Sometimes Latin dispenses with connectives for special emphasis or to point a contrast: *veni, vidi, vici*; *pepercit militibus, ducem interfecit.* Bear in mind that the effectiveness of this stylistic device depends upon its sparing use.

(iv) Latin writers are particularly fond of long compound sentences, called periods, in which a number of various circumstances logically related to the main sentence are expressed by subordinate clauses. Thus an English writer might say :—

> Servius had already gained an undoubted hold on the crown by exercising its functions. The young Tarquin, however, boastfully declared at times that the rule of Servius had not been approved by the people. The king heard of this and first won the goodwill of the people by dividing amongst them the land won from the enemy. He then took the bold step of submitting to them the question whether they desired and approved of his kingship.

In Livy, however, all the circumstances are related and subordinated to the single main idea: *Servius ausus est ferre ad populum*, thus :—

> *Servius quamquam iam usu haud dubie regnum possederat, tamen, quia interdum iactari voces a iuvene Tarquinio audiebat se iniussu populi regnare, conciliata prius voluntate plebis agro capto ex hostibus viritim diviso, ausus est ferre ad populum, vellent iuberentne se regnare.*

Considerable skill is needed before one can write such a period; but if the student aims from the first at a periodic style in Latin, he will be well repaid by a growing sense of mastery over the language and by the satisfaction which accompanies all intellectual achievement.

(ix) **Observe the practice of Latin authors.** In several of the previous paragraphs stress has been laid on careful observation of the way Latin writers use their own language.

Such advice cannot be too often repeated; for more can be learned by the patient reading of authors such as Cicero and Livy than can be taught by any number of hints. It is only from the Romans themselves that we can learn how to use words correctly, what metaphors are appropriate to Latin, and how a period is constructed. Such knowledge cannot be gained at second-hand. Furthermore, this minute study of the great Latin writers, undertaken to improve a mere facility in writing Latin prose, is likely to bring other and still more valuable rewards. It will widen and deepen our appreciation of the writers themselves; it will compel us to think carefully about the many problems of literary expression, in English no less than in Latin; and it will help us to realise that the proper use of language is one of the most delicate and subtle of human faculties.

(x) Beware of the English-Latin dictionary. No English-Latin dictionary has ever been compiled which can offer a student more than the most elementary equipment for Latin composition; and the General Vocabulary at the end of this book does not profess to do more than recall to mind words which may be useful in the Exercises for which it was compiled. There are three main objections to the use of an English-Latin dictionary. (i) It often gives poetic, unusual, or late Latin words as renderings of the English, and so induces the student to violate the principles mentioned in § iii above. (ii) Even when it gives normal Latin words, it does not and cannot possibly help the student to decide which of those words is the most suitable for the context he is translating. (iii) It is a direct incentive to the student to neglect his own powers of memory, and so makes him less able to read Latin authors with ease.

If, in an emergency, you have recourse to any such aid, the information offered should at once be checked in the best Latin-English dictionary available; and no effort should be spared to reduce those emergencies to a minimum.

PASSAGES FOR TRANSLATION

1. The story has often been told of how the Romans, soon after the foundation of the city, seized by force a number of Sabine maidens. The Sabines did not immediately try to rescue their daughters but waited until they had gathered an army, and then marched towards the city with the intention of destroying it. Outside the city a fierce battle took place in which neither side was victorious; and both armies were making ready for a second encounter when they were prevented by a strange spectacle. The women who had been carried off came running in great confusion from the city and with piteous cries placed themselves between the rival forces. 'What have we done,' they shouted to the Sabines, 'that we should suffer so? The Romans took us by violence; but we are now their wives and they are the fathers of our children. You did not save us when we most needed your help; do not now try to separate wives from their husbands and mothers from their children.' Thereupon the Sabines laid down their arms and, after a truce had been made, it was agreed that Romans and Sabines should dwell together in peace in a single city.

2. About the end of Romulus nothing is known for certain. It happened that, as he was addressing the people on the Nones of July outside the city, a great storm suddenly arose. The face of the sun was darkened and day was turned into night; there were terrible thunderings and the winds blew from all quarters. At this, the common people dispersed and fled, but the senators kept close together near Romulus. When the tempest was over and light returned, the people gathered together again and, noticing that the king was no longer there, anxiously enquired for him. The senators, however, would not permit them to make any search or to busy themselves about the matter; Romulus, they said, must now be honoured as one taken up to the gods; he who had been a good prince to the Roman people would for the future be a propitious deity. The multitude hearing this went away, rejoicing in hopes of the prosperity Romulus would now bestow upon them. But there were some who refused to believe this account of the matter

and secretly accused the senators of having murdered Romulus through jealousy of his popularity with the people.

3. Numa was about forty years of age when ambassadors came to the town of Cures to offer him the kingship at Rome. They made only a short speech, supposing that anyone would be easily persuaded to accept an honour so exalted. But, contrary to their expectations, they found that they had to use many entreaties to prevail upon one who had always lived peaceably, to accept the government of a city whose greatness had been won by martial prowess. 'Unlike Romulus,' said Numa, 'I am the son of a mortal father. I dislike all warlike occupations; and I find my greatest pleasures in the society of pious men whose sole concern is the tilling of their lands. Would it not indeed be madness for me to abandon the simple life to which I am accustomed?' To this the ambassadors replied: 'Even though you do not desire riches or authority, will you not consider that government is itself a duty you owe to the gods? Will you not consent to guide the Romans in the arts of peace now that they are satiated with war?' Moved by these words and influenced by certain favourable omens, Numa at last determined to accompany the ambassadors to Rome.

4. During the reign of Numa a terrible pestilence traversed the whole of Italy and ravaged even the city of Rome, so that many died and the citizens were reduced to the depths of despair. When the malady was at its height, a shield of unusual shape is said to have fallen miraculously from the sky into the hands of the king. Numa declared that it had been sent for the cure and safety of the city and that the gods had commanded him to have eleven others made like it; in that way no thief would be able to distinguish the original and steal it. Within a short space the pestilence did indeed cease; but when Numa showed the shield to the most skilled workmen, all except Mamurius Veturius confessed that they could not make others like it. Veturius, however, was so successful that when he had completed his task not even Numa was able to say which was the true shield. The keeping of the twelve shields was then entrusted to certain priests, called Salii ; and from that time onwards it was the custom for these priests, during the month of March, to dance through the streets of the city, carrying the sacred shields and smiting them with short daggers.

5. The third king of Rome, Tullus Hostilius, being of a warlike nature, devoted all his energies to extending the power of the city. Above all, he was ill-disposed towards the neighbouring city of Alba Longa, which had been founded many years before Rome itself, and deliberately provoked her to war. But when the two armies were already facing each other in battle array, Tullus agreed that the issue should be decided by the combat of three of the best warriors on each side. So in the presence of both armies three brothers named Horatii fought for Rome and three brothers named Curiatii for Alba. At first the contest seemed to favour the Albans, who succeeded in killing two of the Horatii. But the remaining Horatius who was unharmed resolved to win a victory for Rome by a trick. He pretended to flee and then, when the three wounded Curiatii were separated from one another in their pursuit, he turned and slew them one by one. Thereafter the people of Alba were loyal for a time to Rome ; but when they began to give aid secretly to the enemies of Rome, Tullus removed all the citizens of Alba to Rome and completely destroyed their ancient city.

6. In the midst of this distress, when King Porsena was sending in his demands to the Romans, as though to a people unable to resist, there occurred a deed of daring which brought hope to the besieged. A young man named Mucius, with the assent of the senate, swam the Tiber and made his way into the enemy's camp with a dagger concealed in the folds of his dress. Seeing a man clad in purple transacting business on a high tribunal, Mucius had no doubt that he was Porsena; and seizing a favourable opportunity, stabbed him to the heart. The man thus slain was not the king and Mucius was at once arrested. When he was brought before Porsena, he boldly declared that his intention had been to kill the king himself; but he promised, on condition of being spared the tortures with which he was threatened, to impart to the king important information. The assurance being given, he told Porsena that three hundred youths in Rome, no less bold than himself and equally careless of their lives, had sworn to slay him; and though he who had been chosen first had failed, the king must expect a similar danger day and night.

7. The Romans under Valerius marched forth to meet the Etruscans and a fierce battle took place a few miles outside the city; but before either side could rout their opponents, a violent storm arose and separated the two armies. Neither general was harsh enough to call upon his weary troops to renew the fight that day; and as Valerius surveyed the scene he was as much dismayed by the sight of his own dead as he rejoiced at the losses of the enemy; for the slaughter on either side seemed to have been equal. During the night, after the armies had laid themselves down to rest, it is said that a strange voice was heard declaring that the Etruscans had lost one man more than the Romans. This divine pronouncement was received by the Romans with shouts of joy; but the Etruscans, in fear and amazement, deserted their tents and most of them dispersed to their own land. The Romans fell upon the remainder, amounting to nearly five thousand, took them prisoners, and plundered the

camp. They then counted the dead lying upon the field of battle and found, as they expected, that what they had heard the previous night was nothing but the truth.

8. After Coriolanus had many times led the Roman armies to victory, the tribunes determined to bring him to trial on the ground that he wished to establish himself as a despot. They also accused him of having distributed unfairly the booty which had been taken from the enemy and ought to have been handed over to the public treasury. The tribunes so worked upon the passions of the populace that he was condemned and the penalty of banishment was pronounced. At this calamity all his friends were as deeply distressed as the populace was joyful; but Coriolanus alone seemed to be unmoved. He returned home from the forum and after saluting his mother and his wife, who were full of loud lamentations, he exhorted them not to make his lot more painful by their expressions of grief. He then proceeded to the city gates, and taking only a few dependants with him, retired to the country where for a few days he debated with himself how best he might satisfy his desire for revenge against his countrymen. In the end he resolved to offer his services to the Volscians and lead them, if they so desired, against the Romans.

9. Coriolanus arrived at Antium, one of the chief towns of the Volscians, about evening; and though several met him in the streets, he passed along without being noticed and went directly to the house of Tullus Aufidius. He entered with his head covered and seated himself without a word. Those who were present could not but wonder, yet they were afraid to question him. But when Tullus had been summoned and had asked him who he was and for what business he had come, Coriolanus uncovered his countenance and said: 'If you cannot call me to mind, Tullus, I must be my own accuser. I am Gaius

Marcius, the author of so much mischief to the Volscians. The one recompense I have received from my countrymen for all the hardships I have undergone is the name Coriolanus which proclaims my former enmity to you and your nation. Of all other honours I have been deprived by the envy of the Roman people. Driven out as an exile I have become a humble suppliant at your hearth, not so much for safety as to seek vengeance. If I can be of help to your cause, make what use of me you think best; for I consider myself a Roman no longer.'

10. Coriolanus was sitting in the camp of the Volscians when he noticed a number of women approaching, with Volumnia his mother and Vergilia his wife at their head. After he had come to meet them and embraced them, Volumnia addressed him. 'Though we should say nothing, you may judge from our dress and from our faces how miserably we have lived since your banishment. Are we not the most unfortunate of women, that I should see my son and Vergilia her husband in arms against Rome? We know not for what we should entreat the gods, who cannot grant both your safety and a Roman victory. But if I cannot prevail upon you to forget your enmity and be the benefactor of both Romans and Volscians rather than the destroyer of one of them, I am resolved that you shall not enter Rome unless you trample first on the corpse of her who gave you life. Never will I see the day when a child of mine shall be either led in triumph by his countrymen or triumph over them.' Thereupon she threw herself down at his feet. But Coriolanus raised her up saying: 'Fortunate it is for the city that you came; for of all the Romans you alone have been able to overcome me.'

11. When the Romans wished to appoint Camillus as tribune for the sixth time, he refused the honour on the ground of ill-health. But the people protested that they did not want his strength for service on horse or foot, but only his wise guidance; and moved by their entreaties, he at last agreed to accompany another of the tribunes who was to lead an army against the Volscians. It was the plan of Camillus to avoid a pitched battle and wear out the enemy by waiting; but his colleague, Lucius Furius, carried away by the desire for glory, was impatient to give battle. Camillus therefore, fearing lest he should seem through envy to be robbing a younger man of a chance of gaining distinction, finally consented. Leaving Camillus behind in the camp with a few men, Lucius engaged the enemy with the main part of the forces so rashly that he was all but defeated and could not prevent his men from running in disorder back towards the camp. When he heard of this, Camillus, despite his sickness, rose from his bed, ran to the gate of the camp, rallied the fugitives, and led them victoriously against the foe.

12. When the Gauls under their leader Brennus were besieging the Etruscan city of Clusium, the Romans sent ambassadors to the barbarians to enquire why they were making war against a neighbouring city. Brennus received them courteously; but he laughed at their question and said: 'We consider that the Clusians do us an injury because, while they themselves are able to till only a small domain, they possess much territory and will not yield any to us who are many in number and poor. In former times you Romans made war upon those who would not share their possessions with you. Like you, we do but follow the most ancient of laws which declares that the feeble shall bow before the strong. Cease therefore to pity the Clusians.' The ambassadors, perceiving that the Gauls were intent upon conquest, entered Clusium and persuaded the inhabitants to attack the besiegers. In the fight one of the Romans was slain; and when Brennus recognised his dead body, he was so angry that a man who had so recently come as an ambassador should take up arms against him, that he drew off his men from Clusium and marched against Rome itself.

13. Appius Claudius was much distressed when he heard that the senate was ready to make peace with King Pyrrhus. Because of his great age and the loss of his sight he had given up the fatigue of public business; but he now commanded his servants to carry him in his chair to the senate house. 'I bore,' he said, 'until this time the misfortune of my eyes with some patience; but now, when I hear of these dishonourable proposals of yours, I wish I were deaf also. When I was young we Romans used to boast that if the great Alexander had dared to cross over to Italy, he would not have been invincible but would have made Rome more glorious. Is Pyrrhus, a general much inferior to Alexander, to come to Italy and be allowed undefeated to leave our shores? Do not persuade yourselves, either, that if you make him your friend you will save yourselves; that is rather the way to bring over other invaders from Greece who will despise you if he is not punished for his outrages on you.' These words of Appius so moved the senate that they sent messages to Pyrrhus telling him that never, so long as he remained in Italy, would they make peace with him.

14. During the second war which the Romans waged against the Samnites they suffered the worst disgrace in their history at a place called the Caudine Forks. The leader of the Samnites, who were encamped near Caudium, caused the Romans to be informed that he and his army had marched to besiege Luceria, the chief town of Apulia. The loss of this town would have been a severe misfortune for the Romans; and the consuls, believing the news they had received, determined to march in pursuit. Their way lay through a valley closed at both ends by narrow passes; and since they had no reason to fear danger at this point, they marched boldly onwards. But no sooner had they entered the valley than they discovered that the exit was blocked by felled trees and other obstacles ; and when they tried to retrace their steps they found that the entrance too was now guarded by the forces of the enemy. To fight would have been useless and the consuls were compelled to surrender. The whole army passed under the yoke as a sign of their submission and six hundred hostages were handed over to the Samnites.

15. After the death of Hasdrubal, Hannibal, the son of Hamilcar, became the leader of the Carthaginian forces in Spain. Though he was at this time only twenty-six years of age, he was well experienced in the arts of warfare and had long since been inspired by his father's example to wage war relentlessly against Rome and her possessions. His first action after he was put in charge of the army was to attack the town of Saguntum which was an ally of Rome. The Saguntines immediately sent messengers to Rome imploring aid ; but the Romans were too busily occupied with their own affairs to do more than remind Hannibal that the Carthaginians had promised not to cross the river Ebro, and warn him of the danger of injuring their allies. Hannibal, however, paid no heed to the Roman ambassadors who were sent to him, but conducted the siege of the town with the utmost vigour and skill. As for the Saguntines, when they realised that they could expect no assistance from Rome, they set fire to their own houses, since they preferred to perish by their own hands rather than become the victims of the Carthaginians' cruelty.

16. When Hannibal, on his journey from Spain to Italy, arrived at the Rhone, he found that barbarian forces were gathered on the other side of the river to hinder his passage. It seemed impossible to cross the river and yet, if he waited where he was, he might be surprised and even defeated by the Roman army which was marching towards him. In this situation of considerable danger he resolved upon a plan which proved successful. He sent a detachment ten miles higher up stream, where there was a small island, and instructed them to construct rafts on which they might reach the other side of the river. Then, when he thought sufficient time had passed for the detachment to have carried out their orders, he himself, with the main body of the army, prepared to cross from the spot where he was encamped. As the first companies began to cross, the barbarians raised a shout of triumph; for they felt sure that the Carthaginians would fall easy victims as they tried to land. But just at this moment the other detachment fell upon their rear, burned their camp, and drove them off in such confusion that Hannibal was able to reach the other bank unmolested.

17. Hannibal, realising that a battle with the forces of Scipio was imminent, called together his soldiers and brought before them some Roman captives who had been recently taken in a skirmish. He then asked these poor wretches in the presence of his army whether they wished to undergo imprisonment in fetters and endure a grievous slavery, or fight in single combat with one another on condition that the victors should be released without ransom. When they had chosen the second alternative and had fought bravely with each other, Hannibal turned and addressed his men. 'Is it not shameful,' he said, 'when these men who have been captured are so brave as to prefer even death to slavery, that we should shrink from incurring a little toil and danger in order to win power and rule for ourselves? All the sufferings that we have ever endured when defeated by the enemy we will inflict upon them if we are victorious. For you can be well assured that by conquering we shall obtain many benefits; but if conquered we, who are now so far from our native land, shall not have even a safe means of escape.'

18. While in Spain, Scipio fell ill; and one of the legions under his command, complaining that their pay had been delayed, drove away their tribunes and elected leaders for themselves. When he heard of this, Scipio sent a letter to the mutinous legion, in which he affected to pardon them for revolting and actually praised those who, by accepting the leadership, had been able to prevent the troops from doing unnecessary violence. The soldiers thereupon made no further trouble and willingly accepted Scipio's command that they should come to his own camp. When they arrived, Scipio arranged that they should be generously supplied with provisions, but only the bolder spirits amongst them were allowed to enter the camp, where they were immediately arrested. On the following morning, however, Scipio addressed the rest of the legion. 'You all deserve to die for your past conduct; yet I will not put you all to death, but will punish only the few whom I have already arrested.' The prisoners were then brought out, bound to stakes, and scourged to death; and though the remainder were indignant at the trick which had been played on them, they made no further attempt at rebellion.

19. While the Syracusans were celebrating a feast of Diana and were entirely given over to wine and revelry, Marcellus gained possession of a tower which was carelessly guarded, and posted his men on the walls. When day broke the inhabitants perceived what had happened; and in the tumult which resulted Marcellus had no difficulty in making himself master of the principal points in the city. As he looked down from an eminence upon the spacious city below him he is said to have wept; for he realised that in a few hours it would all be sacked, and the riches which had been gathered during many years of prosperity would become the prey of the soldiers. But by nothing was he more moved than by the death of the mathematician Archimedes. It so happened that this man, whose knowledge was the admiration of all who knew him, was engaged upon certain calculations so intently that he did not notice that the Romans had entered and taken the city. While he was thus occupied, a Roman soldier commanded him to come to Marcellus and, when he asked to be allowed to complete his task, drew his sword and slew him on the spot.

20. In all the arts of warfare Hannibal was the undoubted superior of every Roman general; but his army was small, it contained many Gauls, and it was left in Italy without any support from home. On the other hand, Rome had great reserves of men, especially if the allies remained faithful to her. This difference between the rival powers was well understood by Fabius, who urged that Hannibal should not be encountered in pitched battles, in which his skill would almost certainly decide the result; he was rather to be followed, harassed, and kept, so to speak, in a state of perpetual anxiety. Furthermore, if he were compelled to live on plunder and devastation, the allies would feel no sympathy for him and would remain faithful to Rome. His army too would grow more restless the longer they were kept away from their native lands; and by continually pursuing an enemy who refused to stay and fight, their spirits would become depressed. 'Wear out the enemy by patience' was the whole plan of Fabius; and if we remember that a daring offensive had always been the tradition of Rome in war, we may realise what courage he needed to give such unusual advice.

21. In gratitude for the many benefits Fabius had conferred in peace and in war on the state, the Romans appointed his son to the consulship. Shortly after he had entered upon his office and had invited some of the chief men in the city to consult with him about military matters, his father, either by reason of age and infirmity or in order to test him, approached him on horseback.

The young consul observed this while he was still at a distance, and sent one of his lictors to command his father to alight and show the respect which was due to a consul by coming to him on foot. The bystanders seemed offended at the imperiousness of the son towards a father so venerable, and turned their eyes in silence towards Fabius. He, however, instantly descended from his horse, and with open arms came up, almost running, and embraced his son, saying: 'Yes, my son, you act rightly and understand well what authority you have received and over whom you are to use it. I should have thought the worse of you had you done otherwise. This was the way by which we and our forefathers advanced the dignity of Rome, preferring always her honour and service even to our own fathers and children.'

22. While the elder Cato was engaged in Spain in reducing some of the tribes to allegiance by force and others by pleading with them and offering them good advice, a large army of barbarians fell upon him, and there was serious danger that he would be overwhelmed and even driven out of the country. He therefore called upon some of the neighbouring tribes to help him. When they demanded two hundred talents for their assistance everyone thought it intolerable that Romans should be willing to pay it; but Cato said there was no disgrace: for if they were victorious they would pay out of the booty taken from the enemy, and if they were overcome there would be no one left to demand the payment or make it. However, he won the ensuing battle decisively, and for the rest of his time in Spain he suffered no reverse, and took many cities by storm. In the fighting the soldiers secured much plunder, yet Cato gave in addition a pound of silver to every man, saying that it was better that many of the Romans should return home with silver than a few with gold. But for himself he refused to benefit in any way from his successes.

23. Tiberius and Gaius Gracchus were brought up by their mother Cornelia, who was unwilling to entrust their training to any of her servants; and though in natural ability they were the first amongst the Romans of their time, they seemed to owe more to their education than to their birth. There were, however, many differences between them. Tiberius, who was the elder by nine years, was of a mild temperament and his countenance was gentle; he dressed plainly and lived frugally; and when he addressed the people, his voice was quiet and he preferred to persuade them by reason rather than move them by appealing to their emotions. Gaius, on the other hand, was of a much more vehement nature; and it is related that when making a speech he would walk about in his excitement and even pull his cloak off his shoulders. Though, as compared with other men, he was temperate at table, he was fonder of good fare than his brother, and he was noteworthy for his ready acceptance of new fashions in dress. Yet the two brothers showed an equal valour in war against their country's enemies, an equal justice and industry in office, and the same deep desire to serve their country in the way they thought best for her welfare.

24. The conduct of the war against Numantia was entrusted to the consul Mancinus, and Tiberius Gracchus was appointed as quaestor. After a number of unsuccessful battles, Mancinus abandoned his camp and was so closely pursued by the Numantines that he was forced into difficult ground from which there could be no possibility of escape. Tiberius was sent to the Numantines, at their own request, to discuss with them the arrangements for a truce and the terms of peace; and he showed so reasonable a spirit that there is no doubt that to him not less than twenty thousand Romans owed their safety. The Numantines naturally retained possession of all the property they had taken in the Roman camp, and amongst it were the account books of Tiberius. These he was anxious to recover so that he should be able to prove that he had wisely and properly spent the money entrusted to him for the campaign. He accordingly went to Numantia himself, accompanied by only a few friends, and asked for the return of his books. Admiring his courage and remembering the skill with which he had conducted the recent negotiations, the Numantines received him courteously and gladly granted his request.

25. The opponents of Tiberius Gracchus, observing that his supporters on the Capitol were already armed, hastened to the senate house and declared that he wished the people to bestow a crown upon him. This news created great consternation amongst the senators and Nasica at once called upon the consul to defend the constitution and punish the tyrant. The consul mildly replied that he would not be the first to do any violence; and just as he would not suffer any free man to be put to death before sentence had been lawfully passed upon him, so he would resist any unlawful action on the part of Gracchus; but nothing had happened as yet which called for his intervention. But Nasica, rising from his seat, cried out: 'Since the consul has no regard for the safety of the commonwealth, let every one who will defend the law follow me.' Then he and his friends and their attendants armed themselves with clubs and staves, rushed to the Capitol, and made towards Tiberius. In the struggle which ensued, many of the party of Gracchus were killed and he himself received a fatal blow from the hand of one of the tribunes who was his colleague in that office.

26. When Gaius Gracchus came forward as a candidate for the tribuneship, many of the nobles opposed his election; but so many came from all parts of Italy to vote for him that lodgings could scarcely be found for them in the city. The nobility were successful to this extent that

Gaius was elected not as the first but as the fourth tribune. Yet when he entered on his office it was at once seen which of the tribunes was the most important; for he was by far the best orator of them all and the resentment he felt at his brother's murder made him all the bolder in his speeches. He used on all occasions to remind the people of what happened on that terrible day. 'The nobles,' he was wont to say, 'slew my brother and dragged his slaughtered body through the city to be cast into the river. His friends too were put to death without a trial, in defiance of all our ancient customs. In this way the rights of freeborn citizens of Rome are being trampled upon; and if we take no steps to defend them we shall soon be no better than slaves. But if I can rely on your support, the power of the nobles can and shall be broken and our freedom saved.'

27. The Teutones soon came in sight, in numbers beyond belief, terrible to look on, and uttering strange cries. Taking up a great part of the plain with their camp, they challenged Marius to battle; but he refused to be enticed into an encounter before he judged the time was suitable. Instead, he placed his men by turns on the ramparts of his camp that they might become familiar with the appearance of the enemy and observe what kind of arms they possessed and how they used them. After a while the soldiers' fears diminished and they became so used to seeing their foes that they complained of their commander's inaction. When small bands of the barbarians even dared to approach the camp of Marius with taunts and threats, some of the Romans could not endure it but ventured outside and were involved in skirmishes. Marius, however, severely censured them for their conduct. 'You who now thus needlessly risk your lives,' he said, 'are no better than traitors to your country. It is our duty to fight, not at the first opportunity, but at a time when the enemy is least prepared for it. In that way alone shall we be able to save Italy from the invasion of these barbarian hordes.'

28. Sulla was especially eager to take the city of Athens because some of the citizens had written jeeringly about him and had mocked at his wife Metella. Traitors within gave him warning of intended sorties and of the plans for obtaining provisions, so that he had no difficulty in warding off attacks upon his siege works or in reducing the city to starvation. Finally he heard that the walls were weakly defended at one point and determined to take the place by assault. The few sentries fled on the approach of the Roman soldiers and a sufficient breach was made in the walls for Sulla to march in at the head of his troops. For a while the city was given over to plunder; the streets flowed with blood, and the air resounded with the screams of the dying. Some of the citizens, however, who had previously helped Sulla now threw themselves at his feet and implored him to spare the town. Their entreaties were supported by many Romans, too, who were moved by the fame of a city in which they themselves had studied in their youth; and after a time Sulla yielded to their pleas, saying that he granted the present inhabitants their lives only because of the glory of their ancestors.

29. The morning after the battle at the Colline gate, which had made him master of Rome, Sulla summoned the senate to the temple of Bellona. Since he was an imperator commanding a military force, the law forbade him to enter the city and it was thus necessary for the senators to meet outside the walls. While Sulla was addressing them and explaining his plans for the government of the city, loud and piteous cries were heard in the distance. 'Do not be alarmed,' he said to his audience; 'it is only some rascals whom I have found it necessary to punish.' In actual fact, the noise which the senators heard came from the eight thousand Samnite prisoners whom Sulla had brought to be butchered by his soldiers in the Campus Martius. Nor was it long before he turned his blows from the Italians upon the Romans themselves; for as soon as he realised that his position was secure, he made his intentions plain in a speech from the rostra. After boasting of his own greatness and power, he assured the people that he would be good to them if they obeyed him; but to his foes he would give no quarter, no matter whether they were of lowly rank or were praetors, quaestors, or tribunes.

30. After his victory, Sulla, who seemed to be wholly bent on slaughter, caused many men within the city to be killed. In the senate a certain Metellus was bold enough to ask him when these evils would come to an end. 'We do not ask you,' he said, 'to pardon any whom you have resolved to destroy, but to free from doubt those whom you are pleased to save.' In reply Sulla said that he did not yet know whom to spare and immediately published a list of eighty persons whom he had determined to proscribe. Despite the general indignation, he announced the names of two hundred and twenty more on the next day, and in an address to the people he declared that he had put up as many names as he could think of and those which had escaped his memory he would publish at a future time. Many of those who were killed had committed no offence against Sulla or his friends but were slain simply for the sake of their riches. Amongst such was Quintus Aurelius, who, coming into the forum to read the list and finding his own name there, cried out: 'It is my Alban farm that causes my death'; and he had not gone far before he was despatched by a ruffian sent on that errand.

31. Of all those who tried to withstand the power of Rome, one of the most remarkable was Spartacus. This man, a Thracian by birth, put himself at the head of a number of gladiators who escaped from Capua where they were being kept in custody. When they had encamped upon the slopes of Vesuvius and had been joined by a great number of run-away slaves, the military forces in Capua found it impossible to dislodge them and the troops sent from Rome were no more successful. As his adherents increased, Spartacus became bolder and marched over a great part of Italy, plundering wherever he went; but, though he gradually acquired a stock of arms and ammunition, he was wise enough to avoid a pitched battle. For more than a year he inspired terror in the countryside and might have continued to do so had not his followers insisted at last on his attacking a Roman army. In the battle Spartacus fought fiercely and fell amongst such heaps of slain that his body was never recovered. Many of his followers, too, were killed in the battle; but no less than six thousand of them were captured and crucified along the road that leads from Capua to Rome.

32. While Lucullus was conducting his campaigns against Mithridates in Asia, he had with him in his army his wife's brother, Publius Clodius by name. This man, thinking that he had not as high a rank as he deserved and feeling an enmity against Lucullus, began to stir up some of the soldiers by professing sympathy with their hard lot. 'Is there to be no end of wars and toils for you,' he used to say to them, 'and are you to wear out your lives wandering over the world and fighting all nations? Is there to be no other reward for you than to guard the waggons of Lucullus laden as they are with gold and precious goblets? The soldiers of Pompey are living safely at home, with their wives and children, on fertile lands or in towns. They have served for but a brief while in Spain and have not overturned the royal cities of Asia. Why should your rewards be less than theirs?' Such words as these so influenced the soldiers

that they refused to follow Lucullus any longer. Even when he entreated them one by one to perform their duties faithfully, they turned away from his salutes and threw down their empty purses, bidding him engage alone with the enemy since he alone gained advantage from it.

33. After his success in Africa, where his army had saluted him as imperator, the young Pompey desired the honour of a triumph. But Sulla was unwilling for it to be granted on the ground that if a man whose beard was not yet fully grown and who was not of an age to be a senator should have a triumph, many would be envious. Pompey, however, was not daunted and bade Sulla remember that more men worshipped the rising than the setting sun, as if to tell him that his own power was increasing whereas that of Sulla was on the wane. Sulla did not hear these words clearly, but observing a look of amazement on the faces of those near him, he asked what it was that Pompey had said. Then, astounded at Pompey's boldness and admiring his courage, he cried out: 'Let him have his triumph.' As Sulla had predicted, many expressed their disapproval; but to gall them the more, Pompey announced his intention of having his triumphal chariot drawn by four elephants which he had brought over with him from Africa. Nor is there any doubt that he would have persisted in his plan had it not been for the fact that the gates of the city were too narrow for such huge beasts to enter.

34. It will perhaps seem strange to some that when Cicero had clear information of Catiline's treason, instead of seizing him in the city, he not only permitted but even urged him to escape and so forced him, as it were, to begin the war. But there were good reasons for what Cicero did. He himself had many personal enemies amongst the nobility, while Catiline had many secret friends; and though he knew quite well the progress and extent of the plot, he had not in his possession the kind of proof which could easily be laid before the people. If, therefore, he had imprisoned Catiline at this time, as he deserved, there were many who would have blamed Cicero and censured his actions as those of a despot. But by driving Catiline into open rebellion, he made all men see the reality of their danger. He was well aware of the number and kind of troops on which Catiline was relying, and he believed that they were so inferior to the forces of the state that there was no doubt of Catiline's defeat in open battle. In this policy Cicero showed true wisdom; for shortly after Catiline left Rome the whole plot was disclosed and the republic was saved from a most serious danger.

35. After Cicero had delivered the conspirators to the officer whose task it was to execute them, he announced their fate to the people and returned from the forum to his own house. As he passed along he was received with applause and the citizens saluted him as the saviour of his country. He was accompanied by a splendid train of the principal citizens, amongst whom were many who had added to the possessions of the Roman empire by land and sea. With one consent they agreed that though the Roman people was indebted to many great commanders for riches and power, yet to Cicero alone they owed thanks for rescuing them from an imminent danger at home; and his service to the state was all the more remarkable because it had been accomplished with so little confusion. For a time nothing but gratitude for Cicero found expression; but there were some who thought the action he had taken against the conspirators was illegal and they were determined to attack him. Nor had they long to wait; for Cicero speedily did harm to himself by continually extolling his own merits whenever he had occasion to speak in public.

36. When Pompey was returning from Asia there were many rumours that he intended to march with his army into the city and establish himself as the sole ruler. Crassus actually withdrew from the city, either because he was really afraid or because he wished to create ill-feeling against Pompey by pretending that he believed the rumour. Pompey, therefore, as soon as he reached Italy, called his men together and commanded them to depart each to his own home. When the news was spread abroad that his army had been thus disbanded, not only was the anxiety in Rome allayed, but a wonderful result ensued. For when the cities through which he passed saw Pompey the Great travelling unarmed and with a small train of friends only, as if he were returning from a journey of pleasure and not from the conquest of Asia, the inhabitants poured out to display their affection for him and received him with every show of honour. Many of them indeed accompanied him to Rome itself, and when he arrived there he had more men at his disposal than he had disbanded; and if he had wished to overthrow the constitution and set up a despotism, he could have done so without the aid of his army.

37. Before he entered upon political life, Cato the Younger visited Asia to observe the manners and customs and strength of the Roman provinces there. His arrangements during his journey were as follows. Every morning he sent his baker and cook towards the place where he intended to stay the next night. They went quietly to the town, and if there happened to be no friend or acquaintance of Cato there, they provided for him in an inn; but if there was no inn, they then asked the assistance of the magistrates and took, without complaint, any lodgings which were allotted to them. Since these servants made as little trouble as possible and never used threats of any kind, it often happened that when Cato arrived he found nothing had been provided for him. Nor was any account taken of Cato himself; for the magistrates, seeing him sitting on his baggage, put him down at once as a person of no importance. Yet sometimes Cato would call them to him and say: 'Foolish people, lay aside this inhospitality. All your visitors will not be Catos. There are men enough who desire but a pretext to take from you by force what you give with such reluctance.'

38. Soon after his return from Asia, Pompey desired the senate to postpone the elections for the consulship so that he could be present to assist a friend who was a candidate. This request was successfully opposed in the senate by Cato, who thought that Pompey's expectations and designs should be curbed. Consequently Pompey resolved to make an attempt to win over Cato to his side by means of a marriage alliance; and he sent Munatius to Cato, offering to marry one of Cato's daughters himself and wed the other to his son. Cato's wife was present when Munatius brought this proposal and was full of joy at the prospect of an alliance with so great and important a person as Pompey. Cato, however, without reflecting, formed his decision at once. 'Go,' he said to Munatius, 'and tell Pompey that Cato cannot be won over on such terms. I am grateful indeed for the intended kindness, and so long as Pompey's actions are upright, I promise him a friendship more sure than any marriage alliance; but I will not give my daughters as hostages to Pompey's glory nor will I pledge myself to anything except the safety of the state and the defence of it against all foes.'

39. When Crassus saw that his army was almost surrounded by the Parthians at Carrhae, he ordered his son Publius to lead an attack against them, in the hope that he would gain a means of escape for the rest of his forces. The Parthians who were facing Publius did not await his charge but, designing to entice him as far away as possible from his father, turned and fled. The young man, crying out that the enemy dared not withstand him, pursued them. For a while he pressed forward, filled with hope and joy; for he believed that he had won an easy victory. But when he had gone too far, he perceived the trick as the fugitives halted, turned again, and began to attack him. The Romans fought bravely, since they knew that they could expect no mercy if they fell into the hands of so cruel an enemy. Some grappled hand to hand with their opponents, pulled them off their horses, and slew them; others struck at the horses who, maddened with pain, trampled on friend and foe alike. Nevertheless, the Romans were overcome by an enemy who greatly outnumbered them and against whom not even the greatest courage could avail.

40. For a while Crassus felt confident that his son would be victorious; but when no news came of the battle he was distracted and, scarcely knowing what counsel to take, he decided to move his forces. He had no sooner formed this resolution than some of the enemy came riding by with his son's head on the point of a spear. They approached so near indeed that they could be heard asking who were the young man's parents: for, they said, it was impossible that so brave a warrior should be the son of so pitiful a coward as Crassus. This sight dismayed the Romans, but Crassus himself showed an admirable fortitude. As he passed along the ranks he cried out to them: 'This, my countrymen, is my own peculiar loss; but the fortune and glory of Rome is safe and untainted so long as you are safe. Yet if any one is grieved at my loss of the best of sons, let him show it by revenging him upon the enemy. Take away their joy, punish their cruelty, and do not be downcast at what has happened. Our ancestors were not always victorious at the first blow or in the first campaign; and Rome became pre-eminent not by fortune but by virtue in confronting danger.'

41. While Crassus was exhorting his men he saw but few that gave much heed to him, and when he ordered them to shout for battle he could no longer mistake the despondency of his army. Though it was clear to every man how great was the danger, they resisted the assaults of the Parthians with little vigour and they would have been utterly routed had not night come on. The enemy camped near by and, flushed with victory, boasted that they would end the business on the morrow. But the Romans passed the night in terror and despair. They neither buried their own dead nor cared for the wounded; for each man bewailed his own fate. Crassus himself, who was largely responsible for the disaster, wrapped his cloak round him and hid himself in his tent. Octavius his lieutenant tried to comfort him; but when he found that was impossible, he called the centurions and tribunes together to discuss what had best be done. Seeing that their only hope lay in flight, they ordered the army to steal away as silently as possible. The wounded they did not dare take with them for fear of hindering their progress; and when morning came the Parthians put no less than four thousand helpless victims to the sword.

42. When the enemy had taken refuge on the top of the hill, all Caesar's officers gathered round him and urged him to fight at once. The soldiers, they said, were ready and eager, the enemy was in despair, and even if he shrank from storming the hill, want of water would soon force the enemy to descend. Caesar calmly listened. He did not intend to fight at all; for he had no doubt that having cut off the enemy's supplies, he would be able to end the campaign without bloodshed. 'Why,' he exclaimed, 'should I sacrifice my men even to win a battle? Is it right for me to expose to wounds the soldiers who have served me well? A general's business is to conquer not by the sword alone but by wisdom also. I am moved, too, by pity for my countrymen who, though I am victorious, will probably be slain.' The soldiers, however, complained and declared that if this chance was thrown away they would not obey when they were commanded to fight. Caesar adhered to his resolve, and by withdrawing his army from its position so reassured his adversaries that they gladly seized the opportunity and returned to their camp.

43. After the battle of Pharsalia and the defeat of the Republican forces, Pompey resolved to flee to Egypt. He sent a messenger to acquaint the king with his arrival and to crave his protection; but Ptolemy himself was young and it was a council of the chief men, and not the king, who deliberated whether this request should be granted. So Pompey, who had thought it dishonourable to live in subjection to Caesar, was forced to wait in his ship some distance from the shore until the sentence of this tribunal was known. Some were for receiving him in Egypt, others thought he should be sent away; but one member of the council argued that neither course was safe for them to pursue. If they received him, they would be sure to make Caesar their enemy and Pompey their master; yet if they dismissed him, they would incur the hatred of Pompey for their lack of hospitality and the anger of Caesar for letting him escape. But if they had him brought ashore and slew him, they would earn the gratitude of Caesar and would have no reason to fear Pompey. This advice won general approval and the execution of the dastardly plot was entrusted to a certain Septimius who had previously served under Pompey.

44. As the Egyptian boat drew near to the ship of Pompey, Septimius stood up and addressed him in Latin and called him by the title of imperator; and an Egyptian, speaking in Greek, invited him to come aboard the boat since the sea was too shallow for a large ship to approach nearer to land. So bidding his wife farewell, Pompey entered the boat with two centurions, a freedman, and a favourite slave. Though there was a considerable distance between the ship and the shore, none in the boat addressed any words of friendliness or welcome to Pompey; and when he asked Septimius if he had not formerly been his fellow soldier, the latter only nodded his head. When they drew nearer to the shore, a company of soldiers was seen to be approaching as if to afford Pompey a more honourable welcome. But as Pompey rose to step ashore, Septimius struck him from behind with his sword and the Egyptians also drew their weapons. Realising too late that he had been betrayed, Pompey threw his cloak over his face and, groaning only a little, endured the wounds they gave him. So he ended his life in the fifty-ninth year of his age.

45. Late in the evening, news reached Utica that there had been a great battle near Thapsus, that Caesar had taken his opponents' camp, and the Republican army had been destroyed. The inhabitants were so alarmed that they were almost out of their wits and could scarce keep themselves within the walls of the city. But Cato came forward and meeting the people in this hurry and clamour, did all he could to comfort and encourage them; he even appeased their fear by telling them that the report was in all probability exaggerated. Next morning he assembled the three hundred Romans who acted as his council and addressed them. He pointed out that they could not hope for safety by separating from each other and trying to make their escape; on the contrary, they must either consult together how best they might oppose Caesar or make their submission in a body. Whichever course they adopted, he would not blame them. If they thought fit to bow to fortune, he would not regard them as cowards; but if they resolved to stand firm and undertake danger for the sake of liberty, he was ready to be their leader and companion.

46. When Brutus and Cassius were soliciting the help of friends whom they could trust in their design of removing Caesar, the name of Antony was mentioned. Most of the conspirators were in favour of including him amongst their number, but Trebonius dissuaded them. He told them that when he and Antony were travelling together to meet Caesar on some matter of business, he had cautiously let fall a few remarks to see how well or how ill Antony was disposed to Caesar. It had been clear that Antony understood the purpose of the remarks, but he had given Trebonius no encouragement to continue or to speak more plainly. All that was in their favour was that Antony had not divulged the conversation, as far as was known, to Caesar himself. Some were then for killing Antony along with Caesar; but Brutus would not give his consent, for he insisted that an action undertaken in defence of right and the laws must not itself be marred by injustice to any man. Consequently it was settled that, since Antony was formidable not only for the high position he held as master of the horse but also for his bodily strength, he should be deliberately detained outside the senate house when the deed was to be done.

47. After Brutus had been persuaded by Cassius to join the conspiracy against Caesar, he betrayed no sign of uneasiness during the daytime when he was engaged in the forum; but at night he would often start out of his sleep and spend many hours in meditating on the difficulties which confronted him and his friends. His wife Portia, as one might expect, was distressed by these signs of her husband's anxiety; but though she well knew that he could not be contemplating anything dishonourable, she resolved not to enquire into his secrets until she had put her own courage to the test. She therefore took a sword and made a deep gash in her thigh; and despite the intense pain, she uttered no cry. When Brutus discovered what she had done, Portia did not conceal the motive of her action but proudly declared that she now had the right to share his counsels. 'I know,' she said, 'that women seem to be of too weak a nature to be entrusted with secret matters. But I am the daughter of Cato and from him I could not fail to learn that pain is no evil; and if you will but trust me, you will find that in constancy and fortitude I am inferior to none of your many friends.'

48. Everything happened in the senate house in accordance with the plans of the conspirators; and Antony, who had been detained outside, hastened to hide himself when he heard of the murder of Caesar. Then, understanding that the conspirators had no further designs against anyone, he showed himself willing to come to terms with them. Next day he spoke in the senate, urging that no measures should be taken against those who regarded themselves as the liberators of the state. Thereby he gained much praise; for it was thought that he prevented a civil war by his reluctance to avenge his dead friend. But, on the day of the funeral, when he was making an oration in the forum over the body of Caesar, he perceived how great was the affection of the common people for the dictator; and as he was ending his speech he so aroused the passions of the crowd by showing to them the clothes of Caesar, bloodstained and pierced by the holes of many daggers, that they there and then made a pyre in the forum and burned Caesar's body. Brutus and the other conspirators saved themselves from the fury of the mob only by leaving the city in which, for the time being, Antony was undoubtedly the most influential man.

49. Octavius was at Apollonia when the news arrived that his uncle Julius Caesar had been killed and that he himself had been named in the will as his heir. He hurried as speedily as possible to Rome and went first to Antony, whom he knew as his uncle's friend. At first Antony laughed when so young a man wished to discuss with him the money of Caesar which was now in his possession, and reminded him of the legacy which Caesar had promised to every Roman citizen; and all the answer he gave was that he hoped Octavius was in good health. No matter how much Octavius insisted and demanded his rightful property, Antony opposed him and insulted him; and there was nothing for the young man to do but to turn to others who might help him. Thus it came about that he obtained the support of Cicero and, through him, that of the senate. Furthermore, he grew popular with the people and with the soldiers, many of whom had served under Caesar. As his influence grew day by day, Antony became alarmed and feared that his own power might be undermined by the young man whom he had so mistakenly despised. He therefore consented to satisfy the demand of Octavius and treat him as his equal.

50. The estates of the proscribed found few purchasers and the prices offered were so low that the Triumvirs received much less money than they had expected. To supply the deficiency, they published an edict requiring fourteen hundred wealthy ladies to declare the value of their properties and to contribute whatever proportion they might demand. Any false declaration was to be punished by a fine, and rewards were promised to informers. The ladies induced the mother of Antony, and Octavia, the younger sister of Octavian, to intercede for them; and as no man dared plead their cause, Hortensia, a daughter of the illustrious advocate who had been the professional rival of Cicero, presented herself, accompanied by the ladies, before the tribunal of the Triumvirs in the forum and made an indignant speech. The Triumvirs ordered their attendants to remove the petitioners; but the sympathetic crowd raised such a clamour that they thought it prudent to postpone the matter till the following day; and when they had given more consideration to the matter, they decided that the number of those required to pay should be reduced to four hundred.

51. Of the many who suffered in that year of sorrow, there was only one whose fate has touched the hearts of all mankind. Cicero, when he heard of the proscription, was in his country house near Tusculum where he had spent his happiest hours. Intending to sail for Macedonia and there join Marcus Brutus, he hurried to the coast and embarked; but he soon landed, after a stormy voyage, and took shelter in his villa at Formiae. Those who have read his letters may well believe the story that he was heard to say: 'I will die in the Fatherland which I have so often saved.' Soon afterwards, as he was being carried in a litter by slaves who were ready to fight for a kind master, some soldiers, led by an officer, Popillius Laenas, whom he had defended in a trial for parricide, discovered him. Cicero forbade his slaves to resist, and met death as those who revered him would have wished. His head and the hand with which he had written the orations against Antony were displayed by the order of his enemy upon the rostra from which he had so often addressed the populace.

52. The next morning, while the soldiers were making their preparations for the oncoming battle, Cassius met Brutus and addressed him as follows: 'It is your hope, no less than mine, Brutus, that we shall be victorious this day and spend the rest of our lives in peace and happiness. But human fortunes are always uncertain and especially so in war; and since we may never meet again, if the battle should go against us, tell me your resolution concerning flight and death.' 'In my youth,' Brutus replied, 'I held that it was cowardly to take one's own life and that a man should fearlessly undergo any evil that befalls him and not try to evade the divine course of things.

But now I am of a different opinion; and if our cause is destined not to prevail this day, I am resolved, whether I perish by the sword of an enemy or by my own, to live no longer. We are fighting to defend the liberty of our country and her laws; should we fail, only slavery or death awaits us.' Cassius thereupon embraced Brutus, saying: 'I too am determined not to be a suppliant for life at the hands of our foe. Let us then lead our forces out to battle; for either we ourselves shall conquer or have no cause to fear those that do.'

53. During the rout, a certain Lucilius, seeing some horsemen pursuing Brutus, resolved to stop them even at the risk of his own life. Placing himself in their way, he persuaded them that he himself was Brutus and pleaded to be taken alive to Antony. When he was brought before Antony, who had come with a great crowd to receive the prisoner, the trick was discovered; but the courage of Lucilius did not fail him. 'Be assured,' he said to Antony, 'none of his enemies has either taken or will ever take Marcus Brutus alive; and as for me, I am ready to suffer on his behalf any severities you may inflict upon me.' Antony, however, so far from being angry, turned to those who had captured Lucilius and said: 'I perceive that you take it ill that you have been thus deceived; but you have met with a booty better than you sought. You were in search of an enemy, but you have brought me, I hope, a friend. I am uncertain how I should have treated Brutus if you had captured him alive; but of this I am sure, it is better to have loyal men like Lucilius as our friends than as our enemies.' Indeed, he treated Lucilius with such kindness that in later years he counted him amongst his most trustworthy supporters.

54. Antony, who for some time had felt that he had not received, during his campaigns in Asia, the assistance he expected from Cleopatra, now summoned her to meet him and explain her conduct. The story is told that Antony's envoy, his friend and comrade, Dellius, assured her that she need not fear: she would find the general the most chivalrous of men, who would treat her with due honour. Indeed, many years before, when she was a girl of fourteen, Antony, as a young cavalry officer, had cast amorous eyes upon her in her father's court; she must have met him also while she was living with Caesar in his suburban villa; and she doubtless knew his temperament by repute. Fresh from the victory which his skill had won, he was the foremost man in the Roman world and with his aid she might well hope to secure and exalt her dynasty. Even if she had lost a little of the beauty which had delighted Caesar, she had gained much in knowledge of men. The result of her interview was that not only was her explanation accepted but Antony hastened to join her in Alexandria for the winter. There she not only kept him constantly amused but, what is more important, even shared his counsels when his mood was serious.

55. Plancus and Titius, who both had reasons of their own for detesting Cleopatra, immediately went to Rome, called upon Octavian, and informed him that Antony's will, which they had themselves witnessed and sealed, and with the contents of which they acquainted him, was in the custody of the Vestal Virgins. When Octavian requested the Virgins to deliver it to him, they flatly refused, and added that, if he insisted, he must come and take it. He did so, and read it aloud, first in the senate and then in the forum. His hearers in this way learned that Antony had bequeathed large legacies to the children whom Cleopatra had borne to himself, and that he had directed that his body should be interred side by side with hers. If some were scandalised by the violence which Octavian had done to the Vestals, the disclosure which it enabled him to make strengthened his hands. Such was the general indignation at the un-Roman conduct of Antony that a rumour found credence that he intended to make Cleopatra Queen of Rome and to transfer the seat of Roman government to Egypt; and the senate, amid popular approval, deprived Antony of the consulship to which he had been designated.

56. The fortune of the day was still undecided when Cleopatra's sixty ships were suddenly seen to hoist sail and make out to sea in full flight; and as the first part of their course lay through the midst of Antony's ships, they caused much confusion and contributed to the victory of Octavian. Antony now showed to all the world that he was no longer a great commander, and what was once said in jest, that a lover's soul lives in another's body, he proved to be a truth. For as soon as he saw her ships sailing away, he abandoned the men that were fighting and spending their lives for him, and put himself aboard a galley to follow Cleopatra. When he reached her ship he was taken aboard; but without seeing her or letting himself be seen by her, he went forward to the prow and sat there alone, covering his face with his hands. For three days he refused to meet the queen; either, as some thought, because he was angry with her for leaving in the midst of the battle, or because he was overwhelmed by the downfall of his hopes. At the end of that time, however, he was reconciled to her and began to plan how they could recover what they had lost.

57. Accompanied by two of her women, Cleopatra had shut herself up in a mausoleum which she had recently built. Dreading the resentment of Antony, she sent a messenger to tell him that she was dead, in the hope that he would commit suicide. When he heard this, Antony called in vain upon a faithful servant to fulfil a long-standing promise and despatch him, plunged a sword into his own body, collapsed upon a couch, and begged bystanders to put him out of his misery. Almost at that very moment another messenger from Cleopatra entered the room and told Antony that the queen wished to see him. Rising, but unable to walk, he had himself carried to the mausoleum. Cleopatra, who would not allow the gate to be opened, caused a rope to be lowered through the window of her room, and when it had been fastened round his body, she and her two women with desperate efforts hauled him up and laid him upon a bed. He asked for wine, and while the queen stood beside him and called him by endearing names, he tried, so long as he remained conscious, to console her; and with his dying breath he urged her, in any dealings she might have with the followers of Octavian, to put her trust in Proculeius alone.

58. Some few days after the death of Antony, Octavian himself came to visit Cleopatra and console her. At his entrance she flung herself at his feet, her hair disordered and her voice quivering; and then, when she was more composed, she tried to justify her actions on the ground that whatever she had done had been through the persuasions of Antony. Her old charm had not entirely left her and other men might have accepted her excuses; but Octavian showed, by the way he refuted all her arguments, that he was no easy victim for a woman's wiles. Perceiving this, the queen resorted once more to entreaties, as if she desired nothing more than to prolong her life. She handed to him a list of her treasure and explained that the few articles which she had omitted were intended to be sent as presents to his wife and sister in the hope that they would intercede for her. Octavian told her that she might dispose of such things as she saw fit, and that he himself proposed to treat her with more honour than she perhaps expected. Indeed, he went away from the interview very well satisfied, little suspecting that in expressing a desire to live the queen had completely deceived him.

59. When Cleopatra had gained permission from Octavian to visit the tomb of Antony, she had herself carried there and spoke in this manner: 'O dearest Antony, it is not long since that with these hands I buried you; now I am a captive and pay these last duties to you under the eyes of a guard; for my enemies fear that my grief may make my servile body less fit to appear in their triumph. These are the last honours I can pay to your memory, for I am to be hurried away far from you. Nothing could part us while we lived, but death threatens to divide us. You, a Roman born, have found a grave in Egypt; I, an Egyptian, am to seek that favour, and none but that, in your own country. But if the gods below, with whom you now are, either can or will do anything, suffer not your living wife to be abandoned, let me not be led in triumph to your shame, but hide me and bury me here with you.' Then having wept for a time, she returned and wrote a letter to Octavian in which she entreated him to permit her burial within the same tomb as Antony. When he read this letter Octavian guessed that she designed to take her own life, and sent messengers to keep a closer watch upon her; but they arrived too late.

60. When Varus became governor of Germany he issued orders to the inhabitants as if they were slaves of the Roman people, and exacted money from them as he would from subject nations. To this they were in no mood to submit, for their leaders longed for their former ascendancy and the masses were oppressed by the burden of taxation. Nevertheless they did not openly revolt but pretended to do all Varus demanded of them and led him to believe that they would live submissively without the presence of soldiers. Consequently Varus did not keep all his legions together in one place, and became so confident that he not only refused to believe all those who suspected treachery and advised him to be on his guard, but actually rebuked them for slandering a friendly people. Then there came an uprising in the furthest part of the province, deliberately so arranged that Varus should march through what he supposed was friendly territory; and when he was already in the midst of almost impenetrable forests and could obtain no help from his scattered legions, the Germans fell upon him and inflicted one of the worst defeats that Roman arms ever suffered.

61. The body of Augustus was borne forth from his house to the forum on a couch adorned with coverings of purple and gold. Behind it were carried the images of his ancestors and of his deceased relatives; but there was no image of Caesar because he had already been numbered amongst the gods. When the couch had been placed on the rostra, in full view of the people, Tiberius delivered an oration in which he praised the character of the dead emperor and recounted the many benefits he had conferred on the Roman people. The couch was then carried to the Campus Martius, followed by the senate, the equestrian order, the praetorian guard, and practically every man and woman who was in the city at the time. There it was placed on the pyre, around which first marched the priests and then the knights. The infantry too ran round it, and as they did so they cast upon it all the triumphal decorations that any of them had ever received from him for any deed of valour. Next the centurions took torches and lighted the pyre from beneath; and as it was consumed, an eagle was seen to fly aloft, appearing to bear his spirit to heaven.

62. When the troops of Germanicus reached the town they did not meet with immediate success; for the enemy set fire of their own accord to the encircling wall and to the houses adjoining it, but contrived to keep it from blazing up at once so that it was unnoticed for some time. After doing this, they retired to the citadel, and the Romans rushed in after them, expecting to sack the whole place without striking a blow. Thus they got inside the circle of fire, and, with their minds intent upon the enemy, saw nothing of it until they were surrounded by it on all sides. Then they found themselves in the direst peril, being pelted by the men from above and injured by the fire from without. They could neither remain where they were safely nor force their way out anywhere without danger. For if they stood out of the range of the missiles, they were scorched by the fire; or, if they leaped back from the flames, they were destroyed by the missiles; and some who got caught in a tight place perished from both causes at once. The majority of those who had rushed into the town met this fate; but some few escaped by casting corpses into the flames and made a passage for themselves by using the bodies as a bridge.

63. When Caligula had resolved to set up his own statue in the Temple at Jerusalem, he entrusted Petronius, the governor of Syria, with the task of seeing that his commands were carried out. As soon as the Jews heard of this they sent a deputation of their leading men to plead with Petronius. They had come with no warlike intentions, they declared; but nevertheless they would rather die than permit this terrible injury to be done to their ancestral land, which would immediately be struck by a curse and never recover if the Temple were thus defiled. They said that as men they acknowledged their allegiance to Rome; there could be no complaints against them for any disloyalty to the emperor or for failure to pay all the taxes that were demanded of them. But their principal allegiance was to the God of their fathers, Who had always preserved them in the past, as long as they had obeyed His laws, and had strictly forbidden the worship of any other gods in His domain. In the face of such obstinacy Petronius could not do otherwise than lead his troops into Judaea and hope that he would not have to employ them.

64. When Petronius had moved his forces into Judaea, he told the Jews that it was his duty to keep the oath he had sworn to the emperor and obey him in every particular. They could see, he said, that with the armed forces at his disposal he was perfectly capable of fulfilling the orders he had received. Nevertheless, he praised the Jews for their firmness and for their abstention from any act of violence. He confessed, too, that though as governor of Syria he knew where his duty lay, yet as a humane man he found it next to impossible to carry out his instructions. It was not a Roman act to kill unarmed old men merely because they persisted in worshipping their own god. He said further that he would write to Caligula and present their case in as favourable a light as possible. It was more than likely that the emperor would reward him with death, but if, by sacrificing his own life, he could save the lives of many thousands of inoffensive provincials, he was willing to do so. He did indeed keep his promise to write to Rome; and the emperor himself relented when he learned that the Jews were determined to abandon the cultivation of their land rather than submit to the violation of their Temple.

65. When Gaius reached the ocean and had drawn up all the soldiers on the beach as if he were going to lead a campaign into Britain, he embarked on a ship and then, after putting out a little from the land, sailed back again. Next he took his seat on a lofty platform and gave the soldiers the signal for battle, bidding the trumpeters urge them on; then of a sudden he ordered them to gather up the shells on the shore. Having secured these spoils—

for he needed booty for his triumphal procession—he became greatly elated as if he had enslaved the very ocean and gave his soldiers many presents. The shells he took back to Rome to exhibit to the people as the booty he had gained in his conquest. The senate knew not how it could remain indifferent to these acts of a madman, nor yet how it could bring itself to praise him as he expected. For if anyone bestows great praise or extraordinary honours for a trivial exploit, he is suspected of making a mockery of the affair. Nevertheless, when Gaius entered the city he came very near destroying the whole senate because it had not voted him divine honours; but on the assembled populace he showered quantities of silver and gold.

66. There was one occasion in which the senate, after seventy years of patience, made an ineffectual attempt to re-assume its long-forgotten rights. When the throne was vacant by the murder of Caligula, the consuls convoked that assembly in the Capitol, condemned the memory of the Caesars, gave the watchword 'liberty' to the few cohorts who adhered to their standard, and during eight-and-forty hours acted as the independent chiefs of a free commonwealth. But while they deliberated, the praetorian guards had resolved. The stupid Claudius, brother of Germanicus, was already in their camp and prepared to support his election by arms. The dream of liberty was at an end; and the senate awoke to all the horrors of inevitable servitude. Deserted by the people and threatened by a military force, that feeble assembly was compelled to ratify the choice of the praetorians, and to embrace the benefit of an amnesty which Claudius had the prudence to offer and the generosity to observe.

67. Towards the end of his reign, the Emperor Claudius, in order to amuse himself and his friends, conceived the idea of exhibiting a naval battle on a certain lake not far from Rome. He had seats erected for the spectators and assembled an enormous throng of people there. He himself, as was appropriate for the occasion, was arrayed in military dress; but the rest of the spectators wore whatever pleased their fancy and the scene was one of unusual gaiety and splendour. The combatants, who were condemned criminals, were divided into two squadrons, each of which manned fifty ships. As the unfortunate men passed in front of the emperor before taking their places, they implored him to have pity on them; but since such great preparations had been made for the spectacle, no attention could be paid to their appeal and they were ordered to begin the fight at once. When the fleets approached each other from opposite sides of the lake, the spectators were amazed to see that they did not engage but sailed harmlessly past their opponents. Several times this happened, until the emperor angrily declared that the men should all be soundly flogged if they continued to make such a mockery of his plans.

68. During the reign of Nero a terrible disaster occurred in Britain; two important cities were sacked and eighty thousand of the Romans and of their allies perished. An excuse for the uprising was found in the fact that the governor of the island demanded the repayment of money which the Emperor Claudius had given to the foremost inhabitants. But it was a woman of the royal family, Boudicca by name, who was chiefly responsible for rousing the natives and persuading them to fight the Romans. She was a person of great intelligence and so highly respected that she was thought worthy to direct the conduct of the entire war. She assembled an army of a hundred and twenty thousand whom she led fearlessly against any Roman forces that came to meet her. For a time she was able to wreak indescribable slaughter, and those who were taken captive were subjected to every known outrage. But at last, when her army had already suffered a signal defeat, she herself fell sick and died. The Britons mourned her deeply and gave her a costly burial; but the Romans were bitterly ashamed that so much ruin had been caused by a woman.

69. When Paulinus heard of the rebellion of Boudicca he hurried with his troops from Mona and within a short time he was able to confront the barbarian hordes. Before the battle began he arranged his men and recalled to their minds the duty of a Roman soldier. 'Up, Romans,' he cried; 'show these accursed wretches how far we surpass them even in the midst of our evil fortune. It would be shameful, indeed, for you now to lose ingloriously what but a short time ago you won by your valour. Many a time have both we ourselves and our fathers, with far fewer numbers than we have at present, conquered far more numerous antagonists. Fear not, then, their numbers or their spirit of rebellion; for their boldness rests on nothing more than headlong rashness unaided by arms or training. Do not fear them because they have burned two cities; for they did not capture them by force nor after a battle, but one was betrayed and the other abandoned to them. Exact from them now, therefore, the proper penalty for these deeds, and let them learn the difference between us, whom they have wronged, and themselves. If you show yourselves brave men today, you will recover all you have lost.'

70. 'You have heard,' said Paulinus, 'what outrages these men have committed against us; nay more, you have even witnessed some of them. Choose, then, whether you wish to suffer the same treatment yourselves as our comrades have suffered, or whether you will avenge those that have perished and at the same time furnish to the rest of mankind an example of severity towards the rebellious. For my part, I hope, above all, that victory will be ours; first, because the gods are our allies and they almost always side with those who have been wronged; secondly, because of the courage that is our heritage, since we are Romans and have triumphed over all mankind by our valour; thirdly, because of our experience, since we have defeated and subdued these very men who are now arrayed against us. But if the outcome should prove contrary to our hope, it would be better for us to fall fighting bravely than to be captured and suffer as though we had been thrown to wild beasts. Let us therefore either conquer or die on the spot. Britain will be a noble monument for us, even though all the other Romans should be driven out; for our own bodies in any case shall for ever possess this land.'

71. Ascending a tribunal which had been constructed of earth in the Roman fashion, Boudicca addressed her troops in words well calculated to rouse their warlike spirit. 'You have learned,' she said, 'by actual experience how different freedom is from slavery. Since these Romans made their appearance in Britain, what shameful treatment have we not suffered? We have been robbed entirely of most of our possessions, and those the greatest; while for what remains we are compelled to pay the heaviest taxes. Yet it is we who have made ourselves responsible for these evils by allowing these men to set foot on the island instead of expelling them at once as we did their famous Julius Caesar. Although we inhabit so large an island and are so separated by the ocean from all the rest of mankind that we have been believed to dwell on a different earth, yet, notwithstanding all this, we have been despised and trampled underfoot by men who know nothing else than how to secure gain. However, even at this late day, let us do our duty while we still remember what freedom is, that we may leave to our children a land in which no oppressor can have a home.'

72. Nero now set his heart on accomplishing what had doubtless always been his desire, namely to make an end of the whole city during his lifetime. Accordingly he secretly sent out men who set fire to one or two or even several buildings in different parts of the city, so that the people were at their wits' end, not being able to find any beginning of the trouble nor having the means to put an end to it. Extraordinary excitement laid hold on all the citizens in all parts of the city, and they ran about in all directions distracted. Some, while assisting their neighbours, would learn that their own premises were afire; others, before word reached them that their own houses were in danger, heard that they were destroyed. Many who were carrying out their goods and many, too, who were stealing the property of others, kept running into one another and falling over their burdens, so that many were suffocated or trampled underfoot. While the whole population was in this state of mind, Nero ascended to the roof of the palace from which there was the best view, and assuming the lyre-player's garb sang the 'Capture of Troy.'

73. Paetus Thrasea was noteworthy for his fearless opposition to Nero and his refusal to approve of the emperor's evil deeds. 'If,' he used to say, 'I were the only one that Nero was going to put to death, I could more easily pardon the rest who load him with flatteries. But since even amongst those who praise him to excess there are many whom he will destroy, why should I degrade myself to no purpose and then perish like a slave?' Never did he show more courage than in the events which followed the death of Nero's mother Agrippina. Almost as soon as he learned of it, Nero sent a letter to the senate in which he enumerated the various offences of which, in his opinion, his mother had been guilty, and even declared that she had committed suicide because her plots against him had been detected. Scarcely a single senator doubted that Nero himself had planned his mother's murder; but as a body they pretended to rejoice at what had taken place and congratulated the emperor on his escape from such a peril. Thrasea, however, at once rose from his seat when the letter had been read and left the senate house, thereby boldly expressing his anger and disgust.

74. When Nero perceived that he had been deserted even by his bodyguard, he sought to flee. Putting on shabby clothing, and mounted on a horse no better than his attire, he rode while it was yet night towards the estate of one of his freedmen. Being recognised in spite of his disguise and saluted as emperor by someone who met him, he turned aside from the road and hid himself in a place full of reeds. There he waited till daylight, lying flat on the ground so as to run the least risk of being seen. Everyone who passed he suspected had come for him; he started at every voice and was terrified if a dog barked anywhere. After a long time, as no one was seen to be searching for him, he went over to a cave where in hunger he ate bread such as he had never before tasted. But it was inevitable that his hiding-place should be discovered, and when he saw horsemen approaching he commanded his companions to kill him. As no one seemed willing to do him even this service, and to avoid a worse fate, he tried to put an end to his own life. 'Jupiter,' he cried as he was dying, 'what an artist perishes in me.'

75. After his forces had been defeated, a horseman brought word of the disaster to Otho. When the bystanders refused to credit his report, he exclaimed: 'Would that this news were false, Caesar; for most gladly would I have died hadst thou been victor. As it is, I shall perish in any case, that no one may think that I fled hither to secure my own safety.' With these words, he slew himself. This act caused all to believe him and they were ready to renew the conflict, but Otho restrained them. 'Enough,' he said, 'quite enough has already happened. I hate civil war, even though I conquer; I love all Romans, even though they do not side with me. Let Vitellius be victor, since this has pleased the gods; and let the lives of his soldiers also be spared, since this pleases me. Surely it is far better and far more just that one should perish for all than many for one. Betake yourselves, therefore, to the victor and pay your court to him. As for me, let all men learn that you chose for your emperor one who would not give you up to save himself, but rather himself to save you.'

76. Vitellius entrusted the conduct of the war against the forces of Vespasian to Alienus, who marched towards Cremona and successfully occupied the town. But seeing that his soldiers, as a result of their luxurious life in Rome and their lack of military drill, were not yet fitted for the conflict which probably lay before them, he felt afraid. Consequently, when friendly proposals came from the leader of Vespasian's troops, he called his men together, and by pointing out to them the weakness of Vitellius and the strength of Vespasian and by contrasting the characters of the two men, he persuaded them to change sides. With the briefest delay the soldiers removed the images of Vitellius from their standards and took an oath that they would serve Vespasian. But after the meeting had broken up and the men had retired to their tents, they again changed their minds and, suddenly rushing together in great haste and excitement, they once more saluted Vitellius as their emperor. But for Alienus, even though he was of consular rank, they showed no respect and of their own accord threw him into prison for having attempted to seduce them from their duty.

77. Though the Romans under Titus had made a breach in the inner wall of the city, Jerusalem did not immediately fall into their hands. On the contrary, the defenders killed great numbers who tried to crowd through the opening, and they set fire to some buildings near by, hoping thus to check the further progress of the Romans. In this way they not only damaged still further the inner wall, but at the same time unintentionally burned down the barrier around the sacred precinct so that the entrance to the temple was now laid open. Nevertheless, the soldiers, because of their superstition, did not immediately rush in; but at last, under compulsion from Titus, they made their way inside. Then the Jews defended themselves much more vigorously than before, as if they had discovered a piece of rare good fortune in being able to fight near the temple and fall in its defence. Though they were but a handful fighting against a far superior force, they were not overcome until a part of the temple was set on fire. Then they met death willingly, some throwing themselves on the swords of the Romans, some slaying one another, others taking their own lives, and still others leaping into the flames.

78. While Trajan was in Antioch a terrible earthquake occurred. Since the emperor himself was passing the winter there with part of his army, and civilians had flocked thither from all sides for law-suits, business, or sight-seeing, there was no nation that went entirely unscathed. First there came, on a sudden, a great roar, and this was followed by a tremendous quaking. The whole earth seemed to be upheaved, buildings leaped into the air, wreckage was spread out over a great extent even of the open country, and an inconceivable amount of dust arose so that it was impossible for one to see anything or to speak or hear a word. Human beings were tossed violently about and then dashed to the earth as if falling from a cliff, and many of those who were not killed outright were maimed. The number of those trapped in the houses was past finding out; those who lay with a part of their body buried under the stones or timbers suffered terribly. Trajan himself made his way out through a window of the room in which he was staying; and the story became current that a being of greater than human stature had come to him and miraculously led him forth to safety.

79. At Jerusalem, Hadrian founded a new city in place of the one which had been razed to the ground; and on the site of the holy temple of the Jews he raised a new one to Jupiter. This brought on a war of no slight importance nor of brief duration; for the Jews deemed it intolerable that foreign races should be settled in their city and strange religious rites planted there. So long, indeed, as Hadrian was close at hand they remained quiet, save in so far as they purposely made of poor quality such weapons as they were called upon to furnish, in order that the Romans might reject them and they themselves might thus have the use of them. But when the emperor went further away, they openly revolted. To be sure, they did not dare try conclusions with the Romans in pitched battles; but they occupied advantageous positions in the country as places of refuge. Julius Severus, who was despatched from Britain to quell the outbreak, did not venture to attack his opponents in the open; but by intercepting small groups and by cutting off supplies of food he was able, rather slowly but with comparatively little danger, to crush, exhaust, and exterminate them.

80. One evening as Commodus was returning to his palace, an assassin awaited him and rushed upon him with a drawn sword, loudly exclaiming: 'The senate sends you this.' The menace prevented the deed; the assassin was seized by the guards and immediately revealed the authors of the conspiracy. But the words of the assassin sank deep into the mind of Commodus and left an indelible impression of fear and hatred against the whole body of the senate. Those whom he had dreaded as importunate ministers, he now suspected as secret enemies. The informers, a race of men discouraged and almost extinguished under the former reigns, again became formidable as soon as they discovered that the emperor was desirous of finding disaffection and treason in the senate. Distinction of every kind soon became criminal; suspicion was equivalent to proof, trial to condemnation. The execution of a considerable senator was attended with the death of all who might lament or revenge his fate; and when Commodus had once tasted human blood, he became incapable of pity or remorse.

81. A spirit of desertion began to prevail among the troops; and the deserters, instead of seeking their safety in flight or concealment, infested the highways. Maternus, a private soldier, collected these bands of robbers into a little army, set open the prisons, invited the slaves to assert their freedom, and plundered with impunity the rich and defenceless cities of Gaul and Spain. The governors of the provinces, who had long been the spectators and perhaps the partners of his depredations, were at length roused from their supine indolence by the threatening commands of the emperor. Maternus found that he was encompassed, and foresaw that he must be overpowered. A great effort of despair was his last resource. He ordered his followers to disperse, cross the Alps in small parties and various disguises, and to assemble at Rome during the licentious tumult of the festival of Cybele. To murder Commodus and to ascend the vacant throne was the ambition of no vulgar robber; and his measures were so ably concerted that his concealed troops filled the streets of Rome. But the envy of an accomplice discovered and ruined the enterprise in the moment when it was ripe for execution.

82. On the twenty-eighth of March, eighty-six days only after the death of Commodus, a general sedition broke out in the camp of the Praetorian guards, which the officers wanted either power or inclination to suppress. Two or three hundred of the most desperate soldiers marched at noon-day, with arms in their hands and fury in their looks, towards the Imperial palace. The gates were thrown open by their companions on guard there, who had already formed a secret conspiracy against the life of the emperor. On the news of their approach, Pertinax, disdaining either flight or concealment, advanced to meet his assassins, and recalled to their minds his own innocence and the sanctity of their recent oath of allegiance. For a few moments they stood in silent suspense, ashamed of their atrocious design and awed by the venerable aspect of their sovereign. But at length one of their number, despairing of pardon, levelled the first blow against Pertinax, who was instantly despatched with a multitude of wounds. His head, separated from his body and placed on a lance, was carried in triumph to the Praetorian camp in the sight of a mournful and indignant people.

83. After the murder of Pertinax, Sulpicianus the prefect of the city thought that by offering bribes to the Praetorians he could obtain the empire for himself; but the more prudent of them ran out upon the ramparts of their camp and proclaimed that the Roman world was to be disposed of to the highest bidder. This infamous offer at length reached the ears of Didius Julianus, a wealthy senator, who, regardless of the public calamities, was indulging himself in the luxury of the table. His wife and daughter easily persuaded him that he deserved the throne and earnestly conjured him to embrace so fortunate an opportunity. Hastening to the camp, where Sulpicianus was still in treaty with the guards, he began to bid against him from the foot of the rampart. The unworthy negotiation was transacted by faithful emissaries who passed alternately from one candidate to the other and acquainted each of them with the offers of his rival. Within a short time Julianus named a price which Sulpicianus could not equal; the gates of the camp were thrown open and he was declared emperor and received an oath of allegiance from the soldiers.

84. The army of Pannonia was at this time commanded by Septimius Severus, a native of Africa, whose ambition was never diverted by the allurements of pleasure, the apprehension of danger, or the feelings of humanity. On the first news of the murder of Pertinax, he assembled his troops, told them of the crime which had been committed, and exhorted them to arms. He concluded his speech by promising to every soldier a reward; and the total sum which he thus offered them was greater than that by which Julianus had purchased the empire. Remembering the saying of Augustus that a Pannonian army might in ten days appear in sight of Rome, he set forth in the hope that he might receive the homage of the senate and people as their lawful emperor before his competitors were even aware of his movements. During the whole expedition he scarcely allowed himself any moments for sleep or food; marching on foot and in complete armour at the head of his columns, he won the confidence and the affection of his troops and was content to share the hardships of the meanest soldier. He had no need, however, to employ force; for when he reached Rome he entered the city without opposition and won power without bloodshed.

85. The news of war in Britain and of the invasion of the province by the barbarians of the North was received with pleasure by Severus. Notwithstanding his advanced age (for he was above threescore) and his gout, which obliged him to be carried in a litter, he transported himself in person to that remote island, attended by his two sons and a formidable army. He immediately passed the walls of Hadrian and Antoninus and entered the enemy's country with a design of completing the conquest of the island. He penetrated to the northern extremity without meeting an enemy. But the ambuscades of the Caledonians, who hung unseen on the rear and flanks of his army, the coldness of the climate, and the severity of a winter march across the hills and morasses of Scotland are reported to have cost the Romans above fifty thousand men. The Caledonians at length yielded to the powerful and obstinate attack and surrendered a part of their arms and a large tract of territory. But their apparent submission lasted no longer than their present terror. As soon as the Roman legions had retired, they resumed their hostile independence.

86. While the emperor Alexander Severus was at Antioch, the punishment of some soldiers excited a sedition in the legion to which they belonged. Alexander faced the armed multitude and, despite their clamour, insisted on addressing them. 'Reserve your shouts,' he said, 'till you take the field against your enemies. Be silent in the presence of your sovereign and benefactor, who bestows upon you the corn, the clothing, and the money of the provinces. Be silent or I shall no longer call you soldiers, but citizens, if those indeed who disclaim the laws of Rome deserve to be ranked even amongst the meanest of the people.' His menaces inflamed the fury of the legion and their brandished arms already threatened his person. 'Your courage,' resumed the intrepid Alexander, 'would be more nobly displayed in the field of battle; you may destroy, but you cannot intimidate me; severe justice would punish your crime and revenge my death.' The legion still persisted in clamorous sedition when the emperor pronounced with a loud voice: 'Citizens, lay down your arms.' The soldiers, suddenly filled with grief and shame, yielded up their arms and retired in confusion not to their camp but to the city.

87. The partial success with which the besieged had repelled the attackers made them a little presumptuous and careless. The watchmen deserted their posts on the walls and went to warm themselves in neighbouring houses, being driven in by a bitterly cold wind. Their opponents saw this, and promptly took advantage of it. They crept up, without noise or clamour, till a sufficient number was collected to begin the attack. They then detached some of their body to the work of forcing the gates of the castle, against which their opponents had heaped quantities of stones. One gate which they found without this obstruction they soon burst open; and immediately a surging multitude rushed in, some to fight, and some to plunder whatever they could find. Those in the castle were as yet ignorant that the courtyard was in the possession of their enemies; but the noise and tumult soon revealed to them the loss they had sustained. Some yielded at once; others, hoping for no quarter, flung themselves from the walls and were dashed to pieces; but others, seizing their arms, prepared to offer a stout resistance. The invaders, however, speedily proved their superiority and compelled an unconditional surrender.

88. At last, when he felt that he was strong enough to launch an attack, Zenghis laid siege to Edessa with a force of chosen warriors. He invested the town on every side, so as to cut off all relief from the besieged, even if any were sent. He erected battering-rams to demolish the walls and he undermined the towers. The inhabitants, including the women, showed the greatest courage, serving the soldiers with stones and other missiles, and bringing them food and water. But Zenghis' archers sent such a constant shower of arrows into the town that the defenders had scarcely any rest by day or night. Terms were offered to the inhabitants, if they would capitulate; but they rejected the proposals with scorn, being convinced that help would soon come. No help came; and on the twenty-

eighth day after the commencement of the siege Edessa was successfully stormed. The troops of Zenghis poured into the city uttering their ferocious battle-cry, and for three whole days the carnage and devastation continued. But the prudent Zenghis saw the advantages that Edessa offered as a fortification; he caused the walls to be repaired and ordered his officers to treat the surviving inhabitants with mercy and justice.

89. After a short rest, the Latins began their long journey to Attalia. The intricate defiles of the Phrygian mountains had to be passed and they knew that they were surrounded both in front and rear by hostile Greeks who had become more open in their enmity as the Latins grew weaker. On the second day of their march they came to a pass by which they hoped to emerge from the valley in which they were. A picked band was sent forward to secure the summit of the mountain so that the main army could ascend in safety; but, unfortunately, they either misunderstood or disobeyed their orders, and instead of taking possession of the summit they pushed onwards until they had reached the other side. When the steep and rocky sides of the mountain were already covered with the Latin squadrons, the enemy, who had been cleverly concealed, rushed down upon them. A scene of awful confusion followed. The packhorses fell on the slippery rocks and rolled with increasing velocity down the mountain sides; men and animals were hurled into the abyss below; and the Greeks, leaving their safe elevation, now rushed in upon the bewildered Latins and slaughtered them like sheep.

90. When the king, alone, exhausted, and splashed with blood, got back to the main body of the army, he had no need to explain what had happened. His knights saw at a glance that his escort had been cut to pieces, and that he had escaped only by his own prowess. With silent grief they mourned over their lost comrades. They burned with a desire to avenge them; but the enemy had retired to the fastnesses of his own mountains, quite out of reach. Few slept that night. Some in anxious watchfulness expected a friend whom they were destined never to see again; others experienced all the ecstasy of joy in the return of one for whom they had lost all hope. Sorrow for the dead was soon replaced by anger against the living; for the small advance party, whose excessive zeal and disobedience had contributed not a little to the disaster, overhearing the clamour of the battle, had retraced their steps, and now at last regained the camp. The general opinion was that they should be hanged. But when the morning dawned and revealed the opposite hill-sides crowded with the enemy, the imperative necessity of taking active measures to save the remainder of the army dispelled all feelings of anger and of sorrow.

91. The voyages of Prince Henry to the coasts of Africa were not undertaken, in the first instance, for the purpose of securing slaves, but to discover what lands there were in the southern seas. Such captives as were brought back to Spain were treated, under his orders, with all kindness; and his own wish seems to have been to civilise the natives and to win over whole tribes to friendship by the education of a few prisoners. But his captains and later explorers had not such noble motives; hardly a capture was made without violence and bloodshed and the destruction of entire villages; and the natives, whatever they might gain when they reached Spain, did not give themselves up very readily to be taught but, whenever they had the chance, killed the men who pretended to have come to do them good. It was not long before many realised that the trade in slaves was a profitable business and they stopped at no cruelty, provided they could obtain a large cargo. It is hardly wonderful then that the natives, who believed that the explorers carried off their people to cook and eat them, put up a determined resistance to any who tried to land on their shores.

92. The next morning at dawn, Cortes divided his forces into three divisions of one hundred men, each under the command of a captain, provided a rear-guard of one hundred more, and so marched out towards the village where a multitude of Indian warriors were waiting. The Indians rushed courageously to the fray and, by sheer force of numbers, overwhelmed the invaders in such a manner that it was hardly possible to distinguish friend from foe, and the battle became a hand-to-hand fight at the closest possible quarters. Though fighting against a civilised force for the first time, the warriors showed little fear of the strange weapons that dealt death amongst them. But when a cavalry squadron, which Cortes had concealed in a wood, suddenly fell upon the rear of the enemy, the appearance of the horses, which the Indians beheld for the first time, struck terror amongst them. For the horse and rider seemed to them to be one irresistible creature; they were amazed at their quick movements and at the glancing armour of the cavaliers. Within a few moments they began to retreat and the horsemen pursued the fugitives across the plain until the survivors disappeared into the impenetrable forests.

93. The early career of Montezuma was that of a successful soldier; from which he passed into the priesthood, rising to the high rank of pontiff. At that time he was held in great veneration by the people as one who received revelations from the gods, and his strict life was a model to his fellows. It is related that, when the news of his election to the imperial throne was brought to him, he was found sweeping the steps of the temple whose altars he served. He ruled sternly, and ill brooked opposition or even counsel; but he was princely in recompensing faithful service. He had greatly embellished his capital; but the liberality that built an aqueduct or new temples in the city cost the subject provinces dear, and Montezuma was more feared than loved by his people. He understood the science of government; but his finer qualities were marred by his inordinate pride, and most of all by superstition, which finally lost him his throne and his life. The news of the approach of the Spaniards seemed to him to be the fulfilment of an old prophecy whose effect he tried to avoid by putting to death all those diviners who confirmed his forebodings.

94. Amongst the officers in Cortes' camp there were some who were unwilling to acquiesce in his bold designs. They claimed that the expedition had been sent out by those in authority for the definite purpose of discovering whether there was any gold in the Indians' territory or not. They had achieved that purpose, and not only had they established trading relations with the natives but they had amassed an imposing quantity of treasure which it was now their duty to carry back to Cuba. They urged that thirty-five men were dead of wounds and the pestilential climate, that others were ill, while all were without provisions and exposed to the certainty of an attack by the Indians. Cortes replied to these representations with great moderation. His opinion was that they would be ill-advised to abandon the country now that they had obtained a foothold in it; it was necessary to explore further, so as to make a satisfactory report concerning the land, its resources, and its inhabitants. As for the loss of thirty-odd men, he reminded his opponents that this was a surprisingly small number, since in all warfare some must fall.

95. When his invitation to a parley was rejected and it was clear that the Indians were determined not to listen to reason, Cortes gave the order to charge and the Spaniards plunged into the fray. After some hours of sharp fighting, the Indians began to draw off in an orderly fashion, while the Spaniards, pressing after them, were artfully drawn into a narrow defile intersected by a water-course, where the ground rendered the cavalry unavailable. The crafty Indians had decoyed them into an ambush; for, all of a sudden, their astonished eyes beheld a countless multitude of warriors whose number was estimated at one hundred thousand. With shrill cries this vast host which, by its numbers alone, might well hope to engulf the little group of Spaniards, rushed to the attack. Many would doubtless have been killed had it not been for the fact that the Indians in this, as in countless later battles, were determined to capture them alive for sacrifice to their native gods. When all seemed lost, however, Cortes managed to shift the action to more level ground where he brought his cavalry into action and so dispersed the enemy.

96. During their first days in Montezuma's capital, the Spaniards were the object of every attention and were visited daily by the great nobles of the country. Despite such outward appearances, however, the Spanish captains were disquieted by reports that treachery was brewing. It was asserted that they had finally been allowed to enter the city because it would be more easy to annihilate them there than elsewhere. Surrounded as they were by innumerable hordes of Montezuma's warriors and vassals, to whom his word was law, the gravity of their situation became daily more evident. Their stay could not be indefinitely prolonged, but it was not clear how it was to terminate felicitously. If it had been difficult to get into the capital, it seemed even more of an undertaking to get out of it alive. The city was so planned that exit from it could be cut off by raising bridges; and once this were done, the little handful of Spaniards would find themselves isolated. The imminence of their danger prompted their leader to put into operation the daring plan of seizing Montezuma himself and holding him as a hostage for the good conduct of his subjects.

97. Despite the success which had attended his military operations, there were some of the followers of Cortes who were so opposed to his plans of conquest that they formed a conspiracy to kill him. Whether too many men were involved in this plot, or too much time was allowed to elapse between its conception and its execution, is not clear; in any case, one of the men privy to it repented, and the day previous to that fixed for carrying it out, he revealed everything to the commander. Calling his officers together, Cortes related what he had just heard, and then going all together to the quarters of the ringleader they surprised him there with several confederates. Realising that he was discovered, the traitor attempted to destroy a slip of paper that lay on the table; but Cortes was too quick for him; and glancing down the list of names written on it, he was pained to find some whom he had considered his friends inscribed amongst his would-be assassins. The chief conspirator was immediately tried, found guilty, and punished with such promptness that the sight of his dead body hanging from his own doorway was the first intimation to his associates that the conspiracy had been discovered.

98. Under the leadership of their young sovereign, who kept his serenity throughout, these naked barbarians, weakened by famine and confronted by inevitable defeat, fought fearlessly. Never did they so much as name surrender, even though Cortes daily renewed his offer of honourable terms for the emperor and his people if they would submit. Time after time, Cortes wasted hours in waiting for better counsels to prevail; but nothing he could say or do sufficed to allay the distrust of the enemy. Their choice was made; they had had enough of the Spaniards, in whose semi-divine character they no longer believed, and whose presence in the land they so deeply detested. Cortes protested throughout the greatest reluctance to destroy the city, and repeatedly declared that the necessity of so doing filled him with inexpressible grief. The fate known to be in store for every Spaniard taken alive, and stories of the hideous rites of sacrifice followed by cannibal feasts, were certainly sufficient to arouse the Spaniards to a frenzy ; yet never, so far as we know, did the spirit of vengeance prompt reprisals on the prisoners who fell into their hands.

99. The execution of the Duke of Somerset was fixed for the morning of the 22nd of January. Since an attempt at rescue was anticipated, all inhabitants of the city were commanded to keep to their houses and a thousand men-at-arms were brought in from the country. But as the day dawned, despite the proclamation, the great square and every avenue of approach to it were thronged with spectators, pressing on all sides against the circle of armed men. A little before eight o'clock Somerset was led out by the guard. He stepped forward, said a short prayer, and bowing to the people, addressed them bareheaded. 'I am come hither to die ; but as true and faithful a man as any unto the King's Majesty and to his realm. I am condemned by a law whereunto I am subject, as are we all ; and therefore to show obedience I am content to die.' Many in the crowd expected that at the very last moment the king would send a pardon, and there was a rumour that a messenger had indeed arrived. But such hopes were groundless ; and within a few minutes of Somerset's first appearance, the executioner had completed his grim task.

100. On the day after the expiration of the truce an enterprising officer performed a service of great importance by surprising the castle of Dumbarton. This was the only fortified place in the kingdom of which the queen had kept possession ever since the commencement of the civil wars. Its situation, on the top of a high and almost inaccessible rock, rendered it extremely strong and, in the opinion of that age, impregnable. As it commanded the river, it was of great importance, and was deemed the most likely place for the landing of any foreign troops that might come to Mary's aid. It was this fortress which a small but gallant band determined to assault. Arriving at midnight, when the moon was already set, they attempted to climb the rock where it was highest and where there were few sentinels. Many were the difficulties they encountered, as their ladders proved to be insecure and the darkness prevented them from seeing each other clearly. It was indeed nearly daybreak before they were at the top of the steep ascent; but fortunately, as they had expected, the sentinels were lulled into a false sense of security, and after a short conflict they made themselves masters of the castle.

101. Next morning the messengers delivered a letter from their sovereign to Mary in which, after the bitterest reproaches and accusations, she informed her that regard for the happiness of the nation had at last rendered it necessary to make a public enquiry into her conduct. She was therefore required, as she had so long lived under the protection of the laws of England, to submit to trial. Mary, though surprised at this message, was neither appalled at the danger nor unmindful of her own dignity. She protested in the most solemn manner that she was innocent and had never countenanced any attempt against the life of the queen of England; but, at the same time, she refused to acknowledge the right of English judges to try her. 'I came into the kingdom,' she said, 'an independent sovereign, to implore the queen's assistance, not to subject myself to her authority. My spirit is not broken by past misfortunes, nor so intimidated by present dangers as to stoop to anything unbecoming the majesty of a crowned head or to anything that will disgrace the ancestors from whom I am descended and the son to whom I shall leave my throne. If I must be tried, princes alone shall try me.'

102. Information soon reached the colonists in America that a scheme was on foot for enforcing their subjugation by means of a body of troops who did not speak their language, and who came from countries where the idea of liberty, as Anglo-Saxons understood it, was totally unknown. The tidings were everywhere received with surprise, indignation, and anxiety. Those feelings were strongest in the well-ordered homesteads in districts which, ever since the Indians had retreated westwards, had been exempt from the terror of rapine, conflagration, and outrage. The German officers who were to be sent against them and a great majority of their men might be respectable and law-abiding, in so far as military law was any protection to the inhabitants of a rural district which had been proclaimed rebellious ; but a considerable percentage of the rank and file in some of the regiments was composed of refuse from all the barrack-rooms in Europe. The near future proved only too well that the apprehensions entertained by the dwellers in the sea-board were not exaggerated.

103. When Charles Fox rose to oppose the measure which the government proposed, he spoke with the ease of private conversation and all the charm and force of oratory. 'I have always said that the war is unjust, and the object of it unattainable. But, admitting it to be a just and practicable war, I now say that the means employed are not such as will secure the desired ends. In order to induce the Americans to submit, you pass laws against them, tyrannical and cruel in the extreme. When they complain of one law, your answer is to pass another more rigorous than the former. You tell us that you have no choice in the matter, because they are in rebellion. Then treat them as rebels are wont to be treated. Send out your fleets and armies, and subdue them ; but show them that your laws are mild, just, and equitable, and that they therefore are in the wrong. The very contrary of this has been your wretched policy. I have ever understood it as a first principle that in rebellion you punish the individuals but spare the country. In a war against a foreign enemy you spare individuals and do your utmost to injure and impoverish the country. Your conduct has in all respects been the reverse of this.'

104. Colonel Markham served until the end of the war, and at different times was entrusted with the command of a brigade. We are told that some singularities appeared in his character, but all tending to his honour. When at the head of his regiment, he always made some tired soldier ride his horse, and he himself marched on foot through every kind of bad ground and partook of every awkwardness of situation to which his men were exposed. His cool courage and contempt of personal danger were almost proverbial in the army. On one occasion, when under a heavy fire, he heard talking in the ranks. He turned his back upon the enemy, commanded silence, and harangued the men upon the discipline of the Lacedaemonians. Upon another occasion his regiment, while advancing amid a shower of bullets, was brought up short by a wooden fence. Colonel Markham went up to the palings, pulled at them and found that they might be forced. After the action, some of his officers represented to him the imminent danger to which he had exposed himself unnecessarily, as he might have sent a private upon the same service. He answered with warmth: 'Good God! Do you suppose I would send any man on a service of danger where I would not go myself?'

105. Toulon still appeared secure. Not one of the great fortresses which protected it was seriously threatened and, judging from the distance at which the Republican forces still remained from the walls, the inhabitants might have believed in the indefinite duration of the siege. But the English fleet began to withdraw from the harbour and the inhabitants learned with dismay that vessels were offered for those who wished to fly. A multitude, struck with despair and beside themselves with terror, rushed to the ships to escape from Republican vengeance. More than fifteen thousand inhabitants thus abandoned their homes; the town was soon deserted and given up to the convicts who had broken their chains. Night came on and increased the confusion. All at once a flame rose from the arsenal, and soon after, a sudden blaze shot into the air from the middle of the harbour; it was the vessels of the Republicans which the English set on fire before leaving. Next day the besieging troops entered the mute and terror-stricken town. Many hundreds of those who had not supposed it needful to take to flight, were publicly shot without any other form of trial than the simple denunciation of their fellow-citizens.

106. Bonaparte's proclamation on taking the field was utterly opposed to the spirit which had hitherto animated the Republican armies. It was an appeal to their ambition, and no longer to their patriotism; it was a war of conquest and not a war of liberty that his words announced. 'Soldiers,' he said, 'you are hungry and nearly naked. The government owes you much, but it can do nothing for you; your patience and courage do you honour, but cannot procure for you either profit or glory. I am come to lead you into the most fertile plains in the world. There you will find rich provinces and great towns; there you will find glory, honour, and—riches.' These seductive promises, so often to be repeated in his later proclamations, were then heard for the first time. The Republican soldiers had often listened to addresses about tyranny to destroy, about liberty to avenge, about chains to break; but no one had yet thought of inflaming their valour by kindling their cupidity. In reading these first words addressed to the army of democrats by this powerful tempter, we think with sadness of the subsequent mad adventures into which he was destined to draw them.

107. After the battle of Lodi, Bonaparte received despatches informing him that he was henceforth to share the command of the army with Kellermann. Nothing could have been more galling to a man of his pride and ambition; but with the decision of one who knows that he is indispensable, he did not hesitate to send in his resignation, fully convinced that it would not be accepted. His letter was firm, but full of deference and courtesy. He began by announcing the news of his victory and the conquest of a fertile province of Italy, which was certainly the best introduction he could have chosen to give weight to his words. 'But,' he continued, 'if I have to refer everything to Ministers at home, if they have the right to change my movements, to send me troops or withdraw them at their pleasure, do not expect any further success. In the present state of affairs it is indeed necessary that you should have one general who has your entire confidence. If it is not I, I shall not complain; I shall only redouble my zeal in order to deserve your esteem. General Kellermann has had more experience and will make war better than I; but both together we shall make it ill.'

108. After he had made himself master of the plain of Lombardy, Bonaparte addressed his soldiers in words which later generations have thought too full of boasting and bombast. 'Much,' he said, 'you have done, my soldiers; but is there nothing more to do? Shall it be said of us that we knew how to conquer, but not how to profit by victory? Shall posterity reproach us with having halted before our final goal is won? No! I see you ready to fly to arms; for you know that every day lost for glory is lost too for your happiness. Let us be stirring, then! We still have forced marches to make, enemies to subdue, laurels to win, and wrongs to avenge. But the people through whose land we shall pass have nothing to fear. We are the friends of them all; we are especially friendly towards the descendants of the Brutuses and Scipios, and those great men whom we have taken for our models. To rebuild the Capitol, and place there with all honour the statues of heroes of renown, to rouse the Roman people, whom so many centuries of bondage have enthralled, such will be the fruit of your victories. And you will have the glory of having changed the face of the most beautiful country in Europe.'

109. From eight to ten thousand peasants had shut themselves up in Pavia and manned the ramparts, when the French column led by Bonaparte came in sight. The summons of the general, calling upon the besieged rabble to surrender, produced no effect, and the order was given to take the ramparts, if possible, by storm and to batter down the gates of the city with axes. Within a short space the peasants, realising that resistance was hopeless, dispersed precipitately into the country, where many of them fell easy victims to the pursuing cavalry. The soldiers, finding themselves masters of the town, loudly demanded permission to pillage, and Bonaparte granted it, thus yielding to a barbarous tradition long proscribed by the code of civilised nations. He also gave orders that those who had been responsible for leading the peasants in their ill-fated defence should be immediately executed; but fortunately for his memory, the order was not carried out at once, and the general was glad enough a few days later to show them a mercy which was no more than justice.

110. The French army was in a most critical situation, but by a rapid concentration of its forces it could regain its lost advantages; for if it was a third less in number than the whole of the troops which surrounded it, it was stronger than each of the enemy detachments taken separately, and could beat them one after another before they had effected their junctions. Bonaparte saw at a glance the necessity of following this plan, and he carried it out with that incomparable decision which in these difficult moments astonished the most resolute and made people say that a god was in him. As he required all his forces, he did not hesitate to raise the siege of Mantua on which he was engaged. This sacrifice has undoubtedly gained him more praise than it deserved, for it was a matter of necessity; but it was a sacrifice that none but he would have made with the same promptitude. Indeed, the besiegers retired with such speed that the enemy leader, who had been hastening by forced marches to bring assistance, found no one to fight with when he arrived; and because of this well-planned but wasted effort he was absent from a battle which decided the fate of his principal army.

111. Mantua had for some time been reduced to the severest extremities; the garrison had eaten all the horses and were now on half rations. It is not surprising that they were compelled to ask for terms; for the resistance could not in fact be prolonged. Nevertheless, the deputation from Mantua to the French camp enumerated, with the exaggeration usual in such cases, the means of defence which the garrison still possessed. While they were conducting their negotiations with the officer in charge of the blockade, they scarcely noticed a stranger wrapped in a large cloak who was writing at a table without saying a word. When he had finished he rose, and extending a paper to the leader of the deputation he said: 'Here are my conditions. If your general still had provisions for twenty-five days and spoke of surrender, he would be unworthy of honourable terms; but I respect his age, his courage, and his misfortunes. If he opens his gates to-morrow, or if he waits three months, the conditions will be the same.' The Mantuans now recognised Bonaparte and, after admitting that they had provisions for only three days more, they agreed to surrender.

112. If the king had been a despot, he might at least have controlled the petty chieftains and kept the right of plundering in his own hand ; but his selfish indifference was worse than any tyranny. No regular government existed. Those who nominally governed the various districts, were in fact collectors of revenue, who had to pay a fixed sum to the king and reimbursed themselves as best they could. This revenue was collected by armed force and no land-owner ever dreamed of paying unless he was compelled. The strong gathered their clansmen around them, shut themselves up in their forts, and received the chieftain and his army with a discharge of artillery. The weak were mercilessly plundered, sometimes killed, and sometimes forced to take to brigandage for a living. The soldiers too were let loose upon the country to realise their pay, so that peasants and small traders never felt secure for a single night. No pen could faithfully describe the sins of the oppressors or the miseries of the oppressed ; and, if the picture could be painted, no humane man would suffer himself to look upon it. For the worst of Roman proconsuls would have blushed at the iniquities.

113. Maddened by repeated taunts, and suffering from a sense of injustice, the Indian soldiers plotted to murder their officers in the dead of night, seize the fortress, and hold it while their brethren in the south were following their example. The English were taken wholly by surprise. Some were shot down at their posts, others were murdered in their beds ; and all must have been overpowered if there had not been a solitary officer outside the fort who heard the tumult and hurried to Arcot for help. Fortunately the commandant of that station was a man equal to any emergency. In less than a quarter of an hour after he had heard the news, he was galloping at the head of a squadron towards the scene of the mutiny. Finding the gate closed against his force, he had himself drawn up alone by a rope over the walls, assumed command of the remnant of the garrison, and kept the mutineers at bay until his men forced their way in, completed the rescue, and took terrible vengeance upon all the delinquents, except those who escaped or who were reserved for more formal punishment.

114. When it was known in the government camp that a battle was to be fought on the morrow, even the sick rose painfully from their beds and swore that they would remain there no longer. Before daybreak the troops were led out to meet the enemy, but it was not until midday that the rebels, unable any longer to hold their ground, were forced to retreat towards the city. The victors, though fearfully exhausted, were still eager for more blood and their general resolved to follow up his success lest the enemy should have time to rally; consequently it was evening before the victorious army laid aside its weapons. Their losses had been severe; but the victory was worth the price paid for it; for the enemy had sustained a crushing defeat. They had been forced to surrender to their conqueror a commanding position from which he would attack them to the greatest advantage while keeping open his communications; and they had been driven ignominiously, by a force far smaller than their own, to take refuge within the walls of the very city from which they had but lately expelled every inhabitant whom they had not destroyed. No wonder then that the victors lay down to rest with light hearts.

115. Then the commander, seeing no hope of succour, and reflecting that his ammunition was fast failing, that many of his best men had fallen, and that the survivors were worn out by the sleepless labour of defence, resolved to attempt an escape. In the river which ran beneath the walls of the fort there were three boats moored, and into these the garrison were ordered to descend. Night was almost over when the men had taken their places, and there was already enough light for the enemy to see that their prey was escaping. With fierce yells they started in pursuit on foot; but the current carried the fugitives away so swiftly that their pursuers, stumbling along the uneven bank, could not gain upon them. But by an unfortunate mischance, two of the boats grounded and only a few of their occupants could be transferred to the remaining boat, which was now uncomfortably loaded. Those who were left behind made their way as best they could to the bank, where they fell easy victims to the enemy. Yet their fate was no worse than that of those in the third boat, which capsized and precipitated them into the river. Of the eighty-five who set out from the fort only three survived to tell the tale.

116. Meanwhile the women in the city had been anxiously waiting for the issue of the battle upon which they believed their safety depended. The distress of those whose husbands were in action was terrible; and after listening for three long hours to the confused noise of the battle, some of them hurried to an eminence within the city, from which they knew they would be able to discern the movements of the two armies. Then their suspense was terminated indeed, but by despair; for they could plainly see their countrymen retreating, hotly pursued by the enemy's cavalry. Within a short time a disorderly mob of their own soldiers, covered with dust and stained with the blood of their wounds, came rushing into the city, clamouring for water. Now that they knew the worst, the women forgot their own sorrows. Some of them went about ministering to the needs of the defeated and exhausted troops; others watched over the bedsides of the wounded and the dying; and there were many who showed a more than womanly fortitude and shared the task of barricading the gates against the enemy, who were now clamouring outside as if they expected to take the city as easily as they had won the battle outside its walls.

117. Grant, whose career had been one of unbroken success, was now called upon to command an army and suppress a rebellion. But he declined the honour which was thrust upon him. If he had believed that he was not the fittest man that could be found, his resolve would have been worthy of respect. But there is no evidence to show that he thought so humbly of his own powers. He declared that he could best serve his country by remaining at headquarters and thence directing the movements of the troops whose glory he refused to share in the field. Others, he said, might have ability enough for crushing a rebellion ; he had to meditate for the future. No matter how gloomy were the messages that came from the scene of the conflict, he was never dismayed ; for he alone failed to realise how serious was the situation. Indeed, the one great service he conferred on his country came about more by accident than design ; for the officer whom he carelessly selected to quell the trouble proved to be a man of genius whose military exploits in later years were destined to win the gratitude of a whole nation.

118. Never since wars began had a besieged garrison been called upon to do or to suffer greater things than were appointed for the garrison of Cawnpore. The besieging army numbered some three thousand trained soldiers, well fed, well lodged, well armed, supplied with all the munitions of war, and supported by the sympathies of a large portion of the civil population. The besieged were few in number, and had to contend against almost every disadvantage that could have been arrayed against them. They could only muster about four hundred fighting men, more than seventy of whom were invalids. Wholly insufficient in itself, this small force was encumbered by the charge of a helpless throng of women and children.

Furthermore, combatants and non-combatants alike experienced now for the first time the unmitigated fierceness of a tropical summer ; without the most ordinary comforts, they were huddled together in two stifling buildings which offered them their only shelter. In such circumstances, it is a matter for wonder and surprise that the defenders did not at once despair of holding the town against the overwhelming numbers of their enemy.

119. The most trying period of the siege had now begun. There was so little food left that the daily ration of each person had to be reduced to a handful of flour ; and whereas fresh hosts of rebels were daily swarming to swell the ranks of the enemy, the numbers of the defenders were greatly diminished. Some were struck down by fever ; others pined away from exposure, from hunger, or from thirst. More wretched still was the fate of the wounded ; for there were no longer any medical supplies of any kind ; and death, which came too slowly, was their only healer. But most to be pitied were those women who still survived. Their only resting place was the hard earth, their only protection a crumbling wall ; they were begrimed with dirt and their dresses were in rags. A skilful pen might describe the acuteness of their bodily sufferings ; but who can imagine the intensity of their mental tortures ? They lacked the consolation of fighting against desperate odds, which may even then have sustained the heart of the soldier. Yet they never despaired and they cheered all by their uncomplaining spirit and their tender, gracious kindness.

120. Two battles had now been won ; but there was no rest for the victors ; for before noon news was brought that the enemy had rallied near an unfordable river six miles distant and were preparing to destroy the bridge. Knowing that if they succeeded in their design his progress would be retarded, the general called upon his troops for a fresh effort. Exhausted by a five hours' march, they were lying down waiting for breakfast; but full of confidence in their leader and inspired by his self-denying example, they sprang to their feet at the word of command and marched forward. When they reached the river they found the enemy massed on its banks; but the bridge was still intact. Undaunted by the numbers confronting them, they rushed into the conflict and after a sharp hand-to-hand encounter they succeeded in driving the enemy in confusion over the bridge. Satisfied that the road was now clear, the general had not the heart to call upon his men to pursue the bewildered foe. The soldiers indeed were so overcome by fatigue that they threw themselves on the ground; and many of them, caring for nothing but rest, even rejected the food which was offered them.

121. It is generally agreed that if Campbell had known how to use his opportunities, or if he had accepted the counsel of one of his lieutenants, he might have gained a far more splendid and decisive success; he might indeed have achieved at one stroke the subjugation not only of a single city but of a whole province. Outram, his second in command, was eager to strike another blow at the rebels while they were confused and demoralised by the loss of their citadel; and in pursuit of this aim he applied for permission to cross the river and attack them. If he had been allowed to do so he might have cut off their retreat. Campbell's answer was one which, if it had proceeded from a less sagacious man, might have been regarded as a symptom of insanity. Influenced by his almost miserly reluctance to expend the lives of his soldiers, even for the attainment of a great object, he forbade Outram to execute his plan if he thought that by doing so he would lose a single man. Others might have dared to disobey so absurd an order. Outram, however, was not a man to act in opposition to his instructions; and thus a great opportunity was lost.

122. After the destruction of his stronghold, Kunwar Singh pursued the career of a freebooter far away from the land of his birth. In the spring, however, he saw an opportunity of proving his claim to rank amongst the heroes of his race. He knew that the British garrison in the province of Oudh had been seriously weakened by the necessity of concentrating troops elsewhere : now was the time for him to strike a crushing blow at the Government. At first his venture was attended by signal successes ; he surprised and captured several villages and eventually blockaded an important town where several detachments of British troops were stationed. The lack of provisions in the town made the plight of the defenders serious in the extreme ; yet after several weeks the town was still in British possession, and there were many rumours that a strong force was marching rapidly to its relief. Though Kunwar Singh now suspected that he must abandon his designs against the garrison, his presence of mind did not forsake him. He posted the flower of his troops to oppose the relieving force, and there is no knowing what the issue would have been had not old age ended the career of this redoubtable warrior.

123. When Lord Dalhousie proclaimed that the state of Jhansi had now become the possession of the British, the widow of the late ruler protested against his action. She might in time have learned to reconcile herself to a not uncommon fate, if the Government had not called upon her to pay debts which her husband had left. At first she could not conceal her indignation at such meanness ; but when she found that her remonstrances were disregarded, she cunningly resolved to wear a smiling face in the presence of her masters, while secretly waiting for an opportunity to gratify the bitter resentment which she harboured against them. She was indeed a woman whom it was dangerous to provoke. Tall of stature and comely in person, she was capable of pursuing a policy with an unconquerable resolution. Moreover, while brooding over her own grievances, she knew how to avail herself of the discontent which British rule had awakened in the minds of all her former subjects; and when news reached her that the peoples in other parts of the peninsula had risen against their oppressors, she felt that her day had come at last and speedily organised a revolt in the territory where her husband had once ruled.

124. The besieged had no thought of yielding without a struggle; but they could not hide from themselves or their enemies that ammunition and supplies of every kind were almost entirely lacking. Their assailants, however, were led by a man who was not trained in warfare and who was unwilling to ask his subordinates what course he ought to pursue; opportunities which a more skilful general would have turned to advantage were let slip. Day after day passed by, and the plight of those in the city was growing more desperate when messengers arrived from the besiegers to say that if the garrison would surrender the city they would be conducted to a place of safety. Trusting to the solemn oaths which the messengers swore, the garrison walked out of the city. It would have been better if they had remained within, destroyed their women and children with their own hands, and then died at their posts. Then at least they would have sold their lives dearly; for the moment they had quitted the city, the enemy fell treacherously upon them, dragged them off to a garden close by, and there murdered nearly every man, woman, and child among them.

125. At three o'clock in the morning the columns marched silently to their positions. The moon was very bright and the men, fearful of being discovered, waited for some time in suspense for the signal. At length the order to advance was whispered along the ranks and the troops moved on. As they approached the city gate, they heard a warning cry from the walls and immediately they were assailed by a shower of missiles of every kind. Undaunted, they pushed on and within a brief space they had gained the rampart where the enemy, paralysed by their opponents' courage, fell back in confusion. Then began a grim struggle for the possession of the streets of the city. House after house was desperately defended and resolutely stormed. Many of the defenders whose retreat was cut off jumped down into the shallow wells rather than face their foes ; but the infuriated soldiers dragged them out and slew them on the spot. The fiercest struggle took place round the palace until the rebels, realising that their chief had abandoned them to their fate, broke and fled. Before dawn every street was in the hands of the attackers and there was scarcely a house that was not ablaze.

GENERAL VOCABULARY

CAUTION.—It should be understood that the Latin words given in this Vocabulary are not necessarily equivalent to the English words when the latter are used with a meaning different from that which they have in the Exercises. (See **17-19**.)

N.B.—The references given in brackets to the various sections of the book are intended to supplement the information given in the Vocabulary. The student should therefore not neglect to make use of such references.

Figures in heavy type refer to sections. Figures in ordinary type refer to declensions and conjugations, except where p. (=page) or Ex. (=Exercise) or Intr. (=Introduction) is prefixed.

abandon, (*a person*) dēser-ō[1] (3, -uī, -tum); dē-sum (-esse, -fuī; with *dat.*; **251**); dēstitu-ō (3, -ī); dē-scīscō (3, -scīvī; with *ab*=*withdraw from a party*).

abandon (*a thing or work*), omittō (3, -mīsī, -missum; see note under *undone, I leave*); dē-sistō (3, -stitī; with *ab* or *abl.*).

abandoned=*wicked,* perditus.

abandonment *of,* use o-mittō (3, -mīsī, -missum). (**417**.)

abide by, stō (1, stetī; with *abl.*).

ability, or **abilities,** ingenium, *n.* (See note under *character.*)

able, possum (posse, potuī).

abound in, abundō (1), circum-fluō (3, -flūxī). (**284**.)

about (*adv.*), circā, circiter; ferē, fermē.

about (*prep.* = concerning), dē. (**332, 4**.)

about (*prep.*=near), circum, circā. (**331, 5**.)

absence, *in my.* (**61**, and **420**.)

absent, absum (abesse, āfuī); *from,* ā, ab.

absolutely, plānē; *or superl. of adj.*

absolutely impossible. (**127**.)

abstain from. (**264**.)

abundance of, plūrimum. (**294**.)

abuse, maledicta, *n. pl.* (**51**, *b.*)

accept, ac-cipiō (3, -cēpī, -ceptum).

acceptable to, grātus. (See note under *delightful.*)

accident, cāsus, 4, *m.*

accident, *by,* cāsū; forte; fortuitō.

accomplish, ef- *or* cōn-ficiō (3, -fēcī, -fectum).

accordance with, *in,* perinde ac, etc. (**491**); prō (**332, 7**).

account of, *on,* propter (with *acc.*).

account, *on no,* nūllō modō; minimē.

account, *take into,* ratiōnem habeō (2; with *gen.*).

accuracy, *with more,* vērius. (**64**.)

accuse, accūsō, 1.

accuser,=*he who accuses.* (**76**.)

accustomed, *am,* soleō (2, solitus sum).

achievements, rēs gestae.

achievements, *perform,* rēs gerō (3, gessī, gestum).

acquire, ad-ipīscor (3, -eptus sum). (**19**.)

[1] *Relinquō,* I abandon, in a neutral and general sense of 'leaving behind'; *dēserō,* I quit a place or person where or with whom duty bids me stay; *dēstituō,* I leave 'in the lurch' one who without me will be unaided; *dēsum,* I fail to be present where my presence is desirable or right; *dēficiō* (with *ab* or, when the subject is not a person, with the acc.), 'I fail' or 'fall off from,' those whom I have hitherto stood by.

acquit, absol-vō (3, -vī, -ūtum). (306.)
across, trāns (with *acc.*).
act (=*behave*), mē gerō (3, gessī).
act rightly, rēctē faciō (3, fēcī).
act thus, haec faciō (3, fēcī).
action, *by,* agendō (398); *nom.* agere (95, 99).
acts, facta, *n. pl.* (51, *b.*)
address (=*speech*), ōrāti-ō, -ōnis, *f.*
address (*the people*), verba (apud populum) faciō (3, fēcī).
adequate, iūstus.
administering the government, reī pūblicae prōcūrāti-ō, -ōnis, *f.*; rempūblicam gubernāre.
administration, prōcūrāti-ō, -ōnis, *f.*
admire, admīror, 1.
advance, prō-cēdō (3, -cessī, -cessum); prō-gredior, (3, -gressus sum).
advance in learning, doctior fīō.
advanced age, prōvecta aetās. (303, *Note* (i).)
advanced in life or years. (303, *Note* (i).)
advance guard, primum ag-men, -minis, *n.*
advantage, ēmolumentum, *n.* (294.)
adverse, adversus (*adj.*).
adversity, rēs adversae.
advice, *against your,* use *pres. part. of* dis-suādeō (2, -suāsī). (420.)
advise, moneō, 2.
advocate of (*peace*), auctor (pācis).
advocate of, *am an,* suādeō (2, suāsī, suāsum); with *acc. of thing.* (See 248.)
advocate, *am your,* tē dēfen-dō (3, -dī).
affair, rēs, 5, *f.*
affected (=*agitated*), *am,* com-moveor (2, -mōtus sum).
affirmative, *to reply in the.* (162.)
afflict with, af-ficiō (3, -fēcī). (283.)
afraid, *am,* timeō, 2.
afraid of, *am,* =*fear* (25), per-timēscō (3, -timuī; with *acc.*, or nē, ut, 137).
after (*prep.*), post (with *acc.*). (322.)
after (*with verbal subst.*), *use* cum.
again, rūrsus. (328, *g.*)
again (*with neg.*), posthāc; posteā.
again and again, saepe, saepissimē. (57, *a*; see also 533, *b.*)
against, contrā (with *acc.*).
against (*my wishes*)=*in spite of.* (420.)
age (=*time of life*), ae-tās, -tātis, *f.*
age (=*of things*), vetus-tās, -tātis, *f.*
age, *old,* senec-tūs, -tūtis, *f.*
age, *of that.* (238, iii.)
age, *those of his own,* aequālēs. (51, *a.*)
age of, *at the.* (327.)
aged, exāctae aetātis (*gen.*). (303, *Note* (i).)
aggressive, *take the,* ultrō arma (*or* bellum) īn-ferō (-ferre, -tulī, illātum).
agitation, *there is,* trepidātur. (218.)
ago. (324.)
agree with, *do not,* parum (=*but little*) cōn-sentiō (4, -sēnsī) cum (with *abl.*).
agreed by (*all*), *it is,* cōnstat inter (omnēs).
agreed on by, *it is,* convenit inter (with *acc.*).
agreement, pactum, *n.*
agreement *is come to, an,* convenit (*impers.*).
agreement with, *am in,* cōn-sentiō (4, -sēnsī) cum (with *abl.*)
aid, auxilium, *n.*
aid, opem ferō (ferre, tulī; with *dat.*).
aid, *come to,* sub-veniō (4, -vēnī, -ventum; with *dat.*). (See also 259.)
aid, *by your,* operā tuā.
aim at, pet-ō (3, -īvī, -ītum); ap-petō. (23.)
aim at (*doing, etc.*), id agō (3, ēgī) ut... (118.)
alarmed, *am,* timeō, 2.
alarmed (=*anxious*) *for,* timeō, 2 (with *dat.*; 248).
Alexander, Alexan-der, -drī.
alien (*adj.*), externus.
alien (*noun*), peregrīnus, *m.*

alike (*adv.*), pariter.
alive, *am*, vīvō (3, vīxī).
all, *pl. of* omnis; *also* cūnctus, ūniversus.[1]
all (*things*), *n. pl. of* omnis.
all is lost, dē summā rē āctum est.
allegiance, fidēs, 5, *f.*
alliance with, *make,* societātem in-eō (-īre, -īvī) cum...
allow (=*let*), per-mittō (3, -mīsī, -missum; with *dat.*; 123).
allow (=*grant*), con-cēdō (3, -cessī, -cessum).
allow (=*confess, admit*), fateor, (2, fassus sum), con-cēdō (3, -cessī).
allow myself to, *will not,* nōn committam ut...
allowed, *am,* licet mihi. (198.)
allowed, *it is* (=*admitted, or agreed on*), cōnstat (*impers.*); *allowed by*, cōnstat inter (with *acc.*).
ally, socius, *m.*
almost, ferē,[2] paene, prope.
aloft, altē.
alone in *doing this, am,* sōlus (*or* ūnus 529 *d*) hoc faciō. (62.)
along. (331, 5 and 21.)
already, iam.
also, quoque (Intr. 89); *or* (*sometimes*) īdem, īdemque. (396.)
altars and hearths, ārae atque focī.
altering, *am* (*intrans.*), mūtor, 1. (21, *a.*)
always, semper.
ambassador, lēgātus.
ambush, ambuscade, īnsidiae, *f. pl.*
amiss, secus.
among, inter (with *acc.*).
ancestors, maiōrēs. (51, *a.*)
ancient, prīstinus[3]; vetus (*gen.* veteris); vetustus (*superl.* vetustissimus); antīquus. (See *note.*)
and, et, -que, atque, ac (Intr. 48; see also 110).
anew, dē integrō. (328, *g.*)
anger, īra; *cherish anger,* succēnseō (2; with *dat.*).
angry with, *am,* īrā-scor (3, -tus sum; with *dat.*).
angry mood, īrācundia, *f.*
angry outcries. (See *outcries.*)
annihilate, dēl-eō (2, -ēvī, -ētum).
announcement, use nūntiō, 1. (417, i.)
another (=*a second*), alter (*gen.* alterīus). (368.)
answer, re-spondeō (2, -spondī, -spōnsum).
answer, *make no=answer nothing.*
answer to, *in.* (331, 1.)
antiquity (*of a thing existing*), vetus-tās, -tātis, *f.*
anxiety, sollicitūd-ō, -inis, *f.*
anxiety, *free from,* sēcūrus.
anxious for, *feel,* dif-fīdō (3, -fīsus sum; with *dat.*).
anxious to, *am,* cup-iō (3, -īvī; with *inf.*).
any (*after negat.*), quisquam, quidquam; ūllus. (See 358.)
any? (*impassioned interrogative*), ecquis; (*adjectival*) ecquī.
any longer, ultrā. (See also 328, *a.*)
any man may, cuiusvīs est. (292, 4.)
any one (*in final and consec. clauses*). (109.)

[1] *Universī*, all as a body, opposed to *singulī*; *omnēs*, all without exception, opposed to *nēmō* or to *ūnus*: *cūnctī*, is stronger than *omnēs*, 'all together.'

[2] *Ferē* (*fermē* often in Livy) is 'more or less,' 'about'; *paene, prope,* 'less than, but bordering on.' Hence *quod ferē fit,* 'as generally happens'; but, *prope dīvīnus,* 'all but divine,' 'heroic.'

[3] *Antīquus* is 'old and no longer existing'; *vetus* and *vetustus* 'old and still existing.' Thus *domus antīqua,* 'what was long ago my home'; *domus* (*vetus* or) *vetusta,* 'what has long been my home'; *mōs antīquus,* 'an old custom now obsolete'; *vetere mōre,* 'in accordance with long-established custom.' *Antīquus* = 'of the good old times,' often used in praise. *Prīscus* = 'old-fashioned,' 'rarely seen now'; *prīstinus,* simply 'earlier' as opposed to 'the present.'

anything (*you please*), quidvīs. (359.)
anywhere (*after negat.*), ūsquam.
Apiolae, Apiolae, -ārum, *pl. f.*
apologise for, veniam pet-ō (3, -īvī; with *quod*-clause or *gen.* of noun).
apparently. (64.)
appeal to, obtestor, 1 (with *acc.*); *to you not to*, tē obtestor (1) nē... (See 118.)
appeal to, *solemnly*, fidem tuam implōrō (1) ut *or* nē...
appeal to fear, dēterreō, 2. (25.)
appear (=*seem*), videor (2, vīsus sum). (43.)
applaud, plau-dō (3, -sī, -sum; with *dat.*).
apprehension, metus, 4, *m.*
approach, adventō, 1 (*intrans.*); appropinquō, 1 (with *dat.*).
approval for *this, get your*, hoc tibi probō.
approved of (*by you*), *it is*, (tibi) probātur.
apt to, *am*=*am wont*, soleō, 2, solitus sum.
ardently, vehement-er, -ius, -issimē.
ardour for, studium, *n.* (with *gen.*). (300.)
argue, dis-serō (3, -seruī).
aright, rēctē.
aristocratic party, optimāt-ēs, *m. pl.* (*gen.* -um *or* -ium). (See 51, *a, and note.*)
arm, bracchium, *n.*
armed, armātus.
armistice, indūtiae, *f. pl.*
arms, arma, *n. pl.*
army, exercitus, 4, *m.*
arrival, adventus, 4, *m.*
arrive, per-veniō (4, -vēnī, -ventum) ad (with *acc.*).
arrow, sagitta, *f.*
art, ars (*gen.* artis), *f.*
as, or *as . . . so*, sīcut (*with* ita *in main clause*); et . . . et.
as (=*as though*), tamquam. (494.)
as (=*while*), dum. (180.)
as often as, quotiēns; cum. (See 193, 432.)
as regards, or *as to* (=*about*), dē (with *abl.*). (332, 4.)
as to (e.g. *free from care as to*), ab. (332 1.)
ascend *the throne*, (see 17), rēx fīō, *or* rēgnum accipiō.
ascertain, cog-nōscō (3, -nōvī, -nitum); certior fīō (factus sum).
ascribe *to you*, tibi acceptum referō. (See *indebted to you.*)
ask (*a question*), rogō, interrogō, 1 (with *acc.*); quaerō (3, quaesīvī; with *ex* or *ā*). (See 231.)
ask (=*request, beg*), rogō, ōrō, 1, ut...; pet-ō (3, -īvī, -ītum; with *ab*) ut... (See 122.)
ask for, poscō (3, poposcī).
ask your opinion, tē cōnsul-ō (3, -uī, -tum). (248.)
aspect *of affairs*, rērum faciēs, 5, *f.*
assailants=*those who assail* (aggredior). (See 175.)
assassin, sīcārius, *m.*
assault. (See *attack.*)
assemble (*intrans.*), convenīre.
assembly, conventus, 4, *m.*
assert (=*pretend*), dictitō, 1.
assert (*as a fact*), affirmō, 1.
assert (=*maintain*), vindicō, 1.
assert *my country's freedom*, patriam in lībertātem vindicō.
assertors *of* (*freedom*)=*those who have asserted, etc.* (175.)
assist, ad-iuvō (1, -iūvī, -iūtum). (246.)
assistance, *bring you*, tibi opem ferō (ferre, tulī).
assistance, *come to his*, eī sub-veniō (4, -vēnī).
assured, *am.* (240.)
Athenians, Athēniēnsēs.
Athens, Athēnae, *pl. f.*
atone for, luō (3, luī; with *acc.*); poenās dō (with *gen.*).
attached to me, meī amantissimus. (302.)
attack (*in general sense*), ag-gredior (3, -gressus sum; with *acc.*); (*a city or place*), oppugnō, 1 (see 24); (*suddenly*), ad-orior (4, -ortus sum).

attack (*in words*), in-vehor (3, -vectus sum; with *in* and *acc.*).
attack (*of a pestilence, panic*), in-vādō (3, -vāsī, -vāsum).
attain to (=*arrive at*), per-veniō (4, -vēnī) ad. (19.)
attain to (=*obtain*), ad-ipīscor (3, -eptus sum). (19.)
attempt, cōnor, 1; id agō ut...
attempt (*noun*), inceptum, *n.*; cōnātus, 4, *m.*
authority, potes-tās, -tātis, *f.* (See *influence*, note.)
avail myself of, ūtor (3, ūsus sum; with *abl.*).
avail with, *am of no*, nihil valeō apud. (331, 4.)
avarice, avāritia, *f.*
avert from, prohibeō (2) ab...
avoid (*a burden, etc.*), dē-fugiō (3, -fūgī).
avoid (*a danger*), vītō, 1.
avoid, *to* (=*in order not to, etc.*). (See 101.)
avow, prae mē ferō (ferre, tulī).
aware of, *am*, or *become*, sentiō, (4, sēnsī, sēnsum).

backs, *they turn their*, terga dant.
band (*of soldiers, etc.*), manus, 4, *f.*
banish, cīvitāte pellō, expellō; in exsilium pellō (3, pepulī, pulsum) *or* exigō (3, exēgī, exāctum).
banishment, exsilium, *n.*
bank, rīpa, *f.*
banquet, *a*, epulae, *pl. f.*
barbarian, *a*, barbarus, *m.*
barbarous, use *superl. of* crūdēlis. (57, *a.*)
base (*adj.*), turpis.
baseness, turpitūd-ō, -inis, *f.*; *the baseness of*=*how base it is*. (174.)
battle, proelium, *n.*
battle, *in*, in aciē.
bear, ferō (ferre, tulī, lātum).
beautiful, pulch-er, -rior, -errimus.[1]
because, quia, quod.
become, fīō (fierī, factus sum).
becomes (*us*), *it*, (nōs) decet (234); *or gen. with* est. (291, *Note* 3.)
befalls, *it*, accidit. (247, 487, *a.*)
before (*adv.*), anteā; antehāc; ante (322).
before (*prep.*), ante (with *acc.*)
before long=*soon* or *shortly*.
beg, rogō, ōrō, etc. (See *ask.*)
begin, in-cipiō (3, -cēpī, -ceptum); coepī (coeptum est; 219); *often expressed by imperf. tense* (185); *begin anew*, redintegrō, 1 (with *acc.*).
begin with. (332, 1.)
beginning, initium, *n.*
behalf of, *on*, prō (with *abl.*).
behave, mē gerō (3, gessī, gestum). (See 241, *Notes* 1, 2.)
behold, a-spiciō (3, -spexī, -spectum).
belief, opīni-ō, -ōnis, *f.*
believe, crē-dō (3, -didī, -ditum). (See 248.)
belong *to the class of*, ūnus sum ex... (529, *a.*)
beneficial, salūtāris; ūtilis.
benefit *you*, tibi prōsum (prōdesse, prōfuī).
beseech, ōrō, 1. (118.)
besiege (*blockade*), ob-sideō (2, -sēdī, sessum); (*by actual attack*), oppugnō, 1.
best, *the very*. (529, *f.*)
bestow (*these things on you*), haec tibi larg-ior (4, -ītus sum).
betake *myself to*, mē cōn-ferō (-tulī) ad...
betray, prō-dō (3, -didī, -ditum); *betrayers*=*those who had betrayed*. (See 175.)
better, *for the*, in melius.
better, *it would have been*, satius *or* melius fuit. (153.)
between. (331, 10.)
bewail, complōrō, 1.
bid, iubeō (2, iussī, iussum). (120.)
bidding, *at the*, iussū. (270, *Note* 3.)

[1] *Pulcher* is 'beautiful' in a general sense; *amoenus*, 'lovely to look on,' is applied to natural objects such as a landscape.

bill (=*proposal for a law*), rogāti-ō, ōnis, *f.*
bind myself, mē ob-stringō (3, -strīnxī).
black (*metaph. of crime*), *simply* tantus; *or* tam atrōx.
blame, culpa, *f.*
blame, vituperō, 1; reprehen-dō (3, -dī, -sum).
blessing, bonum, *n.* (51, *c*).
blind, caecus.
blockade. (See *besiege*.)
blood, sangui-s, -nis, *m.*; cru-or, ōris, *m.*; *so much*, (205, *c*).
bloodshed, caed-ēs, -is, *f.*
bloody, cruentus.
blow, *a* (*metaph.*), calami-tās, -tātis, *f.*
blunder, err-or, -ōris, *m.*
blush at, or *for*, mē pudet, with *inf.* or *gen.* (309 and *Notes*.)
boast, *make a*, glōrior, 1. (282, *Note*.)
body, *the whole*, ūniversī. (380, *b*.) (See note under *all*.)
body-guard, satell-es, -itis, *m.*
boldly, audācter; ferōciter; *or use adj.* (61) ferōx.[1]
book, lib-er, -ri, *m.*
born, nātus (*from* nāscor).
born and brought up, nātus ēdūcātusque.
both, uterque; ambō. (See 378.)
both . . . and, et . . . et, vel . . . vel (Intr. 48, 49).
bound (*in duty*) (p. 123, *note*).
bow to (*metaph.*), ob-sequor (3, -secūtus sum; with *dat.*).
boy, pu-er, -erī.
boy, *from a*, or *from boyhood*, ā puerō; *when used of more than one*, ā puerīs.
boyhood, *in*. (63.)
brand (*you*) *with dishonour*, ignōminiae notam (tibi) in-ūrō (3, -ussī, -ustum).
brandish, iactō, 1.
brave (*adj.*), fortis; *adv.* fortiter.
brave *the worst*, ultima ex-perior, (4, -pertus sum).
break (*metaph.*), violō, 1.
break *my word*, fidem fallō (3, fefellī, falsum).
break up (*trans.*), dissipō, 1.
break up (*intrans.*), dissipor, 1.
breathing space. (399, *Note* 2.)
bribery, ambitus, 4, *m.*[2]
brigand, latr-ō, -ōnis, *m.*
bring, dūcō (3, dūxī, ductum).
bring (*you this*), hoc tibi af-ferō. (-ferre, attulī, allatum.)
bring back word, renūntiō, 1.
bring (*a person*) **before you**, ad tē ad-dūcō (3, -dūxī, -ductum).
bring credit *to*=*be creditable to*. (260.)
bring forward (*a law*), ferō (ferre, tulī, lātum).
bring help, opem ferō (ferre, tulī).
bring loss *on you*, tibi damnum īn-ferō (-ferre, -tulī, illātum).
bring out (*persons*), prō-dūcō (3, -dūxī, -ductum).
bring to an end, fīnem faciō (3, fēcī) with *gen.*
bring under, faciō, with *gen. of* iūs (iūris) *or* arbitrium. (See 290, *Note* 3.)
bring up (*supplies, etc.*), subvehō (3, -vēxī, -vectum); supportō, 1; *of soldiers*, ad-dūcō (3, -dūxī, -ductum).
broad, lātus.
brother, frāt-er, -ris.
brought up (=*bred*), ēdūcātus (*from* ēdūcō, 1).
bugbears, terrōrēs, *m. pl.*; terricula, *n. pl.* (Livy).
burden (e.g. *of administering*), *use* rēs labōriōsissima *in appos.* (223, *Note* 1.)
burdensome, molestus; gravis.

[1] *Ferōx* is not used in the sense of 'ferocious' (which is rather *crūdēlis* or *saevus*); it denotes 'high spirit' carried to excess.

[2] From *ambiō*, lit. 'I go round,' 'I canvass'; hence both verb and noun are used for 'illegal canvassing' or 'bribery.'

business, rēs, 5, *f.*
but, sed; vērum (*emphatic*).
butcher, trucīdō, 1.
bystander, *use* adstō *or* circumstō. (See 71, 78, 175.)

calamity, calami-tās, -tātis, *f.*
call away, āvocō, 1.
call to me, ad mē vocō, convocō, 1.
call to mind, see *recall.*
called, *am*, vocor, 1. (7.)
calm, (*adj.*) tranquillus.
calmly, aequō animō.
camp, castr-a, -ōrum, *n. pl.*
campaign=*year*, annus, *m.*
campaign *was disastrous, was prosperous*, rēs īnfēlīciter (*or superl.*), prosperē, gesta est.
can, possum (posse, potuī).
candid, līber.
candidate for, *am a*, pet-ō (3, -īvī, -ītum). (22, 23.)
cannot, nequ-eō (-īre, -īvī).
caprice, libīd-ō, -inis, *f.*
care, cūra, *f.*
care, *free from*, sēcūrus.
care to, volō (velle, voluī).
careful for (*your safety*), tibi caveō (2, cāvī). (248.)
carry across, trānsportō, 1. (229, *Note* 3.)
carry on=*wage*, gerō (3, gessī, gestum).
carry out (=*perform*), ex-sequor (3, -secūtus sum); cōn-ficiō (3, -fēcī).
carry out (*of the country*), exportō, 1.
Carthage, Karthāg-ō, (*loc.* -inī).
case, *in our*, in nōbīs.
case, *it is the*, fit ut...; accidit ut... (123.)
cast, con-iciō (3, -iēcī, -iectum).
catch, capiō (3, cēpī, captum).
cause, causa, *f.*
cause (*loss*), (damnum) īn-ferō (-ferre, -tulī).
cause (*panic*) (pavōrem) in-iciō (3, -iēcī).
cause of, *am the*, per mē fit ut...; per mē stat quōminus... (131.)
caution, *want of*, temeri-tās, -tātis, *f.*
caution, *with*, caut-ē, -ius.
cavalry, equit-ēs, -um, *m. pl.*
cease, dē-sinō (3, -īvī, -itum), *or* dē-sistō (3, -stitī).
certain (=*definite*), certus.
certain (=*sure*, e.g. *victory*), explōrātus.
certain, *consider as*, prō certō habeō. (240, *Note* 2.)
certain, *am*, certō (*adv.*) scio, 4.
certainly (=*I grant that*), sānē.
centre of, *the*. (60.)
centre (*of army*), media (60) aciēs, 5, *f.*
centurion, centuri-ō, -ōnis, *m.*
chain (*general term*), vinculum, *n.*, and see *fetters.*
Chance (*personified*), Fortūna, *f.*
chance, *by mere*, forte ac cāsū. (270, *Note* 1.)
change (*trans.*), mūtō, commūtō, 1, (see 20, 21); (*intrans.*), mūtor, 1.
change (*of purpose*), incōnstantia, *f.*
change (*of sides*), trānsiti-ō, -ōnis, *f.*
channel, fretum, *n.*
character, *often turned* (*as in Ex.* 22) *by a dependent clause.* (See 174.)
character (*natural*), ingenium,[1] *n.*
character (*good*), vir-tūs, -tūtis, *f.* (See *note.*)
character (*mode of life*), mōr-ēs, -um, *pl. m.* (See *note.*)
character, *highest*, optimī mōrēs; virtūs summa.

[1] *Ingenium* is 'one's inborn disposition or natural gifts.' It often = 'abilities,' but is never used in the plural of a single person. *Ingenium mōrēsque* may be used to express the whole idea of 'character' as natural and acquired by habit. *Indolēs* (a rarer word) also denotes 'one's natural disposition,' but it has reference more to moral qualities and less to intellectual ones than *ingenium*. Cicero joins the two words: *summa ingenī indolēs*, 'the highest natural gifts.' When 'character' = 'good character,' *virtūs* should be used.

character, *of the same, as,* tālis, . . . quālis. (See **84.**)
characteristic of, *it is the.* (**291.**)
charge (*of troops*), impetus, 4, *m.*
charge, *make a,* invā-dō (3, -sī, -sum) in... ; impetum faciō (3, fēcī) in...
charged, *am* (*with*), in crīmen veniō (4, vēnī ; with *gen.*).
charm (*noun*), dulcēd-ō, -inis, *f.*
chastisement *on, inflict,* animad-vert-ō (3, -ī ; with *in* and *acc.*).
check, *keep in* (*temper, etc.*), moderor, 1 (**249**) ; (*troops*), contineō, 2.
cheer, clām-or, -ōris, *m.*
cheer, *am of good,* bonō animō sum. (**303,** *Note* ii.)
cheer on, hortor, adhortor, 1.
cheerful, hilaris.
cheerfully, facile.
cherish, tueor, 2.
choose to (or *like*), mihi libet. (**247.**)
choose (*as*), ē-ligō (3, -lēgī, -lēctum) (See **259,** *Note* 3.)
chief (*chieftain*), rēgulus.
chief (*chief man*), prin-ceps, -cipis.
child, pu-er, -erī.
children (*offspring*), līber-ī, -ōrum.
circumstance, rēs, 5, *f.*
circumstances, temp-us, -oris, *n.* (**292,** 7.)
citadel, arx (*gen.* arcis), *f.*
city, urb-s, -is, *f.*
civilisation, *advance in,* hūmānior fīō (fierī, factus sum).
clamour for, flāgitō (1, with *acc.*).
class, gen-us, -eris, *n.*
clear, certus; manifēstus; clārus.
clear, *it is,* appāret (2; see **46,** *c*); *or* manifēstum est.
clear (*myself of*) (mē) pūrgō, 1, *with* dē (**306,** *Note*), *or with abl. simply.*
clemency, clēmentia, *f.*
clement, clēmēns.
client, *my,* hic. (**338,** *Note* 1.)
Clitus, Clitus, 2.
close (*friend*), *superl. of* amīcus. (**55.**)
close (*shut up*), inter-clūdō, **3,** -clūsī, -clūsum.
close *at hand, is,* prope (*or* haud procul) est.
close *to.* (**331, 13** or **19**).
closely *resembling, use superl. of* similis.
clothing, vestītus, 4, *m.*
coast along, (nāve) praeter-vehor, 3, -vectus sum (*acc.*); *but* nāve *is often omitted.*
cold (*noun*), frīg-us, -oris, *n.*
colleague, collēga, *m.*
collision (*with*), *come into,* cōn-flīgō, 3, -flīxī, -flīctum (cum).
colony, colōnia, *f.*
combination, *in,* coniūnctī.
comfort, commoda, *n. pl.*
command (*an army*), praesum (*dat.* 251); dūcō, 3, dūxī (*acc.*).
command myself, mihi imperō, 1.
commander (*of garrison, etc.*), praefectus. (**408.**)
commanders (*general sense*)=*those who lead* (dūcō).
commencement *of,* initium, *n.*; *or part. pass. of* incipiō. (See **417.**)
commit (*a crime*), com-mittō (3, -mīsī, -missum); faciō (3, fēcī, factum).
commit *a fault,* peccō, 1. (**25.**)
common (*belonging to many*), commūnis; *common to you and me,* commūnis tibi mēcum.
commonwealth, rēspūblica.
communicate *to* (=*impart to*), commūnicō, 1, cum. (**253,** v.)
community (*civil*), cīvi-tās, -tātis, *f.*
companions, *his,* suī. (**354,** iii.)
compare, cōn-ferō, -ferre (cum).
compassion, misericordia, *f.*
compel, cōgō (3, coēgī, coāctum).
competent, *am*=*am able.*
competition *for,* contenti-ō, -ōnis, *f.* (*with gen.,* **300.**)
complain, *make complaints,* queror (3, questus sum); conqueror.
compliments *to, pay,* collaudō, **1.** (25.)
comply with, ob-sequor (3, secūtus sum; with *dat.*). (See **253,** i.)

compulsion, *under,* coāctus.
comrades, *his.* (See *companions.*)
conceal, cēlō, 1. (See 230.)
concerning (*prep.*), dē (with *abl.*).
concerns, *it,* pertinet (253, ii) ad; interest, rēfert (310).
condemn, condemnō, 1. (306, 307.)
condemnation, condemnāti-ō, -ōnis, *f.*
condign (*punishment*), gravissimus.
condition (=*lot*), fortūna, *f.*; (=*term, agreement*), condici-ō, -ōnis, *f.*; *condition of slavery,* (58.)
conduct myself (*of soldiers*), rem gerō (3, gessī).
conference (*with*), *have a,* col-loquor, 3, -locūtus sum (cum).
confess, fateor (2, fassus sum); cōn-fiteor (2, -fessus sum).
confidence, fīdūcia, *f.*; *put confidence in,* cōn-fīdo (2, -fīsus sum; see 282, *Note*); fidem (tibi) habeō.
confiscate, pūblicō, 1.
confusion, trepidāti-ō, -ōnis, *f.*
confusion *reigns, etc.*; *use impers. pass. of* trepidō, 1. (See 218.)
congratulate *you on this,* hoc (*acc.*), hanc rem, *or* ob hanc rem, *or* dē hāc rē, tibi grātulor, 1.
conquer, vincō, 3, vīcī, victum.
conqueror, vict-or, -ōris.
conscience, *with a good.* (See 64.)
consciousness, sēnsus, 4, *m.*
consent (*noun*), cōnsēns-us, 4, *m.*
consent to, volō, velle, voluī.
consider, arbitror, 1. (See note under *fancy.*)
considerations, *all*=*everything.* (53, 54.)
considering, ut in (332, 9; 492, v, *b*); *considering the greatness of,* ut in tantō...
consist of, cōn-stō (1, -stitī, *with* ē, ex).
consolation, *is a great,* magnō est sōlāciō (*dat.*). (260.)
conspire (*against*), coniūrō (1, with contrā and *acc.*).
conspirator, *turn by* quī-*clause.* (175.)
Constantinople, Cōnstantīnopol-is, *acc.* -im, *loc.* -ī.
constantly, semper *or* numquam nōn.
constitution, *the,* rēspūblica. (See 292, 10, and *footnote.*)
constitutional; unconstitutional, ē rēpūblicā (332, 4); contrā rempūblicam.
consul, cōn-sul, -sulis, *m.*
consulship, cōnsulātus, 4, *m.*
consult (=*ask the opinion of*), cōnsul-ō (3, -uī, -tum; with *acc.*).
consult *the good or interest of,* cōnsulō, *with dat.* (See 248.)
consummate. (See *statesman.*)
contemporary, *a,* aequālis. (51, *a.*)
contempt *for,* contemptus, 4, *m.* (*with gen.,* 300.)
contemptible, *far from,* haud (169, *footnote*) contemnendus (393).
content *with, am,* contentus sum (*abl.*).
contest, *a,* certām-en, -inis, *n.*; or *use impers. pass. of* certō, 1. (218.)
continent, contin-ēns, -entis (*i.e.* terra).
contrary (*adj.*), contrārius.
contrary *to,* contrā quam. (491.)
convenience, commoda, *n. pl.*
conversation, *have,* col-loquor (3, -locūtus sum).
converse (*with*), colloquor (cum); (*of two or more,* inter sē, 353).
convinced, *am* = *am persuaded.* (See 124.)
convinced of *this, am,* or *feel,* hoc mihi persuāsum habeō. (240.)
corn, frūmentum, *n.*
Cortes, Cortesius.
cost, cōn-stō (1, -stitī; see 280, *Note* 2); *costs too much, it,* nimiō cōnstat.
council, cōnsilium, *n.*
count (=*number*), numerō, 1.
count (=*hold, consider as*), habeō, 2; dūcō (3, dūxī).
count among. (240, *Note* 2.)

countenance, vultus, 4, *m.*
country (*one's*), patria, *f.* (see **16,** *a*); (*the*), rēspūblica.
country (=*territory*), fīn-ēs, -ium, *m.* (See **16,** *a.*)
country (*as distinct from the town*), rūs (*gen.* rūris), *n.* (see **16,** *a*); *in the country,* rūrī.
countryman (*fellow*), cīv-is, -is.
courage, vir-tūs, -tūtis, *f.*; cōnstantia, *f.*; fortitūd-ō, -inis, *f.*
courage, *a man of.* (**58,** *Note.*)
courage, *show.* (**240,** *Note* 1.)
courage *to, have the=venture* (**25**); audeō (2, ausus sum).
course, *take this,* haec faciō; hanc ratiōnem ineō (inīre, inīvī.)
course *which,* id quod. (**67.**)
court, iūdicium, *n.*
cover (*with armies or fleets*), īnfēstum habeō. (**240.**)
coward, timidus, ignāvus; *cowards,* ignāvī.
cowardice, ignāvia, *f.*; timidi-tās, -tātis, *f.*
cowardly, ignāvus; timidus.
crave *for,* dēsīderō, 1 (*acc.*) (*mostly for what I have had and have lost*); *in Ex.* 48 B *use* appet-ō (3, -īvī, -ītum).
craving *for,* appetēns (*partic.*) (*with gen.*). (**302.**)
credible, *it is scarcely,* vix crēdī potest. (**197.**)
credit, *a,* or *creditable, it is.* (**260.**)
crime, facin-us, -oris, *n.*; flāgitium, *n.*; scel-us,[1] -eris, *n.*; dēlictum, *n.* (See *note.*)
criminal, scelerātus.
criminally, nefāriē.
crisis, discrīm-en, -inis, *n.*; temp-us, -oris, *n.*
critical *moment* (*such a*), *use simply* temp-us, -oris, *n.*, *or* occāsi-ō, -ōnis, *f.*

cross, trā-iciō, 3, -iēcī, -iectum.
crowd, *a,* multitūd-ō, -inis, *f.*
crowd, *to* (*intrans.*), congregārī, 1.
crowds, *in.* (**61.**)
crown (*kingly*), rēgnum, *n.* (See **17.**)
crown (=*circlet*), corōna, *f.*
cruel, crūdēlis.
cruelly, crūdēl-iter, -ius, -issimē.
cruelty, crūdēli-tās, -tātis, *f.*; *show,* saeviō, 4.
crush, op-primō, 3, -pressī, -pressum; *crushed* (*pass. part.*), oppressus.
crushing (e.g. *calamity*), *use* tantus *or* tantus tamque gravis.
cry, *raise a,* conclāmō, 1.
cultivated, *to be* (=*sought for*), expetendus.
custom, mōs (*gen.* mōris), *m.*
cut off (*destroy*), ab-sūmō, 3, -sūmpsī, -sūmptum.
cut off (*destroyed*), *am,* inter-eō, -īre.

dagger, pugi-ō, -ōnis, *m.* (not *f.*).
daily, cottīdiē; *with comparatives and certain verbs,* in diēs. (See **328,** *c.*)
danger, perīculum, *n.* (See also **137-8.**)
dangerous, perīculōsus.
Danube, Dānuvius, *m.*
dare, see *venture*; *daring* (*adj.*), audāx.
daringly, audācter.
dark (*metaph. applied to crime*), atrōx.
dark, *keep you in the,* tē cēlō (1, with *acc.,* **230,** *or* dē; **231**).
darkness, tenebrae, *f. pl.*
dart, iaculum, *n.*; tēlum, *n.*
dash (*of*), *a,* nōn nihil. (**294.**)
dash *into,* mē im-mittō (3, -mīsī) in.

[1] *Scelus,* a crime; offence against a fellow-creature (ἀδίκημα); also the guilt which causes overt crimes (ἀδικία); *vitium,* a fault, that which marks imperfection; *peccātum,* a sin or offence which deserves blame or punishment; *dēlictum,* an omission, or contravention, of some duty; *flāgitium,* a crime as a breach of duty towards oneself; *facinus,* an *act* of heinous crime (sometimes a great exploit); *nēquitia,* wickedness in the sense of 'worthlessness.'

dash *over*, (*intrans.*, see **20, 21**), īn-fundor, (3, -fūsus sum; with *dat.*).
date, temp-us, -oris, *n.*
day, diēs, 5, *m.*
day *after day*. (**328**, *c.*)
day *before*, prīdiē.
day *before, of the*, hesternus.
day, *for the*, in diem.
day, *in my=in my time* (*pl.*).
daybreak, prīma lūx (*gen.* lūcis).
deadly (=*hostile*), īnfēnsus.
dear, cārus.
dear *friends*, hominēs amīcissimī. (**224**, *Note* 2.)
death, mor-s, -tis, *f.*; *after his*, (**61**.)
debt, aes aliēnum; *gen.* aeris aliēnī, *n.*
deceive, dē-cipiō (3, -cēpī, -ceptum).
decide (=*resolve*) *to*, or *on*, cōn-stituō (3, -stituī, -stitūtum). (**45**.)
decide (=*pass judgment*), iūdicō, 1; *on* (*a fact*), dē.
decide (*let others, etc.*). (**146**.)
decision, *come to a*, dē-cernō (3, -crēvī, -crētum).
decision, *depends on my*. (**292**, 9.)
declare (*war*), (bellum) in-dīcō (3, -dīxī, -dictum). (**253**, iii.)
decline, (*trans.*) dētrectō, 1.
decline (*to*), nōlō, nōlle, nōluī.
decree, dē-cernō, 3, crēvī, -crētum.
decree, *a*, dēcrētum, *n.* (See **51**, *b.*)
deed. (See **51**, *b.*)
deep (*of feelings*), gravis.
deeper (*impression*). See *impression*.
defeat, clād-ēs, -is, *f.*; *of Cannae*, Cannēnsis (*adj.*, **58**).
defend, dēfen-dō, 3, -dī, -sum.
defendant, iste. (**338**, *Note* 1.)
defiance *of, in*, contrā, contrā quam. (**491**.)
defile, saltus, 4, *m.*
degrading, indignus (=*unmerited*); humilis (=*abject*).
delay, cūnctor, 1.
delay, *by, gerund of* cūnctor. (**99**.)
delay, *without*, cōnfestim.
deliberate, dēlīberō, 1.
deliberation, *need of*. (**286**.)
deliberation, *with*, cōnsultō, (*adv.*).
delightful, iūcundus.[1]
demand, postulō,[2] 1.
demand (=*exact*) *this from you*, hoc tibi imperō (1).
demeanour, habitus, 4, *m.* (*i.e.* corporis).
denied *this, am*, hōc (*abl.*) careō, 2.
denounce (=*upbraid*), in-crepō, (1, -crepuī).
deny, negō, 1.
depart (=*go away*), ab-eō (-īre); dis-cēdō (3, -cessī).
departure, *take my*. (**25**.)
depend *on*, pendeō, (2, pependī) ē, with *abl.*
depends *on you, this*. (**331**, 15.)
deplore, dēplōrō, 1.
deprecate, dēprecor, 1.
deprive *of*, prīvō, 1, (**264**); ad-imō, 3, -ēmī, -ēmptum (**244**, *Note* 2.)
depth. (**318**, *Note*.)
depth *of, such a, use* tantus; *or* eō *with gen.* (**294**, *Note*.)
descend, dēscend-ō (3, -ī).
desert, dēser-ō (3, -uī, -tum); dēstitu-ō (3, -ī). (See note under *abandon*.)
deserter, trānsfuga, *m.*
desertion, dēserō. (**417**.)
deserts, *in accordance with his*, (**490**, ii. 3).
deserve, mereor (2, meritus sum); *also* mere-ō (2, -uī).

[1] *Iūcundus*, that which causes joy or delight; *grātus*, what is acceptable, deserves gratitude; *ista vēritās etiamsī iūcunda nōn est, mihi tamen grāta est*.—(CICERO.)

[2] *Poscō*, I call for, make a sharp, peremptory demand; often used of what is unjust; *postulō*, I claim in accordance with, or as though in accordance with, what is right.

deserve *well of.* (332, 4.)
deservedly, meritō.
deserving *of,* dignus. (285.)
design (*noun*), cōnsilium, *n.*; *by design,* or *designedly,* cōnsultō.
desire; *am desirous to,* cupiō (3, cupīvī) *or* studeō, 2 (with *inf.*).
desire (*noun*)=*that which* (*you*) *desire.* (76.)
desire *for, with little,* parum appetēns (*with gen.,* 302).
despair, dēspērō, 1; *of,* dē (*abl.*).
despatch, *a,* litterae, *f. pl.*
desperately, atrōciter.
despicable. (See 276.)
despise, contem-nō, 3, -psī, -ptum; dē-spiciō, 3, -spexī, -spectum.[1]
despot, dominus.
despotism, rēgnum, *n.*; dominātī-ō, -ōnis, *f.*
destitution, eges-tās, -tātis, *f.*
destined, fātālis; *for* or *to,* ad. (331, 1.)
destiny, fātum, *n.*
destroy, ex-scindō (3, -scidī, -scissum).
destruction (*general sense*), exitium. *n.*; perniciēs, 5, *f.*; (=*massacre*), interneci-ō, -ōnis, *f.*
destruction *of* (*tends to the*). (See 292, 10.)
detach (*troops*)=*send.*
detain, retineō, 2.
determine *on.* (45.)
detraction, obtrectātī-ō, -ōnis, *f.*
detrimental, *it is.* (260.)
devastate, vastō, 1.
devote *myself to,* operam dō (with *dat.*); *or* (*stronger*), in-cumbō (3, -cubuī) in...
devoted *to,* studiōsus (*gen.,* 301, ii.).
dictate *terms to you,* lēgēs tibi im-pōnō (3, -posuī).
dictator, dictāt-or, -ōris.
die, morior (3, mortuus sum); vītā ex-cēdō (3, -cessī).
die *out* (*metaphor*), ex-cidere (3, -cidī) ē (ex).
difference *between, there is this,* (331, 10); *there is all the,* (92).
difference, *it makes no,* nihil interest (310).
different, alius; *to,* ac. (91; see also 92, and 370, 371.)
different *times, at,* alius aliō tempore. (371.)
differently *from,* aliter ac. (491.)
difficult, difficilis.
difficulty *in persuading, find a*=*persuade this* (illud) *with difficulty* (aegrē).
difficulty, *with,* aegrē; vix; difficulter, *comp.* difficilius.
din, strepitus, 4, *m.*
dire, *use* tantus.
directions, *in both,* utrimque; *in opposite,* dīversī. (See also 371, and *Note* 3.)
disaffected, male sentiō (4, sēnsī).
disagree *with,* dis-sentiō (4, -sēnsī) ab *or* cum.
disagreement *on,* dissēnsi-ō, -ōnis, *f.* (*with gen.,* 300).
disappear (=*am destroyed*), ex-stinguor, 3, -stīnctus sum.
disappoint. (332, 4.)
disapproval (*expressed by clamour*), acclāmō,[2] 1.
disaster, cāsus,[3] 4, *m.*; calami-tās, -tātis, *f.*
disastrous, *most, use the adv.,* īnfēlīciter. (218, *Note.*)
discharge *the duties of,* fungor (3, fūnctus sum). (281.)
discipline, disciplīna, *f.*
discontinue, inter-mittō (3, -mīsī). (See note under *undone.*)

[1] *Dēspiciō,* I look down on as beneath myself; *contemnō,* I think lightly of in itself, =*parvī faciō*; *spernō,* I put from me; *aspernor,* the same, with idea of strong dislike; *repudiō,* I put from me with contempt; *neglegō,* I am indifferent to.

[2] *Acclāmō* always in Cicero of disapproval; in later writers, of approval.

[3] *Cāsus,* properly an accident, that which *falls* out, is mostly used in a bad sense, as misfortune or disaster; but is not so strong a word as *calamitās.*

discussion, *by (in), gerund of* dis-serō, 3, -seruī. (99.)
disdain *to, use* nōlō, nōlle, nōluī.
disease, *a,* morbus.
disembark. (331, 26.)
disgrace, ignōminia, f.
disgraceful, turpis. (See 57.)
disgraceful, *it is.* (260, and *Note* 1.)
disheartened, *am.* (See 118, *example.*)
dishonour (*noun*), ignōminia, *f.*
dishonourable, inhonestus.
dishonourable, *it is.* (260.)
dislike, haud multum amō.
disloyal, īnfīdus.
dismayed, *am,* perterreor, 2.
dismiss, dī-mittō (3, -mīsī, -missum).
dispense *with,* careō, 2 (284); *or* carēre volō (velle, voluī).
disperse (*intrans.*), dī-lābī (3, -lāpsus sum). (See 20.)
displease, displiceō (2; with *dat.*).
disposed to (*a quality*), *use comparative of adj.* (57, *b.*)
dissatisfied *with oneself, one is,* suī paenitet.
dissemble (= *hide*), dissimulō, 1.
distance, *from a,* ē longinquō.
distance *from, am at a,* absum ā. (318.)
distant, longinquus.
distasteful, ingrātus.
distinction (=*mark of difference*), discrīm-en, -inis, *n.*
distinction (*honourable*), hon-ōs, -ōris, *m.*
distinguished (*adj.*), praeclārus. (224.)
district, ag-er, -rī, *m.*
distrust, dif-fīdō (3, -fīsus sum). (245, *c.*)
ditch, fossa, *f.*
divine, dīvīnus.
do, faciō (3, fēcī, factum).
doom, fātum, *n.*
doomed *to, am,* dēstinor, 1, *with dat.* or *ad.*
doors, for-ēs, -um, *pl. f.*
Doria, Doria, *f.*
doubt, dubitō, 1.
down *from,* dē (with *abl.*).
down-trodden, afflīctus.
drag (*to prison*), trahō (3, trāxī, tractum) in vincula *or* carcerem.
draw (=*drag*), trahō.
draw *up* (*a law*), scrībō (3, scrīpsī).
draw *up* (*soldiers*), īn-struō (3, -strūxī, -strūctum).
dread, reformīdō, 1.
dreadful, atrōx.
dress, vest-is, -is, *f.* (303, ii.)
drive *from,* ex-igō (3, -ēgī, -āctum); pellō (3, pepulī, pulsum).
drive *on shore,* ē-iciō (3, -iēcī, -iectum).
drowned (*metaph., of words*). (332, 6.)
dull, hebetō, 1.
duration (*its future*)=*how lasting* (diūturnus) *it will,* or *would, be.* (174.)
duty, *it is my,* dēbeō. (199.)
duty *of, it is the, use gen.* (291.)
duty (*as opposed to expediency*), hones-tās, -tātis, *f.*; *or* honesta, *n. pl.* (51, *c.*)
dwelling, domicilium, *n.*

each *and every,* ūnus quisque. (529 *e.*)
each *other, one another,* alius alium; *of two,* alter alterum (see 371, iv.); inter sē (353).
eager *for,* cupidus (*gen.*, 301, ii.).
eager *to,* gestiō, 4.
early *manhood.* (See *manhood.*)
earlier (*adv.*), matūrius.
earlier *than* (=*before*), ante. (331, 3.)
earliest=*first.*
earnestly, magnopere.
earnestly *implore,* ōrō atque obsecrō.
ears, *with my own.* (355, *Note* 1.)
earth, *the,* tell-ūs, -ūris, *f.*
easy, facilis.
easily (*readily*), facile; nūllō negōtiō (*without effort*).
echo *with,* person-ō (1, -uī; with *abl.*).

effect, ef-ficiō (3, -fēcī, -fectum).
effect *on, have but little*, parum valeō apud.
eight, octō (*indecl.*).
eighteenth. (530.)
either . . . or, aut . . . aut; **vel . . .** **vel** (Intr. 49).
elected, fīō, fierī, factus sum.
eloquence, ēloquentia, *f.*
else, *or*, **aut.**
embark (*intrans.*), **nāvem** cōnscend-ō (3, -ī).
emergency, **temp-us**, -oris, *m.*; *in the present*, **see** (for *in*) **273**, *Note* 2.
Emperor, **rēx** (*gen.* **rēgis**) *or* **prīn**-ceps, -cipis.
empire, imperium, *n.*
empty, **inānis.**
enacted, *get* (*a law*), **per-ferō**, -ferre, -tulī.
encamp, **castra** pōnō (3, posuī).
encounter (*death*), op-petō (3, īvī, -ītum); (*evil*), **exper-ior** (4, -tus sum).
encourage, co-, *or* ad-hortor, 1, (*acc. and* ut, 118).
encouragement, *words of*, **adhortantis vōx.** (414.)
end, fīn-is, -is, *m.*
endanger, **perīclitor**, 1.
endeavour, cōnor, 1.
endure, per-ferō (-ferre, -tulī).
enemy (*private*), inimīcus.
enemy (*public*), host-is, -is.
energy, *with some want of*, **paulō** (279) **remissius.**
engage (*an enemy*), con-gredior (3, -gressus sum) cum.
engage *in* (=*take part in*), intersum (251); *in battle*, proelium com-mittō (3, -mīsī, -missum); *in conflict*, **manūs cōnser-ō** (3, -uī, -tum).
England (*the people*), **Anglī.** (See 319.)
engrafted, īnsitīvus.
enjoy, fruor (3, frūctus **sum** ; **see** 281) ; *the friendship of*, amīcō ūtor (3, ūsus sum; see 282); *praise, etc.*, flōreō, 2 (with *abl.*).
enjoy *happiness*, **beātus sum.**
enmity, inimīcitia, *f.*
enormity, flāgitium, *n.* (See **note** under *crime*.)
enormous, *such*, **tantus.**
enough *and to spare*, **satis** superque (*with gen.*, 294).
enquire, quaerō (3, quaesīvī) ā *or* ex; (tē) rogō, inter-rogō, 1, (231); percūnctor, 1 (with *acc.*).
entail *this upon you*, hoc tibi **in**- *or* af-ferō (252).
enter, in-gredior (3, -gressus sum); veniō (4, vēnī) in.
enter *political life*. (See *political life*.)
enterprise. (See **54.**)
enthusiasm, **alacri-tās**, -tātis, *f.*
entire *innocence*. (See *innocence*.)
entirely, **tōtus** (*with verbs*, 61); *for adjs., use superl.*
entreat, ōrō, 1. (122.)
entreat *for, earnestly*, flāgitō, 1. (122.)
entreaty, **obsecrāti-ō**, -ōnis, *f.*
entrust, **per-mittō** (3, -mīsī, -missum); mandō, 1. (See 123.)
enumerate, ēnumerō, 1.
envoy (*embassy*), lēgāti-ō, -ōnis, *f.*
envy, in-videō (2, -vīdī, -vīsum; with *dat.*). (See **5.**)
equal *to, use* **tantus . . . quantus.** (490, i.)
err, errō, 1.
error, err-or, -ōris, *m.*; *or* errāre.[1] (94, 99.)
escape, ef-fugiō (3, -fūgī).
establish, stabiliō, 4.
estimate, aestimō, 1. (305.)
eternal, sempiternus.
evade (=*shirk*), subter-fugiō (3, -fūgī; with *acc.*); *a law*, lēgī fraudem faciō (3, fēcī).
even, etiam; quoque; *before adj.*, vel; *not even*, nē . . . quidem. (Intr. 90.)

[1] *Errāre*, error generally, in the abstract *error*, an error or blunder.

even now (*i.e. at the present time*), hodiē.
evening, *in the*, vesperī.
events, *at all*, certē. (See note under *least*.)
ever (=*always*), semper; *with negat.* (=*at any time*), umquam.
every (=*all*), *pl.* of omnis; *everything*, omnia, *n. pl.* (53.)
evident, *it was*, (satis) appārēbat. (46, *c*.)
evil, *an*, incommodum, *n.*; malum, *n.* (51, *b*.)
exact *from* (=*make requisition of*), imperō (1; with *acc.* and *dat.*; see **248**, **253**, iii).
exact (*punishment*), sūmo (3, sūmpsī) ab, dē, *or* ex.
exasperate, irrītō, 1.
excellent, optimus (see **57**, *a*); *for use with proper noun or person, see* **224**.
except *to*, nisi ut.
exception, *without*, =*all*.
excessive, nimius.
exchange *for*, mūtō, 1; permūtō 1. (See **280**.)
exclaim, ex- *or* con-clāmō, 1.
execrable (*by*), *considered*, exsecrābilis (*with dat.*).
execution (=*punishment*), supplicium, *n.*
exertion, *make* (*some*), (paulum) ad-nītor (3, -nīsus sum).
exertions=*toils*.
exhausted, fatīgātus; cōnfectus; *am*, or *become*, fatīgor, 1.
exhort, hortor, 1. (118.)
exile, *an*, ex-sul, -sulis.
exile, *am driven into*, in exsilium pellor (3, pulsus sum). (See *banish*.)
exile, *am in*, or *endure*, exsulō 1.
exist, sum, esse, fuī. (Intr. 35, *Note*.)
existence, *use* sum (*no Latin noun*); est Deus=*God exists*.
expect, exspectō, 1.
expedient, ūtilis.
expediency, ūtili-tās, -tātis, *f*.
experience, exper-ior (4, -tus sum).
experience *of life*, rērum perītia, *f*.
experienced (*adj*.), (rērum) perītus. (301, ii.)
explain, ex-pōnō (3, -posuī).
exploit, rēs gesta.
expose (*to danger, etc*.), ob-iciō (3, -iēcī).
expose (=*confute*), coargu-ō (3, -ī).
express *myself, to*, ut (ita) dīcam.
extent. (**174**, *b*.)
extortion, (rēs) repetundae, *f. pl.*
extreme, extrēmus.
extremely, *use superl. of adj.*
extremity *of*, extrēmus (*adj*.). (**60**.)
exult in, exsultō, 1. (With *abl*.).
eye, oculus, *m*.
eyes, *with my own*, ipse (**355**, *Note*); *before our*, (**332**, 9).

face (=*meet*), obviam eō (īre, īvī; with *dat*.).
face (=*put to the proof*), ex-perior (4, -pertus sum).
face, faciēs, 5, *f*.; *in the face of*, in (*with abl*., **273**, *Note* 2).
fact, rēs, 5, *f*.
faction, facti-ō, -ōnis, *f*.
fail (=*am wanting to*), dēficiō (*used absolutely or with acc*.); dēsum (*dat*., **251**). (See note under *abandon*).
fain, *would*; or *would fain have* (*done*), velim, vellem. (See **152**, *c*.)
fair (*adj*.), pulcher; amoenus. (See note on *beautiful*.)
fair (=*fair amount of*), satis. (**294**.)
faith, *good*, fidēs, 5, *f*.
faith *in you, put*, fidem tibi habeō.
faithful, fidēlis.
fall (*in battle*), per-eō, -īre, -iī.
fall *into*, in-cidō (3, -cidī) in (*acc*.); *or* praecipitō, 1 (*fall headlong*); *into ruin*, cor-ruō (3, -ruī).
fallen, afflictus.
falls *out, it*, accidit ut.
falls *to* (*my*) *lot*. (See *lot*.)
false (*of persons*), mend-āx, -ācis; (*of things*), falsus; fictus.
false *to*, dēsum (*dat*., **251**). (See note under *abandon*.)

falsehood, mendācium, *n.*
falsehood (*abstract*), mentīrī. (98, *a.*)
falsehood, *tell a*; *speak falsely*, mentior, 4. (54.)
fame, glōria, *f.*
family, meī; tuī; suī. (354, iii.)[1]
family (*adj.*), domesticus.
famine, cibī inopia, *f.*
famous, praeclārus. (19.)
fancy, puto,[2] 1; opīnor, 1.
far, *by*, multō. (279.)
far *from* (*adv.*), parum.
far *removed from*, aliēnus (*superl.*) ab.
fare (*noun*), vīctus, 4, *m.*
fare, mihi ēvenit (*impers.*).
farmhouse, vīlla, *f.*
fatal, perniciōsus; fūnestus.[3]
Fate, Fortūna (*personified*).
father, pat-er, -ris.
fatigue, lassitūd-ō, -inis, *f.*
fault, culpa, *f.*
fault, *commit a*, peccō, 1. (25.)
favour (=*kindness*), beneficium, *n.*
favour, faveō (2, fāvī, fautum; with *dat.*, 5).
favour, *do you this*, hoc (*acc.*, 237) tibi grātificor, 1.
favour, *win your*, apud tē grātiam in-eo (-īre, -īvī).
favourable (=*suitable*), idōneus. (255, 507.)
fawn upon, adūlor, 1. (With *acc.*)
fear, metus, 4, *m.*; tim-or, -ōris, *m.*
fear, metu-ō (3, -ī); vereor, 2; (see 138, 139)[4]; *have fears for*, timeō (2) *with dat.* (248.)
fear *for my safety*, salūtī meae dif-fīdō, (3, -fīsus sum).
feasting (*noun*), epulae, *f. pl.*
features, vultus, 4, *m. sing.*
feel, sentiō (4, sēnsī, sēnsum).
feelings, animus, *m.*
fellow-*subject*, cīv-is, -is, *m.*
ferocity (*of an act*), atrōci-tās, -tātis, *f.*
fertile, fertilis.
fetters, catēnae, *f. pl.*
few, paucī; perpaucī (*very few*).
fickle, levis.
fictitious, fīctus.
field *of battle*, aciēs,[5] 5, *f.*
field, *in the* (*in war*), mīlitiae, *opposed to* domī. (312, *Note* 1.)
fiercely (*boldly*), ferōciter; ācriter.
fifth, quīntus.
fight, pugnō, 1; *a battle*, proelium com-mittō (3, -mīsī, -missum).
fill *with* (*panic*), in-cutiō (3, -cussī, -cussum).
find, reperiō (4, repperī, repertum) (*by search*); in-veniō (4, -vēnī, -ventum) (*by chance*).
find *fault with*, vituperō, 1.
fine, pulcher. (See note on *beautiful.*)
finish, cōn-ficiō (3, -fēcī, -fectum).
fire *and sword*, ferrum et ign-is (*abl.* -ī).
firm, cōnstāns.
first (*adv.*); *first . . . then*; *first . . . secondly, etc.* (534, and *Note.*)
first *of June*, Kalendae Iūniae (538); *by the*, (326).

[1] *Familia* means the household establishment, the domestic slaves; not the blood relations of the *paterfamiliās*.

[2] *Puto*, 'I incline to think,' 'I fancy,' 'I suspect,' I think without having as yet any full clearly reasoned grounds for thinking; *opīnor*, 'I conjecture,' with still less clear grounds; *reor*, rather 'I calculate,' 'I come to a conclusion'; *arbitror*, I form my own personal judgement; *cēnseō*, I form and express a clear view or judgement.

[3] *Fātālis* means destined, fated.

[4] *Timēre*, the feeling of fear, causing a wish to flee; *metuere*, the sense of danger, causing us to take precautions; *verērī*, often, to look on with respect or awe.

[5] *Aciēs*, the *edge* or *line* of battle, often answers to the English 'field,' or even 'battle.'

first *to*; *first who*. (62.)
five, quīnque.
fix (*my eyes*) *on*, dēfīgō (3, -fīxī, -fīxum) in (*acc.*).
flag, signum, *n*.
flank, lat-us, -eris, *n*.
flatter, assentor, 1. (253, i.)
fleet, class-is, -is, *f*.
flight, fuga, *f*.
fling *away*, prō- *or* ab-iciō (3, -iēcī, -iectum).
flock (*noun*), grex (*gen.* gregis), *m*.
flock *together*, congregārī, 1.
flourishing, opulentus (*use superl.*, 57, *a*).
flow *down*, dē-fluō (3, -flūxī).
fly, fugiō (3, fūgī).
foe, host-is, -is, *m*.
follow, sequor (3, secūtus sum); *follow up*, īnsector, 1 (*acc.*).
follow *that, it does not*, nōn idcircō.
folly, stultitia, *f.*; *or use adj.* stultus.
food, vīctus, 4, *m*.
food, *get* (*of soldiers*), frūmentor, 1.
food, *take*, cibum capiō.
food, *want of*, (=*fasting*), inedia, *f*.
foolish, īnsipiēns; *it is foolish*. (291, *Note* 1.)
foot *of* (*a mountain*) īmus. (60.)
foot-soldier, ped-es, -itis.
for (*prep.*), prō. (With *abl.* See 6 and 332, 7.)
for (*conj.*), nam; enim (Intr. 89); quippe.
for *some time* (*past*), iamdūdum. (181.)
forage, *get*, pābulor, 1.
force, vīs, *f*. (*abl.* vī).
force *of arms, by*, vī et armīs.
force *from*, dēturbō (1) dē (*abl.*); *force out of* (=*wrench from*), extor-queō, 2, -sī, -tum. (257.)
forces (=*troops*), cōpiae, *f. pl*.
forefathers, maiōr-ēs, -um. (See 51, *footnote* 3.)
foreign, externus.
foreigner (*opposed to* cīvis), peregrīnus, *m*.
foremost, prīmus.
foresee, prae-sentiō (4, -sēnsī, -sēnsum); prō-spiciō (3, -spexī, -spectum); prō-videō (2, -vīdī, -vīsum). (248.)
forest, silva, *f*.
foretell, prae-dīcō (3, -dīxī, -dictum); praesāgiō, 4.
forget, oblīvīscor (3, oblītus sum; with *gen.*, 308).
forgive, ig-nōscō (3, -nōvī, -nōtum; *dat.*, see 5); veniam dō (*dat. of person, gen. of thing*); *or* condōnō, 1 (*dat. of person, acc. of thing*).
forgotten, *become*, or *am*, in oblīviōnem veniō (4, vēnī).
form *line* (*of battle*), aciem īn-struō (3, -strūxī, -strūctum).
former, prīstinus (see note under *ancient*), *often joined with* ille. (339, i.)
formidable, formīdandus (393); *comp.* magis formīdandus.
fortress, arx (*gen.* arcis), *f*.
fortunate, fēl-īx, -īcis.
fortunate, *it was most*, peropportūnē accidit ut. (126.)
fortune, fortūna, *f.*; *fortunes*, fortūnae, *pl*.
fortune, *good*, fēlīci-tās, -tātis, *f*.
Fortune's *favourites*. (529, *b*.)
foul, foedus.
foully, nefāriē.
found (*a colony*), dē-dūcō (3, -dūxī, -ductum).
fourteen, quattuordecim.
fourth, quārtus.
free (*adj.*), līber; *free from*, vacuus (265); *free from blame*, extrā culpam (331, 9); *free from care*, sēcūrus (19).
free; *give freedom to*; or *set at liberty* (*from*), līberō (1) ab *or abl.* (264); *freed from, am*, līberor, 1.
freedom, līber-tās, -tātis, *f*.
freedom, *in*, līber. (61.)
fresh, recēns.
friend, amīcus (51 *a*, and 55, 256); *close friend*, amīcissimus.

friend *here, my*; *your friend there.* (338, *Notes* 1 and 2.)
friend, *make my,* amīcōrum in numerō habeō, 2. (240, *Note* 2.)
friendliness, benevolentia, *f.*
friendship, amīcitia, *f.*; *friendship of, enjoy the,* amīcō ūtor. (282.)
from, ā, ab (with *abl.*). (332, 1.)
front, *in,* ā fronte, (332, 1); adversus, *adj.* (see 61); *in the front of* (=*before*), ante (with *acc.*; 331, 3).
fuel, *add* (*metaph.*), facēs sub-iciō (3, -iēcī; with *dat.*).
fugitives, *use pres. part. of* fugiō.
full (=*the whole of*), tōtus. (60.)
full of, plēnus (*abl.*).
funds, pecūniae, *f. pl.*
funeral, fūn-us, -eris, *n.*
further, ultrā.
fury, īra,[1] *f.*
fury, *with the utmost,* vehementissimē.
future, *the,* futūra, *n. pl.* (52, 408.)
future, *in,* or *for, the,* in futūrum; in posterum. (331, 26.)

gain, ēmolumentum, *n.*; ūtili-tās, -tātis, *f.*; (*for*) *a source of gain,* quaestuī. (260.)
gain by=*it is profitable to me,* (260.)
gained, partus (from pariō, peperī, *I produce*).
gallant, fortis (use *superl.*); for usage with *proper noun* or word denoting a *person,* see 224.
gallantly, fortiter.
gallop, *at full,* equō concitātō.
games, lūdī, *m. pl.*
garrison, praesidium, *n.*
gate, porta, *f.*
gather (*together*) (*intrans.*), con-veniō (4, -vēnī, -ventum). (20.)
Gauls, *the,* Gallī.
gaze on, intueor, 2.
general, dux (*gen.* ducis).
general (*adj.*)=*of all.* (59.)
generally (*believed*)=*by most men.*
generation, ae-tās, -tātis, *f.*
Genoa, Genua, *f.*
gentle, mītis; mītissimī ingenī (*gen.*; 303, *Note,* ii.); *so gentle as* (224, *Note* 3.)
gentle, lēniter.
gentlemen *of the jury,* iūdicēs.
gentleness, lēni-tās, -tātis, *f.*; *show gentleness* (240, *Note* 1); *such,* tam *or* adeō mītis, etc.
German, *a,* Germānus.
Germany, Germānia, *f.*
gesture, gestus, 4, *m.*
get *over* (*danger*), fungor (3, fūnctus sum) *or* dēfungor. (281.)
get *ready for,* mē parō (1) ad *with gerund.* (396.)
get *to.* (See *reach.*)
give, dō, dare, dedī, datum; *a verdict,* sententiam dīcō (3, dīxī); *a name,* nomen in-dō (3, -didī, -ditum); *my word* (*formally*), fidem inter-pōnō (3, -posuī).
gladly, libenter; *or use adj.,* libēns. (61.)
globe, *the,* orbis terrārum, *m.*
glorious, praeclārus.
glory, glōria, *f.*
gluttony, gula, *f.* (lit. *the gullet*).
go away, ab-eō, -īre, -iī, -iturus.
go *down to meet,* obviam dēscend-ō (3, -ī; with *dat.*).
go *out,* ex-cēdō (3, -cessī); ex-eō, -īre, -īvī, -iī (*abl., with* or *without* ē, ex.)
God, Deus; *nom. pl.* Dī.
gold, *of,* aureus.
good *fortune, enjoy,* fēlīx sum.
good *name,* exīstimāti-ō, -ōnis, *f.*; fāma, *f.*
good *old times.* (339, i.)
good *sense,* prūdentia, *f.*
good-will, benevolentia, *f.*
goodness, vir-tūs, -tūtis, *f.*
gossip, rūmōrēs, *m. pl.*
govern, praesum. (251.)

[1] *Furor* means 'frenzy,' 'madness'; it never means 'fury' in the sense of mere 'anger.'

government, *the*. (175.)
governor (*of city*), praefectus.
gradually, paulātim.
grandfather, avus.
grandson, nepō-s, -tis.
grateful, grātus; *am most grateful*, maximam habeō grātiam. (98, *b*.)
gratitude, *show*, grātiam re-ferō, -ttulī; *feel*, habeō. (98, *b*.)
great, magnus, *comp*. maior, *superl*. maximus; *great men*, summī virī; virī praestantissimī.
greater (=*more of*), plūs. (294.)
greatly, magnopere; vehementer; maximē; *with comparatives*, multō. (279.)
greatness *of* (*your*) *debt*=*how much* (*you*) *owe* (dēbeō). (174.)
Greeks, *the*, Graecī.
greet, salūtō, 1.
groans (*angry*), convīcium, *n*. (*sing*.).
ground, *on the*, humī. (312.)
ground, *perilous*, *on which they stood*, tale tempus; tantum perīculum.
groundless, falsus.
grounds (=*reason*), causa, *f*.; *on grounds of*, propter. (331, 20.)
grow=*become*.
grudge *against you*, *have a*, tibi succēnseō, 2.
guard, custō-s, -dis, *m*.
guard, *off his*, incautus. (61.)
guard, custōdiō, 4; *guard against*, caveō (2, cāvī, cautum). (248.)
guest, hosp-es, -itis.
guide, dux (*gen*. ducis).
guilt, scel-us, -eris, *n*. (See note under *crime*.)
guilty, nocēns.
guilty *deed*, facin-us, -oris, *n*. (See note under *crime*.)
guilty, *find*, condemnō, 1; *am found*, condemnor.
guilty *of*, *am* (*not*), (nōn) id committō (3, -mīsī) ut.

habit *of*, *am in the*, soleō (2, solitus sum; with *inf*.).
hackneyed, trītus, lit. '*well worn*' (terō).
hair, *white*, cānī capillī (*pl*.).
half *as many*, *as large*, *again*. (535, *d*.)
halt; *come to a halt*, cōn-sistō (3, -stitī).
hand, manus, 4, *f*.
hand, *am at*, ad-sum, -esse, -fuī.
hand *in*, afferō, afferre, attulī, allātum.
hand *over to*, per-mittō (3, -mīsī).
handful *of*=*so small a band of*.
hang *back*, cessō,[1] 1.
happens, *it*, accidit. (126.)
happily (see 64), deōrum beneficiō (*or* peropportūnē) accidit.
happiness, vīta beāta; beātē vīvere; beātum esse (98, *b*); *enjoy h*., beātus sum.
happy, beātus.
hard *pressed*, *am*, premor (3, pressus sum).
hard *to say*, difficile dictū. (404.)
hardly, vix.
hardship, incommodum, *n*.; *hardships*, molestiae, *pl*.
harm, *do*. (See *injure*.)
harsh, asper, asperior, asperrimus.
harvest, mess-is, -is, *f*.
haste (*noun*), celeri-tās, -tātis, *f*.; *there is need of haste*, properātō opus est. (See 286 and 416.)
hasten, properō (1; *absolutely or with inf*.); contend-ō (3, -ī).
hate, ōd-ī (*perf. with pres. meaning*), -isse, -eram; *am hated*, odiō sum. (260, *Note* 2.)
hatred, odium, *n*.
haughty, superbus. (57, *a*.)
have *you*, *would*. (152, *c*.)
he *himself*, ipse (355); *he* (11, *a*, *d*.)
head, cap-ut, -itis, *n*.
head *of*, *am the*, prae-sum. (251.)
headlong, prae-ceps, -cipitis (*adj*.).
health, *am in good*, valeō, 2.

[1] *Cessō*, I hang back from something which I have begun or have to do; *differō*, I put off action, adjourn it to another time; *cūnctor*, I delay from caution or indecision.

heap (*abuse*) *on you*, tē (maledictīs) onerō, 1.
hear; *hear of*, audiō, 4; ac-cipiō (3, -cēpī).
heard *of by, have been*. (**258**, ii.)
hearing, *in my, use abl. abs.* (*pres. partic.*) (**420**); *without a hearing* (**425**).
hearing, *sense of*, aur-ēs, -ium, *f. pl.*
heart (*affections, spirit*), animus, *m.*; (*disposition*), ingenium, *n.*
heat, aestus, 4, *m.*
heave *a groan*, ingem-īscō (3, -uī).
Heaven (*metaph.*), Dī immortālēs. (See **17.**)
heaven *and earth, appeal to*, deōrum hominumque fidem implōrō.
heavy, gravis; *or, in metaphorical sense only*, labōriōsus (*use superl.* **57**, *a*).
height *of*, summus. (**60.**)
heir, hēr-ēs, -ēdis.
help, *can* (*not*). (**134.**)
help *you*, auxiliō tibi sum. (**259.**) tibi opem ferō.
helplessness, *in*, in-ops, -opis (*adj.*). (See **61.**)
henceforth, iam.
herdsman, bubulc-us, -i, *m.*
here, hīc.
here, ad-sum, -esse, -fuī.
hesitate *to*, dubitō, 1 (with *inf.*; but see **136**); cūnctor, 1 (with *inf.*)
hidden, occultus.
hide (*by silence*),[1] dissimulō, 1.
high, altus; *high hopes*, (see **54**).
high-spirited, ferōx. (See note under *boldly*.)
highest, summus.
hill, coll-is, -is, *m.*
himself, ipse. (**355.**)
his, eius; illīus; suus. (See **11.**)
his *own* (*enemy*), sibi *or* suī (**55**) ipse (inimīcus).
historian, rērum scrīpt-or, -ōris.
hoist (*a flag*), ē-dō (3, -didī, -ditum)
hold, obtineō, 2; (**19**); habeō, 2.
hold (=*think*), dūcō (3, dūxī, ductum); *hold* (=*count*) *as*, habeō (**240**); habeō prō (**240**, *Note* 2).
hold *my peace*, contic-ēscō (3, -uī). (See **17.**)
home, *at*, domī (**312**); *at his own home* (**316**, iii.); *from home* (*with verb of motion*), domō (**9**, *b*); *home* (*return*), domum (**9**, *b*).
home-*sickness*, suōrum dēsīderium.
homes *and hearths, for*, prō ārīs et focīs.
honest, probus.
honesty, probi-tās,[2] -tātis, *f.*
honour (=*good faith*), fid-ēs, **5**, *f.*
honour (=*distinction*), hon-ōs, -ōris, *m.*
honour (=*self-respect*), digni-tās, -tātis, *f.*
honour (*as opposed to expediency*), hones-tās, -tātis,[2] *f.* (**51**, *c*).
honour, *pay* (*you*), or *honour* (*you*), honōrem (tibi) habeō; tē in honōre habeō; *honour highly*, in summō honōre habeō.
honour (*with*) (*publicly*), ōrnō (1, with *abl.*); *or* prō-sequor (3, -secūtus sum).
honourable, honestus; *to be honourable* (*creditable*) *to*, honōrī esse. (**260.**)
hope *for*, spērō, 1. (**23.**)
hopes, spēs,[3] **5**, *f.*; *form hopes*, spērō. (**54.**)
horrified *at*, perhorrēscō (3, perhorruī).
hospitality, *rights of*, iūs hospitī.
host (opp. to *guest*), hosp-es, -itis, *m.*

[1] *Dissimulō* is used of a person who tries to conceal something which exists *simulō* of one who pretends that something exists which does not.

[2] *Honestās* is not 'honesty,' but the *abstract term* for what is honourable (*honestum*) in a general sense.

[3] *Spēs* is rarely used in the plural of the 'hopes' of a single person, or even of many. Cf. *ingenium, memoria*.

host, multitūd-ō, -inis, *f.*
hostage, obs-es, -idis.
hour, hōra, *f.*; *of victory*, (63).
house, *in my*, apud mē (331, 4); domī meae (316, iii.).
household, familia, *f.*
how. (See 157, ii.)
how (*disgraceful, etc.*) (260, *Note* 1.)
how *much* (*adv.*), quantum.
how *much* (*with comparat.*), quantō.
how *often*, quotiēns. (157, ii.)
human, hūmānus; *or gen. pl. of* homō. (59.)
human *beings*, hominēs.
humble *means*, tenuis fortūna.
humble *origin*, *of*, humilī locō nātus.
humour, grātificor, 1 (with *dat.*).
hundred *thousand*. (527.)
hurl, con-iciō (3, -iēcī, -iectum); *at*, in (with *acc.*).
hurry *away from*, āvolō, 1.
hurry *to*, conten-dō (3, -dī); festīnō, 1.
husband, vir (*gen.* virī).

I, ego. (See 11, *a* and *b*; also 334.)
idle (=*vain, groundless*), vānus.
if, sī. (See Conditional Clauses and 171.)
if not . . . yet. (466, *c.*)
ignorant *of*, ignōrō,[1] 1 (*trans.*); nescio, 4. (174, *e.*)
ill, *am*, aegrōtō, 1.
ill-starred, īnfēlīx, *comp.* īnfēlīcior. (57, *b.*)
illustrious, **praeclārus**; **praestāns**. (57, *a.*)
ill-will, malevolentia, *f.*
imagine, (=*think*), puto, 1. (See note under *fancy*.)
imagine (=*conceive*), animō concipiō (3, -cēpī).
imitate, imitor, 1.
immediately *after*. (332, 1, *or* 331, 21.)
immensely, quam plūrimum.

impart *to*, commūnicō, 1 (cum). (253, v.)
impiety, impie-tās, -tātis, *f.*
implore, obsecrō, 1.
importance *of the matter*, tanta rēs.
importance *to me*, *it is of*, meā interest (310).
important, gravis.
impose *upon you* (*conditions*), tibi im-pōnō (3, -posuī).
impossible, *it is* (*quite*). (127.)
impress (*affect*) *you*; *make an impression on you*, tē, *or oftener* animum tuum, moveō *or* commoveō (2, -mōvī, -mōtum); *where more than one person is implied*, *pl.* animōs.
impression (*of*), opīni-ō, -ōnis, *f.*
imprisonment, vincula, *n. pl.*
improvident, imprōvidus.
impulse, *of its own*, suā sponte. (See note under *voluntarily*.)
impunity, *with*, impūne (*adv.*).
impute *this to you as a fault*, hoc tibi vitiō ver-tō (3, -tī, -sum); culpae dō (dare, dedī, datum). (260.)
in; *in a time of*, in (with *abl.*). (See 332, 9; 273, *Note* 2.)
incapable *of* (*morally*), abhorreō (2) ab; aliēnissimus sum ab. (See *unable*.)
inclination, volun-tās, -tātis, *f.*
incline. (See 152, *Note* 2, and 169.)
incompetence (*ignorance*), īnscītia, *f.*
inconsiderable (*of danger*), parum gravis.
inconsistent *with*, aliēnus ab.
incorruptibility, integri-tās, -tātis, *f.*
increase (*trans.*), augeō (2, auxī, auctum).
increase (*intrans.*), crēscō (3, crēvī).
incur, in-currō (3, -currī) in (with *acc.*); *incur loss*, damnum capiō (3, cēpī).
indebted *to you for this*, hoc tibi acceptum re-ferō (-ferre, -ttulī · *metaph. from account-book*).

[1] *Nescio*, 'I am absolutely ignorant of,' opposed to *scio*; *ignōrō*, 'I have not made myself acquainted with,' opposed to *nōvī*; *illum ignōrō* (not *nescio*), 'I do not know him.'

indecisive, an-ceps, -cipitis.
India, India, *f.*; *an Indian*, Indus.
indict, reum faciō; accūsō, 1. (306.)
indictment, crīm-en, -inis, *n.*
indifferent *to*, neglegēns (*with gen.*, 301); *am indifferent to*, parvī *or* nihilī (365) faciō.
indignation, *use* indignor, 1. (416.)
indispensable, necessārius.
individuals; *as individuals*, singulī. (380, *b.*)
induced, *am*, mihi persuādētur.
indulge, indul-geō (2, -sī, with *dat.*).
indulgence (=*forgiveness*), venia, *f.*
inexperience, *use adj.*, imperītus.
infallible, certissimus.
infamous, *am declared*, ignōminiā notor, 1.
infant, īn-fāns, -fantis.
infantry, pedit-ēs, -um, *m. pl.*
inferior *to*. (278.)
infest, īnfēstum habeō. (240.)
inflict *loss on you*, damnō (*abl.*) tē af-ficiō (3, -fēcī; 283).
inflict *death on you* (*judicially*), morte tē multō, 1.
inflict *punishment on*, poenās sūm-ō (3, -psī, -ptum) dē (*abl.*).
influence, auctōri-tās,[1] -tātis, *f.*
influence *with, have* (*much, etc.*), possum apud. (331, 4.)
information, *give*, doceō (2, docuī.) (231.)
inhuman, inhūmānus.
injure, noc-eō (2; *dat.*)
injury (=*harm*), damnum, *n.* (See note under *wrong*.)
innocence, *entire, use superl. of* innocēns.
innocent, extrā culpam sum. (331, 9.)
innocent, *the*, innocentēs. (50.)
inspiration, afflātus, 4, *m.*
instantly, continuō.
instead *of* (*doing, etc.*), adeō nōn . . . ut; nōn modo . . . sed; tantum āfuit ut . . . ut (128); *or* cum posset (*or* dēbēret), (434).
instigation, *use* auctor (424), *or* suādeō, moneō (420).
institution, īnstitūtum. (51, *b.*)
instrumentality, *by your*. (267, *Note* 2.)
insult, contumēlia, *f.*
intellect, mēns (*gen.* mentis), *f.*
intend *to*, *use fut. tense, or* in animō habeō *with infin.*
intent *on*, dō operam. (397.)
intention *of, with the*. (108.)
intentionally, cōnsultō; cōnsiliō, (270.)
interest, grātia, *f.* (See note under *influence*.)
interest (*advantage*), ūtili-tās, -tātis, *f.* (51, *c.*)
interest or *interests of, consult*, cōnsul-ō (3, -uī, -tum) with *dat.* (See 248.)
interest *of, in the*, causā. (290, *Note* 1.)
interfere *with*, inter-veniō (4, -vēnī; with *dat.*).
interpose (*intrans.*)=*interfere*.
interposition, *miraculous*. (64.)
interpreter, interpr-es, -etis.
intervene, inter-veniō (4, -vēnī; with *dat.*).
interview *with, have an*, con-veniō (4, -vēnī; *trans.*; 24 and 229); col-loquor (3, -locūtus sum) cum.
intimate *terms with, live on*. (282.)
into, in. (331, 26.)
intolerable (*to*), *almost*, vix ferendus. (394 and 258, i.)
invade, bellum, *or* arma, īn-ferō (-ferre, -tulī, illātum) in (with *acc.*).
invasion, *use* bellum īnferō (and see 417.)

[1] *Auctōritās*, moral influence as distinct from authority in the sense of *power*; *potestās*, legal or legitimate authority or power; *imperium*, military authority or power; *potentia*, 'power,' 'might,' in a more general sense; *rēgnum*, kingly or despotic power; *grātia*, 'interest' with the powerful; *favor*, 'popularity' with the masses.

inveigh *against*. (331, 6.)
invent (=*fabricate*), fingō (3, fīnxī, fīctum).
inventor, invent-or, -ōris : *fem. form* invent-rīx, -rīcis.
invest (*a city*), circum-sedeō (2, -sēdī, -sessum; *trans.*; 229).
invite, invītō, 1. (331, 26.)
involved *in*, versor (1) in (with *abl.*).
involves, *it* (=*implies*), habet.
irruption, incursi-ō, -ōnis, *f.*
island, īnsula, *f.*
issue, *the*, ēventus, 4, *m.*; but see 174, *d.*
Isthmus, *the*, Isthm-us, -ī, *m.*
Italy, Italia, *f.*
itself, ipse. (355.)

January, Iānuārius.
javelin (*Roman soldier's*), pīlum, *n.*
jealous *of you*, tibi in-videō (2, -vīdī).
jewel (*metaph.*), *use* rēs. (223, *Note* 1.)
join (*you*), mē (tibi, *or* ad tē) ad-iungō (3, -iūnxī, -iūnctum); *join the ranks of*, mē adiungō ad.
journey, it-er, -ineris, *n.*; *am on a journey*, iter faciō.
joy, laetitia, *f.*; *shouts of joy*, laetantium (*gen. pl. of part. pres. of* laetor) clāmor. (See 414 and *Note*.)
joyful, laetus.
judge (=*think*), reor, 2, ratus sum. (See note under *fancy*.)
judgement (=*decision*), iūdicium, *n.*
judgement (=*will*), arbitrium, *n.*
judgement (*good*), cōnsilium, *n.*
judgement *is different*, *my*, aliter iūdicō, 1. (54.)
June (*month of*) (mēnsis) Iūnius : *first of*, Kalendae Iūniae. (538.)
juniors, iūniōrēs; nātū minōrēs.
jury (*judges*), iūdicēs.[1]
just (*adj.*), iūstus.
just (*lately*), nūperrimē.
just (*then*), iam tum.
justification, causa, *f.*
justly, iūre. (See note under *rightly*.)

keenness, aciēs, 5, *f.* (lit. *edge*).
keep (*promises*), stō, stāre, stetī (with *abl.*).
keep (*within*), contineō, 2, intrā.
keep *anxious about*, sollicitum habeō dē. (240.)
keep *back from*, prohibeō, 2; arceō, 2 (*abl.*).
keep *in the dark*, or *secret*, cēlō, 1. (230, 231.)
keep *my word*, fidem prae-stō (-stāre, -stitī).
kill, inter-ficiō[2] (3, -fēcī, -fectum); oc-cīdō (3, -cīdī, -cīsum).
kind *deed*, beneficium, *n.*; officium, *n.*
kind *of*, *every*, omnis.
kind *of man*, *the*, *use* quālis. (174, *c.*)
kind, *of this*, huius modī;[3] *of that kind*, *that kind of*, eius modī.[3] (See 87.)
kindly (*adj.*), benignus; hūmānus.
kindly *disposed to*, bene-volus (-volentior) in. (255.)
kindness, boni-tās, -tātis, *f.*; (*act of*), beneficium, *n.*; *return k.* (see *gratitude*).
king, rēx (*gen.* rēgis); *king's*, rēgius (*adj.*, 58).
know (*a fact*), scio (4, scīvī); (*a person*), nōvī, nōsse, nōveram (nōram); nōtum habeō (188).
knowledge (=*learning*), doctrīna, *f.*
knowledge, *to* (or *within*) *my*. (508.)

lack, mihi dēest. (251.)
laden, onustus.
laggard, ignāvus.

[1] Plural because each *iūdex* gave his own *sententia*, 'opinion' or 'vote.'

[2] *Interficere*, general word for to kill; *occīdere*, to kill with a weapon, as in war *necāre*, to put to death cruelly; *trucīdāre*, to murder inhumanly, to butcher.

[3] *Huius modī* and *eius modī* are often used contemptuously; *tālis* rarely so.

lamentations, *make,* lāmentor, 1.
land, terra, *f.*; ag-er, -rī, *m.*
land, *our* (=*territory*), agrī nostrī. (See *country* and **16** *a.*)
land *on,* (*trans.*) ex-pōnō (3, -posuī, -positum) in (with *abl.*).
landing *of, use partic. of* expōnō. (**417.**)
language (=*conversation*), serm-ō, -ōnis, *m.*
language, *use this,* haec loquor. (See **25** and **54.**)
large. (See *great.*)
last (*to*), *the,* ultimus. (**62.**)
last (*of past time*), proximus; *for* (or *within*) *the last* (*days, etc.*) (**325,** *Note* 2).
last, *at,* tandem.
lasting, diūturnus.
late (=*recent*), recēns.
late *in life,* iam senex (**63**); prōvectā iam aetāte (*abl. abs.*).
late, *too* (*adv.*), sērō.
lately, nūper, *superl.*, nūperrimē; *but lately,* paulō ante. (**279,** *Note.*)
launch *against,* im-mittō (3, -mīsī) in (*acc.*).
law, lēx (*gen.* lēgis), *f.* (See p. 58, *n.* 1.)
lawful, lēgitimus.
lay *before,* dē-ferō (-ferre, -tulī) ad.
lay *down my arms* (=*disband or surrender*), ab armīs dis-cēdō (3, -cessī).
lay *violent hands on myself.* (**253,** iii.)
lay *waste.* (See *waste.*)
lazy, ignāvus.
lead, dūcō (3, dūxī, ductum).
lead *a life.* (**237.**)
lead *across, or through,* trāns-dūcō (3, -dūxī). (**229,** *Note* 3.)
lead *back,* re-dūcō (3, -dūxī, -ductum).
lead *out,* ēdūcō.
leadership. (**424.**)
learn, discō (3, didicī).
learn *fresh* (*additional*), ad-discō (3, -didicī).
learning, doctrīna, *f.*; but *advance in learning,* doctior fīō; and see **279** for *superior in learning.*
least, *at,* saltem; *I at least,* ego certē.[1]
leave; *leave behind,* re-linquō (3, -līquī, -lictum; see note under *abandon*); (*a place*), ex-cēdō (3, -cessī; with *abl. or* ex); pro-ficīscor (3, -fectus sum; with *abl.*, see **314**); *leave my country* (**264**).
leave *you* (*free*) *to.* (**198,** *Note* 4.)
leave *alone,* missum faciō. (**240.**)
leave *nothing* (**298,** *b*); *leave nothing undone,* nihil praeter-mittō (3, -mīsī) quīn.
leave, *you have my.* (**331,** 16.)
left (*adj.*), sinist-er, -ra, -rum.
legion, legi-ō, -ōnis, *f.*
leisure, ōtium, *n.*; *at leisure,* ōtiōsus (*adj.*).
Lemnos, Lēmn-os, *gen.* -i; *f.*
less (*adv.*) minus; *less than* (*with numerals*), (**275,** *Note*).
let (*you*), (tibi) trā-dō (3, -didī, -ditum *with gerundive*). (**400.**)
let *slip* (*an opportunity*), dēsum. (**251.**)
letter, litter-ae, -ārum, *f. pl.*; *from,* ā, ab.
level *plain,* plānitiēs, 5, *f.*
levy (*noun*), dēlēctus, 4, *m.*; *hold a levy,* dēlēctum habeō, 2.
levy *contributions on you,* pecūniās tibi imperō, 1.
liar, mend-āx, -ācis (*adj.*).
liberties, līber-tās, -tātis, *f.* (sing.); = *exemptions,* immūnitāt-ēs, -ium, *f. pl.*
life, vīta, *f.*
lifetime, *in his* (**61**); *in your father's*=*your father being alive* (vīvus), *abl. abs.* (**424**).
like (*adj.*), similis. (**254, 255.**)

[1] *Certē*, when it follows a word, means 'at least,' and is equivalent to *saltem*; more emphatic than *quidem*.

likely *to, use fut. tense, or* fierī potest ut.
line (*of battle*), aciēs, 5, *f.* (see note under *field*); *line of march,* agm-en, -inis, *n.*; *lines* (*fortified*), mūnīmenta, *n. pl.*; *line* (*metaph. for* '*opinion*'), iūdicium, *n.*
linger, cūnctor, 1.
list *of, write a,* per-scrībō (3, -scrīpsī; *trans.*).
listen *to,* audiō, 4. (23.)
listen *to* (=*comply with* or *obey*) obtemperō, 1, (*dat.*). (See *obey,* note.)
literature, litterae, *f. pl.*
little (see 53); *little of,* parum (294).
live, vīvō (3, vīxī, vīctum).
load, onerō, 1.
load (*noun*), on-us, -eris, *n.*
locality, loc-a, -ōrum, *n. pl.*
lofty, praealtus.
London, Londinium, *n.*
long (*in distance*), longus; *in time,* diūtinus, diūturnus.
long (*adv.*), diū, *or* iam diū; *long ago,* iam prīdem; *long continued,* diūtinus; *long tried,* spectātus, (57, *a*).
longer (*adv.*), diūtius; *no longer,* or *any longer* (*after a negative*), nōn iam *or* nōn diūtius (328, *a*); *how much longer?* quoūsque, *or* quoūsque tandem? (157, *Note* 5.)
look *at,* spectō, 1 (see note under *see*); intueor, 2 (*perf. rare*).
look *down on,* dē-spiciō, 3, -spexī, -spectum (*trans.*).
look *for* (=*wait for*), exspectō, 1. (23.)
look *for* (*in vain*), dēsīderō, 1.
look *forward to,* prō-videō (2, -vīdī; with *acc.*).
look *round for,* circum-spiciō (3, -spexī. (22, 23.)
look *up at,* suspiciō, 3.
looked *for, than I had,* spē, *or* exspectātiōne, meā. (277.)
lose, ā-mittō (3, -mīsī, -missum).
lose (*opportunity*), dē-sum, -esse. (251.)
lose *heart,* animō dēficiō, 3; *of more than one person,* animīs.
lose *my labour,* (=*effect nothing*), nihil agō (3, -ēgī).
lose *time,* tempus terō (3, trīvī, trītum).
lose *the day,* (=*am conquered*), vincor (3, victus sum).
loss, damnum, *n.*; dētrīmentum, *n.*
loss *of, without the, use* ā-mittō, 3. (425.)
loss *what to do, at a.* (172.)
lost, *all is,* dē summā rē āctum est.
lot (*metaph.*), *lot in life,* fortūna, *f.*
lot, *it falls to* (*my*), (mihi) contingit: [1] *it is men's lot to,* hominibus contingit ut. (123.)
love, dī-ligō (3, -lēxī, -lēctum); amō,[2] 1.
lovely, pulcherrimus.
low, abiectus; *very low,* īnfimus. (57, *a.*)
low (or *lowly*) *birth,* ignōbili-tās, -tātis, *f.*
lowest *part of,* īmus. (60.)
loyal, fidēlis.
loyalty, fidēs, 5, *f.*
luxury, luxuria, *f.*

mad, *am* (*quite*), furō (3; perf. rare).[3]
made, *am being,* fīō, fierī, factus sum.
magnificent, praeclārissimus.
magnitude, *use* quantus. (174, *a.*)

[1] *Contingit,* 'happens' by a natural process; oftener, but not always, of what is desirable: *accidit,* 'happens,' 'falls out,' by chance; often, but not always, of what is undesirable; *ūsū venit,* 'falls within my experience'; *ēvenit,* 'happens,' 'turns out,' as the result of previous circumstances.

[2] *Amāre* expresses greater warmth of feeling than *dīligere*: it is 'to love passionately,' 'to be enamoured of.'

[3] *Furō* is a stronger term than *īnsāniō.* See note on 'fury.'

mainly, potissimum.
maintain, sustineō, 2.
make, faciō (3, fēcī, factum); *make war*, bellum īnferō (253, iii.); *make my way*, iter faciō.
make *fast* (=*bind*), cōn-stringō (3, -strīnxī, -strictus).
malice, malitia;[1] malevolentia.
Malta, Melita, *f.*
man, vir; hom-ō, -inis (for the difference see p. 131, *footnote* 2); *to a man*, (331, i.).
management, prōcūrātiō, -ōnis, *f.*
manhood, *in quite early*, admodum adulēscēns. (63, and p. 51, *footnote* 1.)
manifestly=*obviously*, (64.)
mankind, hominēs; *or* genus hūmānum.
manliness, *with*, virīliter.
manner, *in this*. (See 270, *Note* 3.)
manner *of life*. (174, *c.*)
manner, mōr-ēs, -um, *m. pl.*
many, multī.
marble (*adj.*), marmoreus.
march (*noun*), it-er, -ineris, *n.*
march, iter faciō.
Marseilles, Massilia, *f.*
marsh, pal-ūs, -ūdis, *f.*
mass, mōl-ēs, -is, *f.*
mass (*of the people*), vulgus, -ī, *n.*; see p. 146, *footnote*.
massacre, caed-ēs, -is, *f.*; *am present at the*, *use gerundive*. (387.)
massacre, trucīdō, 1. (See *kill*.)
master, dominus, *m.*
matter, rēs, 5, *f.*
matters *little, it*, parvī rēfert (310); *it matters not*, nihil rēfert (*ibid.*).
mature *life, in*, iam adultus. (63.)
May (*month of*) (mēnsis) Maius. (538, *footnote*.)
may. (198, *Note* 3.)
mean (*adj.*), sordidus; abiectus.
means, *by no*, nēquāquam; haudquāquam; nūllō modō; minimē.
means, *by this*. (268.)
means, *humble*, tenuis fortūna.
meantime, intereā.
meddle *with*, at-tingō (3, -tigī).
Medes, *the*, Mēdī, -ōrum.
meditate *on*, cōgitō, 1, dē (*abl.*).
meet, obviam fīō (with *dat.*); *come* (*go, go down*) *to meet*, obviam veniō (eō, dēscendō).
meet (=*endure*), ex-perior (4, -pertus sum).
meet (*doom*), ob-eō (-īre, -iī; with *acc.*).
meet (*together*) *at*, convenīre ad. (331, i.)
member *of the nation* (or *state*), cīv-is, -is, *m.*
memory, memoria, *f.*
menace *with*, dēnūntiō, 1 (*acc. of thing, dat. of person*).
mention, mentiōnem faciō (with *gen.*).
mention, *not to*, nē dīcam. (100, *footnote* 3.)
merchant *vessel*, nāvis onerāria.
mercy, misericordia, *f.*; *place myself entirely at your*, tōtum mē tibi trādō ac permittō.
mere (*from the*), ipse (*use abl. of cause, or* propter : see also 355); '*mere*' and '*merely*' *are often expressed by emphatic order simply.*
message, nūntium, *n.*
messenger, nūntius, *m.*
method, rati-ō, -ōnis, *f.*
mid-day, merīdiēs, 5, *m.*
middle *of, midst of*. (60.)
midst *of, in the*. (332, 9.)
mighty, *superl. of* magnus.
Milan, Mediōlānum, *n.*
mile, mīlle, *pl.* mīlia (*i.e.* passuum; 1000 *paces of* 5 *feet*).
mind, animus, *m.*; (=*intellect*), mēns (*gen.* mentis), *f.*; *his whole mind*,=*all that he thinks* (sentiō).
mind (*verb imperat.*), fac (*or* cūrā) ut. (141.)

[1] *Malevolentia*, ill-will; *malitia*, the same feeling shown in underhand attacks or schemes; *malignitās*, ill-will shown in a desire to defraud, niggardliness.

mind, *am out of my,* īnsāniō, 4. (See 25.)
mind, *am of one (with),* cōn-sentiō (4, -sēnsī) cum.
mingle *with (intrans.),* im-misceor (2, -mixtus sum ; with *dat.*).
mingled . . . *and,* et . . . et.
miraculous *interposition.* (See 64.)
miserable, mis-er, -era, -erum.
mislead, dēcipiō.
missile, tēlum, *n.*
missing, *am,* dēsideror, 1.
mistake, *a,* err-or, -ōris, *m.* ; *mistake in,* use *gen.* (300).
mistake, *make a* ; *am mistaken,* errō, 1.
Mithridates, Mithridāt-ēs, -is.
mob, multitūd-ō, -inis, *f.*
mode, rati-ō, -ōnis, *f.*
moderate (*not too great*), modicus ; mediocris (' *middling* ').
moment *when, at the.* (431.)
money, pecūnia, *f.*
monstrous (=*wicked*), nefārius.
monument, monumentum, *n.*
moon, lūna, *f.*
morals, mōr-ēs, -um, *m.*
more (*adv.*), plūs (*of quantity*) ; magis (*of degree*). *As noun* (294), plūs, *n. pl.* (54) plūra ; *more than* (=*rather than*), magis quam ; *more than once,* see *once.*
moreover, praetereā.
morning, *in the,* māne (*adv.*).
morrow, *the (still in future),* diēs crāstinus ; *on the morrow (of a past date),* diē posterō.
mortal (e.g. *wound*), morti-fer, -fera, -ferum. (18, 19.)
most (*used loosely in comparing two only*), plūs. (See *more.*)
most *men,* plērīque.
motive, *from,* or *with, a, use* ob with *acc.* (331, 14); *my only motive is,* (483, *Note* 1).
mount *up,* ascend-ō (3, -ī).
mountain, mōns (*gen.* montis), *m.*
mournfully, maestus. (61.)
move (*intrans.*), moveor (2, mōtus sum). (20.)

much, multus ; *as noun* (see 53) ; *much of,* (294) ; *with comparat.,* multō (279).
multitude, multitūd-ō, inis, *f.*
murder, caed-ēs, -is, *f.*
murder, necō, 1.
murderer. (See 175.)
must *be, use gerundive* (200).
mutiny, sēditi-ō, -ōnis, *f.*
my, *meus.* (See 11, *c.*)
myself (*emphatic*), ipse (355) ; (*reflexive*), mē, mē ipsum ; *for myself,* ego *or* equidem (11, *a,* and 334, i. and iv.).

name, nōm-en, -inis, *n.* ; *in name (nominally),* (274, *Note*).
name, *good,* fāma, *f.*
Naples, Neāpol-is, -is, *loc.* -ī.
Narbonne, Narbō, -ōnis, *m.*
nation, populus, *m.* ; cīvi-tās, -tātis, *f.*, *or* cīv-ēs, -ium ; rēs pūblica. (See 19.)
national, commūnis ; *or gen. of* rēs pūblica. (58.)
national *cause, the,* rēs pūblica ; commūnis reī p. causa.
natural *powers,* nātūra, *f.*, and see note under *character.*
naturally (*by nature*), nātūrā.
nature, *use* quālis *or* quis. (174, *b.*)
native *land,* or *country* (see 16, *a*) ; *leave my,* patriā cēdō (264).
nearly, prope, paene. (See note under *almost.*)
necessary, necessārius ; *is necessary,* (see 286).
necessaries (*of life*). (286.)
necessity (=*emergency*), temp-us, -oris, *n.*
need *of* ; *is needed, etc.,* opus. (286.)
needs *must,* necesse est. (201.)
neglect, neg-legō (3, -lēxī, -lēctum).
neighbour (*actual*), vīcīnus ; *in sense of ' fellow man ' or ' men,'* alter ; cēterī. (372.)
neighbouring, fīnitimus.
neither . . . *nor,* neque . . . neque.
neither *of the two.* (340, ii.)
never, numquam ; *and never,* nec umquam. (110.)

new, novus.
news *of, use* nūntiō, 1 (417); *news has been brought*, (46, *a*).
next, proximus; īnsequēns; *next* (*day*), posterus; or (*on the*), postrīdiē (*adv.*).
next *to* (*prep.*). (331, 21.)
niceties (*of argument*), argūtiae, *f. pl.*
night, nox (*gen.* noctis), *f.*
nineteen, ūndēvīgintī. (527.)
ninety-second. (See 530 and 531.)
no (162); *say* or *answer* 'no,' negō, 1.
no, *none* (*adj.*), nūllus.
no (*not*) *more* (*adv.*) *than*, nihilō magis quam.
no *one, none*, nēmō, *gen.* nullīus (see 223, *Note* 2); *and no one, none*, nec quisquam (110).
no *sooner . . . than*, ubi prīmum; simul atque. (428.)
noble (*morally*), praeclārus (p. 51, *footnote* 2); pulcherrimus (57, *a*); *for usage with proper nouns and persons, see* 224.
nobles. (51, *a*, and *note*.)
noon, *noon-day*. (See *mid-day*.)
nor, neque; *in final clauses*, neu.
not *yet*, nōndum.
nothing, nihil.
now, iam (=*by this time; can be used of the past*); nunc (*at the present, at the moment of speaking*); hodiē (*to-day*).
now . . . *long*, iamdiū; iamprīdem. (181.)
now . . . *now*, modo . . . modo.
number (*proportion* or *part*), par-s, -tis, *f.*
number *of, the* (*interrog.*). (174, *a.*)
numbers, *great*, multī; complūrēs; *superior*, multitūd-ō, -inis, *f.*
numerous, *more*, plūrēs; *such numerous*, tot.

oath, iūsiūrandum, *gen.* iūrisiūrandī, *n.*
obedient *to*=*obey*.
obey, pār-eō,[1] 2 (*dat.*, 5); obtemperō, 1 (*dat.*); *the orders of*, dictō audiēns sum (with *dat. of person*).
object, recūsō, 1 (130).
object (*noun*), *objects* (see 54); *object of unpopularity with you*, invidiā flagrō (1) apud vōs.
obligation, *am under*, grātiam dēbeō. (98, *b.*)
obstacle, (id) quod obstat.
obstinate, pertin-āx, *comp.*, -ācior.
obtain, adipīscor [2] (3, adeptus sum; cōn-sequor (3, -secūtus sum; 18, 19); *a request*, impetrō, 1.
obviously. (64.)
occasion, *on that*, tum.
occupy (=*hold*), teneō, 2.
ocean, ōceanus, *m.*
off (=*am at a distance of*), absum. (318.)
offence, peccātum, *n.* (403.)
offensive, *take the*, see *aggressive*.
offend (*annoy*), offen-dō (3, -dī, -sum; with *acc.*).
offer, dē-ferō (-ferre, -tulī, -lātum); *offer* (*terms*), ferō.
office, magistrātus, 4, (18, 19); *am in*, in magistrātū sum; *hold*, m. habeō, obtineō.
officers (*military*), tribūnī (mīlitum) centuriōnēsque.
often, saepe; *so often*, totiēns.
old. (See *ancient*, and note.)
old *age*, senec-tūs, -tūtis, *f.*; *in my*. (63.)
old *man*, sen-ex, -is.

[1] *Pāreō*, the general word for 'I obey,' applied often to habitual obedience of any kind: *obtemperō*, I obey as from a sense of reason and right; *oboediō*, I obey a single command; *obsequor*, 'I comply with,' 'I suit myself to'; *dictō audiēns sum*, I render implicit obedience, as that of a soldier.

[2] *Nancīscor*, I obtain, often without effort, by circumstances or chance; *cōnsequor*, I obtain a thing which I follow after as a good; *adipīscor*, I obtain after effort; *impetrō*, by entreaty.

old-world, *old-fashioned,* priscus; antīquus. (See note under *ancient.*)
oldest, nātū maximus.
once, semel; *often exp. by tense of verb; more than once,* semel ac saepius. (533, *b.*)
once (*=formerly*), quondam; ōlim.[1]
once, *at* (*=immediately*), statim.
once, *at* (*=at the same time*), *use* īdem. (366.)
one (*numeral*), ūnus; *of,* ex (529 *a*); *one of the best,* (529, *f*); *one or two*; *one, two, several,* (529, *g*).
one (*indefinite*), *one who,* (see 72); *one so,* (224, *Note* 3).
one, *not,* nēmō (223, *Note* 2); nē ūnus quidem (529, *g*).
one, . . . *the other.* (368.)
one *and all,* cūnctī (see under *all*); omnēs (*placed last*).
one *by one,* singulī. (380, *b.*)
one *day* (*=at some time or other*), aliquandō. (See note under *once.*)
one *thing . . . another, it is.* (92.)
only, sōlum, modo, tantum (*placed after the word qualified*); *this and only this,* (347, *example*); *not only,* nōn sōlum, nōn modo.
onset, impetus, 4, *m.*
open; *throw open*; *open wide*; *cause to be opened,* pate-faciō (3, -fēcī, -factum).
open, *to be,* patēre (*no fut. in* -rus).
open *to question, is=can be doubted,* dubitārī potest.
opening, *first possible.* (377.)
openly, palam.
opinion, *good,* exīstimāti-ō, -ōnis, *f.*
opinion *on, your=what you think of* (cēnseō dē).
opponent. See *oppose.*
opportunity, occāsi-ō, -ōnis, *f.*; facul-tās, -tātis, *f.*; *first possible,* (377.)
oppose, adversor, 1 (*dat.,* 245, *b*); ob-stō, 1, -stitī (253, i.).
opposite *to.* (331, 2.)
opposition, *in spite of your, use partic. of* adversor, 1 (420.)
oppress, vexō, 1. (19.)
oppressive, inīquus.
or, aut, vel (see Intr. 49); *in final and consec. clauses,* 103, 110; *interrog.,* 159, 160; 168, *and Note.*
orator, ōrāt-or, -ōris.
order, iubeō, 2, iussī, iussum. (120.)
orders, iussa, *n. pl.* (51, *b.*)
orders, *give,* imperō, 1; ē-dīcō (3, -dīxī, -dictum). (122.)
origin (*=extraction*), gen-us, -eris, *n.*; *of humble origin,* humilī locō nātus.
originally (*sprung*). (See *sprung.*)
orphan, orbus.
other, *the,* ille (339, iv.); (*of two*), alter (368); *others,* aliī, *or* (*=other men, the rest*) cēterī (372).
other *men's,* or *persons',* aliēnus (*adj.,* 58).
ought. (199.)
our, nost-er, -ra, -rum.
our *men,* nostrī. (50.)
out *of,* ē, ex (332, 5), *or* dē (*abl.*).
outcries, *angry,* maledicta, *n. pl.* (408.)
outdo (*far*) (facile) vincō (3, vīcī), superō, 1.
outnumber, *we,* plūrēs sumus quam.
outrage *on, use gerundive or partic. of* violō, 1. (417.)
outside (*the city*). (318, *Note.*)
outstrip=*outdo.*
over (*=more than*), plūs. (275, *Note.*)
over *with, all.* (332, 4.)
over-*reach,* circum-veniō (4, -vēnī). (229.)
overwhelm, ob-ruō (3, -ruī, -rutum) op-primō (3, -pressī, -pressum).
owe, dēbeō, 2.

[1] *Ōlim,* at a distant *point,* in the past or (sometimes) in the future; *quondam,* only of the past, and generally during some *space* of time in the past; *aliquandō,* at some time or other, past, present or future, opposed to 'never.'

owing *to*, propter (*acc.*, 331, 20).
own, *his*, suus (11, *e*); *my own*, meus.

pacify, plācō, 1.
pain, dol-or, -ōris, *m.*
painful, *is*. (260.)
palace, domus (*decl.* 2 *and* 4; *gen.* domūs), *f.*; *the king's*, domus rēgia. (58.)
panic, pav-or, -ōris, *m.*
pardon, ig-nōscō (3, -nōvī, -nōtum; *dat.*, 5); *pardon* (*you*) *for* (*this*), hoc tibi condōnō, 1; *wish you pardoned*; tibi ignōtum volō (240); *by pardoning*, *gerund of* ignōscō (99).
parent, parēns.
park (=*pleasure grounds*), hortī, *m. pl.*
Parliament=*Senate*.
part, *for my*, equidem. (See also 334, i.)
part, *it is our*. (291, *Note* 3.)
part, *the greater*, plērīque.
part *from*, dis-cēdō (3, -cessī) ab.
part *in*, *take*, mē im-misceō (2, -miscuī, -mixtum; with *dat.*); *a battle*, intersum (*dat.*); *politics*, at-tingō (3, -tigī).
part *in*, *without*, exper-s, -tis (*gen.*, 301, ii.).
partly, partim.
party, par-s, -tis, *f.*; and see *popular* and *aristocratic*.
party, *one . . . the other*. (340, iii.)
pass (*a law*), per-ferō, -ferre, -tulī.
pass (*time*), dēgō (3, dēgī); agō (3, ēgī, āctum).
pass, (*intrans.*, *of intervals of time*), inter-cēdere (3, -cessit).
pass *by*, praeter-eō, -īre, -iī.
passion (=*anger*), īra, *f.*
passionate, īrācundus.
passionateness, īrācundia, *f.*
past (*adj.*), praeteritus; *the past*, praeterita, *n. pl.*, (52); tempus praeteritum.
pathless, invius.
patience, *with*, aequō animō, *or* patienter.
patriot; *true patriot*, bonus cīvis, cīvis optimus; *patriots*, *every patriot*, *all true patriots*, optimus quisque (375); *best patriot*, optimus cīvis.
pay *attention to*, ratiōnem habeō (*with gen.*); *pay* (*you*) *honour*; honōrem (tibi) habeō, 2; *pay my respects to*, salūtō, 1 (*acc.*); *pay the penalty* (see *penalty*).
peace, pāx (*gen.* pācis), *f.*
peace (*of mind*), sēcūri-tās, -tātis, *f.*
peculiarity, *special*, proprium, *n.* (255.)
penalty, poena, *f.*; supplicium, *n.*; *pay the penalty of*, poenās dō (with *gen.*). (See note under *punishment*.)
people (=*men*), hominēs; *a people* (=*nation*), populus, *m.*
perceive, intel-legō (3, -lēxī, -lēctum.) (19.)
perhaps, nescio an (see 169, i.), *or* haud scio an (*the latter should always be used before an adj. when no verb is expressed*); fortasse; forsitan (169, ii.).
perilous, perīculōsus. (57, *a.*)
period, *at that*. (294, *Note*.)
perish, per-eō, -īre.
permission, *with your kind*; *without his*, (270, *Note* 3).
permit, per mē licet (331, 16); *am permitted*, mihi licet (198).
perpetrate, com-, *or* ad-, mittō (3, -mīsī, -missum); faciō (3, fēcī, factum).
perpetrator (*of*)=*he who perpetrated*. (175.)
persecute, īnsector, 1.
persevere or *persist*, persevērō, 1.
person, hom-ō, -inis. (224, *Note* 3.)
person, *a single* (*after a negat.*), quisquam. (358, i.)
person (*your own*), caput, *n.*
personal *appearance*, corporis (59) habitus, 4, *m.*
persuade, persuā-deō (2, -sī, -sum) (5); *cannot be persuaded*, persuādērī mihi nōn potest. (219, i.)

pestilence, pestilentia, *f*.
philosopher, philosophus.
philosophy, philosophia, *f*.
pierce, cōn-fodiō (3, -fōdī, -fossum).
pitch *of, to such a*, eō (with *gen*., 294, *Note*).
pity *for, feel*, mē miseret (*gen*., 309).
place, locus, *m*. (*pl*. generally loca, *n*.) ; *in the place* (*where*), ibi ; *to the place* (*whence*), eō. (89.)
place, pōnō (3, posuī, positum).
plain, campus, *m*.
plain (*adj*.), manifēstus.
plan, cōnsilium, *n*.
plead (*as excuse*), excūsō, 1 ; *my cause*, causam ōrō (1), *or* dīcō (3, dīxī), *or* agō (3, ēgī).
pleasantly (*speak*), iūcunda, *n. pl*.
please (e.g. *you*), placeō, 2 (*dat*., 5).
please (= *it pleases me*), mihi libet (libuit *or* libitum est) (247) ; *if you please*, sī libet.
pleasing *to*, grātus (*dat*.).
pleasure, volup-tās, -tātis, *f*. (*often in pl., when used for pleasure in the abstract*).
pledge *myself*, spondeō (2, spopondī).
plunder, praeda, *f*.
poet, poēta, *m*.
point (*in every*), rēs (*pl*.).
point *of, on the, use fut. in* -ūrus ; (418, *d*).
point (*whence*), *to the*, eō. (89.)
point *out*, mōnstrō, 1 ; ostend-ō (3, ī, ostēnsum).
poison, venēnum, *n*.
policy, cōnsilia, *n. pl*.
political, use *gen. of* rēs pūblica (see 59).
political *life*, rēs pūblica ; *I enter political life* ; ad rem p. mē cōnferō (-ferre, -tulī) *or* ac-cēdō (3, -cessī).
politicians. (175.)
politics, rēspūblica (*never pl*.).
poor, paup-er, -eris ; *the poor*, pauper-ēs, -um. (51, *a*.)
popular (*party*), populāris ; or *the popular party*, populār-ēs, -ium, *m. pl*. (p. 51, *footnote* 2).
popularity, fav-or, -ōris, *m*. (See note under *influence*.)
populous, frequēns.
position, locus, *m*.
possible (*with superlatives*), vel.
possible, *it is*. (127.)
possibly, *use* fierī potest ut. (64 and 127.)
post *up*, fīgō, 3, fīxī, fīxum.
posterity. (See 51, *a*, *and footnote* 3.)
postpone, dif-ferō (-ferre, distulī). (See note under *hang back*.)
poverty, pauper-tās, -tātis, *f*.
power, potentia, *f*. ; potes-tās, -tātis, *f*. (See note under *influence*.)
power, *under his own, gen. of* diciō sua, arbitrium suum. (290, *Note* 3.)
powerful, potēns ; *the powerful*, potentissimus quisque (*sing*., 375) ; *am most powerful*, plūrimum possum.
powerless, *am*, nihil possum.
praise (*noun*), lau-s, -dis, *f*.
praise, laudō, 1.
praised, *to be* (*adj*.), laudandus.
praiseworthy, laudābilis.
pray *for* (= *desire much*), optō, 1 (*acc*.) ; *make one prayer*, ūnum optō.
prayers, prec-ēs, -um, *f*.
preceding, proximus.
precious, pretiōsus (*superl*., 57, *a*.)
predecessors. (175.)
prefer, mālō (mālle, mālu ; with *inf*.).
prefer (*him to you*) (eum tibi) prae-, *or* ante-pōnō (3, -posuī, -positum) (253, iii.) ; *or* prae-ferō, (-ferre, -tulī).
preparations, *make*, parō, 1. (54.)
prepare (*trans*.) (*for* or *against you*) (tibi) in-tendō (3, -tendī)
preparing *to* (= *about to*), *use partic. in* -ūrus.
presence, *in his, my, etc*., praesēns. (61, *or* 420.)
presence *of, in the*, in (273, *Note* 2) ; cōram (*abl. of persons*).

present (*adj.*), hic (337); but *your present*, iste (338).
present, *am*, ad-sum (-esse, -fuī); *present at*, intersum. (251.)
present, *at*, or *for the*, in praesēns. (331, 26.)
present, *as a*. (260.)
present *you with this*, hōc (*abl.*) tē (*acc.*) dōnō, 1.
presently, mox; brevī.
preservation *of, the, use* cōnservō, 1. (292, 10.)
preserve, servō, 1; cōnservō, 1.
press *on*, īn-stō (1, -stāre, -stitī; with *dat.*); *by pressing on*, *gerund*. (99.)
pretend, simulō, 1; (=*assert*) dictitō,[1] 1; fingō, 3, fīnxī, fīctum.
pretty (*adv.*); *pretty well*, satis.
prevail *by prayer*, impetrō, 1, *upon*, ab. (122.)
prevent (*from*), ob-stō (1, -stāre, -stitī (with *dat.*) quōminus. (129.)
prevent, *to* (*in order that . . . not*), nē. (101.)
priceless, pretiōsissimus.
prince, rēx (*gen.* rēgis).
principle, *want of*, levi-tās, -tātis, *f.*
prison, vincula, *n. pl.*, car-cer, -ceris, *m.*
prisoner, captīvus, *m.*; *am being taken*, capior (3, captus sum).
private (*person*), prīvātus; *private property*, rēs familiāris.
privilege, iūs (*gen.* iūris), *n.*
procrastinate, differō (differre, distulī.) (See note under *hang back*.)
procrastination, cūnctāti-ō, -ōnis, *f.*; *or use verb*, cūnctor, 1 (98, *a.*)
profess, pro-fiteor (2, -fessus sum).
progress *in, make* (*much, more*), (multum, plūs) prōficiō in (*abl.*).
project (*noun*), cōnsilium, *n.*
prolonged, diūtinus.
promise, pollic-eor (2, -itus sum); prō-mittō (3, mīsī, -missum). (37.)
promise, prōmissum, *n.* (51, *b*); *make promises*=*promise.*
proof, indicium, *n.*; *is a proof* (260.)
proof *against*, invictus ab (with *abl.*) *or* adversus (with *acc.*).
proper (=*one's own*), suus.
property, bona, *n. pl.* (51, *b*); fortūnae, *f. pl.*; rēs, 5, *f.*
prophet, vāt-ēs, -is, *m.*
prophetic=*of him foretelling the future.*
proportion *to, in* (332, 7; 376); *exact proportion to* (*with verbs of valuing*), tantī . . . quantī.
prosecuted *for, am*, reus fīō (factus sum); accūsor, 1 (306).
prospect, or *prospects*, spēs, 5, *f.* (*sing.*). (See note under *hope.*)
prosperity, rēs prosperae, *or* secundae.
protect *your interests*, tibi (248) caveō (2, cāvī, cautum).
protest *against*. (130.)
protract (*war*), trahō (3, trāxī).
proud, superbus.
proud *of*, glōrior, 1. (282, *Note.*)
prove (*intrans.*). (259, *Note* 1.)
provide *against*, caveō (2, cāvī, cautum) nē, *or with acc. of noun.*
provide *for*, prō-videō (2, -vīdī, -vīsum). (248.)
provided *that*, modo, modo nē. (468.)
provision, *make no*, nihil prōvideō.
provisions (*for army*), frūmentum, *n.*; rēs frūmentāria, *f.*
provocation, *without*=*no one provoking, abl. abs.* (See 332, 8.)
provoke, lacess-ō (3, -īvī, -ītum), irrītō, (1).
prudence, prūdentia, *f.*
prudence, *want of*, imprūdentia, *f.*

[1] *Simulō*=I pretend something exists which does not; *dissimulō*=I try to conceal something which does exist. When the pretence is applied to words rather than to conduct, *dictitō* (a frequentative form of *dīcō*) is common in the sense of 'I assert, allege.' *Fingō*, and still more *mentior*, emphasises the falsehood of the allegation.

public (*services*)=*to the people*; *public interest*, rēspūblica; *public life*, see *political life*.

punish, poenās sūmō (3, sūmpsī) dē (332, 4); *am punished for*, poenas dō, *with gen. of the crime*.

punishment, poena,[1] *f.*; supplicium, *n.* (*heavy*).

purpose, prōpositum, *n.* (51, *b*); cōnsilium, *n.*

purposely, cōnsultō.

pursue, sequor (3, secūtus sum).

pursuit, studium, *n.*

put *off*, differō (differre, distulī).

put *to death*, caedō (3, cecīdī, caesum). (See also under *kill*.)

put *to the test*, perīclitor, 1.

put *up with*, tolerō, 1 (with *acc.*).

Pyrrhus, Pyrrhus.

quail *before*, pertim-ēscō (3, -uī; with *acc.*).

qualities, *good*, virtūt-ēs, -um, *f. pl.*

quantity, vīs (*acc.* vim). (See also 174.)

quarter, *ask for*, ut mihi parcātur precor, 1; mortem *or* victōris īram dēprecor; *I obtain*, ut mihi parcātur impetrō, 1; *or* mihi parcitur.

question (*ask*), interrogō, 1; *it is questioned* (*doubted*), dubitātur; *may be questioned*, dubitārī potest.

question, *my*, *his*, *the*; *to my*, *etc.*, *pres. part. of* interrogō (346); *the real question* (see *real*).

question (=*matter*), rēs, 5, *f.*

quiet (*noun*), tranquilli-tās, -tātis, *f.*

quietly, *use adj.* (61), sēcūrus.

quit, ex-cēdō (3, -cessī) (*with or without* ē, ex, 314).

quite, *not*, parum; vix.

race (=*nation*), gēns (*gen.* gentis), *f.*; *the human race*, hominum (*or* hūmānum) gen-us, -eris, *n.*

rage, īra, *f.*

raid *upon*, *make a*, incursiōnem faciō in (*acc.*).

raise, tollō (3, sustulī, sublātum); (*an army*) (exercitum) comparō, 1; (*a cheer*) (clāmōrem) tollō.

raise *up*, attollō (3, sustulī, sublātum).

rally (*intrans.*), mē col-ligō (3, -lēgī); *to rally* (*of a number*), concurrere.

rank (=*position*), status, 4, *m.*; (*of army*), ōrd-ō, -inis, *m.*; *ranks* (*metaph. of a party*), part-ēs, -ium, *f. pl.*; *high rank*, digni-tās -tātis, *f.*

rare (=*remarkable*), singulāris.

rarely, rārō, *comp.* rārius.

rash, temerārius.

rashness, temeri-tās, -tātis, *f.*

rather (*adv.*), potius.

rather, *had*, or *would*, mālō (mālle, māluī).

ravage, populor, 1.

reach, perveniō ad (253, ii.); *reach such a pitch of*, eō prō-cēdō (3, -cessī) (294, *Note*); *to reach* (*of letters*), perferrī ad.

reach (*of darts*), *the*, iactus, 4, *m.*

read *through*, per-legō (3, -lēgī, -lēctum).

ready *to*, volō (velle, voluī; with *inf.*).

real (*question*) *is*, *the*, illud (341) quaeritur (218).

realise (=*conceive*), animō (*or* mente) con-cipiō (3, -cēpī, -ceptum).

reality, *in*; *really*, rē; rē ipsā; rē vērā. (274.)

reap (=*gain*), per-cipiō (3, -cepī, -ceptum); *the fruit of*, frūctum percipiō (*gen.*).

rear, tergum, *n.*; *in the*, ā tergō (332, 1), *or* āversus. (See 61.)

reason, causa, *f.*; *for* (*both*) *reasons* (378, i.); *the reason* (*of*), quās ob causās *or* cūr (174); *the reason* (*of*) . . . *was* (483, *Note* 1).

[1] *Poena*, 'requital'; *supplicium* is used mainly of the punishment of death.

rebel,[1] quī contrā rēgem arma sūmpsit. (**175.**)
rebel *to* (*invite*)=*to* ***rebellion.***
rebellion (***renewal of war after submission***), rebelli-ō, -ōnis, *f.*; (***revolt***), dēfecti-ō, -ōnis, *f.*
rebuke (***noun***), ***use*** increp-ō, (1, -uī), (**414**, *Note*).
recall (***to***), revocō, 1 (ad); ***to mind***, in animum.
receive, ac-cipiō (3, -cēpī, -ceptum) (19); ***without receiving*** (**425, 420.**)
recent, recēns.
reckon ***up***, ēnumerō, **1.**
recognise, cog-nōscō (**3**, -nōvī, -nitum).
reconciled ***with you***, tēcum in grātiam red-eō (-īre, -iī).
reconciliation (***you delay your***)=***to be reconciled with.***
recover (***trans.***), recuperō, 1; re-cipiō (3, -cēpī, -ceptum); ***recover myself***, mē recipiō; ***recover*** (***intrans.***) ***from***, ēmer-gō (3, -sī) ē (ex).
recruit, tīr-ō, -ōnis; ***army of recruits***, (223, *Note* 2).
reflect *on*, recordor, 1.
refrain (***from***), facere nōn possum (quīn).
refuge ***with, take***, cōn-fugiō (3, -fūgī) ad.
refuse, nōlō (nōlle, nōluī).
refute (***an opponent***), redargu-ō (3, -ī); ***a charge***, dīlu-ō (3, -ī); ā mē re-moveō (2, -mōvī).
regard ***for*** or ***to, have***, ratiōnem habeō (2, with *gen.*).
regiment, ***use*** cohor-s, -tis, *f.*
regret, mē pud-et (2, -uit). (**309.**)
regular ***engagement***, iūstum proelium, *n.*
reign, rēgnō, 1.
reinforcements, subsidia, ***n. pl.***
reject, repudiō, 1.
rejoice, gaudeō (2, gāvīsus sum).
rejoicing (***noun***), laetitia, *f.*

relates ***to***, spectat **ad.**
relation, propinquus, ***m.*** (**256.**)
reliance ***on*** (***you***), ***place***, fidem (tibi) habeō, 2.
relief, ***bring you***, tibi succurr-ō (3, -ī).
relieve, sublevō, 1 (***acc.***); ***relieve of***, levō, 1 (***abl. of thing***).
relinquish, o-mittō (3, -mīsī, -missum). (See note under ***undone.***)
reluctant, nōlō (nōlle, nōluī).
reluctantly; ***with reluctance.*** (**61.**)
rely ***on***, cōn-fīdō (3, -fīsus sum; 282, *Note*, **245**, *Note* **4**); fidem habeō (2, with *dat.*).
relying ***on*** (*adj.*), frētus. (**285.**)
remain ***behind***, re-maneō (**2**, -mānsī).
remain ***firm***, permaneō.
remains, ***it***, restat ut. (See **126.**)
remarkable, singulāris.
remember, memin-ī (-isse; ***imperative*** mementō; ***for pres. subj.***, meminerim).
Remi, ***the***, Rēm-ī, -ōrum.
remorse ***for, feel***, mē (**234**) paenit-et (2, -uit; *gen.*, **309**).
remove (***my home***), commigrō, **1** (***intrans.***).
removed ***from, far.*** (**264**, ***Note.***)
renown, glōria, *f.*
repeatedly, saepe; saepissimē (**57**, *a*); persaepe.
repel, prōpulsō, 1; ***from***, **ab.**
repent ***of***, mē paenit-et (2, -uit). (**309.**)
reply, respond-eō (2, -ī).
repose, ōtium, ***n.***; ***enjoy***, ōtiōsus sum.
reproach, ***it is a.*** (**260.**)
reputation, exīstimāti-ō, -ōnis, ***f.***; fāma, *f.*; ***reputation for***, lau-s, -dis, *f.* (with *gen.*).
request, ***make a***, petō (**3**, petīvī) (122), poscō (3, poposcī) (231). (See note under ***demand***); ***make this***, hoc (***acc.***) petō; ***my request***, quae petō. (**175.**)

[1] A 'rebel' might also be '*quī ā fidē dēscīvit*' or *dēfēcit*; or *rem pūblicam* might be substituted for *rēgem*, according to the context.

require, *use* opus. (286.)
resemble (*closely*), similis (*superl.*) sum. (255.)
resentment, dol-or, -ōris, *m.*
resident, *am,* domicilium habeō; *at* (see 312).
resignation, *with,* aequō animō.
resist, repugnō, 1 (*dat.*).
resistance, *use inf. pass. of* re-sistō, (3, -stitī); *in spite of resistance,* (420).
resolution (=*design*), cōnsilium, *n.*
resolution, *pass a,* dēcernō (3, dēcrēvī).
resolve, statu-ō (3, -ī); dēcernō (3, -crēvī, -crētum). (45.)
resources, op-ēs, -um, *f.*
respect, observantia, *f.*
respectable, honestus.
responsible (*for*), *make you,* ratiōnem ā tē reposcō (*with gen.*).
rest, qui-ēs, -ētis, *f.*
rest (*of*), *the,* cēterī; *or* (372) reliquus (*in agreement,* 60, *or with gen.*); *rest of the world,* (see *world*).
rest *on,* nī-tor (3, -sus sum) (*abl.,* 282, *Note*).
rest *with,* penes (331, 15) esse.
restore (*strength, etc.*), redintegrō, 1.
restrained *from, cannot be,* retinērī nōn possum quīn.
result, rēs, 5, *f.*; (*of toil*), frūctus, 4, *m.*; *the result is, was, etc.,* ēvenit (ēvēnit, ēventūrum); *without result,* (332, 8).
retain, retineō, 2.
retake, re-cipiō (3, -cēpī, -ceptum).
retire *from,* ab-eō (-īre, -iī). (264.)
retreat, mē re-cipiō (3, -cēpī); pedem re-ferō (-ferre, rettulī).
retrieve, sānō, 1.
return (*noun*), reditus, 4, *m.*
return (*intrans.*), red-eō (-īre, -iī).
return *kindness,* grātiam referō (referre, rettulī). (98, *b.*)
revolt, dēfecti-ō, -ōnis, *f.*
reward (=*prize*), praemium, *n.*; (=*pay, fee*), merc-ēs, -ēdis, *f.*; (=*fruit*), frūctus, 4, *m.*
reward, praemiīs afficiō (3, affēcī).
rich (*of persons*), dīv-es, -itis; *of cities,* opulentus; *the rich* (51, *a*).
riches, dīvitiae, *pl. f.*
ride *past,* (equō) praeter-vehor (3, -vectus sum) (*trans.,* 24); cf. *coast along.*
ridge, iugum, *n.*
ridiculed, *am,* irrīdeor (2, irrīsus sum). (253, iv.)
right (*noun*), iūs (*gen.* iūris), *n.*; *am in the right,* vērē (*or* rēctē) sentiō (4, sēnsī).
right *hand,* dextra, *f.*
rightly, *rightfully,* iūre.[1] (270, *Note* 1.)
rigour, sēvēri-tās, -tātis, *f.*
ring *with,* (=*echo with*), person-ō (1, -uī; with *abl.*).
rising, sēditi-ō, -ōnis, *f.*
rising *ground,* tumulus, *m.* (*use pl.*).
rival, invidus, *m.*
river, flūm-en, -inis, *n.*; fluvius, *m.*
road, via.
roar *out,* vōciferor, 1; magnā vōce conclāmō, 1.
rock, saxum, *n.*
roll (*intrans.*), volvor (3, volūtus sum). (21, *a.*)
Rome (*the city*), Rōma, *f.*; (*the nation*) populus Rōmānus. (319.)
roof, *under my.* (331, 4.)
round (*prep.*), circā *or* circum (*acc.,* 331, 5).
rout, fundō (3, fūdī, fūsum).
royal, rēgius.
ruin, interitus,[2] 4, *m.*; exitium, *n.*; perniciēs, 5, *f.*; clād-ēs, -is, *f.*; calami-tās, -tātis, *f.*; *without ruin to, use* salvus (*abl. abs.,* 424).

[1] *Iūre* is 'rightly' in the sense of 'rightfully,' 'deservedly'; *rēctē,* 'correctly,' 'accurately'; *rīte,* in accordance with religious usage or ceremonial.

[2] *Ruīna* is the fall (literal) of a building, etc., and is only occasionally used in a metaphorical sense. (See 17-19.)

ruin, pessum dō ; *ruined*, afflīctus.
ruler *of*, imperō, 1 (*dat.*).
rumour, rūm-or, -ōris, *m.*
run *forward*, prō-currō (3, -currī).
run, *into*, incurrō in (with *acc.*).
rural, rūsticus.
rustic (*adj.*), agrestis.

sack (*a city*), dī-ripiō (3, -ripuī, -reptum).
sacrifice *to* (*metaph.*) = *place behind*, posthabeō, 2. (253, iii.)
sad, maestus.
safe, tūtus ; incolumis (*safe and sound*) ; salvus (*of things as well as persons*). *For adv.* 'safely' *use* tūtus *or* incolumis. (61.)
safety, sal-ūs, -ūtis, *f.* ; *in safety*, tūtō (*adv.*) ; incolumis (*adj.*, 61); *wish for your safety*, tē salvum volō (velle, voluī). (240.)
sail, nāvigō, 1 ; *sail round*, circumnāvigō, 1 (*trans.*)
sailor, nauta, *m.*
sake *of*, *for the*, causā *or* grātiā, *with gen. or pronominal adj.* (289) ; *or* ad *with gerund* (396) ; *for its own sake*, propter sē (331, 20).
sally, ērupti-ō, -ōnis, *f.* ; *make a*, ēruptiōnem faciō.
sally *out*, ē-rumpō (3, -rūpī).
salute, salūtō, 1.
same *as*, *the*. (84, 365.)
satisfactory, *use* ex sententiā 'in accordance with one's views.'
satisfied *with*, contentus (*abl.*, 285).
save *you*, tibi salūtem afferō (afferre, attulī).
say, dīcō (3, dīxī, dictum) ; *said he* (*parenthetic*) (40) ; *it is said* (43). (See also under *speak*.)
saying, *a*, dictum (see 51, *b* ; 55) ; *the saying*, illud (341).
scale, cōnscen-dō (3, -dī).
scanty, exiguus.
scarcely, vix.
scatter (*intrans.*), dissipārī, 1. (20, 21, *a*.)
scene, *come on the*, inter-veniō (4, -vēnī).
scenes (= *places*), loc-a, -ōrum, *n.*
schemes, īnsidiae, *f.* ; art-ēs, -ium, *f.*
science *of war*, rēs mīlitāris.
scout, explōrāt-or, -ōris.
sea. mar-e, -is, *n.* ; *by sea and land*, terrā marīque (*note the order*).
sea-*sickness*, nausea, *f.*
second, alter (531, *a*) ; (*for*) *a second time*, iterum (533, *b*) ; **secondly**, deinde (534, *Note*.)
secret *from*, *keep*, cēlō, 1 (230) ; *make a secret of*, dissimulō, 1. (See footnote on *pretend*.)
secretly, sēcrētō (*adv.*).
secure (= *safe*), tūtus. (19.)
secure ; *make secure* ; cōnfirmō, 1.
see, videō [1] (2, vīdī, vīsum) ; (*as a spectator*) spectō, 1 ; (*in sense of perceive*), intel-legō (3, -lēxī, -lēctum) ; *am seen*, cōn-spicior (3, -spectus sum).
seek *for*, pet-ō (3, -īvī, -ītum).
seem, videor (2, vīsus sum) (43, *Note* 2).
seize, comprehen-dō (3, -dī, -sum) ; (*an opportunity*), ūtor (3, ūsus sum). (281.)
seldom, rārō.
self, ipse (355, 356).
self-*confidence*, suī fīdūcia, *f.* (300.)
self-*control*, modestia ; (animī) moderāti-ō, -ōnis, *f.*
self-*control*, *want of*, impotentia, *f.* ; *adj.* impotēns, *adv.* impotenter.
Senate, senātus, 4, *m.*
Senate *house*, cūria, *f.*
send, mittō (3, mīsī, missum) ; *to*, ad (6) ; *send back* (*to*), remittō (ad) ; *send for*, arcess-ō (3, -īvī, -ītum) (*acc.*).
sense, *good*, prūdentia, *f.*

[1] *Vidēre*, the general word, to see ; *spectāre*, to look long at, to watch as a spectacle ; *cernere*, to see clearly, to decern ; *cōnspicere*, to get sight of ; *aspicere*, to turn the eye towards ; *intuērī*, to gaze at earnestly or steadfastly.

sensible, or *of sense*, prūdēns; *one so sensible as* (**224**, *Note* 3); *adv.*, prūdenter.
sentenced *to*, multor, 1. (**307**.)
sentiments, *hold the same*, eadem (**365**) sentiō (4, sēnsī) (**54**).
separately, singulī. (**380**, *b.*)
serious, grav-is (-ior, -issimus).
serpent, serpēns (*gen.* serpentis), *f.*
service, *military*, mīlitia, *f.*
service *to, do* (*good, the best, such good*) (bene, optimē, tam bene) mereor (2, meritus sum) dē (**332**, 4); but *services to*, merita (**51**, *b*) in (**331**, 26).
set (e.g. *spurs*), sub-dō (3, -didī) (*dat.*).
set *at liberty*, līberō, 1.
set *at naught*, con-temnō (3, -tempsī, -temptum); parvī (minimī, nihilī) faciō *or* habeō (**305**).
set *before* (*you*), (tibi) ex-pōnō (3, -posuī, -positum).
set *fire to*, incen-dō (3, -dī, -sum) (*acc.*).
set *out*, pro-ficīscor (3, -fectus sum).
settle, cōnstit-uō (3, -uī) (*trans.*).
several (= *some*), aliquot (*indecl.*); = *respective*, suus *with* quisque. (**354**, i.).
severe, gravis.
sex, sexus, 4, *m.*
shake (*trans.*), labefactō, 1.
shamelessness, impudentia, *f.*
share (*with*), commūnicō, 1 (cum; **253**, v.).
shatter, quassō, 1.
shelter, tegō (3, tēxī, tēctum).
shelter, perfugium, *n.*; *under shelter of*, tēctus (with *abl. of instrument*).
shew. (See *show.*)
shield, scūtum, *n.*
ship *of war, a*, nāvis longa; *merchant ship*, nāvis onerāria.
short, *in*, dēnique.
short-*lived* (*panic*) = *of the shortest time.* (**303**, *Note* 1.)
shortly, brevī.
shout, clām-or, -ōris, *m.*
show (=*point out*), mōnstrō, 1; *show* (=*display*) *clemency, etc.*, or *show myself* (=*prove*), (see **240**. *Note* 1); *show such cruelty to*, adeō saeviō (4) in (*abl.*); *show gratitude*, (**98**, *b*).
shrewd, acūtus (*superl.*, **57**, *a*).
shrink *from*, dētrectō (1) (*acc.*).
sick, aeg-er, -ra, -rum; *am sick*, aegrōtō, 1; *his sick-bed*=*him whilst sick and failing.*
side (*of a river*), rīpa, *f.*
side, *by your*, tibi praestō (*adv.*) sum; *on your*, ā tē stō (1, stetī). (**332**, i.)
side, *on no*, nūsquam; nec ūsquam; *on this side* (*of*), *prep.*, cis (**331**, 6); *on the other*, ultrā (**331**, 25); *on all sides*, undique.
sigh *for* (*metaph.*), dēsīderō, 1, (*trans.*, **22**, **23**).
signal, signum, *n.*
silence, *in.* (**61**.)
silent, *am*, taceō, 2.
sin, peccō, 1.
since (*adv.*), posteā; *as prep.* (=*from*), ex *or* ab. (**326**.)
single *combat, in*, comminus.
single, *a*, ūnus; *not a single*; *not one*, nē ūnus quidem. (**529**, *g.*)
sink (*trans.*), dēmer-gō (3, -sī, -sum); *intrans.* (*metaph.*), dēscend-ō (3, -ī); *am sinking* (*fainting*) *under*, exanimor, 1, (*abl.*, **268**, *Note* 2).
sister, sor-or, -ōris.
sit, sedeō (2, sēdī); *sit down*, cōn-sīdō (3, -sēdī).
situation, situs, 4, *m.*
six, sex; *sixth*, sextus.
size, magnitūd-ō, -inis, *f.*; and see **174**.
slander, maledicta, *n. pl.* (**51**, *b.*)
slaughter, *use* oc-cīdō (3, -cīdī, -cīsum).
slave, servus, *m.*; *am a slave*, serviō, 4.
slavery, servi-tūs, -tūtis, *f.*
slay. (See *kill.*)
sleep, dormiō, 4; *in his sleep, use pres. partic.*

sleep, somnus, *m.*
sleep, *want of*, vigiliae, *f. pl.*
so, ita : *with verbs*, adeō; *so little*, adeō nōn : *with adjs. and advs. only*, tam : *so=accordingly*, itaque : *so great, so many*, (84) : *so small*, tantulus: *so far from*, tantum abest ut (128) : *so*, or *as, long as*, (420).
society, *as a.* (380, *b.*)
soften (*metaph.*), exōrō, 1.
soldier, mīl-es, -itis.
solemnly *appeal*. (See *appeal*.)
solitude (*of a place*), īnfrequentia, *f.*
Solon, Sol-ōn, -ōnis.
some *one*, aliquis (360); nescio quis (362); *some . . . others*, aliī . . . aliī (369).
some (*amount of*), aliquantum (*gen.*, 294); *for some time*, aliquantum temporis.
somehow. (363.)
something (*opposed to nothing*), aliquid (360).
sometimes, nōnnumquam;[1] interdum.
son, fīlius.
soon, mox; brevī; iam (328, *b*); *sooner than he had hoped= quicker* (celerius) *than his own hope* (277).
sore (*of famine*), gravis.
sorrows, incommoda, *n. pl.*, aerumnae, *f. pl.*, (*stronger*).
soul (*not*) *a*, quisquam (358, i.); *in Livy* ūnus *is sometimes added*; nē ūnus quidem. (529, *g.*)
sound *your praises*, laudibus tē ferō (ferre, tulī).
sounds *incredible, it*, incrēdibile dictū est. (404.)
source *of* (*metaph.*), *the, use* unde (174, *e*); *a source of* (*gain*) (260).
sovereign, rēx (*gen.* rēgis).
sovereignty, prīncipātus, 4, *m.*
Spaniard, *a*, Hispānus; *Spain* (*=the nation*), Hispānī. (319.)
spare, parcō (3, pepercī; *dat.*); *for perf. pass., use* temperātum est (249.)
speak, loquor[2] (3, locūtus sum); dīcō (3, -dīxī); *speak out*, ēloquor; *in speaking, abl. of gerund.*
special *peculiarity of.* (See *peculiarity*.)
speech, ōrāti-ō, -ōnis, *f.*; if to *soldiers* or *multitude*, conti-ō, -ōnis, *f.*; *my speech is over*; *I have done my speech*, dīxī. (187.)
speed, celeri-tās, -tātis, *f.*
spirit, animus, *m.*; *of more than one person*, animī; *with spirit*, ferōciter. (See note under *boldly*.)
spite *of, in*, in (273, *Note* 2); *of your resistance, etc., abl. abs.* (420); *in spite of his innocence* (224, *Note* 2).
spoil, praeda, *f.*
spotless, integer, innocēns; *or use superl.*
spread *beneath* (*trans.*), sub-iciō, (3, -iēcī, -iectum); *intrans.*, subicior. (20.)
spring, *the*, vēr (*gen.* vēris), *n.*
spring (*=am sprung*), orior (4, ortus sum); *sprung from*, ortus (*abl.*); *originally sprung from*, oriundus ab.
spur, calc-ar, -āris, *n.*; *put spurs to*, calcāria sub-dō (3, -didī) (*dat.*).
spy, speculāt-or, -ōris, *m.*
staff (*military*), lēgātī, *m. pl.*
stand, stō (stāre, stetī); *stand by*, ad-stō (1, -stitī) (*dat.*); *stand round*, circum-stō (1, -stetī) (*acc.*).

[1] *Nōnnumquam*, 'fairly often'; approaches *saepius*. *Interdum*, 'now and then,' more rarely than *nōnnumquam*. *Aliquandō*, 'on certain occasions,' opposed to 'never,' almost=*rārō*.

[2] *Dīcō*, I 'speak' or 'say,' i.e. I give expression to thoughts or views which I have formed; *loquor*, I 'speak,' use the organs of speech to utter articulate words. Hence *dīcō*=I make a formal speech, *loquor*=I utter informal or casual words.

stand *for* (=*am a candidate for*), petō (3, petīvī) (*acc.*).
stand *in need of*, indigeō, 2. (**284**, *Note* 1.)
stand *in your way*, tibi ob-stō (1, -stitī). (**253**, i.)
standard, signum, *n.*; vexillum, *n.*
start (=*set out*), pro-ficīscor (3, -fectus sum).
state (=*condition*), status, 4, *m.*
state (*adj.*), pūblicus.
statesman, *a consummate*, reīpūblicae gubernandae perītissimus. (**301**, ii.)
stay *with* (=*visit*), commoror (1) apud (**331**, 4); *stay at home*, domī maneō (2, mānsī).
steadily, turn by *did not cease to* (dē-sistō, 3, -stitī).
steadiness, *want of*, incōnstantia, *f.*
steal *away* (*intrans.*), dī-lābor (3, -lāpsus sum).
stern, sēvērus.
sternly, *act*, saeviō, 4. (**25**.)
still (*adv.*), adhūc; etiam nunc (*of the present*); etiam tum (*past or fut.*).
stony-*hearted*, ferreus.
storm, tempes-tās, -tātis, *f.*
storm (=*take by storm*), expugnō, 1.
story, rēs, 5, *f.*; and see **54**; *there is a story*, ferunt (**44**).
strangely, nescio quō pactō. (See **169**, v.)
stream, rīvus, *m.* (See *river*.)
strength, vīr-ēs, -ium, *f. pl.*; *strength of mind*, cōnstantia, *f.*
stretch *forth*, por-rigō (3, -rēxī, -rēctum).
strike *off*, ex-cutiō (3, -cussī, -cussum).
strikingly, graviter.
strive (*to*), cōnor, 1 (with *inf.*).
stronghold, arx (*gen.* arcis), *f.*
struck (*partic.*), ictus; *am struck*, per-cutior (3, -cussus sum).
study, *a*, ar-s, -tis, *f.*; *study* (*of*), cogniti-ō, -ōnis, *f.*
study, operam dō (*dat.*); *study my own interest*, mihi (**248**) cōn-sulō (3, -suluī).
subject, *a*, cīv-is, -is, *m.*
submit *to*, per-ferō (-ferre, -tulī) (*acc.*).
substantial, solidus, *comp.*, magis solidus.
succeed *in*, (*a design, etc.*), perficiō (*trans.*); efficiō ut. (**125**.)
succeed *to* (*the throne*), (rēgnum) ex-cipiō (3, -cēpī, -ceptum) (**17**); *succeed you*, tibi suc-cēdō (3, -cessī, -cessum).
success (**98**, *a*); *without success*, īnfectā rē (**332**, 8; **425**).
successfully, prosperē.
successive, continuus.
successors (*his*)=*those who reigned after* (*him*); or *those who will succeed* (*him*). (See **175**; and p. 197, *footnote*.)
succour, sub-veniō (4, -vēnī) (*dat.*).
such (=*of such a kind*), tālis; (=*so great*), tantus; *as*, quālis *or* quantus (see **86**): *such . . . as this*, huius modī (**87**), *or* hic tālis, hic tantus (**88**, *Note*): *such as to, of such a kind that* (**108**): *such* (*adv.*), *such a* (*with adj.*), tam, tālis (*or* tantus) tamque (**88**): *where English subst. is expressed by Latin verb, use* adeō; *I show such cruelty*, adeō saeviō (4).
sudden, subitus; repentīnus (*unexpected.*)
suddenly, subitō.
suddenness *of, the*=*how sudden it was*. (**174**, *e*.)
suffer *from*, labōrō, 1 (*abl.*).
suffering (*adj.*), afflictus (*from* afflīgō).
suffices, *it*, satis est.
sufficient, satis, *with gen.*
suggest, auctor sum (**399**, *Note* 2); admoneō, 2.
suggestion, *at* (*my*), (mē) auctōre (*abl. abs.*, **424**).
suicide (*commit*), mortem mihi cōn-scīscō (3, -scīvī). (**253**, iii.)
summer, aes-tās, -tātis, *f.*
summit. (**60**.)
summon, vocō, 1; *to*, ad.
sun, sōl (*gen.* sōlis), *m.*

sunlight, lūx (*gen.* lūcis), *f.* (sōlis *may be added*).
superior *to*=*surpass*; (*in courage, etc.*), *use comparat. of adj.* (278, 279); *superior numbers* (see *numbers*).
superstition, superstiti-ō, -ōnis, *f.*
supper, cēna, *f.*; *to*, ad.
supplies, commeātus, 4, *m.* (*sing. and pl.*).
supply *with*, suppeditō, 1. (244.)
support (*noun*), subsidium, *n.*
suppose, puto, 1. (See note under *fancy*.)
supreme *power*, imperium, *n.*
sure, *am* or *feel*, certō scio; prō certō habeō, 2; *have made sure of*, compertum habeō (188): *be sure to*, fac (*or* cūrā) ut. (See 141.)
surpass, superō, 1.
surprise (*as a foe*), op-primō (3, pressī).
surrender (*trans.*), dē-dō (3, -didī, -ditum); (*intrans.*), mē dēdō (see 21, *b*); *surrender my arms*, arma trādō (3, trādidī).
surround, circum-veniō (4, -vēnī) (*trans.*); *surrounded*, *use pres. partic. of* circum-stō (1, -stetī) (*abl. abs.*, 420); *surrounded* (*by defences*), cīnctus (*from* cingō): *to be surrounded* (*as by water*), circum-fundī (3, -fūsus sum).
survive, supersum; *from*, ē (ex); *so long as you survive*, tē superstite (*abl. abs.*, 424).
suspect, suspicor, 1; (=*I think*), puto, 1 (see note under *fancy*); *am* (*become*) *suspected of*, in suspīciōnem veniō (4, vēnī) (*gen.*).
suspend, inter-mittō (3, -mīsī, -missum). (See note under *undone*.)
suspicion, suspīci-ō, -ōnis, *f.*; *have no*=*suspect nothing*.
sustain (*onset*), sustineō, 2.
swallow, *a*, hirund-ō, -inis, *f.*
swarm *out of*, ef-fundor (3, -fūsus sum) (*abl.*).
swear, iūrō, 1.
sweep (*metaph.*), volitō, 1.
sword, gladius, *m.*; *in metaphorical sense*, arma, *n. pl.*; ferrum, *n.*; *with fire and sword*, ferrō et ignī; *by sword and violence*, vī et armīs: *note the order*.
Syracuse, Syrācūsae, *f. pl.*

take (*a city*), capiō (3, -cēpī, captum); *by assault*, expugnō, 1.
take *advantage of*, ūtor (3, ūsus sum). (281.)
take *care that*, faciō ut. (125.)
take *from you*, tibi ad-imō (3, -ēmī, -ēmptum). (244, *Note* 2.)
take *part in*. (See *part in*.)
take *place, to*, fierī.
take *prisoner*, capiō (3, cēpī, captum).
take *the same view*. (See *view*.)
take *up* (*arms*), sūm-ō (3, -psī, -ptum; (=*spend*), cōnsūmō.
talk, loquor (3, locūtus sum).
talkative, loqu-āx, *comp.*, -ācior.
tall, prōcērus.
task, op-us, -eris, *n.*
taste, *a* (*metaph.*), studium, *n.*
taunt *you with this*, id tibi ob-iciō (3, -iēcī). (253, iii.)
tax *with*, incūsō,[1] 1, īnsimulō, 1 (*acc. of person, gen. of thing*).
teacher, magist-er, -rī: *fem. form*, magistra.
teaching, *the*, praecepta, *n. pl.*
tear, lacrima, *f.*
tedious, longus.
teeth *of, in the*. (420.)
tell (=*bid*), iubeō (2, iussī). (120.)
tell (*a story*), nārrō, 1.
temper, animus, *m.*
temperament, indol-ēs, -is, *f.* (See note under *character*.)

[1] *Incūsō*, 'I tax with,' 'charge with,' but informally, not as *accūsō* (with gen. 'bring a charge in court.' *Īnsimulō*, 'I hint charges without proof.' *Arguō*, 'I try to prove guilty.'

temple, templum, *n.*
ten, decem; (*a piece*), dēnī. (532.)
tenacious *of*, tenāx. (301, i.)
tends *to*, *use gen. with* est. (291, *Note* 3.)
tent, tabernāculum, *n.*
terms, condiciōn-ēs, -um, *f. pl.*
terrible, *so*, tantus.
territory, fīn-ēs, -ium, *m.*
terror, *am in such*, adeō pertim-ēsco (3, -uī).
testify (=*show*), dēclārō, 1.
than, quam; *or abl.* (275, 493.)
thank *you* (*for*), grātiās (tibi) agō (3, ēgī) ob (*or* prō).
thanks, *return*, grātiās agō (98, *b*); *thanks to*, propter (331, 20, *b*).
that (*demonstrative*), ille (339).
that, *after verbs of saying*, see Ōrātiō Oblīqua; (=*in order that, so that*), see Final, Consecutive, Clauses.
themselves (*reflexive*), sē (349).
then, tum, tunc; *then and there*, īlicō. (See also *therefore*.)
thence, inde.
there, ibi; illīc; *after verb of motion*, eō, illūc.
therefore, igitur; *in narrative*, itaque.
thereupon, tum.
thick *of*, *the*=*the midst of*. (60.)
think (=*reflect*), cōgitō, 1.
third, tertius (*adj.*).
thirst, sit-is, -is, *f.*, *abl.* sitī.
thirty, trīgintā (*indecl.*).
this, hic, haec, hoc. (337.)
thoroughly (*with adj.*), *use superl.*
though, *use pres. part.* (412, *Note*.)
thousand, mīlle, *pl.* mīlia; *to die a thousand deaths*=*a thousand times*, mīliēns (*adv.*).
threaten, īn-stō (1, -stitī); (*of things*), immineō, 2; impend-eō (2, -ī) (253, i.); *threaten with*, minor (1; see 244, *Note* 1); dēnūntiō (1), (244, *Note* 1); *threaten to*, minor, 1. (See 37.)
threats, minae, *f. pl.*; *make threats* (=*threaten*), (minor).
three, trēs, tria; *three days* (*space of*), trīduum, *n.*; *three years*, triennium, *n.*
thrice, ter.
throne, rēgnum, *n.*, *or* imperium, *n.*; *am on the throne*, rēgnō, 1. (See 17.)
throng, multitūd-ō, -inis, *f.*
throughout, per (*acc.*); *throughout* (*the city*)=*in the whole*, use *abl.*
throw, con-iciō (3, -iēcī, -iectum); *into*, in (*acc.*); *myself* (*at the feet of*), mē prōiciō (257, ii.); *throw across*, trāiciō; *throw away*, prōiciō; *throw down* (*arms*), abiciō.
tie (*noun*), necessitūd-ō, -inis, *f.*
till, col-ō (3, -uī, cultum).
till (440, 441); *not till* (443, *Note*).
time, temp-us, -oris, *n.*; *at that time*, tum; eā tempestāte; tum temporis (294, *Note*); *at his own time*, (354, iv.); *in good time*, ad tempus (326).
timid, timidus.
to, ad (331, 1); in (331, 26). (See 6.)
to-day, hodiē.
toil, lab-or, -ōris, *m.*
toilsome=*of such toil*. (303, i.)
tomb, sepulcrum, *n.*
to-morrow, crās.
tongue, lingua, *f.*
too (*also*), quoque. (Intr. 89.)
too, *with adjectives*. (See 57, *b*.)
too *little* (*of*), parum. (294.)
too *much*, 294; nimiō (280, *Note* 2).
torture, cruciātus, 4, *m.*
touch (*his heart*) (animum eius) flectō (3, flexī); *am touched by*, moveor (*abl.*).
towards, ad (331, 1).
town, oppidum, *n.*
townsman, oppidānus.
traditions, *hand down*, trādō (3, trādidī, trāditum); *there is a tradition*. (44.)
train, exerceō, 2; exercitō, 1; *trained in*, exercitātus (with *abl.*).
training, disciplīna, *f.*

traitors, cīvēs impiī.
transact, agō (3, ēgī, āctum).
tranquillity, ōtium, *n.*
transported, *am* (*metaph.*), ex-ardēscō (3, -arsī) (lit. *become hot*).
travel, iter faciō; (=*go abroad*), peregrīnor, 1; *travel over*, perlūstrō, 1 (*acc.*).
treachery, perfidia, *f.*
treat *as a source of gain.* (260.)
treat *lightly*, parvī faciō. (305.)
treat *with success* (*heal*), medeor, 2 (*dat.*).
treaty, foed-us, -eris, *n.*
tree, arb-or, -oris, *f.*
tribe, nāti-ō, -ōnis,[1] *f.*; gēns (*gen.* gentis), *f.*
trifling (*adj.*), levissimus (57, *a*); incōnstāns, incōnstantissimus.
triumph (=*success*), victōria, *f.*; (*a Roman general's*), triumphus; *in triumph*, victor (63); *in the very hour of*, in ipsā victōriā; *shouts of triumph*, exsultantium clāmor (414).
triumph (*metaph.*), exsultō,[2] 1; *triumph over*, superō, 1 (*acc.*).
troops, cōpiae, *f.*; mīlit-ēs, -um, *m.*
trouble, *without*, nūllō negōtiō (270, *Note* 3); *troubles*, molestiae, *f. pl*; *troublesome*, molestus.
truce, indūtiae, *f. pl.*
true, vērus; *it is true, use* ille (334, iv.); *truest patriot* (see *patriot*).
trust (*that*), cōn-fīdō (3, -fīsus sum); *trust your word*, fidem tibi habeō.
truth, *the*, vēra, *n. pl.* (53); *but in truth* (*opposed to a supposition*), nunc vērō.
try (*to*), cōnor, 1 (with *inf.*).
trying (*adj.*), difficilis. (57, *a.*)
tumult, tumultus, 4, *m.*
turn (*trans.*), vert-ō (3, -ī); *my back on you*, tergum tibi vertō.
turn (*intrans.*), vertor (3, versus sum); convertor (20); *to*, ad; *turn back*, revertor.
turn, *each in*, prō sē quisque.
turn *out* (=*prove*), ēvā-dō (3, -sī); *it turns out*, ēvenit; ūsū venit (see note under *lot*); *turns out so*, eō ēvādit.
twelve *hundred*, mīlle ducentī. (527, 528.)
twentieth, vīcēnsimus.
twenty, vīgintī (*indecl.*).
twice *over*, semel atque iterum; *twice two*, bis bīna.
two, du-o, -ae, -o; *two a-piece*, bīnī (532, *a*); *two-thirds*, duae partēs (535, *c*); *two years* (*space of*), biennium, *n.*
tyrant, tyrannus.
tyranny, dominātī-ō, -ōnis, *f.*

unable *to*, nequ-eō (-īvī); nōn possum (posse, potuī).
unanimous; *unanimously, use* omnis. (59.)
unarmed, inermis.
unawares, imprūdēns (*adj.*, 61).
uncertain, *it is*, incertum est.
uncle, avunculus.
uncomplaining *under*, patiēns (57, *a*), *with gen.* (302).
unconstitutional, *unconstitutionally*, contrā rempūblicam. (331, 7.)
uncultivated, rudis.
undaunted, intrepidus (*for usage with proper nouns and persons, see* 224.)
under (e.g. *disgrace*), cum. (269.)
understand, intel-legō (3, -lēxī, -lēctum).
undertake, sus-cipiō (3, -cēpī, -ceptum).
undertaking, *an*, inceptum, *n.* (51, *b.*)
undeserved, immeritus.

[1] *Nātiō* is not to be used of a civilized and organized nation (which is called a *cīvitās*); it means a people or tribe and carries with it an implication of contempt.

[2] *Triumphō* is rarely used metaphorically, or in any other sense than that of celebrating a *triumphus*, i.e. of a general entering the city in triumphal procession.

undiminished=*the same as before.* (84.)
undone, *leave,* o-mittō [1] (3, -mīsī, -missum).
undoubtedly=*indisputably.* (64.)
unequalled, tantus . . . quantus (*followed by* nēmō etc.). (See 490, i.)
unhappy, mis-er, -era, -erum.
unharmed, incolumis.
unhealthy, pestilentus.
unheard, indictā causā (*abl. abs.*).
union, *in,* coniūnctī.
universal, *use* omnis. (59.)
unjust, inīquus.
unlucky, īnfēl-īx (*comp.*, -īcior).
unmoved, immōtus.
unnatural, nefārius.
unpatriotic, *the,* malī (*or* improbī) cīvēs. (50, *footnote.*)
unpopularity, invidia, *f.*; *object of* (see *object*).
unprincipled, nēqu-am (-ior, -issimus) (lit. *worthless*). (See 224.)
unquestionable, *it is*=*it cannot be doubted.* (See 135.)
unrivalled. (358, ii., *or* 490, i.)
until. (See *till.*)
untimely, immātūrus.
untouched, integ-er, -ra, -rum.
unusual, inūsitātus.
unversed *in,* imperītus (301, ii.).
unwilling, use nōlō (nōlle, nōlui).
unwillingly. (61.)
unwise, īnsipiēns.
unworthy *of,* indignus. (See 274.)
unwounded, integ-er, -ra, -rum.
up *to,* ad; *up to this day,* ūsque ad hunc diem.
uphold, sustineō, 2.
uproar, tumultus, 4, *m.*
urge (*to do*), suā-deō (2, -sī), īn-stō (1, -stitī) (*both with dat. and* ut *or* nē *clause*): *urge to* (*crime*), ad (scelus) im-pellō (3, -pulī); *urge this upon you,* hoc tibi suādeō; huius reī auctor tibi ac suāsor sum.
urgently, vehementer.
use *of, make,* ūtor (3, ūsus sum). (282.)
use *to, am of,* prōsum (prōdesse, prōfuī). (251.)
usefulness, *public, use verb*: reīpūblicae (plūs, maximē) prōsum.
useless, *is,* nihil prōdest.
utmost (*to*), *will do my,* quantum in mē est *or* erit (332, 9), *with fut. indic.*
utmost *value.* (See *value.*)

vain, *in,* frūstrā,[2] nēquīquam.
valley, vall-is, -is, *f.*
value (*to*), *of* (*the utmost*) (maximē) prōsum. (251.)
value *highly* (*more highly*), magnī (plūris) aestimō, 1 (*or* faciō); *am highly valued by,* magnī fīō apud; *estimate you at your proper value,* tantī tē quantī dēbeō faciō (see 305): *value above*=*prefer to* (253, iii.).
vanquish, vincō (3, vīcī, victum).
variance *with, to be at,* pugnāre (1) cum (*abl.*).
various. (371.)
vast, maximus; ingēns.
vehement, *use adv.* vehement-er (*superl.*, -issimē).
Veii, Veiī, *m. pl.*
venture, audeō (2, ausus sum; 152, *Note* 2); *by venturing on something,* audendō aliquid. (99, 360, i.)
verdict, sententia, *f.* (*use pl.*: see footnote on *jury*); *give my,* dīcō.
versed *in,* perītus (*gen.*, 301, ii.).
very, *this,* hic ipse (see 355): for '*very*' *with adjs. see* 57, *a.*
veteran (*adj.*), veterānus.
victorious, *when he was,* victor (*noun,* 63).

[1] *Omittō* is I give up, or do not begin, something, *designedly*; *intermittō,* I leave alone *for a time*; *praetermittō,* I pass by, omit, *undesignedly.*

[2] *Frūstrā,* 'in vain,' of the *person* who fails in his object; *nēquīquam,* 'in vain,' of the *attempt* which has produced no result.

victory, victōria, *f.*; vincere. (See 98, *a.*)
view (=*opinion*), sententia, *f.*
view, *take the same*, idem (eadem) sentiō quod (quae), *or* ac (365); *a different*, aliter sentiō ac (367).
vigour (*spirit*), ferōcia, *f.*; (*force*), vīs (*acc.* vim), *f.*
vile, turpis, e. (19.)
vileness, turpitūd-ō, -inis, *f.*
violating, *without*, *use* salvus (424).
violation *of*, *partic.* *of* violō, 1 (417); *in violation of*, contrā quam (491).
violence, vīs (*abl.* vī), *f.*
virtue, vir-tūs, -tūtis, *f.*; *in virtue of*, prō (332, 7.)
virtuously, honestē.
visible, *am*, appāreō, 2.
visit, vīs-ō (3, -ī).
voice, vōx (*gen.* vōcis), *f.*
voluntarily, ultrō.[1]
vote (*of elector*), suffrāgium, *n.*; (*of judge or senator*), sententia, *f.*
voyage, nāvigāti-ō, -ōnis, *f.*, *have or make*, *a*, nāvigō, 1.

wage, gerō (3, gessī, gestum); *with*, cum *or* contrā.
wailing, plōrātus, 4, *m.*
wait (*for*), exspectō, 1 (*acc.*, 22); *wait to see*, (174, *d*).
walk *in*, inambulō, 1 (*abl.*).
wall (*general term*), mūrus, *m.*; *walls* (*of city or fortress*), moenia, *n. pl.*, *3rd decl.*
want (*to*), volō (velle, voluī).
wanting *to*, *am* (=*fail*), dē-sum, (-esse, -fuī) (251); *wanting in* (*nothing*), (nihil) mihi deest.
war, bellum, *n.*; *make war against*, bellum (*or* arma) īnferō (253, iii.); *declare*, indīcō (*ibid.*); *ship of war* (see *ship*).
warfare, mīlitia, *f.*
warmth, *with*, vehementer.
warn, moneō, 2; admoneō, 2.
waste, *lay*, populor, 1; vastō, 1; *waste* (*time*), terō (3, trīvī).
wave, flūctus, 4, *m.*
way, via, *f.*; *in this way* (270, *Note* 3).
weak (*morally*), levis.
weakness, īnfirmi-tās, -tātis, *f.*; *in his weakness*, imbēcillus (*adj.*, 61).
wealth, dīvitiae, *f. pl.*
wealthy (*of cities*), opulentus.
weapon, *a*, tēlum, *n.*
weariness, lassitūd-ō, -inis, *f.*
weary (*trans.*), fatīgō, 1: *am wearied with*, langueō (2) dē (332, 4) *or* ē (ex).
weary *of*, *am*, mē taedet (2, pertaesum est). (309.)
weather, *the*, tempes-tās, -tātis, *f.*
week, *substitute approximate number of days*; *at the end of a*, *within a*,=*after*, *before*, *the 7th day*.
weep *over*, illacrimō, 1 (*dat.*).
weight, *have great* or *no*, multum *or* nihil valeō (apud.) (331, 4.)
welfare, sal-ūs, -ūtis, *f.*
well (*adv.*), bene; *well enough*, satis: *know well*, certō scio; *well known*, satis nōtus.
well-*disposed to*, bene-volus (-volentior) in (*or* ergā). (255.)
well-*earned*, meritus.
well-*trained*, exercitātus.
well-*wishers*. (175.)
what. (157, *Note* 1; and see *who*.)
when (*interrogat.*), quandō (157, *Note* 7); *conj.*, cum. (See Temporal Clauses, I.)
whence, unde; *interrogat.*, (157, ii.); *correlat.*, (89).
whenever. (432.)
where, ubi; *where . . . from* (=*whence*), unde; (=*whither*), quō; *where in the world?* ubi gentium? (294, *Note*.)
whether . . . *or*. (168; see also 171 and 467.)

[1] *Ultrō*, before receiving, without waiting for, provocation, solicitation, etc.: *suā* (*meā*, etc.) *sponte*, of one's own impulse, without external pressure or advice.

which (see *who*); *which of two*, uter (157, i.).
while (*conj.*), dum. (180.) (See also Temporal Clauses, II.)
while, *for a*, paulisper.
whither, quō. (157, ii.)
who, *which* (*that*), *what* (*relat.*), quī, quae, quod. (See Relative.)
who, *which*, *what* (*interrogat.*), quis, quae, quid (*noun*); quī, quae, quod (*adj.*). (See 157, i.)
whoever, quīcumque.
whole, tōt-us, a, um; *whole of.* (60.)
wholly (61); *wholly despair*, dē summā rē dēspērō, *i.e. of our most important interests.*
why, cūr, quam ob rem (157, ii.). (See also 174.)
wicked, *the*, improbī. (50, and *footnote.*)
wickedness, nēquitia, *f.* (See note under *crime.*)
widow, vidua.
will, *against my*, mē invītō, *abl. abs.* (420.)
willing, *use* volō (velle, voluī).
win (=*obtain*), cōn-sequor (3, -secūtus sum); *win the day*, vincō (3, vīcī).
wind, ventus, *m.*
wing (*of army*), cornū, *n.*; *on the*, (332, 1).
winter (*adj.*), hībernus.
winter (=*pass the winter*), hiemō, 1.
wisdom, sapientia, *f.*
wise, sapiēns; *all the wisest men.* (375.)
wish, volō (velle, voluī): *could have wished* (153): *do not wish*, nōlō (nōlle, nōluī).
wish *for this*, hoc optō (1), volō (velle, voluī).
wishes (*against your*). (424.)
with (see 332, 2); *weight with* (see *weight*).
withdraw *from*, mē re-cipiō (3, -cēpī) ē (ex).
within, intrā (331, 12); *of time*, 325; *within memory*, post (331, 17); *within a little of* (134).
without (*prep.*), sine; *more often exp. by abl. abs.* (332, 8, and 425); ita ut (111); quīn (134, *Note*).
withstand, ob-stō (1, -stitī) (*dat.*, 253).
woman, muli-er, -eris.
wonder, mīror, 1.
wonderful, mīrificus.
word, verbum, *n.*; *words*, dicta. (55.)
word (*of honour*), fidēs, 5, *f.*
work, *a*, op-us, -eris, *n.*
work *upon* (*your feelings*), flectō (3, flexī, flexum).
world (see 16, *b*); *all the world*, nēmō est quīn (80); *in the, in the whole, world*, ūsquam; *the rest of the*, cēterī hominēs; cēterae gentēs.
worse, peior; dēterior; *for the worse*, in dēterius.
worst *foe, enemy, superl. of* inimīcus (*dat.*, 256).
worth *seeking, gerundive of* appetō, 3. (393.)
worthless, nēqu-am (-ior, -issimus).
worthy *of*, dignus. (285, *Note* 2.)
would *that.* (150.)
wound, vuln-us, -eris, *n.*; *national*, reīpūblicae. (58.)
wound, vulnerō, 1; *wounded*, saucius (*adj.*); *am wounded*, vulneror, 1; saucior, 1 (*severely*).
wrench *from* (*you*), (tibi) extorqueō (2, -torsī, -tortum). (257.)
write, scrī-bō (3, -psī, -ptum); *write you word*, ad tē scrībō.
wrong, *a*, iniūria,[1] *f.*; *do wrong*, peccō, 1; *wrongdoing*, peccāre (98, *a*).

year, annus, *m.*; (*space of*) *two, three, years.* (See *two, three.*)
yes (see 162); *say yes*, aiō.

[1] *Iniūria* is never used for 'injury' in the sense of mere *harm* or *damage*; this must be expressed by *damnum*.

yesterday, heri; *of yesterday*, hesternus (*adj.*).

yet (*nevertheless*), tamen; vērō (*emphatic*).

yet, *not*, nōndum.

yield *to*, cēdō (3, cessī) (*dat.*).

you, tū, *pl.* vōs. (See 11, *a*, *b*; 334.)

young, iuvenis, iūnior. (51, *a*, *note*.)

your, *your own* (*sing.*), tuus: (*pl.*), vester (see 11, *c*); *that of yours*, iste (338).

yourself, tē, *pl.* vōs.

youth (*time of*), adulēscentia, *f.*; *in my*, (63). (See also 51 *a*, *footnote*.)

zeal, studium, *n.*

INDEX OF SUBJECTS

Ablative, main use of, **212**; syntax of, **262-86**; ablative absolute, **14**, **419-26**; of *accompaniment*, **269**; with certain adjectives, **265**, **285**; of *agent*, **8**, **267**, **391**; of *cause*, **268** *n* 2; of *comparison*, **276**; of gerund and gerundive, **398**; of *instrument*, **8**, **268**, **280-1**, **282** *n*, **284** *n* 2, **286**; of *limitation*, **274**; local, **272** *n*, **312**, **320**; of *manner*, **270**; of *measure of difference*, **279**, **318**, **322**; with *opus*, **286**; of *origin*, **266** *n*; of *place* (at which), **272-3**, **311**, **316**; of *place* (from which), **9**, **314-15**; of *price*, **280**; of *quality*, **271**, **303** *n*; of *respect*, **274**; of *separation*, **264-6**, **276** *n* 1, **284** *n* 2, **314**; of *time* (when), **9**, **272-3**, **320**; of *time* (within which), **9**, **325**; with *usus*, **286**; with certain verbs, **281-4**.

Abstract, see Noun.

Accusative, main use of, **209**; syntax of, **228-41**; with *abhinc*, **324**; adverbial use, **238**; *cognate*, **236-8**; of direct object, Intr. 20, **4**, **228**; of *exclamation*, **241**; of *extent*, *i.e.* space covered, dimension, **318**, **324**; with impersonal verbs, **309**; and infinitive, **31-41**, **96**, **445-6**, **517**; of *motion towards*, **9**, **235**, **313**, **402**, **402** *n* 1; with *natus*, **327**; *predicative*, **239**; retained with passive voice, *p.* 133 *footnote*; of *specification* or *respect*, **233**; of *time* (during *or* for which), **9**, **238**, **321**.

Active, see Verbs.

Adjectival clauses, Intr. **72**; and see Relative clauses.

Adjectives, Intr. 8-12, **47-62**; in ablative absolute, **424**; with ablative of manner, **270**; with ablative of quality, **271**; with cognate accusative, **237**; with predicative dative, **259** *n* 2; *attributive*, Intr. 10, **49**; use of comparative, **57**, **493** *n* 2, **507**; used where English has adverb, **61**; used where English has *of*, **60**; used where English has relative clause, **62**; with genitive of quality, **303**; with names of towns, **317**; how combined with proper names, **224**; used as nouns, **50-55**; of number, Intr. 9, **527-36**; *possessive*, **11**, **290** *n* 1, **291** *n* 2, **515**; *predicative*, Intr. 11, **47-8**; of *quality*, Intr. **9**; of *quantity*, Intr. **9**; use of superlative, **57**, **69**, (with *quisque*) **375-6**, (with *unus*) **529**; of third decl., **291** *n* 1, **295**.

Adverbs, Intr. 38-9, 87, **516**; correlative, **89**; interrogative, **157**; numeral, **533-4**; in *oratio obliqua*, **516**; of time, **328**.

Adverbial clauses, Intr. **73-6**, **94**; participle as substitute, **406**; see Final, Consecutive clauses, *etc.*

Adverbial phrases, **64**.

Adversative clauses, Intr. **74** conjunctions, Intr. **47**.

Affirmative answer, **162**.

Age, how expressed, **327**.

Agent, see Ablative and Dative; secondary, **267** *n* **2**; words denoting agent in English, **76**, **175**, *p.* 197 *footnote* **1**.

Agreement, of adjectives and pronouns, **2**, **47-9**, **83** *n*.; of nouns in apposition, **3**, **221-2**;

of relative, 12, 65-6, 83; of verb, 1, 26-30, 226.
Ambiguity, rare in Latin, 52; avoided by change of voice, 216 *n*; in use of gerund and gerundive, 395.
Answers to questions, 162.
Antecedent, Intr. 72, 12.
Apodosis, 450, 475, 494.
Apposition, 3, 221-7, 317, 406.
Approximation, in numbers, 536.
Article, English, Intr. 3, 348.
Assertions, modest, 152 *n* 2.
Attraction, of gender, 83, 227, 347.
Attributive use of adjectives, Intr. 10.
Auxiliary, see Verbs.

Calendar, the Roman, 537-40.
Cases, remarks on, Intr. 41, 203-7, 329; see also Nominative, etc.
Causal clauses, Intr. 74, 482-6; introduced by *cum*, 430 *n*, 434; introduced by *qui*, 500, 510-13.
Characterising clauses, 503 *n*-506.
Clauses, subordinate, defined, Intr. 69; types of, Intr. 71-4; see also Final, Consecutive, etc.
Commands, 140-2, 149; indirect, Intr. 71, 117-19, 149 *n* 1, 349 *n* 2; in *orat. obl.*, 522.
Commanding, see Verbs.
Comparative clauses, Intr. 74, 108 *n* 2, 488-97.
Comparative degree, 57, 275-8, 507; in final clause, 102; with *quisque*, 376; double, 493 *n* 2.
Compound, see Verbs.
Concessive clauses, Intr. 74, 412 *n*, 477-81; introduced by *cum*, 434; introduced by *qui*, 500, 510-12.
Conditional clauses, Intr. 74, 450-468, 494; Open, Type I, 451-454; Open in *orat. obl.*, 470; Ideal, Type II, 455-6; Ideal in *orat. obl.*, 471; Unreal, Type III, 457-8; Unreal in *orat. obl.*, 472-3; Unreal, which are also clauses of result, etc., 474; indicative in apodosis of Types II and III, 153, 460-3.
Conjunctions, Intr. 44-5; co-ordinating, Intr. 45, 47; subordinating, Intr. 46, 51; see also *et*, *aut*, *ut*, *ne*, *cum*, etc., in Latin Index.
Consecutive clauses, Intr. 74, 106-116, 126 *n* 1, 134; used in a limiting sense, 111, 134 *n*; negatives used in, 109; introduced by *qui*, 500, 502-9; sequence of tenses in, 112-15.
Contrast, how indicated, Intr. 83, 91; marked by place of relative clause, 75; by use of personal pronoun, 334; by *idem*, 366; by repeated *alius*, 370.
Co-ordinate sentences, Intr. 66-8.
Copulative, see Verbs.
Correlatives, 84-93.

Dates, how expressed, 531, 537-540.
Dative, main use of, 211; syntax of, 242-61; with adjectives and adverbs, 254-5; of *agent*, 258; of gerund and gerundive, 397; with gerundive, 390; of indirect object, Intr. 23, 5, 242-4; of *possessor*, 257; *predicative*, 259; of *purpose*, 259; with certain classes of verbs, 245, 248, 251; with compound verbs, 252-3.
Demonstrative, see Pronouns.
Deponent, see Verbs.
Difference, how expressed, 91-2, 367, 370-1; measure of, 279, 318, 322; and see Comparative clauses.
Duty, how expressed, 195, 199-200.

Emphasis, expressed by use of pronouns, 11; see also Order of Words.

Enclitics, Intr. 89.
Entreaties, see Commands.
Explanatory clauses, **487**.

Factitive, see Verbs.
Final clauses, Intr. 74, **100-3**, **106** *n*, **117** *n* 2, **149** *n* 1, 349 *n* 2, **396**; negative used in, **101**. **103**, **109**; introduced by *qui*, **101** *n* 1, **500**, **501**, **509**; introduced by *quo*, **102**.
Fractions, **535**.
Frequentative action, how expressed, 432.
Future, see Tenses of Indicative.

Genitive, main use of, **10**, **214**; syntax of, **287-9**; and adjectives, **58-60**; *appositional*, **304**; of *characteristic*, **291**; of *charge*, **306**; of *definition*, **304**; of gerund and gerundive, **399**; *objective*, **300-2**, **407**; *partitive*, **290** *n* 3, **293-8**, **536**; *possessive*, **290**, **345**; of *punishment*, **307**; of *quality*, **58** *n*, **303**, **318** *n*, **327** *n* 3; *subjective*, **299**; of *value*, **305**; with certain verbs, **305-10**; with impersonal verbs, **234**, **309**.
Geographical expressions in Latin, **223**, **304** *n*; and see Place.
Gerund, **382-5**, **395-9**; ablative of, **398**; with *ad*, **396**; dative of, **397**; and direct object, **385**, **395**; genitive of, **399**; origin of, *p*. 215 *footnote* 1; supplies cases to substantival infinitive, **99**, **384**.
Gerundive, **386-400**; with dative of agent, **258**, **390**; expresses *duty*, *obligation*, **149** *n* 3, **200-201**, **392-3**; in impersonal construction, **389**; in indirect questions, **172**; substitute for final clause, **101** *n* 1; expresses *possibility*, **394**; with indicative of *sum*, **153**, **461**.

Historic tenses, see Tenses of Indicative and Subjunctive.
Historic present, **179-80**.
Historic infinitive, **186**.

Imperative, **140-1**, **143** *n* **4**, **147**; future imperative, so-called, *p*. 93 *footnote* 7.
Imperfect, see Tenses of Indicative and Subjunctive.
Impersonal construction of intransitive verbs, Intr. 28, **5**, **208**, **217**, **217** *n*; of *coepi*, *desino*, *possum*, **198** *n* 2, **219**; of verbs of *saying*, etc., avoided, **43**, **43** *n* 1 and *n* 2, **46**.
Impersonal verbs, see Verbs.
Indicative mood, **147**; in conditional sentences, Types II, III, **153**, **460-3**; in *dum*-clauses in *orat. obl.*, **438** *n* 1; used parenthetically in *orat. obl.*, **449**.
Infinitive, **94-9**, **382** *n*, **384**; never used in final sense, **101**; future without *esse*, *p*. 43 *footnote* 1; so-called future passive, **403**; English infinitive turned by a Latin noun clause, **117**; historic, **186**; *prolative*, as object of certain verbs, *possum*, etc., Intr. 34 *footnote*, and see **42**; after some verbs of *commanding* and *wishing*, **120**; tenses of, **35**.
Interjections, Intr. **53**.
Interrogative, particles and pronouns, **156-7**; clauses distinguished from adjectival, **176**; for English abstract nouns, **174**; see also Questions.
Intransitive, see Verbs.

Latin and English usage compared: abstract nouns, **98**, **174-5**, **218**, **417**; accusative and infinitive construction, **31**; adjectives, **54** *n*, **56**, **58-62**, **81**; adverbs,

63-4; ambiguity, 52, **216** *n*, **515** *n* 2; English 'it,' 82, 96 *n*, 156 *n*; meanings of words, 16-25; metaphors, **17**, **361** *n* 2; noun clauses, 117; participles, **14**, **407** *n*, **411-12**, **414** *n*; personification, 319; indirect questions, 166; relative clauses, **13**, **78**; result clauses, **107** *n*; tense of dependent infinitive, **153** *n* 2; verbs of *fearing*, **137** *n* 2; verbs, transitive and intransitive, Intr. 24; use of voices, **43**, **216** *n*; words denoting agent, **76**, **175**; word order, Intr. 77, 82, 155.

Locative, **213**, **272** *n*, **312-16**.

Metaphors, English, **17**; qualified by *quidam*, **361**; qualified by *tamquam*, etc., **494** *n* 2.

Moods, **147**; see also Indicative, Subjunctive, Imperative.

Motion, *from*, **9**, **314-15**; *to*, **9**, **235**, **313**.

Necessity, how expressed, **195**, **201**, **387-93**.

Negative, after *say* expressed by *nego*, **33**; in final clauses, **101**; in consecutive clauses, **109**; second negative, **103**, **145**; negative answer, **162**; virtual negative, **132**.

Neuter adjective for English abstract nouns, **51**.

Nominative, **208**, **216-21**; with infinitive, **42-5**.

Nouns, Intr. 5-7; classified, Intr. 7; adjective in agreement with, **48**; adjective used as noun, **50-5**, **256**; collective with singular verb, **30**; English abstract, **98**, **174-5**, **218**, **417**; predicative, Intr. 64; English verbal, **94** *n*, **181** *n*, **218**; in *-tor*, *-sor*, *p*. 197 *footnote* 1.

Noun clauses, Intr. 71; introduced by *ut*, *ne*, **117-28**; by *quominus*, *quin*, **129-35**; by interrogatives, **163-9**, **174**; and see Oratio Obliqua.

Numerals, **293** *n*, **296**, **373**, **377**, **527-36**; cardinals, **527-9**, **536**; distributive, **532-3**; ordinal, **321** *n* 2, **325** *n* 1, **530-1**, **534**; numeral adverbs, **533**; omission of *quam*, **275** *n*; with *quisque*, **377**.

Object, direct, Intr. 20, **4**, **228**; indirect, Intr. 23, **5**, **242**-6.

Obligation, how expressed, **195**, **199-200**.

Oratio Obliqua, **31-4**, **444-7**, **514-526**; commands in, **522**; conditional clauses in, **469-75**; prohibitions in, **522**; coordinate *qui* clause in, **79** *n*, **517** *n*; subordinate clauses in, **523**; wishes in, **522**; virtual, **448-9**, **475**, **484**.

Order of words in Latin sentences, Intr. 77-91, **82**, **156** *n*; of personal pronouns, *p*. 36 *footnote* 5; of clauses, Intr. 92-8; of *qui* clauses, **75**; of correlative clauses, **85** *n*.

Parataxis, **129** *n*, **149** *n* 1.

Participles, **14**, **346**, **405-18**; oblique cases of, **73-4**; used as adjectives, **407**; for finite verb, **15**, **406**; present, **302**, **407**, **409-14**; present of *sum*, **224** *n* 2 and *p*. 271 *footnote* 1; past, **407**, **409**, **415-17**, **422**; future, **409**, **418**, **423**; future, with *sum* in conditional clauses, **463**.

Parts of Speech, Intr. 1-4.

Perfect, see Tenses of Indicative and Subjunctive.

Periphrastic construction, see *fore* in Latin Index.

Permission, how expressed, **195**, **198**.

Personification of country, avoided, **319**.

Place, how expressed, 311-17; see also Ablative and Accusative.
Pluperfect, see Tenses of Indicative and Subjunctive.
Possessive, see Adjective, Genitive, Dative.
Possibility, how expressed, 195-7, 394.
Predicate, Intr. 55, 61.
Predicative adjective, Intr. 11; noun, Intr. 64.
Prepositions, Intr. 40-3; list of, **330**; assist case-system, 205, **329**; with accusative, **331**; with ablative, **332**; origin of, Intr. 42.
Present, see Tenses of Indicative and Subjunctive.
Price, see Ablative and Genitive.
Primary, see Tenses.
Prohibitions, 143-5, 149; in *orat. obl.*, **522**; see also Commands, indirect.
Pronouns, Intr. 13-16; demonstrative, **290** *n* **4, 335-48, 504**; demonstrative in *orat. obl.*, **515**; intensifying, **355-6**; indefinite, **357-64, 505**; interrogative, **505**; personal, Intr. 55, **11, 26** *footnote*, **34, 225, 291** *n* 2, **334, 515**; reciprocal, supplied by *inter se*, **353**, or by repeated *alius*, **371**; reflexive, **349-53**; relative, see Relative; and predicative noun, **83** *n*; in *orat. obl.*, **515.**
Pronominal adjectives, Intr. 9.
Proportion, 376, 497.
Protasis, 450; suppressed, **152.**
Proviso, clauses of, 439, 468.

Questions, 154, 176; deliberative, **149** *n* **2, 520, 521** *n*; direct single, **154-7**, direct alternative, **158-61**; distinguished from relative clauses, **176**; indirect, Intr. 71, **163-6, 173-174, 349** *n* 2; indirect single, **167**; indirect alternative, **168-9**; in *orat. obl.*, **519-21**; rhetorical, **521.**

Qui-clauses, see Relative clauses.
Quotation introduced by *illud*, 341.

Relative clauses, Intr. 72, **77-83, 500-13**; instead of co-ordinate sentence, **13, 78, 499**; co-ordinate in *orat. obl.*, **79** *n*, **517** *n*; explanatory, **487.**
Relative pronoun, Intr. 14-15; gender attracted, **83**; has *is* as its antecedent, **84, 336, 342**; co-ordinating use, Intr. 50, **13**; prefixed to conditional clause, **459** *n*; introducing final clause, **102, 501, 501** *n* 2; introducing explanatory clause, **487**; introducing consecutive clause, **502-8**; introducing causal clause, **510-13**; introducing concessive clause, **510-12.**
Repraesentatio, 525.
Restrictive clause, 11, 134 *n*, **468, 492, 508.**

Sentence, defined, Intr. 54; simple, Intr. 54-64; complex, Intr. 69-76; compound, Intr. 65-68; co-ordinate, Intr. 66; main, Intr. 69.
Space, how expressed, 318-19.
Statement, indirect, Intr. 71; and see Oratio Obliqua.
Subject, Intr. 55, 58; compound, Intr. 59, 26-8.
Subjunctive mood, 147-52; anticipatory, **441** *n* 2; of conditioned futurity, **151-2, 154**; deliberative, **149** *n* 2, **154**; of desire, **150**; jussive, 149, **439**; prospective, **441** *n* 2, **495** *n*; and indefinite second person, **442** *n*.
Substantives, Intr. 6; and see Nouns.
Superlative degree, 57; of adjective in relative clause, **69**; with *quisque*, **375-6**; with *unus*, **529.**
Supines, 101 *n* 1, **235, 401-4**; in *-um* with *iri*, **470** *n* **3, 471** *n* **2.**

Temporal clauses, **427-43**.

Tenses, primary, **104**, **177** *n* **2**; secondary, **104**, **177** *n* 2; normal sequence of, **104-5**; unusual sequence, 112,173 *n* 1, **470** *n* 1, **474**, **494** *n* 1; sequence in *orat. obl.*, **524-5**.

Tenses of the Indicative, **177-94**; present, **177-82**; historic present, **179-80**, **438**, **523** *n* 2; imperfect, **177**, **183-5**; future, **177**, **189-91**, **453**; future perfect, **177**, **189-90**, **192**, **447** *n* 1, **453**, **470** *n* 2; perfect, **104** *n*, **105** *n* 1, **177**, 181, 187-8, **428** *n*; pluperfect, **177**, **181**, **193**, **428** *n*.

Tenses of the Infinitive, **35**.

Tenses of the Subjunctive: present, **105**, **112**, **142**, **143** *n* 3, **144**, **151**, **456**; imperfect, 105, 151, **458**; perfect, **105**, **113**, **143**, **151**, **456** *n*, **470** *n* 2; perfect with future participle, **474**, **474** *n*; pluperfect, **105**, **151**, **458**, **470** *n* 2.

Time, expressions of, **320-8**; *at which*, **9**, and see Ablative; *during which*, **9**, and see Accusative; adverbs of, **328**.

Transitive, see Verbs.

Verbs, Intr. 17-37; with ablative, **281-4**; auxiliary, Intr. 33; of *commanding*, **118**; compounded with preposition, Intr. 43, **24**, **252**; copulative, Intr. 35, **7**, **239** *n*; with dative, **245**, **248**, **251-3**; deponent, Intr. 29, **415-16**, **423**; desiderative, *p*. 46 *footnote* 1; of *doubting*, **135-6**; factitive, Intr. 36, **95**, **239**; of *fearing*, **137-9**, **150** *n*; finite, Intr. 37; with genitive, **234**, **305-10**; of *hoping, promising*, **37**; impersonal, Intr. 32, **95**, **126**, **247**, **309**; inchoative, *p*. 46 *footnote* 2; intransitive, Intr. 22-4, **5**, **20**, **229**, **252**, **422**; modal, *p*. 6 *footnote* 1; of *preventing, hindering*, **129-31**; of *saying, thinking*, **31**, and see Oratio Obliqua; semi-deponent, Intr. 30, **415-16**, **423**; of *teaching, concealing*, **230-1**; transitive, Intr. 19-21, 27, **4**, **20**, **229**, **252**; of *will* and *wish*, **118**; with two constructions, **124**, **165** *n*; used absolutely, Intr. 21, **20**.

Vocative, **215**.

Voice, active, Intr. 25; passive, Intr. 26; middle, **233**.

Wishes, **150**; indirect, Intr. 71, **137**, **349** *n* 2.

LATIN INDEX

ā, ab, 8, 264-7, 314, 326, 332, 391.
abeō, 264.
abest (tantum), 128.
abhinc, 324.
abhorreō, 264 *n*.
abs, 332.
absolvō, 306.
absque, 333.
abstineō, 264.
absum, 251; see abest.
abundō, 284.
ac (Intr. 48), 90, 91, 488, 491.
accēdit, 487.
accidit, 126, 247, 487, 487 *n*. 2; see Vocab., *lot*.
aciēs, see Vocab., *field*.
accipiō, 19.
acclāmō, see Vocab., *disapproval*.
accūsō, 306, 448 *n*.; see Vocab., *tax with*.
acquīrō, 19.
ācta (*n. pl.*), 408.
ad, 235 *n*, 313 *n*, 326, 331; used adverbially, 536.
addō, 487.
adeō (*adverb*), 108 *n*, 128.
adhūc, 328.
adimō, 244 *n* 2.
adipīscor, 19; see Vocab., *obtain*.
adiuvō, 246.
admīror, 484 *n*.
admoneō, 308.
adsum, 251; see *p*. 143, *footnote* 6.
adulēscēns, 51, 63, 408; see *p*. 51, *footnote* 1.
adversor, 245
adversus, -um (*prep*.), 331.
aegrē, 132.
aequālis, 51, 256.
aestimō, 305.
afficiō, 283.
affinis, 255-6, 301.
agō (id), 118.
aiō, 40.
aliēnus, 255, 265, 354.
aliquandō, see Vocab., *once, sometimes*.
aliquātenus, 333.
aliquis, 360, 381.
aliquī (*adj*.), 360.
aliter, 91, 371 *n* 1, 488, 491, 491 *n* 2.
aliunde, 371 *n* 1.
alius, 91-2, 367-71.
alloquor, 253.
alter, 368, 369 *n*, 378 *n* 1, 530-1.
ambō, 378.
amicus, 256.
amō, see Vocab., *love*.
amoenus, see Vocab., *beautiful*.
amplius, 275 *n*.
an, 159-61, 169.
animī pendeō, 312 *n* 2.
anne, 159, 168.
annōn, 159.
ante, 320 *n* 1, 322, 331, 443.
antepōnō, 253.
antequam, 322 *n*, 442-3.
antīquus, see Vocab., *ancient*.
appāreō (Intr. 35 *n*).
appāret, 31.
appellor (Intr. 36).
Aprīlis, see *p*. 295, *footnote* 1.
aptus, 255.
apud, 331; see *p*. 45, *footnote* 1.
arbitror, 492; see Vocab., *fancy*.
argūmentum, 260.
arguō, 306; see Vocab., *tax with*.
aspernor, see Vocab., *despise*.
aspiciō, see Vocab., *see*.
assentor, 253.
assuēscō, 42.
assuēfactus, 255.
assuētus, 255.
at, 464 *n* 1.
atque, see ac.
attineō, 19.
attingō, 19, 253.
auctōritās, see *p*. 280, *footnote* 1, and Vocab., *influence*.
audeō, 42, 416.
audiō (Intr. 35 *n*), 23, 410 *n*.
augeō, 21.
Augustus, see p. 295, *fn*. 1.
ausim, 152 *n* 2.
aut (Intr. 49), 29, 171, 467 *n*.
autem (Intr. 89).
auxiliō (*dat*.), 259.
auxilior, 245.
āversor, 253, 416.
avi, see *p*. 51, *footnote* 3.

beātē vīvere, beātum esse, 98.
bellī (*locative*), 312 *n* 1.
bene, 252.
benevolus, 255.
bīnī, 532.
bis, 533.
bona (*n. pl*.), 51.
bonī, 50; see *p*. 50, *footnote* 1, and *p*. 282, *footnote* 6.

calamitās, see Vocab., *disaster*.
candidātus, 408.
capāx, 301.
careō, 284.
cāsus, 206; see Vocab., *disaster*.
cāsū, 270 *n* 1.
causam ob eam, 108 *n* 1.
causā (*abl*.), 290 *n* 2, 329 *n*, 396 *n* 1, 399.
caveō, 118, 143, 143 *n* 2, 248.
cēdō (patriā), 264.
cēlō, 230-1.
cēnseō, 118; see Vocab., *fancy*.
cernō, see Vocab., *see*.
certē, 464 *n* 1; see Vocab., (*at*) *least*.
certiōrem faciō, 301 *n* 2.
cessō, see Vocab., *hang back*.
cēterī, 372.
circā, 331.
circiter, 331.
circum, 331.
circumdō, 250.
circumsedeō, 229 *n* 1.
circumveniō, 229 *n* 1.
cis, 331.
citrā, 331.
cīvitās, 19; see Vocab., *tribe*.
clam, 333.
cliēns, see *p*. 195, *footnote* 1.
coepī, 42, 219.
cognōmen, 224 *n* 1, 261.
colligō, 21.
comitia, 397.
commodum, 51.
commonefaciō, 308.
commūnicō, 253.
commūnis, 255.
compleō, 284, 284 *n* 1.
concēdō, 118, 122.
condemnō, 306.
condōnō, 244 *n* 1.
cōnfīdō, 245 *n* 4, 253, 282*n*. 416.

cōnor, 42, 475 *n*.
cōnscīscō, 253.
cōnsequor, 19 ; see Vocab., *obtain*.
cōnsiliō (*abl.*), 270 *n* 1 ; eō cōnsiliō, 108 *n* 1.
cōnspiciō, see Vocab., *see*.
cōnstat, 31.
cōnstituō, 42, 45, 118.
cōnstō, 280 *n* 2.
cōnsuēvī, 42.
cōnsulō, 248, 389 *n* 2.
cōnsultō (*abl.*), 270 *n* 1.
cōnsultum (senātūs), 408.
contemnō, see Vocab., *despise*.
contingit, 247 ; see Vocab., *lot*.
contrā, 91, 331.
conveniō, 21, 24, 229 *n* 1.
conversus (*participle*), 416.
cōram, 332.
corōna, 19.
cottīdiānus, 328.
cottīdiē, 328.
crās, 516.
crēdibilis, 404.
crēdiderim, 152.
crēdō, 248, 492.
creor (Intr. 36).
crēscō, 21.
crimine, see *p.* 174, *footnote*.
crūdēlis, see Vocab., *boldly*.
culpa, 260.
cumulō, 283-4.
cūnctī, see Vocab., *all*.
cūnctor, 98 ; see Vocab., *hang back*.
cupidus, 301.
cupiō, 41-2, 118, 120, 150 *n*.
cūr, 157, 174.
cūrō, 118, 121, 141, 246, 400.
cum (*prep.*), 8, 332 ; -cum, 8 *n*.
cum (*conjunction*), 157 *n* 7, 406 *n*, 429-35, 486 ; cum prīmum, 428 ; cum *inversum*, 433 *n* 2.

damnō, 306.
damnum, 260 ; see Vocab., *wrong*.
dē, 206 *n*, 332.
dē integrō, 328.
dēbeō, 42, 153, 199, 461.
dēcēdō, see *p.* 225, *footnote* 1.
December, see *p.* 295, *footnote* 1.
dēcernō, 118.
decet, 234.
dēclāror (Intr. 36).
dēclīnātiō, 206.
decumae, 535.
dēdecet, 234.
dēdecus, 260.
dēdō, 21.
dēfector, see *p.* 197, *footnote* 1.
dēficiō, see Vocab., *abandon*.
deinceps, 534 *n*.
deinde (Intr. 88), 534 *n*.
dēlectō, 246.
dēlictum, 408 ; see Vocab., *crime*.
dēmum, 347, 443 *n*.
dēnique, 534 *n* ; see *p.* 210, *footnote* 6.
dēserō, see Vocab., *abandon*.
dēsīderō, 23.
dēsinō (Intr. 34), 42, 219.
dēsistō, 42, 264.
dēspiciō, see Vocab., *despise*.
dēstituō, see Vocab., *abandon*.
dēsum, see Vocab., *abandon*.
dēterreō, 129.
dētrīmentum, 260.
dēvolvō, 21.
dextrā (*abl.*), 273 *n*. 1.
dīcat aliquis, 152.
diciōnis faciō, 290 *n* 3.
dīcō, 244, 444 ; see Vocab., *speak*.
dictitō, see Vocab., *pretnde*.
dīcunt, 44.
differō, see Vocab., *hang back*.
difficilis, 404.
diffīdō, 245, 416.
dignus, 274, 285, 285 *n* 2, 507.
diem dē diē, 328 ; in diēs, 328.
dīligō, see Vocab., *love*.
dīmidium, 535.
discernō, 264 *n*.
discō, 42.
displiceō, 245.
dissēnsiō, 300.
dissimulō, see Vocab., *hide*, *pretend*.
dissipō, 21.
diurnus, 328.
diūtius, 328.
dīversus, 371 *n* 3.
dō, 400 ; operam dō, 118, 397 ; vēnum dō, 235.
doceō, 42, 230-1.
doctus, 407.
documentum, 260.
doleō, 487.
dolor, 260.
domus, 9, 235 ; domum (*accus.*), 313 ; domī (*loc.*), 312 *n* 1, 316 ; domō (*abl.*), 314.
dōnec, 437, 440, 441.
dōnō (*verb*), 250.
dubitō, 42, 135-6 ; see *p.* 46, *footnote* 3.
dubium (non est), 135.
ducentī, 527-8.
dūcō, 245 *n* 3, 259.
dum, 180, 406 *n*, 437-41.
dummodo, 439 *n*.
duo, 527-8.

eā (*abl.*), 89.
ecquis, 157.
ēdīcō, 118, 122-3.
efficiō, 125.
egeō, 284, 284 *n* 1.
ego, 334, 515.
eius modī, 87 ; see Vocab., *kind*.
ēligō, 259.
emō, 305.
enim (Intr. 89).
eō (*verb*), 402 *n* 2 ; īnfitiās eō, 235 ; obviam eō, 253.
eō (*abl.*), 279 *n*, 483 *n* 1 ; (*adverbial*), 89 ; eō . . . quō, 376, 497 ; eō tempore, 431.
equidem, 334.
ērēctus, 407.
ergā, 255, 331.
ēruditus, 407.
est, 505 *n* 3 ; est quī (sunt quī), 360, 506.
et (Intr. 48) ; see *p.* 59 *footnote* 5.
etiam, 162.
etiamsī, 477-8.
etsī, 477-8.
ēvenit, 126 ; see Vocab., *lot*.
ex, 326, 332.
exhortor, 118, 122.
expedit, 247.
expers, 301.
expugnō, 229 *n* 1.
exspectātiōne, 277.
exspectō, 22, 23.
extrā, 331.
extrēmum, 534 *n*.

fac, 141.
facilis, 404.
facinus, see Vocab., *crime*.
faciō, 125, 305 ; see certiōrem and fac.
facta (*n. pl.*), 408.
fāma, 277.
familia, see Vocab., *family*.
fāmōsus, 19.
fās, 404.
fātālis, see Vocab., *fatal*.
faveō, 5, 245.
favor, see Vocab., *influence*.
Februārius, see *p.* 295, *footnote* 1.
fēlīcitās, 347 *n*.
ferē, fermē, see Vocab., *almost*.

feror (Intr. 36).
ferōx, see Vocab., *boldly*.
ferunt, 44.
festīnō, 42.
fīdō, 245.
fidūcia, 300.
fingō, see Vocab., *pretend*.
fīnitimus, 256.
fīō (Intr. 36), 42, 305 *n*; fit, 126; fierī potest, 126, 197.
flāgitium, 122; see Vocab., *crime*.
flāgitō, 230.
forās, 235.
fore, 38, 403, 470 *n* 3, 471 *n* 2.
forsitan, 169, 170, 197.
fortasse, 170.
forte (*abl.*), 170, 270 *n* 1.
fraude, 270 *n* 1.
fraudō, 284.
frētus, 285.
fruor, 281; see *p*. 216, *footnote* 1.
frūstrā, see Vocab., *vain*.
fungor, 281; see *p*. 216, *footnote* 1.
furō, see Vocab., *mad*.

gaudeō, 41, 487.
gerō, 240 *n* 1.
glōrior, 282 *n*.
grātia, see Vocab., *influence*; grātiā (*abl.*), 290 *n* 2, 329 *n*, 396 *n* 1, 399; grātiam habēre, etc., 98.
grātus, 254; see Vocab., *delightful*.
gubernātor, see *p*. 197, *footnote* 1.

habeō, 188, 240, 259, 305; pēnsī habeō, 298.
hāc, 89.
hāctenus, 333.
haud (Intr. 90); see *p*. 109, *footnote* 1.
haud scio, 169, 170, 197.
herī, 516.
hērōs, see *p*. 282, *footnote* 4.
hiberna, see *p*. 235, *footnote* 1.
hic, 325 *n* 2, 337, 338 *n* 1, 340, 515; see *p*. 195, *footnote* 1.
hīc, 89, 516.
hinc, 89, 516.
hodiē, 516.
homō, 52, 224; see *p*. 131, *footnote* 2.
honestās, 51; see Vocab., *honesty*.
honestus, 51.
honor, 260.
horreō, 232.
hortor, 118, 122, 246.
hostis, see *p*. 28, *footnote* 1.
hūc, 89, 516; see *p*. 58, *footnote* 4.
huius modī, 87; see Vocab., *kind*.
humī, 312 *n* 1.

iam, 328.
iamdiū, 181.
iamdūdum, 181, 328.
iampridem, 181, 328.
Iānuārius, see *p*. 295, *footnote* 1.
ibi, 89, 516.
id aetātis, 294 *n*.
id agō, 118.
id locōrum, 294 *n*.
id temporis, 238.
idcircō, 108 *n* 1, 483 *n* 1.
īdem, 84, 90, 365-6.
Īdūs, 538.
idōneus, 255, 507.
ignārus, 301.
ignōrō, see Vocab., *ignorant*.
ignōscō, 5, 245.
ille, 11, 70, 325 *n* 2, 334, 339, 340-1, 346, 348, 515, 515 *n* 3.
illīc, 89
illūc, 89, 516.
immemor, 301.
immineō, 253.
impār, 397.
impedimentō (*dat.*), 260.
impediō, 129.
impellō, 118, 122, 253.
imperītus, 301.
imperium, see Vocab., *influence*.
imperō, 118, 121-23, 245, 245 *n* 2.
impetrō, 118, 122; see Vocab., *obtain*.
improbī, see *p*. 50, *footnote* 1, and *p*. 282, *footnote* 6.
īmus, 60.
in, 255, 273 *n* 2, 320 *n* 2, 326, 330, 331, 332.
in-, 407.
incipiō, 42.
incūsō, 306; see Vocab. *tax with*.
inde, 89.
indicō (bellum), 253.
indigeō, 284 *n* 1.
indignātus (*participle*), 416.
indignus, 274, 507.
indolēs, see Vocab., *character*.
indulgeō, 245.
induō, 233.
īnfāns, 408.
īnferō, 253.
īnfēstus, 254.
īnfitiās eō, 235.
īnfrā, 331.
ingenium, see Vocab., *character*.
inimīcus, 256, 290 *n* 2.
iniūria, 270 *n* 1; see Vocab., *wrong*.
iniussū, 270 *n* 3.
inquam, inquit, 40.
inrīdeō, 253.
īnsāniō, see Vocab., *mad*.
īnsimulō, see Vocab., *tax with*.
īnsistō, 253.
īnstitūtum, 408.
īnstō, 253.
īnsuētus, 255, 301.
īnsula, 304 *n*.
īnsum, 251.
intellegō, 19.
inter, 306 *n*, 331; inter sē, 353.
intercēdō, 253.
interdīcō, 129.
interdum, see Vocab., *sometimes*.
interest, 310, 378 *n* 3.
interficiō, see Vocab., *kill*.
interitus, 19.
intermittō, see Vocab., *undone*.
interrogō, 230-1.
intersum, 251; see interest.
intrā, 331.
intueor, see Vocab., *see*.
invideō, 245.
ipse, 349 *n* 1, 350 *n*, 355-6.
īrāscor, 245.
is, 11, 67, 70-6, 84, 336, 339, 342, 346, 348, 504, 515, 515 *n* 3.
isque, 344.
iste, 338 and *n* 1 and *n* 2, 515.
istīus modī, 87.
ita, 108 *n* 1, 488, 491, 497; ita . . . ut, 376; ita vērō, 162.
iterum, 328, 533-4.
iubeō, 41, 120, 123, 246.
iūcundus, 404; see Vocab., *delightful*.
iūdex, see Vocab., *judge*.
Iūlius, see *p*. 295, *footnote* 1.
Iūnius, see *p*. 295, *footnote* 1.
iūre, 270 *n* 1; see Vocab., *rightly*.
iūris cōnsultus, 302 *n* 2.
iūris suī, 290 *n* 3.
iūrō, 37.
iussū, 270 *n* 3.
iūstō (*abl.*), 277.
iuvenis, see *p*. 51, *footnote* 1.
iuvō, 246.
iuxtā, 331, 491.

Kalendae, 538.

laedō, 246.

laevā (*abl.*), 273 *n* 1.
laudō, 484 *n*.
legor (Intr. 36).
lēx, see *p*. 58, *footnote* 1.
līber (*adj.*), 265.
līberō, 264 *n*.
libet, 31, 247.
licet, 198, 202, 247, 261, 478, 480.
longum est, 153; longius (quam), 275 *n*.
loquor, see Vocab., *speak*.

magistrātus, 19.
magnī (*gen.*), 305; magnō (*abl.*), 280 *n* 2.
maiōrēs, 51; see *p*. 51, *footnote* 3.
Maius, see *p*. 295, *footnote* 1.
male, 252.
maledīcō, 253.
malevolentia, malignitās, malitia, see Vocab., *malice*.
mālō, 41, 42, 188, 120; mālim, 121.
mandō, 188, 122-3, 244 *n* 1.
manifēstum (est), 31.
Mārtius, see *p*. 295, *footnote* 1.
mātūrō, 42.
maximī (*gen.*), 305.
mē, 349 *n* 1.
medeor, 245.
medius, 60, 295.
melius est, 153.
meminī, 228 *n*, 308, 308 *n* 1.
memor, 301.
memoria, see *p*. 282, *footnote* 3.
mentior, 98; see Vocab., *pretend*.
merita (*n. pl.*), 408.
metuō, 137, 165 *n*; see Vocab., *fear*.
meus, 515.
mīlitiae (*loc.*), 312 *n* 1.
mīlle, mīlia, 527-8, 536.
minimē, 162.
minimī (*gen.*), 305.
minor (*verb*), 37, 244 *n* 1.
minōris (*gen.*), 305.
minōrēs, see *p*. 51, *footnote* 3.
minus (quam), 275 *n*.
mīror, 41, 484 *n*.
misereor, 308.
miseret, 234, 309.
miserēscō, 308.
miseror, 308, *n* 5.
moderor, 249.
modō (*abl.*), 270 *n* 3.
modo, 439 *n*.
moneō, 118, 121, 124, 165 *n*.
mōnstrō, 244.
mōrēs, see Vocab., *character*.
mortālis, 19.
mortifer, 19.
moveō, 21.
multī, 293 *n*, 296.
multī sunt quī, 506 *n* 1.
multō (*abl.*), 279 *n*.
mundus, 19.
mūnus, 260.
mūtō, 21.

nancīscor, see Vocab., *obtain*.
nātiō, 19; see Vocab., *tribe*.
nātū (maior, minor), 274 *n*.
nātus (*participle*), 266, 327.
nāvis longa, 56.
nē, 101, 117, 119, 129-31, 137, 149, 150, 357.
nē dicam, see *p*. 74, *footnote* 3.
nē . . . nōn (=ut), 137 *n* 3.
nē . . . quidem (Intr. 90).
-ne (Intr. 89), 156, 159-60.
nec (Intr. 90), 29, 110.
necdum, 328.
necesse est, 118, 121, 201, 202.
necne, 168.
necō, see Vocab., *kill*.
nefās, 404.
neglegō, see Vocab., *despise*.
negō, 33.
negōtiō (*abl.*), 270 *n* 3.
nēmō, 223 *n* 2, 293 *n*, 296, 358 *n*, 505; see *p*. 130, *footnote* 2.
nepōtēs, see p. 51, *footnote* 3.
nēquāquam, 162.
neque, see nec.
nequeō (Intr. 34), 42.
nēquīquam, see Vocab., *vain*.
nēquitia, see Vocab., *crime*.
nescio, see Vocab., *ignorant*.
nescio quis (and quī), 169, 362-3.
nēve (and neu), 103, 119 *n*, 145.
nī, 464 *n* 2.
nihil, 294, 505; nihilī (*gen.*), 305.
nimiō, 280 *n* 2.
nimis, 294.
nisi, 357, 450, 464, 466.
nītor, 282 *n*.
nōbilēs, see *p*. 51, *footnote* 2.
noceō, 245.
nōlō, 41, 42, 118, 120; nōlī, 143, 145 *n*; nōlim, 121.
nōmen, 261; nōmine, 274 *n*; see *p*. 174, *footnote* 1.
nōn (Intr. 90), 109, 149, 151, 162; see *p*. 32, *footnote* 4.
nōn modo nōn, 128.
Nōnae, 538.
nōn diūtius, nōn iam, 328.
nōndum, 328.
nōnne, 156, 167.
nōn nūllī, 360.
nōn numquam, see Vocab., *sometimes*.
nōn quin, 485.
nōn quō, 485; nōn quod, 485.
nōs, 515.
noster, 515.
November, see *p*. 295, *footnote* 1.
novī hominēs, see *p*. 51, *footnote* 2.
novissimus, 60.
nūbō, 245 *n* 3.
nūllus, 505, 529; see *p*. 130, *footnote* 2.
num, 156, 157 *n* 2, 161, 167, 357.
nunc, 328, 516.

ob, 268 *n* 3, 331.
obiciō, 253.
oblīvīscor, 308.
oboedientia, 300.
oboediō, 245; see Vocab., *obey*.
obsecrō, 118, 122, 141.
obsequor, 245, 253; see Vocab., *obey*.
obsideō, 24, 229 *n* 1.
obsistō, 129.
obstō, 129, 245, 253.
obtemperō, see Vocab., *obey*.
obtineō, 19.
obviam eō, 253.
occīdō, see Vocab., *kill*.
occurrō, 253.
Octōber, see *p*. 295, *footnote* 1.
ōdī, 260 *n* 2.
odium, odiō (*dat.*) sum, 260.
offendō, 246.
officium, 18, 19.
ōlim, see Vocab., *once*.
omittō, 487; see Vocab., *undone*.
omnēs, 297, 373; see Vocab., *all*.
onerō, 284.
operā (*abl.*), 267 *n* 2.
operam dō, 118, 397.
opere (*abl.*), 270 *n* 3.
opīniō, 300; opīniōne, 277.
opīnor, see Vocab., *fancy*.
opitulor, 245.
oportet, 31, 118, 121, 122, 199.
oppidum, 223, 226 *n*, 304 *n*, 316-17.
opprimō, 19.

opprobrium, 260.
oppugnō, 229 *n* 1.
optimātēs, 51; see *p.* 51, *footnote* 2.
optimus quisque, see *p.* 211, *footnote* 2.
optō, 23, 42, 118, 150 *n*.
opus, 286, 286 *n*
orbis terrārum, 16.
orbō, 284.
ōrō, 118, 122.
ortus, 266.

pactō (*abl.*), 270 *n* 3.
paene, see Vocab., *almost*.
paenitet, 31, 234, 309; see *p.* 168, *footnote* 3.
palam, 333.
pār, 255.
parātus, 407.
parcō, 5, 245.
pāreō, 5, 228 *n*, 245; see Vocab., *obey*.
pariter, 488, 491.
pars, 535.
particeps, 301.
parum, 294.
parvī (*gen.*), 305; parvō (*abl.*), 280 *n* 2.
patior, 41, 120.
patrēs, see *p.* 51, *footnote* 3.
patria, 16; patriā cēdō, 264.
paucī, 293 *n*, 296.
paulō, 279 *n*.
peccātum, 408; see Vocab., *crime*.
pellō, 264.
pendeō animī, 312 *n* 2.
penes, 331.
pēnsī habeō, 298.
per, 267 *n* 2, 321 *n* 1, 331.
percipiō, 19.
pergō, 42.
perhorrēscō, 232.
perinde, 488, 491.
perītus, 301.
permittō, 118, 122-3, 244 *n* 1.
perniciēs, 19.
persevērō, 42.
persuādeō, 5, 188, 122, 124, 245.
perveniō, 19, 253.
petō, 23, 118, 122, 231.
piget, 31, 234, 309.
placeō, 5, 245.
placet, 247.
placēre sibi, 98.
plēnus, 285 *n* 1, 301 *n* 1.
plērique, see *p.* 294, *footnote* 2.
plūs, 275 *n*, 294; plūris (*gen.*) 305.
poena, see Vocab., *punishment*.
polliceor, 37, 244.
pōne, 331.
populārēs, see *p.* 51, *footnote* 2.
populus, 19.
poscō, 122, 230-1; see Vocab., *demand*.
possum (Intr. 34), 39, 42, 153, 196, 219, 461.
potest (*impersonal*), 196 *n* 2.
post, 320 *n* 1, 322, 331, 534 *n*.
posterī, 51.
posthabeō, 253.
postquam, 428.
postrēmō (*adverb*), 534 *n*.
postulō, 118, 122, 231; see Vocab., *demand*.
potentia, potestās, see Vocab., *influence*.
potior (*verb*), 281-2; see *p.* 216, *footnote* 1.
potius, 488, 495.
prae, 332.
praecipiō, 118, 122-3, 245.
praeclārus, 19.
praeditus, 285.
praefectus, 408.
praeficiō, 253, 397.
praestō (*verb*), 240 *n* 1; see *p.* 137, *footnote* 1.
praesum, 397.
praeter, 331.
praetereō, 487.
praetermittō, see Vocab., *undone*.
praetervehor, 24.
precor, 118, 122, 231.
prīdiē, 516.
prīmus, 62, 530-1; prīmum (*adverbial*), 328, 534; prīmō (*adverb*), 534 *n*.
prior, 62, 530-1.
prīscus, prīstinus, see Vocab., *ancient*.
prius, 443, 495.
priusquam, 442-3.
prīvō, 284.
prō, 6, 332, 398 *n*.
prō eō, 488, 491.
probō, 244 *n* 1.
prōgressus (*participle*), 416.
prohibeō, 41, 129, 130.
prōiectus, 416.
prōmittō, 37.
prope, 331; see Vocab., *almost*.
properō, 42.
propinquus, 256.
propius, 331.
proprius, 255.
propter, 268 *n* 3, 331; see *p.* 186, *footnote* 6.
prōsequor, 283.
prōspiciō, 248.
prōvolūtus, 416.
proximē, 331.
proximum est, 127.
prūdēns, 301 *n* 1.
pudet, 31, 234, 309.
puer, 63.
pulcher, see Vocab., *beautiful*.
pūrgō, 306.
puto, see Vocab., *fancy*; putor (Intr. 36).

quā, 89.
quaerō, 167.
quaesō, 141.
quaestus, 260.
quālis, 84, 86, 157, 174.
quam, 91, 157, 275, 443, 488, 491, 493, 495, 507; (*omitted*), 275 *n*, 536.
quam ob rem, 157.
quam sī, 494.
quam ut, 496.
quamdiū, 157, 437.
quamquam, 478, 479.
quamvīs, 478, 480.
quandō, 157, 174, 483-4.
quantus, 84, 86, 157, 174, 294; quantī (*gen.*), 305; quantō (*abl.*), 280 *n* 2, 357, 376, 497.
quantopere, 157.
quārē, 157.
quasi, 488, 494.
-que (Intr. 48, 89).
quem ad modum, 157, 488.
queror, 484 *n* 1.
quī (*rel. pronoun*), (Intr. 50), 12, 78, 84, 336, 339, 342, 432 *n*, 498-513.
quī (*pronominal adj.*), 157, 157 *n* 1, 357.
quī (*abl.*), 127, 157 *n* 5.
quia, 483-4.
quīcumque, 364, 432 *n*.
quīdam, 361-2.
quidem, 334.
quīlibet, 359.
quīn, 80, 129-35, 505 *n* 2.
Quīntīlis, see *p.* 295, *footnote* 1.
quippe, 513.
quis (*interrogative*), 157, 157 *n* 1, 174; (*indefinite*), 357.
quisnam, 157.
quispiam, 360.
quisquam, 293 *n*, 358.
quisque, 157 *n* 4, 293 *n*, 354, 373-77, 432 *n*, 529.
quisquis, 364.
quīvīs, 359.
quō (*abl.*), 357, 376, 497; (=ut eō), 102, 501 *n* 2.
quō (*adverb of place*), 89, 157.
quoad, 437, 440.
quod (*conjunction*), 32, 459 *n*, 483-4, 487.
quōminus, 129-31.
quōmodo, 157.
quondam, see Vocab., *once*.

quoniam, 483-4.
quoque (Intr. 89).
quot, 84, 157, 174, 527.
quotēni, 532.
quotiēns, 157, 428, 533.
quotus, 157, 157 *n* 4, 377, 530.
quoūsque, 157.

ratiōne, 270 *n* 3.
ratus, 416.
re-, 252.
recipiō, 19.
recordor, 308 *n* 3.
rēctē, see Vocab., *rightly*.
recūsō, 129, 130.
referciō, 284.
rēfert, 310.
rēgnum, see Vocab., *influence*.
relinquō, see Vocab., *abandon*.
reliquī, 372.
reliquum est, 127.
remedium, 300.
reor, see Vocab., *fancy*.
repleō, 284 *n* 1.
repudiō, see Vocab., *despise*.
repugnō, 245, 253.
rēs, 52, 67, 223 *n* 1; rē ipsā, 274 *n*.
respondeō, 444.
rēspūblica, 19; see *p.* 165, *footnote* 1.
restat, 127.
retineō, 129.
reum faciō, 306.
rēx, see *p.* 131, *footnote* 1.
rīte, see Vocab., *rightly*.
rogō, 118, 121-2, 230-1.
rudis, 301, 301 *n* 1.
ruīna, 19; see Vocab., *ruin*.
rūrsus, 328.
rūs, 9, 235; rūs (*accus.*), 313; rūre (*abl.*), 314; rūrī (*loc.*) 312 *n* 1.

saepe, 328.
saepissimē, 533.
sānē, 162, 481.
satis, 252, 294.
satisfaciō, 253.
satius est, 153.
scelus, see Vocab., *crime*.
scio, 42; see *p.* 46, *footnote* 4, and Vocab., *ignorant*.
scribō, 124.
sē, 11, 34, 349-53, 515.
secundus, 530-1.
secundum (*prep.*), 331.
sēcūrus, 19.
secus, 488, 491.
semel, 328, 533.
senex, 63.
sententia, see *p.* 133, *footnote* 1.
sēparō, 264 *n*.
September, see *p.* 295, *footnote* 1.
sequitur, 127.
serviō, 245.
sescentī, 536.
seu, see sīve.
Sextīlis, see *p.* 295, *footnote* 1.
sī, 167 *n*, 171, 357-8, 450, 459, 459 *n*, 465-6; see *p.* 109, *footnote* 2.
sī minus, 465 *n*, 466.
sī nōn, 464, 464 *n* 1, 465 *n*, 466.
sī quandō, 432 *n*.
sīc, 488, 491.
sīcut, 488.
silentiō (*abl.*), 270 *n* 1.
similis, 254-5, 290 *n* 2.
simul ac, 428.
simulō, see Vocab., *hide*, *pretend*.
sīn, 465.
sine, 332, 398 *n*.
singulāris, 381 *n*.
singulī, 380, 532.
sinō, 41, 120, 123.
sīs (=sī vīs), 141.
sitiō, 232.
sīve, 171, 467, 467 *n*.
soleō, 42.
solium, 17.
solvō, 264.
solvendō nōn sum, 397 *n*.
sōlus, 62, 505, 529.
speciē, 274 *n*.
spectō, see Vocab., *see*.
spernō, see Vocab., *despise*.
spērō, 23, 37.
spēs, see *p.* 190, *footnote* 10, and Vocab., *hope*; spē, 277.
sponte, see Vocab., *voluntarily*.
statuō, 42.
studeō, 245.
studiōsus, 301.
studium, 300.
suādeō, 118, 121-2, 245.
sub, 330, 331, 332.
subsidiō (*dat.*), 259.
subter, 330, 331, 332.
subveniō, 245.
succēnseō, 245.
sum (Intr. 33, 35 *n*, 81), 195 *n*, 251, 292, 305 *n*, 424; see est, fore.
summus, 60.
super, 330, 331, 332.
superstes, 255.
suppeditō, 244.
supplicium, see Vocab., *punishment*.
suprā, 331.
suspiciō (*verb*), 23.
suus, 11, 349-54, 515.
suī (*nom. pl.*), 354; suum (*neut.*), 399 *n* 1.

taedet, 31, 234, 309.
tālis, 84, 86, 88, 108 *n* 1; see *p.* 155, *footnote* 8, and Vocab., *kind*.
tam, 88, 108 *n* 1.
tamen, 464 *n* 1, 479 *n* 1, 512 *n*.
tametsī, 477-8.
tamquam, 361 *n* 2, 488, 494.
tamquam sī, 488, 494.
tandem, 157 *n* 5.
tantus, 84, 86, 88, 108 *n* 1; see *p.* 67, *footnote* 1; tantī (*gen.*), 305; tantō (*abl.*), 279 *n*, 376, 497.
tellūs, 16.
temperō, 249.
tenus, 333; see *p.* 186, *footnote* 6.
ter, 533.
terrā marīque, 273 *n* 1.
tertium (*adverbial*), 534.
timeō, 137, 248; see Vocab., *fear*.
tīrō, 223 *n* 2.
tot, 84.
tōtus, 295.
trādō, 400; trādunt, 44.
trāns, 331.
trāns-, 229 *n* 3.
trānsdūcō, 229 *n* 3.
trāiciō, 229 *n* 3.
trēs, 527-8.
triumphō, see Vocab., *triumph*.
trucīdō, see Vocab., *kill*.
tū, 334, 515; tē, 349 *n* 1.
tum (Intr. 88), 328, 431, 435, 534 *n*.
tunc, 516.
turpis, 19.
tūtus, 19.
tuus, 515.

ubi, 89, 428, 432 *n*, 509; ubi gentium, 294 *n*.
ūllus, 358.
ultimus, 62.
ultrā, 331.
ultrō, see Vocab., *voluntarily*.
umquam, 328.
unde, 89, 157, 509.
ūniversī, 380; see Vocab., *all*.
ūnus, 62, 293 *n*, 296, 378 *n* 2, 381, 505, 527-9, 531; ūnī (*pl.*), 532.
urbs, 223, 226 *n*, 304 *n*, 316-17.

ūsquam, 16.
ūsus (*participle*), 416.
ūsus (*noun*), 286; see Vocab., *lot*.
ut (*introducing subj. clause*), 101, 107, 108 *n* 1, 117, 137; (*introducing indic. clause*), 108 *n* 2, 376, 428, 432 *n*, 488, 491-2, 497; (*omitted*), 121, 125 *n*; ut ita dīcam, see *p.* 74, *footnote* 3.
ut quī, 513.
ut quisque, 376, 432 *n*.
ut sī, 494.
uter, 157, 379.
uterlibet, 379.
uterque, 293 *n*, 298, 378-9.
utervis, 379.
ūtilis, 254-5; ūtile, ūtilitās, 51.
utinam, 150.
ūtor, 228 *n*, 281-2; see *p.* 216, *footnote* 1.
utpote, 513.
utrum, 159-61, 467 *n*.

vacō, 248 *n*, 284.
vacuus, 265.
varius, 371 *n* 3.
-ve (Intr. 49, 89).
vel (Intr. 49, 89), 171.
velim, 121, 141, 150 *n*, 152.
velut, velut sī, 488, 494.
venia, 270 *n* 3.
veniō, 402 *n* 2.
vēnum dō, 235.
vēndō, 305.
vereor, 137; see Vocab., *fear*.
veritus, 416.
vērō (Intr. 89); ita vērō, 162.
versus (*prep.*), 331; see *p.* 186, *footnote* 6.
vertō, 259.
vēscor, 281; see *p.* 216, *footnote* 1.
vester, 515.
vetō, 41, 130.
vetus, vetustus, see Vocab., *ancient*.
vexō, 19.
vī, 270 *n* 1.
vicem tuam, 238.
vīcīnus, 256.
videō, 118, 143, 410 *n*; see Vocab., *see*; videor (Intr. 35 *n*), 43 *n* 2; vīderis, 146; vidētur, 46, 492.
vīgintī, 527-8.
vīlis, 19.
vir, 52, 224; see *p.* 131, *footnote* 2.
vitium, 260; see Vocab., *crime*.
vix, 132, 358.
vocor (Intr. 36).
volō (Intr. 34), 41-2, 45, 118, 120; see velim.
vōs, 515.
vulgus, see *p.* 146, *footnote* 1.